The Translation Studies Reader

Second Edition

Edited by

Lawrence Venuti

Routledge
Taylor & Francis Group

NEW YORK AND LONDON

First published 2000 by Routledge
Reprinted in 2000 and twice in 2002

Second edition first published 2004 in the USA and Canada
by Routledge
270 Madison Ave, New York, NY 10016

Simultaneously published by Routledge
2 Park Square, Milton Park, Abingdon, Oxon, OX14 4RN

Reprinted 2005, 2006 (twice), 2007, 2008

Routledge is an imprint of the Taylor & Francis Group, an informa business

Typeset in Perpetua and Bell Gothic by
Florence Production Ltd, Stoodleigh, Devon
Printed and bound by
TJ International Ltd, Padstow, Cornwall

Library of Congress Cataloging in Publication Data
The translation studies reader / [edited by] Lawrence Venuti –
2nd ed.
    p. cm
  Includes bibliographical references and index.
  1. Translating and interpreting – History.   I. Venuti, Lawrence.
  P306.T7436 2004
  418'.02–dc22   2003022335

British Library Cataloguing in Publication Data
A catalogue record for this book is available from the
British Library

ISBN 10: 0–415–31919–6 (hbk)
ISBN 10: 0–415–31920–X (pbk)
ISBN 13: 978–0–415–31919–5 (hbk)
ISBN 13: 978–0–415–31920–1 (pbk)

For Julius David Venuti

ma tu ci hai trovato

e hai scelto nel gatto
quei miagolii che
non lo fanno apposta!

Contents

Acknowledgments

I am grateful to the following copyright holders for allowing me to use the materials that comprise this book:

Kwame Anthony Appiah, "Thick Translation," *Callaloo* 16: 808–19. Copyright © 1993 by Charles H. Rowell. Reprinted by permission of the author and the Johns Hopkins University Press.

Walter Benjamin, "The Task of the Translator" (1923) from *Illuminations*, copyright © 1955 by Suhrkamp Verlag, Frankfurt a.M., English translation by Harry Zohn, copyright © 1968 and renewed 1996 by Harcourt, Inc., reprinted by permission of Harcourt, Inc. and by the publisher from *Walter Benjamin: Selected Writings Volume I, 1913–1926* edited by Marcus Bullock and Michael Jennings, Cambridge, Mass.: The Belknap Press of Harvard University Press, copyright © 1998 by the President and Fellows of Harvard College.

Antoine Berman, "La Traduction comme épreuve de l'étranger," *Texte* (1985): 67–81. "Translation and the Trials of the Foreign": Translation copyright © 2000 by Lawrence Venuti. Published by permission of Isabelle Berman.

Shoshana Blum-Kulka, "Shifts of Cohesion and Coherence in Translation." In Juliane House and Shoshana Blum-Kulka (eds), *Interlingual and Intercultural Communication: Discourse and Cognition in Translation and Second Language Acquisition Studies*, Tübingen: Narr, 1986 (Tübinger Beiträge zur Linguistik 272), pp. 17–35. Reprinted by permission of the author and the publisher.

Jorge Luis Borges, "The Translators of *The Thousand and One Nights*," trans. Esther Allen, from *Selected Non-Fictions* by Jorge Luis Borges, edited by Eliot Weinberger. Copyright © 1999 by Maria Kodama; translation copyright © 1999 by Penguin Putnam Inc. Used by permission of Viking Penguin, a division of Penguin Putnam Inc.

Annie Brisset, "The Search for a Native Language: Translation and Cultural Identity." Chapter 4 in Annie Brisset, *A Sociocritique of Translation: Theatre and Alterity in Quebec, 1968–1988*, trans. Rosalind Gill and Roger Gannon, Toronto: University of Toronto Press, 1996, pp. 162–94. Copyright © 1996 by Rosalind Gill and Roger Gannon. Used by permission of the author and the translators.

Lori Chamberlain, "Gender and the Metaphorics of Translation," *Signs* 13: 454–72. Copyright © 1988 by The University of Chicago. Reprinted by permission of the author and the publisher.

Jacques Derrida, "What Is a 'Relevant' Translation?" trans. Lawrence Venuti, *Critical Inquiry* 27: 174–200. Copyright © 2001 by The University of Chicago. Reprinted by permission of the author and the publisher.

Itamar Even-Zohar, "The Position of Translated Literature within the Literary Polysystem," *Poetics Today* 11 (1990): 45–51. Reprinted by permission of the author and Duke University Press.

Johann Wolfgang von Goethe, "Translations" (1819), trans. Sharon Sloan. In Rainer Schulte and John Biguenet (eds) *Theories of Translation: An Anthology of Essays from Dryden to Derrida*, Chicago: University of Chicago Press, 1992, pp. 60–3. Copyright © 1992 by The University of Chicago. Reprinted by permission of the publisher.

Keith Harvey, "Translating Camp Talk: Gay Identities and Cultural Transfer," *The Translator* 4(2): 295–320. Copyright © 1998 by St Jerome Publishing. Reprinted by permission of the author and the publisher.

James S. Holmes, "The Name and Nature of Translation Studies." From James S. Holmes, *Translated! Papers on Literary Translation and Translation Studies*, second edition, Amsterdam and Atlanta: Editions Rodopi, 1994. Reprinted by permission of the estate of James S. Holmes and the publisher.

Roman Jakobson, "On Linguistic Aspects of Translation." Reprinted by permission of the publisher from *On Translation* by Reuben Brower (ed.), Cambridge, Mass.: Harvard University Press, Copyright © 1959 by the President and Fellows of Harvard College.

Jerome, "Letter to Pammachius." Translation copyright © 2004 by Kathleen Davis. Published by permission of the translator.

André Lefevere, "Mother Courage's Cucumbers: Text, System and Refraction in a Theory of Literature," *Modern Language Studies* 12:4 (1982): 3–20. Reprinted by permission of the Northeast Modern Language Association and Ria Vanderauwera.

Philip E. Lewis, "The Measure of Translation Effects." In *Difference in Translation*, ed. Joseph Graham, pp. 31–62. Copyright © 1985 by Cornell University Press. Used by permission of the author and the publisher.

Ian Mason, "Text Parameters in Translation: Transitivity and Institutional Cultures." In Eva Hajicova, Peter Sgall, Zuzanna Jettmarova, Annely Rothkegel, Dorothee Rothfuß-Bastian, and Heidrun Gerzymisch-Arbogast (eds) *Textologie und Translation* (Jahrbuch Übersetzen und Dolmetschen 4/2), Tübingen: Narr, 2003. Reprinted by permission of the author and the publisher.

Vladimir Nabokov, "Problems of Translation: *Onegin* in English," *Partisan Review* 22 (1955): 496–512. Reprinted by permission of the Estate of Vladimir Nabokov.

Eugene Nida, "Principles of Correspondence." From Eugene Nida, *Toward a Science of Translating*, Leiden: E.J Brill, 1964, pp. 156–71. Reprinted by permission of the author and the publisher.

Friedrich Nietzsche, "Translation." From Friedrich Nietzsche, *The Gay Science*, trans. Walter Kaufmann, New York: Vintage, 1974, pp. 136–8. Reprinted by permission of the publisher and the estate of Walter Kaufmann.

Abé Mark Nornes, "For an Abusive Subtitling," *Film Quarterly* 52 (3): 17–34. Copyright © 1999 by the Regents of the University of California. Reprinted by permission of the author and the University of California Press.

Ezra Pound, "Guido's Relations." From *Literary Essays* by Ezra Pound. Copyright 1918, 1920, 1935 by Ezra Pound. Used by permission of New Directions Publishing Corporation and Faber and Faber Ltd.

Katharina Reiss, "Type, Kind and Individuality of Text: Decision Making in Translation," trans. Susan Kitron, *Poetics Today* 2:4 (1981): 121–31. Reprinted by permission of the author and Duke University Press.

Steven Rendall, "A Note on Harry Zohn's Translation." An extract from "Notes on Zohn's translation of Benjamin's 'Die Aufgabe des Übersetzers'," *TTR Traduction, Terminologie, Rédaction: Etudes sur le texte et ses transformations* 10:2 (1997): 191–206. Reprinted by permission of the author and Professor Annick Chapdelaine, editor of *TTR*.

Friedrich Schleiermacher, "On the Different Methods of Translating." Translation copyright © 2004 by Susan Bernofsky. Published by permission of the translator.

Gayatri Chakravorty Spivak, "The Politics of Translation." In Gayatri Spivak, *Outside in the Teaching Machine*, London and New York: Routledge, 1993. Reprinted by permission of the author and the publisher.

George Steiner, "The Hermeneutic Motion." In George Steiner, *After Babel: Aspects of Language and Translation*, Oxford: Oxford University Press, 1975, pp. 296–303. Copyright © 1975 by George Steiner. Reprinted by permission of the publisher.

Gideon Toury, "The Nature and Role of Norms in Translation." In Gideon Toury, *Descriptive Translation Studies – and Beyond*, Amsterdam and Philadelphia: Benjamins, 1995, pp. 53–69. Copyright © 1995 by John Benjamins B.V. Reprinted by permission of the author and the publisher.

Hans J. Vermeer, "Skopos and Commission in Translation Theory." In *Readings in Translation Theory*, ed. and trans. Andrew Chesterman (Helsinki: Oy Finn Lectura Ob, 1989), pp. 173–87. Used by permission of the author, the translator, and the publisher.

Jean-Paul Vinay and Jean Darbelnet, "A Methodology for Translation." In Jean-Paul Vinay and Jean Darbelnet, *Comparative Stylistics of French and English: A Methodology for Translation*, trans. and eds. Juan C. Sager and M.-J. Hamel, Amsterdam and Philadelphia: Benjamins, 1995, pp. 31–42. Copyright © 1995 by John Benjamins B.V. Reprinted by permission of the publisher.

I am indebted to Richard Sieburth and Elena Reeves for their incisive and useful comments on my translation of Antoine Berman's essay.

My essay, "Translation, Community, Utopia," benefited from readings by Jean Boase-Beier, Terry Hale, and Susan Wells, as well as questions and comments from appreciative audiences where I delivered it in various stages of completion. For these opportunities to speak in lecture series, seminars and conferences, I thank Mohammed Abdel Aatty and the organizing committee of the Fifth International Symposium on Comparative Literature at Cairo University, David Bellos (Princeton University), Peter Bush (British Centre for Literary Translation, University of East Anglia, and the Institute of Translation and Interpreting), Maria González Davies (Universitat de Vic), Geoffrey Harris (European Studies Research Institute, University of Salford), Michael Henry Heim and Katherine King (University of California at Los Angeles), Serena Jin and Chan Sin Wai (The Chinese University of Hong Kong), Alberto Alvarez Lugrís and Maria Teresa Caneda (Universidad de Vigo), Millicent Marcus (University of Pennsylvania), Marta Mateo Martínez-Bartolomé (Universidad de Oviedo), Susan Matthias (New York University), Ramon Ribé (Universidad de Barcelona), and Nicholas Round (University of Sheffield).

Louisa Semlyen, my editor at Routledge, gave her unflinching encouragement and helpful advice throughout this project (and patiently waited for its delivery). Katharine Jacobson, Jody Ball and, in its early stages, Miranda Filbee were superbly efficient in getting a very complicated book into production. Hannah Hyam copy-edited the print-out with her customary precision and Susan Dunsmore proofread the galleys with care.

The Italian verse in the dedication is drawn from Milo De Angelis's poem "Un maestro" in *Millimetri* (Torino: Einaudi, 1983).

I must acknowledge, finally, the forebearance and inspiration of Lindsay Davies, Gemma Leigh Venuti, and Julius David Venuti, who endured my absences during many months of work and were most helpful in distracting me from it.

For the second edition, I relied on the assistance of a number of people. The new translations were expertly vetted by Margaret Devinney (Susan Bernofsky's Schleiermacher), Janet Martin (Kathleen Davis's Jerome), and Steven Rendall (my D'Ablancourt). Richard Sieburth gave my version of Jacques Derrida's essay a painstakingly close reading that led to many improvements. Patricia Crouch and Miriam Fried helpfully spotted typographical errors in the first edition.

Louisa Semlyen not only saw the need for this revision, but believed in the value of the form I wanted to give it. Christy Kirkpatrick greatly facilitated an onerous production process. Kate Parker efficiently took care of permission payments.

For working conditions that were essential to my timely completion of this project – apart from being generally enjoyable – I remain grateful to Martha Tennent.

L.V.
New York City
September 2003

INTRODUCTION

Translation studies: an emerging discipline

THIS READER GATHERS documents that represent many of the main approaches to understanding translation in the West from antiquity to the present. It concentrates on approaches that have been developed during the twentieth century, focusing particularly on the past thirty years. It was during this period that translation studies emerged as a new academic field, at once international and interdisciplinary. The need for a reader is thus partly institutional, created by the rapid growth of the discipline, especially as evidenced by the proliferation of translator training programs worldwide. Recent surveys indicate more than 250, offering a variety of certificates and degrees, undergraduate and graduate, training not only professional translators, but also scholar-teachers of translation and of foreign languages and literatures (Caminade and Pym 1995, periodically updated at www.fut.es/~apym; Harris 1997).

This growth has been accompanied by diverse forms of translation research and commentary, some oriented toward pedagogy, yet most falling within – or crossing – traditional academic disciplines, such as linguistics, literary criticism, philosophy, and anthropology. The principal aim of the reader is to bring together a substantial selection from this varied mass of writing, but in the form of a historical survey that invites sustained examination of key theoretical developments.

Of course, edited volumes always work to define a field, a body of knowledge, a textbook market, and so they create as much as satisfy institutional needs, especially in the case of emergent disciplines. In translation studies, the broad spectrum of theories and research methodologies may doom any assessment of its current state to partial representation, superficial synthesis, optimistic canonization. This reader is intended, nonetheless, to be an introduction to the field recognizable to the scholars who work within it.

But recognition must not be construed as mirror reflection. The intention is also to challenge any disciplinary complacency, to produce a consolidation that interrogates the ways in which translation is currently researched and taught by revealing – even if implicitly – the limitations of scholarly knowledge and pedagogical practices, to show what translation studies have been and to suggest what they might be. Perhaps the most effective way to issue this challenge is to enable a historical perspective. "A translator without a historical consciousness," wrote the French translator and translation theorist Antoine Berman, remains "a prisoner to his or her representation of translating and to those representations that convey the 'social discourses' of the moment" (Berman 1995: 61, my translation). In assembling this reader, I am suggesting that scholars of translation, as well as translators, can significantly advance their work by taking into account the historical contexts in which translation has been practiced and studied.

The readings are organized into six chronological sections; the date of publication for each reading appears at the foot of its first page. The documents gathered in the first section, all predating the twentieth century, have exerted such a powerful influence on later practices and commentary as to warrant the term "foundational." The next five sections are divided into decades of the twentieth century. Whether a decade stands on its own or is combined with others depends, in the first instance, on the volume of translation commentary published within it, sheer bibliographical quantity (cf. the bibliographies in Morgan 1959, Steiner 1975, Schulte and Biguenet 1992). But there is also a qualitative standard: as the readings move towards the present, the level of sophistication and inventiveness does in fact rise, and new concepts, methods, and research projects are developed, justifying separate sections for the 1980s and the 1990s and beyond.

The sections are each prefaced by introductory essays which describe main trends in translation studies, establishing a context for concise expositions of the readings and calling attention to the work of influential writers, theorists, and scholars who are not represented by a reading. The section introductions are historical narratives that refer to theoretical and methodological advances and occasionally offer critical evaluations. Yet the stories they tell avoid any evolutionary model of progress, as well as any systematic critique. I wanted to outline, however rapidly, the history of the present moment in translation studies. And to some degree this meant asking questions of the past raised by the latest tendencies in theory and research.

The map of translation studies drawn here, its centers and peripheries, admissions and exclusions, reflects the current fragmentation of the field into subspecialties, some empirically oriented, some hermeneutic and literary, and some influenced by various forms of linguistics and cultural studies which have resulted in productive syntheses. The effort to cast a wide net has not encompassed certain areas of translation research, whose volume and degree of specialization demand separate coverage regardless of their importance to translation studies (e.g. inter-preting and machine translation). And breadth of coverage has limited depth of representation for particular theories and approaches. The section introductions aim, in brief space, to supply some omissions and to sketch a historical setting. And the bibliography not only identifies parenthetical references made throughout the book, but lists additional publications by particularly influential or prolific authors. It will be clear that I have tried to cover much – for some, no doubt, too much – in an effort to suggest the variety of translation studies.

The image of the field fashioned by this reader reflects the contemporary scene all the more closely because it has been produced in consultation with many leading writers and translators, theorists and scholars. They commented on various versions of the table of contents, responded to questions about particular translation tradi-tions and forms of research, suggested specific texts, made lists of names, and criticized my rationale and principles of selection and organization. Any author or text that received a relatively large number of recommendations earned some sort of representation here. In some cases, my consultants encouraged me to collect research that fell outside their specialty. And some helped simply, but most tangibly, by allowing their work to be reprinted without charge.

Their names and locations: Kwame Anthony Appiah (USA), Rosemary Arrojo (USA), Isabelle Berman (France), Annie Brisset (Canada), Peter Bush (Spain), Andrew Chesterman (Finland), Kathleen Davis (USA), Dirk Delabastita (Belgium), Jacques Derrida (France), Itamar Even-Zohar (Israel), Peter Fawcett (UK), Peter France (UK), Sean Golden (Spain), Jean-Marc Gouanvic (Canada), Basil Hatim (United Arab Emirates), Michael Henry Heim (USA), Juliane House (Germany), David Katan (Italy), Suzanne Jill Levine (USA), Philip E. Lewis (USA), Ian Mason (UK), Rachel May (USA), Eugene Nida (Belgium), Christiane Nord (Germany), Abé Mark Nornes (USA), Alexis Nouss (Canada), Anthony Pym (Spain), Elena Reeves (USA), Katharina Reiss (Germany), Steven Rendall (France), Richard Sieburth (USA), Sherry Simon (Canada), Gayatri Spivak (USA), Gideon Toury (Israel), Harish Trivedi (India), Maria Tymoczko (USA), Margherita Ulrych (Italy), Hans Vermeer (Germany), Luise von Flotow (Canada), and Patrick Zabalbeascoa (Spain).

Those who evaluated the project for Routledge also came from the international community of translation scholars: for the first edition, Neus Carbonell (Spain), Michael Cronin (Ireland), Keith Harvey (UK), Theo Hermans (UK), Efrain Kristal (USA), Carol Maier (USA), Kirsten Malmkjaer (UK), Mark Shuttleworth (UK), and Martha Tennent (Spain); for the second edition, Susan Bernofsky (USA), Stefan Herbretcher (UK), Lars Ole Sauerberg (Denmark), Corinne Scheiner (USA), Daniel Simeoni (Canada), and Carmen Valero-Garces (Spain).

The first edition was decisively shaped by my Advisory Editor, Mona Baker (UK), who evaluated every decision I made, every document I wrote. She is a trans-lation scholar who was trained as a linguist and whose field of research is corpus linguistics, computerized analysis of text collections; my work has fallen within literary criticism and cultural studies. We began with some shared ideas, but also with large differences – theoretical, methodological, pedagogical. What we had in common was a set of basic assumptions: that translation studies constitutes an emergent academic discipline; that research and commentary on translation from other disciplines might be useful to translation studies, but does not necessarily fall within it; that many cultures have strong translation traditions in the twentieth century, but that to be influential internationally, writing about translation needs to be written in or translated into an internationalized language such as English (cf. the rich traditions of translation commentary in Russian, Chinese, Brazilian Portuguese, and Catalan, among many other languages, major and minor). These assumptions did not make any easier the difficult process of selecting texts. On the contrary, they led to an effort to limit the inevitable drift toward English-language traditions by considering various untranslated materials, by gathering previously published translations, and by presenting new and improved translations of classic documents. In the end, this reader shows that native speakers of English wrote relatively little of the Western translation theory that has proved influential during the twentieth century and certainly before it.

The differences between me and my advisory editor were equally, if not more, significant because they resulted in many debates over the range of current approaches to translation. These differences and debates reflected the institutional divisions of academic labor, testing the notion of interdisciplinarity by showing that many interdisciplines are possible in translation studies, and that even if disciplines do not share conceptual paradigms and research methods, they might nonetheless be joined together to advance a project on translation. The first edition of the reader was the fruit of such a collaboration, although its final form remained my sole responsibility. For the second edition, I have worked alone.

What is a translation theory?

The increasingly interdisciplinary nature of translation studies has multiplied theories of translation. A shared interest in a topic, however, is no guarantee that what is acceptable as a theory in one field or approach will satisfy the conceptual requirements of a theory in others. In the West, from antiquity to the late nineteenth century, theoretical statements about translation fell into traditionally defined areas of thinking about language and culture: rhetoric, literary theory, philosophy. And the most frequently cited theorists comprised a fairly limited group. One such catalogue might include: Cicero, Horace, Quintilian, Jerome, Augustine, Dryden, Goethe, Schleiermacher, Arnold, Nietzsche. Twentieth-century translation theory reveals a much expanded range of fields and approaches reflecting the differentiation of modern culture: not only varieties of linguistics, literary criticism, philosophical speculation, and cultural theory, but experimental studies and anthropological fieldwork, as well as translator training and translation practice. Any account of theoretical concepts and trends must acknowledge the disciplinary sites in which they emerged in order to understand and evaluate them. At the same time, it is possible to locate recurrent themes and celebrated topoi, if not broad areas of agreement.

Louis Kelly has argued that a "complete" theory of translation "has three components: specification of function and goal; description and analysis of operations; and critical comment on relationships between goal and operations" (Kelly 1979: 1). Kelly is careful to observe that throughout history theorists have tended to emphasize one of these components at the expense of others. The component that receives the greatest emphasis, I would add, often devolves into a recommendation or prescription for good translating.

The Roman poet Horace asserted in his *Ars Poetica* (c. 10 BC) that the poet who resorts to translation should avoid a certain operation – namely, word-for-word rendering – in order to write distinctive poetry. Here the function of translating is to construct poetic authorship, and the immediate goal is a good poem in Horatian or Roman terms. In a lecture entitled "On the Different Methods of Translating" (1813), the German philosopher and theologian Friedrich Schleiermacher advocated word-for-word literalism in language that "departs from the quotidian" to produce an effect of foreignness in the translation: "for the more precisely the translation adheres to the turns and figures of the original, the more foreign it will seem to its reader" (Schleiermacher, this volume). For Schleiermacher, textual operations produce cognitive effects and serve cultural and political functions. These operations, effects and functions are described and judged according to values that are literary and nationalist, according to whether the translation helps to build a German language and literature during the Napoleonic wars. Even with modern approaches that are based on linguistics and tend to assume a scientific or value-free treatment of language, the emphasis on one theoretical component might be linked to prescription. During the 1960s and 1970s, linguistics-oriented theorists emphasized the description and analysis of translation operations, producing typologies of equivalence that act as normative principles to guide translator training.

The surveys of theoretical trends in the section introductions have both benefited from and revised Kelly's useful scheme. To my mind, however, the key category in any translation research and commentary is what I shall call the relative **autonomy** of translation, the textual features and operations or strategies that distinguish it from the foreign text and from texts initially written in the translating language. These complicated features and strategies are what prevent translating from being unmediated or transparent communication; they both enable and set up obstacles to cross-cultural understanding by working over the foreign text. They substantiate the arguments for the impossibility of translation that recur throughout the twentieth century. Yet without some sense of distinctive features and strategies, translation never emerges as an object of study in its own right.

The history of translation theory can in fact be imagined as a set of changing relationships between the relative autonomy of the translated text, or the translator's actions, and two other categories: **equivalence** and **function**. Equivalence has been understood as "accuracy," "adequacy," "correctness," "correspondence," "fidelity," or "identity"; it is a variable notion of how the translation is connected to the foreign text. Function has been understood as the potentiality of the translated text to release diverse effects, beginning with the communication of information and the production of a response comparable to the one produced by the foreign text in its own culture. Yet the effects of translation are also social, and they have been harnessed to cultural, economic, and political agendas: evangelical programs, commercial ventures, and colonial projects, as well as the development of languages, national literatures, and avant-garde literary movements. Function is a variable notion of how the translated text is connected to the receiving language and culture. In some periods, such as the 1960s and 1970s, the autonomy of translation is limited by the dominance of thinking about equivalence, and functionalism becomes a solution to a theoretical impasse, the impossibility of fixing relations of equivalence for every text type and every translation situation. In other periods, such as the 1980s and 1990s, autonomy is limited by the dominance of functionalisms, and equivalence is rethought to embrace what were previously treated as shifts or deviations from the foreign text.

The changing importance of a particular theoretical category, whether autonomy, equivalence or function, may be determined by various factors, linguistic and literary, cultural and social. Yet the most decisive determination is a particular theory of language or textuality. George Steiner has argued that a translation theory "presumes a systematic theory of language with which it overlaps completely or from which it derives as a special case according to demonstrable rules of deduction and application" (Steiner 1975: 280–1). He doubted whether any such theory of language existed. But he nevertheless proceeded to outline his own "conviction" before offering his reflections on translation.

A translation theory always rests on particular assumptions about language use, even if they are no more than fragmentary hypotheses that remain implicit or unacknowledged. For centuries the assumptions seem to have fallen into two large categories: instrumental and hermeneutic (cf. Kelly 1979: chap. 1). Some translation theories have assumed an instrumental concept of language as communication, expressive of thought and meaning, where meanings are either based on reference to an empirical reality or derived from a context that is primarily linguistic, but may also encompass a pragmatic situation. Other theories have assumed a hermeneutic concept of language as interpretation, constitutive of thought and meaning, where meanings shape reality and are inscribed according to changing cultural and social situations. An instrumental concept of language leads to translation theories that privilege the communication of objective information and formulate typologies of equivalence, minimizing and sometimes excluding altogether any question of function beyond communication. A hermeneutic concept of language leads to translation theories that privilege the interpretation of creative values and therefore describe the target-language inscription in the foreign text, often explaining it on the basis of social functions and effects.

These concepts of language and translation are obviously no more than abstractions. Before they can contribute to any explanation or interrogation of translation theories and practices, they require analysis in specific historical contexts. In the section introductions they have been used as heuristic devices to describe and distinguish among different theoretical texts and trends.

Classroom applications

The primary audience imagined for this reader is academic: instructors and students in advanced undergraduate or graduate courses in translation theory, as well as theorists and scholars of translation and practitioners with a theoretical inclination. The institutional sites of such courses vary widely today, including not only trans-lator training programs, but various other departments and programs, such as linguistics, foreign languages, comparative literature, philosophy, and cultural studies. Instructors will of course have their own ideas about how to use a book they decide to require or recommend. In selecting and mulling over the texts that compose the reader, I thought often about potential uses in the classroom. Here are a few suggestions.

Read historically

The chronological organization encourages historical surveys of theoretical trends by focusing on particular traditions, disciplines, or conceptual discourses. Selections spanning decades within the twentieth century can be grouped to show the important impact of the German translation tradition (Benjamin, Steiner, Berman), Czech and Russian formalism (Jakobson, Even-Zohar, Toury, Lefevere), semiotics (Jakobson, Lewis), linguistics (Blum-Kulka, Harvey, Mason), poststructuralism (Lewis, Chamberlain, Spivak, Derrida).

Theoretical trends can be constructed according to different, even opposing narratives of development. The narratives might be problem-solving: earlier theor-ists pose problems that are reformulated more precisely and possibly solved by later theoretical advances (Nida's "dynamic equivalence" is recast in practical terms by Vermeer's emphasis on the translator's goal and commission); or theoretical approaches based on seemingly incompatible assumptions are joined in an innova-tive synthesis (Lewis combines comparative discourse analysis and deconstruction). The emphasis on continuity and progress in such historical narratives can be replaced by an emphasis on discontinuity and present insufficiencies. Thus, a later theorist might be seen as posing a problem for which earlier theories provide a viable solu-tion (Pound recommends that the translator construct a stylistic analogue with literary texts in the receiving culture to compensate for the very loss of foreign textual features that Nabokov laments). Or a theoretical advance in one field might be treated as a limitation in another (Grice's conversational "maxims" enable Blum-Kulka's discourse analysis but undergo Appiah's philosophical critique). Historical groupings are most productive, in other words, when they are accompanied by an awareness of the different narratives that might structure the critical reading of the selections.

Read thematically

The chronological organization can also be set aside in favor of tracing specific themes in translation studies. Selections can be grouped to explore assumptions about language use (instrumental vs. hermeneutic), theoretical concepts (translata-bility and relative autonomy, equivalence and shifts, reception and function), translation strategies (free vs. literal, sense-for-sense vs. word-for-word, domesti-cating vs. foreignizing), particular genres or text types (humanistic, pragmatic), and various cultural and political issues (identity and ideology, power and minority, disciplines and institutions).

A particular theme will bring together a spectrum of differing approaches. The genre of poetry, for example, is at the center of the texts by Benjamin, Pound, and Nabokov, but also those by Dryden and Goethe. Schleiermacher, Lewis, and Derrida address the translation of philosophy. A theme can also provide a cross-section of work in a specific period. Political agendas for translation are described and theor-ized in the 1990s from different perspectives and situations (Brisset, Spivak, Appiah, Harvey, Nornes). Selections can be made contrapuntally, bringing together diverging treatments. Both D'Ablancourt's practices and Vinay and Darbelnet's methodology raise ethical questions when juxtaposed to Berman; Chamberlain includes a feminist critique of Steiner; Mason's examination of European Union documents suggests that Vermeer's functionalism becomes ideologically complicated in political institutions.

Use supplementary readings

Any approach to this reader will be strengthened by a fuller historical or theoret-ical context. Histories of translation theory and practice now exist for many languages, traditions and periods (e.g. Ballard 1992, Copeland 1991, Cronin 1996, Pym 2000, Starke 1999, Tymoczko 1999, van Hoof 1991, Vermeer 1992). Theoretical texts in particular translation traditions have also been collected (e.g. Störig 1963, Horguelin 1981, Bacardí, Fontcuberta and Parcerisas 1998). Reference works, such as Baker's encyclopedia (1998) and Shuttleworth and Cowie's dictionary (1997), can be useful in situating particular texts in the disci-pline of translation studies: they provide detailed entries on theoretical concepts and research methodologies and include historical surveys of translation traditions in various linguistic communities. An instructor might create more language-specific contexts with such reference works as France's guide (2000) to literary translating in English, and Chan and Pollard's encyclopedia (1995) of theories and practices focusing on translation between Chinese and English.

Supplementary readings can be strategic in deepening the representation of a tradition, concept, or theme. The philosophical debates on translatability are repre-sented in the reader by Appiah and Derrida. They might be developed further with texts by Quine (1960), Davidson (1984), and MacIntyre (1988). Meschonnic's hermeneutic orientation (1973) is important for understanding Berman, and Brown and Levinson's politeness theory (1987) for Harvey. Spivak's postcolonial reflec-tions can be extended through the historical and theoretical links between translation and colonial discourse established by Niranjana (1992) and Bhabha (1994). And of course an instructor might assign influential theorists who are not represented here by a text, but nonetheless discussed in the section introductions. Sperber and

Wilson's revelance theory (1986) informs the approach to translation in Gutt (1991), which might be productively studied in relation to Derrida's notion of relevant translation.

The lists of "Further reading" that conclude each introduction can be useful in initiating classroom debates. These very selective lists refer to critical commentary on theoretical trends and concepts and on the work of specific theorists.

Anthologies are always judged by what they exclude as well as include. This reader, given its space limitations and selection criteria, will prove no exception. I am keen, therefore, to hear from instructors who have adopted it for classroom use, whether successfully or with frustration. Information concerning actual reading assignments, the helpfulness of the introductory material, and the usefulness of particular texts will be invaluable in considering revisions for subsequent editions. Please direct any comments to me care of Routledge.

Foundational statements

TRANSLATION THEORY AS WE know it today, the formulation of concepts designed to illuminate and to improve the practice of translation, did not exist in classical antiquity. When commentary about translation first appears in the West, it tends to take the form of passing remarks, not systematic arguments, and it is situated in the academic discipline of rhetoric. Indeed, the first influential commentators – Cicero, Pliny the Younger, Quintilian – are all distinguished Roman orators who consider translation as a pedagogical exercise for aspirants to their profession.

In *De optimo genere oratorum* (46 BC), Cicero describes how, in order to "be useful to students," he composed Latin versions of speeches by the Greek orators, Aeschines and Demosthenes (Cicero 1949: 365). "I did not translate them as an interpreter [*nec converti ut interpres*]," he writes,

> but as an orator, keeping the same ideas and the forms, or as one might say, the "figures" of thought, but in language which conforms to our usage. And in so doing I did not hold it necessary to render word for word, but I preserved the general style and force of the language.
>
> (Ibid.)

Here translation serves the study and imitation of rhetorical models, it is a springboard for the invention of new and better speeches, and this function requires a discursive strategy that is free, paraphrastic, focused on the meaning of the foreign text while adhering to Latin norms.

Cicero's remarks point to another discipline in which translation is practiced at this time: grammar. The grammarian or "interpreter" likewise uses translation to serve an academic function, which in this case is limited to linguistic analysis and textual exposition. Roman education is bilingual, students are taught Greek as well as Latin, and translation exercises are routinely implemented in language learning and literary study. Because of such uses, the grammarian favors a rather different discursive strategy, interpreting the foreign text much more closely, rendering it "word for word."

In ancient Rome, the sparse comments about translation reflect the peculiar institutional status of this writing practice. It is subordinated to the procedures and educational aims of two academic disciplines, rhetoric and grammar. Yet it is also imprinted by their rivalry for cultural authority. In distinguishing his use of translation from that of the grammarian, Cicero suggests that grammatical translation is not useful to the orator. It is rhetoric, moreover, that achieves dominance, mainly because of its capacity to deploy various kinds of knowledge for social and political purposes. Orators argue legal cases and occupy government office; grammarians work in a strictly academic capacity.

The use that Cicero assigns to translation makes clear that it enacts another, more emulative rivalry between Roman and Greek culture. In the Republic and early Empire, Roman authors sought to capitalize on the cultural prestige of Greece by submitting Greek texts to various forms of translation and adaptation. Thus they implicitly expressed their admiration for those texts while aggressively rewriting them to create a distinctively Latin literature. Horace's *Ars Poetica* not only assumes the disciplinary rivalry that informed Roman translation (he sides with the orators), but also indicates how the free translation of Greek texts might aid poetic composition:

> It is difficult to treat common matter in a way that is particular to you; and you would do better to turn a song of Troy into dramatic acts than to bring forth for the first time something unknown and unsung. Public material will be private property if you do not linger over the common and open way, and if you do not render word for word like a faithful translator [*interpres*].
>
> (Trans. in Copeland 1991: 29)

Horace advocates a rhetorical imitation of the foreign text whereby the Homeric epics ("a song of Troy") become sites of invention for the Latin poet, the "public material" from which "private" poems are produced, possibly through a change in genre. These poems are not so much "new" as different in a way that exhibits the poet's individual talent.

The cultural functions of Roman translation stress the relative autonomy of the translated text, minimizing the importance of equivalence by defining it as a general semantic and stylistic correspondence. In late antiquity, however, patristic commentary moves equivalence to the center of thinking about translation because the foreign texts at issue are often key religious documents, notably the Bible. In *De doctrina Christiana* (428 AD), Augustine argues for the authoritative accuracy of the Septuagint, the Greek version of the Hebrew Scriptures prepared in the third century BC. He rehearses the legend of how seventy Hellenistic Jews working independently, "separated in various cells," nonetheless wrote the exact same translations (Augustine 1958: 49). "In all the more learned churches," Augustine observes, "it is now said that this translation was so inspired by the Holy Spirit that many spoke as if with the mouth of one," leading him to conclude that "even though something is found in Hebrew versions different from what they have set down, I think we should cede to the divine dispensation by which they worked" (ibid.). Augustine's standard of accuracy is not so much close adherence to the foreign text as an institutional validation that the translation is divinely inspired regardless of its deviations.

Early Christian commentators take up the paraphrastic translation typical of their Roman predecessors, but it is detached from the disciplinary and cultural rivalries that determined its value for orators, poets, and playwrights. Translating that focuses on the sense of the foreign text, when that text is the Bible, inevitably assumes a religious significance: the resulting translation is seen as a transparent representation of divine meaning. Word-for-word renderings come to be stigmatized not simply because they contain infelicities, given the lexical and syntactical differences between languages, but because they interfere with the transmission of God's word. Nonetheless, the Christian appropriation of the Roman tradition mystifies the extent to which meaning-oriented translation actually revises foreign texts.

This mystification can be glimpsed in the first reading that appears below, **Jerome**'s indignantly defensive *Letter to Pammachius* (395 AD). His treatment of Bible translation turns contradictory in its attempt to synthesize pagan and Christian sources. In justifying his "sense for sense" version of a papal letter, he evinces his respect for the Roman commentators while reserving a "word for word" method for Scripture because, as he states, "the very order of the words is a mystery." Yet he also relies on the authority of the Gospels, which are shown to contain various free renderings of the Hebrew Bible that differ from the Septuagint. Ultimately he asserts that "in Scripture one must consider not the words, but the sense."

Behind this contradiction lies the close connection between sense-for-sense translation and Biblical exegesis. Jerome's examples from the Gospels include renderings of the Old Testament that do not merely express the "sense" but rather fix it by imposing a Christian interpretation. Thus Matthew's version of a sentence from the Book of Hosea –"Out of Egypt I have called my son"– inscribes a prophetic meaning that refers to the Holy Family's flight from Herod, whereas the Hebrew text reads quite differently: "When Israel was a child I loved him, and out of Egypt I called my son." Jerome's Latin version of the Bible, the Vulgate, similarly Christianizes Judaic themes (Kelly 1975: 162). It finally replaces the Septuagint and becomes the translation authorized by the Catholic Church.

With few exceptions, commentators follow Jerome's validation of sense-for-sense translation through the Middle Ages and into the Renaissance, so that when the translating language is no longer classical but vernacular, his precepts are still echoed. His influence extends even to heretical sects who challenge the authority of the Vulgate. The prologue to the Wycliffite Bible (c.1395) asserts that "the beste translating is, out of Latyn into English, to translate aftir the sentence and not oneli aftir the wordis, so that the sentence be as opin either openere in English as in Latyn" (Hudson 1978: 68). The emphasis on intelligibility, on making the language of the translation even more "opin" than Jerome's Latin, shows that the avoidance of word-for-word translation is a proselytizing move designed to increase access to the sacred text. Martin Luther's version of the Bible (1522, 1534) sought to displace the Vulgate by relying on High German, a dialect that is spoken by "the mother in the home, the children on the street, the common man in the marketplace" (Luther 1960: 189). Yet he applies Jerome's sense-for-sense strategy and inscribes Protestant theology through subtle revisions. In his 1530 letter on translating, for example, Luther admits that he inserted a word (*allein*, meaning "alone" or "only") in Jerome's version of a Pauline epistle, arguing that the addition "conveys the sense of the text" (ibid.: 188). In effect, however, the apostle is transformed into an advocate of the Lutheran doctrine of justification by faith alone.

The spread of humanist curricula ensures that during the sixteenth and seventeenth centuries the classical commentators will dominate the discussion and practice of literary translation. Occasionally citing Cicero and Horace as their models, poets produce free versions that are not always distinguished from original compositions and would today fall into the category of adaptations. This development derives partly from a prevalent conception of authorship as imitation (Greene 1982). Hence the versions of Petrarch's sonnets written by Tudor courtiers like Sir Thomas Wyatt and Henry Howard, earl of Surrey, are not identified as translations when they initially circulate in manuscript or finally see print in Richard Tottel's *Miscellany* (1557). Meanwhile translation is regarded as a practice that can be useful in the construction of a national culture. Elizabethan translators such as Sir Thomas Hoby and Philemon Holland display a deep nationalist investment in their work: by making available classical and contemporary texts such as Castiglione's *The Courtier* (1561) and Pliny's *Natural History* (1601), they see themselves as performing the public service of educating their countrymen (Ebel 1969).

The functionalism that accompanies sense-for-sense translation since antiquity is now redefined to fit different cultural and social realities. Translators are forthright in stating that their freedoms are intended not merely to imitate features of the foreign texts, but to allow the translation to work as a literary text in its own right, exerting its force within native traditions. As a result, translation is strongly domesticating, assimilating foreign literatures to the linguistic and cultural values of the receiving situation. The French translator **Nicolas Perrot d'Ablancourt** is exemplary in elevating acceptability in the translating culture over adequacy to the foreign text.

In the prefaces that are included in this volume, D'Ablancourt rationalizes his substantial revisions of Tacitus (1640) and Lucian (1654) by appealing to the canons of French literary taste that his translations help to form. "Diverse times," he argues, "require not only different words, but different thoughts." This view results in translations that are clearer and more stylistically felicitous than the foreign texts, but also bowdlerized. D'Ablancourt tells his reader that he wishes to avoid both "offending the delicacy of our Language" and causing moral offense. He is very much aware that his discursive strategies flout conventional notions of equivalence. Yet he makes clear that his domesticating choices are not arbitrary, but based on an interpretation that displays an acute sense of historical difference. He just does not feel that this difference is worth preserving in itself and certainly not at the cost of departing from an elegant style as he conceives it.

D'Ablancourt initiates a translation tradition whose products are soon labelled "les belles infidèles," beautiful but unfaithful. His ideas gain prestige from his membership in the Académie Française, and throughout the eighteenth century they are given diverse formulations and applications, some more extreme than others. Antoine Houdar de la Motte prefaces his version of the *Iliad* (1714) by frankly describing his many revisions in accordance with neoclassical values. "I have tried to ensure continuity of character," he writes, "since it is this point – which has become so well established in our time – to which the reader is most sensitive, and that also makes him the sternest judge" (Lefevere 1992a: 30). Pierre le Tourneur similarly introduces his version of Edward Young's *Night Thoughts* (1769) by stating his "intention to distill from the English Young a French one to be read with pleasure and interest by French readers who would not have to ask themselves whether the book they were reading was a copy or an original" (ibid.: 39).

Le Tourneur's comment is remarkable for its conceptual sleight of hand. It does not distinguish between a translation that produces an effect equivalent to that of the foreign text and a translation that produces the illusion of originality by effacing its translated status. The tradition of *les belles infidèles* repeatedly collapses this distinction, asserting a correspondence to the foreign author's intention or to the essential meaning of the foreign text while performing revisions that answer to what is intelligible and interesting in French culture. The sheer familiarity of the translation, of its language and style, enables it to seem transparent and thereby pass for the original.

English commentary during the seventeenth and eighteenth centuries is decisively influenced by French developments. Poets such as Abraham Cowley, Sir John Denham, and Sir Richard Fanshawe most likely encounter D'Ablancourt's work in France, where they follow the exiled court of Charles I after the Civil War. Denham's preface to *The Destruction of Troy* (1656), his version of the second book of the *Aeneid*, announces his allegiance to a sense-for-sense strategy that avoids literal renderings, "the vulgar error" of "being *Fidus Interpres*," and instead rewrites the foreign text in English cultural terms (Denham 1656: A2v). "If *Virgil* must needs speak English," Denham asserts, "it were fit he should speak not only as a man of this Nation, but as a man of this age" (ibid.: A3r). Denham makes good his pronouncement by casting the unrhymed Latin verse in the heroic couplets that are beginning to dominate English poetry, while likening Trojan architecture to the royal buildings in England.

After the Restoration, **John Dryden** revises the classical distinction between rhetorical and grammatical translation to take into account the practices employed by his English predecessors. The extract reprinted here, drawn from the preface to his anthology *Ovid's Epistles* (1680), shows him tracing an English tradition of notable poet-translators which stretches back to the start of the seventeenth century. Dryden situates himself in this tradition, although he is careful to declare his preference for a moderately free strategy, "Paraphrase, or Translation with Latitude," which seeks to render meanings. He rejects not only word-for-word versions as lacking fluency or easy readability ("either perspicuity or gracefulness will frequently be wanting"), but also "Imitations" that adapt the foreign text so as to serve the translator's own literary ambitions.

All the same, Dryden underestimates the extent to which paraphrase falls short of maintaining a semantic correspondence and is actually transformative. He suggests that when structural differences between languages complicate the translator's task, the goal should be "to vary but the dress, not to alter or destroy the substance" – as if a change in the means of expression did not change the substance expressed, especially with literary genres such as poetry. The clothing metaphor assumes an instrumental concept of language whereby communication is untroubled by linguistic and cultural differences.

It is precisely this assumption that underlies Alexander Fraser Tytler's *Essay on the Principles of Translation* (1791), the first systematic treatise in English. For Tytler, intercultural communication is possible because he relies on the Enlightenment notion of an essential human nature endowed with reason. Thus he defines "good" translation as producing an equivalent effect that transcends the differences between languages and cultures:

> the merit of the original work is so completely transfused into another language, as to be as distinctly apprehended, and as strongly felt, by a native of the country to which that language belongs, as it is by those who speak the language of the original work.
>
> (Tytler 1978: 15)

To achieve this effect, Tytler recommends paraphrastic translation that imitates the "ideas" and "style" of the foreign text and possesses the "ease of original composition," or such fluency as to seem untranslated (ibid.).

Yet the "merit" of the foreign text is judged, not according to universal reason, but according to the standards of the receiving culture, pre-empting any equivalent effect. Tytler applauds Alexander Pope's translations of the Homeric epics (1715–1726) for deleting passages that "offend, by introducing low images and puerile allusions" (ibid.: 79). Tytler's standards are not simply British; they also reflect the taste of the cultural elite of which he is a member. He urges the translator to "prevent that ease [of original composition] from degenerating into licentiousness" by refusing to render classical literature into popular dialects and discourses:

> If we are justly offended at hearing Virgil speak in the style of the Evening Post or the Daily Advertiser, what must we think of the translator, who makes the solemn and sententious Tacitus express himself in the low cant of the streets, or in the dialect of the waiters of a tavern.
>
> (ibid.: 119)

Tytler's "principles" entail the inscription of the foreign text with linguistic and cultural values that prevail in the receiving situation, starting with the current standard dialect of the translating language.

During the eighteenth century, a growing body of German commentary presents a striking alternative to the French and English traditions. In 1766, Johann Gottfried Herder complains that "the French, who are much too proud of their own taste, adapt all things to it, rather than try to adapt themselves to the taste of another time" (Lefevere 1992a: 74). Language is conceived, not as expressing thought and meaning transparently, but as shaping them according to linguistic structures and cultural traditions which are in turn shaped by language use. Consequently, translation is viewed less as communicating the foreign text than as offering an interpretation that can take diverse forms according to the translator's aims, the genre, and the cultural and social situation in which the translating is done.

Among the German writers who adopt this view, the function that is most often assigned to translating is the improvement of the German language. Johann Heinrich Voss's versions of the *Odyssey* (1781) and the *Iliad* (1793) are frequently cited as exemplary: they are the first in German to recreate the hexameter. Wilhelm von Humboldt includes an homage to Voss in the preface to his own version of Aeschylus' *Agamemnon* (1816). "What strides has the German language not made," writes Humboldt, "since it began to imitate the meters of Greek, and what developments have not taken place in the nation, not just among the learned, but also among the masses, even down to women and children, since the Greeks really did become the nation's reading matter in their true and unadulterated shape?" (Lefevere 1992a: 137).

The fullest theoretical statement in this German trend is **Friedrich Schleiermacher**'s 1813 lecture to the Berlin Academy of Sciences (included here). For Schleiermacher, the ideal translation creates an "image" that incorporates the knowledge and taste of "an amateur and connoisseur, a man who is well acquainted with the foreign language, yet to whom it remains nonetheless foreign." In assigning importance to a sense of foreignness, Schleiermacher excludes not only commercial and pragmatic uses of translation, but the sorts of paraphrase and imitation that long prevailed in translation practice and commentary. He most values humanistic genres and disciplines, especially literature and philosophy. And he at once revives and rehabilitates literalizing strategies. There can be no doubt that he speaks for an elite cultural taste and aims to set it up as a standard for translators and readers of translations. Like Humboldt, he imagines foreignizing translation as a nationalist practice that can build a German language and literature and overcome the cultural and political domination that France exercises over German-speaking lands.

In the passage from the *West-Easterly Divan* (1819) that appears below, **Johann Wolfgang von Goethe** surveys the emerging German tradition by distinguishing between three different kinds of translation. Goethe describes them not in terms of how closely the translator's strategies adhere to the form and meaning of the foreign text, as Dryden had done, but rather in terms of how much the translation preserves the linguistic and cultural differences that constitute the foreignness of that text. Although he observes that the three kinds may occur in the same period, his treatment is both historical and progressive: he moves from Luther to Voss and beyond, so that foreignizing translation becomes "the final and highest" of the three "epochs." For Goethe, this kind of translation issues from a Romantic transcendence in which the translator loses his national self through a strong identification with a cultural other.

In the history of western translation theory, the German tradition marks an important watershed. It abandons the conceptual categories that were repeatedly used since antiquity and develops others that are not only linguistic and literary, but cultural and political. Given **Friedrich Nietzsche**'s incisive critique of western thinking, it is not surprising that he too should display an acute awareness of how translators might efface the differences of foreign texts. The pithy reflections from *The Gay Science* (1882) that conclude this section return to ancient Rome, describing how poets like Horace and Propertius appropriated their Greek predecessors and linking their rhetorical use of translation to Roman imperialism. "What was past and alien was an embarrassment for them," writes Nietzsche, "and being Romans, they saw it as an incentive for a Roman conquest."

Yet Nietzsche might have levelled a similar criticism at the German tradition as well. For although German theorists and practitioners bring an increased self-awareness to translation, treating it as a decisive encounter with the foreign, they translate to appropriate, enlisting foreign texts in German cultural and political agendas. The social functions they assign to their work reveal the imperialistic impulse that may well be indissociable from translation.

Further reading

Amos 1920, Berman 1985 and 1992, Copeland 1991, Daniell 2003, Kelly 1979, Lefevere 1977, Norton 1984, Rener 1989, Robinson 1991 and 1992, Steiner 1975a, Venuti 1995, Zuber 1968

Chapter 1

Jerome

LETTER TO PAMMACHIUS

Translated by Kathleen Davis

I. **T**HE APOSTLE PAUL, when in the presence of King Agrippa to
answer criminal charges in a way his listener would understand, immediately rejoiced, sure of victory for his cause; and he began by saying, "I consider
myself fortunate today, O King Agrippa, because I am to make my defense against
the accusations of the Jews before you who are especially familiar with Hebrew
customs and controversies" [Acts 26:2–3]. Surely he had read the saying in
Ecclesiasticus – "fortunate is he who speaks to attentive ears" [Ecclesiasticus 25:9]
– for he knew that the words of an orator can succeed only so much as the intellect of the judge can perceive. Hence I too, Pammachius, consider myself fortunate
in this affair, since your educated ears will hear my answer to a foolish tongue that
slings allegations of ignorance or deceit at me, claiming that either I was unable or
I refused to translate [*interpretari*]¹ a letter accurately from Greek. Now of these,
the first is an error, the second a crime! So, taking no chance that my accuser –
through a slickness of tongue that exceeds all bounds and an impunity that usurps
all license – might vilify me before you, just as he has accused Pope Epiphanius of
crime, I send this letter in order that you, and through you others who deem me
worthy of their love, may know how the situation came about.²

II. About two years ago Pope Epiphanius sent a letter to Bishop John of
Jerusalem, rebuking him about certain principles of doctrine and afterwards mildly
urging him to repent. Copies of this letter were eagerly snatched up throughout
Palestine, either because of the merit of its author or the elegance of its composition. There was in our monastery a man by no means undistinguished among his
own people, Eusebius of Cremona, who, when this letter was on everyone's lips,

admired by the learned and unlearned alike for its doctrine and flawless style, began ardently to beseech me to turn it into Latin for him and, for ease of understanding, to explain it clearly and simply, since he was entirely ignorant of the Greek language. I did just as he asked: summoning a scribe I dictated swiftly and hastily, briefly annotating in the margins of the page the sense within each main section. Now, here is the case: he had earnestly requested that I make the copy only for himself, and I asked in return that he keep it at home and not willingly make it public. Eighteen months passed thus before the translation [*interpretatio*] – by some novel trick – migrated from his desk to Jerusalem. A certain fraudulent monk, either for a bribe (as the evidence suggests) or out of gratuitous malice (as his corruptor struggles in vain to argue), proved himself another Judas by plundering and seizing Eusebius's papers, thus affording my adversaries a chance to howl against me. Among the uneducated crowd they declare me false, claiming that I did not translate word for word, but wrote "dearest one" for "honorable one," and that – monstrous to say – through a malicious interpretation I chose not to carry over the title αἰδεσιμώτατον [most reverend] for Bishop John. These, and trivialities of this sort, are my crimes.

III. But first, before I address the issue of translation, I wish to question those who call prudence malice. Where did you get a copy of the letter? Who supplied it? By what affrontery do you publish what you have purchased through crime? What among men will be safe, when we cannot keep secrets even within our own walls and desks? If I were to press these charges against you before a tribunal, I would invoke the civil laws that, even in financial cases, decree punishment for informers and, while they accept the betrayal, condemn the betrayer. The gain obviously pleases, but the intent disgusts. Not long ago the consul Hesychius, against whom the patriarch Gamaliel maintained a most grave hostility, was condemned to death by the Emperor Theodosius, because by corrupting a secretary he had confiscated documents. In the ancient histories we read about the double-dealing teacher who betrayed the Faliscan children, and – because the Roman people would not accept shamefully bought victory – was bound and delivered back to his pupils, returned to those whom he had betrayed. When Pyrrus, King of Epirus, was in camp being healed of his wounds, his own doctor treacherously offered to murder him; but his enemy Fabricius preferred to return the doctor in chains to his master, rather than sanction such a heinous crime, even in an enemy. This principle, which public laws and enemies preserve, which is sacred even in the midst of war, has been upheld among the monks and priests of Christ. And does any of them now dare, with raised eyebrows and a snap of the fingers, to belch and say, "So what if he did bribe or extort? He did what served his interest." What an amazing defense of wickedness! As if bandits and thieves and pirates do not do what profits them. Certainly Annas and Caiphas, in seducing the wretched Judas, judged it useful to themselves.

IV. I wish to write trifles in my notebook as I please, to comment upon Scripture, to strike back at those who insult me, to settle my ire, to exercise my writing style in rhetorical commonplaces, and to store arrows as if polished for battle: as long as I do not publish my thoughts they are merely abusive, not criminal; indeed, something never aired in public cannot even be abusive. You may corrupt servants, harass companions and, as we read in fables, rape Danae disguised as a shower of gold. Dissimulating your actions you declare me false, but do you not at the same time confess yourself guilty of more serious crimes than those you charge against me? One man accuses you of heresy, another of perverting dogma: you are silent; not daring to answer the charge itself, you tear the translator [*interpretatem*] to pieces, deprecating mere syllables, and deem your defense complete if you drag down one who remains silent. Suppose I have erred or omitted something in translating: this is the hinge whereon your entire case turns, this your defense! On that account are you not a heretic if I am a poor translator [*interpres*]? I am not reviving the charge of heresy against you – he who made the accusation knows what he wrote – but when accused by one man it is most foolish to charge another and, your body gaping with wounds, to seek comfort in wounding one who sleeps peacefully.

V. Up to now I have spoken as if I did change the letter somewhat, arguing that a simple translation can have mistakes without being criminal. But truly, since the letter shows the sense has not been changed in the least, nor anything added that counters orthodox doctrine, my accusers, as Terence says, "seeking to understand, understand nothing" [*Andria*, prologue] and, wishing to prove another's ignorance, expose their own. Indeed, I not only admit, but freely proclaim that in translation [*interpretatione*] from the Greek – except in the case of Sacred Scripture, where the very order of the words is a mystery – I render not word for word, but sense for sense. In this matter I have the guidance of Cicero, who translated Plato's *Protagoras* and Xenophon's *Oeconomicus* and the two most beautiful orations that Aeschines and Demosthenes delivered against each other. How much he omitted, how much he added, and how much he changed in order to display the properties of another language through the properties of his own, there is not enough time to say. It suffices for me to quote the authority of this translator, who writes in his prologue:

> I have judged it right to undertake a labor useful to students, although certainly not necessary for myself. That is, I have converted the most celebrated orations of two of the most eloquent Attic orators, Aeschines and Demosthenes, which they delivered in debate against each other, not recasting them as a translator [*interpres*], but as an orator, keeping the same meanings but with their forms – their figures, so to speak – in words adapted to our idiom. I have not thought it necessary to pay out one word for another in this process, but have conserved the character and the force of the language. Nor have I thought it fitting to count them out to the reader, but to weigh them out.

Then again in his conclusion he writes:

> If, as I hope, I succeed in expressing these speeches by retaining all their virtues – that is, their meanings and their figures and the order of topics, following the wording only so long as it does not conflict with our idiom – if all are not literally from the Greek, I have at least endeavored to match them according to type . . . etc.

And then there is Horace, a wise and learned man, who likewise advises the skilled translator [*interpretati*] in his *Ars Poetica*: "Do not strive to render word for word like a faithful translator [*interpres*]." Terence has translated Menander, and Plautus and Caecilius have translated the ancient comic poets: now, do they simply cling to the words or rather conserve the greater beauty and elegance in their translations? What you call truthfulness in translation [*interpretationis*], the educated call κακοζηλίαν or "overzealousness." Twenty years ago, having been educated in this tradition of overzealousness and likewise deceived by its error, and certainly not anticipating your accusations against me, I turned the *Chronicle* of Eusebius of Caesarea into Latin. Even then I urged in my preface:

> It is difficult, when following the lines of another, not to overshoot somewhere and arduous, when something is well put in another language, to preserve this same beauty in translation. To a degree signification is one with the very property of a word: I do not have a comparable word in my language with which to express it, and in seeking to satisfy the meaning, I take a long way around to cover barely the space of a few words. Joined to this difficulty are the twists of hyperbaton, the differences in grammatical cases, the varieties of rhetorical figures and, finally, what I might call the peculiar native character of the language: if I translate [*interpretor*] word by word, it sounds absurd; if out of necessity I alter something in the order or diction, I will seem to have abandoned the task of a translator [*interpretis*].

After discussing much else that would be tedious to follow here, I added:

> If anyone does not think that translation [*interpretatione*] alters the charm of a language, let him force Homer word for word into Latin. Better yet, let him translate [*interpretatur*] Homer into prose. He will see that the syntax becomes ridiculous, and the most eloquent poet barely articulate.

VI. Now, there may be little authority in my words – by this example I wished only to prove that from adolescence I have transferred not the words, but the meaning – yet as an example of the same type read and consider this short preface to a life of St. Anthony:

> A translation expressed word for word from one language into another conceals the sense just as an overabundant pasture strangles the crops. Since speech observes cases and figures, this method takes a long way around to cover barely the space of a few words. Therefore, I have shunned this method in translating, at your request, the life of St. Anthony, so that nothing is lost from the sense when I have had to change the words. Let others chase after syllables and letters, you seek the meaning.

Time will run out if I repeat the testimony of all those who have translated according to the sense. It suffices for the present to cite Hilary the Confessor, who in turning some homilies on Job and many commentaries on the psalms from Greek into Latin, did not attend to the drowsy letter nor contort himself by translating [*interpreta-tione*] the boorish style of rustics, but by right of victory carried the sense captive into his own language.

VII. Nor should it seem surprising that secular and ecclesiastical writers translate [*interpretes*] in this way, when the Seventy Translators, the Evangelists, and the Apostles did likewise with the Sacred Books.[3] We read in Mark that the Lord said, "*talitha cumi*," and immediately added "which is translated [*interpretatur*]: young woman, I say to you, arise" [Mark 5:41]. The Evangelist might be denounced for deceit in adding "I say to you," when the Hebrew had merely "young woman, arise." Yet to make it ἐμφατικώτερον [more emphatic] and to express the sense of calling and commanding, he added "I say to you." Again in Matthew, when the thirty pieces of silver are returned by Judas and the potter's field bought with them, it is written: "Then was fulfilled as written what had been spoken by the prophet Jeremiah: and they took the thirty pieces of silver, the price of him on whom a price had been set by the sons of Israel, and they gave them for the potter's field, as the Lord directed me" [Matthew 27:9–10]. Now this is not to be found in Jeremiah, but in Zechariah, in far different words and in an entirely different order. Indeed, the Greek of the Septuagint has "And I will say to them: if in your heart it seems good to you, give me my wages; otherwise, refuse them. And they weighed out my wages as thirty pieces of silver. And the Lord said to me: cast them into the furnace, and consider if it has been tried as I was tried by them. And I took the thirty pieces of silver and threw them into the furnace in the house of the Lord" [Zechariah 11: 12–13]. Here it is certainly evident how much the testimony of the Evangelist departs from the Septuagint translation. And, in the Hebrew, while the sense is the same, the words are turned about and nearly contradictory. It reads: "And I said to them: If to your eyes it seems good to you, bring forth my wages; and if not, do nothing. And they weighed out my wages as thirty pieces of silver. And the Lord said to me: cast them to the potter, a suitable price, for it is the price they set upon me. And I took the 30 pieces of silver, and cast them to the potter in the house of the Lord." One might accuse the Apostle of falsehood, since he agrees neither with the Hebrew nor with the Septuagint translators, and, what is worse, he errs in the attribution, saying Jeremiah instead of Zechariah. But far be it from me to say such a thing about a follower of Christ, whose care it was not to chase after words and syllables, but to set forth the meaning of doctrine.

Let us give another example of the same sort from Zechariah, which John the Evangelist takes from the Hebrew truth: "They will gaze upon him whom they have pierced" [John 19–37]. For this the Septuagint reads: "They will look upon me, because they have mocked me," which the Latin version translates [*interpretati*] as "And they will gaze upon me because of those things they have mocked" or "insulted." The Evangelist, the Septuagint and our Latin translation of Zechariah each differ, yet the various modes of expression unite in one spirit. In Matthew we also read of the Lord foretelling the flight of the Apostles, and confirming this with a quotation from Zechariah: "It is written," he says, "I will strike the shepherd, and the sheep will be scattered" [Matthew 26:31; Zechariah 13:7]. But in the Septuagint and the Hebrew it is much different, for this is not said by the person of God himself, as the Evangelist would have it, but by the prophet entreating God the Father: "strike the shepherd, and the sheep will be scattered." Here, I believe, as do certain other prudent men, the Evangelist might stand accused of sacrilege for daring to attribute the words of a prophet to the person of God. The same Evangelist, Matthew, writes that Joseph, warned by an angel, took the infant and his mother, went into Egypt and there remained until the death of Herod, so that God's word spoken through the prophet Hosea would be fulfilled: "Out of Egypt I have called my son" [Matthew 2:15]. Our Greek and Latin translations of Hosea do not have it this way, but according to the Hebrew truth it is written: "When Israel was a child I loved him, and out of Egypt I have called my son" [Hosea 11:1]. For this the Septuagint translates, "When Israel was an infant I loved him, and out of Egypt I have called his sons." Now, are all those to be scorned who differ in translating this passage, which pertains to the mystery of Christ, or rather be granted indulgence, in the spirit of the following passage from James: "We all offend in many things, and he who never offends in speaking is a perfect man and can restrain the entire body" [James 3:2]? Another example appears in Matthew where it is written: "He came and lived in a city called Nazareth, so that what was spoken by the prophets might be fulfilled, that he would be called a Nazarene" [Matthew 2:23]. Let the word-smiths and the fastidious judges of all things written answer where they have read this, and let them discover its place in Isaiah. Now, in this place, where we have read and translated: "There shall come forth a shoot out of the root of Jesse, and a bough shall grow from its roots" [Isaiah 11:1], the Hebrew, according to the ιδίωμα [idiom] of that tongue, has "There shall come forth a shoot out of the root of Jesse, and a Nazarene shall spring from its roots." Why is the word Nazarene omitted in the Septuagint? If it is not permitted to replace one word with another, then certainly it is a sacrilege to conceal or to ignore a mystery of God.

VIII. We should proceed to other examples – a brief letter forbids one to dwell on a single point. Matthew also says, "All this took place in order to fulfill what the Lord had spoken through the prophet: behold a virgin shall have in her womb [*in utero habebit*] and bear a son and they shall call his name Emmanuel" [Matthew 1:22–23; Isaiah 7:14]. Which the Septuagint translates as "Behold a virgin shall receive in her womb [*in utero accipiet*] and bear a son, and you shall call his name Emmanuel." Can mere words defame us? Well then, certainly "She shall have" and "she shall receive" and "they shall call" and "you shall call" are not the same thing. Moreover, in the Hebrew we read it written thus: "Behold a virgin shall conceive [*concipiet*] and bear a son, and she shall call his name Emmanuel." It is not Achaz, who was charged with infidelity, nor the Jews, who would deny the Lord, but she herself who shall name him, the virgin herself, who will conceive and bear him. Elsewhere in this Evangelist we read how Herod was disturbed by the arrival of the Magi, and, gathering his scribes and priests, he inquired of them where Christ would be born. And they responded, "In Bethlehem of Judea; for so it was written by the prophet: 'and you, Bethlehem, the land of Judah, are not the least among the rulers of Judah; for from you shall come a ruler to govern my people Israel'" [Matthew 2:5–6]. This passage the Septuagint renders: "And you, Bethlehem, house of Ephratah, are small to be among the thousands of Judah; from you one shall come forth to me to be prince of Israel." The degree of difference between Matthew and the Septuagint, in both words and syntax, will amaze you even more if you look at the Hebrew, where it is written, "And you, Bethlehem Ephratah, are little among the thousands of Judah; yet out of you one will come forth to me, who will be a ruler in Israel" [Micah 5:2]. Consider phrase by phrase what is set forth by the Evangelist: "And you, Bethlehem, land of Judah": for "land of Judah" the Hebrew has "Ephratah," and the Septuagint has "the house of Ephratah." Consider next, the Evangelist's phrase "you are not the least among the leaders of Judah." In the Septuagint this reads, "you are small to be among the thousands of Judah," and in the Hebrew, "you are little among the thousands of Judah." Here the Evangelist gives a contrary sense to the Septuagint and to the Hebrew, which in this passage agree closely. For the Evangelist says that Bethlehem is not small among the leaders of Judah, even though it is directly stated: "you are indeed little and small; but little and small as you are, out of you will come forth to me a leader of Israel" – which follows the saying of the Apostle Paul: "God chose what is weak in the world in order to confound the strong" [1 Corinthians 1:27]. Lastly, what follows in Matthew: "who shall govern" or "who shall support" my people Israel clearly differs from the words of the prophet.

IX. I reveal these things, not to declare the Evangelists guilty of falsehood – indeed, such an accusation is reserved for the impious, like Celsus, Porphyry and Julian the Apostate – but to convince my accusers of their ignorance and to seek indulgence from them, so they will concede to me in the matter of this simple letter that which, like it or not, they must concede to the Apostles in the matter of Sacred Scripture. Here is a telling example. Mark, the disciple of Peter, begins his gospel: "The beginning of the Gospel of Jesus Christ, as it is written in Isaiah the prophet: Behold, I send my messenger before your face, who shall prepare your way. A voice of one crying in the wilderness; prepare the way of the Lord, make straight his paths" [Mark 1:1–3]. This passage is a composite from two prophets – Malachi, obviously, and Isaiah. The first part, which says "Behold I send my messenger before your face, who shall prepare your way," is from the end of Malachi; the second part, however, which is interpolated, "a voice of one crying in the wilderness" etc., we read in Isaiah. How then does Mark, at the very opening of his text, state "as it was written in Isaiah the prophet: Behold I send my messenger," when this is not in Isaiah, as I have said, but in Malachi, the last of the twelve prophets? Let the ignorant in their presumption solve this little puzzle, and I in turn will seek indulgence for my deviations from Epiphanius's letter. The same Mark, moreover, also introduces the Saviour speaking to the Pharisees thus: "Have you never read what David did when he and his followers were needy and hungry: how he entered the house of God, then under the high-priest Abiathar, and ate the bread of presentation, which is not lawful for any except the priests to eat?" [Mark 2:25–26]. Reading Samuel – or, as it is commonly known, the Book of Kings – we will discover that the high priest was not Abiathar but Achimelech, whom afterward Saul ordered killed by Doeg, along with the other priests.

We can go on to the Apostle Paul, who writes to the Corinthians: "If they had known, they would never have crucified the Lord of glory. But, as it is written, no eye has seen, nor ear heard, nor the heart of man conceived, what God has prepared for those who love him" [1 Corinthians 2:8–9]. Commentators on this passage typically root through the ravings of the apocrypha and claim that it is taken from the Apocalypse of Elijah, but in the Hebrew text of Isaiah we read: "From the beginning, none have heard nor perceived by the ear. No eye has seen, God, besides you, what you have prepared for those who wait for you" [Isaiah 64:4]. The Septuagint translates this much differently: "From the beginning, we have not heard, nor have our eyes seen a God besides you and your true works, and you will provide mercy for those who wait for you." We can plainly understand the source of this passage, yet the Apostle does not translate word by word, but παραφραστικῶς [through periphrasis], as it is said in Greek, he expressed the same sense in different phrasing. In his epistle to the Romans the same blessed apostle, taking a passage from Isaiah, says: "Behold, I lay in Zion a stumbling stone and a rock of scandal" [Romans 9:33; Is. 8:14]. He differs here from the Septuagint and yet agrees with the Hebrew truth, for the Septuagint has the contrary sense: "So that you do not fall upon a stumbling stone or a rock of destruction." And when Peter cites this passage he agrees with both Paul and the Hebrew text: "But for the unbelieving a stumbling stone and a rock of scandal" [1 Peter 2:8]. All these examples make clear that in interpreting the Old Testament the Apostles and Evangelists sought the sense, not the words, and did not particularly take pains with the syntax and style, so long as the truth lay open to understanding.

X. Luke, Apostle and Evangelist, writes that Stephen, Christ's first martyr, in dispute with the Jews said: "With seventy-five souls Jacob went down into Egypt, and he died, he himself and our fathers, and they were carried back to Shechem; and they were laid in the tomb that Abraham had bought with silver from the sons of Hamor, the son of Shechem" [Acts 7:14–16]. This passage takes a very different form in Genesis, where clearly Abraham purchased from Ephron the Hittite, son of Zohar, a double tomb and a field near Hebron for 400 *didrachma* of silver and afterward buried his wife Sarah there [Genesis 23:8–16]. But later in Genesis we read that Jacob, returning from Mesopotamia with his wives and his sons, pitched his tent near Salem, the city of Shechem in the land called Canaan, and dwelled there, purchasing the field where he had pitched his tents from Hamor, father of Shechem, for 100 lambs; and raising an altar there he called upon the God of Israel [Genesis 36:18–20]. So, in this chapter, Abraham did not buy a tomb from Hamor whose father was Shechem, but from Ephron son of Zohar; the tomb is not in Shechem, but in Hebron, mistakenly called Arboc. The twelve patriarchs are not buried in Arboc but in Shechem, and the field was not purchased by Abraham, but by Jacob. I will put off solving this little puzzle so my detractors may themselves inquire and understand that in Scripture one must consider not the words, but the sense.

Yet another example. The twenty-first psalm in the Hebrew text begins with the same words that the Lord spoke on the cross: "*heli heli lama zabtani*," which is translated [*interpretatur*] as "My God, my God, why have you forsaken me?" [Psalm 21:1]. Can my detractors in turn explain why the Seventy Translators added "look upon me"? For they render it: "God, my God, look upon me, why have you forsaken me?" Surely they will answer that none of the meaning is damaged if these few words are added. So then let them grant that I have not imperiled the position of the churches by letting a few words slip in swift dictation.

XI. It would be tedious to disclose how much the Septuagint added and deleted, which in Church copies is marked off by daggers and asterisks. Indeed, the Jews inevitably laugh when they hear what we read in Isaiah, "Blessed is he who has seed in Sion and a household in Jerusalem," and laugh no less at the passage in Amos after the description of *luxuria*: "They have regarded these things as permanent rather than fleeting." This is actually fine rhetoric with a Ciceronian flair. But what shall we do with the authoritative books, in which these and so many similar passages do not appear, when the publication of such differences would fill countless volumes? Formerly, as I have said, omissions were marked by an asterisk, or diligent readers compared our translation [interpretatio] to older ones. But despite all this, the Septuagint rightly remains the church edition – either because it is the original, made before Christ's coming, or because it was used by the Apostles – but only in those places where it does not conflict with the Hebrew. However, we rightly reject Aquila, a proselyte and a contentious translator [interpres], who attempts to transfer not just single words, but their etymology. Who can accept or comprehend for "corn and wine and oil" his χεῦμα, ὀπωρισμόν, στιλπνότητα or, as we would say, "profusion, fruitfulness, and brightness"? Or that, because the Hebrew marker for the accusative corresponds to the preposition "with," this man must – κακοζήλως – interpret by syllables and letters and therefore say σὺν τὸν οὐρανὸν καὶ σὺν τὴν γῆν or "[God created] with the heaven and with the earth" [Genesis 1:1], which makes no sense in either Greek or Latin? We could give examples of this in our own idiom. For so much that is beautifully expressed by the Greeks does not, if transferred literally, resound in Latin; and conversely, what sounds pleasing to us, if converted by strict word order, would displease them!

XII. But in order to bypass this endless discussion and show you, most Christian of nobles, and most noble of Christians, the kind of falsehood they rebuke in my translation of Epiphanius's letter, I give the beginning of this letter with the Greek wording, so that through a single accusation others may be understood, Ἔδει ἡμᾶς, ἀγαπητέ, μὴ τῇ οἰήσει τῶν χλήρων φέρεσθαι, which I recall having converted to "It is fitting, dearest one, that we not abuse our privilege as clergy out of pride." "Look," they cry, "how many lies in one short line! First, ἀγαπητός is 'dear one,' not 'dearest one'; then, οἴησις means 'esteem,' not 'pride' – for it says not οἰήματι but οἰήσει, of which the former means 'a swelling' and the latter signifies 'a judgment'; and the rest of the sentence is your own interpolation." What do you say, O pillar of literature and Aristarchus[4] of our times, you who pass judgment on all writers? In vain, then, have we studied so long and, as Juvenal says, "often winced under the rod" [Satires I]? Sailing from port, we shipwreck immediately. And so, since to err is human and to admit error is prudent, I beg you, my critic, whoever you are, to amend the error – O teacher – and render word for word. "You ought to have said," you tell me, 'It is fitting, dear one, that we not overestimate the clergy'." This the eloquence of Plautus, this the Attic charm worthy of the Muses! The well-worn proverb is fulfilled in me: He loses both his ointment and his money, who sends a bull into a wrestling match.

All this is not the fault of my accusers, who are like actors playing roles in a tragedy, but of their teachers, who for a high price have taught them to know nothing. By no means do I criticize uncultivated speech in a Christian – if only we would have that Socratic wisdom, "I know what I do not know," and that of another wise man, "Know yourself!" My deepest respect has always been not for crude verbosity but for holy simplicity: those who say that they imitate the apostles in speech must first imitate them in life. Their simplicity of speech was vindicated by the abundance of their sanctity; and the resurrection of the dead confuted the syllogisms of Aristotle and the contrivances of Chrysippus. We must admit, however, that it would be absurd for any one of us living here amidst the wealth of Croesus and the delights of Sardanapalus to boast himself a simple rustic, as if to claim that bandits and criminals become something else if they hide their bloody swords in philosophy books instead of tree trunks.

XIII. This has exceeded the measure of a letter, but has not exceeded the depth of my offense. Yet although I am called a liar and shredded upon a shuttle by girls in a weaver's shop, I am content to absolve it without retaliation. I leave the whole matter to your judgment, as you read the letter both in Greek and in my Latin, and instantly perceive the extravagant dirges and lamentations of my accusers. Satisfied that I have instructed my dearest friend, I await the Judgment Day concealed in my cell. And I hope, if possible, although my enemies may rage, to write commentaries on Scripture rather than philippics like Demosthenes and Cicero.

Translator's notes

1　Jerome uses two sets of terms to refer to the agent, process and product of translating: one relating to *interpres*, which follows classical authors such as Cicero and Horace, and the other relating to *translator*. When the former is rendered here as "translate," the Latin will be enclosed in brackets.

2　Pammachius was a Roman senator who abandoned his political career to become a monk. Jerome is writing to him about the accusations made by a former friend, Rufinus, with whom he was involved in a dispute concerning the Origenistic heresy. Bishop Epiphanius of Salamis had written a letter to Bishop John of Jerusalem, charging him with preaching the heresy. After Jerome's Latin translation of this letter was published, his enemies, including Rufinus, accused him of inserting deliberate falsifications for the purpose of disparaging John. Rufinus is probably the "heretic" occasionally mentioned here.

3　The lengthy discussion of Biblical translation that follows forms part of a broader campaign by Jerome. He had become dissatisfied with the Greek Septuagint and Old Latin translations, which he frequently critiqued. At the time of this letter he was in the process of retranslating the Hebrew (which he often calls the "Hebrew truth") directly into Latin. His version, known as the Vulgate, gradually displaced the Old Latin and eventually became the official Church version.

4　Jerome is referring to Aristarchus of Samothrace, head of the Alexandrian Library (*c.* 180–145 BC) and a prolific textual critic. He produced editions of Homer, Hesiod, Alcaeus, Anacreon, and Pindar, as well as voluminous commentaries on literary and grammatical subjects.

Chapter 2

Nicolas Perrot d'Ablancourt

PREFACE TO TACITUS

Translated by Lawrence Venuti

I WOULD NEVER HAVE VENTURED to divide this Work into two Parts had not Fortune rent it asunder before me. Although Tacitus bequeathed us the history of four Emperors in his *Annals*, only the first and last remain, the second is entirely lost, and of the third we possess no more than half. I have therefore deemed it appropriate to devote one volume to the Reign of Tiberius, reserving those of Claudius and Nero for a second Part – should I some day be seized by the desire to continue.[1] The present volume is, nevertheless, Tacitus's masterpiece, as well as the life of a great Politician, which is the métier wherein our Author excels. The rest of his History might have been composed by someone else; nor did Rome lack its Ranters to depict the vices of Caligula, the stupidity of Claudius, and the cruelties of Nero. But to write the life of a Prince like Tiberius required a Historian like Tacitus, who could unravel all the intrigues in the Cabinet, assign genuine causes to events, and distinguish pretense and appearance from truth. For here one never encounters, as one does in other Histories, a long succession of wars and battles; and if you except the military exploits of Germanicus treated in the first and second Books, you will find no others that are not disposed of within thirty lines and are not more commendable for the consequences that the Author draws from them, and the circumstances that he notes in them, than for the grandeur or beauty of the events. All the same, as he often considers things from some strange angle, he occasionally leaves his narratives incomplete, a quality which, together with the multitude of errors that appear in them and the dim light that presently shines upon most things whereof they treat, engenders the obscurity in his works. One need not marvel, therefore, that he is so difficult to translate, seeing that he is difficult even to understand. He is, furthermore, wont to mix in the same sentence, sometimes in the same phrase, diverse thoughts which bear not the slightest relation to each other, and of which a part is inevitably lost (as when one polishes a work) in the effort to express the rest without offending the delicacy of our Language and the correctness of the argument. For people do not have the same respect for my French as for his Latin; and they would not forgive me things that they often admire in him and even – if it might be put thus – revere. Everywhere else I have followed him step by step, and rather as a slave than as a companion, although I might have allowed myself more freedom since I was not translating a passage, but a Book, every part of which must be linked together and fused as in the same body. Furthermore, the diversity that one finds amongst languages is so great, in the construction and shape of periods as well as in figures and other ornaments, that at every turn one must adopt a different air and visage, unless one wishes to create a monstrous body, such as those of ordinary translations, which are either dead and listless or confused and muddled, without any order or charm. Hence one must take heed that an Author's grace not be lost through too much scrupulousness, and that the fear of being unfaithful to him in some one thing not result in infidelity to the whole: principally when one is creating a work that is to take the place of the original, and one is not endeavoring to help young people understand Greek or Latin. For one knows that bold phrases are not exact, because correctness is the enemy of grandeur, as can be seen in painting and writing. Yet a bold stroke supplies the want of correctness, and such phrases are deemed more beautiful than if they were more in conformity with the rules. It is difficult, moreover, to be very exact when translating an Author who is not himself exact. One is often forced to add something to his thought in order to clarify it; at times it is necessary to retrench one part in order to give birth to all the rest. This means, however, that the best translations seem to be the least faithful. Indeed, a Critic of our time has noted two thousand errors in Amyot's Plutarch,[2] while another found almost as many in Erasmus's translations,[3] perhaps because they did not know that the diversity of Languages and styles obliges the use of completely different expressions, since eloquence is such a delicate thing that sometimes a mere syllable is enough to spoil it. For after all it is hardly likely that such great Men were mistaken in so many places, even though it is not unusual for a mistake to be made here and there. But not everyone is capable of judging a translation, although everyone is of the opinion that he is. Here as elsewhere, Aristotle's maxim should serve as the rule: one must needs trust each man concerning his own Art.[4] It is time, however, to proceed to other considerations, and to conclude this Preface.

One should not be surprised, first of all, to hear mention of Centurions and Cohorts, the Angrivariens and the Cattes. The translator has been forced to retain these terms because ancient armies do not correspond to ours, and Germany has undergone so many changes that it no longer contains the same Provinces or the same Peoples. As for the ancient system of money, I would not have retained it had I not found great disadvantages in the one used today. For since Roman money differs from ours, sometimes when we need a round sum, it comes out quite contrary. For example, Arminius promises one hundred sesterces per day to the soldiers who surrender to him; if I insert seven livres ten sous, which is pretty near the same amount, I would render the thing ridiculous. For who would ever conceive of making such a promise? One might offer soldiers a pistole or an écu, or something of the kind, but seven livres ten sous, or six livres fifteen, would be absurd. I have therefore retained the ancient form, and I contented myself with putting the value in the margin to prevent obscurity. It remains to speak of proper nouns, with which I have not followed any particular rule because none in fact exists. We say Marc Antoine and Marc Aurele, but we do not say, in my view, Marc Agrippa or Marc Ciceron. We say Quinte-Curce, but not Quinte-Ligaire. As for the Ancients' custom of designating days as Nones, Ides, and Calends, I had initially followed it because it adds some majesty, but in the end I abandoned it to avoid making a mystery of a thing that is naught, and that is marvelous only in its extravagance. That is virtually all I have felt obliged to explain in this Preface. I shall add only that I have not observed any of these rules so exactly that I did not occasionally exempt myself from it, either to avoid the awkward pronunciation of a word, or for some other reason. Truly the Latins were even more religious than we in this respect, taking pains to prevent any offense to the delicacy of their language by barbaric and foreign terms. Our own Fathers said Naples and the Tiber, not Napoli and the Tevere, in order to accommodate things to their pronunciation. But before concluding, to provide some information regarding our Author, I shall say that he descended from Roman Knights, that he flourished under Vespasian's Empire and the following reigns, and that after having passed through all the great Offices of the Republic, cherished by the foremost men of his century, he finally enjoyed the glory of having an Emperor who bore his name and belonged to his family.[5]

PREFACE TO LUCIAN

To Monsieur Conrart, Counselor and Secretary to the King[6]

Monsieur,

As things return to their origin and ordinarily end where they commenced, it was only just that I dedicate my final Translation to him who enjoyed my first fruits; and so Minucius Felix[7] having given birth to our friendship, Lucian was to bring about its perfection. It was necessary, furthermore, not merely that affixed to the frontispiece should be a name that banishes every ill opinion which might sully this Work, but that the Author's libertinage should be overshadowed by Monsieur Conrart's virtue. I would add that this Book could not honorably appear in public under any auspices but your own, since you have done so much to bringing it into the world, and your sound advice is the reason that it sees the light in a more perfected state. This is not, then, so much a gift as an act of grateful recognition, although an interested recognition, since it begs the protection of him whom it would recognize as its benefactor. And truly, Monsieur, since it is principally you who moved me to undertake this Version, you ought to share the censure or praise that may attend it – apart from the fact that it will meet with monsters enough at its birth to justify the search for a Protector. But that you might not reproach me for rashly implicating you in a quarrel which you were better off without, I aim to equip you with weapons to defend yourself, and to shield us both from Calumny.

Every complaint that may be lodged against me falls under two Heads: Design and Way of Proceeding. For some will say that this Author ought not to have been translated, whilst others will say that he ought to have been translated otherwise. I wish therefore to respond to these two objections, after having said something about Lucian which will serve as my justification and clarify the reasons that led me to translate him.

Lucian was a native of Samosata, capital of Commagene, and he was not of gentle birth, for his father, lacking the means to maintain him, resolved that he should learn a métier; but since his first efforts did not show promise, he threw himself into Letters, after a dream which is reported at the beginning of this Work. He himself says that he embraced the profession of Barrister; but since he abhorred wrangling and the other vices of the Bar, he resorted to Philosophy as to a refuge. To judge from his Writings, he was a Rhetor who made Eloquence his profession and composed Declamations and Harangues on diverse subjects, even Pleas for Law Courts, although none of his work in this vein survives. He first took up residence in Antioch, whence he shifted to Ionia and Greece, then to Gaul and Italy, and afterwards returned to his country via Macedonia. Yet he clearly lived a stretch of time in Athens, where he also acquired its vices and virtues. He finally withdrew from the activities of which I have spoken, in order to devote himself to Philosophy; this is why he complains somewhere that people want him to embark on them anew in his old age. He lived ninety years, being born before Trajan's reign and outlasting Marc Aurele, under whom he was held in great esteem and became the Emperor's Administrator in Egypt. Suidas, the Byzantine lexicographer, maintains that dogs had torn him to pieces; but this is apparently calumny, a gesture of revenge because in his raillery he did not spare the first Christians any more than others. Yet what he said of them can be related, in my view, to their charity and simplicity, which is more praise than injury; besides, one should not expect a eulogy of Christianity from a Pagan. Some believed that he was a Christian; but it is not evident in this Book. True, for a Foreigner he knows many of our mysteries, although Judea's nearness and dealings with Christians, along with his natural curiosity, might have enabled him to come by all this knowledge. Others have sought to represent him as a paragon of wisdom and learning. But in addition to the love of Boys, to which he was inclined, and his scant awareness of the Deity, he cannot be pardoned for having vilified the reputations of the most eminent Men on the strength of Rumor – or rather their enemies' tales. For even though one might excuse him by arguing that his sights were not trained on them, but on those who misuse their names to hide their vices, he obviously let slip no opportunity to traduce them and always made some biting remark *en passant*. Furthermore, the manner in which he treated the most significant matters makes abundantly clear that he was not deeply learned in Philosophy, and that he had acquired only what was of use for his profession of Rhetor, which was to speak pro and con on all kinds of subjects. Yet it cannot be denied that he was one of the readiest Wits of his century, who is everywhere delicate and charming, with a gay and playful humor and that gallant air which the ancients termed *urbanity*, not to mention the cleanness and purity of his style as well as his elegance and civility. I find him only a bit coarse in matters of Love, whether that should be imputed to the spirit of his time or to his own. Indeed, when he wishes to speak of it, he leaps the bounds of decency and forthwith tumbles into the obscene, which is the mark of a debauched rather than a gallant wit. He also displays the mark of a Ranter when he wishes to say everything and does not conclude when he must needs do, a vice that springs from too much wit and learning. Nevertheless, it is a great proof of the merit and excellence of his Works that they have been preserved down to our day, seeing the little affection that people have felt for their Author and the wreck of so many other vessels of Antiquity which have been lost through mischance or negligence; and obviously Christians as well must have found that he could be much more profitable than injurious. More, never did a man so effectively lay bare the vanity and imposture of false Gods, or the pride and ignorance of Philosophers, along with the frailty and inconstancy of human things; and I doubt that there exist better Books in this respect. For he sweetly steals into the intellect through raillery; and his Moral is all the more useful as it is pleasing. Herein too one can learn a thousand most curious things; it is like a bouquet of flowers selected from the finest specimens of the Ancients. I leave aside the point that the Myths are treated in an ingenious fashion that is most conducive to impressing them on the memory and contributes not a little to the understanding of Poets. One need not find strange, then, my decision to translate this Book, following the example of several learned Persons who have produced Latin Versions, whether of one Dialogue or another; and I am the less blameworthy as I have retrenched what was most obscene and, in some passages, tempered what was too loose. Thus have I entered upon the justification of my way of proceeding, for my design is well justified by the many advantages that the public can derive from reading this Author. I shall say only that I have left his opinions wholly intact, since otherwise this would not have been a Translation, but I respond to the most intemperate in the Argument or in the Remarks, so that no injury might result.

As the greatest number of things found herein consists only of polite turns of phrase and raillery, which are different in every Language, a Translation in accord with the rules was impossible. There are even some Pieces, like *The Vowels' Judgment*,[8] which could not be translated at all, and two or three others which hinge on the distinctive quality of Greek terms and will not be understood outside of that context. All comparisons drawn with Love address the Love of Boys, which was not foreign to the morals of Greece, but which is abhorrent to ours. At every turn, the Author cites some verses from Homer, which would now be pedantry, to say nothing of the old, too banal Myths, the Proverbs, the Examples and the antiquated Comparisons, which would today produce an effect completely contrary to his design; for here it is a question of Gallantry, not erudition. It was therefore necessary to change all that, in order to make something pleasing; otherwise, it would not be Lucian; and what pleases in his Language would not be tolerable in ours. Furthermore, as the most beautiful visages always contain something that one wishes were not there, so the best Authors contain passages that must needs be altered or clarified, particularly when things are done solely to please; for then one cannot permit the slightest flaw; and should there be any want of delicacy, one will not divert, but bore. Hence I do not always cleave to the words or thoughts of this Author; whilst keeping in sight his purpose, I fit things to our air and manner. Diverse times require not only different words, but different thoughts; and

Ambassadors are accustomed to dress in the fashion of the country where they have been sent for fear of appearing ridiculous to those whom they endeavor to please. Nevertheless, this is not properly a Translation; but it rates more highly than a Translation; and the Ancients did not translate otherwise. Terence deployed this very method with the Comedies that he took from Menander, even though Aulus Gellius does not leave off calling them Translations; the name is of no importance, provided that we have the thing. Cicero resorted to the same method in his *Offices*, which are scarcely but a Version of Panaetius; and in those Versions that he had made from the Orations of Demosthenes and Aeschines, he says that he worked not as an Interpreter, but as an Orator; which is the very thing that I want to say of Lucian's Dialogues, although I did not permit myself the same freedom throughout. I have translated many passages word for word, at least as much as one can do so in an elegant Translation; there are also passages wherein I have heeded more what should be said, or what I could say, than what he had said, following the example of Virgil in those passages that he took from Homer and Theocritus. But I have restrained myself almost everywhere without descending into details, a practice that is not followed in our time. I am well aware, however, that this will not please everyone, particularly those who idolize every word and every thought of the Ancients and do not believe that a Work can be good if its Author is still living. For these sorts of people will carp as they did in Terence's time,

Contaminari non decere Fabulas,

That one must not corrupt one's Author, or in any way tamper with his subject; but I shall respond with Terence's help,

Faciunt nae intelligendo, ut nihil intelligant,
Qui cum hunc accusant, Naevium, Plautum, Ennium
Accusant, quos hic noster authores habet.
Quorum aemulari exoptat negligentiam
Potius, quam istorum obscuram diligentiam.[9]

How well "obscuram diligentiam" articulates the defect of scrupulous Translations, which require one to read the Original to understand the Version!

Thus have I presented, Monsieur, what I had to say in my defense. I leave to your valor and shrewdness, not to mention your zeal and affection, how best to employ these weapons which are more strong than bright – should your name not suffice to disperse my enemies and prevent them from showing themselves. Come what may, I shall attribute every favorable outcome to the glory of my defender, and I shall remain all my life,

Monsieur,

Your most humble and obedient servant,

Perrot Ablancourt

Translator's notes

1   D'Ablancourt published the second volume in 1644.

2   Jacques Amyot (1513–1593), professor of Greek and Latin at the University of Bourges, produced French versions of such works as Longus's *Daphnis and Chloe* (1559) and Plutarch's *Lives* (1559, 1565).

3   The translations produced by the scholar and theologian Desiderius Erasmus (?1466–1536) include a Latin version of the New Testament.

4   The "maxim" is actually not Aristotle's, but attributed to the followers of Pythagoras by Montaigne in his *Apology for Raymond Sebonde* (D'Ablancourt 1972: 122–123n.24).

5   The emperor is Marcus Claudius Tacitus, who reigned briefly in the third century AD and claimed descent from the historian.

6   With the support of Cardinal Richelieu, Valentin Conrart (1603–1675) founded the Académie Française in 1635 and for the next four decades served as its secretary.

7   Marcus Minucius Felix, an early Latin apologist for Christianity, wrote the dialogue *Octavius* which D'Ablancourt translated anonymously in 1637. His version of Lucian did not prove to be his last translation; he subsequently rendered Thucydides (1662) and a collection of ancient apophthegms (1663).

8   In this rhetorical work, a jury of vowels judges a suit brought by the Greek letter sigma against tau. D'Ablancourt replaced it with an original composition, *Dialogue des Lettres de l'Alphabet*, a fantasy on French spelling assigned to Frémont d'Ablancourt.

9   D'Ablancourt drew these lines from the prologue to Terence's play *Andria* (ll.16–21). In a note he provided a French translation that is generally faithful while omitting the Latin authors' names: "They undo reason by dint of reasoning. For by upbraiding it, they upbraid the Ancients, who serve as its surety, and whose negligence he would rather imitate, than the obscure exactitude of others" (the French version is quoted in D'Ablancourt 1972: 188n.25; my translation).

Chapter 3

John Dryden

FROM THE PREFACE TO
OVID'S EPISTLES

IT REMAINS THAT I SHOULD say somewhat of Poetical Translations in general, and give my opinion (with submission to better Judgments) which way of Version seems to me most proper.

All Translation I suppose may be reduced to these three heads.

First, that of Metaphrase, or turning an Authour word by word, and Line by Line, from one Language into another. Thus, or near this manner, was *Horace* his Art of Poetry translated by *Ben. Johnson*.[1] The second way is that of Paraphrase, or Translation with Latitude, where the Authour it kept in view by the Translator, so as never to be lost, but his words are not so strictly follow'd as his sense, and that too is admitted to be amplyfied, but not alter'd. Such is Mr. *Wallers* Translation of *Virgils* Fourth *Æneid*.[2] The Third way is that of Imitation, where the Translator (if now he has not lost that Name) assumes the liberty not only to vary from the words and sence, but to forsake them both as he sees occasion: and taking only some general hints from the Original, to run division on the ground-work, as he pleases. Such is Mr. *Cowleys* practice in turning two odes of *Pindar*, and one of *Horace* into *English*.[3]

Concerning the first of these Methods, our Master *Horace* has given us this Caution,

> Nec verbum verbo curabis reddere, fidus
> Interpres—

Nor word for word too faithfully translate. As the *Earl* of *Roscommon* has excellently render'd it.[4] Too faithfully is indeed pedantically: 'tis a faith like that which proceeds from Superstition, blind and zealous: Take it in the Expression of Sir *John Denham*, to Sir *Rich. Fanshaw*, on his Version of the *Pastor Fido*.[5]

> That servile path, thou nobly do'st decline,
> Of tracing word by word and Line by Line;
> A new and nobler way thou do'st pursue,
> To make Translations, and Translators too:
> They but preserve the Ashes, thou the Flame,
> True to his Sence, but truer to his Fame.

'Tis almost impossible to Translate verbally, and well, at the same time; For the *Latin*, (a most severe and Compendious Language) often expresses that in one word, which either the Barbarity, or the narrowness of modern Tongues cannot supply in more. 'Tis frequent also that the Conceit is couch'd in some Expression, which will be lost in *English*.

> atque idem venti vela fidemque ferent[6]

What Poet of our Nation is so happy as to express this thought Literally in *English*, and to strike Wit or almost Sense out of it?

In short the Verbal Copyer is incumber'd with so many difficulties at once, that he can never disentangle himself from all. He is to consider at the same time the thought of his Authour, and his words, and to find out the Counterpart to each in another Language: and besides this he is to confine himself to the compass of Numbers, and the Slavery of Rhime. 'Tis much like dancing on Ropes with fetter'd Leggs: A man may shun a fall by using Caution, but the gracefulness of Motion is not to be expected: and when we have said the best of it, 'tis but a foolish Task; for no sober man would put himself into a danger for the Applause of scaping without breaking his Neck. We see *Ben. Johnson* could not avoid obscurity in his literal Translation of *Horace*, attempted in the same compass of Lines: nay *Horace* himself could scarce have done it to a *Greek* Poet.

> Brevis esse laboro, obscurus fio.[7]

Either perspicuity or gracefulness will frequently be wanting. *Horace* has indeed avoided both these Rocks in his Translation of the three first Lines of *Homers Odysses*, which he has Contracted into two.

> Dic mihi Musa Virum captæ post tempora Trojæ
> Qui mores hominum multorum vidit & urbes.
> Muse, speak the man, who since the Siege of Troy,   } *Earl of*
> So many Towns, such Change of Manners saw.   } *Rosc.*

But then the sufferings of *Ulysses*, which are a Considerable part of that Sentence are omitted.

> "Ος μάλα πλλά πλάγχθη[8]

The Consideration of these difficulties, in a servile, literal Translation, not long since made two of our famous Wits, Sir *John Denham*, and Mr. *Cowley* to contrive another way of turning Authours into our Tongue, call'd by the latter of them, Imitation. As they were Friends, I suppose they Communicated their thoughts on this Subject to each other, and therefore their reasons for it are little different: though the practice of one is much more moderate. I take Imitation of an Authour in their sense to be an Endeavour of a later Poet to write like one who has written before him on the same Subject: that is, not to Translate his words, or to be Confin'd to his Sense, but only to set him as a Patern, and to write, as he supposes, that Authour would have done, had he liv'd in our Age, and in our Country. Yet I dare not say that either of them have carried thir libertine way of rendring Authours (as Mr. *Cowley* calls it) so far as my Definition reaches. For in the *Pindarick Odes*, the Customs and Ceremonies of Ancient *Greece* are still preserv'd: but I know not what mischief may arise hereafter from the Example of such an Innovation, when writers of unequal parts to him, shall imitate so bold an undertaking; to add and to diminish what we please, which is the way avow'd by him, ought only to be granted to Mr. *Cowley*, and that too only in his Translation of *Pindar*, because he alone was able to make him amends, by giving him better of his own, when ever he refus'd his Authours thoughts. *Pindar* is generally known to be a dark writer, to want Connexion, (I mean as to our understanding) to soar out of sight, and leave his Reader at a Gaze: So wild and ungovernable a Poet cannot be Translated litterally, his Genius is too strong to bear a Chain, and *Sampson* like he shakes it off: A Genius so Elevated and unconfin'd as Mr. *Cowley*'s, was but necessary to make *Pindar* speak *English*, and that was to be perform'd by no other way than Imitation. But if *Virgil* or *Ovid*, or any regular intelligible Authours be thus us'd, 'tis no longer to be call'd their work, when neither the thoughts nor words are drawn from the Original: but instead of them there is something new produc'd, which is almost the creation of another hand. By this way 'tis true, somewhat that is Excellent may be invented perhaps more Excellent than the first design, though *Virgil* must be still excepted, when that perhaps takes place: Yet he who is inquisitive to know an Authours thoughts will be disapointed in his expectation. And 'tis not always that a man will be contented to have a Present made him, when he expects the payment of a Debt. To state it fairly, Imitation of an Authour is the most advantagious way for a Translator to shew himself, but the greatest wrong which can be done to the Memory and Reputation of the dead. Sir *John Denham* (who advis'd more Liberty than he took himself,) gives this Reason for his Innovation, in his admirable Preface before the Translation of the second *Æneid*: "Poetry is of so subtil a Spirit, that in pouring out of one Language into another, it will all Evaporate; and if a new Spirit be not added in the transfusion, there will remain nothing but a *Caput Mortuum*". I confess this Argument holds good against a litteral Translation, but who defends it? Imitation and verbal Version are in my Opinion the two Extreams, which ought to be avoided: and therefore when I have propos'd the mean betwixt them, it will be seen how far his Argument will reach.

No man is capable of Translating Poetry, who besides a Genius to that Art, is not a Master both of his Authours Language, and of his own: Nor must we understand the Language only of the Poet, but his particular turn of Thoughts, and of Expression, which are the Characters that distinguish, and as it were individuate him from all other writers. When we are come thus far, 'tis time to look into our selves, to conform our Genius to his, to give his thought either the same turn if our tongue will bear it, or if not, to vary but the dress, not to alter or destroy the substance. The like Care must be taken of the more outward Ornaments, the Words: when they appear (which is but seldom) litterally graceful, it were an injury to the Authour that they should be chang'd: But since every Language is so full of its own proprieties, that what is Beautiful in one, is often Barbarous, nay sometimes Nonsense in another, it would be unreasonable to limit a Translator to the narrow compass of his Authours words: 'tis enough if he choose out some Expression which does not vitiate the Sense. I suppose he may stretch his Chain to such a Latitude, but by innovation of thoughts, methinks he breaks it. By this means the Spirit of an Authour may be transfus'd, and yet not lost: and thus 'tis plain that the reason alledg'd by Sir *John Denham*, has no farther force than to Expression: for thought, if it be Translated truly, cannot be lost in another Language, but the words that convey it to our apprehension (which are the Image and Ornament of that thought) may be so ill chosen as to make it appear in an unhandsome dress, and rob it of its native Lustre. There is therefore a Liberty to be allow'd for the Expression, neither is it necessary that Words and Lines should be confin'd to the measure of their Original. The sence of an Authour, generally speaking, is to be Sacred and inviolable. If the Fancy of *Ovid* be luxuriant, 'tis his Character to be so, and if I retrench it, he is no longer *Ovid*. It will be replyed that he receives advantage by this lopping of his superfluous branches, but I rejoyn that a Translator has no such Right: when a *Painter* Copies from the life, I suppose he has no priviledge to alter Features, and Lineaments, under pretence that his Picture will look better: perhaps the Face which he has drawn would be more Exact, if the Eyes, or Nose were alter'd, but 'tis his business to make it resemble the Original. In two Cases only there may a seeming difficulty arise, that is, if the thought be notoriously trivial or dishonest; But the same Answer will serve for both, that then they ought not to be Translated.

—Et quae
Desperes tractata nitescere posse, relinquas.[9]

Thus I have ventur'd to give my opinion on this Subject against the Authority of two great men, but I hope without offence to either of their Memories, for I both lov'd them living, and reverence them now they are dead. But if after what I have urg'd, it be thought by better Judges that the praise of a Translation Consists in adding new Beauties to the piece, thereby to recompence the loss which it sustains by change of Language, I shall be willing to be taught better, and to recant. In the mean time it seems to me, that the true reason why we have so few Versions which are tolerable, is not from the too close persuing of the Authours Sence: but because there are so few who have all the Talents which are requisite for Translation: and that there is so little praise and so small Encouragement for so considerable a part of Learning.

To apply in short, what has been said, to this present work, the Reader will here find most of the Translations, with some little Latitude or variation from the Authours Sence: That of *Oenone* to *Paris*, is in Mr. *Cowleys* way of Imitation only. I was desir'd to say that the Authour who is of the *Fair Sex*,[10] understood not *Latine*.

But if she does not, I am afraid she has given us occasion to be asham'd who do.

For my own part I am ready to acknowledge that I have transgress'd the Rules which I have given; and taken more liberty than a just Translation will allow. But so many Gentlemen whose Wit and Learning are well known, being Joyn'd in it, I doubt not but that their Excellencies will make you ample Satisfaction for my Errours.

Editor's notes

1   The poet and dramatist Ben Jonson (1572–1637) translated Horace's "Art of Poetrie" around 1605 and then revised his version after 1610 when a new edition of the Latin text appeared.

2   In 1658 Edmund Waller (1606–1687) completed the version of the fourth *Aeneid* begun by Sidney Godolphin (1610–1643), who died in the Civil War. Both poets were associated with the court of Charles I. Waller's smooth prosody was much admired in his lifetime and during the eighteenth century.

3   The poet Abraham Cowley (1618–1667) first published his *Pindarique Odes* in 1656.

4   Wentworth Dillon (1633–1685), the fourth Earl of Roscommon, translated Horace's *Ars Poetica* into blank verse (1680) and wrote a treatise in couplets, *Essay on Translated Verse* (1684).

5   The poet Sir John Denham (1615–1669) wrote an influential translation of the second *Aeneid*, entitled *The Destruction of Troy* (1656). In 1648 Sir Richard Fanshawe (1608–1666) produced an English version of Battista Guarini's pastoral drama, *Il pastor fido* (The Faithful Shepherd), to which Denham contributed a commendatory poem.

6   This line, taken from Ovid's *Heroides* ("Dido Aeneae," 7.8), may be rendered closely as follows: "And will the same winds carry away your sails and your fidelity?"

7   Jonson's version of this line from Horace's *Ars Poetica* (l.25) reads: "My selfe for shortnesse labour, and am stil'd/Obscure."

8   Dryden is quoting a portion of *Odyssey* 1.1–2. Robert Fagles's 1996 version renders the phrase as "driven time and again off course." Here are Fagles's opening lines:

> Sing to me of the man, Muse, the man of twists and turns
> driven time and again off course, once he had plundered
> the hallowed heights of Troy.
> Many cities of men he saw and learned their minds,
> many pains he suffered, heartsick on the open sea.

9   Jonson's version of these lines from Horace (ll.149–150) reads: "letting goe/What he despaires, being handled might not show."

10   Dryden is referring to the novelist and dramatist Aphra Behn (1640–1689), who also translated La Rochefoucauld's maxims (1685) and Bernard de Fontenelle's *A Discovery of New Worlds* (1688).

Chapter 4

Friedrich Schleiermacher

ON THE DIFFERENT METHODS OF TRANSLATING

Translated by Susan Bernofsky

THAT UTTERANCES ARE TRANSLATED from one language to another is a fact we meet with everywhere, in the most diverse forms. If, on the one hand, men are thus brought together who were originally separated perhaps by the span of the earth's diameter, and if one language can become the receptacle of works written many centuries before in a tongue long since deceased, we need not, on the other hand, even go beyond the bounds of a single language to encounter the same phenomenon. For not only do the dialects of the different clans that make up a people, and the different ways a language or dialect develops in different centuries, already constitute different languages in a stricter sense, between which it is often enough necessary to translate; even contemporaries who share a dialect but belong to different classes that rarely come together in social intercourse and diverge substantially in their education are commonly unable to communicate save through a similar mediation. Yea, are we not often compelled to translate for ourselves the utterances of another who, though our compeer, is of different opinions and sensibility? Compelled to translate, that is, wherever we feel that the same words upon our own lips would have a rather different import than upon his, or at least weigh here the more heavily, there the more lightly, and that, would we express just what he intended, we must needs employ quite different words and turns of phrase; and when we examine this feeling more closely so that it takes on the character of thought, it would appear that we are translating. Indeed, we must sometimes translate our own utterances after a certain time has passed, would we make them truly our own again. This ability is employed not only to transplant to foreign soil the scientific and rhetorical accomplishments of a given tongue, thus enlarging the sphere of their influence; it also enters into business transactions between different individual peoples and in diplomatic relations between independent governing bodies, each of which, by custom, speaks only its own language when addressing the others so as to maintain strict equality without their availing themselves of a dead language.

Still, not all that lies within this broad realm should play a role in our present inquiry. The compulsion to translate in response to a more or less momentary need will always be too confined to the moment in its effects to require other guidance than that of feeling; and if rules for this were to be given, they would have to be such as to produce a purely moral state of mind in which the spirit remains receptive even to what is most unlike itself. Let us set this case aside and restrict ourselves for the nonce to considering only translations from a foreign tongue into our own; here too we will be able to distinguish two separate areas – not clearly defined, to be sure, for that is rarely possible, but even these blurred boundaries will appear distinct enough if one examines the ultimate goals in either case. The interpreter plies his trade in the area of business, while the translator proper works above all in the areas of science and art. If these definitions appear arbitrary, interpretation being commonly understood to refer more to oral translation and translation proper to the written sort, may we be forgiven for choosing to use them thus out of convenience in the present instance, particularly as the two terms are not at all distant from one another. The areas of art and science are best served by the written word, which alone can make their works endure; and interpreting scientific or artistic products aloud would be just as useless as, it seems, impossible. For business transactions, however, writing is only a mechanical means; verbal negotiation is their original mode, and every written interpretation should be seen only as the record of a spoken exchange.

Bordering this area are two others closely akin to it in spirit and nature, yet given the great variety of objects embraced by them, they already form a transition to the areas of art, in the one case, and of science, in the other. For every negotiation involving an interpreter is an event whose particulars are set down in two different tongues. But even the translation of purely narrative or descriptive writings which merely transmits a previously described sequence of events into another tongue can still have much about it of the interpreter's trade. The less obvious the author's presence was in the original, and the more he served merely as an organ of apperception guided by his object's spatial and temporal organization, the more the translation will be a matter of mere interpreting. Thus the translator of newspaper articles and ordinary travel literature tends to make common cause with the interpreter, and it will soon become ridiculous if he claims for his work too high a status and wishes to be respected as an artist. The more, however, the author's own particular way of seeing and drawing connections has determined the character of the work, and the more it is organized according to principles that he himself has either freely chosen or that are designed to call forth a particular impression, the more his work will partake of the higher realm of art, and so too the translator must bring different powers and skills to his work and be familiar with his author and the author's tongue in a different sense than the interpreter. Every negotiation that uses an interpreter involves, as a rule, setting down a particular state of affairs within a specific framework; the interpreter is working only for the benefit of participants sufficiently familiar with these affairs, and the phrases that express them in both languages are determined in advance either by law or by usage and mutually agreed-upon conventions. Quite a different matter are the sorts of negotiations that, although often similar in form to the conventional ones, are intended to establish new frameworks. The less the latter can themselves be considered specific instances of a recognized general principle, the more scientific knowledge and care will be required in their very composition, and the greater the knowledge of technical details and terminology needed for the translator to carry out his task. Upon this twofold ladder, then, the translator ascends higher and higher above the interpreter until he reaches the realm most properly his, namely, those works of art and science in which the author's free individual combinatory faculties, on the one hand, and the spirit of the language along with the entire system of views and sentiments in all their shadings represented in it, on the other, count for everything; the object no longer dominates in any way, but rather is governed by thought and feeling; indeed, it often comes into existence only through being uttered and exists only in this utterance.

Yet what is the basis for this important distinction that is visible even in these borderline regions but shines forth most brilliantly at the furthest extremes? Business dealings generally involve a matter of readily apparent, or at least fairly well defined objects; all negotiations are, as it were, arithmetical or geometrical in nature, and numbers and measures come to one's aid at every step; and even in the case of notions that, as the ancients already observed, encompass the greater and lesser within themselves and are indicated by a graded series of terms that vary in ordinary usage, making their import uncertain, habit and convention soon serve to fix the usage of the individual terms. So long as the speaker does not smuggle in hidden vaguenesses with intent to deceive, or err out of carelessness, he will be perfectly comprehensible to anyone with knowledge of both the matter under discussion and the language, and in any given case only slight variations in language use will be encountered. Even so there will be scarcely any doubt that cannot easily be remedied as to which expression in the one language corresponds to any given expression in the other. Thus is translation in this realm little more than a mechanical task which can be performed by anyone who has moderate knowledge of the two languages, with little difference to be found between better and lesser efforts as long as obvious errors are avoided. When, however, artistic and scientific works are to be transplanted from one language to another, two sorts of considerations arise which alter the situation. For if in any two languages each word in the one were to correspond perfectly to a word in the other, expressing the same idea with the same range of meaning; if their declensions displayed the same relationships, and the structures of their periods coincided so that the two languages in fact differed only to the ear: then all translation in the areas of art and science, assuming the sole matter to be communicated was the information contained in an utterance or piece of writing, would be as purely mechanical as in business transactions; and, setting aside the effects produced by tone and intonation, one might claim of any given translation that it placed the foreign reader in the same relationship to the author and his work as was the reader of the original. As it happens, however, just the opposite is true for all languages that are not so closely related as to count almost as different dialects of a single tongue, and the further removed they are from one another in etymology and years, the more it will be seen that not a single word in one language will correspond perfectly to a word in another, nor does any pattern of declensions in the one contain precisely the same multiplicity of relationships as in another. Since this irrationality, as I would like to call it, permeates all elements of two languages, it must also, to be sure, affect that sphere of bourgeois affairs we have mentioned. Yet it is obviously less of a hindrance here, having little or no effect. All words that stand for objects and actions that can be of consequence are, as it were, gauged according to a standard measure, and even if, out of unfounded faint-hearted oversubtlety, one were to protest that the words were being inconsistently applied, the simple facts of the matter should serve to resolve all quibbles. Quite different is the case in the arts and sciences, and indeed in every sphere in which thought that is one with speech predominates and it is not the facts that make of the word a perhaps arbitrarily determined and then irrevocably fixed sign. For how infinitely laborious and knotty the business becomes here! What firm knowledge and mastery of the two languages does it require! And how often, where it is generally acknowledged that a perfect equivalent for an expression cannot be found, do even the most knowledgeable scholars, well-versed in both the language itself and the subject matter, diverge significantly in their attempts to choose the most fitting word. This is equally true of the vivid picturesque expressions of poetic works and of the most abstract works of the noblest sciences that show us the most profound and universal nature of things.

The second matter, however, that makes translation proper a quite different activity from ordinary interpreting is this. Wherever utterances are not bound by readily apparent objects or external circumstances which it is merely their task to name — wherever, in other words, the speaker is engaged in more or less independent thought, that is, self-expression, he stands in a twofold relationship to language, and his words will be understood aright only insofar as this relationship itself is correctly grasped. Every human being is, on the one hand, in the power of the language he speaks; he and all his thought are its products. He cannot think with complete certainty anything that lies outside its boundaries; the form of his ideas, the manner in which he combines them, and the limits of these combinations are all preordained by the language in which he was born and raised: both his intellect and his imagination are bound by it. On the other hand, every free-thinking, intellectually independent individual shapes the language in his turn. For how else if not by these influences could it have gained and grown from its raw beginnings to its present, more perfect state of development in the sciences and arts? In this sense, then, it is the living force of the individual that causes new forms to emerge from the tractable matter of language, in each case with the initial aim of passing on a fleeting state of consciousness, but leaving behind now a greater, now a fainter trace in the language that, taken up by others, continues to have an ever broader shaping influence. Indeed, one can say that only to the extent that a person influences language in this way does he deserve to be heard outside his immediate sphere of activity, whatever it may be. Every utterance will quickly pass away if it is such that any one of a thousand voices might reproduce it; only that one is able and entitled to endure which constitutes a new moment in the life of language itself. For this reason, every nobler, free utterance must be grasped in two different senses, first in terms of the genius of the language from whose elements it was derived, as an expressive means tied to and determined by this spirit that brought it to life within the speaker; yet it must also be understood in terms of the speaker himself, as an act that can only have emerged out of, and be explained as a product of, his particular being. Indeed, every utterance of this sort will be understood in the higher sense of the word only when these two sets of relationships are conceived of both together and in their true connection to one another, so that no question remains concerning which of the two dominates in the utterance as a whole and in its individual parts. One understands an utterance as an action of the speaker only if, at the same time, one can feel where and how he was seized by the force of the language, where along its path the lightning flashes of thought snaked their way, where and how in its forms errant imagination was held fast. One understands speech both as a work of language and as an expression of its spirit only if, while feeling that only a Hellene, for instance, can have thought and spoken thus, that only this language can have influenced a human spirit thus, one at the same time feels that only thus can *this man* have thought and spoken in a Hellenic manner, only thus can he have seized and worked to shape this language, and what is here manifested is only his living grasp on the richness of the language, his keen sense of rhythm and euphony, and his capacity to think and to fashion. Now if understanding works of this sort is already difficult even in the same language and involves immersing oneself in both the spirit of the language and the writer's characteristic nature, how much yet nobler an art must it be when we are speaking of the products of a foreign, far distant tongue! To be sure, whoever has mastered this art of understanding by studying the language with diligence, acquiring precise knowledge of the entire historical life of a people and picturing keenly before him the individual works and their authors – *he*, to be sure, and he alone is justified in desiring to bring to his countrymen and contemporaries just this same understanding of these masterworks of art and science. But his scruples must needs multiply when he prepares to approach the task, when the time comes for him to specify his goals and he begins to survey the means at his disposal. Should he really venture to take two men who are as far distant from one another as his countryman who speaks only his own language and the writer himself, and to bring them together in so immediate a relationship as that between a writer and his original reader? Or if he wishes to give his readers only the same understanding and the same pleasure which he himself enjoys, one marked, to be sure, with the traces of his effort, and with the feeling of the foreign admixed with it, how can he achieve even this, let alone provide the understanding and pleasure of the original reader, by the means available to him? If his readers are to understand, then they must grasp the genius of the language that was native to the writer, they must be able to observe his characteristic manner of thinking and sensibility; and all he can offer them as a help for achieving these two things is their own language, corresponding in none of its parts to the other tongue, along with himself, as he has recognized his writer now the more, now the less lucidly, and as he admires and applauds the writer's work now more, now less. Does not translation appear, viewed in this way, an utterly foolish undertaking? Therefore, in despair of reaching this goal, or, if one prefers, before the thought of a goal was even fully formed, two new methods were devised for making the acquaintance of foreign works – not for the sake of genuine artistic and linguistic virtuosity, but rather to fill a spiritual need, on the one hand, and to serve a spiritual art, on the other — methods that eliminate by force some of the difficulties mentioned above, cunningly circumvent others, and in any case altogether abandon the notion of translation we have been proposing; these methods are paraphrase and imitation. Paraphrase sets out to overcome the irrationality of languages, but only in a mechanical way. Its approach is to say: even if I cannot find a word in my language to correspond to the one in the original, I will attempt to approximate its value by adding restrictive and amplifying modifiers. Thus caught between a burdensome too-much and a tormenting too-little, it laboriously works its way through a great mass of individual details. Through this approach it can perhaps reproduce the contents of a work with some accuracy, but the impression made by the work must be dispensed with altogether; for living speech hereby perishes irrevocably, it being clear that all these words could not have sprung originally thus from a human mind. The paraphrast treats the elements of the two languages as though they were mathematical signs that can be reduced to the same value by means of addition and subtraction, and neither the genius of the language being subjected to transformation nor that of the original tongue becomes apparent under this procedure. If, moreover, paraphrase seeks to mark psychologically the traces of the connections between thoughts — wherever these are indistinct and threaten to disappear — with the help of interpolated sentences pounded in like notice stakes, then in the case of more difficult works it is striving at the same time to take the place of a commentary, making it all the less apt to be considered a form of translation. Imitation, on the other hand, surrenders to the irrationality of languages; it concedes that one cannot possibly produce in another tongue a replica of a work of rhetorical art that in its individual parts would correspond perfectly to the individual parts of the original, but that given the differences between languages, with which so many other differences are essentially caught up, we have no other recourse but to contrive a copy, an entire work comprised of parts that differ noticeably from the parts of the original, yet which in its effect comes so close to the original as the differences in the material permit. Now such a copy is no longer the work itself, and it makes no pretense to be showing us the spirit of the original language as an effective force in its own right, particularly as the foreignness this spirit has produced now appears with different underpinnings; rather, a work of this sort, taking into account the differences in language, morals and education, strives to be for its readers, as far as possible, everything the original provided its original readers; for the sake of preserving the unity of the impression made by the work, its identity is sacrificed. The imitator, then, considering impossible any sort of unmediated relationship between the writer and the reader of the imitation, makes no effort to bring the two together; rather, he strives only to give the reader an impression similar to the one received by readers who shared a language and an age with the author of the original. Paraphrase is more commonly found in the sciences, and imitation in the fine arts; and as everyone will concede that a work of art loses its tone, its luster, indeed its very character as art once it is paraphrased, surely no one has yet been so foolish as to attempt to produce an imitation of a scientific masterpiece that rendered its contents loosely. Both these procedures, however, will fail to satisfy someone who, filled with admiration for the excellence of a foreign masterpiece, wishes to enlarge the sphere of its influence to include fellow speakers of his language and has in mind a stricter notion of translation. Neither procedure, then, as they diverge from this notion, can receive more detailed consideration here; they have been named only as landmarks showing the boundaries of the region with which we shall concern ourselves.

Now as for the translator proper who truly wishes to bring together these two quite separate persons, his writer and his reader, and to help the reader, though without forcing him to leave the bounds of his own native tongue behind him, to acquire as correct and complete an understanding of and take as much pleasure in the writer as possible – what sorts of paths might he set off upon to this end? In my opinion, there are only two possibilities. Either the translator leaves the author in peace as much as possible and moves the reader toward him; or he leaves the reader in peace as much as possible and moves the writer toward him. These two paths are so very different from one another that one or the other must certainly be followed as strictly as possible, any attempt to combine them being certain to produce a highly unreliable result and to carry with it the danger that writer and reader might miss each other completely. The difference between these two methods, as well as their relationship to one another, should be obvious at once. For in the first case the translator is endeavoring, in his work, to compensate for the reader's inability to understand the original language. He seeks to impart to the reader the same image, the same impression that he himself received thanks to his knowledge of the original language of the work as it was written, thus moving the reader to his own position, one in fact foreign to him. Yet if the translation wants to make its Roman author, say, speak as he would have spoken and written as a German to Germans, this would not merely move the author as far as the position of the translator – for to him as well the author speaks not German, but Latin – but rather thrust him directly into the world of the German readers and turn him into one of them; this, then, is the second case. The first translation will be perfect in its way if one can say that if the author had learned German just as well as the translator has learned Latin, then he would have translated his work, written originally in Latin, no differently than the translator has done. The other method, however, showing the author not as he himself would have translated but the way that he as a German would have written originally in German, can hardly have any other standard of perfection than if one could claim for certain that, if the German readers were transformed one and all into connoisseurs and contemporaries of the author, the work itself would appear just the same to them as now, the author having been transformed into a German, the translation does. This is no doubt the method imagined by all those who like to say that one should translate an author just as he himself would have written in German. From this juxtaposition it is immediately clear how different a procedure is required in each particular instance, and how, were one to tergiversate within a single work, the whole would become unintelligible and profitless. Yet I will continue to insist that beside these two methods there can exist no third one that might serve some particular end. For there are no other possible ways of proceeding. The two separate parties must be united either at some point between the two – and that will always be the position of the translator – or else the one must betake itself to the other, and only one of these two possibilities lies within the realm of translation, for the other could occur only if, in our case, the German readers were to achieve complete mastery of the Roman tongue or rather would themselves be mastered by it to the point of their ultimate metamorphosis. So whatever else one hears said about translations that adhere to the letter or to the meaning of a work, that are faithful or free, and whatever other expressions might now be in common use – if these too are supposed to be different methods, it must be possible to derive them from the original two; but if failings and virtues are to be described in these terms, then what is faithful and true-to-meaning in the one method, or too literal or too free, will differ in the other. It is therefore my intention, setting to one side all the various questions regarding this subject that have already been treated by the cognoscenti, to examine only the most general characteristics of these two methods so as to prepare for a more general understanding of the characteristic advantages and difficulties of each, the extent to which each most fully achieves the goals of translation, and the limits of applicability in each case. After such a comprehensive survey, there will remain two matters to be treated, for which this discourse is merely the introduction. For each of the two methods one might outline a set of instructions referring to the different rhetorical genres, and one might compare and judge the most admirable efforts that have been made according to both views, and by these means elucidate the matter even further. Both of these tasks I must leave to others, or at least to another occasion.

The method whose aim it is to give the reader, through the translation, the impression he would have received as a German reading the work in the original language, must, to be sure, first decide what sort of understanding of the original language it intends, as it were, to imitate. For there is one sort of understanding that it may not imitate, and another that it cannot. The first is a schoolboyish understanding that bungles its way with great effort and all but distaste through line after line, and yet nowhere arrives at a clear survey of the whole, a living grasp of its contents. As long as the educated part of a nation still has, on the whole, no experience of a deeper knowledge of foreign tongues, then may even those who are further advanced be preserved by their guardian spirits from undertaking translations of this sort. For if they wished to take their own understanding as a standard, they themselves would be little understood and would achieve little; but if their translation aimed to represent ordinary understanding, then the clumsy work could not be booed quickly enough from the stage. During such a period, then, free imitations should first awaken and whet readers' appetites for foreign works, and paraphrase prepare for a more general understanding, so as to pave the way for future translations.[1] There is another understanding, however, that no translator can imitate. For let us consider those extraordinary men such as Nature is in the habit sometimes of producing, as if to show herself able to destroy even the barriers of national particularity in individual cases, men who feel such natural affinity to a foreign state of being that they immerse themselves, in both their lives and their thoughts, in a foreign language and its works, and as they occupy themselves entirely with a foreign world, they allow their native world and their native tongue to become quite foreign to them; or else those other men who are destined to represent the power of speech in all its glory and for whom all the languages they can somehow acquire are equally serviceable and suit them as if made for them: these men stand upon a point at which the value of translation approaches zero; since they are able to grasp foreign works free from the influence of their mother tongue, and to perceive their own understanding not in their mother tongue but with perfectly native ease in the original language of the work, and as they feel no incommensurability at all between their thought and the language they are reading, no translation can ever attain or depict their understanding. And just as it would mean pouring water into the sea, or into wine, if one wished to translate for them, so too are they wont to smile in certainly not unjustified condescension, even pity, at the exertions being made in this area. For, to be sure, if the audience for which the translations are being made resembled them, these efforts would be needless. Translation, then, concerns a state that lies midway between these two, and the translator must take it as his goal to furnish his reader with just such an image and just such enjoyment as reading the work in the original language would have provided the well educated man whom we are in the habit of calling, in the best sense of the word, an amateur and connoisseur, a man who is well acquainted with the foreign language, yet to whom it remains nonetheless foreign, who must no longer think each detail through in his mother tongue like a schoolboy before he is able to grasp the whole, yet who, even where he can take pleasure unhindered in the beauty of a work, remains ever conscious of the differences between this language and his mother tongue. To be sure, the domain of this sort of translation and its purpose remain uncertain enough even after these points have been settled. Only this much do we see, that just as the inclination to translate cannot arise until a certain foreign language ability has been established among the educated, so too will the art of translation grow and its aim be set higher and higher when connoisseurship and the taste for foreign works become more widespread and more advanced among those who have trained and educated their ears, without, however, having made the study of languages their primary occupation. Yet at the same time we cannot deny that the more receptive the readers who might avail themselves of such translations, the more towering become the difficulties of the task, above all if one considers the most characteristic works of art and science produced among a people, these naturally being the translator's principal objects. For just as language is a historical entity, so too is it impossible to appreciate it rightly without an appreciation of its history. Languages are not invented, and all arbitrary work one might undertake to perform on and in them would be folly; rather, they are gradually discovered, and science and art are the forces by means of which this discovery is furthered and perfected. Every preeminent spirit in whom some portion of a nation's views takes characteristic shape in one of these two forms must necessarily labor within his language to make this come about, and the works he produces must therefore also contain part of the history of the language. This, to be sure, causes the translator of scientific works considerable, yea, often insurmountable difficulties; for whoever, armed with adequate knowledge, reads a preeminent work of this sort in its original tongue will not fail to note the influence this work has had on the language. He will note which words and associations of ideas appear to him there in the first splendor of novelty; he will see how they have insinuated themselves into the language by way of the specific needs of this spirit and its expressive powers; and what he thus notes will largely determine the impression he receives. Therefore it belongs to the task of translation to communicate just these things to the reader; else he will be missing an often quite significant part of what was intended for him. But how is this to be achieved? Even on a small scale, how often will it happen that the term best corresponding to a new word in the original will be one that in our language is already old and worn out, so that the translator, would he show the work's contribution to the development of the language, will be forced to introduce foreign content into the passage, deviating into the realm of imitation! How often, even where he is able to replace new with new, will the term that is most similar in etymology and form not give the most faithful account of the meaning, finally obliging him to call up other associations – if he would preserve the immediate context! He will have to console himself that he will be able to make up for the loss in other passages where the author used only old, familiar words, and thus he may still achieve at large what cannot be accomplished in each individual case. If we consider, however, a master's power to shape the language in a larger context, his use of related words and their roots in great quantities of works that make reference to one another, how is the translator to find his way, given that the system of ideas and the signs for them in his language are completely different than in the original, and the roots of the words, instead of neatly corresponding to one another, rather overlap in the most curious patterns? It is therefore impossible that the language use of the translator could cohere everywhere in exactly the same way as that of his author. Here, then, he will have to be content to achieve in the particular what he cannot on the whole. He will stipulate as a condition for his readers that they do not compare each work with others by the same author with the same rigor as would be applied by readers of the original, but rather consider each more on its own terms, indeed, that they should praise him when he succeeds within individual works, or even only within their several subsections, in preserving a certain uniformity in the intention of the more important objects so that a given word is not matched with a host of different proxies, or the translation marked by a miscellany of expressions where the orig-inal confined itself to a select few. These difficulties are found above all in scientific works; other difficulties, and certainly not lesser ones, occur in the areas of poetry and artistical prose, in which the musical element of language that reveals itself in rhythm and alterations of tone is itself expressive and holds a higher meaning. It is sensible to all that the finest spirit, the highest magic of art in its most perfect works is lost when these things are disregarded or destroyed. Whatever, therefore, strikes the judicious reader of the original in this respect as characteristic, as intentional, as having an influence on tone and feeling, as decisive for the mimetic or musical accompaniment of speech: all these things our translator must render. But how often – indeed, that we are not obliged to say "always" borders on the miraculous – does one find fidelity to rhythm and melody caught in irreconcilable conflict with fidelity to dialectic and grammar! How difficult it is to prevent, in the eternal back and forth of what is to be sacrificed here and what there, a result that often is precisely the least fitting! How even more difficult that the translator must always compel himself to replace impartially, wherever the opportunity presents itself, that of which he has had to deprive the reader, not letting himself slip, even unconsciously, into a pertinacious one-sidedness because his inclinations bid him favor one artis-tical element above all the others! For if what he loves in the work of art is more the ethical subject matter and its treatment, then he will be the less likely to note how often he has done an injustice to the metrical and musical elements of the form and, rather than thinking of how to compensate for the loss, content himself with a rendering that tends ever more to lightness and, as it were, to paraphrase. Should it happen, however, that the translator is a musician or skilled in metrical verse, then he will neglect the logical element so as to seize hold of the musical, and as he becomes ever more deeply caught up in this one-sidedness, he will find his labors increasingly bootless; and when comparing his translation as a whole to the original, one will find that, without his remarking it, he will have approached nearer and nearer to that schoolboy inadequacy that loses sight of the whole for the sake of the part, for when in the interest of the material likeness of tone and rhythm what is expressed in one language with lightness and naturalness is replaced by clumsy, displeasing expressions in the other, then a quite different overall impression must result.

Yet other difficulties emerge when the translator considers his relationship to the language in which he writes and the relationship of his translation to his other works. Excepting those extraordinary masters who have equal command of several languages, or even find that one they have learned comes more naturally to them than their mother tongue, men for whom, as has been said, it is not possible to translate – excepting them, all other people, as fluently as they might read a foreign tongue, will yet retain while doing so a feeling of the foreign. Now how shall the translator contrive to disseminate among his readers this sense of encountering the foreign when he presents them with a translation in their own tongue? Surely one can reply that the solution to this riddle has long been obvious, and that, moreover, it has been solved, all too often perhaps, more than well enough; for the more precisely the translation adheres to the turns and figures of the original, the more foreign it will seem to its reader. By all means, it is easy enough to smile at this practice in general. Yet if one is wary of purchasing this pleasure too cheaply, of throwing out the most masterful attempts and the worst schoolboy efforts with the same bathwater, one must admit that an indispensable requirement for this method of translating is a disposition of the language that not only departs from the quotidian but lets one perceive that it was not left to develop freely but rather was bent to a foreign likeness; and it must be confessed that achieving this with art and measure, with detriment neither to oneself nor to the language, is perhaps the greatest diffi-culty our translator must confront. This undertaking would appear to be the most extraordinary form of humiliation to which a writer of some quality can subject himself. Who would not like to make his native tongue appear everywhere displaying the most splendid characteristic beauty allowed by each genre? Who would not prefer to beget children who would purely represent their fathers' lineage, rather than mongrels? Who would suffer himself to be seen moving with far less lightness and grace than that of which he is capable, and to appear at least occasionally harsh and stiff so as to displease the reader just enough to keep him conscious of what one is about? Who would gladly consent to be considered ungainly for striving to adhere so closely to the foreign tongue as his own language allows, and to being criticized, like parents who entrust their children to tumblers for their education, for having failed to exercise his mother tongue in the sorts of gymnas-tics native to it, instead accustoming it to alien, unnatural contortions! And who, finally, would wish to see himself smiled upon with utmost condescension by precisely the greatest masters and connoisseurs, who assure him that they would be entirely unable to understand his laborious, ill-considered German if they had not their knowledge of Greek and Latin to come to their aid! These are the sacrifices every translator of this sort is obliged to make, these the dangers to which he exposes

himself if, in his attempt to preserve a foreign tone in the language of his translation, he does not observe that finest of lines, and these are dangers and sacrifices
he cannot possibly avoid outright, as every person draws this line in a slightly
different spot. If he thinks now of the inevitable influence habit must have – well,
then, may he fear that even his own freely composed, original writings could be
invaded by coarse and improper elements originating in his own translations, and
his delicate sensibility for the native well-being of his own language blunted. And
should he dare to consider that great army of imitators and the indolence and
mediocrity that prevail in literary circles, then surely he must be seized with terror
at the thought of the slovenly disregard for the rules of euphony, the genuine wood-
enness and dissonance, the detriment to the language in various forms for which he
may now be held jointly responsible; for almost only the very best and the very
worst will not strive to profit falsely from his efforts. The cries that translation of
this sort must necessarily have a detrimental effect from within on the purity of the
language and the peaceful course of its development have often been heard. Even
if we choose to dismiss them for the moment with the perhaps empty promise that
advantages are sure to accompany these detriments, and that even as all good things
come with an admixture of bad, the wise course of action will always be to acquire
as much as possible of the former while taking along as little as possible of the latter,
the difficult task of representing the foreign in one's own mother tongue will most
certainly bring with it certain consequences. First, it is clear that this method of
translating cannot flourish equally well in all tongues, but rather only in those that
are not confined within the narrow bounds of a classical style beyond which all else
is deemed reprehensible. Let these bounded languages seek to expand their terri-
tories by inducing foreigners who require more than their native tongues to speak
them, something to which these languages are no doubt admirably suited; and let
them appropriate foreign works by means of imitations or perhaps translations of
that other sort: but this sort of translation they must leave to the freer languages
in which deviations and innovations are more readily tolerated, such that these
deviations may, in the end, combine to produce a new characteristic mode of
expression. It also follows clearly enough that this sort of translation has no value
at all if it is practiced only randomly in individual cases in a given tongue. For what
is being aimed at is plainly far more than merely causing some indifferent sort of
foreign spirit to waft in the reader's direction; rather, he is to be given an inkling,
if only a distant one, of the original language and what the work owes to it, and
thus some of what he loses for not understanding the original tongue is here compensated: he is not only to have a vague sense that what he is reading does not
sound unquestionably native to his own tongue; rather, it should sound foreign
in a quite specific way; this, however, is only possible if he is able to make comparisons on a large scale. If he has read several works that he knows were translated
from modern languages, and others from ancient ones, and if all of them were translated in this way, then surely he will develop an ear for the differences between
the ancient and the modern. He will have to have read a great deal more, however,
before he can differentiate between works of Hellenic and Roman origin, or Italian
and Spanish. And yet even this would hardly be the highest goal; rather, the reader
of the translation will be a match for the better reader of the original work only
when he is able to sense and eventually grasp with confidence not only the spirit

of the language but also the author's characteristic spirit, for which, to be sure, the talent of intuitive perception is the only possible organ, yet to this end, too, a far greater number of comparisons are utterly necessary. These comparisons cannot be made if only individual masterpieces in individual genres are translated. Even the most educated readers will acquire in this way only a highly imperfect knowledge of the foreign through translation; it is inconceivable, then, that they might rise to the level of forming actual judgments, be it about translations or originals. This sort of translation, then, clearly requires a large-scale operation, the transplanting of entire literatures into a single tongue, and it has meaning and value only in a nation whose people are favorably disposed to appropriate the foreign. Individual works of this sort have value only as forerunners of a more generally developing and burgeoning inclination. If they cannot arouse the desire to follow this practice, then there must be something against them in the spirit of the language and of the time; they will appear simply as failed attempts and enjoy little or no success. Yet even if this business prevails, it can hardly be expected that a work of this sort, splendid as it might be, will enjoy general approbation. Given all that must be taken into consideration, all the difficulties to be surmounted, different views will develop as to which parts of the task are to be emphasized and which deemed subordinate. And so different schools, as it were, will form among the master practitioners, and different parties of their adherents among the reading public; and even though it is the same method that forms the basis of each school, different translations of the same work made from different points of view will be able to coexist, and it would be difficult to say that any one of them is as a whole more perfect than the others or falls short in merit; rather, certain passages will prove more successful in one version, and other passages in another version, and only the sum of all these taken together and in relation to each other – the way one places particular value on approximating the original language, while the other rather insists that no violence be done to its own – will fulfill the task completely, and each in its own right will always have only relative and subjective value.

These are the difficulties that oppose this method of translating, and the flaws inherent in it. Yet even given these, one must still acknowledge the legitimacy of the undertaking itself, whose achievements cannot be denied. It is founded on two basic conditions: that the understanding of foreign texts be acknowledged as a known and desirable state, and that a certain flexibility be granted to our native tongue. Where both conditions are met, translation of this sort will appear a quite natural phenomenon that influences the entire intellectual development of a nation, and even as it is given a certain value, it will not fail to give pleasure as well.

But what of the opposite method, which, wishing to spare its reader all exertion and toil, sets out to summon the foreign author as if by magic into his immediate presence and to show the work as it would be had the author himself written it originally in the reader's tongue? This demand has often been cited as one that should be made of a true translator, representing a far nobler and more perfect aim than the one previously described; and individual attempts have been undertaken, perhaps even masterpieces, that have clearly enough assigned it as their goal. Let us now look at how matters stand with regard to this other method, and whether it might not perhaps be good if this practice, till now indisputably less common, were to be more frequently encountered and were to replace the questionable one that is in so many ways lacking.

It is immediately obvious that the translator's language has nothing at all to fear from this method. His foremost rule, given the relation in which his work stands to a foreign tongue, must be to allow himself nothing that would not also be allowed in any original work of the same genre written in his native tongue. Indeed, as much as anyone he has the duty to heed at least the same concern for the purity and perfection of his language and to attempt to achieve the same lightness and naturalness of style for which his author might be extolled in the original. This too is certain: that if we wish to make clear to our compatriots what a writer's work meant for the language in which he wrote it, we can find no better formula than to introduce him into our language speaking in such a way as we must assume he would have spoken had our language been his own, particularly if the stage of development that his language occupied when he came to it bears some similarity to the one currently occupied by ours. In a certain sense, it is possible for us to think of how Tacitus might have spoken had he been German, or, to be more precise, how a German would speak whose relationship to our language was the same as that of Tacitus to his own; and happy is he who is able to imagine this so vividly that he can really make him speak! Yet whether this would succeed if the translator had him say just the same things as the Roman Tacitus said in Latin is quite a different question, one difficult to answer in the affirmative. For it is one thing to grasp correctly and somehow represent the influence that a man has had upon his language, and another thing altogether to guess at the turns that his thoughts and their expression would have taken had he originally been used to thinking and expressing himself in some other tongue! Whoever is convinced of the inner, essential identity between thought and expression – and this conviction forms the basis for the entire art of understanding speech and thus of all translation as well – can he wish to sever a man from his native tongue and still believe that this man, or even so much as a train of thought, might turn out the same in two languages? Or if the train of thought is then in some way different, can he presume to break down speech to its inmost core so as to separate out that part played by language and then through a new and, as it were, chemical process conjoin the inner core of speech with the being and force of another tongue? For would it not seem that to carry out this task one must first eliminate everything in a man's written work that showed, even to the slightest extent, the influence of all he had spoken and heard in his mother tongue from childhood on, and then add, as it were, to his naked characteristic way of thinking in its approach to a particular object all that would have resulted from all he would have spoken and heard in the foreign tongue from either the beginning of his life or his first acquaintance with this language until he had acquired the skill necessary to think and write originally in it? This will not be possible until we have succeeded in assembling organic products through an artificial chemical process. Indeed, one can say that the goal of translating just as the author himself would have written originally in the language of the translation is not only unattainable, but is also in itself null and void; for whoever acknowledges the formative power of language, which is one with the particular nature of a people, must also concede that the entire knowledge of even the most exceptional man, as well as his ability to represent it, has come to him with and through language, and that no one has his language mechanically attached to him from the outside as if by straps, so that one might, as easily as one would unharness a team of horses and replace it with another, harness up a new language as it happened to suit one's frame of mind; but rather that each person produces originally only in his mother tongue, and that the question of how he would have written his works in another language ought not even to be raised. To be sure, two cases that are commonly enough met can be offered here to counter my examples. First, there is clearly such a thing as the ability to write in languages other than one's native tongue, even in the areas of philosophy and poetry, and this not only appears in isolated cases, although such cases continue to occur, but is quite common. Why, then, should one not, to avail oneself of a more reliable point of reference, suppose this ability in every author one intends to translate? What speaks against this is that the ability is so constituted as to appear only in those cases in which the same thing could either not be said at all in a man's native tongue or at least not by him. If we go back in time to when the Romance languages were beginning to emerge, who could say what language was native to the people living then? And who would want to deny that for those with scholarly aspirations Latin was more a native tongue than the vernacular? This goes much deeper for specific intellectual activities and needs. As long as the mother tongue has not yet grown to fit these needs, the language in which endeavors of the spirit first announced themselves to a people still undergoing development remains their partial mother tongue. Grotius and Leibnitz could not, at least without having been other people entirely, have written philosophy in German and Dutch. Indeed, even if the root has shriveled up altogether and the runner been torn away from the old trunk, whoever is not himself a being simultaneously engaged in shaping and uprooting his language will often be forced to cleave to some foreign language either chosen arbitrarily or dictated by secondary considerations. All the noblest and finest thoughts of our great king[2] came to him in a foreign language, which he had made his most intimate property. He could not possibly have written in German the philosophy and poetry he set down in French. It is regrettable that the great love certain members of his family held for England did not result in his having been instructed in English from an early age, a tongue far closer to German, and one whose last golden age was then in full flower. But we can certainly hope that if he had enjoyed a more rigorous scholarly education, he would rather have written his philosophy and poetry in Latin than in French. Since, therefore, special conditions adhere in this instance, it being only in a particular foreign language and not in some arbitrarily chosen one that each person achieves some particular aim that could not have been realized in his mother tongue, it cannot serve as evidence for a method of translation that means to show us how someone might have written in some other language what he in fact has written in his mother tongue. The second case, however, which concerns reading and writing originally in foreign languages, would appear more promising for this method. For who would wish to belittle our courtiers and men of the world by denying that the pretty speeches that trip from their tongues in various languages were not also conceived from the outset in these languages and not, say, first translated in their heads from the shabby German? And just as they are famed for being able to utter these sugarplums of eloquence equally well in various languages, they no doubt think them in all these languages with equivalent ease, and each of them will no doubt be instantly in a position to say how the other would have formulated in Italian what he has just finished saying in French. Yet these speeches, to be sure, do not lie in a sphere in which thoughts shoot up forcefully from the deep roots of a particular language; they are rather like the watercress that an artful man causes to sprout without soil on a white cloth. These speeches represent language neither in all its sacred gravity nor in its pleasant, well-measured play; rather, just as the people of different nations have begun to intermingle in a way formerly not often seen, so do we find a marketplace all around us, and these conversations are market talk, be they political or literary in content, or merely convivial, and they truly fall not within the domain of the translator, but rather – shall we say? – that of the interpreter. Now when speech of this sort, as sometimes happens, is interwoven into a piece of writing, such writing, which disports itself entirely in the bright and gay reaches of life without delving into the profundities of existence or capturing the characteristic nature of a people, may well be translated according to this rule; but only writing of this sort, for it alone might just as well have been set down originally in another language. And this rule may extend no further than, say, the prefaces and preambles of more splendid and profound works, which often are constructed entirely in the realm of light social intercourse. For the more the specific nature of a people leaves its mark on the individual thoughts that appear in a work and the connections drawn between them, to which perhaps may even be added the stamp of an age long past, the more this rule will cease to have meaning. For, true as it remains in many respects that only through the knowledge of several languages does a man become educated in a certain sense and a cosmopolite, we must all the same confess that just as we cannot accept as true cosmopolitism one that at critical moments supplants a man's love of his fatherland, so too with regard to languages is a general love not the proper, truly educational sort if, in both quotidian and nobler contexts, it would just as soon substitute some other language, ancient or modern, for the paternal tongue. One must be loyal to one language or another, just as to one nation, or else drift disoriented in an unlovely in-between realm. It is fitting that Latin should still be used among us for official business, lest we forget that this was the sacred scientific mother tongue of our forebears; it is salutary, too, that this practice should continue throughout the European scientific community so as to facilitate interchange; yet even in this case it will succeed only to the extent that in these works the subject matter is everything and the writer's views and special manner of making connections count for little. The same holds true of Romance languages. Whoever is forced to write such a language in some official capacity will certainly be well aware that his thoughts, as they are first conceived, are German: he merely begins to translate them while the embryo is still in an early stage of development; and whoever makes the sacrifice of writing in another language for the sake of scientific inquiry will be able to write freely and without constraint, rather than secretly translating as he goes along, only when he can lose himself in his subject matter. To be sure, there are those who write in Latin and French for their own amusement, and if the aim of this activity were truly to write equally as well and as originally in the foreign tongue as in one's own, then I would not hesitate to declare this a wicked and magical art like the trick of doubling oneself, an attempt not only to mock the laws of nature but also to bewilder. This, however, is clearly not its design; rather, this activity is only a sort of tasteful mimetic game that allows one to while away a pleasant hour in the antechambers of science and art. What one produces in a foreign tongue is not original; rather, memories of some particular writer or perhaps the style of a certain period, representing, as it were, some general personage, appear before the mind's eye almost like a living image in the outside world, and the imitation of this image guides and defines what one produces. Thus rarely does anything come about by this means that might have true worth beyond mimetic precision; and one's pleasure in this popular trick is all the more innocuous as the person being imitated is readily visible throughout. But if someone has turned against nature and custom and deserted, as it were, his mother tongue, devoting himself instead to another, it need not be affectation or mockery when he assures us he is no longer in a position to move freely in his native language; rather, by this justification he is seeking to convince himself that his nature really is a natural wonder that subverts all hierarchies and laws, and to reassure others that he is at least not walking about double like a ghost.

Yet too long have we tarried over matters foreign to our inquiry, creating the impression that we meant to speak of works written in foreign tongues rather than translations from them. In fact, it is as follows. If it is impossible to write originally in a foreign language something that at once requires and is worthy of translation, insofar as translation is an art, or if this must at least be seen as a rare and wondrous exception, then one cannot put forth as a rule for translation that it must think of how the author himself would have written just the same thing in the translator's tongue; for there are all too few examples of bilingual writers from whom we might derive an analogy which the translator might follow; rather, in accordance with the foregoing, he will have little more than his imagination to assist him in dealing with works that resemble neither light entertainment nor the style of business transactions. Indeed, what objection can be made if a translator says to his reader: Here I bring you the book as the man would have written it had he written in German; and the reader responds: I am just as obliged to you as if you had brought me the picture of a man the way he would look if his mother had conceived him by a different father? For if in all works belonging in the higher sense to the realms of science and art the author's characteristic spirit is the mother, then the father is his paternal tongue. Each of these artifices would lay claim to mysterious insights to which no one is privy, and only in play can one enjoy the one or the other of them without reserve.

That the applicability of this method is greatly limited, being indeed well-nigh zero where translation is concerned, is best borne out when one observes the insurmountable difficulties with which it so often becomes entangled in certain branches of the sciences and arts. Since one must concede that even in everyday usage there are only a very few words in any given tongue that correspond perfectly to words in any other such that these latter can be employed in any context suitable to the former, and that in corresponding contexts each will produce just the same effect as the other, this is more true of terms the more they have a philosophical import, which is above all the case in philosophy proper. Here more than anywhere is it the case that any language, despite the different concurrently and consecutively held views expressed in it, encompasses within itself a single system of ideas which, precisely because they are contiguous, linking and complementing one another within this language, form a single whole – whose several parts, however, do not correspond to those to be found in comparable systems in other languages, and this is scarcely excluding "God" and "to be," the noun of nouns and the verb of verbs. For even universals, which lie outside the realm of particularity, are illumined and colored by the particular. This language system subsumes the wisdom of all individuals. Each draws from what is present, and helps to bring to light what is not yet present but only prefigured. Only thus can the wisdom of the individual come alive, and only thus can it govern his existence, which he sets down entirely within this language. If, then, the translator of a philosophical author is not resolved to bend the language of his translation to accord to the greatest possible extent with the language of the original so as to give as full a sense as possible of the system of ideas inherent in this other language, if he seeks, rather, to have his author speak as though he had originally formed his thoughts and formulated his utterances in another language, what choice will this translator have, given the unlikeness of the elements in the two languages? Either he must paraphrase – which will not fulfill his purpose, for a paraphrase can and will never appear to have been composed originally in the same language – or else he must transform his man's entire wisdom and knowledge into the system of ideas in the other language, transforming all its parts accordingly, in which case it is hard to see how the wildest arbitrariness could be kept within bounds. Indeed, it must be said that whoever has the slightest respect for philosophical aspirations and developments will hardly be found engaging in such cavalier play. Let Plato answer for it if I now proceed from my discussion of philosophers to the writers of comedies.[3] This literary genre lies, as regards its use of language, closest to the realm of society conversation. The entire representation draws its breath from the customs of the age and of a particular nation, and these in turn find themselves most aptly reflected in its language. Lightness and naturalness in grace are its principal virtues; and precisely for this reason the difficulties of translation according to the method we have been considering are formidable. For every attempt to approximate one's language to a foreign tongue is detrimental to these virtues as they exist within a work. And if the translation now sets out to make a playwright speak as though he had written originally in the language of the translation, then there will be many things he cannot be allowed to utter, as they are not native to this particular nation, for which reason the language contains no signs to express them. The translator, then, must excise whole passages, destroying the power and form of the whole, or else place others in their stead. In this area, then, strictly following this formula will lead, it seems, either to imitation plain and simple or to an even more disagreeably conspicuous and disconcerting mixture of translation and imitation, which mercilessly tosses the reader back and forth like a ball between his world and the foreign one, between the inventive powers and wit of the author, on the one hand, and of the translator, on the other, which is certain to bring him no true pleasure but instead result, in the end, in dizziness and fatigue. The translator who works according to the other method, by contrast, is not called upon to undertake such single-handed transformations, since his reader is always to remain aware that the author lived in another world and wrote in another tongue. He is bound only to the admittedly difficult art of supplying this knowledge of the foreign world by the swiftest, most efficacious means, while allowing the greater lightness and naturalness of the original to shine through everywhere. These two examples taken from the farthest reaches of science and art show clearly how little the true goal of all translation, the fullest possible unadulterated enjoyment of foreign works, can be achieved through a method that insists on breathing into the translated work the spirit of a language foreign to it. Moreover, every language has its own characteristic features, including the rhythms of its prose as well as its poetry, and if the fiction is to be put forth that the author might also have written in the language of the translator, one would have to make him appear in the rhythms of this language, which would disfigure his work even more and limit to a far greater extent the knowledge of his particular character, which the translation was to preserve.

And in fact this fiction, which alone provides the basis for the theory of translating we are at present considering, goes far beyond the aim of this endeavor. Translation as regarded from the first point of view is a matter of necessity for a people of whom only a small number are able to acquire sufficient knowledge of foreign languages, while a larger number are receptive to the enjoyment of foreign works. If this latter group could be subsumed entirely into the former, then all translation would be in vain and scarcely anyone could be found who might be willing to undertake so thankless a task. Not so with the second method. It has nothing to do with need but rather is the work of wantonness and presumption. Even were the knowledge of foreign languages as widely distributed as possible and their noblest works readily accessible to any capable person, still it would remain a peculiar undertaking, one certain to draw all the more eager listeners, if someone promised to show us a work by Cicero or Plato just as these gentlemen would have written it themselves directly in German. And if someone were to succeed in achieving this not only in his own native tongue but in one foreign to him, we would certainly then hail him as a great master of the difficult, all but impossible art of making the spirits of different tongues intermingle. But one can see that this would not be translation in the strictest sense, and its aim would not be to facilitate the most direct enjoyment of the works themselves; rather, it would become more and more an imitation, and only he who had acquired direct knowledge of the writers in question by other means would be in a position to enjoy such works of art, or of sleight of hand. And its true aim could be only to reveal the similarities between different tongues in the way specific expressions and phrases relate to certain essential features of the language, and, in general, to illumine the language using the distinctive spirit of a foreign master, who, however, has been entirely cut off from and separated from his language. As the former is merely an artful and agreeable pastime, and the latter based upon a fiction that would be all but impossible to bring about, one can understand why translation of this sort is practiced only seldom, in experiments which themselves show clearly enough that this method is impracticable on a large scale. One might also say by way of explanation that only the most accomplished masters who may judge themselves capable of marvelous feats are able to work according to this method; and only those are truly justified in doing so who have already paid their dues to the world and thus can afford themselves the leisure of this charming and somewhat dangerous pastime. All the more comprehensible is it that these masters who feel themselves capable of attempting such a thing should with some degree of pity look down upon the activities of other translators. For they believe themselves alone to be engaged in that fine and free art, whereas the others, so they suppose, stand much closer to the interpreter's work, though it remains true that they too are working to fulfill a need, albeit a rather higher one. And these others also appear to them worthy of pity for the reason that they expend far more labor and art than is meet upon a lowly, thankless task. For which reason they have always ready at hand the counsel that one should, whenever possible, have recourse to paraphrase such as interpreters employ in difficult, contentious cases, instead of translations of this sort.

And what now? Should we adopt this view and follow this counsel? The ancients, it would seem, translated very little in this most authentic sense, and even among the moderns, most have been disheartened by the difficulties of authentic translation and content themselves with imitation and paraphrase. Who would claim that anything has ever been translated, whether from an ancient or a Germanic tongue, into French! But we Germans, while we might willingly give ear to such counsel, will surely not follow it. An inner necessity, in which a peculiar calling of our people asserts itself clearly enough, has driven us to translation *en masse*; there is no turning back, we must keep forging on. Just as it is perhaps only through the cultivation of foreign plant life that our soil has become richer and more fertile, and our climate more pleasing and milder, so too do we feel that our language, since our Nordic lassitude prevents us from exercising it sufficiently, can most vigorously flourish and develop its own strength only through extensive contact with the foreign. And we must add to this, it seems, that our people, because of its esteem for the foreign and its own mediating nature, may be destined to unite all the jewels of foreign science and art together with our own in our own language, forming, as it were, a great historical whole that will be preserved at the center and heart of Europe, so that now, with the help of our language, everyone will be able to enjoy all the beautiful things that the most different ages have given us as purely and perfectly as possible for one who is foreign to them. Indeed, this seems to be the true historical goal of translation as a whole, as it is now native to us. But this goal is served only by one method of translation, the one we first noted. Art must learn to conquer its difficulties, of which we have made no secret, to the greatest extent possible. A good beginning has been made, but the greater part still remains. Many experiments and exercises will still have to pave the way before a few excellent works are achieved; and much that initially glitters will thereafter be surpassed by a better. The extent to which individual artists have in part overcome these difficulties, in part skillfully evaded them, can be observed in various examples. And even if some of lesser skill also work in this field, we will not be so fainthearted as to fear that great harm might come to our language through their efforts. For it must first of all be established that in a language in which translation is practiced on so large a scale there must be an area of the language reserved for translations, and to them certain concessions will be made that would not be tolerated elsewhere. He who nonetheless transplants such novelties without license will find few or no followers, and if we agree not to tally up the accounts too soon, we will be able to rely on the fact that the assimilating process of the language will cast out everything that was taken up only to fulfill a temporary need and is not truly in accordance with its nature. On the other hand, we must not fail to realize that much in our language that is beautiful and strong was developed, or restored from oblivion, only through translation. We speak too little and engage in relatively too much idle chatter; and it cannot be denied that for some time now even our manner of writing has displayed this tendency to far too great an extent – and translation has contributed not a little to promoting a more rigorous style. When the time comes wherein we have a public life that will give us, on the one hand, a society of more substance more attentive to language and, on the other, a freer space for the talents of the speaker to unfold, then will we perhaps have less need of translation for the development of our language. And may this time arrive before we have come full circle in our survey of the translator's travails!

Notes

1   This was, on the whole, the condition of the Germans at the time of which Goethe eloquently says that prose translations, even of poetic works, and these will always have to be more or less paraphrases, are more beneficial for educating young people, and thus far I can agree with him entirely; for in such an age foreign literature can be made comprehensible only in its substance, and there cannot yet be any acknowledgement of its metrical and musical value. Yet I cannot believe that even now Voss's Homer and Schlegel's Shakespeare should serve only for the entertainment of the learned among themselves; and just as little that even today a prose translation of Homer might aid in promoting taste and an aesthetic sensibility; rather, there should be for children an adaptation like Becker's, and for adults young and old a metrical translation such as, to be sure, we perhaps do not yet possess; between these two, I know nothing that might profitably be included. [Schleiermacher is referring to Goethe's comments on translation in his auto-biographical work *Dichtung und Wahrheit (Poetry and Truth)*. For an English translation of these comments, see Lefevere 1992a: 74–75. Johann Heinrich Voss (1751–1826) published translations of Homer's *Iliad* (1793) and *Odyssey* (1781) in hexameter verse – an unprecedented feat in German. They were much discussed, first widely lauded but later reviled. August Wilhelm Schlegel (1767–1845) translated seventeen of Shakespeare's plays, all but one between 1796 and 1800. Trans.]

2   [Frederick II of Prussia (1712–1786), known as Frederick the Great, was raised speaking only French at the will of his father, Frederick William I, and became a great amateur of poetry and philosophy. Voltaire was a frequent guest of his at Sanssouci Castle outside Potsdam. Trans.]

3   [Schleiermacher himself translated the collected works of Plato into German. His translations were published between 1804 and 1828. Trans.]

Chapter 5

Johann Wolfgang von Goethe

TRANSLATIONS

Translated by Sharon Sloan

THERE ARE THREE KINDS of translation. The first acquaints us with the foreign country on our own terms; a plain prose translation is best for this purpose. Prose in and of itself serves as the best introduction: it completely neutralizes the formal characteristics of any sort of poetic art and reduces even the most exuberant waves of poetic enthusiasm to still water. The plain prose translation surprises us with foreign splendors in the midst of our national domestic sensibility; in our everyday lives, and without our realizing what is happening to us – by lending our lives a nobler air – it genuinely uplifts us. Luther's Bible translation will produce this kind of effect with each reading.

Much would have been gained, for instance, if the *Nibelungen* had been set in good, solid prose at the outset, and labeled as popular literature. Then the brutal, dark, solemn, and strange sense of chivalry would still have spoken to us in its full power. Whether this would still be feasible or even advisable now is best decided by those who have more rigorously dedicated themselves to these matters of antiquity.

A second epoch follows, in which the translator endeavors to transport himself into the foreign situation but actually only appropriates the foreign idea and represents it as his own. I would like to call such an epoch *parodistic*, in the purest sense of that word. It is most often men of wit who feel drawn to the parodistic. The French make use of this style in the translation of all poetic works: Delille's translations provide hundreds of examples.[1] In the same way that the French adapt foreign words to their pronunciation, they adapt feelings, thoughts, even objects; for every foreign fruit there must be a substitute grown in their own soil.

Wieland's translations are of this kind;[2] he, too, had his own peculiar understanding and taste, which he adapted to antiquity and foreign countries only to the
extent that he found it convenient. This superb man can be seen as the representative of his time; he exercised an inordinate amount of influence in that, no matter
what appealed to him, no matter how he absorbed and passed it on to his contemporaries, it was received by them as something pleasant and enjoyable.

Because we cannot linger for very long in either a perfect or an imperfect state
but must, after all, undergo one transformation after another, we experienced the
third epoch of translation, which is the final and highest of the three. In such periods,
the goal of the translation is to achieve perfect identity with the original, so that
the one does not exist instead of the other but in the other's place.

This kind met with the most resistance in its early stages, because the translator identifies so strongly with the original that he more or less gives up the
uniqueness of his own nation, creating this third kind of text for which the taste of
the masses has to be developed.

At first the public was not at all satisfied with Voss[3] (who will never be fully
appreciated) until gradually the public's ear accustomed itself to this new kind of
translation and became comfortable with it. Now anyone who assesses the extent
of what has happened, what versatility has come to the Germans, what rhythmical
and metrical advantages are available to the spirited, talented beginner, how Ariosto
and Tasso, Shakespeare and Calderon have been brought to us two and three times
over as Germanized foreigners, may hope that literary history will openly acknowledge who was the first to choose this path in spite of so many and varied obstacles.

For the most part, the works of von Hammer indicate a similar treatment of
oriental masterpieces;[4] he suggests that the translation approximate as closely as
possible the external form of the original work. How much more convincing the
passages of a translation of Firdausi prove to be when produced by our friend himself
compared to those reworked by an adaptor whose examples can be read in the
Fundgruben.[5] Disfiguring a poet in this way is, in our opinion, the saddest mistake a
diligent and quite capable translator can make.

Since, however, in every literature all of these three epochs are found to repeat
and reverse themselves, as well as exist simultaneously, a prose translation of the
Shahnama[6] and the works of Nizami would still be in order. It could be used for a
quick reading, which would open up the essential meaning of the work: we could
enjoy the historical, the legendary, the larger ethical issues, and we would gradually become familiar with the attitudes and ways of thinking, until we could at last
feel a kinship with them.

Think only of the undisputed applause we Germans have attributed to such
a translation of the *Sakuntala*,[7] whose success we can most definitely ascribe to its
plain prose, into which the poem has been dissolved. Now would be the proper
time for a new translation of the third type that would not only correspond to the
various dialects, rhythms, meters, and prosaic idioms in the original but would also,
in a pleasant and familiar manner, renew the poem in all of its distinctiveness for
us. Since a manuscript of this eternal work is available in Paris, a German living
there could earn undying gratitude for undertaking such a work.

Similarly, the English translator of *Messenger of the Clouds*[8] deserves every honor,
simply because our first acquaintance with this kind of a work is always such a

momentous occasion in our lives. But his translation really belongs to the second epoch; using paraphrase and supplementary words, the translation flatters the Northern ear and senses with its iambic pentameter. I owe a debt of thanks to our own Kosegarten[9] for translating a few lines directly from the original source language, which indeed give a totally different impression. The Englishman took certain liberties as well, transposing motifs, which the trained aesthetic eye immediately discovers and condemns.

The reason why we also call the third epoch the final one can be explained in a few words. A translation that attempts to identify itself with the original ultimately comes close to an interlinear version and greatly facilitates our understanding of the original. We are led, yes, compelled as it were, back to the source text: the circle, within which the approximation of the foreign and the familiar, the known and the unknown constantly move, is finally complete.

Translator's notes

1   Abbé Jacques Delille (1738–1813) was a well-known and prolific translator who rendered Virgil's *Georgics* (1770) and *Aeneid* (1805) as well as Milton's *Paradise Lost* (1805).

2   Christoph Martin Wieland (1733–1813) translated twenty-two of Shakespeare's plays into German between 1762 and 1766.

3   Johann Heinrich Voss (1751–1826) was the German translator of Homer into hexameters.

4   Joseph von Hammer-Purgstall (1774–1856) was the Viennese Orientalist.

5   *Fundgruben des Orients* was a review of Oriental studies edited by von Hammer.

6   Goethe is referring to *The Book of Kings*, an epic poem by the Persian poet Firdausi (*c*. 940–1020). The poet Nizami (*c*. 1141–1209), an Azerbaijan who wrote in Persian, is the author of *Layla and Majnun*.

7   The *Sakuntala* is a verse drama in Sanskrit by the Indian poet and dramatist Kalidasa (fl. 5th century).

8   In 1813 Horace Hayman Wilson published his English version of Khalidasa's *Meghaduta* under the title *Messenger of the Clouds*.

9   Johann Gottfried Ludwig Kosegarten (1792–1860) was an Orientalist at the University of Jena from 1817 to 1824.

Chapter 6

Friedrich Nietzsche

TRANSLATIONS

Translated by Walter Kaufmann

T HE DEGREE OF THE HISTORICAL SENSE of any age may be
inferred from the manner in which this age makes *translations* and tries to absorb
former ages and books. In the age of Corneille[1] and even of the Revolution, the
French took possession of Roman antiquity in a way for which we would no longer
have courage enough – thanks to our more highly developed historical sense. And
Roman antiquity itself: how forcibly and at the same time how naively it took
hold of everything good and lofty of Greek antiquity, which was more ancient! How
they translated things into the Roman present! How deliberately and recklessly they
brushed the dust off the wings of the butterfly that is called moment! Thus Horace
now and then translated Alcaeus or Archilochus; and Propertius did the same with
Callimachus and Philetas (poets of the same rank as Theocritus, if we *may* judge).[2]
What was it to them that the real creator had experienced this and that and written
the signs of it into his poem? As poets, they had no sympathy for the antiquarian
inquisitiveness that precedes the historical sense; as poets, they had no time for all
those very personal things and names and whatever might be considered the costume
and mask of a city, a coast, or a century: quickly, they replaced it with what was
contemporary and Roman. They seem to ask us: "Should we not make new for
ourselves what is old and find ourselves in it? Should we not have the right to breathe
our own soul into this dead body? For it is dead after all; how ugly is everything
dead!" They did not know the delights of the historical sense; what was past and
alien was an embarrassment for them; and being Romans, they saw it as an incentive for a Roman conquest. Indeed, translation was a form of conquest. Not only
did one omit what was historical; one also added allusions to the present and, above

1882

all, struck out the name of the poet and replaced it with one's own – not with any sense of theft but with the very best conscience of the *imperium Romanum*.

Editor's notes

1   The French poet and dramatist Pierre Corneille (1606–1684) based many of his plays on classical themes.
2   Alcaeus (*c.* 600 BC), Archilochus (fl.*c.* 650 BC), Callimachus (fl.*c.* 260 BC), and Philetas (*c.* 330–275 BC) were Greek lyric poets whose writing was imitated and in some cases freely translated by such Roman poets as Catullus, Horace, Ovid, and Propertius. The Greek poet Theocritus (*c.* 310–250 BC) wrote pastoral verse that was imitated by Virgil.

1900s–1930s

THE MAIN TRENDS in translation theory during this period are rooted in German literary and philosophical traditions, in Romanticism, hermeneutics, and existential phenomenology. They assume that language is not so much communicative as constitutive in its representation of thought and reality, and so translation is seen as an interpretation which necessarily reconstitutes and transforms the foreign text. Nineteenth-century theorists and practitioners like Friedrich Schleiermacher and Wilhelm von Humboldt treated translation as a creative force in which specific translation strategies might serve a variety of cultural and social functions, building languages, literatures, and nations. At the start of the twentieth century, these ideas are rethought from the vantage point of modernist movements which prize experiments with literary form as a way of revitalizing culture. Translation is a focus of theoretical speculation and formal innovation.

An important assumption in this development is the autonomy of translation, its status as a text in its own right, derivative but nonetheless independent as a work of signification. In **Walter Benjamin**'s 1923 essay (included in this volume), a translation participates in the "afterlife" (*Überleben*) of the foreign text, enacting an interpretation that is informed by a history of reception ("the age of its fame"). This interpretation does more than transmit messages; it recreates the values that accrued to the foreign text over time. And insofar as the linguistic differences of this text are signalled in the translating language, they ultimately convey a philosophical concept, "pure language," a sense of how the "mutually exclusive" differences among languages coexist with "complementary" intentions to communicate and to refer, intentions that are derailed by the differences. For Benjamin, translation offers a utopian vision of linguistic "harmony."

This speculative approach is linked to a particular discursive strategy. The pure language is released in the translation through literalisms, especially in syntax, which result in departures from current standard usage. Benjamin is reviving Schleiermacher's notion of foreignizing translation, wherein the reader of the translated text is brought as close as possible to the foreign one through close renderings that transform the translating language. Benjamin quotes Rudolf Pannwitz's likeminded commentary on the German translation tradition, which complains about translations that "germanize hindu greek english instead of hinduizing grecizing anglicizing german" (Pannwitz 1917: 240; trans. John Zilcosky). Pannwitz sees translation as an experimental literary practice, where the translator "must broaden and deepen his own language with the foreign one" – just as Pannwitz's own prose tampers with conventional German syntax, capitalization, and punctuation.

Ezra Pound's translation theories and practices share the German interest in literary experimentalism. His rare, mostly unfavorable comments on German poetry nonetheless include praise for Rudolf Borchardt's innovative version of Dante, which begins to appear in 1908 (Pound 1934: 55). Borchardt's use of archaic German dialects resembles Pound's own work with another thirteenth-century Italian poet, Guido Cavalcanti. In the 1929 essay reprinted here, Pound sees archaism as a discursive strategy that might go some way toward registering the literary and historical differences of Cavalcanti's Italian.

The experiment answers to Pound's search for a stylistic equivalent or analogue, "a verbal weight about equal to that of the original." But he is perfectly aware that the translation discourse he chose for Cavalcanti – "pre-Elizabethan" English poetry – doesn't match medieval Tuscan in any chronological sense. The relation Pound establishes between his translations and the foreign text is partial, both incomplete and slanted toward what interests him. "We are preserving one value of early Italian work," he observes of one rendering, "the cantabile."

In Pound's view, the autonomy of translation takes two forms. A translated text might be "interpretive," a critical "accompaniment," usually printed next to the foreign poem and composed of linguistic peculiarities that direct the reader across the page to foreign textual features, like a lexical choice or a prosodic effect. Or a translation might be "original writing," in which literary "standards" in the translating culture guide the rewriting of the foreign poem so decisively as to seem a "new poem" in that language. The relation between the two texts doesn't disappear; it is just masked by an illusion of originality, although in target-language terms.

Pound's standards are modernist; they include philosophical and poetic values like positivism and linguistic precision. And so he translates to recover foreign poetries that might advance these values in English. Pound's experimental versions of Cavalcanti challenge previous English attempts, Victorian translations which seem to him "obfuscated" by pre-Raphaelite medievalism. He also wants to invigorate the English language by overcoming the "six centuries of derivative convention and loose usage [that] have obscured the exact significances of such phrases as: 'The death of the heart,' and 'The departure of the soul'" (Anderson 1983: 12).

Translation theory and practice in the early twentieth century are marked by two competing tendencies: on the one hand, a formalist interest in technique, usually expressed as innovative translation strategies that match new interpretations of foreign texts; and on the other hand, a strong functionalism, a recurrent yoking of translation projects to cultural and political agendas. During the 1920s Martin Buber and Franz Rosenzweig hope to contribute to a renaissance of German Jewish culture through a close rendering of the Hebrew Bible that evokes the oral quality of the Hebrew. To distinguish their Jewish reading of the text from the fluency of Luther's Christian version, they deviate from standard usage, not only by Hebraicizing the syntax of their German, but also by inserting archaisms and stylistic devices (e.g. Buber's "Leitworte," comparable to the modernist technique of creating recurrent patterns in a work of art: "leitmotifs").

Not every account of these tendencies is enthusiastic, even within the German tradition. In 1925 the philosopher Karl Vossler argues that translation is instrumental in the preservation and development of national languages, especially highly literary projects like Borchardt's experimental *Deutsche Dante*, where "the sense of language produces its final and rarest flowers" (Vossler 1932: 177). But Vossler also sees an "aesthetic imperialism" in these projects which casts doubt on their claims to register the foreignness of the foreign text in the translating language. "The artistically perfect translations in a national literature," he writes, "are the means by which the linguistic genius of a nation defends itself against what is foreign by cunningly stealing from it as much as possible" (Lefevere 1977: 97). In the German tradition, foreignizing strategies are intensely nationalistic, a fortification of the language against such forces as French cultural domination during the Napoleonic wars. Vossler recognizes that imperialism might be the dark underside of translation driven by a vernacular nationalism.

More conservative theorists who reject stylistically innovative translations still imagine a social function for translating. In Hilaire Belloc's 1931 Taylorian lecture at Oxford, "any hint of foreignness in the translated version is a blemish" since the "social importance of translation" is to preserve "our cultural unity in the west," currently threatened because "the tradition of Latin" has "lost its efficacy" as "a common bond of comprehension" (Belloc 1931: 9, 22).

During the 1920s, the philologist Ulrich von Wilamowitz-Moellendorff urged translators of classical literature to "spurn the letter and follow the spirit" so as "to let the ancient poet speak to us clearly and in a manner as immediately intelligible as he did in his own time" (Lefevere 1992a: 34, 169). This suggests, not the literalism of German translation, but the freedom so esteemed in the French and English traditions, not Hölderlin, but D'Ablancourt, Dryden, and Matthew Arnold. In Wilamowitz's case, clarity and intelligibility are important because he feels that translations of the "Greek ideal" can "check the moral and spiritual decline our nation is moving toward" (ibid.: 167).

With the Argentine writer **Jorge Luis Borges**, these theoretical issues undergo a subtle and incisive development. His 1935 essay on the translators of the *Arabian Nights* (reprinted here) shows that literary translations produce varying representations of the same foreign text and culture, and their "veracity" or degree of equivalence is always in doubt, regardless of their impact or influence. Antoine Galland's eighteenth-century version is "the least faithful," but "the mostly widely read" for the next two hundred years. Such facts of translation are not to be lamented, however, but celebrated, studied historically, and interrogated for their ideological implications. Borges argues that "it is [the translator's] infidelity, his happy and creative infidelity, that must matter to us."

Of course, not all infidelities are equal to Borges. In his detailed discussion of the different translations, he performs ideological critiques that expose their investment in various cultural values and political interests, Orientalist and anti-Semitic, masculinist and puritanical, middle-class and academic. His approach is exemplary: he analyzes textual features, such as lexicon and syntax, prosody and discourse, and explains them with reference to the translator's "literary habits" and the literary traditions in the translating language. Borges most appreciates translations that are written "in the wake of a literature" and therefore "presuppose a rich (prior) process." This leads him to value "heterogeneous" language, a "glorious hybridization" that mixes archaism and slang, neologism and foreign borrowings. What he misses in a scholarly German translation is precisely the foreignizing impulse of the Romantic tradition, "the Germanic distortion, the *Unheimlichkeit* of Germany."

At the end of the 1930s, translation is regarded as a distinctive linguistic practice, "a literary genre apart," writes the Spanish philosopher José Ortega y Gasset, "with its own norms and its own ends" (Ortega y Gasset 1992: 109). It attracts the attention of leading writers and thinkers, literary critics and philologists. It becomes the topic of scholarly monographs that survey translation theory and practice in particular periods and languages (e.g. Amos 1920, Matthiessen 1931, Bates 1936). And it generates a range of theoretical issues that are still debated today.

In 1937 Ortega takes up these issues in "The Misery and the Splendor of Translation," a striking philosophical dialogue that argues for the continuing importance of the German translation tradition. The "misery" of translation is its impossibility, because of irreducible differences which are not only linguistic, but cultural, incommensurabilities that stem from "different mental pictures, from disparate intellectual systems." The "splendor" of translation is its manipulation of these differences to "force the reader from his linguistic habits and oblige him to move within those of the [foreign] author" (Ortega y Gasset 1992: 108) For Ortega, translating is useful in challenging the complacencies of contemporary culture because it fosters a "historical consciousness" (ibid: 110) that is lacking in the mathematical and physical sciences. "We need the ancients precisely to the degree that they are dissimilar to us," (ibid: 111) he writes, so that translating can introduce a critical difference into the present.

Further reading

Benjamin 1989, Blanchot 1997, Jacobs 1975, Kelly 1979, Kristal 2002, Nouss 1997, Reichert 1996, Robinson 1991, Steiner 1975, Venuti 1995

Chapter 7

Walter Benjamin

THE TASK OF THE TRANSLATOR: AN INTRODUCTION TO THE TRANSLATION OF BAUDELAIRE'S *TABLEAUX PARISIENS*

Translated by Harry Zohn

IN THE APPRECIATION of a work of art or an art form, consideration of the receiver never proves fruitful. Not only is any reference to a certain public or its representatives misleading, but even the concept of an "ideal" receiver is detrimental in the theoretical consideration of art, since all it posits is the existence and nature of man as such. Art, in the same way, posits man's physical and spiritual existence, but in none of its works is it concerned with his response. No poem is intended for the reader, no picture for the beholder, no symphony for the listener.

Is a translation meant for readers who do not understand the original? This would seem to explain adequately the divergence of their standing in the realm of art. Moreover, it seems to be the only conceivable reason for saying "the same thing" repeatedly. For what does a literary work "say"? What does it communicate? It "tells" very little to those who understand it. Its essential quality is not statement or the imparting of information. Yet any translation which intends to perform a transmitting function cannot transmit anything but information – hence, something inessential. This is the hallmark of bad translations. But do we not generally regard as the essential substance of a literary work what it contains in addition to information – as even a poor translator will admit – the unfathomable, the mysterious, the "poetic," something that a translator can reproduce only if he is also a poet? This, actually, is the cause of another characteristic of inferior translation, which consequently we may define as the inaccurate transmission of an inessential content. This will be true whenever a translation undertakes to serve the reader. However, if it were intended for the reader, the same would have to apply to the original. If the original does not exist for the reader's sake, how could the translation be understood on the basis of this premise?

Translation is a mode. To comprehend it as mode one must go back to the original, for that contains the law governing the translation: its translatability. The question of whether a work is translatable has a dual meaning. Either: Will an adequate translator ever be found among the totality of its readers? Or, more pertinently: Does its nature lend itself to translation and, therefore, in view of the significance of the mode, call for it? In principle, the first question can be decided only contingently; the second, however, apodictically. Only superficial thinking will deny the independent meaning of the latter and declare both questions to be of equal significance. . . . It should be pointed out that certain correlative concepts retain their meaning, and possibly their foremost significance, if they are referred exclusively to man. One might, for example, speak of an unforgettable life or moment even if all men had forgotten it. If the nature of such a life or moment required that it be unforgotten, that predicate would not imply a falsehood but merely a claim not fulfilled by men, and probably also a reference to a realm in which it *is* fulfilled: God's remembrance. Analogously, the translatability of linguistic creations ought to be considered even if men should prove unable to translate them. Given a strict concept of translation, would they not really be translatable to some degree? The question as to whether the translation of certain linguistic creations is called for ought to be posed in this sense. For this thought is valid here: If translation is a mode, translatability must be an essential feature of certain works.

Translatability is an essential quality of certain works, which is not to say that it is essential that they be translated; it means rather that a specific significance inherent in the original manifests itself in its translatability. It is plausible that no translation, however good it may be, can have any significance as regards the original. Yet, by virtue of its translatability the original is closely connected with the translation; in fact, this connection is all the closer since it is no longer of importance to the original. We may call this connection a natural one, or, more specifically, a vital connection. Just as the manifestations of life are intimately connected with the phenomenon of life without being of importance to it, a translation issues from the original — not so much from its life as from its afterlife. For a translation comes later than the original, and since the important works of world literature never find their chosen translators at the time of their origin, their translation marks their stage of continued life. The idea of life and afterlife in works of art should be regarded with an entirely unmetaphorical objectivity. Even in times of narrowly prejudiced thought there was an inkling that life was not limited to organic corporeality. But it cannot be a matter of extending its dominion under the feeble scepter of the soul, as Fechner tried to do, or, conversely, of basing its definition on the even less conclusive factors of animality, such as sensation, which characterize life only occasionally. The concept of life is given its due only if everything that has a history of its own, and is not merely the setting for history, is credited with life. In the final analysis, the range of life must be determined by history rather than by nature, least of all by such tenuous factors as sensation and soul. The philosopher's task consists in comprehending all of natural life through the more encompassing life of history. And indeed, is not the continued life of works of art far easier to recognize than the continual life of animal species? The history of the great works of art tells us about their antecedents, their realization in the age of the artist, their potentially eternal afterlife in succeeding generations. Where this last manifests itself, it is called fame. Translations that are more than transmissions of subject matter come into being when in the course of its survival a work has reached the age of its fame. Contrary, therefore, to the claims of bad translators, such translations do not so much serve the work as owe their existence to it. The life of the originals attains in them to its ever-renewed latest and most abundant flowering.

Being a special and high form of life, this flowering is governed by a special, high purposiveness. The relationship between life and purposefulness, seemingly obvious yet almost beyond the grasp of the intellect, reveals itself only if the ultimate purpose toward which all single functions tend is sought not in its own sphere but in a higher one. All purposeful manifestations of life, including their very purposiveness, in the final analysis have their end not in life, but in the expression of its nature, in the representation of its significance. Translation thus ultimately serves the purpose of expressing the central reciprocal relationship between languages. It cannot possibly reveal or establish this hidden relationship itself; but it can represent it by realizing it in embryonic or intensive form. This representation of hidden significance through an embryonic attempt at making it visible is of so singular a nature that it is rarely met with in the sphere of nonlinguistic life. This, in its analogies and symbols, can draw on other ways of suggesting meaning than intensive – that is, anticipative, intimating – realization. As for the posited central kinship of languages, it is marked by a distinctive convergence. Languages are not strangers to one another, but are, a priori and apart from all historical relationships, interrelated in what they want to express.

With this attempt at an explication our study appears to rejoin, after futile detours, the traditional theory of translation. If the kinship of languages is to be demonstrated by translations, how else can this be done but by conveying the form and meaning of the original as accurately as possible? To be sure, that theory would be hard put to define the nature of this accuracy and therefore could shed no light on what is important in a translation. Actually, however, the kinship of languages is brought out by a translation far more profoundly and clearly than in the superficial and indefinable similarity of two works of literature. To grasp the genuine relationship between an original and a translation requires an investigation analogous to the argumentation by which a critique of cognition would have to prove the impossibility of an image theory. There it is a matter of showing that in cognition there could be no objectivity, not even a claim to it, if it dealt with images of reality; here it can be demonstrated that no translation would be possible if in its ultimate essence it strove for likeness to the original. For in its afterlife – which could not be called that if it were not a transformation and a renewal of something living – the original undergoes a change. Even words with fixed meaning can undergo a maturing process. The obvious tendency of a writer's literary style may in time wither away, only to give rise to immanent tendencies in the literary creation. What sounded fresh once may sound hackneyed later; what was once current may someday sound quaint. To seek the essence of such changes, as well as the equally constant changes in meaning, in the subjectivity of posterity rather than in the very life of language and its works, would mean – even allowing for the crudest psychologism – to confuse the root cause of a thing with its essence. More pertinently, it would mean denying, by an impotence of thought, one of the most powerful and fruitful historical processes. And even if one tried to turn an author's last stroke of the pen into the *coup de grâce* of his work, this still would not save that dead theory of translation. For just as the tenor and the significance of the great works of literature undergo a complete transformation over the centuries, the mother tongue of the translator is transformed as well. While a poet's words endure in his own language, even the greatest translation is destined to become part of the growth of its own language and eventually to be absorbed by its renewal. Translation is so far removed from being the sterile equation of two dead languages that of all literary forms it is the one charged with the special mission of watching over the maturing process of the original language and the birth pangs of its own.

If the kinship of languages manifests itself in translations, this is not accomplished through a vague alikeness between adaptation and original. It stands to reason that kinship does not necessarily involve likeness. The concept of kinship as used here is in accord with its more restricted common usage: in both cases, it cannot be defined adequately by identity of origin, although in defining the more restricted usage the concept of origin remains indispensable. Wherein resides the relatedness of two languages, apart from historical considerations? Certainly not in the similarity between works of literature or words. Rather, all suprahistorical kinship of languages rests in the intention underlying each language as a whole – an intention, however, which no single language can attain by itself but which is realized only by the totality of their intentions supplementing each other: pure language. While all individual elements of foreign languages – words, sentences, structure – are mutually exclusive, these languages supplement one another in their intentions. Without distinguishing the intended object from the mode of intention, no firm grasp of this basic law of a philosophy of language can be achieved. The words *Brot* and *pain* "intend" the same object, but the modes of this intention are not the same. It is owing to these modes that the word *Brot* means something different to a German than the word *pain* to a Frenchman, that these words are not interchangeable for them, that, in fact, they strive to exclude each other. As to the intended object, however, the two words mean the very same thing. While the modes of intention in these two words are in conflict, intention and object of intention complement each of the two languages from which they are derived; there the object is complementary to the intention. In the individual, unsupplemented languages, meaning is never found in relative independence, as in individual words or sentences; rather, it is in a constant state of flux – until it is able to emerge as pure language from the harmony of all the various modes of intention. Until then, it remains hidden in the languages. If, however, these languages continue to grow in this manner until the end of their time, it is translation which catches fire on the eternal life of the works and the perpetual renewal of language. Translation keeps putting the hallowed growth of languages to the test: How far removed is their hidden meaning from revelation, how close can it be brought by the knowledge of this remoteness?

This, to be sure, is to admit that all translation is only a somewhat provisional way of coming to terms with the foreignness of languages. An instant and final rather than a temporary and provisional solution of this foreignness remains out of the reach of mankind; at any rate, it eludes any direct attempt. Indirectly, however, the growth of religions ripens the hidden seed into a higher development of language. Although translation, unlike art, cannot claim permanence for its products, its goal is undeniably a final, conclusive, decisive stage of all linguistic creation. In translation the original rises into a higher and purer linguistic air, as it were. It cannot live there permanently, to be sure, and it certainly does not reach it in its entirety. Yet, in a singularly impressive manner, at least it points the way to this region: the predestined, hitherto inaccessible realm of reconciliation and fulfillment of languages. The transfer can never be total, but what reaches this region is that element in a translation which goes beyond transmittal of subject matter. This nucleus is best defined as the element that does not lend itself to translation. Even when all the surface content has been extracted and transmitted, the primary concern of the genuine translator remains elusive. Unlike the words of the original, it is not translatable, because the relationship between content and language is quite different in the original and the translation. While content and language form a certain unity in the original, like a fruit and its skin, the language of the translation envelops its content like a royal robe with ample folds. For it signifies a more exalted language than its own and thus remains unsuited to its content, overpowering and alien. This disjunction prevents translation and at the same time makes it superfluous. For any translation of a work originating in a specific stage of linguistic history represents, in regard to a specific aspect of its content, translation into all other languages. Thus translation, ironically, transplants the original into a more definitive linguistic realm since it can no longer be displaced by a secondary rendering. The original can only be raised there anew and at other points of time. It is no mere coincidence that the word "ironic" here brings the Romanticists to mind. They, more than any others, were gifted with an insight into the life of literary works which has its highest testimony in translation. To be sure, they hardly recognized translation in this sense, but devoted their entire attention to criticism, another, if a lesser, factor in the continued life of literary works. But even though the Romanticists virtually ignored translation in their theoretical writings, their own great translations testify to their sense of the essential nature and the dignity of this literary mode. There is abundant evidence that this sense is not necessarily most pronounced in a poet; in fact, he may be least open to it. Not even literary history suggests the traditional notion that great poets have been eminent translators and lesser poets have been indifferent translators. A number of the most eminent ones, such as Luther, Voss, and Schlegel, are incomparably more important as translators than as creative writers; some of the great among them, such as Hölderlin and Stefan George, cannot be simply subsumed as poets, and quite particularly not if we consider them as translators. As translation is a mode of its own, the task of the translator, too, may be regarded as distinct and clearly differentiated from the task of the poet.

The task of the translator consists in finding that intended effect [*Intention*] upon the language into which he is translating which produces in it the echo of the original. This is a feature of translation which basically differentiates it from the poet's work, because the effort of the latter is never directed at the language as such, at its totality, but solely and immediately at specific linguistic contextual aspects. Unlike a work of literature, translation does not find itself in the center of the language forest but on the outside facing the wooded ridge; it calls into it without entering, aiming at that single spot where the echo is able to give, in its own language, the reverberation of the work in the alien one. Not only does the aim of translation differ from that of a literary work – it intends language as a whole, taking an individual work in an alien language as a point of departure – but it is a different effort altogether. The intention of the poet is spontaneous, primary, graphic; that of the translator is derivative, ultimate, ideational. For the great motif of integrating many tongues into one true language is at work. This language is one in which the independent sentences, works of literature, critical judgments, will never communicate – for they remain dependent on translation; but in it the languages themselves, supplemented and reconciled in their mode of signification, harmonize. If there is such a thing as a language of truth, the tensionless and even silent depository of the ultimate truth which all thought strives for, then this language of truth is – the true language. And this very language, whose divination and description is the only perfection a philosopher can hope for, is concealed in concentrated fashion in translations. There is no muse of philosophy, nor is there one of translation. But despite the claims of sentimental artists, these two are not banausic. For there is a philosophical genius that is characterized by a yearning for that language which manifests itself in translations. "*Les langues imparfaites en cela que plusieurs, manque la suprême: penser étant écrire sans accessoires, ni chuchotement mais tacite encore l'immortelle parole, la diversité, sur terre, des idiomes empêche personne de proférer les mots qui, sinon se trouveraient, par une frappe unique, elle-même matériellement la vérité.*"* If what Mallarmé evokes here is fully fathomable to a philosopher, translation, with its rudiments of such a language, is midway between poetry and doctrine. Its products are less sharply defined, but it leaves no less of a mark on history.

If the task of the translator is viewed in this light, the roads toward a solution seem to be all the more obscure and impenetrable. Indeed, the problem of ripening the seed of pure language in a translation seems to be insoluble, determinable in no solution. For is not the ground cut from under such a solution if the reproduction of the sense ceases to be decisive? Viewed negatively, this is actually the meaning of all the foregoing. The traditional concepts in any discussion of translations are fidelity and license – the freedom of faithful reproduction and, in its service, fidelity to the word. These ideas seem to be no longer serviceable to a theory that looks for other things in a translation than reproduction of meaning. To be sure, traditional usage makes these terms appear as if in constant conflict with each other. What can fidelity really do for the rendering of meaning? Fidelity in the translation of individual words can almost never fully reproduce the meaning they have in the original. For sense in its poetic significance is not limited to meaning, but derives from the connotations conveyed by the word chosen to express it. We say of words that they have emotional connotations. A literal rendering of the syntax completely demolishes the theory of reproduction of meaning and is a direct threat to comprehensibility. The nineteenth century considered Hölderlin's translations of Sophocles as monstrous examples of such literalness. Finally, it is self-evident how greatly fidelity in reproducing the form impedes the rendering of the sense. Thus no case for literalness can be based on a desire to retain the meaning. Meaning is served far better – and literature and language far worse – by the unrestrained license of bad translators. Of necessity, therefore, the demand for literalness, whose justification is obvious, whose legitimate ground is quite obscure, must be understood in a more meaningful context. Fragments of a vessel which are to be glued together must match one another in the smallest details, although they need not be like one another. In the same way a translation, instead of resembling the meaning of the original, must lovingly and in detail incorporate the original's mode of signification, thus making both the original and the translation recognizable as fragments of a greater language, just as fragments are part of a vessel. For this very reason translation must in large measure refrain from wanting to communicate something, from rendering the sense, and in this the original is important to it only insofar as it has already relieved the translator and his translation of the effort of assembling and expressing what is to be conveyed. In the realm of translation, too, the words ἐν ἀρχῇ ἦν ὁ λόγος [in the beginning was the word] apply. On the other hand, as regards the meaning, the language of a translation can – in fact, must – let itself go, so that it gives voice to the *intentio* of the original not as reproduction but as harmony, as a supplement to the language in which it expresses itself, as its own kind of *intentio*. Therefore it is not the highest praise of a translation, particularly in the age of its origin, to say that it reads as if it had originally been written in that language. Rather, the significance of fidelity as ensured by literalness is that the work reflects the great longing for linguistic complementation. A real translation is transparent; it does not cover the original, does not black its light, but allows the pure language, as though reinforced by its own medium to shine upon the original all the more fully. This may be achieved, above all, by a literal rendering of the syntax which proves words rather than sentences to be the primary element of the translator. For if the sentence is the wall before the language of the original, literalness is the arcade.

Fidelity and freedom in translation have traditionally been regarded as conflicting tendencies. This deeper interpretation of the one apparently does not serve to reconcile the two; in fact, it seems to deny the other all justification. For what is meant by freedom but that the rendering of the sense is no longer to be regarded as all-important? Only if the sense of a linguistic creation may be equated with the information it conveys does some ultimate, decisive element remain beyond all communication – quite close and yet infinitely remote, concealed or distinguishable, fragmented or powerful. In all language and linguistic creations there remains in addition to what can be conveyed something that cannot be communicated; depending on the context in which it appears, it is something that symbolizes or something symbolized. It is the former only in the finite products of language, the latter in the evolving of the languages themselves. And that which seeks to represent, to produce itself in the evolving of languages, is that very nucleus of pure language. Though concealed and fragmentary, it is an active force in life as the symbolized thing itself, whereas it inhabits linguistic creations only in symbolized form. While that ultimate essence, pure language, in the various tongues is tied only to linguistic elements and their changes, in linguistic creations it is weighted with a heavy, alien meaning. To relieve it of this, to turn the symbolizing into the symbolized, to regain pure language fully formed in the linguistic flux, is the tremendous and only capacity of translation. In this pure language – which no longer means or expresses anything but is, as expressionless and creative Word, that which is meant in all languages – all information, all sense, and all intention finally encounter a stratum in which they are destined to be extinguished. This very stratum furnishes a new and higher justification for free translation; this justification does not derive from the sense of what is to be conveyed, for the emancipation from this sense is the task of fidelity. Rather, for the sake of pure language, a free translation bases the test on its own language. It is the task of the translator to release in his own language that pure language which is under the spell of another, to liberate the language imprisoned in a work in his re-creation of that work. For the sake of pure language he breaks through decayed barriers of his own language. Luther, Voss, Hölderlin, and George have extended the boundaries of the German language. – And what of the sense in its importance for the relationship between translation and original? A simile may help here. Just as a tangent touches a circle lightly and at but one point, with this touch rather than with the point setting the law according to which it is to continue on its straight path to infinity, a translation touches the original lightly and only at the infinitely small point of the sense, thereupon pursuing its own course according to the laws of fidelity in the freedom of linguistic flux. Without explicitly naming or substantiating it, Rudolf Pannwitz has characterized the true significance of this freedom. His observations are contained in *Die Krisis der europäischen Kultur* and rank with Goethe's Notes to the *Westöstlicher Divan* as the best comment on the theory of translation that has been published in Germany. Pannwitz writes: "Our translations, even the best ones, proceed from a wrong premise. They want to turn Hindi, Greek, English into German instead of turning German into Hindi, Greek, English. Our translators have a far greater reverence for the usage of their own language than for the spirit of the foreign works. . . . The basic error of the translator is that he preserves the state in which his own language happens to be instead of allowing his language to be powerfully affected by the foreign tongue. Particularly when translating from a language very remote from his own he must go back to the primal elements of language itself and penetrate to the point where work, image, and tone converge. He must expand and deepen his language by means of the foreign language. It is not generally realized to what extent this is possible, to what extent any language can be transformed, how language differs from language almost the way dialect differs from dialect; however, this last is true only if one takes language seriously enough, not if one takes it lightly."

The extent to which a translation manages to be in keeping with the nature of this mode is determined objectively by the translatability of the original. The lower the quality and distinction of its language, the larger the extent to which it is information, the less fertile a field is it for translation, until the utter preponderance of content, far from being the lever for a translation of distinctive mode, renders it impossible. The higher the level of a work, the more does it remain translatable even if its meaning is touched upon only fleetingly. This, of course, applies to originals only. Translations, on the other hand, prove to be untranslatable not because of any inherent difficulty, but because of the looseness with which meaning attaches to them. Confirmation of this as well as of every other important aspect is supplied by Hölderlin's translations, particularly those of the two tragedies by Sophocles. In them the harmony of the languages is so profound that sense is touched by language only the way an aeolian harp is touched by the wind. Hölderlin's translations are prototypes of their kind; they are to even the most perfect renderings of their texts as a prototype is to a model. This can be demonstrated by comparing Hölderlin's and Rudolf Borchardt's translations of Pindar's Third Pythian Ode. For this very reason Hölderlin's translations in particular are subject to the enormous danger inherent in all translations: the gates of a language thus expanded and modified may slam shut and enclose the translator with silence. Hölderlin's translations from Sophocles were his last work; in them meaning plunges from abyss to abyss until it threatens to become lost in the bottomless depths of language. There is, however, a stop. It is vouchsafed to Holy Writ alone, in which meaning has ceased to be the watershed for the flow of language and the flow of revelation. Where a text is identical with truth or dogma, where it is supposed to be "the true language" in all its literalness and without the mediation of meaning, this text is unconditionally translatable. In such case translations are called for only because of the plurality of languages. Just as, in the original, language and revelation are one without any tension, so the translation must be one with the original in the form of the interlinear version, in which literalness and freedom are united. For to some degree all great texts contain their potential translation between the lines; this is true to the highest degree of sacred writings. The interlinear version of the Scriptures is the prototype or ideal of all translation.

A note on Harry Zohn's translation

Steven Rendall

In 1968 Harry Zohn published a pioneering translation of Walter Benjamin's "Die Aufgabe des Übersetzers," entitled "The Task of the Translator." Because of copyright restrictions, Zohn's version continues to be the main form in which Benjamin's famous essay is known to English-language readers. These notes examine certain problems raised by Zohn's version.

The most obvious are four glaring omissions. One of these has been noted by a number of critics:

> gewisse Relationsbegriffe ihren guten, ja vielleicht besten Sinn behalten, wenn sie nicht von vorne herein ausschliesslich auf den Menschen bezogen werden.
> (Benjamin 1923: 10)

> certain correlative concepts retain their meaning, and possibly their foremost significance, if they are referred exclusively to man.
> (Benjamin 1968: 70)

Here the omission of the negative completely inverts Benjamin's meaning and makes it impossible to follow the logic of his argument at this point. Paul de Man, in his commentary on Zohn's translation, regarded this omission as particularly crucial because it conceals what de Man saw as Benjamin's assertion of the inhuman, mechanical operation of language, of the essential *inhumanity* of language (de Man 1986).

A second omission I have not seen mentioned by critics occurs later in the essay:

> Wenn aber diese derart bis ans messianische Ende ihrer Geschichte wachsen . . .
> (Benjamin 1923: 14)

> If, however, these languages continue to grow in this manner until the end of their time . . .
> (Benjamin 1968: 74)

Here Zohn neglects to translate the word "messianisch," and this again cannot be considered insignificant, particularly with regard to the intense debates about the role of messianism in Benjamin's thought in general and in this essay in particular.

The third omission, which also seems to have passed unnoticed, occurs in the crucial passage where Benjamin is discussing the "wesenhafte Kern" that is the true translator's chief concern, and whose ripening points towards the (messianic) "realm of reconciliation and fulfillment of languages" without ever quite reaching or realizing it:

> Den erreicht es nicht mit Stumpf und Stiel, aber in ihm steht dasjenige, was an einer Übersetzung mehr ist als Mitteilung. Genauer lässt sich dieser wesenhafte Kern als dasjenige bestimmen, was an ihr selbst nicht wiederum übersetzbar is.
>
> (Benjamin 1923: 15)

> The transfer can never be total, but what reaches this region is that element in a translation which goes beyond transmittal of subject matter. This nucleus is best defined as the element that does not lend itself to translation.
>
> (Benjamin 1968: 75)

In this case, Zohn fails to translate the words "an ihr" and "wiederum" in the second sentence, with the result that it seems Benjamin is suggesting that the object of the translator's chief concern lies completely outside his reach. Although in one sense this may be true (as Paul de Man has argued), the point here is surely that whatever aspect of the "wesenhafte Kern" is echoed in a translation ("an ihr" clearly refers back to "die Übersetzung" in the preceding sentence) cannot be translated again. This presupposes, of course, that the "wesenhafte Kern" can be translated a first time. The reason it cannot be translated again – that is, the reason a translation of a translation gives no access to this essential nucleus of language – is, as Rodolphe Gasché's reading of the essay suggests, that this "wesenhafte Kern" of language consists of communicability or translatability itself, that which within language exceeds any given use, situation – or "language" (Gasché 1988). A translation of the kind Benjamin is defining makes perceptible the element of "pure language" simultaneously hidden and designated in the text to be translated – and which is precisely its translatability. One may find Benjamin's explanation of this point in the rest of this paragraph less than wholly clear, but the problem is not solved by merely eliding the words that cause it.

A fourth omission, which also seems to have gone unnoticed, occurs in a passage where Benjamin is discussing the traditional concepts of freedom and fidelity in translation:

> Treue und Freiheit – Freiheit der sinngemässen Wiedergabe und in ihrem Dienst Treue gegen das Wort – sind die althergebrachten Begriffe in jeder Diskussion von Übersetzungen.
>
> (Benjamin 1923: 17)

> The traditional concepts in any discussion of translations are fidelity and license – the freedom of faithful reproduction, and in its service, fidelity to the word.
>
> (Benjamin 1968: 77–78)

Zohn's translation omits the words *sinngemässen Wiedergabe* ("rendering in accord with the meaning"), thus making it hard for the reader to see that the "freedom" Benjamin refers to is the freedom – demanded by translation theorists from Horace to Dryden and beyond – to deviate from the letter of the text in order to render its spirit.

This omission is apparently connected with a fundamental misunderstanding of Benjamin's text reflected in Zohn's translation of the following passage:

Wenn Treue und Freiheit der Übersetzung seit jeher als widerstrebende Tendenzen betrachtet wurden, so scheint auch diese tiefere Deutung der einen beide nicht zu versöhnen, sondern im Gegenteil alles Recht der andern abzusprechen. Denn worauf bezieht Freiheit sich, wenn nicht auf die Wiedergabe des Sinnes, die aufhören soll, gesetzgegebend zu heissen?

(Benjamin 1923: 18–19)

Fidelity and freedom have traditionally been regarded as conflicting tendencies. This deeper interpretation of the one apparently does not serve to reconcile the two; in fact, it seems to deny the other all justification. For what is meant by freedom but that the rendering of the sense is no longer to be regarded as all important?

(Benjamin 1968: 79)

Zohn's rendering makes it appear that the reinterpreted concept is freedom, and that the reinterpretation deprives the concept of fidelity of any justification. This is precisely the reverse of what Benjamin's text says. The preceding passage has offered a reinterpretation of fidelity to the word (*Wörtlichkeit*) that disconnects it from the translation of meaning, and it is clearly this reinterpretation to which Benjamin is referring here. Thus the concept that is deprived of any justification by this reinterpretation is freedom, and the last sentence should read: "For what can the point of freedom be, if not the reproduction of meaning, which is no longer to be regarded as normative?"

Note

*   "The imperfection of languages consists in their plurality, the supreme one is lacking: thinking is writing without accessories or even whispering, the immortal word still remains silent; the diversity of idioms on earth prevents everybody from uttering the words which otherwise, at one single stroke, would materialize as truth."

Chapter 8

Ezra Pound

GUIDO'S RELATIONS

THE CRITIC, NORMALLY A BORE and a nuisance, can justify his existence in one or more minor and subordinate ways: he may dig out and focus attention upon matter of interest that would otherwise have passed without notice; he may, in the rare cases when he has any really general knowledge or "perception of relations" (swift or other), locate his finds with regard to other literary inventions; he may, thirdly, or as you might say, conversely and as part and supplement of his activity, construct cloacae to carry off the waste matter, which stagnates about the real work, and which is continuously being heaped up and caused to stagnate by academic bodies, obese publishing houses, and combinations of both, such as the Oxford Press. (We note their particular infamy in a recent re-issue of Palgrave.)

Since Dante's unfinished brochure on the common tongue, Italy may have had no general literary criticism, the brochure is somewhat "special" and of interest mainly to practitioners of the art of writing. Lorenzo Valla somewhat altered the course of history by his close inspection of Latin usage. His prefaces have here and there a burst of magnificence, and the spirit of the Elegantiae should benefit any writer's lungs. As he wrote about an ancient idiom, Italian and English writers alike have, when they have heard his name at all, supposed that he had no "message" and, in the case of the Britons, they returned, we may suppose, to Pater's remarks on Pico. (Based on what the weary peruser of some few other parts of Pico's output, might pettishly denounce as Pico's one remarkable paragraph.)

The study called "comparative literature" was invented in Germany but has seldom if ever aspired to the study of "comparative values in letters".

1929

The literature of the Mediterranean races continued in a steady descending curve of renaissanceism. There are minor upward fluctuations. The best period of Italian poetry ends in the year 1321. So far as I know one excellent Italian tennis-player and no known Italian writer has thought of considering the local literature in relation to the rest of the world.

Leopardi read, and imitated Shakespeare. The Prince of Monte Nevoso has been able to build his unique contemporary position because of barbarian contacts, whether consciously, and *via* visual stimulus from any printed pages, or simply because he was aware of, let us say, the existence of Wagner and Browning. If Nostro Gabriele started something new in Italian. Hating Barbarism, teutonism, never mentioning the existence of the ultimate Britons, unsurrounded by any sort of society or milieu, he ends as a solitary, superficially eccentric, but with a surprisingly sound standard of values, values, that is, as to the relative worth of a few perfect lines of writing, as contrasted to a great deal of flub-dub and "action".

The only living author who has ever taken a city or held up the diplomatic crapule at the point of machine-guns, he is in a position to speak with more authority than a batch of neurasthenic incompetents or of writers who never having swerved from their jobs, might be, or are, supposed by the scientists and the populace to be incapable of action. Like other serious characters who have taken seventy years to live and to learn to live, he has passed through periods wherein he lived (or wrote) we should not quite say "less ably", but with less immediately demonstrable result.

This period "nel mezzo", this passage of the "selva oscura" takes men in different ways, so different indeed that comparison is more likely to bring ridicule on the comparer than to focus attention on the analogy – often admittedly far-fetched.

In many cases the complete man makes a "very promising start", and then flounders or appears to flounder for ten years, or for twenty or thirty (cf. Henry James's middle period) to end, if he survive, with some sort of demonstration, discovery, or other justification of his having gone by the route he has (apparently) stumbled on.

When I "translated" Guido eighteen years ago I did *not* see Guido at all. I saw that Rossetti had made a remarkable translation of the *Vita Nuova*, in some places improving (or at least enriching) the original; that he was undubitably the man "sent", or "chosen" for that particular job, and that there was something in Guido that escaped him or that was, at any rate, absent from his translations. A *robustezza*, a masculinity. I had a great enthusiasm (perfectly justified), but I did not clearly see exterior demarcations – Euclid inside his cube, with no premonition of Cartesian axes.

My perception was not obfuscated by Guido's Italian, difficult as it then was for me to read. I was obfuscated by the Victorian language. If I hadn't been, I very possibly couldn't have done the job at all. I should have seen the too great multiplicity of problems contained in the one problem before me.

I don't mean that I didn't see dull spots in the sonnets. I saw that Rossetti had taken most of the best sonnets, that one couldn't make a complete edition of Guido simply by taking Rossetti's translations and filling in the gaps, it would have been too dreary a job. Even though I saw that Rossetti had made better English poems than I was likely to make by (in intention) sticking closer to the direction of the original. I began by meaning merely to give prose translation so that the reader ignorant of Italian could see what the melodic original meant. It is, however, an illusion to suppose that more than one person in every 300,000 has the patience or the intelligence to read a foreign tongue for its sound, or even to read what are known to be the masterworks of foreign melody, in order to learn the qualities of that melody, or to see where one's own falls short.

What obfuscated me was not the Italian but the crust of dead English, the sediment present in my own available vocabulary – which I, let us hope, got rid of a few years later. You can't go round this sort of thing. It takes six or eight years to get educated in one's art, and another ten to get rid of that education.

Neither can anyone learn English, one can only learn a series of Englishes. Rossetti made his own language. I hadn't in 1910 made a language, I don't mean a language to use, but even a language to think in.

It is stupid to overlook the lingual inventions of precurrent authors, even when they are fools or flapdoodles or Tennysons. It is sometimes advisable to sort out these languages and inventions, and to know what and why they are.

Keats, out of Elizabethans, Swinburne out of a larger set of Elizabethans and a mixed bag (Greeks, *und so weiter*), Rossetti out of Sheets, Kelly, and Co. plus early Italians (written and painted); and so forth, including *King Wenceslas*, ballads and carols.

Let me not discourage a possible reader, or spoil anyone's naïve enjoyment, by saying that my early versions of Guido are bogged in Dante Gabriel and in Algernon. It is true, but let us pass by it in silence. Where both Rossetti and I went off the rails was in taking an English sonnet as the equivalent for a sonnet in Italian. I don't mean in overlooking the mild difference in the rhyme scheme. The mistake is "quite natural", very few mistakes are "unnatural". Rime looks very important. Take the rimes off a good sonnet, and there is a vacuum. And besides the movement of *some* Italian sonnets *is* very like that in some sonnets in English. The feminine rhyme goes by the board . . . again for obvious reasons. It had gone by the board, quite often, in Provençal. The French made an ecclesiastical law about using it 50/50.

As a bad analogy, imagine a Giotto or Simone Martini fresco, "translated" into oils by "Sir Joshua", or Sir Frederick Leighton. Something is lost, something is somewhat denatured.

Suppose, however, we have a Cimabue done in oil, not by Holbein, but by some contemporary of Holbein who can't paint as well as Cimabue.

There are about seven reasons why the analogy is incorrect, and six more to suppose it inverted, but it may serve to free the reader's mind from preconceived notions about the English of "Elizabeth" and her British garden of song-birds. – And to consider language as a medium of expression.

(Breton forgives Flaubert on hearing that Father Gustave was trying only to give "l'impression de la couleur jaune" (*Nadja*, p. 12).)

Dr Schelling has lectured about the Italianate Englishman of Shakespeare's day. I find two Shakespeare plots within ten pages of each other in a forgotten history of Bologna, printed in 1596. We have heard of the effects of the travelling Italian theatre companies, *commedia dell'arte*, etc. What happens when you idly attempt to translate early Italian into English, unclogged by the Victorian era, freed from sonnet obsession, but trying merely to sing and to leave out the dull bits in the Italian, or the bits you don't understand?

I offer you a poem that "don't matter", it is attributed to Guido in Codex Barberiniano Lat. 3953. Alacci prints it as Guido's; Simone Occhi in 1740 says that Alacci is a fool or words to that effect and a careless man without principles, and proceeds to print the poem with those of Cino Pistoia. Whoever wrote it, it is, indubitably, not a *capo lavoro*.

> "Madonna la vostra belta enfolio
> Si li mei ochi che menan lo core   MS. *oghi*
> A la bataglia ove l' ancise amore
> Che del vostro placer armato uscio;   *usio*
>
> Si che nel primo asalto che asalio
> Passo dentro la mente e fa signore,
> E prese l' alma che fuzia di fore
> Planzendo di dolor che vi sentio.
>
> Però vedete che vostra beltate
> Mosse la folia und e il cor morto
> Et a me ne convien clamar pietate,
>
> Non per campar, ma per aver conforto
> Ne la morte crudel che far min fate
> Et o rason sel non vinzesse il torto."

Is it worth an editor's while to include it among dubious attributions? It is not very attractive: until one starts playing with the simplest English equivalent.

> "Lady thy beauty doth so mad mine eyes,
> Driving my heart to strife wherein he dies."

Sing it of course, don't try to speak it. It thoroughly falsifies the movement of the Italian, it is an opening quite good enough for Herrick or Campion. It will help you to understand just why Herrick, and Campion, and possibly Donne are still with us.

The next line is rather a cliché; the line after more or less lacking in interest. We pull up on:

> "Whereby thou seest how fair thy beauty is
> To compass doom".

That would be very nice, but it is hardly translation.

Take these scraps, and the almost impossible conclusion, a tag of Provençal rhythm, and make them into a plenum. It will help you to understand some of M. de Schloezer's remarks about Stravinsky's trend toward melody. And you will also see what the best Elizabethan lyricists did, as well as what they didn't.

My two lines take the opening and two and a half of the Italian, English more concise; and the octave gets too light for the sestet. Lighten the sestet.

> "So unto Pity must I cry
> Not for safety, but to die.
> Cruel Death is now mine ease
> If that he thine envoy is."

We are preserving one value of early Italian work, the cantabile; and we are losing another, that is the specific weight. And if we notice it we fall on a root difference between early Italian, "The philosophic school coming out of Bologna", and the Elizabethan lyric. For in these two couplets, and in attacking this sonnet, I have let go the fervour and the intensity, which were all I, rather blindly, had to carry through my attempt of twenty years gone.

And I think that if anyone now lay, or if we assume that they mostly *then* (in the expansive days) laid, aside care for specific statement of emotion, a dogmatic statement, made with the seriousness of someone to whom it mattered whether he had three souls, one in the head, one in the heart, one possibly in his abdomen, or lungs, or wherever Plato, or Galen, had located it; if the anima is still breath, if the stopped heart is a dead heart, and if it is all serious, much more serious than it would have been to Herrick, the imaginary investigator will see more or less how the Elizabethan modes came into being.

Let him try it for himself, on any Tuscan author of that time, taking the words, not thinking greatly of their significance, not baulking at clichés, but being greatly intent on the melody, on the single uninterrupted flow of syllables – as open as possible, that can be sung prettily, that are not very interesting if spoken, that don't even work into a period or an even metre if spoken.

And the mastery, a minor mastery, will lie in keeping this line unbroken, as unbroken in sound as a line in one of Miro's latest drawings is on paper; and giving it perfect balance, with no breaks, no bits sticking ineptly out, and no losses to the force of individual phrases.

> "Whereby thou seest how fair thy beauty is
> To compass doom."

Very possible too regularly "iambic" to fit in the finished poem.

There is opposition, not only between what M. de Schloezer distinguishes as musical and poetic lyricism, but in the writing itself there is a distinction between poetic lyricism, the emotional force of the verbal movement, and the melopœic lyricism, the letting the words flow on a melodic current, realized or not, realizable or not, if the line is supposed to be sung on a sequence of notes of different pitch.

But by taking these Italian sonnets, which are not metrically the equivalent of the English sonnet, by sacrificing, or losing, or simply not feeling and understanding their cogency, their sobriety, and by seeking simply that far from quickly or so-easily-as-it-looks attainable thing, the perfect melody, careless of exactitude of idea, or careless as to which profound and fundamental idea you, at that moment, utter, perhaps in precise enough phrases, by cutting away the apparently non-functioning phrases (whose appearance deceives) you find yourself in the English *seicento* song-books.

Death has become melodious; sorrow is as serious as the nightingale's, tomb-stones are shelves for the reception of rose-leaves. And there is, quite often, a Mozartian perfection of melody, a wisdom, almost perhaps an ultimate wisdom, deplorably lacking in guts. My phrase is, shall we say, vulgar. Exactly, because it fails in precision. Guts in surgery refers to a very limited range of internal furnish-ings. A thirteenth-century exactitude in search for the exact organ best illustrating the lack, would have saved me that plunge. We must turn again to the Latins. When the late T. Roosevelt was interviewed in France on his return from the jungle, he used a phrase which was translated (the publication of the interview rather annoyed him). The French at the point I mention ran: "Ils ont voulu me briser les *reins* mais je les ai solides."

And now the reader may, if he like, return to the problem of the "eyes that lead the heart to battle where him love kills". This was not felt as an inversion. It was 1280, Italian was still in the state that German is to-day. How can you have "PROSE" in a country where the chambermaid comes into your room and exclaims: "Schön ist das Hemd!"

Continue: who is armed with thy delight, is come forth so that at the first assault he assails, he passes inward to the mind, and lords it there, and catches the breath (soul) that was fleeing, lamenting the grief I feel.

"Whereby thou seest how thy beauty moves the madness, whence is the heart dead (stopped) and I must cry on Pity, not to be saved but to have ease of the cruel death thou puttest on me. And I am right (?) save the wrong him conquereth."

When the reader will accept this little problem in melopœia as substitute for the cross-word puzzle I am unable to predict. I leave it on the supposition that the philosopher should try almost everything once.

As second exercise, we may try the sonnet by Guido Orlando which is supposed to have invited Cavalcanti's *Donna mi Prega*.

"Say what is Love, whence doth he start	?
Through what be his courses bent	?
Memory, substance, accident	?
A chance of eye or will of heart	?
Whence he state or madness leadeth	?
Burns he with consuming pain	?
Tell me, friend, on what he feedeth	?
How, where, and o'er whom doth he reign	?
Say what is Love, hath he a face	?
True form or vain similitude	?
Is the Love life, or is he death	?
Thou shouldst know for rumour saith:	
Servant should know his master's mood –	
Oft art thou ta'en in his dwelling-place."	

I give the Italian to show that there is no deception, I have invented nothing, I have given a *verbal* weight about equal to that of the original, and arrived at this equality by dropping a couple of syllables per line. The great past-master of pastiche has, it would seem, passed this way before me. A line or two of this, a few more from Lorenzo Medici, and he has concocted one of the finest gems in our language.

"Onde si move e donde nasce Amore
qual è suo proprio luogo, ov' ei dimora
Sustanza, o accidente, o ei memora?
E cagion d' occhi, o è voler di cuore?

Da che procede suo stato o furore?
Come fuoco si sente che divora?
Di che si nutre domand' io ancora,
Come, e quando, e di cui si fa signore?

Che cosa è, dico, amor? ae figura?
A per se forma o pur somiglia altrui?
E vita questo amore ovvero e morte?

Ch 'l serve dee saver di sua natura:
Io ne domando voi, Guido, di lui:
Odo che molto usate in la sua corte."

We are not in a realm of proofs, I suggest, simply, the way in which early Italian poetry has been utilized in England. The Italian of Petrarch and his successors is of no interest to the practising writer or to the student of comparative dynamics in language, the collectors of bric-à-brac are outside our domain.

There is no question of giving Guido in an English contemporary to himself, the ultimate Britons were at that date unbreeched, painted in woad, and grunting in an idiom far more difficult for us to master than the Langue d'Oc of the Plantagenets or the Lingua di Si.

If, however, we reach back to pre-Elizabethan English, or a period when the writers were still intent on clarity and explicitness, still preferring them to magnilo-quence and the thundering phrase, our trial, or mine at least, results in:

"Who is she that comes, makying turn every man's eye
And makying the air to tremble with a bright clearenesse
That leadeth with her Love, in such nearness
No man may proffer of speech more than a sigh?

Ah God, what she is like when her owne eye turneth, is
Fit for Amor to speake, for I cannot at all;
Such is her modesty, I would call
Every woman else but an useless uneasiness.

No one could ever tell all of her pleasauntness
In that every high noble vertu leaneth to herward,
So Beauty sheweth her forth as her Godhede;

Never before so high was our mind led,
Nor have we so much of heal as will afford
That our mind may take her immediate in its embrace."

The objections to such a method are: the doubt as to whether one has the right to take a serious poem and turn it into a mere exercise in quaintness; the "misrepresentation" not of the poem's antiquity, but of the proportionate feel of that antiquity, by which I mean that Guido's thirteenth-century language is to twentieth-century Italian sense much less archaic than any fourteenth-, fifteenth-, or early sixteenth-century English is for us. It is even doubtful whether my bungling version of twenty years back isn't more "faithful", in the sense at least that it tried to preserve the fervour of the original. And as this fervour simply does not occur in English poetry in those centuries there is no ready-made verbal pigment for its objectification.

In the long run the translator is in all probability impotent to do *all* of the work for the linguistically lazy reader. He can show where the treasure lies, he can guide the reader in choice of what tongue is to be studied, and he can very materially assist the hurried student who has a smattering of a language and the energy to read the original text alongside the metrical gloze.

This refers to "interpretative translation". The "other sort", I mean in cases where the "translater" is definitely making a new poem, falls simply in the domain of original writing, or if it does not it must be censured according to equal standards, and praised with some sort of just deduction, assessable only in the particular case.

Chapter 9

Jorge Luis Borges

THE TRANSLATORS OF *THE THOUSAND AND ONE NIGHTS*

Translated by Esther Allen

1 Captain Burton

AT TRIESTE, IN 1872, in a palace with damp statues and deficient hygienic facilities, a gentleman on whose face an African scar told its tale – Captain Richard Francis Burton, the English consul – embarked on a famous translation of the *Quitab alif laila ua laila*, which the *roumis* know by the title, *The Thousand and One Nights*. One of the secret aims of his work was the annihilation of another gentleman (also weatherbeaten, and with a dark Moorish beard) who was compiling a vast dictionary in England and who died long before he was annihilated by Burton. That gentleman was Edward Lane, the Orientalist, author of a highly scrupulous version of *The Thousand and One Nights* that had supplanted a version by Galland. Lane translated against Galland, Burton against Lane; to understand Burton we must understand this hostile dynasty.

I shall begin with the founder. As is known, Jean Antoine Galland was a French Arabist who came back from Istanbul with a diligent collection of coins, a monograph on the spread of coffee, a copy of the *Nights* in Arabic, and a supplementary Maronite whose memory was no less inspired than Scheherazade's. To this obscure consultant – whose name I do not wish to forget: it was Hanna, they say – we owe certain fundamental tales unknown to the original: the stories of Aladdin; the Forty Thieves; Prince Ahmad and the Fairy Peri-Banu; Abu al-Hasan, the Sleeper and Waker; the night adventure of Caliph Harun al-Rashid; the two sisters who envied their younger sister. The mere mention of these names amply demonstrates that Galland established the canon, incorporating stories that time would render indispensable and that the translators to come – his enemies – would not dare omit.

Another fact is also undeniable. The most famous and eloquent encomiums of *The Thousand and One Nights* – by Coleridge, Thomas De Quincey, Stendhal, Tennyson, Edgar Allan Poe, Newman – are from readers of Galland's translation. Two hundred years and ten better translations have passed, but the man in Europe or the Americas who thinks of *The Thousand and One Nights* thinks, invariably, of this first translation. The Spanish adjective *milyunanochesco* [thousand-and-one-nights-esque] – *milyunanochero* is too Argentine, *milyunanocturno* overly variant – has nothing to do with the erudite obscenities of Burton or Mardrus, and everything to do with Antoine Galland's bijoux and sorceries.

Word for word, Galland's version is the most poorly written of them all, the least faithful, and the weakest, but it was the most widely read. Those who grew intimate with it experienced happiness and astonishment. Its Orientalism, which seems frugal to us now, was bedazzling to men who took snuff and composed tragedies in five acts. Twelve exquisite volumes appeared from 1707 to 1717, twelve volumes that were innumerably read and that passed into various languages, including Hindi and Arabic. We, their mere anachronistic readers of the twentieth century, perceive only the cloying flavor of the eighteenth century in them and not the evaporated aroma of the Orient which two hundred years ago was their novelty and their glory. No one is to blame for this disjunction, Galland least of all. At times, shifts in the language work against him. In the preface to a German translation of *The Thousand and One Nights*, Doctor Weil recorded that the merchants of the inexcusable Galland equip themselves with a "valise full of dates" each time the tale obliges them to cross the desert. It could be argued that in 1710 the mention of dates alone sufficed to erase the image of a valise, but that is unnecessary: *valise*, then, was a sub-species of saddlebag.

There have been other attacks. In a befuddled panegyric that survives in his 1921 *Morceaux choisis*, André Gide vituperates the licenses of Antoine Galland, all the better to erase (with a candor that entirely surpasses his reputation) the notion of the literalness of Mardrus, who is as *fin de siècle* as Galland is eighteenth-century, and much more unfaithful.

Galland's discretions are urbane, inspired by decorum, not morality. I copy down a few lines from the third page of his *Nights*: "*Il alla droit à l'appartement de cette princesse, qui, ne s'attendant pas à le revoir, avait reçu dans son lit un des derniers officiers de sa maison.*" [He went directly to the chamber of that princess, who, not expecting to see him again, had received in her bed one of the lowliest servants of his household.] Burton concretizes this nebulous *officier*: "a black cook of loathsome aspect and foul with kitchen grease and grime." Each, in his way, distorts: the original is less ceremonious than Galland and less greasy than Burton. (Effects of decorum: in Galland's measured prose, "*recevoir dans son lit*" has a brutal ring.)

Ninety years after Antoine Galland's death, an alternate translator of the *Nights* is born: Edward Lane. His biographers never fail to repeat that he is the son of Dr. Theophilus Lane, a Hereford prebendary. This generative datum (and the terrible Form of holy cow that it evokes) may be all we need. The Arabized Lane lived five studious years in Cairo, "almost exclusively among Moslems, speaking and listening to their language, conforming to their customs with the greatest care, and received by all of them as an equal." Yet neither the high Egyptian nights nor the black and opulent coffee with cardamom seed nor frequent literary discussions with the Doctors of the Law nor the venerable muslin turban nor the meals eaten with his fingers made him forget his British reticence, the delicate central solitude of the masters of the earth. Consequently, his exceedingly erudite version of the *Nights* is (or seems to be) a mere encyclopedia of evasion. The original is not professionally obscene; Galland corrects occasional indelicacies because he believes them to be in bad taste. Lane seeks them out and persecutes them like an inquisitor. His probity makes no pact with silence: he prefers an alarmed chorus of notes in a cramped supplementary volume, which murmur things like: *I shall overlook an episode of the most reprehensible sort*; *I suppress a repugnant explanation*; *Here, a line far too coarse for translation*; *I must of necessity suppress the other anecdote*; *Hereafter, a series of omissions*; *Here, the story of the slave Bujait, wholly inappropriate for translation*. Mutilation does not exclude death: some tales are rejected in their entirety "because they cannot be purified without destruction." This responsible and total repudiation does not strike me as illogical: what I condemn is the Puritan subterfuge. Lane is a virtuoso of the subterfuge, an undoubted precursor of the still more bizarre reticences of Hollywood. My notes furnish me with a pair of examples. In night 391, a fisherman offers a fish to the king of kings, who wishes to know if it is male or female, and is told it is a hermaphrodite. Lane succeeds in taming this inadmissible colloquy by translating that the king asks what species the fish in question belongs to, and the astute fisherman replies that it is of a mixed species. The tale of night 217 speaks of a king with two wives, who lay one night with the first and the following night with the second, and so they all were happy. Lane accounts for the good fortune of this monarch by saying that he treated his wives "with impartiality" . . . One reason for this was that he destined his work for "the parlor table," a center for placid reading and chaste conversation.

The most oblique and fleeting reference to carnal matters is enough to make Lane forget his honor in a profusion of convolutions and occultations. There is no other fault in him. When free of the peculiar contact of this temptation, Lane is of an admirable veracity. He has no objective, which is a positive advantage. He does not seek to bring out the barbaric color of the *Nights* like Captain Burton, or to forget it and attenuate it like Galland, who domesticated his Arabs so they would not be irreparably out of place in Paris. Lane is at great pains to be an authentic descendant of Hagar. Galland was completely ignorant of all literal precision; Lane justifies his interpretation of each problematic word. Galland invoked an invisible manuscript and a dead Maronite; Lane furnishes editions and page numbers. Galland did not bother about notes; Lane accumulates a chaos of clarifications which, in organized form, make up a separate volume. To be different: this is the rule the precursor imposes. Lane will follow the rule: he needs only to abstain from abridging the original.

The beautiful Newman–Arnold exchange (1861–1862) – more memorable than its two interlocutors – extensively argued the two general ways of translating. Newman championed the literal mode, the retention of all verbal singularities: Arnold, the severe elimination of details that distract or detain. The latter procedure may provide the charms of uniformity and seriousness; the former, continuous small surprises. Both are less important than the translator and his literary habits. To translate the spirit is so enormous and phantasmal an intent that it may well be innocuous; to translate the letter, a requirement so extravagant that there is no risk of its ever being attempted. More serious than these infinite aspirations is the retention or suppression of certain particularities; more serious than these preferences and oversights is the movement of the syntax. Lane's syntax is delightful, as befits the refined parlor table. His vocabulary is often excessively festooned with Latin words, unaided by any artifice of brevity. He is careless; on the opening page of his translation he places the adjective *romantic* in the bearded mouth of a twelfth-century Moslem, which is a kind of futurism. At times this lack of sensitivity serves him well, for it allows him to include very commonplace words in a noble paragraph, with involuntary good results. The most rewarding example of such a cooperation of heterogenous words must be: "And in this palace is the last information respecting lords collected in the dust." The following invocation may be another: "By the Living One who does not die or have to die, in the name of He to whom glory and permanence belong." In Burton – the occasional precursor of the always fantastical Mardrus – I would be suspicious of so satisfyingly Oriental a formula; in Lane, such passages are so scarce that I must suppose them to be involuntary, in other words, genuine.

The scandalous decorum of the versions by Galland and Lane has given rise to a whole genre of witticisms that are traditionally repeated. I myself have not failed to respect this tradition. It is common knowledge that the two translators did not fulfil their obligation to the unfortunate man who witnessed the Night of Power, to the imprecations of a thirteenth-century garbage collector cheated by a dervish, and to the customs of Sodom. It is common knowledge that they disinfected the Nights.

Their detractors argue that this process destroys or wounds the good-hearted naiveté of the original. They are in error; *The Book of the Thousand Nights and a Night* is not (morally) ingenuous; it is an adaptation of ancient stories to the low-brow or ribald tastes of the Cairo middle classes. Except in the exemplary tales of the *Sindibad-namah*, the indecencies of *The Thousand and One Nights* have nothing to do with the freedom of the paradisiacal state. They are speculations on the part of the editor: their aim is a round of guffaws, their heroes are never more than porters, beggars, or eunuchs. The ancient love stories of the repertory, those which relate cases from the Desert or the cities of Arabia, are not obscene, and neither is any production of pre-Islamic literature. They are impassioned and sad, and one of their favorite themes is death for love, the death that an opinion rendered by the *ulamas* declared no less holy than that of a martyr who bears witness to the faith . . . If we approve of this argument, we may see the timidities of Galland and Lane as the restoration of a primal text.

I know of another defense, a better one. An evasion of the original's erotic opportunities is not an unpardonable sin in the sight of the Lord when the primary aim is to emphasize the atmosphere of magic. To offer mankind a new *Decameron* is a commercial enterprise like so many others; to offer an "Ancient Mariner," now, or a "*Bateau ivre,*" is a thing that warrants entry into a higher celestial sphere. Littmann observes that *The Thousand and One Nights* is, above all, a repertory of marvels. The universal imposition of this assumption on every Western mind is

Galland's work; let there be no doubt on that score. Less fortunate than we, the Arabs claim to think little of the original; they are already well acquainted with the men, mores, talismans, deserts, and demons that the tales reveal to us.

In a passage somewhere in his work, Rafael Cansinos Asséns swears he can salute the stars in fourteen classical and modern languages. Burton dreamed in seventeen languages and claimed to have mastered thirty-five: Semitic, Dravidian, Indo-European, Ethiopic . . . This vast wealth does not complete his definition: it is merely a trait that tallies with the others, all equally excessive. No one was less vulnerable to the frequent gibes in *Hudibras* against learned men who are capable of saying absolutely nothing in several languages. Burton was a man who had a considerable amount to say, and the seventy-two volumes of his complete works say it still. I will note a few titles at random: *Goa and the Blue Mountains* (1851); *A Complete System of Bayonet Exercise* (1853); *Personal Narrative of a Pilgrimage to El-Medinah and Meccah* (1855); *The Lake Regions of Central Equatorial Africa* (1860); *The City of the Saints* (1861); *The Highlands of the Brazil* (1869); *On an Hermaphrodite from the Cape de Verde Islands* (1866); *Letters from the Battlefields of Paraguay* (1870); *Ultima Thule* (1875); *To the Gold Coast for Gold* (1883); *The Book of the Sword* (first volume, 1884); *The Perfumed Garden of Cheikh Nefzaoui* – a posthumous work consigned to the flames by Lady Burton, along with the *Priapeia, or the Sporting Epigrams of Divers Poets on Priapus*. The writer can be deduced from this catalogue: the English captain with his passion for geography and for the innumerable ways of being a man that are known to mankind. I will not defame his memory by comparing him to Morand, that sedentary, bilingual gentleman who infinitely ascends and descends in the elevators of identical international hotels, and who pays homage to the sight of a trunk . . . Burton, disguised as an Afghani, made the pilgrimage to the holy cities of Arabia; his voice begged the Lord to deny his bones and skin, his dolorous flesh and blood, to the Flames of Wrath and Justice; his mouth, dried out by the *samun*, left a kiss on the aerolith that is worshipped in the Kaaba. The adventure is famous: the slightest rumor that an uncircumcised man, a *nasráni*, was profaning the sanctuary would have meant certain death. Before that, in the guise of a dervish, he practiced medicine in Cairo – alternating it with prestidigitation and magic so as to gain the trust of the sick. In 1858, he commanded an expedition to the secret sources of the Nile, a mission that led him to discover Lake Tanganyika. During that undertaking he was attacked by a high fever; in 1855, the Somalis thrust a javelin through his jaws (Burton was coming from Harar, a city in the interior of Abyssinia that was forbidden to Europeans). Nine years later, he essayed the terrible hospitality of the ceremonious cannibals of Dahomey; on his return there was no scarcity of rumors (possibly spread and certainly encouraged by Burton himself) that, like Shakespeare's omniverous proconsul,[1] he had "eaten strange flesh." The Jews, democracy, the British Foreign Office, and Christianity were his preferred objects of loathing; Lord Byron and Islam, his venerations. Of the writer's solitary trade he made something valiant and plural: he plunged into his work at dawn, in a vast chamber multiplied by eleven tables, with the materials for a book on each one – and, on a few, a bright spray of jasmine in a vase of water. He inspired illustrious friendships and loves: among the former I will name only that of Swinburne, who dedicated the second series of *Poems and Ballads* to him – "in recognition of a friendship which I must always count among the highest honours of my life" – and who mourned his death in many stanzas. A man of words and deeds, Burton could well take up the boast of Almotanabi's *Divan*:

> The horse, the desert, the night know me,
> Guest and sword, paper and pen.

It will be observed that, from his amateur cannibal to his dreaming polyglot, I have not rejected those of Richard Burton's personae that, without diminishment of fervor, we could call legendary. My reason is clear: the Burton of the Burton legend is the translator of the *Nights*. I have sometimes suspected that the radical distinction between poetry and prose lies in the very different expectations of readers: poetry presupposes an intensity that is not tolerated in prose. Something similar happens with Burton's work: it has a preordained prestige with which no other Arabist has ever been able to compete. The attractions of the forbidden are rightfully his. There was a single edition, limited to one thousand copies for the thousand subscribers of the Burton Club, with a legally binding commitment never to reprint. (The Leonard C. Smithers re-edition "omits given passages in dreadful taste, whose elimination will be mourned by no one"; Bennett Cerf's representative selection – which purports to be unabridged – proceeds from this purified text.) I will venture a hyperbole: to peruse *The Thousand and One Nights* in Sir Richard's translation is no less incredible than to read them in "a plain and literal translation with explanatory notes" by Sinbad the Sailor.

The problems Burton resolved are innumerable, but a convenient fiction can reduce them to three: to justify and expand his reputation as an Arabist; to differ from Lane as ostensibly as possible; and to interest nineteenth-century British gentlemen in the written version of thirteenth-century oral Moslem tales. The first of these aims was perhaps incompatible with the third; the second led him into a serious lapse, which I must now disclose. Hundreds of couplets and songs occur in the *Nights*; Lane (incapable of falsehood except with respect to the flesh) translated them precisely into a comfortable prose. Burton was a poet: in 1880 he had privately published *The Kasidah of Haji Abdu*, an evolutionist rhapsody that Lady Burton always deemed far superior to FitzGerald's *Rubáiyát*. His rival's "prosaic" solution did not fail to arouse Burton's indignation, and he opted for a rendering into English verse – a procedure that was unfortunate from the start since it contradicted his own rule of total literalness. His ear was as greatly offended against as his sense of logic, for it is not impossible that this quatrain is among the best he came up with:

> A night whose stars refused to run their course,
> A night of those which never seem outworn:
> Like Resurrection-day, of lonesome length
> To him that watched and waited for the morn.[2]

And it is entirely possible that this one is not the worst:

> A sun on wand in knoll of sand she showed,
> Clad in her cramoisy-hued chemisette:
> Of her lips honey-dew she gave me drink,
> And with her rosy cheeks quencht fire she set.

I have alluded to the fundamental difference between the original audience of the tales and Burton's club of subscribers. The former were roguish, prone to exaggeration, illiterate, infinitely suspicious of the present and credulous of remote marvels; the latter were the respectable men of the West End, well equipped for disdain and erudition but not for belly laughs or terror. The first audience appreciated the fact that the whale died when it heard the man's cry; the second, that there had ever been men who lent credence to any fatal capacity of such a cry. The text's marvels – undoubtedly adequate in Kordofan or Bûlâq, where they were offered up as true – ran the risk of seeming rather threadbare in England. (No one requires that the truth be plausible or instantly ingenious: few readers of the *Life and Correspondence of Karl Marx* will indignantly demand the symmetry of Toulet's *Contrerimes* or the severe precision of an acrostic.) To keep his subscribers with him, Burton abounded in explanatory notes on "the manners and customs of Moslem men," a territory previously occupied by Lane. Clothing, everyday customs, religious practices, architecture, references to history or to the Koran, games, arts, mythology – all had already been elucidated in the inconvenient precursor's three volumes. Predictably, what was missing was the erotic. Burton (whose first stylistic effort was a highly personal account of the brothels of Bengal) was rampantly capable of filling this gap. Among the delinquent delectations over which he lingered, a good example is a certain random note in the seventh volume which the index wittily entitles "*capotes mélancoliques*" [melancholy French letters]. The *Edinburgh Review* accused him of writing for the sewer; the *Encyclopedia Britannica* declared that an unabridged translation was unacceptable and that Edward Lane's version "remained unsurpassed for any truly serious use." Let us not wax too indignant over this obscure theory of the scientific and documentary superiority of expurgation: Burton was courting these animosities. Furthermore, the slightly varying variations of physical love did not entirely consume the attention of his commentary, which is encyclopedic and seditious and of an interest that increases in inverse proportion to its necessity. Thus Volume Six (which I have before me) includes some three hundred notes, among which are the following: a condemnation of jails and a defense of corporal punishment and fines; some examples of the Islamic respect for bread; a legend about the hairiness of Queen Belkis's legs; an enumeration of the four colors that are emblematic of death; a theory and practice of Oriental ingratitude; the information that angels prefer a piebald mount, while Djinns favor horses with a bright-bay coat; a synopsis of the mythology surrounding the secret Night of Power or Night of Nights; a denunciation of the superficiality of Andrew Lang; a diatribe against rule by democracy; a census of the names of Mohammed, on the Earth, in the Fire, and in the Garden; a mention of the Amalekite people, of long years and large stature; a note on the private parts of the Moslem, which for the man extend from the navel to his knees, and for the woman from the top of the head to the tips of her toes; a consideration of the *asa'o* [roasted beef] of the Argentine gaucho; a warning about the discomforts of "equitation" when the steed is human; an allusion to a grandiose plan for cross-breeding baboons with women and thus deriving a sub-race of good proletarians. At fifty, a man has accumulated affections, ironies, obscenities, and copious anecdotes; Burton unburdened himself of them in his notes.

The basic problem remains: how to entertain nineteenth-century gentlemen with the pulp fictions of the thirteenth century? The stylistic poverty of the *Nights* is well known. Burton speaks somewhere of the "dry and business-like tone" of the Arab prosifiers, in contrast to the rhetorical luxuriance of the Persians. Littmann, the ninth translator, accuses himself of having interpolated words such as *asked*, *begged*, *answered*, in five thousand pages that know of no other formula than an invariable *said*. Burton lovingly abounds in this type of substitution. His vocabulary is as unparalleled as his notes. Archaic words coexist with slang, the lingo of prisoners or sailors with technical terms. He does not shy away from the glorious hybridization of English: neither Morris's Scandinavian repertory nor Johnson's Latin has his blessing, but rather the contact and reverberation of the two. Neologisms and foreignisms are in plentiful supply: *castrato*, *inconséquence*, *hauteur*, *in gloria*, *bagnio*, *langue fourrée*, *pundonor*, *vendetta*, *Wazir*. Each of these is indubitably the *mot juste*, but their interspersion amounts to a kind of skewing of the original. A good skewing, since such verbal – and syntactical – pranks beguile the occasionally exhausting course of the *Nights*. Burton administers them carefully: first he translates gravely "Sulayman, Son of David (on the twain be peace!)"; then – once this majesty is familiar to us – he reduces it to "Solomon Davidson." A king who, for the other translators, is "King of Samarcand in Persia," is, for Burton, "King of Samarcand in Barbarian-land"; a merchant who, for the others, is "ill-tempered", is "a man of wrath." That is not all: Burton rewrites in its entirety – with the addition of circumstantial details and physiological traits – the initial and final story. He thus, in 1885, inaugurates a procedure whose perfection (or whose *reductio ad absurdum*) we will now consider in Mardrus. An Englishman is always more timeless than a Frenchman: Burton's heterogeneous style is less antiquated than Mardrus's, which is noticeably dated.

2 Doctor Mardrus

Mardrus's destiny is a paradoxical one. To him has been ascribed the *moral* virtue of being the most truthful translator of *The Thousand and One Nights*, a book of admirable lascivity, whose purchasers were previously hoodwinked by Galland's good manners and Lane's Puritan qualms. His prodigious literalness, thoroughly demonstrated by the inarguable subtitle "Literal and complete translation of the Arabic text," is revered, along with the inspired idea of writing *The Book of the Thousand Nights and One Night*. The history of this title is instructive; we should review it before proceeding with our investigation of Mardrus.

Masudi's *Meadows of Gold and Mines of Precious Stones* describes an anthology titled *Hazar afsana*, Persian words whose true meaning is "a thousand adventures," but which people renamed "a thousand nights." Another tenth-century document, the *Fihrist*, narrates the opening tale of the series, the king's heartbroken oath that every night he will wed a virgin whom he will have beheaded at dawn, and the resolution of Scheherazade, who diverts him with marvelous stories until a thousand nights have revolved over the two of them and she shows him his son. This invention – far superior to the future and analogous devices of Chaucer's pious cavalcade or Giovanni Boccaccio's epidemic – is said to be posterior to the title, and was devised in the aim of justifying it . . . Be that as it may, the early figure of 1000 quickly increased to 1001. How did this additional and now indispensable night emerge, this prototype of Pico della Mirandola's *Book of All Things and Also Many Others*, so derided by Quevedo and later Voltaire. Littmann suggests a contamination of the Turkish phrase *bin bir*, literally "a thousand and one," but commonly used to mean "many." In early 1840, Lane advanced a more beautiful reason: the magical dread of even numbers. The title's adventures certainly did not end there. Antoine Galland, in 1704, eliminated the original's repetition and translated *The Thousand and One Nights*, a name now familiar in all the nations of Europe except England, which prefers *The Arabian Nights*. In 1839, the editor of the Calcutta edition, W. H. Macnaghten, had the singular scruple of translating *Quitab alif laila ua laila* as *Book of the Thousand Nights and One Night*. This renovation through spelling did not go unremarked. John Payne, in 1882, began publishing his *Book of the Thousand Nights and One Night*; Captain Burton, in 1885, his *Book of the Thousand Nights and a Night*; J. C. Mardrus, in 1899, his *Livre des mille nuits et une nuit*.

I turn to the passage that made me definitively doubt this last translator's veracity. It belongs to the doctrinal story of the City of Brass, which in all other versions extends from the end of night 566 through part of night 578, but which Doctor Mardrus has transposed (for what cause, his Guardian Angel alone knows) to nights 338–346. I shall not insist on this point; we must not waste our consternation on this inconceivable reform of an ideal calendar. Scheherazade-Mardrus relates:

> The water ran through four channels worked in the chamber's floor with charming meanderings, and each channel had a bed of a special color; the first channel had a bed of pink porphyry; the second of topaz, the third of emerald, and the fourth of turquoise; so that the water was tinted the color of the bed, and bathed by the attenuated light filtered in through the silks above, it projected onto the surrounding objects and the marble walls all the sweetness of a seascape.

As an attempt at visual prose in the manner of *The Portrait of Dorian Gray*, I accept (and even salute) this description; as a "literal and complete" version of a passage composed in the thirteenth century, I repeat that it alarms me unendingly. The reasons are multiple. A Scheherazade without Mardrus describes by enumerating parts, not by mutual reaction, does not attest to circumstantial details like that of water that takes on the color of its bed, does not define the quality of light filtered by silk, and does not allude to the Salon des Aquarellistes in the final image. Another small flaw: "charming meanderings" is not Arabic, it is very distinctly French. I do not know if the foregoing reasons are sufficient; they were not enough for me, and I had the indolent pleasure of comparing the three German versions by Weil, Henning, and Littmann, and the two English versions by Lane and Sir Richard Burton. In them I confirmed that the original of Mardrus's ten lines was this: "The four drains ran into a fountain, which was of marble in various colors."

Mardrus's interpolations are not uniform. At times they are brazenly anachronistic – as if suddenly the Fashoda incident and Marchand's withdrawal were being discussed. For example:

They were overlooking a dream city . . . As far as the gaze fixed on hori-
zons drowned by the night could reach, the vale of bronze was terraced
with the cupolas of palaces, the balconies of houses, and serene gardens;
canals illuminated by the moon ran in a thousand clear circuits in the
shadow of the peaks, while away in the distance, a sea of metal contained
the sky's reflected fires in its cold bosom.

Or this passage, whose Gallicism is no less public:

A magnificent carpet of glorious colors and dexterous wool opened its
odorless flowers in a meadow without sap, and lived all the artificial life
of its verdant groves full of birds and animals, surprised in their exact
natural beauty and their precise lines.

(Here the Arabic editions state: "To the sides were carpets, with a variety of birds
and beasts embroidered in red gold and white silver, but with eyes of pearls and
rubies. Whoever saw them could not cease to wonder at them.")

Mardrus cannot cease to wonder at the poverty of the "Oriental color" of
The Thousand and One Nights. With a stamina worthy of Cecil B. de Mille, he heaps
on the viziers, the kisses, the palm trees and the moons. He happens to read, in
night 570:

They arrived at a column of black stone, in which a man was buried up
to his armpits. He had two enormous wings and four arms; two of which
were like the arms of the sons of Adam, and two like a lion's forepaws,
with iron claws. The hair on his head was like a horse's tail, and his eyes
were like embers, and he had in his forehead a third eye which was like
the eye of a lynx.

He translates luxuriantly:

One evening the caravan came to a column of black stone, to which was
chained a strange being, only half of whose body could be seen, for the
other half was buried in the ground. The bust that emerged from the
earth seemed to be some monstrous spawn riveted there by the force
of the infernal powers. It was black and as large as the trunk of an old,
rotting palm tree, stripped of its fronds. It had two enormous black
wings and four hands, of which two were like the clawed paws of a lion.
A tuft of coarse bristles like a wild ass's tale whipped wildly over its
frightful skull. Beneath its orbital arches flamed two red pupils, while
its double-horned forehead was pierced by a single eye, which opened,
immobile and fixed, shooting out green sparks like the gaze of a tiger
or a panther.

Somewhat later he writes:

The bronze of the walls, the fiery gemstones of the cupolas, the ivory terraces, the canals and all the sea, as well as the shadows projected towards the West, merged harmoniously beneath the nocturnal breeze and the magical moon.

"Magical," for a man of the thirteenth century, must have been a very precise classification, and not the gallant doctor's mere urbane adjective . . . I suspect that the Arabic language is incapable of a "literal and complete" version of Mardrus's paragraph, and neither is Latin or the Spanish of Miguel de Cervantes.

The Book of the Thousand and One Nights abounds in two procedures: one (purely formal), rhymed prose; the other, moral predications. The first, retained by Burton and by Littmann, coincides with the narrator's moments of animation: people of comely aspect, palaces, gardens, magical operations, mentions of the Divinity, sunsets, battles, dawns, the beginnings and endings of tales. Mardrus, perhaps mercifully, omits it. The second requires two faculties: that of majestically combining abstract words and that of offering up stock comments without embarrassment. Mardrus lacks both. From the line memorably translated by Lane as "And in this palace is the last information respecting lords collected in the dust," the good Doctor barely extracts: "They passed on, all of them! They had barely the time to repose in the shadow of my towers." The angel's confession – "I am imprisoned by Power, confined by Splendor, and punished for as long as the Eternal commands it, to whom Force and Glory belong" – is, for Mardrus's reader, "I am chained here by the Invisible Force until the extinction of the centuries."

Nor does sorcery have in Mardrus a co-conspirator of good will. He is incapable of mentioning the supernatural without smirking. He feigns to translate, for example:

One day when Caliph Abdelmelik, hearing tell of certain vessels of antique copper whose contents were a strange black smoke-cloud of diabolical form, marveled greatly and seemed to place in doubt the reality of facts so commonly known, the traveller Talib ben-Sahl had to intervene.

In this paragraph (like the others I have cited, it belongs to the Story of the City of Brass, which, in Mardrus, is made of imposing Bronze), the deliberate candor of "so commonly known" and the rather implausible doubts of Caliph Abdelmelik are two personal contributions by the translator.

Mardrus continually strives to complete the work neglected by those languid, anonymous Arabs. He adds Art Nouveau passages, fine obscenities, brief comical interludes, circumstantial details, symmetries, vast quantities of visual Orientalism. An example among so many: in night 573, the Emir Musa bin Nusayr orders his blacksmiths and carpenters to construct a strong ladder of wood and iron. Mardrus (in his night 344) reforms this dull episode, adding that the men of the camp went in search of dry branches, peeled them with knives and scimitars, and bound them together with turbans, belts, camel ropes, leather cinches and tack, until they had built a tall ladder that they propped against the wall, supporting it with stones on both sides . . . In general, it can be said that Mardrus does not translate the book's words but its scenes: a freedom denied to translators, but tolerated in illustrators, who are allowed to add these kinds of details . . . I do not know if these smiling diversions are what infuse the work with such a happy air, the air of a far-fetched personal yarn rather than of a laborious hefting of dictionaries. But to me the Mardrus "translation" is the most readable of them all – after Burton's incomparable version, which is not truthful either. (In Burton, the falsification is of another order. It resides in the gigantic employ of a gaudy English, crammed with archaic and barbaric words.)

I would greatly deplore it (not for Mardrus, for myself) if any constabulary intent were read into the foregoing scrutiny. Mardrus is the only Arabist whose glory was promoted by men of letters, with such unbridled success that now even the Arabists know who he is. André Gide was among the first to praise him, in August 1889; I do not think Cancela and Capdevila will be the last. My aim is not to demolish this admiration, but to substantiate it. To celebrate Mardrus's fidelity is to leave out the soul of Mardrus, to ignore Mardrus entirely. It is his infidelity, his happy and creative infidelity, that must matter to us.

3 Enno Littmann

Fatherland to a famous Arabic edition of *The Thousand and One Nights*, Germany can take (vain) glory in four versions: by the "librarian though Israelite" Gustav Weil – the adversative is from the Catalan pages of a certain Encyclopedia – ; by Max Henning, translator of the Koran; by the man of letters Félix Paul Greve; and by Enno Littmann, decipherer of the Ethiopic inscriptions in the fortress of Axum. The first of these versions, in four volumes (1839–1842), is the most pleasurable, as its author – exiled from Africa and Asia by dysentery – strives to maintain or substitute for the Oriental style. His interpolations earn my deepest respect. He has some intruders at a gathering say, "We do not wish to be like the morning, which disperses all revelries." Of a generous king, he assures us, "The fire that burns for his guests brings to mind the Inferno and the dew of his benign hand is like the Deluge"; of another he tells us that his hands "were liberal as the sea." These fine apocrypha are not unworthy of Burton or Mardrus, and the translator assigned them to the parts in verse, where this graceful animation can be an *ersatz* or replacement for the original rhymes. Where the prose is concerned, I see that he translated it as is, with certain justified omissions, equidistant from hypocrisy and immodesty. Burton praised his work – "as faithful as a translation of a popular nature can be." Not in vain was Doctor Weil Jewish "though librarian"; in his language I think I perceive something of the flavor of Scripture.

The second version (1895–1897) dispenses with the enchantments of accuracy, but also with those of style. I am speaking of the one provided by Henning, a Leipzig Arabist, to Philipp Reclam's *Universalbibliothek*. This is an expurgated version, though the publisher claims otherwise. The style is dogged and flat. Its most indisputable virtue must be its length. The editions of Bûlâq and Breslau are represented, along with the Zotenberg manuscripts and Burton's *Supplemental Nights*. Henning, translator of Sir Richard, is, word for word, superior to Henning, translator of Arabic, which is merely a confirmation of Sir Richard's primacy over the Arabs.

In the book's preface and conclusion, praises of Burton abound – almost deprived of their authority by the information that Burton wielded "the language of Chaucer, equivalent to medieval Arabic." A mention of Chaucer as *one* of the sources of Burton's vocabulary would have been more reasonable. (Another is Sir Thomas Urquhart's Rabelais.)

The third version, Greve's, derives from Burton's English and repeats it, excluding only the encyclopedic notes. Insel-Verlag published it before the war.

The fourth (1923–1928) comes to supplant the previous one and, like it, runs to six volumes. It is signed by Enno Littmann, decipherer of the monuments of Axum, cataloguer of the 283 Ethiopic manuscripts found in Jerusalem, contributor to the *Zeitschrift für Assyriologie*. Though it does not engage in Burton's indulgent loitering, his translation is entirely frank. The most ineffable obscenities do not give him pause; he renders them into his placid German, only rarely into Latin. He omits not a single word, not even those that register – 1000 times – the passage from one night to the next. He neglects or refuses all local color: express instructions from the publisher were necessary to make him retain the name of Allah and not substitute it with God. Like Burton and John Payne, he translates Arabic verse into Western verse. He notes ingenuously that if the ritual announcement "So-and-so pronounced these verses" were followed by a paragraph of German prose, his readers would be disconcerted. He provides whatever notes are necessary for a basic understanding of the text: twenty or so per volume, all of them laconic. He is always lucid, readable, mediocre. He follows (he tells us) the very breath of the Arabic. If the *Encyclopedia Britannica* contains no errors, his translation is the best of all those in circulation. I hear that the Arabists agree; it matters not at all that a mere man of letters – and he of the merely Argentine Republic – prefers to dissent.

My reason is this: the versions by Burton and Mardrus, and even by Galland, can only be conceived of *in the wake of a literature*. Whatever their blemishes or merits, these characteristic works presuppose a rich (prior) process. In some way, the almost inexhaustible process of English is adumbrated in Burton – John Donne's hard obscenity, the gigantic vocabularies of Shakespeare and Cyril Tourneur, Swinburne's affinity for the archaic, the crass erudition of the authors of seventeenth-century chapbooks, the energy and imprecision, the love of tempests and magic. In Mardrus's laughing paragraphs, *Salammbô* and La Fontaine, the *Mannequin d'osier* and the *ballets russes* all coexist. In Littmann, who, like Washington, cannot tell a lie, there is nothing but the probity of Germany. This is so little, so very little. The commerce between Germany and the *Nights* should have produced something more.

Whether in philosophy or in the novel, Germany possesses a literature of the fantastic – rather, it possesses *only* a literature of the fantastic. There are marvels in the *Nights* that I would like to see rethought in German. As I formulate this desire, I think of the repertory's deliberate wonders – the all-powerful slaves of a lamp or a ring, Queen Lab who transforms Moslems into birds, the copper boatman with talismans and formulae on his chest – and of those more general ones that proceed from its collective nature, from the need to complete one thousand and one episodes. Once they had run out of magic, the copyists had to fall back on historical or pious notices whose inclusion seems to attest to the good faith of the rest. The ruby that ascends into sky and the earliest description of Sumatra, details of the court of the Abbasids and silver angels whose food is the justification of the Lord all dwell together in a single volume. It is, finally, a poetic mixture; and I would say the same of certain repetitions. Is it not portentous that on night 602 King Schahriah hears his own story from the queen's lips? Like the general framework, a given tale often contains within itself other tales of equal length: stages within the stage as in the tragedy of *Hamlet*, raised to the power of a dream. A clear and difficult line from Tennyson seems to define them:

Laborious orient ivory, sphere in sphere.

To heighten further the astonishment, these adventitious Hydra's heads can be more concrete than the body: Schahriah, the fantastical king "of the Islands of China and Hindustan" receives news of Tarik ibn Ziyad, governor of Tangiers and victor in the battle of Guadalete . . . The threshold is confused with the mirror, the mask lies beneath the face, no one knows any longer which is the true man and which are his idols. And none of it matters; the disorder is as acceptable and trivial as the inventions of a daydream.

Chance has played at symmetries, contrasts, digressions. What might a man – a Kafka – do if he organized and intensified this play, remade it in line with the Germanic distortion, the *Unheimlichkeit* of Germany?

Notes

1   I allude to Mark Anthony, invoked by Caesar's apostrophe: "on the Alps/It is reported, thou didst eat strange flesh/Which some did die to look on . . ." In these lines, I think I glimpse some inverted reflection of the zoological myth of the basilisk, a serpent whose gaze is fatal. Pliny (*Natural History*, Book Eight, paragraph 33) tells us nothing of the posthumous aptitudes of this ophidian, but the conjunction of the two ideas of seeing (*mirar*) and dying (*morir*) *vedi Napoli e poi mori* [see Naples and die] – must have influenced Shakespeare.

The gaze of the basilisk was poisonous; the Divinity, however, can kill with pure splendor or pure radiation of *manna*. The direct sight of God is intolerable. Moses covers his face on Mount Horeb, "for he was afraid to look on God"; Hakim, the prophet of Khorasan, used a four-fold veil of white silk in order not to blind men's eyes. Cf. also Isaiah 6:5, and 1 Kings 19:13.

2   Also memorable is this variation on the themes of Abulmeca de Ronda and Jorge Manrique: "Where is the wight who peopled in the past/Hind-land and Sind; and there the tyrant played?"

References

Among the volumes consulted, I must enumerate:

Les Mille et une Nuits, contes arabes traduits par Galland. Paris, s.d.
The Thousand and One Nights, commonly called The Arabian Nights Entertainments. A new translation from the Arabic, by E. W. Lane. London, 1839.

The Book of the Thousand Nights and a Night. A plain and literal translation, by Richard
  F. Burton. London (?) n.d. vols. VI, VII, VIII.

The Arabian Nights. A complete (sic) *and unabridged selection from the famous literal translation of R. F. Burton*, New York, 1932.

Le Livre des Mille Nuits et Une Nuit. Traduction littérale et complète du texte arabe, par le
  Dr. J. C. Mardrus, Paris, 1906.

Tausend und eine Nacht. Aus dem Arabischen übertragen von Max Henning. Leipzig,
  1897.

*Die Erzählungen aus den Tausendundein Nächten. Nach dem arabischen Urtext der Calcuttaer
  Ausgabe vom Jahre 1839* übertragen von Enno Littmann. Leipzig, 1928.

1940s–1950s

TRANSLATION THEORY DURING these decades is dominated by the fundamental issue of translatability. Influential figures in philosophy, literary criticism, and linguistics all consider whether translation can reconcile the differences that separate languages and cultures. The obstacles to translation are duly noted, judged either insurmountable or negotiable, and translation methods are formulated with precision. Opinions are shaped by disciplinary trends and vary widely, ranging between the extremes of philosophical skepticism and practical optimism.

The skeptical extreme in Anglo-American analytical philosophy is occupied by Willard Van Orman Quine's concept of "radical translation," or "the translation of the language of a hitherto untouched people," which he first explored in the late 1950s (Brower 1959: 148; Quine 1960). Quine questions the empirical foundations of translating by pointing to a basic semantic "indeterminacy" that cannot be resolved even in the presence of an environmental "stimulus" (Brower 1959: 172). Since he couches his arguments in an imaginary ethnographical encounter between a "linguist" who is "Western" and even "English-bred" and a "native" who speaks a "jungle language" (ibid.: 154, 167), Quine's anti-foundationalism carries larger implications, both anthropological and geopolitical. His discourse, however, adheres to the abstraction of analytical philosophy, and these implications are not pursued, treated instead as the purview of other disciplines.

Quine acknowledges that translating does in fact occur on the basis of "analytical hypotheses," derived from segmentations of foreign utterances which are equated with words and phrases in the translating language (ibid.: 165). And linguists rely on them to produce effective dictionaries, grammars, and manuals. Still, he argues that none of these translating tools can guarantee a correlation between stimuli and meaning. The "conceptual schemes" that shape interpretations of the data may divide the native from the linguist (ibid.: 154–155, 167). These schemes may be not only mutually unintelligible, but incommensurable, likely to use different standards to evaluate translations. Quine's doubt of metaphysical grounds for language leads to more pragmatic views of translation wherein meaning is seen as conventional, socially circumscribed, and the foreign text is rewritten according to the terms and values of the receiving culture. "Most talk of meaning," he observes, "requires tacit reference to a home language in much the way that talk of truth involves tacit reference to one's own system of the world" (ibid.: 171).

Continental philosophical traditions, notably hermeneutics and existential phenomenology, continue to be conscious of the linguistic and cultural differences that impede translation. In 1946, a decade before Quine begins to deliver his challenging papers at American universities, Martin Heidegger's essay "The Anaximander Fragment" sets out a powerful understanding of how competing conceptual schemes complicate modern translations of ancient Greek philosophy. The versions of classical scholars are questionable, Heidegger argues, because they assimilate Anaximander to later metaphysical traditions which follow Plato or Aristotle. These translations carry philosophical assumptions that are either idealist or positivist, giving the Greek text a religious or scientific cast.

Heidegger's anti-metaphysical approach to language, unlike Quine's, comes with a practical solution that is distinctly literary. Reviving Schleiermacher's notion of translation as bringing the domestic reader to the foreign text, Heidegger recommends a "poetizing" strategy that does "violence" to everyday language by relying on archaisms, which he submits to etymological interpretations (Heidegger 1975: 19). The etymologies are motivated by an exacting fidelity, designed to demonstrate a kinship between German and classical Greek culture. But they also inscribe Anaximander with a modern, peculiarly Heideggerian outlook.

When literary criticism addresses the issue of translatability, it emphasizes the impossibility of reproducing a foreign literary text in another language which is sedimented with different literary styles, genres, and traditions. **Vladimir Nabokov** sees national literatures as sites of international influence and affiliation which nonetheless develop in nationally distinct ways, producing unique "masterpieces" that demand from the translator an "ideal version," ultimately unattainable (Nabokov 1941: 161). In the 1955 essay that appears here, Nabokov describes the complicated resonances and allusions of Alexsandr Pushkin's poem *Eugene Onegin* so as to rationalize his own scholarly version of it: close to the Russian, devoid of Anglo-American poetic diction, and heavily annotated. For Nabokov, paraphrastic versions that "conform to the notions and prejudices of a given public" constitute the worst "evil" of translation (Nabokov 1941: 160). Yet he too privileges the values of a given public, even if an elite minority: an academic readership who might want a literal translation by a scholar who can combine native proficiency in the foreign language, historical scholarship in the foreign literature, and detailed commentary on the formal features of the foreign text.

Nabokov's views on translation are very much those of a Russian émigré writer living in the United States after 1940. He nurtures a deep, nostalgic investment in the Russian language and in canonical works of Russian literature and disdains the homogenizing tendencies of American consumer culture. Few English-language literary translators at the time follow Nabokov's uncompromising example. The dominant trend favors just the sort of "poetical" language he detests, free versions that seek to produce poetic effects in the translating language, usually deploying standard usage and canonical styles.

In 1958, a few years after Nabokov's essay appears, the American poet, critic and translator Dudley Fitts criticizes it precisely in these terms, asserting that in poetry translation "we need something at once less ambitious and more audacious: another poem" (Fitts 1959: 34). The poem, moreover, has to be a particular kind, possessing immense fluency, written in the most familiar language: current American English with some socially acceptable colloquialisms. As a translator of classical and Latin American literatures, Fitts inclines toward adaptation, achieving notable success with his modernizing versions of Aristophanes. Nevertheless, he is aware that his translations of ancient Greek poetry might be anachronistic, risking "a spurious atmosphere of monotheism by writing 'God' for 'Zeus'" (Fitts 1956: xviii).

The optimistic extreme in translation theory during these decades is occupied by linguistic analysis. Linguistics addresses the issue of translatability by analyzing specific translation problems and describing the methods that translators have developed to solve them. The optimism derives to some extent from a theory of language that is communicative, not constitutive, of meaning, which in turn is conceived along empiricist lines as referential. Chaim Rabin's essay "The Linguistics of Translation" opens with the assertion that translation "involves two distinct factors, a 'meaning,' or reference to some slice of reality, and the difference between two languages in referring to that reality" (Rabin 1958: 123). But Heidegger and Quine might ask: which version of reality will be used to measure the success of the translation, the adequacy of its reference?

Eugene Nida, drawing on research from the American Bible Society, considers the problem of translating between different realities. He argues that solutions need to be ethnological, based on the translator's acquisition of sufficient "cultural information." Since "it is inconceivable to a Maya Indian that any place should not have vegetation unless it has been cleared for a maize-field," Nida concludes that the Bible translator "must translate 'desert' as an 'abandoned place'" to establish "the cultural equivalent of the desert of Palestine" (Nida 1945: 197). Here translation is paraphrase. It works to reduce linguistic and cultural differences to a shared referent. Yet the referent is clearly a core of meaning constructed by the translator and weighted toward the receiving culture so as to be comprehensible there.

The signal achievement of **Roman Jakobson**'s widely cited 1959 essay (reprinted here) is to have introduced a semiotic reflection on translatability. Jakobson questions empiricist semantics by conceiving of meaning, not as a reference to reality, but as a relation to a potentially endless chain of signs. He describes translation as a process of recoding which "involves two equivalent messages in two different codes." Jakobson underestimates the interpretive nature of translation, the fact that recoding is an active rewording that doesn't simply transmit the foreign message, but transforms it. Still, he is mindful of the differences among cultural discourses, especially poetry, where "grammatical categories carry a high semantic import" and which therefore requires translation that is a "creative transposition" into a different system of signs.

The most influential work of translation studies in this period is first published in 1958 by the Canadian linguists **Jean-Paul Vinay and Jean Darbelnet**. By approaching French–English translation from the field of comparative stylistics, they are able to provide a theoretical basis for a variety of translation methods currently in use. As a result, they produce a textbook that has been a staple in translator training programs for over four decades. Their descriptions of translation methods involve some reduction of linguistic and cultural differences to empiricist semantics: "Equivalence of messages," they write, "ultimately relies upon an identity of situations," where the term "situations" indicates an undefined "reality." But they also encourage the translator to think of meaning as a cultural construction and to see a close connection between linguistic procedures and "metalinguistic information," namely "the current state of literature, science, politics etc. of both language communities" (Vinay and Darbelnet 1995: 42).

The enormous practical and pedagogical value of Vinay and Darbelnet's work overcame any philosophical qualms about translatability – and distracted attention away from their conservative prescriptions about language use in translation. The extract reprinted here is remarkable both for its careful methodological description and for its criticisms of translation in the global political economy.

This period closes with Reuben Brower's anthology (1959), which helpfully gathers together the main trends in commentary on translation. There, notwithstanding great conceptual and methodological differences, linguists, literary critics, and philosophers join in a remarkable unity of interest in translation as a problem of language and culture. And they are joined by translators, both academics in those fields and writers in various genres, who present sophisticated discussions of translation and their own projects.

Valéry Larbaud's "invocation" of St. Jerome (1946), the patron saint of sense-for-sense translation, must be ranked among the most accomplished of translators' commentaries. Larbaud's text is learned but literary, effortlessly conjuring up a range of theorists and practitioners from Quintilian to Alexander Fraser Tytler to Paul Valéry. Larbaud views translation through Aristotelian categories of poetics and rhetoric. Yet his concerns are modernist, including the recommendation that translations be given a "foreign air" despite the protestations of "purists," whose vernacular nationalism he judges "more dangerous to the essence of culture than the most fiercely boorish ignorance" (Larbaud 1946: 164, my translation). For Larbaud, only an approach to translation that combines theory and history can challenge the misunderstanding that greets the translator's work in the present.

Further reading

Gentzler 1993, Hjort 1990, Kelly 1979, Larose 1989, Malmkjær 1993, Robinson 1991, Sturrock 1991, Venuti 1995

Chapter 10

Vladimir Nabokov

PROBLEMS OF TRANSLATION: *ONEGIN* IN ENGLISH

I

I **CONSTANTLY FIND IN REVIEWS** of verse translations the following kind of thing that sends me into spasms of helpless fury: "Mr. (or Miss) So-and-so's translation reads smoothly." In other words, the reviewer of the "translation," who neither has, nor would be able to have, without special study, any knowledge whatsoever of the original, praises as "readable" an imitation only because the drudge or the rhymster has substituted easy platitudes for the breathtaking intricacies of the text. "Readable," indeed! A schoolboy's boner is less of a mockery in regard to the ancient masterpiece than its commercial interpretation or poetization. "Rhyme" rhymes with "crime," when Homer or *Hamlet* are rhymed. The term "free translation" smacks of knavery and tyranny. It is when the translator sets out to render the "spirit" – not the textual sense – that he begins to traduce his author. The clumsiest literal translation is a thousand times more useful than the prettiest paraphrase.

For the last five years or so I have been engaged, on and off, in translating and annotating Pushkin's *Onegin*. In the course of this work I have learned some facts and come to certain conclusions. First, the facts.

The novel is concerned with the afflictions, affections and fortunes of three young men – Onegin, the bitter lean fop, Lenski, the temperamental minor poet, and Pushkin, their friend – and of three young ladies – Tatiana, Olga, and Pushkin's Muse. Its events take place between the end of 1819 and the spring of 1825. The scene shifts from the capital to the countryside (midway between Opochka and Moscow), and thence to Moscow and back to Petersburg. There is a description of a young rake's day in town; rural landscapes and rural libraries; a dream and a duel; various festivities in country and city; and a variety of romantic, satirical and bibliographic digressions that lend wonderful depth and color to the thing.

Onegin himself is, of course, a literary phenomenon, not a local or historical one. Childe Harold, the hero of Byron's "romaunt" (1812), whose "early youth [had been] misspent in maddest whim," who has "moping fits," who is bid to loath his present state by a "weariness which springs from all [he] meets," is really only a relative, not the direct prototype, of Onegin. The latter is less "a Muscovite in Harold's cloak" than a descendant of many fantastic Frenchmen such as Chateaubriand's *René*, who was aware of existing only through a "*profond sentiment d'ennui.*" Pushkin speaks of Onegin's spleen or "chondria" (the English "hypo" and the Russian "chondria" or "*handra*" represent a neat division of linguistic labor on the part of two nations) as of "a malady the cause of which it seems high time to find." To this search Russian critics applied themselves with commendable zeal, accumulating during the last one hundred and thirty years one of the most somniferous masses of comments known to civilized man. Even a special term for Onegin's "sickness" has been invented (*Oneginstvo*); and thousands of pages have been devoted to him as a "type" of something or other. Modern Soviet critics standing on a tower of soapboxes provided a hundred years ago by Belinski, Herzen, and many others, diagnosed Onegin's sickness as the result of "Tzarist despotism." Thus a character borrowed from books but brilliantly recomposed by a great poet to whom life and library were one, placed by that poet within a brilliantly reconstructed environment, and played with by him in a succession of compositional patterns – lyrical impersonations, tomfooleries of genius, literary parodies, stylized epistles, and so on – is treated by Russian commentators as a sociological and historical phenomenon typical of Alexander the First's regime: alas, this tendency to generalize and vulgarize the unique fancy of an individual genius has also its advocates in this country.

Actually there has never been anything especially local or time-significant in hypochondria, misanthropy, ennui, the blues, *Weltschmerz*, etc. By 1820, ennui was a seasoned literary cliché of characterization which Pushkin could toy with at his leisure. French fiction of the eighteenth century is full of young characters suffering from the spleen. It was a convenient device to keep one's hero on the move. Byron gave it a new thrill; René, Adolphe, and their co-sufferers received a transfusion of demon blood.

Evgeniy Onegin is a Russian novel in verse. Pushkin worked at it from May 1823 to October 1831. The first complete edition appeared in the spring of 1833 in St. Petersburg; there is a well-preserved specimen of this edition at the Houghton Library, Harvard University. *Onegin* has eight chapters and consists of 5,551 lines, all of which, except a song of eighteen unrhymed lines (in trochaic trimeter), are in iambic tetrameter, rhymed. The main body of the work contains, apart from two freely rhymed epistles, 366 stanzas, each of fourteen lines, with a fixed rhyme pattern: ababeecciddiff (the vowels indicate the feminine rhymes, the consonants the masculine ones). Its resemblance to the sonnet is obvious. Its octet consists of an elegiac quatrain and of two couplets, its sestet of a closed quatrain and a couplet. This hyperborean freak is far removed from the Petrarchan pattern, but is distinctly related to Malherbe's and Surrey's variations.

The tetrametric, or "anacreontic," sonnet was introduced in France by Scévole de Sainte-Marthe in 1579; and it was once tried by Shakespeare (Sonnet CXLV: "Those lips that Love's own hand did make," with a rhyme scheme "make-hate-sake: state-come-sweet-doom-greet: end-day-fiend-away. Threw-you"). The *Onegin* stanza would be technically an English anacreontic sonnet had not the second quatrain consisted of two couplets instead of being closed or alternate. The novelty of Pushkin's freak sonnet is that its first twelve lines include the greatest variation in rhyme sequence possible within a three-quatrain frame: alternate, paired, and closed. However, it is really from the French, not from the English, that Pushkin derived the idea for this new kind of stanza. He knew his Malherbe well – and Malherbe had composed several sonnets (see, for example, "*A Rabel, peintre, sur un livre de fleurs,*" 1630) in tetrameter, with four rhymes in the octet and asymmetrical quatrains (the first alternately rhymed, the second closed), but of course Malherbe's sestet was the classical one, never clinched with a couplet in the English fashion. We have to look elsewhere for Pushkin's third quatrain and for his epigrammatic couplet – namely in French light verse of the seventeenth and eighteenth century. In one of Gresset's "*Epîtres*" ("*Au Père Bougeant, jésuite*") the Onegin sestet is exactly represented by the lines

> Mais pourquoi donner au mystère,
> Pourquoi reprocher au hazard
> De ce prompt et triste départ
> La cause trop involontaire?
> Oui, vous seriez encore à nous
> Si vous étiez vous-même à vous.

Theoretically speaking, it is not impossible that a complete *Onegin* stanza may be found embedded somewhere in the endless "Epistles" of those periwigged bores, just as its sequence of rhymes is found in La Fontaine's *Contes* (e.g. "*Nicaise,*" 48–61) and in Pushkin's own freely-rhymed *Ruslan i Lyudmila*, composed in his youth (see the last section of Canto Three, from *Za otdalyonnïmi godami* to *skazal mne vazhno Chernomor*). In this Pushkinian pseudo-sonnet the opening quatrain, with its brilliant alternate rhymes, and the closing couplet, with its epigrammatic click, are in greater evidence than the intermediate parts, as if we were being shown first the pattern on one side of an immobile sphere which would then start to revolve, blurring the colors, and presently would come to a stop, revealing clearly again a smaller pattern on its opposite side.

As already said, there are in *Onegin* more than 300 stanzas of this kind. We have moreover fragments of two additional chapters and numerous stanzas canceled by Pushkin, some of them sparkling with more originality and beauty than any in the Cantos from which he excluded them before publication. All this matter, as well as Pushkin's own commentaries, the variants, epigraphs, dedications, and so forth, must be of course translated too, in appendices and notes.

II

Russian poetry is affected by the following six characteristics of language and prosody:

1   The number of rhymes, both masculine and feminine (i.e., single and double), is incomparably greater than in English and leads to the cult of the rare and the rich. As in French, the *consonne d'appui* is obligatory in masculine rhymes and aesthetically valued in feminine ones. This is far removed from the English rhyme, Echo's poor relation, a genteel pauper whose attempts to shine result merely in doggerel garishness. For if in Russian and French, the feminine rhyme is a glamorous lady friend, her English counterpart is either an old maid or a drunken hussy from Limerick.

2   No matter the length of a word in Russian it has but one stress; there is never a secondary accent or two accents as occurs in English – especially American English.

3   Polysyllabic words are considerably more frequent than in English.

4   All syllables are fully pronounced; there are no elisions and slurs as there are in English verse.

5   Inversion, or more exactly pyrrhichization of trochaic words – so commonly met with in English iambics (especially in the case of two-syllable words ending in -er or -ing) – is rare in Russian verse: only a few two-syllable prepositions and the trochaic components of compound words lend themselves to shifts of stress.

6   Russian poems composed in iambic tetrameter contain a larger number of modulated lines than of regular ones, while the reverse is true in regard to English poems.

By "regular line" I mean an iambic line in which the metrical beat coincides in each foot with the natural stress of the word: *Of cloudless climes and starry skies* (Byron). By "modulated line" I mean an iambic line in which at least one metrical accent falls on the unstressed syllable of a polysyllabic word (such as the third syllable in "reasonable") or on a monosyllabic word unstressed in speech (such as "of," "the," "and" etc.). In Russian prosody such modulations are termed "half-accents," and both in Russian and English poetry a tetrametric iambic line may have one such half-accent on the first, second, or third foot, or two half-accents in the first and third, or in adjacent feet. Here are some examples (the Roman figure designates the foot where the half-accent occurs).

I	Make the delighted spirit glow (Shelley);
	My apprehensions come in crowds (Wordsworth);
II	Of forests and enchantments drear (Milton);
	Beyond participation lie (Wordsworth);
III	Do paint the meadows with delight (Shakespeare);
	I know a reasonable woman (Pope);
I+II	And on that unforgotten shore (Bottomly);
II+III	When icicles hang by the wall (Shakespeare);

I+III   Or in the chambers of the sea (Blake);
          An incommunicable sleep (Wordsworth).

It is important to mark that, probably in conjunction with characteristic 3, the half-accent in the third foot occurs three or four times more frequently in Russian iambic tetrameters than in English ones, and that the regular line is more than twice rarer. If, for instance, we examine Byron's *Mazeppa*, Scott's *The Lady of the Lake*, Keats's *The Eve of Saint Mark* and Tennyson's *In Memoriam*, we find that the percentage of regular lines there is around 65, as against only some 25 in *Onegin*. There is, however, one English poet whose modulations, if not as rich in quantity and variety as Pushkin's, are at least an approach to that richness. I refer to Andrew Marvell. It is instructive to compare Byron's snip-snap monotonies such as

One shade the more one ray the less
Had half impaired the nameless grace
Which waves in every raven tress
Or softly lightens o'er her face

with any of the lines addressed by Marvell "To His Coy Mistress":

And you should if you please refuse,
Till the conversion of the Jews
My vegetable love should grow
Vaster than empires and more slow,

– four lines in which there are six half-accents against Byron's single one.

It is among such melodies that one should seek one's model when translating Pushkin in verse.

III

I shall now make a statement for which I am ready to incur the wrath of Russian patriots: Alexandr Sergeyevich Pushkin (1799–1837), the national poet of Russia, was as much a product of French literature as of Russian culture; and what happened to be added to this mixture, was individual genius which is neither Russian nor French, but universal and divine. In regard to Russian influence, Zhukovski and Batyushkov were the immediate predeccessors of Pushkin: harmony and precision – this was what he learned from both, though even his boyish verses were more vivid and vigorous than those of his young teachers. Pushkin's French was as fluent as that of any highly cultured gentleman of his day. Gallicisms in various stages of assimilation populate his poetry with the gay hardiness of lucern and dandelion invading a trail in the Rocky Mountains. *Cœur flétri, essaim de désirs, transports, alarmes, attraits, attendrissement, fol amour, amer regret* are only a few — my list comprises about ninety expressions that Pushkin as well as his predecessors and contemporaries transposed from French into melodious Russian. Of special importance is *bizarre, bizarrerie* which Pushkin rendered as *strannïy, strannost'* when alluding to the oddity of Onegin's nature. The *douces chimères* of French elegies are as close to the *sladkie mechtï* and *sladostnïe mechtaniya* of Pushkin as they are to the "delicious reverie" and "sweet delusions" of eighteenth-century English poets. The *sombres bocages* are Pushkin's *sumrachnïe dubrovï* and Pope's "darksome groves." The English translator should also make up his mind how to render such significant nouns and their derivatives as *toska (angoisse), tomnost' (langueur)* and *nega (mollesse)* which constantly recur in Pushkin's idiom. I translate *toska* as "heart-ache" or "anguish" in the sense of Keats's "wakeful anguish." *Tomnost'* with its adjective *tomnïy* is among Pushkin's favorite words. The good translator will recall that "languish" is used as a noun by Elizabethan poets (e.g., Samuel Daniel's "relieve my languish"), and in this sense is to "anguish" what "pale" is to "dark." Blake's "her languished head" takes care of the adjective, and the "languid moon" of Keats is nicely duplicated by Pushkin's *tomnaya luna*. At some point *tomnost'* (languor) grades into *nega (molle langueur)*, soft luxury of the senses, slumberous tenderness. Pushkin was acquainted with English poets only through their French models or French versions; the English translator of *Onegin*, while seeking an idiom in the Gallic diction of Pope and Byron, or in the romantic vocabulary of Keats, must constantly refer to the French poets.

In his early youth, Pushkin's literary taste was formed by the same writers and the same *Cours de Littérature* that formed Lamartine and Stendhal. This manual was the "*Lycée ou Cours de Littérature, ancienne et moderne*" by Jean François Laharpe, in sixteen volumes, 1799–1805. To the end of his days, Pushkin's favorite authors were Boileau, Bossuet, Corneille, Fénelon, Lafontaine, Molière, Pascal, Racine, and Voltaire. In relation to his contemporaries, he found Lamartine melodious but monotonous, Hugo gifted but on the whole second-rate; he welcomed the lascivious verse of young Musset, and rightly despised Béranger. In *Onegin* one finds echoes not only of Voltaire's "*Le Mondain*" (various passages in Chapter One) or Millevoye's *Elégies* (especially in passages related to Lenski), but also of Parny's *Poésies Erotiques*, Gresset's *Vert-vert*, Chénier's melancholy melodies and of a host of *petits poètes français*, such as Baïf, Gentil Bernard, Bernis, Bertin, Chaulieu, Colardeau, Delavigne, Delille, Desbordes-Valmore, Desportes, Dorat, Ducis, Gilbert, Lattaignant, Lebrun, Le Brun, Legouvé, Lemierre, Léonard, Malfilâtre, Piron, Jean-Baptiste Rousseau, and others.

As to German and English, he hardly had any. In 1821, translating Byron into gentleman's French for his own private use, he renders "the wave that rolls below the Athenian's grave" (beginning of the *Giaour*) as "*ce flot qui roule sur la grève d'Athène*." He read Shakespeare in Guizot's and Amédée Pichot's revision of Letourneur's edition (Paris, 1821) and Byron in Pichot's and Eusèbe de Salle's versions (Paris, 1819–21). Byron's command of the cliché was singularly dear to Russian poets as echoing the minor and major French poetry on which they had been brought up.

It would have been a flat and dry business indeed, if the verbal texture of *Onegin* were reduced to these patterns in faded silks. But a miracle occurred. When, more than a hundred and fifty years ago, the Russian literary language underwent the prodigious impact of French, the Russian poets made certain inspired selections and matched the old and the new in certain enchantingly individual ways. French stock epithets, in their Russian metamorphosis, breathe and bloom anew, so delicately does Pushkin manipulate them as he disposes them at strategic points of his meaningful harmonies. Incidentally, this does not lighten our task.

IV

The person who desires to turn a literary masterpiece into another language, has only one duty to perform, and this is to reproduce with absolute exactitude the whole text, and nothing but the text. The term "literal translation" is tautological since anything but that is not truly a translation but an imitation, an adaptation or a parody.

The problem, then, is a choice between rhyme and reason: can a translation while rendering with absolute fidelity the whole text, and nothing but the text, keep the form of the original, its rhythm and its rhyme? To the artist whom practice within the limits of one language, his own, has convinced that matter and manner are one, it comes as a shock to discover that a work of art can present itself to the would-be translator as split into form and content, and that the question of rendering one but not the other may arise at all. Actually what happens is still a monist's delight: shorn of its primary verbal existence, the original text will not be able to soar and to sing; but it can be very nicely dissected and mounted, and scientifically studied in all its organic details. So here is the sonnet, and there is the sonneteer's ardent admirer still hoping that by some miracle of ingenuity he will be able to render every shade and sheen of the original and somehow keep intact its special pattern in another tongue.

Let me state at once that in regard to mere meter there is not much trouble. The iambic measure is perfectly willing to be combined with literal accuracy for the curious reason that English prose lapses quite naturally into an iambic rhythm.

Stevenson has a delightful essay warning the student against the danger of transferring one's prose into blank verse by dint of polishing and pruning; and the beauty of the thing is that Stevenson's discussion of the rhythmic traps and pitfalls is couched in pure iambic verse with such precision and economy of diction that readers, or at least the simpler readers, are not aware of the didactic trick.

Newspapers use blank verse as commonly as Monsieur Jourdain used prose. I have just stretched my hand toward a prostrate paper, and reading at random I find

Debate on European Army interrupted: the Assembly's
Foreign Affairs Committee by a vote
Of twenty-four to twenty has decided
To recommend when the Assembly
Convenes this afternoon
That it adopt the resolution
To put off the debate indefinitely.
This, in effect, would kill the treaty.

The New York Yankees aren't conceding
The American League flag to Cleveland
But the first seed of doubt
Is growing in the minds of the defending champions.

Nebraska city proud of jail:
Stromsburg, Nebraska (Associated Press).
They're mighty proud here of the city jail,

A building that provides both for incarceration
And entertainment. The brick structure houses
The police station and the jail. The second story
Has open sides and is used as a band stand.

V

Onegin has been mistranslated into many languages. I have checked only the French and English versions, and some of the rhymed German ones. The three complete German concoctions I have seen are the worst of the lot. Of these Lippert's (1840) which changes Tatiana into Johanna, and Seubert's (1873) with its Max-und-Moritz tang, are beneath contempt; but Bodenstedt's fluffy product (1854) has been so much praised by German critics that it is necessary to warn the reader that it, too, despite a more laudable attempt at understanding if not expression, bristles with incredible blunders and ridiculous interpolations. Incidentally, at this point, it should be noted that Russians themselves are responsible for the two greatest insults that have been hurled at Pushkin's masterpiece – the vile Chaykovski (Tschaykowsky) opera and the equally vile illustrations by Repin which decorate most editions of the novel.

Onegin fared better in French – namely in Turgenev and Viardot's fairly exact prose version (in *La Revue Nationale*, Paris 1863). It would have been a really good translation had Viardot realized how much Pushkin relied on the Russian equivalent of the stock epithets of French poetry, and had he acted accordingly. As it is, Dupont's prose version (1847), while crawling with errors of a textual nature, is more idiomatic.

There are four English complete versions unfortunately available to college students: *Eugene Onéguine*, translated by Lieut.-Col. Spalding (Macmillan, London 1881); *Eugene Onegin*, translated by Babette Deutsch in *The Works of Alexander Pushkin*, selected and edited by Abraham Yarmolinski (Random House, New York 1936); *Evgeny Onegin*, translated by Oliver Elton (*The Slavonic Revue*, London, Jan. 1936 to Jan. 1938, and The Pushkin Press, London 1937); *Eugene Onegin*, translated by Dorothea Prall Radin and George Z. Patrick (Univ. of California Press, Berkeley 1937).

All four are in meter and rhyme; all are the result of earnest effort and of an incredible amount of mental labor; all contain here and there little gems of ingenuity; and all are grotesque travesties of their model, rendered in dreadful verse, teeming with mistranslations. The least offender is the bluff, matter-of-fact Colonel; the worst is Professor Elton, who combines a kind of irresponsible verbal felicity with the most exuberant vulgarity and the funniest howlers.

One of the main troubles with would-be translators is their ignorance. Only by sheer unacquaintance with Russian life in the 'twenties of the last century can one explain, for instance, their persistently translating *derevnya* by "village" instead of "country-seat," and *skakat'* by "to gallop" instead of "to drive." Anyone who wishes to attempt a translation of *Onegin* should acquire exact information in regard to a number of relevant subjects, such as the Fables of Krilov, Byron's works, French poets of the eighteenth century, Rousseau's *La Nouvelle Héloïse*, Pushkin's biography, banking games, Russian songs related to divination, Russian military ranks of the time as compared to Western European and American ones, the difference between cranberry and lingenberry, the rules of the English pistol duel as used in Russia, and the Russian language.

VI

To illustrate some of the special subtleties that Pushkin's translators should be aware of, I propose to analyze the opening quatrain of stanza XXXIX in Chapter Four, which describes Onegin's life in the summer of 1820 on his country estate situated some three hundred miles west of Moscow:

> Progúlki, chtén'e, son glubókoy,
> Lesnáya ten', zhurchán'e struy,
> Poróy belyánki cherno-ókoy
> Mladóy i svézhiy potzelúy . . .

In the first line,

> progulki, chten'e, son glubokoy

(which Turgenev-Viardot translated correctly as "*la promenade, la lecture, un sommeil profond et salutaire*"), *progulki* cannot be rendered by the obvious "walks" since the Russian term includes the additional idea of riding for exercise or pleasure. I did not care for "promenades" and settled for "rambles" since one can ramble about on horseback as well as on foot. The next word means "reading," and then comes a teaser: *glubokoy son* means not only "deep sleep" but also "sound sleep" (hence the double epithet in the French translation) and of course implies "sleep by night." One is tempted to use "slumber," which would nicely echo in another key the alliterations of the text (*progulki-glubokoy*, rambles-slumber), but of these elegancies the translator should beware. The most direct rendering of the line seems to be:

> rambles, and reading, and sound sleep . . .[1]

In the next line

> lesnaya ten', zhurchan'e struy . . .

lesnaya ten' is "the forest's shade," or, in better concord "the sylvan shade" (and I confess to have toyed with (Byron's) "the umbrage of the wood"); and now comes another difficulty: the catch in *zhurchan'e struy*, which I finally rendered as "the bubbling of the streams," is that *strui* (nominative plural) has two meanings: its ordinary one is the old sense of the English "streams" designating not bodies of water but rather limbs of water, the shafts of a running river (for example as used by Kyd in "Cornelia": "O beautious Tyber with thine easie streams that glide . . . ," or by Anne Bradstreet in "Contemplations": "a [River] where gliding streams" etc.), while the other meaning is an attempt on Pushkin's part to express the French "*ondes*," waters; for it should be clear to Pushkin's translator that the line

the sylvan shade, the bubbling of the streams . . .

(or as an old English rhymster might have put it "the green-wood shade, the purling rillets") deliberately reflects an idyllic ideal dear to the Arcadian poets. The wood and the water, "*les ruisseaux et les bois*," can be found together in countless "*éloges de la campagne*" praising the "green retreats" that were theoretically favored by eight-eenth-century French and English poets. Antoine Bertin's "*le silence des bois, le murmure de l'onde*" (*Elégie XXII*) or Evariste Parny's "*dans l'épaisseur du bois, au doux bruit des ruisseaux*" (*Fragment d'Alcée*) are typical commonplaces of this kind.

With the assistance of these minor French poets, we have now translated the first two lines of the stanza. Its entire first quatrain runs:

Rambles, and reading, and sound sleep,
the sylvan shade, the bubbling of the streams;
sometimes a white-skinned dark-eyed girl's
young and fresh kiss.

Poroy belyanki cherno-okoy
Mladoy i svezhiy potzeluy

The translator is confronted here by something quite special. Pushkin masks an auto-biographical allusion under the disguise of a literal translation from André Chénier, whom, however, he does not mention in any appended note. I am against stressing the human-interest angle in the discussion of literary works; and such emphasis would be especially incongruous in the case of Pushkin's novel where a stylized, and thus fantastic, Pushkin is one of the main characters.

However, there is little doubt that our author camouflaged in the present stanza, by means of a device which in 1825 was unique in the annals of literary art, his own experience: namely a brief intrigue he was having that summer on his estate in the Province of Pskov with Olga Kalashnikov, a meek, delicate-looking slave girl, whom he made pregnant and eventually bundled away to a second demesne of his, in another province. If we now turn to André Chénier, we find, in a fragment dated 1789 and published by Latouche as "*Epitre VII, à de Pange ainé*" (lines 5–8):

. . . Il a dans sa paisible et sainte solitude,
Du loisir, du sommeil, et les bois, et l'étude,
Le banquet des amis, et quelquefois, les soirs,
Le baiser jeune et frais d'une blanche aux yeux noirs.

None of the translators of Pushkin, English, German or French, have noticed what several Russian students of Pushkin discovered independently (a discovery first published, I think, by Savchenko – "*Elegiya Lenskogo i frantzuskaya elegiya*," in *Pushkin v mirovoy literature*, note, p. 362, Leningrad 1926), that the two first lines of our stanza XXXIX are a paraphrase, and the next two a metaphrase of Chénier's lines.

Chénier's curious preoccupation with the whiteness of a woman's skin (see, for example, "*Elégie XXII*) and Pushkin's vision of his own frail young mistress, fuse to form a marvelous mask, the disguise of a personal emotion; for it will be noted that our author, who was generally rather careful about the identification of his sources, nowhere reveals his direct borrowing here, as if by referring to the literary origin of these lines he might impinge upon the mystery of his own romance.

English translators, who were completely unaware of all the implications and niceties I have discussed in connection with this stanza, have had a good deal of trouble with it. Spalding stresses the hygienic side of the event

> the uncontaminated kiss
> of a young dark-eyed country maid;

Miss Radin produces the dreadful:

> a kiss at times from some fair maiden
> dark-eyed, with bright and youthful looks;

Miss Deutsch, apparently not realizing that Pushkin is alluding to Onegin's carnal relations with his serf girls, comes up with the incredibly coy:

> and if a black-eyed girl permitted
> sometimes a kiss as fresh as she;

and Professor Elton, who in such cases can always be depended upon for grotesque triteness and bad grammar, reverses the act and peroxides the concubine:

> at times a fresh young kiss bestowing
> upon some blond and dark-eyed maid.

Pushkin's line is, by-the-by, an excellent illustration of what I mean by "literalism, literality, literal interpretation." I take literalism to mean "absolute accuracy." If such accuracy sometimes results in the strange allegoric scene suggested by the phrase "the letter has killed the spirit," only one reason can be imagined: there must have been something wrong either with the original letter or with the original spirit, and this is not really a translator's concern. Pushkin has literally (i.e. with absolute accuracy) rendered Chénier's "*une blanche*" by "*belyanka*" and the English translator should reincarnate here both Pushkin and Chénier. It would be false literalism to render *belyanka (une blanche)* as "a white one" – or, still worse, "a white female"; and it would be ambiguous to say "fair-faced." The accurate meaning is "a white-skinned female," certainly "young," hence a "white-skinned girl," with dark eyes and, presumably, dark hair enhancing by contrast the luminous fairness of unpigmented skin.

Another good example of a particularly "untranslatable" stanza is XXXIII in Chapter One:

> I recollect the sea before a storm:
> O how I envied

the waves that ran in turbulent succession
to lie down at her feet with love!

Ya pómnyu móre pred grozóyu:
kak ya zavídoval volnám
begúshchim búrnoy cheredóyu
s lyukóv'yu lech k eyó nogám!

Russian readers discern in the original here two sets of beautifully onomatopoeic alliterations: *begúshchim búrnoy* . . . which renders the turbulent rush of the surf, and *s lyukóv'yu lech* – the liquid lisp of the waves dying in adoration at the lady's feet. Whomsoever the recollected feet belonged to (thirteen-year-old Marie Raevski paddling near Taganrog, or her father's godchild, a young *dame de compagnie* of Tatar origin, or what is more likely – despite Marie's own memoirs – Countess Elise Vorontzov, Pushkin's mistress in Odessa, or, most likely, a retrospective combination of reflected ladies), the only relevant fact here is that these waves come from Lafontaine through Bogdanovich. I refer to "*L'onde pour toucher . . . [Vénus] à longs flots s'entrepousse et d'une égale ardeur chaque flot à son tour s'en vient baiser les pieds de la mère d'Amour* (Jean de la Fontaine. "*Les Amours de Psiche et de Cupidon,*" 1669) and to a close paraphrase of this by Ippolit Bogdanovich, in his "Sweet Psyche" (*Dushen'ka,* 1783–1799) which in English should read "the waves that pursue her jostle jealously to fall humbly at her feet."

Without introducing various changes, there is no possibility whatsoever to make of Pushkin's four lines an alternately-rhymed tetrametric quatrain in English, even if only masculine rhymes be used. The key words are: *collect, sea, storm, envied, waves, ran, turbulent, succession, lie, feet, love*; and to these eleven not a single addition can be made without betrayal. For instance, if we try to end the first line in "before" – *I recollect the sea before* (followed by a crude enjambement) – and graft the rhyme "shore" to the end of the third line (*the* something *waves that storm the shore*), this one concession would involve us in a number of other changes completely breaking up the original sense and all its literary associations. In other words, the translator should constantly bear in mind not only the essential pattern of the text but also the borrowings with which that pattern is interwoven. Nor can anything be added for the sake of rhyme or meter. One thinks of some of those task problems in chess tourneys to the composition of which special restrictive rules are applied, such as the stipulation that only certain pieces may be used. In the marvelous economy of an *Onegin* stanza, the usable pieces are likewise strictly limited in number and kind: they may be shifted around by the translator but no additional men may be used for padding or filling up the gaps that impair a unique solution.

VII

To translate an *Onegin* stanza does not mean to rig up fourteen lines with alternate beats and affix to them seven jingle rhymes starting with pleasure-love-leisure-dove. Granted that rhymes can be found, they should be raised to the level of *Onegin*'s harmonies but if the masculine ones may be made to take care of themselves, what shall we do about the feminine rhymes? When Pushkin rhymes *devï* (maidens) with *gde vï* (where are you?), the effect is evocative and euphonious, but when Byron rhymes "maidens" with "gay dens," the result is burlesque. Even such split rhymes in *Onegin* as the instrumental of Childe Harold and the instrumental of "ice" (*Garol'dom – so-l'dom*), retain their aonian gravity and have nothing in common with such monstrosities in Byron as "new skin" and "Pouskin" (a distortion of the name of Count Musin-Pushkin, a binominal branch of the family).

So here are three conclusions I have arrived at: 1. It is impossible to translate *Onegin* in rhyme. 2. It is possible to describe in a series of footnotes the modulations and rhymes of the text as well as all its associations and other special features. 3. It is possible to translate *Onegin* with reasonable accuracy by substituting for the fourteen rhymed tetrameter lines of each stanza fourteen unrhymed lines of varying length, from iambic dimeter to iambic pentameter.

These conclusions can be generalized. I want translations with copious footnotes, footnotes reaching up like skyscrapers to the top of this or that page so as to leave only the gleam of one textual line between commentary and eternity. I want such footnotes and the absolutely literal sense, with no emasculation and no padding – I want such sense and such notes for all the poetry in other tongues that still languishes in "poetical" versions, begrimed and beslimed by rhyme. And when my *Onegin* is ready, it will either conform exactly to my vision or not appear at all.

Note

1   Cp. Pope's "sound sleep by night, study and ease," in "Solitude," or James Thomson's "retirement, rural quiet, friendship, books," in "The Seasons: Spring."

Chapter 11

Jean-Paul Vinay and Jean Darbelnet

A METHODOLOGY FOR TRANSLATION

Translated by Juan C. Sager and M.-J. Hamel

AT FIRST THE DIFFERENT methods or procedures seem to be countless, but they can be condensed to just seven, each one corresponding to a higher degree of complexity. In practice, they may be used either on their own or combined with one or more of the others.

Direct and oblique translation

Generally speaking, translators can choose from two methods of translating, namely direct, or literal translation and oblique translation. In some translation tasks it may be possible to transpose the source language message element by element into the target language, because it is based on either (i) parallel categories, in which case we can speak of structural parallelism, or (ii) on parallel concepts, which are the result of metalinguistic parallelisms. But translators may also notice gaps, or "lacunae", in the target language (TL) which must be filled by corresponding elements, so that the overall impression is the same for the two messages.

It may, however, also happen that, because of structural or metalinguistic differences, certain stylistic effects cannot be transposed into the TL without upsetting the syntactic order, or even the lexis. In this case it is understood that more complex methods have to be used which at first may look unusual but which nevertheless can permit translators a strict control over the reliability of their work: these procedures are called oblique translation methods. In the listing which follows, the first three procedures are direct and the others are oblique.

1958/1995

Procedure 1: Borrowing

To overcome a lacuna, usually a metalinguistic one (e.g. a new technical process, an unknown concept), borrowing is the simplest of all translation methods. It would not even merit discussion in this context if translators did not occasionally need to use it in order to create a stylistic effect. For instance, in order to introduce the flavour of the source language (SL) culture into a translation, foreign terms may be used, e.g. such Russian words as "roubles", "datchas" and "aparatchik", "dollars" and "party" from American English, Mexican Spanish food names "tequila" and "tortillas", and so on. In a story with a typical English setting, an expression such as "the coroner spoke" is probably better translated into French by borrowing the English term "coroner", rather than trying to find a more or less satisfying equivalent title from amongst the French magistrature, e.g.: *Le coroner prit la parole*.

Some well-established, mainly older borrowings are so widely used that they are no longer considered as such and have become a part of the respective TL lexicon. Some examples of French borrowings from other languages are *"alcool"*, *"redingote"*, *"paquebot"*, *"acajou"*, etc. In English such words as "menu", "carburetor", "hangar", "chic" and expressions like "déjà vu", "enfant terrible" and "rendez-vous" are no longer considered to be borrowings. Translators are particularly interested in the newer borrowings, even personal ones. It must be remembered that many borrowings enter a language through translation, just like semantic borrowings or faux amis, whose pitfalls translators must carefully avoid.

The decision to borrow a SL word or expression for introducing an element of local colour is a matter of style and consequently of the message.

Procedure 2: Calque

A calque is a special kind of borrowing whereby a language borrows an expression form of another, but then translates literally each of its elements. The result is either

i   a lexical calque, as in the first example, below, i.e. a calque which respects the syntactic structure of the TL, whilst introducing a new mode of expression; or

ii   a structural calque, as in the second example, below, which introduces a new construction into the language, e.g.:

> *English–French calque*
> Compliments of the Season!   Compliments de la saison!
> Science-fiction   Science-fiction

As with borrowings, there are many fixed calques which, after a period of time, become an integral part of the language. These too, like borrowings, may have undergone a semantic change, turning them into faux amis. Translators are more interested in new calques which can serve to fill a lacuna, without having to use an actual borrowing (cf. *"économiquement faible"*, a French calque taken from the German language). In such cases it may be preferable to create a new lexical form using

Greek or Latin roots or use conversion (cf. "*l'hypostase*"; Bally 1944: 257 ff.). This would avoid awkward calques, such as:

French calque	*English source*
thérapie occupationnelle	occupational therapy
Banque pour le Commerce et le Développement	Bank for Commerce and Development
les quatre Grands	the four great powers
le Premier Français	The French Premier
Le mariage est une association à cinquante-cinquante. (*Les Nouvelles Littéraires*, October 1955)	Matrimony is a fifty-fifty association
l'homme dans la rue (*Revue des Deux Mondes*, May 1955)	the man in the street [instead of "l'homme de la rue" or "le Français moyen"]
compagnon de route (*Le Monde*, March 1956)	fellow-traveller
La plupart des grandes décisions sur le Proche-Orient ont été prises à un moment où Sir Winston Churchill affectait de considérer comme "vide" la "chaise" de la France sur la scène internationale. (*Le Monde*, March 1956)	Most major decisions regarding the Near-East were taken when Churchill pretended that the chair occupied by France on the international scene was empty. [instead of: "la place" or "le fauteuil"]

Procedure 3: Literal translation

Literal, or word for word, translation is the direct transfer of a SL text into a grammatically and idiomatically appropriate TL text in which the translators' task is limited to observing the adherence to the linguistic servitudes of the TL.

I left my spectacles on the table downstairs.	J'ai laissé mes lunettes sur la table en bas.
Where are you?	Où êtes-vous?
This train arrives at Union Station at ten.	Ce train arrive à la gare Centrale à 10 heures.

In principle, a literal translation is a unique solution which is reversible and complete in itself. It is most common when translating between two languages of the same family (e.g. between French and Italian), and even more so when they also share the same culture. If literal translations arise between French and English, it is because common metalinguistic concepts also reveal physical coexistence, i.e. periods of bilingualism, with the conscious or unconscious imitation which attaches to a certain intellectual or political prestige, and such like. They can also be justified by a certain convergence of thought and sometimes of structure, which are certainly present among the European languages (cf. the creation of the definite article, the concepts of culture and civilization), and which have motivated interesting research in General Semantics.

In the preceding methods, translation does not involve any special stylistic procedures. If this were always the case then our present study would lack justification and translation would lack an intellectual challenge since it would be reduced to an unambiguous transfer from SL to TL. The exploration of the possibility of translating scientific texts by machine, as proposed by the many research groups in universities and industry in all major countries, is largely based on the existence of parallel passages in SL and TL texts, corresponding to parallel thought processes which, as would be expected, are particularly frequent in the documentation required in science and technology. The suitability of such texts for automatic translation was recognised as early as 1955 by Locke and Booth. (For current assessments of the scope of applications of machine translation see Hutchins and Somers 1992, Sager 1994.)

If, after trying the first three procedures, translators regard a literal translation unacceptable, they must turn to the methods of oblique translation. By unacceptable we mean that the message, when translated literally

i   gives another meaning, or
ii   has no meaning, or
iii   is structurally impossible, or
iv   does not have a corresponding expression within the metalinguistic experience of the TL, or
v   has a corresponding expression, but not within the same register.

To clarify these ideas, consider the following examples:

He looked at the map	Il regarda la carte.
He looked the picture of health.	Il paraissait l'image de la santé.
	Il avait l'air en pleine forme.

While we can translate the first sentence literally, this is impossible for the second, unless we wish to do so for an expressive reason (e.g. in order to characterise an Englishman who does not speak very good conversational French). The first example pair is less specific, since "*carte*" is less specific than "map". But this in no way renders the demonstration invalid.

If translators offer something similar to the second example, above, e.g.: "*Il se portait comme un charme*", this indicates that they have aimed at an equivalence of the two messages, something their "neutral" position outside both the TL and the SL enables them to do. Equivalence of messages ultimately relies upon an identity of situations, and it is this alone that allows us to state that the TL may retain certain characteristics of reality that are unknown to the SL.

If there were conceptual dictionaries with bilingual signifiers, translators would only need to look up the appropriate translation under the entry corresponding to the situation identified by the SL message. But such dictionaries do not exist and therefore translators start off with words or units of translation, to which they apply particular procedures with the intention of conveying the desired message. Since the positioning of a word within an utterance has an effect on its meaning, it may well arise that the solution results in a grouping of words that is so far from the original starting point that no dictionary could give it. Given the infinite number of combinations of signifiers alone, it is understandable that dictionaries cannot provide translators with ready-made solutions to all their problems. Only translators can be aware of the totality of the message, which determines their decisions. In the final analysis, it is the message alone, a reflection of the situation, that allows us to judge whether two texts are adequate alternatives.

Procedure 4: Transposition

The method called transposition involves replacing one word class with another without changing the meaning of the message. Beside being a special translation procedure, transposition can also be applied within a language. For example: "*Il a annoncé qu'il reviendrait*", can be re-expressed by transposing a subordinate verb with a noun, thus: "*Il a annoncé son retour*". In contrast to the first expression, which we call the base expression, we refer to the second one as the transposed expression. In translation there are two distinct types of transposition: (i) obligatory transposition, and (ii) optional transposition.

The following example has to be translated literally (procedure 3), but must also be transposed (procedure 4):

Dès son lever . . .	As soon as he gets/got up . . .
As soon as he gets up . . .	Dès son lever . . .
	Dès qu'il se lève . . .

In this example, the English allows no choice between the two forms, the base form being the only one possible. Inversely, however, when translating back into French, we have the choice between applying a calque or a transposition, because French permits either construction.

In contrast, the two following phrases can both be transposed:

Après qu'il sera revenu . . .	After he comes back . . .
Après son retour . . .	After his return . . .

From a stylistic point of view, the base and the transposed expression do not necessarily have the same value. Translators must, therefore, choose to carry out a transposition if the translation thus obtained fits better into the utterance, or allows a particular nuance of style to be retained. Indeed, the transposed form is generally more literary in character.

A special and frequently used case of transposition is that of interchange.

Procedure 5: Modulation

Modulation is a variation of the form of the message, obtained by a change in the point of view. This change can be justified when, although a literal, or even transposed, translation results in a grammatically correct utterance, it is considered unsuitable, unidiomatic or awkward in the TL.

As with transposition, we distinguish between free or optional modulations and those that are fixed or obligatory. A classical example of an obligatory modulation is the phrase, "The time when . . .", which must be translated as "*Le moment où* . . .". The type of modulation which turns a negative SL expression into a positive TL expression is more often than not optional, even though this is closely linked with the structure of each language, e.g.:

> It is not difficult to show . . .   Il est facile de démontrer . . .

The difference between fixed and free modulation is one of degree. In the case of fixed modulation, translators with a good knowledge of both languages freely use this method, as they will be aware of the frequency of use, the overall acceptance, and the confirmation provided by a dictionary or grammar of the preferred expression.

Cases of free modulation are single instances not yet fixed and sanctioned by usage, so that the procedure must be carried out anew each time. This, however, is not what qualifies it as optional; when carried out as it should be, the resulting translation should correspond perfectly to the situation indicated by the SL. To illustrate this point, it can be said that the result of a free modulation should lead to a solution that makes the reader exclaim, "Yes, that's exactly what you would say". Free modulation thus tends towards a unique solution, a solution which rests upon an habitual train of thought and which is necessary rather than optional. It is therefore evident that between fixed modulation and free modulation there is but a difference of degree, and that as soon as a free modulation is used often enough, or is felt to offer the only solution (this usually results from the study of bilingual texts, from discussions at a bilingual conference, or from a famous translation which claims recognition due to its literary merit), it may become fixed. However, a free modulation does not actually become fixed until it is referred to in dictionaries and grammars and is regularly taught. A passage not using such a modulation would then be considered inaccurate and rejected. In his M.A. thesis, G. Panneton, from whom we have borrowed the term modulation, correctly anticipated the results of a systematic application of transposition and modulation:

> La transposition correspondrait en traduction à une équation du premier degré, la modulation à une équation du second degré, chacune transformant l'équation en identité, toutes deux effectuant la résolution appropriée.
>
> (Panneton 1946)

Procedure 6: Equivalence

We have repeatedly stressed that one and the same situation can be rendered by two texts using completely different stylistic and structural methods. In such cases we are dealing with the method which produces equivalent texts. The classical example of equivalence is given by the reaction of an amateur who accidentally hits his finger with a hammer: if he were French his cry of pain would be transcribed as "Aïe!", but if he were English this would be interpreted as "Ouch!". Another striking case of equivalences are the many onomatopoeia of animal sounds, e.g.:

cocorico	cock-a-doodle-do
miaou	miaow
hi-han	heehaw

These simple examples illustrate a particular feature of equivalences: more often than not they are of a syntagmatic nature, and affect the whole of the message. As a result, most equivalences are fixed, and belong to a phraseological repertoire of idioms, clichés, proverbs, nominal or adjectival phrases, etc. In general, proverbs are perfect examples of equivalences, e.g.:

Il pleut à seaux/des cordes.	It is raining cats and dogs.
Like a bull in a china shop.	Comme un chien dans un jeu de quilles.
Too many cooks spoil the broth.	Deux patrons font chavirer la barque.

The method of creating equivalences is also frequently applied to idioms. For example, "To talk through one's hat" and "as like as two peas" cannot be translated by means of a calque. Yet this is exactly what happens amongst members of so-called bilingual populations, who have permanent contact with two languages but never become fully acquainted with either. It happens, nevertheless, that some of these calques actually become accepted by the other language, especially if they relate to a new field which is likely to become established in the country of the TL. For example, in Canadian French the idiom "to talk through one's hat" has acquired the equivalent "*parler à travers son chapeau*". But the responsibility of introducing such calques into a perfectly organised language should not fall upon the shoulders of translators: only writers can take such liberties, and they alone should take credit or blame for success or failure. In translation it is advisable to use traditional forms of expression, because the accusation of using Gallicisms, Anglicisms, Germanisms, Hispanisms, etc. will always be present when a translator attempts to introduce a new calque.

Procedure 7: Adaptation

With this seventh method we reach the extreme limit of translation: it is used in those cases where the type of situation being referred to by the SL message is unknown in the TL culture. In such cases translators have to create a new situation that can be considered as being equivalent. Adaptation can, therefore, be described as a special kind of equivalence, a situational equivalence. Let us take the example of an English father who would think nothing of kissing his daughter on the mouth, something which is normal in that culture but which would not be acceptable in a literal rendering into French. Translating, "He kissed his daughter on the mouth" by "*Il embrassa sa fille sur la bouche*", would introduce into the TL an element which is not present in the SL, where the situation may be that of a loving father returning home and greeting his daughter after a long journey. The French rendering would be a special kind of overtranslation. A more appropriate translation would be, "*Il serra tendrement sa fille dans ses bras*", unless, of course, the translator wishes to achieve a cheap effect. Adaptations are particularly frequent in the translation of book and film titles e.g.:

Trois hommes et un couffin	Three men and a baby. [film]
Le grand Meaulnes	The Wanderer. [book title]

The method of adaptation is well known amongst simultaneous interpreters: there is the story of an interpreter who, having adapted "cricket" into "Tour de France" in a context referring to a particularly popular sport, was put on the spot when the French delegate then thanked the speaker for having referred to such a typically French sport. The interpreter then had to reverse the adaptation and speak of cricket to his English client.

The refusal to make an adaptation is invariably detected within a translation because it affects not only the syntactic structure, but also the development of ideas and how they are represented within the paragraph. Even though translators may produce a perfectly correct text without adaptation, the absence of adaptation may still be noticeable by an indefinable tone, something that does not sound quite right. This is unfortunately the impression given only too often by texts published by international organizations, whose members, either through ignorance or because of a mistaken insistence on literalness, demand translations which are largely based on calques. The result may then turn out to be pure gibberish which has no name in any language, but which René Etiemble quite rightly referred to as "*sabir atlantique*", which is only partly rendered by the equivalent "Mid-Atlantic jargon". Translations cannot be produced simply by creating structural or metalinguistic calques. All the great literary translations were carried out with the implicit knowledge of the methods described in this chapter, as Gide's preface to his translation of *Hamlet* clearly shows. One cannot help wondering, however, if the reason the Americans refused to take the League of Nations seriously was not because many of their documents were un-modulated and un-adapted renderings of original French texts, just as the "*sabir atlantique*" has its roots in ill-digested translations of Anglo-American originals. Here, we touch upon an extremely serious problem, which, unfortunately, lack of space prevents us from discussing further, that of intellectual, cultural, and linguistic changes, which over time can be effected by important documents, school textbooks, journals, film dialogues, etc., written by translators who are either unable to or who dare not venture into the world of oblique translations. At a time when excessive centralization and lack of respect for cultural differences are driving international organizations into adopting working languages sui generis for writing documents which are then hastily translated by overworked and unappreciated translators, there is good reason to be concerned about the prospect that four-fifths of the world will have to live on nothing but translations, their intellect being starved by a diet of linguistic pap.

Application of the seven methods

These seven methods are applied to different degrees at the three planes of expression, i.e. lexis, syntactic structure, and message, For example, borrowing may occur at the lexical level – "*bulldozer*", "*réaliser*", and "*stopover*" are French lexical borrowings from English; borrowing also occurs at the level of the message, e.g. "*O.K.*" and "*Five o'clock*". This range of possibilities is illustrated in Table 11.1, where each procedure is exemplified for each plane of expression.

Table 11.1: Summary of the seven translation procedures (methods in increasing order of difficulty)

	Lexis	*Structures*	*Message*
1 Borrowing	F: *Bulldozer* E: Fuselage	*science-fiction* à la mode	*Five o'Clock Tea* Bon voyage
2 Calque	F: *économiquement faible* E: Normal School (C.E.)	*Lutetia Palace* Governor General	*Compliments de la Saison* Take it or leave it
3 Literal Transl.	F: *encre* ↕ E: ink	*Le livre est sur la table.* The book is on the table.	*Quelle heure est-il?* What time is it?
4 Transposition	F: *Expéditeur* ↕ E: From	*Depuis la revalorisation du bois* As timber becomes more valuable	*Défense de fumer* No smoking
5 Modulation	F: *Peu profond* ↕ E: Shallow	*Donnez un peu de votre sang* Give a pint of your blood	*Complet* No vacancies
6 Equivalence	F: (Mil.) ↕ *la soupe* E, UK: (Mil.) Tea E, US: chow	*Comme un chien dans un jeu de quilles* Like a bull in a china shop	*Château de cartes* Hollow triumph
7 Adaptation	F: *Cyclisme* ↕ E, UK: Cricket E, US: Baseball	*En un clin d'œil* Before you could say Jack Robinson.	*Bon appétit!* US. Hi!

It is obvious that several of these methods can be used within the same sentence, and that some translations come under a whole complex of methods so that it is difficult to distinguish them; e.g., the translation of "paper weight" by "presse-papiers" is both a fixed transposition and a fixed modulation. Similarly, the translation of PRIVATE (written on a door) by DÉFENSE D'ENTRER is at the same time a transposition, a modulation, and an equivalence. It is a transposition because the adjective "private" is transformed into a nominal expression; a modulation because a statement is converted into a warning (cf. Wet paint: Prenez garde à la peinture, though "peinture fraîche" seems to be gaining ground in French-speaking countries); and finally, it is an equivalence since it is the situation that has been translated, rather than the actual grammatical structure.

Chapter 12

Roman Jakobson

ON LINGUISTIC ASPECTS
OF TRANSLATION

ACCORDING TO BERTRAND RUSSELL, "no one can understand the word 'cheese' unless he has a nonlinguistic acquaintance with cheese."[1] If, however, we follow Russell's fundamental precept and place our "emphasis upon the linguistic aspects of traditional philosophical problems," then we are obliged to state that no one can understand the word "cheese" unless he has an acquaintance with the meaning assigned to this word in the lexical code of English. Any representative of a cheese-less culinary culture will understand the English word "cheese" if he is aware that in this language it means "food made of pressed curds" and if he has at least a linguistic acquaintance with "curds." We never consumed ambrosia or nectar and have only a linguistic acquaintance with the words "ambrosia," "nectar," and "gods" – the name of their mythical users; nonetheless, we understand these words and know in what contexts each of them may be used.

The meaning of the words "cheese," "apple," "nectar," "acquaintance," "but," "mere," and of any word or phrase whatsoever is definitely a linguistic – or to be more precise and less narrow – a semiotic fact. Against those who assign meaning (*signatum*) not to the sign, but to the thing itself, the simplest and truest argument would be that nobody has ever smelled or tasted the meaning of "cheese" or of "apple." There is no *signatum* without *signum*. The meaning of the word "cheese" cannot be inferred from a nonlinguistic acquaintance with cheddar or with camembert without the assistance of the verbal code. An array of linguistic signs is needed to introduce an unfamiliar word. Mere pointing will not teach us whether "cheese" is the name of the given specimen, or of any box of camembert, or of camembert in general or of any cheese, any milk product, any food, any refreshment, or perhaps

1959

any box irrespective of contents. Finally, does a word simply name the thing in question, or does it imply a meaning such as offering, sale, prohibition, or malediction? (Pointing actually may mean malediction; in some cultures, particularly in Africa, it is an ominous gesture.)

For us, both as linguists and as ordinary word-users, the meaning of any linguistic sign is its translation into some further, alternative sign, especially a sign "in which it is more fully developed," as Peirce, the deepest inquirer into the essence of signs, insistently stated.[2] The term "bachelor" may be converted into a more explicit designation, "unmarried man," whenever higher explicitness is required. We distinguish three ways of interpreting a verbal sign: it may be translated into other signs of the same language, into another language, or into another, nonverbal system of symbols. These three kinds of translation are to be differently labeled:

1   Intralingual translation or *rewording* is an interpretation of verbal signs by means of other signs of the same language.
2   Interlingual translation or *translation proper* is an interpretation of verbal signs by means of some other language.
3   Intersemiotic translation or *transmutation* is an interpretation of verbal signs by means of signs of nonverbal sign systems.

The intralingual translation of a word uses either another, more or less synonymous, word or resorts to a circumlocution. Yet synonymy, as a rule, is not complete equivalence: for example. "every celibate is a bachelor, but not every bachelor is a celibate." A word or an idiomatic phrase-word, briefly a code-unit of the highest level, may be fully interpreted only by means of an equivalent combination of code-units, i.e., a message referring to this code-unit: "every bachelor is an unmarried man, and every unmarried man is a bachelor," or "every celibate is bound not to marry, and everyone who is bound not to marry is a celibate."

Likewise, on the level of interlingual translation, there is ordinarily no full equivalence between code-units, while messages may serve as adequate interpretations of alien code-units or messages. The English word "cheese" cannot be completely identified with its standard Russian heteronym "сыр" because cottage cheese is a cheese but not a сыр. Russians say: принеси сыру и творогу "bring cheese and [sic] cottage cheese." In standard Russian, the food made of pressed curds is called сыр only if ferment is used.

Most frequently, however, translation from one language into another substitutes messages in one language not for separate code-units but for entire messages in some other language. Such a translation is a reported speech; the translator recodes and transmits a message received from another source. Thus translation involves two equivalent messages in two different codes.

Equivalence in difference is the cardinal problem of language and the pivotal concern of linguistics. Like any receiver of verbal messages, the linguist acts as their interpreter. No linguistic specimen may be interpreted by the science of language without a translation of its signs into other signs of the same system or into signs of another system. Any comparison of two languages implies an examination of their mutual translatability; widespread practice of interlingual communication, particularly translating activities, must be kept under constant scrutiny by linguistic science.

It is difficult to overestimate the urgent need for and the theoretical and practical significance of differential bilingual dictionaries with careful comparative definition of all the corresponding units in their intention and extension. Likewise differential bilingual grammars should define what unifies and what differentiates the two languages in their selection and delimitation of grammatical concepts.

Both the practice and the theory of translation abound with intricacies, and from time to time attempts are made to sever the Gordian knot by proclaiming the dogma of untranslatability. "Mr. Everyman, the natural logician," vividly imagined by B. L. Whorf, is supposed to have arrived at the following bit of reasoning: "Facts are unlike to speakers whose language background provides for unlike formulation of them."[3] In the first years of the Russian revolution there were fanatic visionaries who argued in Soviet periodicals for a radical revision of traditional language and particularly for the weeding out of such misleading expressions as "sunrise" or "sunset." Yet we still use this Ptolemaic imagery without implying a rejection of Copernican doctrine, and we can easily transform our customary talk about the rising and setting sun into a picture of the earth's rotation simply because any sign is translatable into a sign in which it appears to us more fully developed and precise.

A faculty of speaking a given language implies a faculty of talking about this language. Such a "metalinguistic" operation permits revision and redefinition of the vocabulary used. The complementarity of both levels — object-language and meta-language — was brought out by Niels Bohr: all well-defined experimental evidence must be expressed in ordinary language, "in which the practical use of every word stands in complementary relation to attempts of its strict definition."[4]

All cognitive experience and its classification is conveyable in any existing language. Whenever there is deficiency, terminology may be qualified and amplified by loan-words or loan-translations, neologisms or semantic shifts, and finally, by circumlocutions. Thus in the newborn literary language of the Northeast Siberian Chukchees, "screw" is rendered as "rotating nail," "steel" as "hard iron," "tin" as "thin iron," "chalk" as "writing soap," "watch" as "hammering heart." Even seemingly contradictory circumlocutions, like "electrical horse-car" (злектрическая конка), the first Russian name of the horseless street car, or "flying steamship" (*jena paragot*), the Koryak term for the airplane, simply designate the electrical analogue of the horse-car and the flying analogue of the steamer and do not impede communication, just as there is no semantic "noise" and disturbance in the double oxymoron — "cold beef-and-pork hot dog."

No lack of grammatical device in the language translated into makes impossible a literal translation of the entire conceptual information contained in the original. The traditional conjunctions "and," "or" are now supplemented by a new connective — "and/or" — which was discussed a few years ago in the witty book *Federal Prose — How to Write in and/or for Washington*.[5] Of these three conjunctions, only the latter occurs in one of the Samoyed languages.[6] Despite these differences in the inventory of conjunctions, all three varieties of messages observed in "federal prose" may be distinctly translated both into traditional English and into this Samoyed language. Federal prose: 1) John and Peter, 2) John or Peter, 3) John and/or Peter will come. Traditional English: 3) John and Peter or one of them will come. Samoyed: John and/or Peter both will come, 2) John and/or Peter, one of them will come.

If some grammatical category is absent in a given language, its meaning may be translated into this language by lexical means. Dual forms like Old Russian брата are translated with the help of the numeral: "two brothers." It is more difficult to remain faithful to the original when we translate into a language provided with a certain grammatical category from a language devoid of such a category. When translating the English sentence "She has brothers" into a language which discriminates dual and plural, we are compelled either to make our own choice between two statements "She has two brothers" – "She has more than two" or to leave the decision to the listener and say: "She has either two or more than two brothers." Again in translating from a language without grammatical number into English one is obliged to select one of the two possibilities – "brother" or "brothers" or to confront the receiver of this message with a two-choice situation: "She has either one or more than one brother."

As Boas neatly observed, the grammatical pattern of a language (as opposed to its lexical stock) determines those aspects of each experience that must be expressed in the given language: "We have to choose between these aspects, and one or the other must be chosen."[7] In order to translate accurately the English sentence "I hired a worker," a Russian needs supplementary information, whether this action was completed or not and whether the worker was a man or a woman, because he must make his choice between a verb of completive or noncompletive aspect – нанял or нанимал – and between a masculine and feminine noun – работника or работницу. If I ask the utterer of the English sentence whether the worker was male or female, my question may be judged irrelevant or indiscreet, whereas in the Russian version of this sentence an answer to this question is obligatory. On the other hand, whatever the choice of Russian grammatical forms to translate the quoted English message, the translation will give no answer to the question of whether I "hired" or "have hired" the worker, or whether he/she was an indefinite or definite worker ("a" or "the"). Because the information required by the English and Russian grammatical pattern is unlike, we face quite different sets of two-choice situations; therefore a chain of translations of one and the same isolated sentence from English into Russian and vice versa could entirely deprive such a message of its initial content. The Geneva linguist S. Karcevski used to compare such a gradual loss with a circular series of unfavorable currency transactions. But evidently the richer the context of a message, the smaller the loss of information.

Languages differ essentially in what they *must* convey and not in what they *may* convey. Each verb of a given language imperatively raises a set of specific yes-or-no questions, as for instance: is the narrated event conceived with or without reference to its completion? Is the narrated event presented as prior to the speech event or not? Naturally the attention of native speakers and listeners will be constantly focused on such items as are compulsory in their verbal code.

In its cognitive function, language is minimally dependent on the grammatical pattern because the definition of our experience stands in complementary relation to metalinguistic operations – the cognitive level of language not only admits but directly requires recoding interpretation, i.e., translation. Any assumption of ineffable or untranslatable cognitive data would be a contradiction in terms. But in jest, in dreams, in magic, briefly, in what one would call everyday verbal mythology and in poetry above all, the grammatical categories carry a high semantic import.

In these conditions, the question of translation becomes much more entangled and controversial.

Even such a category as grammatical gender, often cited as merely formal, plays a great role in the mythological attitudes of a speech community. In Russian the feminine cannot designate a male person, nor the masculine specify a female. Ways of personifying or metaphorically interpreting inanimate nouns are prompted by their gender. A test in the Moscow Psychological Institute (1915) showed that Russians, prone to personify the weekdays, consistently represented Monday, Tuesday, and Thursday as males and Wednesday, Friday, and Saturday as females, without realizing that this distribution was due to the masculine gender of the first three names (понедѣлъник, торник, четверг) as against the feminine gender of the others (среда, пятница, суббога). The fact that the word for Friday is masculine in some Slavic languages and feminine in others is reflected in the folk traditions of the corresponding peoples, which differ in their Friday ritual. The widespread Russian superstition that a fallen knife presages a male guest and a fallen fork a female one is determined by the masculine gender of ножж "knife" and the feminine of вилка "fork" in Russian. In Slavic and other languages where "day" is masculine and "night" feminine, day is represented by poets as the lover of night. The Russian painter Repin was baffled as to why Sin had been depicted as a woman by German artists: he did not realize that "sin" is feminine in German (*die Sünde*), but masculine in Russian (рпех). Likewise a Russian child, while reading a translation of German tales, was astounded to find that Death, obviously a woman (Russian смерть, fem.), was pictured as an old man (German *der Tod*, masc.). *My Sister Life*, the title of a book of poems by Boris Pasternak, is quite natural in Russian, where "life" is feminine жизнь, but was enough to reduce to despair the Czech poet Josef Hora in his attempt to translate these poems, since in Czech this noun is masculine *život*.

What was the initial question which arose in Slavic literature at its very beginning? Curiously enough, the translator's difficulty in preserving the symbolism of genders, and the cognitive irrelevance of this difficulty, appears to be the main topic of the earliest Slavic original work, the preface to the first translation of the *Evangeliarium*, made in the early 860's by the founder of Slavic letters and liturgy, Constantine the Philosopher, and recently restored and interpreted by A. Vaillant.[8] "Greek, when translated into another language, cannot always be reproduced identically, and that happens to each language being translated," the Slavic apostle states. "Masculine nouns as ποταμός 'river' and ἀστήρ 'star' in Greek, are feminine in another language as рѣка and звѣзда in Slavic." According to Vaillant's commentary, this divergence effaces the symbolic identification of the rivers with demons and of the stars with angels in the Slavic translation of two of Matthew's verses (7:25 and 2:9). But to this poetic obstacle, Saint Constantine resolutely opposes the precept of Dionysius the Areopagite, who called for chief attention to the cognitive values (силѣ разуму) and not to the words themselves.

In poetry, verbal equations become a constructive principle of the text. Syntactic and morphological categories, roots, and affixes, phonemes and their components (distinctive features) – in short, any constituents of the verbal code – are confronted, juxtaposed, brought into contiguous relation according to the principle of similarity and contrast and carry their own autonomous signification.

Phonemic similarity is sensed as semantic relationship. The pun, or to use a more erudite, and perhaps more precise term – paronomasia, reigns over poetic art, and whether its rule is absolute or limited, poetry by definition is untranslatable. Only creative transposition is possible: either intralingual transposition – from one poetic shape into another, or interlingual transposition – from one language into another, or finally intersemiotic transposition – from one system of signs into another, e.g., from verbal art into music, dance, cinema, or painting.

If we were to translate into English the traditional formula *Traduttore, traditore* as "the translator is a betrayer," we would deprive the Italian rhyming epigram of all its paronomastic value. Hence a cognitive attitude would compel us to change this aphorism into a more explicit statement and to answer the questions: translator of what messages? betrayer of what values?

Notes

1   Bertrand Russell, "Logical Positivism," *Revue Internationale de Philosophie*, IV (1950), 18; cf. p. 3.

2   Cf. John Dewey, "Peirce's Theory of Linguistic Signs, Thought, and Meaning," *The Journal of Philosophy*, XLIII (1946), 91.

3   Benjamin Lee Whorf, *Language, Thought, and Reality* (Cambridge, Mass., 1956), p. 235.

4   Niels Bohr, "On the Notions of Causality and Complementarity," *Dialectica*, I (1948), 317f.

5   James R. Masterson and Wendell Brooks Phillips, *Federal Prose* (Chapel Hill, NC, 1948), p. 40f.

6   Cf. Knut Bergsland, "Finsk-ugrisk og almen språkvitenskap," *Norsk Tidsskrift for Sprogvidenskap*, XV (1949), 374f.

7   Franz Boas, "Language," *General Anthropology* (Boston, 1938), pp. 132f.

8   André Vaillant, "Le Préface de l'évangeliaire vieux-slave," *Revue des études Slaves*, XXIV (1948), 5f.

1960s–1970s

THE CONTROLLING CONCEPT for most translation theory during these decades is equivalence. Translating is generally seen as a process of communicating the foreign text by establishing a relationship of identity or analogy with it. In 1963 Georges Mounin argues that equivalence is based on "universals" of language and culture, questioning the notions of relativity that in previous decades made translation seem impossible. At the same time, the literature on equivalence is fundamentally normative, aiming to provide not only analytical tools to describe translations, but also standards to evaluate them. The universal is then shaped to a local situation.

Theorists tend to assume that the foreign text is a fairly stable object, possessing invariants, capable of reduction to precisely defined units, levels, and categories of language and textuality. Equivalence is submitted to lexical, grammatical, and stylistic analysis; it is established on the basis of text type and social function. By the end of the 1970s, so many typologies of equivalence have been devised that Werner Koller can offer a nuanced summary of the possibilities. Equivalence, he writes, may be "denotative," depending on an "invariance of content"; "connotative," depending on similarities of register, dialect, and style; "text-normative," based on "usage norms" for particular text types; and "pragmatic," ensuring comprehensibility in the receiving culture (Koller 1979: 186–91; Koller 1989: 99–104).

The most familiar theoretical move in this period is to draw an opposition between translating that cultivates pragmatic equivalence, drawing on terms that are immediately intelligible to the receptor, and translating that is formally equivalent, designed to approximate the linguistic and cultural features of the foreign text. In his widely cited 1964 book (excerpted below), **Eugene Nida** distinguishes between "dynamic" and "formal" varieties of "correspondence," later replacing the term "dynamic" with "functional" (Nida and Taber 1969). The year 1977 sees the first appearance of similar oppositions from Peter Newmark ("communicative" and "semantic") and Juliane House ("covert" and "overt"). House's distinction contains the added refinement of considering how much the foreign text depends on its own culture for intelligibility. If the significance of a foreign text is peculiarly indigenous, it requires a translation that is overt or noticeable through its reliance on supplementary information, whether in the form of expansions, insertions or annotations.

These varying sets of terms derive from traditional dichotomies between "sense-for-sense" and "word-for-word" translating which date back to antiquity, to Cicero and Horace, Jerome and Augustine. But now they are informed by the ascendancy and sheer proliferation of linguistics-oriented approaches in translation research. The binary oppositions are basically synonymous, despite the variations among the terms. They are not quite identical, however, since each pair emphasizes different translation aims and effects. Pragmatic equivalence communicates the foreign text according to values so familiar in the receiving language and culture as to conceal the very fact of translation. Formal equivalence, in contrast, adheres so closely to the linguistic and cultural values of the foreign text as to reveal the translation to be a translation.

Translation theories that privilege equivalence must inevitably come to terms with the existence of "shifts" between the foreign and translated texts, deviations that can occur at such linguistic levels as graphology, phonology, grammar, and lexis. J. C. Catford's detailed account must "assume some degree of formal correspondence" so that shifts can be detected as "departures" (Catford 1965: 73, 76). Yet he finally questions this assumption by concluding that "translation equivalence does not entirely match formal correspondence" (ibid.: 82).

Instead of raising fundamental doubts about the possibility of equivalence, shifts are used to recommend translating that is pragmatic, functional, communicative. When Anton Popovic asserts that "shifts do not occur because the translator wishes to 'change' a work, but because he strives to reproduce it as faithfully as possible," the kind of "faithfulness" he has in mind is "functional," with the translator locating "suitable equivalents in the milieu of his time and society" (Popovic 1970: 80, 82).

Jirí Levý carries out experiments showing that pragmatic translation involves a "gradual semantic shifting" as translators choose from a number of possible solutions (Levý 1967: 1176). Modern translators, he asserts, intuitively apply the "minimax strategy," choosing the solution "which promises a maximum of effect with a minimum of effort" – short of violating the "linguistic or aesthetic standards" of a particular readership (ibid.: 1179–80). Elsewhere Levý is critical of the results: in an experiment designed to study the language of "average" and "bad" translations, he finds that shifts work to generalize and clarify meaning, "changing the style of a literary work into a dry and uninspiring description of things and actions" (Levý 1965: 78–80).

Katharina Reiss (1971) presents a sophisticated typology that displays the logical tensions among the reigning concepts in the literature. As she argues in the essay reprinted here, the "functionally equivalent" translation needs to be based on a "detailed semantic, syntactic, and pragmatic analysis" of the foreign text. But the pragmatic analysis always risks revising any previous account of meaning because it redefines the object of analysis. The pragmatic translator doesn't simply analyze the linguistic and cultural features of the foreign text, but reverbalizes them according to the values of a different language and culture, often applying what House calls a "filter" to aid the receptor's comprehension of the differences.

The functionalism in so many translation theories at this time casts doubt on elaborate typologies of equivalence by suggesting that they are merely constructions, ideal schemes not realized in actual translations. Or, more precisely, the ideal becomes possible only within a narrow range of texts in specific institutional situations, including translator training programs. Reiss, like so many of her contemporaries, develops her theory while training translators of "informative" texts. With official documents, scholarly articles, operation manuals, and news reports, it is assumed, the translator can choose linguistic forms that correspond directly to communicative functions, securing equivalence on the basis of reference to real objects, persons, and events. Translator training, moreover, creates a demand for analytical tools that can be used to generate translation strategies and solutions in the classroom.

In the case of literary texts, the functionalist trend ultimately displaces equivalence as a central concept in translation research by directing attention to the receptor. During the 1970s, **Itamar Even-Zohar** and **Gideon Toury** set out from the assumption that literary translations are facts of the target system. In often cited essays that are reprinted below in later revised versions, they theorize literature as a "polysystem" of interrelated forms and canons that constitute "norms" constraining the translator's choices and strategies.

Even-Zohar imagines the body of translated literature as a system in its own right, existing in varying relationships with original compositions. Both occupy "positions" in literary systems, whether "central" or "peripheral," and both perform literary "functions," whether "innovative" or "conservatory." A minor literature – minor in relation to longer and more richly developed literary traditions – may assign translation a central role in spurring innovation. In a major literature, translation may be assigned a peripheral role, conservatively adhering to norms rejected by original writing.

Toury shows how the target orientation transforms the concept of equivalence. The "adequacy" of a translation to the source text becomes an unproductive line of enquiry, not only because shifts always occur, but because any determination of adequacy, even the identification of a source text and a translation, involves the application of a target norm. Hence, Toury seeks to describe and explain the "acceptability" of the translation in the receiving culture, the ways in which various shifts constitute a type of equivalence that reflects target norms at a certain historical moment.

Polysystem theory proves to be a decisive advance in translation research. The literature on equivalence formulates linguistic and textual models and often prescribes a specific translation practice (pragmatic, functional, communicative). The target orientation, in contrast, focuses on actual translations and submits them to detailed description and explanation. It inspires research projects that involve substantial corpora of translated texts. A pioneering study of nineteenth-century French translations is conducted by Lieven D'hulst, José Lambert, and Katrin van Bragt.

The expansion of translation research in the 1960s and 1970s coincides with an increased awareness that it represents an emerging academic discipline. Early theorists like Catford feel that translation studies do not deserve the institutional autonomy of linguistics because they are a site, not of theorizing about language, but of applying linguistic theories. When Nida and later Wolfram Wilss call their theoretical works a "science" of translation, they are giving the topic a scholarly coherence and legitimacy that it has so far lacked (Wilss 1977, 1982).

In the influential paper included here (1972), **James Holmes** draws up a disci-plinary map for translation studies, distinguishing "pure" research-oriented areas of theory and description from "applied" areas like training and criticism. The distinction between "pure" and "applied" points to his adoption of a scientific model, not so much from linguistics as from the physical sciences. For Holmes, theoretical concepts derived from empirical description, much like scientific laws, should aim "to explain and predict what translating and translations are and will be." The drive to establish a distinct discipline leaves unanswered the ques-tions of whether the translation scholar will need to rely on other conceptual materials, what they might be, and what disciplines might furnish them. The new disciplinarity also creates an epistemological hierarchy: the knowledge assigned the greatest value is produced by theoretical and descriptive studies of translation products, functions, and processes, whereas applied studies are seen as yielding "data" for the theorist.

Holmes's vision is shared by target-oriented theorists like Even-Zohar and Toury, for whom Russian Formalism is more useful than functional linguistics. Their work responds to his call for empirical data and the search for probabilistic laws of translation. Nonetheless, translation theory remains a heterogeneous field throughout this period. It encompasses both linguists like Catford, whose study is underwritten by Hallidayan analytical concepts, and the eclectic Levý, who synthe-sizes psycholinguistics, semantics, structural anthropology, literary criticism, and game theory.

George Steiner's magisterial 1975 study *After Babel*, continuously in print for more than two decades, is undoubtedly the most widely known work in translation theory since the Second World War. It opposes modern linguistics with a literary and philosophical approach. Whereas linguistics-oriented theorists define transla-tion as functional communication, Steiner returns to German Romanticism and the hermeneutic tradition to view translating as an interpretation of the foreign text that is at once profoundly sympathetic and violent, exploitive and ethically restora-tive. For Steiner, language is not instrumental in communicating meaning, but constitutive in reconstructing it. And it is the individualistic aspects of language, "the privacies of individual usage," that resist interpretation and escape the univer-salizing concepts of linguistics (Steiner 1975: 205). Deepening Schleiermacher's recommendation that German translators signal the foreignness of the foreign text,

Steiner argues that "great translation must carry with it the most precise sense possible of the resistant, of the barriers intact at the heart of understanding" (ibid.: 378).

Linguists like Mounin and Catford assume that universals bridge linguistic and cultural differences. "Translation equivalence," Catford asserts, "occurs when a SL [source-language] and a TL [target-language] text or item are relatable to (at least some of) the same features of substance," where "substance" can signify a relatively fixed range of linguistic features, levels and categories, as well as a potentially infinite series of cultural situations (Catford 1965: 50). Yet Steiner, as the excerpt below makes clear, is also prone to universalizing insofar as his theory of the "hermeneutic motion" threatens to transcend the specific historical moments that inflect every translation. Steiner's discussions of translated texts either focus on the theoretical concept he wants to illustrate or analyze and evaluate a translator's handling of stylistic features. His forte is literary criticism as the appreciation of personal style, which results in suggestive readings of noted translations, especially by poets and philosophers. Historical situations, however, recede behind the innovative performances that occur in them.

For Henri Meschonnic, the German tradition leads in a different direction: he mounts a critique of naturalizing translation for mystifying its appropriation of the foreign text. "The current proposition," he writes, "according to which a translation should not give the impression of being translated," masks a process of "annexation" wherein the translated text "transposes the so-called dominant ideology" under the "illusion of transparency" (Meschonnic 1973: 308, my translation). Like Nietzsche and Vossler before him, Meschonnic is acutely aware of the "imperialism" of any translating that "tends to forget its history" (ibid.: 310). He argues for a more theoretically sophisticated translation practice that questions the main tendency in this period towards the pragmatic, the functional, the communicative.

Further reading

Fawcett 1997, Gentzler 1993, Hatim 1998, Hermans 1995 and 1999, Kelly 1979, Ladmiral 1986, Lambert 1995, Larose 1989, Nord 1997, Pym 1995 and 1997a, Snell-Hornby 1988 and 1990

Chapter 13

Eugene Nida

PRINCIPLES OF
CORRESPONDENCE

S INCE NO TWO LANGUAGES are identical, either in the meanings
given to corresponding symbols or in the ways in which such symbols are
arranged in phrases and sentences, it stands to reason that there can be no absolute
correspondence between languages. Hence there can be no fully exact translations.
The total impact of a translation may be reasonably close to the original, but there
can be no identity in detail. Constance B. West (1932: 344) clearly states the
problem: "Whoever takes upon himself to translate contracts a debt; to discharge
it, he must pay not with the same money, but the same sum." One must not imagine
that the process of translation can avoid a certain degree of interpretation by the
translator. In fact, as D. G. Rossetti stated in 1874 (Fang 1953), "A translation
remains perhaps the most direct form of commentary."

Different types of translations

No statement of the principles of correspondence in translating can be complete
without recognizing the many different types of translations (Herbert P. Phillips
1959). Traditionally, we have tended to think in terms of free or paraphrastic translations as contrasted with close or literal ones. Actually, there are many more grades
of translating than these extremes imply. There are, for example, such ultraliteral
translations as interlinears; while others involve highly concordant relationships, e.g.
the same source-language word is always translated by one – and only one –
receptor-language word. Still others may be quite devoid of artificial restrictions in

form, but nevertheless may be overtraditional and even archaizing. Some translations aim at very close formal and semantic correspondence, but are generously supplied with notes and commentary. Many are not so much concerned with giving information as with creating in the reader something of the same mood as was conveyed by the original.

Differences in translations can generally be accounted for by three basic factors in translating: (1) the nature of the message, (2) the purpose or purposes of the author and, by proxy, of the translator, and (3) the type of audience.

Messages differ primarily in the degree to which content or form is the dominant consideration. Of course, the content of a message can never be completely abstracted from the form, and form is nothing apart from content; but in some messages the content is of primary consideration, and in others the form must be given a higher priority. For example, in the Sermon on the Mount, despite certain important stylistic qualities, the importance of the message far exceeds considerations of form. On the other hand, some of the acrostic poems of the Old Testament are obviously designed to fit a very strict formal "strait jacket." But even the contents of a message may differ widely in applicability to the receptor-language audience. For example, the folk tale of the Bauré Indians of Bolivia, about a giant who led the animals in a symbolic dance, is interesting to an English-speaking audience, but to them it has not the same relevance as the Sermon on the Mount. And even the Bauré Indians themselves recognize the Sermon on the Mount as more significant than their favorite "how-it-happened" story. At the same time, of course, the Sermon on the Mount has greater relevance to these Indians than have some passages in Leviticus.

In poetry there is obviously a greater focus of attention upon formal elements than one normally finds in prose. Not that content is necessarily sacrificed in translation of a poem, but the content is necessarily constricted into certain formal molds. Only rarely can one reproduce both content and form in a translation, and hence in general the form is usually sacrificed for the sake of the content. On the other hand, a lyric poem translated as prose is not an adequate equivalent of the original. Though it may reproduce the conceptual content, it falls far short of reproducing the emotional intensity and flavor. However, the translating of some types of poetry by prose may be dictated by important cultural considerations. For example, Homer's epic poetry reproduced in English poetic form usually seems to us antique and queer – with nothing of the liveliness and spontaneity characteristic of Homer's style. One reason is that we are not accustomed to having stories told to us in poetic form. In our Western European tradition such epics are related in prose. For this reason E. V. Rieu chose prose rather than poetry as the more appropriate medium by which to render The Iliad and The Odyssey.

The particular purposes of the translator are also important factors in dictating the type of translation. Of course, it is assumed that the translator has purposes generally similar to, or at least compatible with, those of the original author, but this is not necessarily so. For example, a San Blas story-teller is interested only in amusing his audience, but an ethnographer who sets about translating such stories may be much more concerned in giving his audience an insight into San Blas personality structure. Since, however, the purposes of the translator are the primary ones to be considered in studying the types of translation which result, the principal purposes that underlie the choice of one or another way to render a particular message are important.

The primary purpose of the translator may be information as to both content and form. One intended type of response to such an informative type of translation is largely cognitive, e.g. an ethnographer's translation of texts from informants, or a philosopher's translation of Heidegger. A largely informative translation may, on the other hand, be designed to elicit an emotional response of pleasure from the reader or listener.

A translator's purposes may involve much more than information. He may, for example, want to suggest a particular type of behaviour by means of a translation. Under such circumstances he is likely to aim at full intelligibility, and to make certain minor adjustments in detail so that the reader may understand the full implications of the message for his own circumstances. In such a situation a translator is not content to have receptors say, "This is intelligible to us." Rather, he is looking for some such response as, "This is meaningful for us." In terms of Bible translating, the people might understand a phrase such as "to change one's mind about sin" as meaning "repentance." But if the indigenous way of talking about repentance is "spit on the ground in front of," as in Shilluk,[1] spoken in the Sudan, the translator will obviously aim at the more meaningful idiom. On a similar basis, "white as snow" may be rendered as "white as egret feathers," if the people of the receptor language are not acquainted with snow but speak of anything very white by this phrase.

A still greater degree of adaptation is likely to occur in a translation which has an imperative purpose. Here the translator feels constrained not merely to suggest a possible line of behavior, but to make such an action explicit and compelling. He is not content to translate in such a way that the people are likely to understand; rather, he insists that the translation must be so clear that no one can possibly misunderstand.

In addition to the different types of messages and the diverse purposes of translators, one must also consider the extent to which prospective audiences differ both in decoding ability and in potential interest.

Decoding ability in any language involves at least four principal levels: (1) the capacity of children, whose vocabulary and cultural experience are limited; (2) the double-standard capacity of new literates, who can decode oral messages with facility but whose ability to decode written messages is limited; (3) the capacity of the average literate adult, who can handle both oral and written messages with relative ease; and (4) the unusually high capacity of specialists (doctors, theologians, philosophers, scientists, etc.), when they are decoding messages within their own area of specialization. Obviously a translation designed for children cannot be the same as one prepared for specialists, nor can a translation for children be the same as one for a newly literate adult.

Prospective audiences differ not only in decoding ability, but perhaps even more in their interests. For example, a translation designed to stimulate reading for pleasure will be quite different from one intended for a person anxious to learn how to assemble a complicated machine. Moreover, a translator of African myths for persons who simply want to satisfy their curiosity about strange peoples and places will produce a different piece of work from one who renders these same myths in a form acceptable to linguists, who are more interested in the linguistic structure underlying the translation than in cultural novelty.

Two basic orientations in translating

Since "there are, properly speaking, no such things as identical equivalents" (Belloc 1931 and 1931a: 37), one must in translating seek to find the closest possible equivalent. However, there are fundamentally two different types of equivalence: one which may be called formal and another which is primarily dynamic.

Formal equivalence focuses attention on the message itself, in both form and content. In such a translation one is concerned with such correspondences as poetry to poetry, sentence to sentence, and concept to concept. Viewed from this formal orientation, one is concerned that the message in the receptor language should match as closely as possible the different elements in the source language. This means, for example, that the message in the receptor culture is constantly compared with the message in the source culture to determine standards of accuracy and correctness.

The type of translation which most completely typifies this structural equivalence might be called a "gloss translation," in which the translator attempts to reproduce as literally and meaningfully as possible the form and content of the original. Such a translation might be a rendering of some Medieval French text into English, intended for students of certain aspects of early French literature not requiring a knowledge of the original language of the text. Their needs call for a relatively close approximation to the structure of the early French text, both as to form (e.g. syntax and idioms) and content (e.g. themes and concepts). Such a translation would require numerous footnotes in order to make the text fully comprehensible.

A gloss translation of this type is designed to permit the reader to identify himself as fully as possible with a person in the source-language context, and to understand as much as he can of the customs, manner of thought, and means of expression. For example, a phrase such as "holy kiss" (Romans 16:16) in a gloss translation would be rendered literally, and would probably be supplemented with a footnote explaining that this was a customary method of greeting in New Testament times.

In contrast, a translation which attempts to produce a dynamic rather than a formal equivalence is based upon "the principle of equivalent effect" (Rieu and Phillips 1954). In such a translation one is not so concerned with matching the receptor-language message with the source-language message, but with the dynamic relationship, that the relationship between receptor and message should be substantially the same as that which existed between the original receptors and the message.

A translation of dynamic equivalence aims at complete naturalness of expression, and tries to relate the receptor to modes of behavior relevant within the context of his own culture; it does not insist that he understand the cultural patterns of the source-language context in order to comprehend the message. Of course, there are varying degrees of such dynamic-equivalence translations. One of the modern English translations which, perhaps more than any other, seeks for equivalent effect is J. B. Phillips's rendering of the New Testament. In Romans 16:16 he quite naturally translates "greet one another with a holy kiss" as "give one another a hearty handshake all around."

Between the two poles of translating (i.e. between strict formal equivalence and complete dynamic equivalence) there are a number of intervening grades, representing various acceptable standards of literary translating. During the past fifty years, however, there has been a marked shift of emphasis from the formal to the dynamic dimension. A recent summary of opinion on translating by literary artists, publishers, educators, and professional translators indicates clearly that the present direction is toward increasing emphasis on dynamic equivalences (Cary 1959).

Linguistic and cultural distance

In any discussion of equivalences, whether structural or dynamic, one must always bear in mind three different types of relatedness, as determined by the linguistic and cultural distance between the codes used to convey the messages. In some instances, for example, a translation may involve comparatively closely related languages and cultures, e.g. translations from Frisian into English, or from Hebrew into Arabic. On the other hand, the languages may not be related, even though the cultures are closely parallel, e.g. as in translations from German into Hungarian, or from Swedish into Finnish (German and Swedish are Indo-European languages, while Hungarian and Finnish belong to the Finno-Ugrian family). In still other instances a translation may involve not only differences of linguistic affiliation but also highly diverse cultures, e.g. English into Zulu, or Greek into Javanese.[2]

Where the linguistic and cultural distances between source and receptor codes are least, one should expect to encounter the least number of serious problems, but as a matter of fact if languages are too closely related one is likely to be badly deceived by the superficial similarities, with the result that translations done under these circumstances are often quite poor. One of the serious dangers consists of so-called "false friends," i.e. borrowed or cognate words which seem to be equivalent but are not always so, e.g. English *demand* and French *demander*, English *ignore* and Spanish *ignorar*, English *virtue* and Latin *virtus*, and English *deacon* and Greek *diakonos*.

When the cultures are related but the languages are quite different, the translator is called upon to make a good many formal shifts in the translation. However, the cultural similarities in such instances usually provide a series of parallelisms of content that make the translation proportionately much less difficult than when both languages and cultures are disparate. In fact, differences between cultures cause many more severe complications for the translator than do differences in language structure.

Definitions of translating

Definitions of proper translating are almost as numerous and varied as the persons who have undertaken to discuss the subject. This diversity is in a sense quite understandable; for there are vast differences in the materials translated, in the purposes of the publication, and in the needs of the prospective audience. Moreover, live languages are constantly changing and stylistic preferences undergo continual modification. Thus a translation acceptable in one period is often quite unacceptable at a later time.

A number of significant and relatively comprehensive definitions of translation have been offered. Procházka (Garvin 1955: 111 ff.) defines a good translation in terms of certain requirements which must be made of the translator, namely: (1) "He must understand the original word thematically and stylistically"; (2) "he must overcome the differences between the two linguistic structures"; and (3) "he must reconstruct the stylistic structures of the original work in his translation."

In a description of proper translation of poetry, Jackson Mathews (1959: 67) states: "One thing seems clear: to translate a poem whole is to compose another poem. A whole translation will be faithful to the *matter*, and it will 'approximate the form' of the original; and it will have a life of its own, which is the voice of the translator." Richmond Lattimore (1959, in Brower 1959: 56) deals with the same basic problem of translating poetry. He describes the fundamental principles in terms of the way in which Greek poetry should be translated, namely: "to make from the Greek poem a poem in English which, while giving a high minimum of meaning of the Greek, is still a new English poem, which would not be the kind of poem it is if it were not translating the Greek which it translates."

No proper definition of translation can avoid some of the basic difficulties. Especially in the rendering of poetry, the tension between form and content and the conflict between formal and dynamic equivalences are always acutely present. However, it seems to be increasingly recognized that adherence to the letter may indeed kill the spirit. William A. Cooper (1928: 484) deals with this problem rather realistically in his article on "Translating Goethe's Poems," in which he says: "If the language of the original employs word formations that give rise to insurmountable difficulties of direct translation, and figures of speech wholly foreign, and hence incomprehensible in the other tongue, it is better to cling to the spirit of the poem and clothe it in language and figures entirely free from awkwardness of speech and obscurity of picture. This might be called a translation from culture to culture."

It must be recognized that in translating poetry there are very special problems involved, for the form of expression (rhythm, meter, assonance, etc.) is essential to communicating the spirit of the message to the audience. But all translating, whether of poetry or prose, must be concerned also with the response of the receptor; hence the ultimate purpose of the translation, in terms of its impact upon its intended audience, is a fundamental factor in any evaluation of translations. This reason underlies Leonard Forster's definition (1958: 6) of a good translation as "one which fulfills the same purpose in the new language as the original did in the language in which it was written."

The resolution of the conflict between literalness of form and equivalence of response seems increasingly to favor the latter, especially in the translating of poetic materials. C.W. Orr (1941: 318), for example, describes translating as somewhat equivalent to painting, for, as he says, "the painter does not reproduce every detail of the landscape" – he selects what seems best to him. Likewise for the translator, "It is the spirit, not only the letter, that he seeks to embody in his own version."

Oliver Edwards (1957: 13) echoes the same point of view: "We expect approximate truth in a translation. . . . What we want to have is the truest possible *feel* of the original. The characters, the situations, the reflections must come to us as they were in the author's mind and heart, not necessarily precisely as he had them on his lips."

It is one thing, however, to produce a generalized definition of translating, whether of poetry or prose; it is often quite another to describe in some detail the significant characteristics of an adequate translation. This fact Savory (1957: 49–50) highlights by contrasting diametrically opposed opinions on a dozen important principles of translating. However, though some dissenting voices can be found on virtually all proposals as to what translating should consist of, there are several significant features of translating on which many of the most competent judges are increasingly in agreement.

Ezra Pound (1954: 273) states the case for translations making sense by declaring for "more sense and less syntax." But as early as 1789 George Campbell (1789: 445 ff.) argued that translation should not be characterized by "obscure sense." E. E. Milligan (1957) also argues for sense rather than words, for he points out that unless a translation communicates, i.e. makes sense to the receptor, it has not justified its existence.

In addition to making sense, translations must also convey the "spirit and manner" of the original (Campbell 1789: 445 ff.). For the Bible translator, this means that the individual style of the various writers of the Scriptures should be reflected as far as possible (Campbell 1789: 547). The same sentiment is clearly expressed by Ruth M. Underhill (1938: 16) in her treatment of certain problems of translating magic incantations of the Papago Indians of southern Arizona: "One can hope to make the translation exact only in spirit, not in letter." Francis Storr (1909) goes so far as to classify translators into "the literalist and the spiritualist schools," and in doing so takes his stand on the Biblical text, "The letter killeth but the spirit giveth life." As evidence for his thesis, Storr cites the difference between the Authorized Version, which he contends represents the spirit, and the English Revised Version, which sticks to the letter, with the result that the translation lacks a *Sprachgefühl*. The absence of literary stylists on the English Revised Committee was, however, corrected in the New English Bible (New Testament, 1961), in which one entire panel was composed of persons with special sensitivity to and competence in English style.

Closely related to the requirement of sensitivity to the style of the original is the need for a "natural and easy" form of expression in the language into which one is translating (Campbell 1789: 445 ff.). Max Beerbohm (1903: 75) considers that the cardinal fault of many who translate plays into English is the failure to be natural in expression; in fact, they make the reader "acutely conscious that their work is a translation. . . . For the most part, their ingenuity consists in finding phrases that could not possibly be used by the average Englishman." Goodspeed (1945: 8) echoes the same sentiment with respect to Bible translating by declaring that: "The best translation is not one that keeps forever before the reader's mind the fact that this is a translation, not an original English composition, but one that makes the reader forget that it is a translation at all and makes him feel that he is looking into the ancient writer's mind, as he would into that of a contemporary. This is, indeed, no light matter to undertake or to execute, but it is, nevertheless, the task of any serious translator." J. B. Phillips (1953: 53) confirms the same viewpoint when he declares that: "The test of a real translation is that it should not read like translation at all." His second principle of translating re-enforces the first, namely a translation into English should avoid "translator's English."

It must be recognized, however, that it is not easy to produce a completely natural translation, especially if the original writing is good literature, precisely because truly good writing intimately reflects and effectively exploits the total idiomatic capacities and special genius of the language in which the writing is done. A translator must therefore not only contend with the special difficulties resulting from such an effective exploitation of the total resources of the source language, but also seek to produce something relatively equivalent in the receptor language. In fact, Justin O'Brien (1959: 81) quotes Raymond Guérin to the effect that: "the most convincing criterion of the quality of a work is the fact that it can only be translated with difficulty, for if it passes readily into another language without losing its essence, then it must have no particular essence or at least not one of the rarest."

An easy and natural style in translating, despite the extreme difficulties of producing it – especially when translating an original of high quality – is nevertheless essential to producing in the ultimate receptors a response similar to that of the original receptors. In one way or another this principle of "similar response" has been widely held and effectively stated by a number of specialists in the field of translating. Even though Matthew Arnold (1861, as quoted in Savory 1957: 45) himself rejected in actual practice the principle of "similar response," he at least seems to have thought he was producing a similar response, for he declares that: "A translation should affect us in the same way as the original may be supposed to have affected its first hearers." Despite Arnold's objection to some of the freer translations done by others, he was at least strongly opposed to the literalist views of such persons as F. W. Newman (1861: xiv). Jowett (1891), on the other hand, comes somewhat closer to a present-day conception of "similar response" in stating that: "an English translation ought to be idiomatic and interesting, not only to the scholar, but to the learned reader. . . . The translator . . . seeks to produce on his reader an impression similar or nearly similar to that produced by the original."

Souter (1920: 7) expresses essentially this same view in stating that: "Our ideal in translation is to produce on the minds of our readers as nearly as possible the same effect as was produced by the original on its readers," and R. A. Knox (1957: 5) insists that a translation should be "read with the same interest and enjoyment which a reading of the original would have afforded."

In dealing with translating from an essentially linguistic point of view, Procházka (in Garvin 1955) re-enforces this same viewpoint, namely, that "the translation should make the same resultant impression on the reader as the original does on its reader."

If a translation is to meet the four basic requirements of (1) making sense, (2) conveying the spirit and manner of the original, (3) having a natural and easy form of expression, and (4) producing a similar response, it is obvious that at certain points the conflict between content and form (or meaning and manner) will be acute, and that one or the other must give way. In general, translators are agreed that, when there is no happy compromise, meaning must have priority over style

(Tancock 1958: 29). What one must attempt, however, is an effective blend of "matter and manner," for these two aspects of any message are inseparably united. Adherence to content, without consideration of form, usually results in a flat mediocrity, with nothing of the sparkle and charm of the original. On the other hand, sacrifice of meaning for the sake of reproducing the style may produce only an impression, and fail to communicate the message. The form, however, may be changed more radically than the content and still be substantially equivalent in its effect upon the receptor. Accordingly, correspondence in meaning must have priority over correspondence in style. However, this assigning of priorities must never be done in a purely mechanical fashion, for what is ultimately required, especially in the translation of poetry, is "a re-creation, not a reproduction" (Lattimore, in Brower 1959: 55).

Any survey of opinions on translating serves to confirm the fact that definitions or descriptions of translating are not served by deterministic rules; rather, they depend on probabilistic rules. One cannot, therefore, state that a particular translation is good or bad without taking into consideration a myriad of factors, which in turn must be weighted in a number of different ways, with appreciably different answers. Hence there will always be a variety of valid answers to the question, "Is this a good translation?"

Principles governing a translation oriented toward formal equivalence

In order to understand somewhat more fully the characteristics of different types of translations, it is important to analyze in more detail the principles that govern a translation which attempts to reproduce a formal equivalence. Such a formal-equivalence (or F–E) translation is basically source-oriented; that is, it is designed to reveal as much as possible of the form and content of the original message.

In doing so, an F–E translation attempts to reproduce several formal elements, including: (1) grammatical units, (2) consistency in word usage, and (3) meanings in terms of the source context. The reproduction of grammatical units may consist in: (a) translating nouns by nouns, verbs by verbs, etc.; (b) keeping all phrases and sentences intact (i.e. not splitting up and readjusting the units); and (c) preserving all formal indicators, e.g. marks of punctuation, paragraph breaks, and poetic indentation.

In attempting to reproduce consistency in word usage, an F–E translation usually aims at so-called concordance of terminology; that is, it always renders a particular term in the source-language document by the corresponding term in the receptor document. Such a principle may, of course, be pushed to an absurd extent, with the result being relatively meaningless strings of words, as in some passages of the so-called Concordant Version of the New Testament. On the other hand, a certain degree of concordance may be highly desirable in certain types of F–E translating. For example, a reader of Plato's Dialogues in English may prefer rigid consistency in the rendering of key terms (as in Jowett's translation), so that he may have some comprehension of the way in which Plato uses certain word symbols to develop his philosophical system. An F–E translation may also make use of brackets, parentheses, or even italics (as in the King James Bible) for words added to make sense in the translation, but missing in the original document.

In order to reproduce meanings in terms of the source context, an F–E translation normally attempts not to make adjustments in idioms, but rather to reproduce such expressions more or less literally, so that the reader may be able to perceive something of the way in which the original document employed local cultural elements to convey meanings.

In many instances, however, one simply cannot reproduce certain formal elements of the source message. For example, there may be puns, chiasmic orders of words, instances of assonance, or acrostic features of line-initial sounds which completely defy equivalent rendering. In such instances one must employ certain types of marginal notes, if the feature in question merits an explanation. In some rare instances one does light upon a roughly equivalent pun or play on words. For example, in translating the Hebrew text of Genesis 2:23, in which the Hebrew word *isshah* "woman" is derived from *ish* "man," it is possible to use a corresponding English pair, *woman* and *man*. However, such formal correspondences are obviously rare, for languages generally differ radically in both content and form.

A consistent F–E translation will obviously contain much that is not readily intelligible to the average reader. One must therefore usually supplement such translations with marginal notes, not only to explain some of the formal features which could not be adequately represented, but also to make intelligible some of the formal equivalents employed, for such expressions may have significance only in terms of the source language or culture.

Some types of strictly F–E translations, e.g. interlinear renderings and completely concordant translations, are of limited value; others are of great value. For example, translations of foreign-language texts prepared especially for linguists rarely attempt anything but close F–E renderings. In such translations the wording is usually quite literal, and even the segments are often numbered so that the corresponding units may be readily compared.

From what has been said directly and indirectly about F–E translations in preceding sections, it might be supposed that such translations are categorically ruled out. To the contrary, they are often perfectly valid translations of certain types of messages for certain types of audiences. The relative value and effectiveness of particular types of translations for particular audiences pose another question, and must not be confused with a description of the nature of various kinds of translations. At this point we are concerned only with their essential features, not with their evaluation.

Principles governing translations oriented toward dynamic equivalence

In contrast with formal-equivalence translations others are oriented toward dynamic equivalence. In such a translation the focus of attention is directed, not so much toward the source message, as toward the receptor response. A dynamic-equivalence (or D–E) translation may be described as one concerning which a bilingual and bicultural person can justifiably say, "That is just the way we would say it." It is important to realize, however, that a D–E translation is not merely another message which is more or less similar to that of the source. It is a translation, and as such must clearly reflect the meaning and intent of the source.

One way of defining a D–E translation is to describe it as "the closest natural equivalent to the source-language message." This type of definition contains three essential terms: (1) *equivalent*, which points toward the source-language message, (2) *natural*, which points toward the receptor language, and (3) *closest*, which binds the two orientations together on the basis of the highest degree of approximation.

However, since a D–E translation is directed primarily toward equivalence of response rather than equivalence of form, it is important to define more fully the implications of the word *natural* as applied to such translations. Basically, the word *natural* is applicable to three areas of the communication process; for a *natural* rendering must fit (1) the receptor language and culture as a whole, (2) the context of the particular message, and (3) the receptor-language audience.

The conformance of a translation to the receptor language and culture as a whole is an essential ingredient in any stylistically acceptable rendering. Actually this quality of linguistic appropriateness is usually noticeable only when it is absent. In a natural translation, therefore, those features which would mar it are conspicuous by their absence. J. H. Frere (1820: 481) has described such a quality by stating, "the language of translation ought, we think, . . . be a pure, impalpable and invisible element, the medium of thought and feeling and nothing more; it ought never to attract attention to itself. . . . All importations from foreign languages . . . are . . . to be avoided." Such an adjustment to the receptor language and culture must result in a translation that bears no obvious trace of foreign origin, so that, as G. A. Black (1936: 50) describes James Thomson's translations of Heine, such renderings are "a reproduction of the original, such as Heine himself, if master of the English language, would have given."

A natural translation involves two principal areas of adaptation, namely, grammar and lexicon. In general the grammatical modifications can be made the more readily, since many grammatical changes are dictated by the obligatory structures of the receptor language. That is to say, one is obliged to make such adjustments as shifting word order, using verbs in place of nouns, and substituting nouns for pronouns. The lexical structure of the source message is less readily adjusted to the semantic requirements of the receptor language, for instead of obvious rules to be followed, there are numerous alternative possibilities. There are in general three lexical levels to be considered: (1) terms for which there are readily available parallels, e.g. *river, tree, stone, knife*, etc.; (2) terms which identify culturally different objects, but with somewhat similar functions, e.g. *book*, which in English means an object with pages bound together into a unit, but which, in New Testament times, meant a long parchment or papyrus rolled up in the form of a scroll; and (3) terms which identify cultural specialties, e.g. *synagogue, homer, ephah, cherubim*, and *jubilee*, to cite only a few from the Bible. Usually the first set of terms involves no problem. In the second set of terms several confusions can arise; hence one must either use another term which reflects the form of the referent, though not the equivalent function, or which identifies the equivalent function at the expense of formal identity. In translating terms of the third class certain "foreign associations" can rarely be avoided. No translation that attempts to bridge a wide cultural gap can hope to eliminate all traces of the foreign setting. For example, in Bible translating it is quite impossible to remove such foreign "objects" as *Pharisees, Sadducees, Solomon's temple, cities of refuge*, or such Biblical themes as *anointing, adulterous generation, living sacrifice*, and *Lamb of God*, for these expressions are deeply imbedded in the very thought structure of the message.

It is inevitable also that when source and receptor languages represent very different cultures there should be many basic themes and accounts which cannot be "naturalized" by the process of translating. For example, the Jivaro Indians of Ecuador certainly do not understand 1 Corinthians 11:14, "Does not nature teach us that for a man to wear long hair is a dishonor to him?", for in general Jivaro men let their hair grow long, while Jivaro adult women usually cut theirs rather close. Similarly, in many areas of West Africa the behavior of Jesus' disciples in spreading leaves and branches in his way as he rode into Jerusalem is regarded as reprehensible; for in accordance with West African custom the path to be walked on or ridden over by a chief is scrupulously cleaned of all litter, and anyone who throws a branch in such a person's way is guilty of grievous insult. Nevertheless, these cultural discrepancies offer less difficulty than might be imagined, especially if footnotes are used to point out the basis for the cultural diversity; for all people recognize that other peoples behave differently from themselves.

Naturalness of expression in the receptor language is essentially a problem of co-suitability – but on several levels, of which the most important are as follows: (1) word classes (e.g. if there is no noun for "love" one must often say, "God loves" instead of "God is love"); (2) grammatical categories (in some languages so-called predicate nominatives must agree in number with the subject, so that "the two shall be one" cannot be said, and accordingly, one must say "the two persons shall act just as though they are one person"); (3) semantic classes (swear words in one language may be based upon the perverted use of divine names, but in another language may be primarily excremental and anatomical); (4) discourse types (some languages may require direct quotation and others indirect); and (5) cultural contexts (in some societies the New Testament practice of sitting down to teach seems strange, if not unbecoming).

In addition to being appropriate to the receptor language and culture, a natural translation must be in accordance with the context of the particular message. The problems are thus not restricted to gross grammatical and lexical features, but may also involve such detailed matters as intonation and sentence rhythm (Ezra Pound 1954: 298). The trouble is that, "Fettered to mere words, the translator loses the spirit of the original author" (Manchester 1951: 68).

A truly natural translation can in some respects be described more easily in terms of what it avoids than in what it actually states; for it is the presence of serious anomalies, avoided in a successful translation, which immediately strike the reader as being out of place in the context. For example, crude vulgarities in a supposedly dignified type of discourse are inappropriate, and as a result are certainly not natural. But vulgarities are much less of a problem than slang or colloquialisms. Stanley Newman (1955) deals with this problem of levels of vocabulary in his analysis of sacred and slang language in Zuñi, and points out that a term such as *melika*, related to English *American*, is not appropriate for the religious atmosphere of the kiva. Rather, one must speak of Americans by means of a Zuñi expression meaning, literally, "broad-hats". For the Zuñis, uttering *melika* in a kiva ceremony would be as out of place as bringing a radio into such a meeting.

Onomatopoeic expressions are considered equivalent to slang by the speakers of some languages. In some languages in Africa, for example, certain highly imitative expressions (sometimes called ideophones) have been ruled out as inappropriate to the dignified context of the Bible. Undoubtedly the critical attitudes of some missionary translators toward such vivid, but highly colloquial, forms of expression have contributed to the feeling of many Africans that such words are inappropriate in Biblical contexts. In some languages, however, such onomatopoeic usages are not only highly developed, but are regarded as essential and becoming in any type of discourse. For example, Waiwai, a language of British Guiana, uses such expressions with great frequency, and without them one can scarcely communicate the emotional tone of the message, for they provide the basic signals for understanding the speaker's attitude toward the events he narrates.

Some translators are successful in avoiding vulgarisms and slang, but fall into the error of making a relatively straightforward message in the source language sound like a complicated legal document in the receptor language by trying too hard to be completely unambiguous; as a result such a translator spins out his definitions in long, technical phrases. In such a translation little is left of the grace and naturalness of the original.

Anachronisms are another means of violating the co-suitability of message and context. For example, a Bible translation into English which used "iron oxide" in place of "rust" would be technically correct, but certainly anachronistic. On the other hand, to translate "heavens and earth" by "universe" in Genesis 1:1 is not so radical a departure as one might think, for the people of the ancient world had a highly developed concept of an organized system comprising the "heavens and the earth," and hence "universe" is not inappropriate. Anachronisms involve two types of errors: (1) using contemporary words which falsify life at historically different periods, e.g. translating "demon possessed" as "mentally distressed," and (2) using old-fashioned language in the receptor language and hence giving an impression of unreality.

Appropriateness of the message within the context is not merely a matter of the referential content of the words. The total impression of a message consists not merely in the objects, events, abstractions, and relationships symbolized by the words, but also in the stylistic selection and arrangement of such symbols. Moreover, the standards of stylistic acceptability for various types of discourse differ radically from language to language. What is entirely appropriate in Spanish, for example, may turn out to be quite unacceptable "purple prose" in English, and the English prose we admire as dignified and effective often seems in Spanish to be colorless, insipid, and flat. Many Spanish literary artists take delight in the flowery elegance of their language, while most English writers prefer bold realism, precision, and movement.

It is essential not only that a translation avoid certain obvious failures to adjust the message to the context, but also that it incorporate certain positive elements of style which provide the proper emotional tone for the discourse. This emotional tone must accurately reflect the point of view of the author. Thus such elements as sarcasm, irony, or whimsical interest must all be accurately reflected in a D–E translation. Furthermore, it is essential that each participant introduced into the message be accurately represented. That is to say, individuals must be properly characterized by the appropriate selection and arrangement of words, so that such features as social class or geographical dialect will be immediately evident. Moreover, each character must be permitted to have the same kind of individuality and personality as the author himself gave them in the original message.

A third element in the naturalness of a D–E translation is the extent to which the message fits the receptor-language audience. This appropriateness must be judged on the basis of the level of experience and the capacity for decoding, if one is to aim at any real dynamic equivalence. On the other hand, one is not always sure how the original audience responded or were supposed to respond. Bible translators, for example, have often made quite a point of the fact that the language of the New Testament was Koine Greek, the language of "the man in the street," and hence a translation should speak to the man in the street. The truth of the matter is that many New Testament messages were not directed primarily to the man in the street, but to the man in the congregation. For this reason, such expressions as "Abba Father," *Maranatha*, and "baptized into Christ" could be used with reasonable expectation that they would be understood.

A translation which aims at dynamic equivalence inevitably involves a number of formal adjustments, for one cannot have his formal cake and eat it dynamically too. Something must give! In general, this limitation involves three principal areas: (1) special literary forms, (2) semantically exocentric expressions, and (3) intraorganismic meanings.

The translating of poetry obviously involves more adjustments in literary form than does prose, for rhythmic forms differ far more radically in form, and hence in esthetic appeal. As a result, certain rhythmic patterns must often be substituted for others, as when Greek dactylic hexameter is translated in iambic pentameter. Moreover, some of the most acceptable translating of rhymed verse is accomplished by substituting free verse. In Bible translating the usual procedure is to attempt a kind of dignified prose where the original employs poetry, since, in general, Biblical content is regarded as much more important than Biblical form.

When semantically exocentric phrases in the source language are meaningless or misleading if translated literally into the receptor language, one is obliged to make some adjustments in a D–E translation. For example, the Semitic idiom "gird up the loins of your mind" may mean nothing more than "put a belt around the hips of your thoughts" if translated literally. Under such circumstances one must change from an exocentric to an endocentric type of expression, e.g. "get ready in your thinking". Moreover, an idiom may not be merely meaningless, but may even convey quite the wrong meaning, in which case it must also be modified. Often, for example, a simile may be substituted for the original metaphor, e.g. "sons of thunder" may become "men like thunder".

Intraorganismic meanings suffer most in the process of translating, for they depend so largely upon the total cultural context of the language in which they are used, and hence are not readily transferable to other language-culture contexts. In the New Testament, for example, the word *tapeinos*, usually translated as "humble" or "lowly" in English, had very definite emotive connotations in the Greek world, where it carried the pejorative meanings of "low," "humiliated," "degraded," "mean," and "base." However, the Christians, who came principally from the lower strata of society, adopted as a symbol of an important Christian virtue this very term, which had been used derisively of the lower classes. Translations of the New Testament into English cannot expect to carry all the latent emotive meanings in the Greek word. Similarly, such translations as "anointed," "Messiah," and "Christ" cannot do full justice to the Greek *Christos*, which had associations intimately linked with the hopes and aspirations of the early Judeo-Christian community. Such emotive elements of meaning need not be related solely to terms of theological import. They apply to all levels of vocabulary. In French, for example, there is no term quite equivalent to English *home*, in contrast with *house*, and in English nothing quite like French *foyer*, which in many respect is like English *home*, but also means "hearth" and "fireside" as well as "focus" and "salon of a theater." Emotively, the English word *home* is close to French *foyer*, but referentially *home* is usually equivalent to *maison, habitation*, and *chez* (followed by an appropriate pronoun).

Notes

1   This idiom is based upon the requirement that plaintiffs and defendants spit on the ground in front of each other when a case has been finally tried and punishment meted out. The spitting indicates that all is forgiven and that the accusations can never be brought into court again.

2   We also encounter certain rare situations in which the languages are related but the cultures are quite disparate. For example, in the case of Hindi and English one is dealing with two languages from the same language family, but the cultures in question are very different. In such instances, the languages are also likely to be so distantly related as to make their linguistic affiliation a matter of minor consequence.

Chapter 14

Katharina Reiss

TYPE, KIND AND INDIVIDUALITY OF TEXT: DECISION MAKING IN TRANSLATION

Translated by Susan Kitron

1 General preliminary remarks

1.1 **I**NTERLINGUAL TRANSLATION MAY BE defined as a bilingual mediated process of communication, which ordinarily aims at the production of a TL [target language] text that is functionally equivalent to an SL text [source language] (2 media: SL and TL + 1 medium: the translator, who becomes a secondary sender; thus translating: secondary communication.)

1.1.1 The use of two natural languages as well as the employment of the medium of the translator necessarily and naturally result in a change of message during the communicative process. The theoretician of communication, Otto Haseloff (1969), has pointed out that an "ideal" communication is rare even when one single language is employed, because the receiver always brings his own knowledge and his own expectations, which are different from those of the sender. H. F. Plett (1975) calls this factor the "communicative difference." In translating, then, such differences are all the more to be expected. At this point I distinguish between "intentional" and "unintentional" changes affecting the translation.

Unintentional changes may arise from the different language structures as well as from differences in translating competence.

> Ex. 1: Je suis allée à la gare (French: information about a female person; no information about the means of travel)

Ich bin zum Bahnhof gegangen (German: no information about
the person; information about the means of travel)
= Linguistically conditioned communicative difference.

Ex. 2:   La France est veuve (Pompidou at the death of de Gaulle)
Frankreich ist Witwe – Frankreich ist Witwe geworden –
Frankreich ist verwitwet – Frankreich ist verwaist [orphaned][1]
Linguistically conditioned: La France – Witwe [Widow]
"Frankreich" is neuter in German. The image of "widow" is
odd to a person ignorant of French. "Waise" [orphan] is also
neuter; the image of an emotional attachment programmed
differently.

Intentional changes frequently occur in translating, if the aims pursued in the translation are different from those of the original; if, besides the language difference of
the TL readers, there is a change in the reading circle, etc. Since this will entail a
change of function in the act of communication, there is now no attempt any more
to strive for a functional equivalence between the SL and the TL text, but for
adequacy of the TL reverbalization in accordance with the "foreign function." It
follows that, besides a text typology relevant to translating, a translation typology
should be worked out.

1.2 Communication comprises linguistic and non-linguistic action

1.2.1 Written texts and texts put in writing (material for translating purposes) are
to be characterized as "one-way communication" (Glinz 1973). This means, on the
one hand, that non-linguistic elements contributing to oral communication
(gestures, facial expressions, speed of speech, intonation, etc.) are partly verbalized
(= alleviation of the text analysis). On the other hand, the text analysis is made
more difficult by the limitation of the possibilities of explicit verbalization of such
elements as well as by the spatio-temporal separation between addresser and
addressee and the lack of feedback during the act of communication; these factors
lead, among other reasons, to a variable understanding of a given text.

1.2.2 Action is *intentional behavior in a given situation* (Vermeer 1972). "Intention"
means here speech purpose, speech aim, motive leading to language communication (Lewandowski 1973–5: 288). Through the intention, verbalized by the author
in his text, this text receives a communicative function for the process of
communication. In order to be able to establish this intention the translator receives
significant assistance if he determines to which text-type and text-variety (relevant
for translating) any given text belongs.
      Written texts may have single or plural intentions. Plural intentions may be of
be same rank and order. Mostly, however, one intention (and, with it, the text
function) is dominant:

Ex. 3:   C vor o und u und a spricht man immer wie ein k; soll es wie
ein c erklingen, lässt man die Cedille springen.
(mnemo-technical rhyme:

> Intention 1 – to convey a rule
> Intention 2 – to facilitate remembering by giving the text an
> artistic form
> Intention 3 – to "sweeten" the learning process by giving the
> text a pleasing form)

Counterexample 3a:

> Ein Wiesel/sass auf einem Kiesel/inmitten Bachgeriesel . . .
> (Christian Morgenstern)
> Intention 1 – the communication of an objective fact
> Intention 2 – artistic creation to convey an aesthetic
> impression

The dominance of intention 2 is established through the text itself: "Das raffinier-te Tier/Tat's um des Reimes Willen." Max Knight gives five English versions, and Jirí Levý regards all of them as equivalent (1969: 103–4):

A weasel	A ferret	
perched on an easel	nibbling a carrot	
within a patch of teasel	in a garret	etc.

1.3 Language is (among other factors) a temporal phenomenon and thus subject to the conditions of time. This also applies to language in written texts and therefore to these texts themselves, a factor which is significant for translating.

1.3.1 A natural consequence of this fact is, firstly, the necessity of re-translating one and the same SL text, if the TL has changed to such an extent, that the TL version reflecting previous language conditions does not guarantee functional equivalence any more (e.g., Bible translations, the translations of classical authors).

1.3.2 A further consequence of this fact may be the loss of understanding of the original SL text functions, because of a change in the situation, in which the SL text fulfilled its function, and/or because of the impossibility of reconstructing this situation (e.g., Caesar, *Commentarii de bello gallico* – electioneering pamphlet = operative text [see 2.1.1 below]. Torn out of its original social context – now a historical report and also translated as such = informative text; Jonathan Swift, *Gulliver's Travels* – satire on contemporary social ills = expressive text with an operative secondary function; today only recognizable in this function by the experts specializing in this period; for the ordinary reader (also of the original) – a fantastic adventure tale = expressive text.)

2 The translating process

Phase of analysis. In order to place a functionally equivalent TL text beside an SL text the translator should clarify the functions of the SL text. This may be done in a three-stage-process, which may, in principle, be carried out either by starting from the smallest textual unit and ending with the text as a whole, or by beginning with the text as a whole and ending with the analysis of the smallest textual unit. For practical as well as for text-theoretical considerations, I have chosen the process of proceeding from the largest to the smallest unit. (In practice, the conscientious translator reads the whole text first to get an impression; from a text-linguistic point of view, the text is nowadays regarded as the primary language sign.) Below, this three-stage process will be presented as a temporal sequence for purely methodological reasons. In practice, the separate stages of analysis dovetail, particularly if the translator is experienced.

2.1 Total function in the framework of written forms of communication

2.1.1 Establishment of the *"text-type"* – a phenomenon going beyond a single linguistic or cultural context, because the following essentially different forms of written communication may be regarded as being present in every speech community with a culture based on the written word and also because every author of a text ought to decide in principle on one of the three forms before beginning to formulate his text.

Question: Which basic communicative form is realized in the concrete text with the help of written texts?

a. The communication of content – informative type
b. The communication of artistically organized content – expressive type
c. The communication of content with a persuasive character – operative type

Aids in orientation: semantic as well as pragmatic ones (content and knowledge of the world), for instance, "pre-signals", i.e., titles or headlines (novel, law, report of an accident, sonnet, strike call, etc.) or "metapropositional expressions" at the beginning of a text (Grosse 1976) (e.g., "Herewith I authorize . . ." in the case of a general power of attorney, etc.); medium: professional periodicals, pamphlets, the news section of a newspaper, etc.

Use of language:

a. The particular frequency of words and phrases of evaluation (positive for the addresser or for the cause to which he has committed himself; negative for any obstacle to his commitment), the particular frequency of certain rhetorical figures may, among other factors, lead to the conclusion that the text is operative. Decisive question: are we dealing with a speech object capable of making an appeal?
b. "The feature that speech elements are capable of pointing beyond themselves to a significance of the whole" (Grosse 1976), "the principle of linkage" (rhymes, leit-motifs, parallelisms, rhythm, etc.) and the "transformation of the material of reality" (Mukařovský) may lead to the conclusion that the text belongs to the expressive type.
c. Should the elements quoted under a. and b. be absent, the conclusion may be that the text is informative.

Thus a "rough grid" has been established for the analysis.

2.1.2 *Mixed forms.* If we accept the three text types, the informative, expressive and the operative type, as the basic forms of written communication (inter-cultural), it should be taken into account that these types are not only realized in their "pure" form, that is, that they do not always appear in their "fully realized form"; and it should also be considered that, for a variety of reasons (change in the conventions of a text variety, or if we have to do with plural intentions) the communicative intention and communicative form cannot be unambiguously adapted to each other. In the first case: texts merely appealing to an affirmative attitude of the addressee without intending to trigger off impulses of behavior, e.g., newspaper articles expressing opinions (no fully realized form of the operative text). In the second case: versified legal texts in the Middle Ages; in order for their content to be acceptable, they had to be presented in verse form = greater dignity of rhymed language! (Mixed form between informative and expressive text type.)

2.1.3 *Additional types?* Bühler's three functions of the linguistic sign, in analogy to which I have isolated the three main text functions, are extended by Roman Jakobson to include the phatic and the poetic functions. Would both of these functions be suitable to isolate text types relevant to the choice of a translating method? Not so, in my opinion! Related to entire texts and not only to single language elements, the phatic function (= the establishment and maintenance of contact) is realized in all three of the basic forms of communication, i.e., the phatic function does not lead to particulars of the text construction.

For instance:

> Picture postcard from a holiday: informative text with phatic function
> Original birthday poem: expressive text with phatic function
> Memory aid in an advertisement slogan: operative text with phatic
>   function

The phatic function does not arise from the text form, but from the use to which the text is put.

Likewise, the poetic function of the language signs is realized in all three of the basic communicative forms:

Soccer reportage:	informative text, partly with poetic language elements, e.g., "der Mann im fahlgrünen Trikot," "Erstaunlich matt war Hölzenbein, fehlerlos Grabowski, eindrucksvoll Neuberger." (rhetorical triple figure)
Lyrical poem:	expressive text – the poetic function determines the whole text
Sales promotion:	(e.g., in verse form) operative text with elements of poetic language "loan structure" (Hantsch 1972)

However, in view of the relevancy for translating purposes, an additional type, a "hyper-type," should be isolated as a super-structure for the three basic types: *the multi-medial text type.* The need for this arises from the fact that the translating material does not only consist of "autonomous" written texts, but also, to a large extent, firstly of verbal texts, which, though put down in writing, are presented orally, and, secondly, of verbal texts, which are only part of a larger whole and are phrased with a view to, and in consideration of, the "additional information" supplied by a sign system other than that of language (picture + text, music and text, gestures, facial expressions, built-up scenery on the stage, slides and text, etc.).

Thus, when the message is verbalized, the multi-medial type possesses its own regularities, which ought to be taken into account in translating, besides – and above – the regularities of the three basic forms of written communication. Therefore I now put this type above the three basic forms, though, formerly, I placed it beside them. However, we should also consider a suggestion made by a research group of the Philips concern, according to which these extra-linguistic conditions should be regarded as the basis for a typology of media relevant to translating.

2.2 The second stage of the analysis aims at the establishment of the *text variety*, i.e., the classification of a given text according to specifically structured socio-cultural patterns of communication belonging to specific language communities. Text variety is still a controversial concept in linguistics. The denotation of text variety as well as that of text type is at present still used for the most variegated textual phenomena. Therefore, I meanwhile define text variety as super-individual acts of speech or writing, which are linked to recurrent actions of communications and in which particular patterns of language and structure have developed because of their recurrence in similar communicative constellations. The *phenomenon* of text variety is not confined to one language. The various kinds of text variety are partly not confined to one language or one culture, but the habits of textualization, the patterns of language and structure often differ from one another to a considerable extent. Hence, the establishment of the text variety is of decisive importance for the translator, so that he may not endanger the functional equivalence of the TL text by naively adopting SL conventions.

Examples:

> Es war einmal: textual opening signal in German for fairy tales
> In the name of the people: for verdicts
> 2 × 4 lines + 2 × 3 lines: structural pattern for the sonnet
> Directions for use in French and German: According to the specific text
> variety there is a distribution of structures common to both languages.
> The passive form and impersonal expressions – conventions in German.
> The indefinite pronoun "on" + infinitive phrase – convention in French.

One single example may not always suffice for the establishment of the text variety.

> Ex. 4:   English death notice:
>   FRANCIS. On Thursday, March 17, Jenny, beloved wife of Tony
>   Francis and mother of Anthony. Service at St. Mary's Church,

Elloughton, 9.50 am, Tuesday, March 22, followed by cremation. No letters or flowers, please.

The translation into German would be more or less as follows (the italicized words and expressions characterize conventions observed in German):

Am 17. März *verstarb meine* geliebte Frau, *meine* liebe Mutter
JENNY *FRANCIS*
Elloughton *Im Namen der Angehörigen* (or: in tiefer Trauer)
Tony Francis
mit Anthony
Trauergottesdienst: Dienstag, den 22.3, 9.50 in St. Marien (Elloughton)
Anschliessend *erfolgt* die Feuerbestattung
Von Kondolenzschreiben und Kranzspenden *bitten wir* höflichst *Abstand zu nehmen.*

2.3 Third stage of the analysis: the analysis of style (the analysis of a particular textual surface). Now the *text individual* is placed in the foreground. This analysis is of supreme importance, because the translator's "decisive battle" is fought on the level of the text individual, where strategy and tactics are directed by type and variety.

Let style in this connection be understood to mean the ad hoc selection of linguistic signs and of their possibilities of combination supplied by the language system. The use of language in a given SL text is investigated in order to clarify in detail, firstly, what linguistic means are used to realize specific communicative functions, and, secondly, how the text is constructed. This detailed semantic, syntactic and pragmatic analysis is necessary, because, as is well known, not even in one single language do form and function show a 1:1 relation. The same phenomenon applies to the relation of SL to TL.

2.4 At this point I see, as it were, a "juncture" between the first phase of the process of translation, the phase of analysis, and the second phase of the process of translation, the phase of reverbalization, for it is already here that the translator, at any rate the experienced translator, pays heed to possible contrasts.

The detailed semantic, syntactic and pragmatic analysis is carried out in small stages of analysis, proceeding from the word, the syntagma, the phrase, the sentence, the section (paragraph or chapter) up to the level of the entire text.

The process of reverbalization is a linear one constructing the TL text out of words, syntagmas, clauses, sentences, paragraphs, etc. During this process of reverbalization a decision has to be made for each element of the text whether the linguistic signs and sequences of linguistic signs selected in the TL in coordination with a sign form and sign function can guarantee the functional equivalence for which a translator should strive, by due consideration of text variety and text type.

3 Phase of reverbalization

Relevance of the classification of text type and text variety to the translating process.

> Thesis: The text type determines the general method of translating;
> The text variety demands consideration for language and text
> structure conventions.

3.1 Normal cases

If functional equivalence is sought during the process of translation, this means:

a. If the SL text is written to convey contents, these contents should also be conveyed in the TL text.

Mode of translating: *translation according to the sense and meaning* in order to maintain the invariability of the content. To this end it may be necessary that what is conveyed implicitly in the SL text should be explicated in the TL and vice versa. This necessity arises, on the one hand, from structural differences in the two languages involved, and, on the other hand, from differences in the collective pragmatics of the two language communities involved.

> Ex. 5a: Vous vous introduisez par l'étroite ouverture *en vous frottant contre
> ses bords* . . . (= explicit)
> Sie *zwängen* sich *durch* die schmale Öffnung (*not* "by rubbing against
> its walls") (= implicit)
> "durchzwängen" in German contains the image of rubbing against an
> edge.

> Ex. 5b: (after Klaus Rülker) A report by a French press agency about the
> presidential elections in France: seulement huit départements
> français votèrent en majorité pour Poher.
> literal translation: Nur acht aller französischen Departements
> stimmten in ihrer Mehrheit für Poher.
> equivalent translation: Nur acht *der hundert* französischen
> Departements stimmten in ihrer Mehrheit für Poher.

b. If the SL text is written in order to convey artistic contents, then the contents in the TL should be conveyed in an analogously artistic organization. Mode of translating: *translating by identification* (not in the sense Goethe uses). The translator identifies with the artistic and creative intention of the SL author in order to maintain the artistic quality of the text.

> Ex. 6: (Ortega y Gasset: *Miseria y Esplendor de la Traducción*)
> Entreveo que es usted una especie de *último abencerraje*, último
> superviviente de una fauna desaparecida, puesto que es usted capaz,
> frente a otro hombre, de creer que es el otro y no usted quien
> tiene razón.

literal translation: "eine Art letzter Abencerraje" (without content for the German reader)

content translation: "eine Art Ausnahmefall" (absence of the artistic components: metaphors and literary allusion)

functionally equivalent translation: "eine Art letzter Ritter ohne Furcht und Tadel"

(One element of the artistic organization in Ortega's essay is the many verbs and nouns alluding to seafaring, either directly or in a figurative sense, in spite of the fact that the subject has nothing to do with seafaring. This is an indication that he is aware of Jakob Grimm's saying, according to which translating resembles a ship manned to sail the seas, but though it safely carries the goods, it must land at shore with a different soil under a different air. The metaphor is obvious because all the images presented by Ortega on the subject of translation derive from what Schleiermacher, Humboldt and Goethe have said about the problem. Thus, he must have known Grimm's metaphor as well. Hence, the translator is satisfied in choosing as shifted equivalents concepts from seafaring, where there are none in the original, if these are easily available in German. The reason is that at other times, when in the Spanish language the association with "seafaring" is implied, an equivalent German expression is not available: *arribar* = *ankommen*, instead of *llegar*. This is one of the examples I mean when referring to "the analogy of artistic form".)

c. If the SL text is written to convey persuasively structured contents in order to trigger off impulses of behavior, then the contents conveyed in the TL must be capable of triggering off analogous impulses of behavior in the TL reader.

> Ex. 7: Black is beautiful
> This slogan appearing in English in a German sales promotion could not be retained in the translation into English of a whole sales promoting text, if that text is intended for South African buyers.

Mode of translating: *adaptive translating*. The psychological mechanisms of the use of persuasive language should be adapted to the needs of the new language community.

3.2 Since form and function of language signs do not show a relation of 1:1, the same SL sequence may be represented in the TL by any other language sequence depending in which text type and text variety they appear and which function they may have to fulfill there.

> Ex. 8: El niño lloraba bajo *el agua del bautismo*.
> Text variety: social news; text type: informative.
> Das Kind weinte unter dem *Taufwasser*.

> Ex. 9: Marcelino lloraba bajo *el agua del bautismo*, como antes callara al advertir *el sabor de la sal*. (Sánchez-Silva, Marcelino, Pan y vino)

Text variety: narrative; text type: expressive (parallelisms; rhythm-elements of artistic organization: retained in the TL)
Marcelino weinte unter dem Wasser der Taufe, wie er zuvor beim Geschmack des Salzes geschwiegen hatte.

Ex. 10: *Souvent femme varie, bien fol est qui s'y fie.*
    a.   This saying of Francis I is mentioned in a history book.
          Text variety: schoolbook; text type: informative.
          Frauen ändern sich oft, wer ihnen traut, ist schön dumm.
    b.   Mentioned in a drama by Victor Hugo (transl. by Georg Büchner), *Maria Tudor.*
          Text variety: drama; text type: expressive.
          Ein Weib ändert sich jeden Tag, ein Narr ist, wer ihr trauen mag (several semantic shifts, rhyme and rhythm retained).
    c.   Item in an advertisement for wine: "Souvent femme varie. Les vins du Postillon ne varient jamais."
          Literary allusion in conjunction with pun-memory aid and the arousal of sympathy in the "connoisseur." The allusion should be re-programmed:
          Text variety: the advertising of products; text type: operative.
          Frauenherzen sind trügerisch. Postillon-Weine betrügen nie.

3.3 Problematic cases

If the three basic forms of communication are not realized in their "pure" form (cf. mixed forms, 2.1.2), then the principles of translating for the three basic types serve as aids for a decision in cases of conflict. In principle, the mode of translating for the entire text applies to all text elements, even if they do not belong to the same type as the dominant type.

    If, for instance, elements of poetic language are used when content is conveyed (informative type) – the so-called loan structures (Hantsch 1972) – the translation ought to strive for an analogously poetic form for those elements. However, if this is not possible in the TL without loss of the unity of content and artistic form, then the retention of content is dominant in informative texts and is to be preferred to the maintenance of an artistic form.

Ex. 11: Nun gibt es freilich moderne Nomaden, für die ein Caravan nur der zweitschönste *Wahn* ist (*Süddeutsche Zeitung*, Streiflicht).
       Text variety: newspaper item; text type: informative.

We have here an item referring to an opinion poll among owners of camping places as regards the behavior of German holiday makers. The "Streiflichter" [a newspaper column] in the *Süddeutsche Zeitung* [a newspaper] are often distinguished by an abundance of entertaining puns and other kinds of play with language. At the same time, however, the subject is invariably a topical state of affairs, and the main function of the text is the communication of content. In translation puns and other kinds of play with language will have to be ignored to a great extent so as to keep the content invariant.

If, however, artistically structured contents in a text of the expressive type have to be conveyed and if, during this process, the artistic organization might be harmed by the retention of the same content elements, then the rule applies for expressive texts that the contents may be changed.

> Ex. 12: . . . une péquerette, ou une primevère, ou un coucou, ou un bouton d'or . . . (Samuel Becket)
> literally: . . . ein Gänse*blümchen*, oder ein Himmels*schlüsselchen*, oder eine *Schlüsselblume* oder eine Butter*blume* . . . (invariance of content)
> Elmar Tophoven: . . . ein Tausendschönchen, eine Primel, eine Schlüsselblume, eine Butterrose . . .

Finally, if, in conveying contents with a persuasive form intended to trigger off impulses of behavior, the unchanged adoption of elements of content or (loaned) elements of artistic structure from the SL texts does not have an operative effect, these elements may be replaced by other elements fulfilling the desired function.

> Ex. 13: Füchse fahren Firestone-Phoenix
> Foxes use Firestone-Phoenix (falsification of association, loss of alliteration; important elements of the operative use of language)
> Pros prefer Firestone-Phoenix (change of content to retain positive association and alliteration)

If operative text elements appear in different text types, then the adapting method of translating also applies to these single elements as long as this is possible without any harm to either the content to be conveyed (in the case of the informative type) or to the artistic organization as a whole (in the case of the expressive text).

3.4 Special cases

If there is a difference between the original text function and the function of the translation, the text typology relevant to translation as well as the establishment of the given text variety are of no significance at all for the question what mode of translating should be adopted to attain functional equivalence. In that case a *typology of translation* should replace the text typology in order to supply suitable criteria for the mode of translating. As has been mentioned above, in changes of function the aim of the translating process is not anymore the attainment of a functionally TL text, but a TL text possessing a form which is adequate to the "foreign function." The criteria are not to be derived from the question "to what end and for whom has the text been *written?*," but from the question "to what end and for whom is the text *translated?*"

> E.g., a "grammar translation"
> — Aim of the translation: to examine whether the pupil is acquainted with vocabulary and grammatical structures of the

foreign language; translated for the teacher. Regardless of which text type is realized by the SL text, only vocabulary and grammar are considered.

E.g., interlinear versions
— Aim of the translation: the reproduction of the SL text for research purposes; translated for the student ignorant of the SL.

E.g., summaries of content
— Aim of the translation: communication of contents relevant for a certain further use; translated upon somebody's order.

Note

1   Translator's remarks in square brackets.

Chapter 15

James S. Holmes

THE NAME AND NATURE OF TRANSLATION STUDIES[1]

1.1

"SCIENCE," MICHAEL MULKAY points out, "tends to proceed by means of discovery of new areas of ignorance."[2] The process by which this takes place has been fairly well defined by the sociologists of science and research.[3] As a new problem or set of problems comes into view in the world of learning, there is an influx of researchers from adjacent areas, bringing with them the paradigms and models that have proved fruitful in their own fields. These paradigms and models are then brought to bear on the new problem, with one of two results. In some situations the problem proves amenable to explicitation, analysis, explication, and at least partial solution within the bounds of one of the paradigms or models, and in that case it is annexed as a legitimate branch of an established field of study. In other situations the paradigms or models fail to produce sufficient results, and researchers become aware that new methods are needed to approach the problem.

In this second type of situation, the result is a tension between researchers investigating the new problem and colleagues in their former fields, and this tension can gradually lead to the establishment of new channels of communication and the development of what has been called a new disciplinary utopia, that is, a new sense of a shared interest in a common set of problems, approaches, and objectives on the part of a new grouping of researchers. As W. O. Hagstrom has indicated, these two steps, the establishment of communication channels and the development of a disciplinary utopia, "make it possible for scientists to identify with the emerging discipline and to claim legitimacy for their point of view when appealing to university bodies or groups in the larger society."[4]

1.2

Though there are no doubt a few scholars who would object, particularly among the linguists, it would seem to me clear that in regard to the complex of problems clustered round the phenomenon of translating and translations,[5] the second situation now applies. After centuries of incidental and desultory attention from a scattering of authors, philologians, and literary scholars, plus here and there a theologian or an idiosyncratic linguist, the subject of translation has enjoyed a marked and constant increase in interest on the part of scholars in recent years, with the Second World War as a kind of turning point. As this interest has solidified and expanded, more and more scholars have moved into the field, particularly from the adjacent fields of linguistics, linguistic philosophy, and literary studies, but also from such seemingly more remote disciplines as information theory, logic, and mathematics, each of them carrying with him paradigms, quasi-paradigms, models, and methodologies that he felt could be brought to bear on this new problem.

At first glance, the resulting situation today would appear to be one of great confusion, with no consensus regarding the types of models to be tested, the kinds of methods to be applied, the varieties of terminology to be used. More than that, there is not even likemindedness about the contours of the field, the problem set, the discipline as such. Indeed, scholars are not so much as agreed on the very name for the new field.

Nevertheless, beneath the superficial level, there are a number of indications that for the field of research focusing on the problems of translating and translations Hagstrom's disciplinary utopia is taking shape. If this is a salutary development (and I believe that it is), it follows that it is worth our while to further the development by consciously turning our attention to matters that are serving to impede it.

1.3

One of these impediments is the lack of appropriate channels of communication. For scholars and researchers in the field, the channels that do exist still tend to run via the older disciplines (with their attendant norms in regard to models, methods, and terminology), so that papers on the subject of translation are dispersed over periodicals in a wide variety of scholarly fields and journals for practising translators. It is clear that there is a need for other communication channels, cutting across the traditional disciplines to reach all scholars working in the field, from whatever background.

2.1

But I should like to focus our attention on two other impediments to the development of a disciplinary utopia. The first of these, the lesser of the two in importance, is the seemingly trivial matter of the name for this field of research. It would not be wise to continue referring to the discipline by its subject matter as has been done at this conference, for the map, as the General Semanticists constantly remind us, is not the territory, and failure to distinguish the two can only further confusion.

Through the years, diverse terms have been used in writings dealing with translating and translations, and one can find references in English to "the art" or "the craft" of translation, but also to the "principles" of translation, the "fundamentals" or the "philosophy". Similar terms recur in French and German. In some cases the choice of term reflects the attitude, point of approach, or background of the writer; in others it has been determined by the fashion of the moment in scholarly terminology.

There have been a few attempts to create more "learned" terms, most of them with the highly active disciplinary suffix -ology. Roger Goffin, for instance, has suggested the designation "translatology" in English, and either its cognate or *traductologie* in French.[6] But since the -ology suffix derives from Greek, purists reject a contamination of this kind, all the more so when the other element is not even from Classical Latin, but from Late Latin in the case of *translatio* or Renaissance French in that of *traduction*. Yet Greek alone offers no way out, for "metaphorology", "metaphraseology", or "metaphrastics" would hardly be of aid to us in making our subject clear even to university bodies, let alone to other "groups in the larger society."[7] Such other terms as "translatistics" or "translistics", both of which have been suggested, would be more readily understood, but hardly more acceptable.

2.2.1

Two further, less classically constructed terms have come to the fore in recent years. One of these began its life in a longer form, "the theory of translating" or "the theory of translation" (and its corresponding forms: "Theorie des Übersetzens", "théorie de la traduction"). In English (and in German) it has since gone the way of many such terms, and is now usually compressed into "translation theory" (*Übersetzungstheorie*). It has been a productive designation, and can be even more so in future, but only if it is restricted to its proper meaning. For, as I hope to make clear in the course of this paper, there is much valuable study and research being done in the discipline, and a need for much more to be done, that does not, strictly speaking, fall within the scope of theory formation.

2.2.2

The second term is one that has, to all intents and purposes, won the field in German as a designation for the entire discipline.[8] This is the term *Übersetzungswissenschaft*, constructed to form a parallel to *Sprachwissenschaft, Literaturwissenschaft*, and many other *Wissenschaften*. In French, the comparable designation, "science de la traduction", has also gained ground, as have parallel terms in various other languages.

One of the first to use a parallel-sounding term in English was Eugene Nida, who in 1964 chose to entitle his theoretical handbook *Towards a Science of*

Translating.[9] It should be noted, though, that Nida did not intend the phrase as a name for the entire field of study, but only for one aspect of the *process* of translating as such.[10] Others, most of them not native speakers of English, have been more bold, advocating the term "science of translation" (or "translation science") as the appropriate designation for this emerging discipline as a whole. Two years ago this recurrent suggestion was followed by something like canonization of the term when Bausch, Klegraf, and Wilss took the decision to make it the main title to their analytical bibliography of the entire field.[11]

It was a decision that I, for one, regret. It is not that I object to the term *Übersetzungswissenschaft*, for there are few if any valid arguments against that designation for the subject in German. The problem is not that the discipline is not a *Wissenschaft*, but that not all *Wissenschaften* can properly be called sciences. Just as no one today would take issue with the terms *Sprachwissenschaft* and *Literaturwissenschaft*, while more than a few would question whether linguistics has yet reached a stage of precision, formalization, and paradigm formation such that it can properly be described as a science, and while practically everyone would agree that literary studies are not, and in the foreseeable future will not be, a science in any true sense of the English word, in the same way I question whether we can with any justification use a designation for the study of translating and translations that places it in the company of mathematics, physics, and chemistry, or even biology, rather than that of sociology, history, and philosophy – or for that matter of literary studies.

2.3

There is, however, another term that is active in English in the naming of new disciplines. This is the word "studies". Indeed, for disciplines that within the old distinction of the universities tend to fall under the humanities or arts rather than the sciences as fields of learning, the word would seem to be almost as active in English as the word *Wissenschaft* in German. One need only think of Russian studies, American studies, Commonwealth studies, population studies, communication studies. True, the word raises a few new complications, among them the fact that it is difficult to derive an adjectival form. Nevertheless, the designation "translation studies" would seem to be the most appropriate of all those available in English, and its adoption as the standard term for the discipline as a whole would remove a fair amount of confusion and misunderstanding. I shall set the example by making use of it in the rest of this paper. A greater impediment than the lack of a generally accepted name in the way of the development of translation studies is the lack of any general consensus as to the scope and structure of the discipline. What constitutes the field of translation studies? A few would say it coincides with comparative (or contrastive) terminological and lexicographical studies; several look upon it as practically identical with comparative or contrastive linguistics; many would consider it largely synonymous with translation theory. But surely it is different, if not always distinct, from the first two of these, and more than the third. As is usually to be found in the case of emerging disciplines, there has as yet been little meta-reflection on the nature of translation studies as such – at least that has made its way into print and to my attention. One of the few cases that I have found is that of Werner Koller, who has given the following delineation of the subject: "Über-setzungswissenschaft ist zu verstehen als Zusammenfassung und Überbegriff für alle Forschungsbemühungen, die von den Phänomenen 'Übersetzen' und 'Übersetzung' ausgehen oder auf diese Phänomene zielen." (Translation studies is to be understood as a collective and inclusive designation for all research activities taking the phenomena of translating and translation as their basis or focus.[12])

3.1

From this delineation it follows that translation studies is, as no one I suppose would deny, an empirical discipline. Such disciplines, it has often been pointed out, have two major objectives, which Carl G. Hempel has phrased as "to describe particular phenomena in the world of our experience and to establish general principles by means of which they can be explained and predicted."[13] As a field of pure research – that is to say, research pursued for its own sake, quite apart from any direct practical application outside its own terrain – translation studies thus has two main objectives: (1) to describe the phenomena of translating and translation(s) as they manifest themselves in the world of our experience, and (2) to establish general principles by means of which these phenomena can be explained and predicted. The two branches of pure translation studies concerning themselves with these objectives can be designated *descriptive translation studies* (DTS) or *translation description* (TD) and *theoretical translation studies* (ThTS) or *translation theory* (TTh).

3.1.1

Of these two, it is perhaps appropriate to give first consideration to *descriptive translation studies*, as the branch of the discipline which constantly maintains the closest contact with the empirical phenomena under study. There would seem to be three major kinds of research in DTS, which may be distinguished by their focus as product-oriented, function-oriented, and process-oriented.

3.1.1.1

Product-oriented DTS, that area of research which describes existing translations, has traditionally been an important area of academic research in translation studies. The starting point for this type of study is the description of individual translations, or text-focused translation description. A second phase is that of comparative translation description, in which comparative analyses are made of various translations of the same text, either in a single language or in various languages. Such individual and comparative descriptions provide the materials for surveys of larger corpuses of translations, for instance those made within a specific period, language, and/or text or discourse type. In practice the corpus has usually been restricted in all three ways: seventeenth-century literary translations into French, or medieval English Bible translations. But such descriptive surveys can also be larger in scope, diachronic as well as (approximately) synchronic, and one of the eventual goals of product-oriented DTS might possibly be a general history of translation – however ambitious such a goal may sound at this time.

3.1.1.2

Function-oriented DTS is not interested in the description of translations in themselves, but in the description of their function in the recipient socio-cultural situation: it is a study of contexts rather than texts. Pursuing such questions as which texts were (and, often as important, were not) translated at a certain time in a certain place, and what influences were exerted in consequence, this area of research is one that has attracted less concentrated attention than the area just mentioned, though it is often introduced as a kind of a sub-theme or counter-theme in histories of translations and in literary histories. Greater emphasis on it could lead to the development of a field of translation sociology for (or – less felicitous but more accurate, since it is a legitimate area of translation studies as well as of sociology – socio-translation studies).

3.1.1.3

Process-oriented DTS concerns itself with the process or act of translation itself. The problem of what exactly takes place in the "little black box" of the translator's "mind" as he creates a new, more or less matching text in another language has been the subject of much speculation on the part of translation's theorists, but there has been very little attempt at systematic investigation of this process under laboratory conditions. Admittedly, the process is an unusually complex one, one which, if I. A. Richards is correct, "may very probably be the most complex type of event yet produced in the evolution of the cosmos."[14] But psychologists have developed and are developing highly sophisticated methods for analysing and describing other complex mental processes, and it is to be hoped that in future this problem, too, will be given closer attention, leading to an area of study that might be called translation psychology or psycho-translation studies.

3.1.2

The other main branch of pure translation studies, *theoretical translation studies* or *translation theory*, is, as its name implies, not interested in describing existing translations, observed translation functions, or experimentally determined translating processes, but in using the results of descriptive translation studies, in combination with the information available from related fields and disciplines, to evolve principles, theories, and models which will serve to explain and predict what translating and translations are and will be.

3.1.2.1

The ultimate goal of the translation theorist in the broad sense must undoubtedly be to develop a full, inclusive theory accommodating so many elements that it can serve to explain and predict all phenomena falling within the terrain of translating and translation, to the exclusion of all phenomena falling outside it. It hardly needs to be pointed out that a *general translation theory* in such a true sense of the term, if indeed it is achievable, will necessarily be highly formalized and, however the scholar may strive after economy, also highly complex.

Most of the theories that have been produced to date are in reality little more than prolegomena to such a general translation theory. A good share of them, in fact, are not actually theories at all, in any scholarly sense of the term, but an array of axioms, postulates, and hypotheses that are so formulated as to be both too inclusive (covering also non-translatory acts and non-translations) and too exclusive (shutting out some translatory acts and some works generally recognized as translations).

3.1.2.2

Others, though they too may bear the designation of "general" translation theories (frequently preceded by the scholar's protectively cautious "towards"), are in fact not general theories, but partial or specific in their scope, dealing with only one or a few of the various aspects of translation theory as a whole. It is in this area of partial theories that the most significant advances have been made in recent years, and in fact it will probably be necessary for a great deal of further research to be conducted in them before we can even begin to think about arriving at a true general theory in the sense I have just outlined. *Partial translation theories* are specified in a number of ways. I would suggest, though, that they can be grouped together into six main kinds.

3.1.2.2.1

First of all, there are translation theories that I have called, with a somewhat unorthodox extension of the term, *medium-restricted translation theories*, according to the medium that is used. Medium-restricted theories can be further subdivided into theories of translation as performed by humans (human translation), as performed by computers (machine translation), and as performed by the two in conjunction (mixed or machine-aided translation). Human translation breaks down into (and restricted theories or "theories" have been developed for) oral translation or interpreting (with the further distinction between consecutive and simultaneous) and written translation. Numerous examples of valuable research into machine and machine-aided translation are no doubt familiar to us all, and perhaps also several into oral human translation. That examples of medium-restricted theories of written translation do not come to mind so easily is largely owing to the fact that their authors have the tendency to present them in the guise of unmarked or general theories.

3.1.2.2.2

Second, there are theories that are area-restricted. *Area-restricted theories* can be of two closely related kinds; restricted as to the languages involved or, which is usually not quite the same, and occasionally hardly at all, as to the cultures involved. In both cases, language restriction and culture restriction, the degree of actual limitation can vary. Theories are feasible for translation between, say, French and German (language-pair restricted theories) as opposed to translation within Slavic languages (language-group restricted theories) or from Romance languages to Germanic languages (language-group pair restricted theories). Similarly, theories might at least hypothetically be developed for translation within Swiss culture (one-culture restricted), or for translation between Swiss and Belgian cultures (cultural-pair restricted), as opposed to translation within western Europe (cultural-group restricted) or between languages reflecting a pre-technological culture and the languages of contemporary Western culture (cultural-group pair restricted). Language-restricted theories have close affinities with the work being done in comparative linguistics and stylistics (though it must always be remembered that a language-pair translation grammar must be a different thing from a contrastive grammar developed for the purpose of language acquisition). In the field of culture-restricted theories there has been little detailed research, though culture restrictions, by being confused with language restrictions, sometimes get introduced into language-restricted theories, where they are out of place in all but those rare cases where culture and language boundaries coincide in both the source and target situations. It is moreover no doubt true that some aspects of theories that are presented as general in reality pertain only to the Western cultural area.

3.1.2.2.3

Third, there are *rank-restricted theories*, that is to say, theories that deal with discourses or texts as wholes, but concern themselves with lower linguistic ranks or levels. Traditionally, a great deal of writing on translation was concerned almost entirely with the rank of the word, and the word and the word group are still the ranks at which much terminologically oriented thinking about scientific and technological translation takes place. Most linguistically oriented research, on the other hand, has until very recently taken the sentence as its upper rank limit, largely ignoring the macro-structural aspects of entire texts as translation problems. The clearly discernible trend away from sentential linguistics in the direction of textual linguistics will, it is to be hoped, encourage linguistically oriented theorists to move beyond sentence-restricted translation theories to the more complex task of developing text-rank (or "rank-free") theories.

3.1.2.2.4

Fourth, there are *text-type* (or discourse-type) *restricted theories*, dealing with the problem of translating specific types or genres of lingual messages. Authors and literary scholars have long concerned themselves with the problems intrinsic to translating literary texts or specific genres of literary texts; theologians, similarly, have devoted much attention to questions of how to translate the Bible and other sacred works. In recent years some effort has been made to develop a specific theory for the translation of scientific texts. All these studies break down, however, because we still lack anything like a formal theory of message, text, or discourse types. Both Bühler's theory of types of communication, as further developed by the Prague structuralists, and the definitions of language varieties arrived at by linguists particularly of the British school provide material for criteria in defining text types that would lend themselves to operationalization more aptly than the inconsistent and mutually contradictory definitions or traditional genre theories. On the other hand, the traditional theories cannot be ignored, for they continue to play a large part in creating the expectation criteria of translation readers. Also requiring study is the important question of text-type skewing or shifting in translation.

3.1.2.2.5

Fifth, there are *time-restricted theories*, which fall into two types: theories regarding the translation of contemporary texts, and theories having to do with the translation of texts from an older period. Again there would seem to be a tendency to present one of the theories, that having to do with contemporary texts, in the guise of a general theory; the other, the theory of what can perhaps best be called cross-temporal translation, is a matter that has led to much disagreement, particularly among literarily oriented theorists, but to few generally valid conclusions.

3.1.2.2.6

Finally, there are *problem-restricted theories*, theories which confine themselves to one or more specific problems within the entire area of general translation theory, problems that can range from such broad and basic questions as the limits of variance and invariance in translation or the nature of translation equivalence (or, as I should prefer to call it, translation matching) to such more specific matters as the translation of metaphors or of proper names.

3.1.2.3

It should be noted that theories can frequently be restricted in more than one way. Contrastive linguists interested in translation, for instance, will probably produce theories that are not only language-restricted but rank- and time-restricted, having to do with translations between specific pairs of contemporary temporal dialects at sentence rank. The theories of literary scholars, similarly, usually are restricted as to medium and text type, and generally also as to culture group; they normally have to do with written texts within the (extended) Western literary tradition. This does not necessarily reduce the worth of such partial theories, for even a theoretical study restricted in every way – say a theory of the manner in which subordinate clauses in contemporary German novels should be translated into written English – can have implications for the more general theory towards which scholars must surely work. It would be wise, though, not to lose sight of such a truly general theory, and wiser still not to succumb to the delusion that a body of restricted theories – for instance, a complex of language-restricted theories of how to translate sentences – can be an adequate substitute for it.

3.2

After this rapid overview of the two main branches of pure research in translation studies, I should like to turn to that branch of the discipline which is, in Bacon's words, "of use" rather than "of light": applied translation studies.[15]

3.2.1

In this discipline, as in so many others, the first thing that comes to mind when one considers the applications that extend beyond the limits of the discipline itself is that of teaching. Actually, the teaching of translating is of two types which need to be carefully distinguished. In the one case, translating has been used for centuries as a technique in foreign-language teaching and a test of foreign-language acquisition. I shall return to this type in a moment. In the second case, a more recent phenomenon, translating is taught in schools and courses to train professional translators. This second situation, that of *translator training*, has raised a number of question that fairly cry for answers: questions that have to do primarily with teaching methods, testing techniques, and curriculum planning. It is obvious that the search for well-founded, reliable answers to these questions constitutes a major area (and for the time being, at least, *the* major area) of research in applied translation studies.

3.2.2

A second, closely related area has to do with the needs for translation aids, both for use in translator training and to meet the requirements of the practising translator. The needs are many and various, but fall largely into two classes: (1) lexicographical and terminological aids and (2) grammars. Both these classes of aids have traditionally been provided by scholars in other, related disciplines, and it could hardly be argued that work on them should be taken over *in toto* as areas of applied translation studies. But lexicographical aids often fall far short of translation needs, and contrastive grammars developed for language-acquisition purposes are not really an adequate substitute for variety-marked translation-matching grammars. There would seem to be a need for scholars in applied translation studies to clarify and define the specific requirements that aids of these kinds should fulfil if they are to meet the needs of practising and prospective translators, and to work together with lexicologists and contrastive linguists in developing them.

3.2.3

A third area of applied translation studies is that of *translation policy*. The task of the translation scholar in this area is to render informed advice to others in defining the place and role of translators, translating, and translations in society at large: such questions, for instance, as determining what works need to be translated in a given socio-cultural situation, what the social and economic position of the translator is and should be, or (and here I return to the point raised above) what part translating should play in the teaching and learning of foreign languages. In regard to that last policy question, since it should hardly be the task of translation studies to abet the use of translating in places where it is dysfunctional, it would seem to me that priority should be given to extensive and rigorous research to assess the efficacy of translating as a technique and testing method in language learning. The chance that it is not efficacious would appear to be so great that in this case it would seem imperative for program research to be preceded by policy research.

3.2.4

A fourth, quite different area of applied translation studies is that of *translation criticism*. The level of such criticism is today still frequently very low, and in many countries still quite uninfluenced by developments within the field of translation studies. Doubtless the activities of translation interpretation and evaluation will always elude the grasp of objective analysis to some extent, and so continue to reflect the intuitive, impressionist attitudes and stances of the critic. But closer contact between translation scholars and translation critics could do a great deal to reduce the intuitive element to a more acceptable level.

3.3.1

After this brief survey of the main branches of translation studies, there are two further points that I should like to make. The first is this: in what has preceded, descriptive, theoretical, and applied translation studies have been presented as three fairly distinct branches of the entire discipline, and the order of presentation might be taken to suggest that their import for one another is unidirectional, translation description supplying the basic data upon which translation theory is to be built, and the two of them providing the scholarly findings which are to be put to use in applied translation studies. In reality, of course, the relation is a dialectical one, with each of the three branches supplying materials for the other two, and making use of the findings with which they in turn provide it. Translation theory, for instance, cannot do without the solid, specific data yielded by research in descriptive and applied translation studies, while on the other hand one cannot even begin to work in one of the other two fields without having at least an intuitive theoretical hypothesis as one's starting point. In view of this dialectical relationship, it follows that, though the needs of a given moment may vary, attention to all three branches is required if the discipline is to grow and flourish.

3.3.2

The second point is that, in each of the three branches of translation studies, there are two further dimensions that I have not mentioned, dimensions having to do with the study, not of translating and translations, but of translation studies itself. One of these dimensions is historical: there is a field of the history of translation theory, in which some valuable work has been done, but also one of the history of translation description and of applied translation studies (largely a history of translation teaching and translator training) both of which are fairly well virgin territory. Likewise there is a dimension that might be called the methodological or meta-theoretical, concerning itself with problems of what methods and models can best be used in research in the various branches of the discipline (how translation theories, for instance, can be formed for greatest validity, or what analytic methods can best be used to achieve the most objective and meaningful descriptive results), but also devoting its attention to such basic issues as what the discipline itself comprises.

This paper has made a few excursions into the first of these two dimensions, but all in all it is meant to be a contribution to the second. It does not ask above all for agreement. Translation studies has reached a stage where it is time to examine the subject itself. Let the meta-discussion begin.

Notes

1   Written in August 1972, this paper is presented in its second pre-publication form with only a few stylistic revisions. Despite the intervening years, most of my remarks can, I believe, stand as they were formulated, though in one or two places I would phrase matters somewhat differently if I were writing today. In section 3.1.2.2.4, for instance, subsequent developments in textual linguistics, particularly in Germany, are noteworthy. More directly relevant, the dearth of meta-reflection on the nature of translation studies, referred to at the beginning of section 3, is somewhat less striking today than in 1972, again thanks largely to German scholars. Particularly relevant is Wolfram Wilss's as yet unpublished paper "Methodische Probleme der allgemeinen und angewandten Übersetzungswissenschaft", read at a colloquium on translation studies held in Germersheim, West Gemany, 31 May 1975.

2   Michael Mulkay, "Cultural Growth in Science", in Barry Barness (ed.), *Sociology of Science: Selected Readings* (Harmondsworth, Middlesex: Penguin; Modern Sociology Readings), pp. 126–141 (abridged reprint of "Some Aspects of Cultural Growth in the Natural Sciences", *Social Research*, 36 [1969], No. 1), quotation p. 136.

3   See e.g. W. O. Hagstrom, "The Differentiation of Disciplines", in Barnes, pp. 121–125 (reprinted from Hagstrom, *The Scientific Community* [New York: Basic Books, 1965], pp. 222–226).

4   Hagstrom, p. 123.

5   Here and throughout, these terms are used only in the strict sense of inter-lingual translating and translation. On the three types of translation in the broader sense of the word, intralingual, interlingual, and intersemiotic, see

Roman Jakobson, "On Linguistic Aspects of Translation", in Reuben A. Brower (ed.), *On Translation* (Cambridge, Mass.: Harvard University Press, 1959), pp. 232–239.

6   Roger Goffin, "Pour une formation universitaire 'sui generis' du traducteur: Réflexions sur certain aspects méthodologiques et sur la recherche scientifique dans le domaine de la traduction", *Meta*, 16 (1971), 57–68, see esp. p. 59.

7   See the Hagstrom quotation in section 1.1. above.

8   Though, given the lack of a general paradigm, scholars frequently tend to restrict the meaning of the term to only a part of the discipline. Often, in fact, it would seem to be more or less synonymous with "translation theory".

9   Eugene Nida, *Towards a Science of Translating, with Special Reference to Principles and Procedures Involved in Bible Translating* (Leiden: Brill, 1964).

10   Cf. Nida's later enlightening remark on his use of the term: "the science of translation (or, perhaps more accurately stated, the scientific *description* of the *processes* involved in translating)", Eugene A. Nida, "Science of Translation", *Language*, 45 [1969], 483–498, quotation p. 483 n. 1; my italics).

11   K.-Richard Bausch, Josef Klegraf, and Wolfram Wilss, *The Science of Translation: An Analytical Bibliography* (Tübingen: Tübinger Beiträge zur Linguistik). Vol. 1 (1970; TBL, No. 21) covers the years 1962–1969; Vol. II (1972; TBL, No. 33) the years 1970–1971 plus a supplement over the years covered by the first volume.

12   Werner Koller, "Übersetzen, Übersetzung und Übersetzer. Zu schwedischen Symposien über Probleme der Übersetzung", *Babel*, 17 (1971), 311, quotation p. 4. See further in this article (also p. 4) the summary of a paper "Übersetzungspraxis, Übersetzungstheorie und Übersetzungswissenschaft" presented by Koller at the Second Swedish-German Translators' Symposium, held in Stockholm, 23–24 October 1969.

13   Carl G. Hempel, *Fundamentals of Concept Formation in Empirical Science* (Chicago: University of Chicago Press, 1967; International Encyclopedia of Social Science, Foundations of the Unity of Sciences, II, Fasc. 7), p. 1.

14   I. A. Richards, "Toward a Theory of Translating", in Arthur F. Wright (ed.), *Studies in Chinese Thought* (Chicago: University of Chicago Press, 1953; also published as *Memoirs of the American Anthropological Association*, 55 [1953], Memoir 75), pp. 247–262.

15   Bacon's distinction was actually not between two types of research in the broader sense, but of experiments: "Experiments of Use" as against "Experiments of Light". See S. Pit Corder, "Problems and Solutions in Applied Linguistics", paper presented in a plenary session of the 1972 Copenhagen Congress of Applied Linguistics.

Chapter 16

George Steiner

THE HERMENEUTIC MOTION

THE HERMENEUTIC MOTION, the act of elicitation and appropriative transfer of meaning, is fourfold. There is initiative trust, an investment of belief, underwritten by previous experience but epistemologically exposed and psychologically hazardous, in the meaningfulness, in the "seriousness" of the facing or, strictly speaking, adverse text. We venture a leap: we grant *ab initio* that there is "something there" to be understood, that the transfer will not be void. All understanding, and the demonstrative statement of understanding which is translation, starts with an act of trust. This confiding will, ordinarily, be instantaneous and unexamined, but it has a complex base. It is an operative convention which derives from a sequence of phenomenological assumptions about the coherence of the world, about the presence of meaning in very different, perhaps formally antithetical semantic systems, about the validity of analogy and parallel. The radical generosity of the translator ("I grant beforehand that there must be something there"), his trust in the "other", as yet untried, unmapped alternity of statement, concentrates to a philosophically dramatic degree the human bias towards seeing the world as symbolic, as constituted of relations in which "this" can stand for "that", and must in fact be able to do so if there are to be meanings and structures.

But the trust can never be final. It is betrayed, trivially, by nonsense, by the discovery that "there is nothing there" to elicit and translate. Nonsense rhymes, *poésie concrète*, glossolalia are untranslatable because they are lexically non-communicative or deliberately insignificant. The commitment of trust will, however, be tested, more or less severely, also in the common run and process of language acquisition and translation (the two being intimately connected). "This means nothing" asserts the exasperated child in front of his Latin reader or the beginner at Berlitz. The sensation comes very close to being tactile, as of a blank, sloping surface which gives no purchase. Social incentive, the officious evidence of precedent – "others have managed to translate this bit before you" – keeps one at the task. But the donation of trust remains ontologically spontaneous and anticipates proof, often by a long, arduous gap (there are texts, says Walter Benjamin, which will be translated only "after us"). As he sets out, the translator must gamble on the coherence, on the symbolic plenitude of the world. Concomitantly he leaves himself vulnerable, though only in extremity and at the theoretical edge, to two dialectically related, mutually determined metaphysical risks. He may find that "anything" or "almost anything" can mean "everything". This is the vertigo of self-sustaining metaphoric or analogic enchainment experienced by medieval exegetists. Or he may find that there is "nothing there" which can be divorced from its formal autonomy, that every meaning worth expressing is monadic and will not enter into any alternative mould. There is Kabbalistic speculation, to which I will return, about a day on which words will shake off "the burden of having to mean" and will be only themselves, blank and replete as stone.

After trust comes aggression. The second move of the translator is incursive and extractive. The relevant analysis is that of Heidegger when he focuses our attention on understanding as an act, on the access, inherently appropriative and therefore violent, of *Erkenntnis* to *Dasein*. *Da-sein*, the "thing there", "the thing that is because it is there", only comes into authentic being when it is comprehended, i.e. translated.[1] The postulate that all cognition is aggressive, that every proposition is an inroad on the world, is, of course, Hegelian. It is Heidegger's contribution to have shown that understanding, recognition, interpretation are a compacted, unavoidable mode of attack. We can modulate Heidegger's insistence that understanding is not a matter of method but of primary being, that "being consists in the understanding of other being" into the more naïve, limited axiom that each act of comprehension must appropriate another entity (we translate *into*). Comprehension, as its etymology shows, "comprehends" not only cognitively but by encirclement and ingestion. In the event of interlingual translation this manoeuvre of comprehension is explicitly invasive and exhaustive. Saint Jerome uses his famous image of meaning brought home captive by the translator. We "break" a code: decipherment is dissective, leaving the shell smashed and the vital layers stripped. Every schoolchild, but also the eminent translator, will note the shift in substantive presence which follows on a protracted or difficult exercise in translation: the text in the other language has become almost materially thinner, the light seems to pass unhindered through its loosened fibres. For a spell the density of hostile or seductive "otherness" is dissipated. Ortega y Gasset speaks of the sadness of the translator after failure. There is also a sadness after success, the Augustinian *tristitia* which follows on the cognate acts of erotic and of intellectual possession.

The translator invades, extracts, and brings home. The simile is that of the open-cast mine left an empty scar in the landscape. As we shall see, this despoliation is illusory or is a mark of false translation. But again, as in the case of the translator's trust, there are genuine borderline cases. Certain texts or genres have been exhausted by translation. Far more interestingly, others have been negated by transfiguration, by an act of appropriative penetration and transfer in excess of the original, more ordered, more aesthetically pleasing. There are originals we no longer turn to because the translation is of a higher magnitude (the sonnets of Louise Labé after Rilke's *Umdichtung*). I will come back to this paradox of betrayal by augment.

The third movement is incorporative, in the strong sense of the word. The import, of meaning and of form, the embodiment, is not made in or into a vacuum. The native semantic field is already extant and crowded. There are innumerable shadings of assimilation and placement of the newly acquired, ranging from a complete domestication, an at-homeness at the core of the kind which cultural history ascribes to, say, Luther's Bible or North's Plutarch, all the way to the permanent strangeness and marginality of an artifact such as Nabokov's "English-language" *Onegin*. But whatever the degree of "naturalization", the act of importation can potentially dislocate or relocate the whole of the native structure. The Heideggerian "we are what we understand to be" entails that our own being is modified by each occurrence of comprehensive appropriation. No language, no traditional symbolic set or cultural ensemble imports without risk of being transformed. Here two families of metaphor, probably related, offer themselves, that of sacramental intake or incarnation and that of infection. The incremental values of communion pivot on the moral, spiritual state of the recipient. Though all decipherment is aggressive and, at one level, destructive, there are differences in the motive of appropriation and in the context of "the bringing back". Where the native matrix is disoriented or immature, the importation will not enrich, it will not find a proper locale. It will generate not an integral response but a wash of mimicry (French neoclassicism in its north-European, German, and Russian versions). There can be contagions of facility triggered by the antique or foreign import. After a time, the native organism will react, endeavouring to neutralize or expel the foreign body. Much of European romanticism can be seen as a riposte to this sort of infection, as an attempt to put an embargo on a plethora of foreign, mainly French eighteenth-century goods. In every pidgin we see an attempt to preserve a zone of native speech and a failure of that attempt in the face of politically and economically enforced linguistic invasion. The dialectic of embodiment entails the possibility that we may be consumed.

This dialectic can be seen at the level of individual sensibility. Acts of translation add to our means; we come to incarnate alternative energies and resources of feeling. But we may be mastered and made lame by what we have imported. There are translators in whom the vein of personal, original creation goes dry. MacKenna speaks of Plotinus literally submerging his own being. Writers have ceased from translation, sometimes too late, because the inhaled voice of the foreign text had come to choke their own. Societies with ancient but eroded epistemologies of ritual and symbol can be knocked off balance and made to lose belief in their own identity under the voracious impact of premature or indigestible assimilation. The cargo-cults of New Guinea, in which the natives worship what airplanes bring in, provide an uncannily exact, ramified image of the risks of translation.

This is only another way of saying that the hermeneutic motion is dangerously incomplete, that it is dangerous because it is incomplete, if it lacks its fourth stage, the piston-stroke, as it were, which completes the cycle. The a-prioristic movement of trust puts us off balance. We "lean towards" the confronting text (every

translator has experienced this palpable bending towards and launching at his target).
We encircle and invade cognitively. We come home laden, thus again off-balance,
having caused disequilibrium throughout the system by taking away from "the other"
and by adding, though possibly with ambiguous consequence, to our own. The
system is now off-tilt. The hermeneutic act must compensate. If it is to be authentic,
it must mediate into exchange and restored parity.

The enactment of reciprocity in order to restore balance is the crux of the
métier and morals of translation. But it is very difficult to put abstractly. The appropriative "rapture" of the translator – the word has in it, of course, the root and
meaning of violent transport – leaves the original with a dialectically enigmatic
residue. Unquestionably there is a dimension of loss, of breakage – hence, as we
have seen, the fear of translation, the taboos on revelatory export which hedge
sacred texts, ritual nominations, and formulas in many cultures. But the residue is
also, and decisively, positive. The work translated is enhanced. This is so at a
number of fairly obvious levels. Being methodical, penetrative, analytic, enumera-
tive, the process of translation, like all modes of focused understanding, will detail,
illumine, and generally body forth its object. The over-determination of the interpretative act is inherently inflationary: it proclaims that "there is more here than
meets the eye", that "the accord between content and executive form is closer, more
delicate than had been observed hitherto". To class a source-text as worth translating is to dignify it immediately and to involve it in a dynamic of magnification
(subject, naturally, to later review and even, perhaps, dismissal). The motion of
transfer and paraphrase enlarges the stature of the original. Historically, in terms
of cultural context, of the public it can reach, the latter is left more prestigious.
But this increase has a more important, existential perspective. The relations of a
text to its translations, imitations, thematic variants, even parodies, are too diverse
to allow of any single theoretic, definitional scheme. They categorize the entire
question of the meaning of meaning in time, of the existence and effects of the
linguistic fact outside its specific, initial form. But there can be no doubt that echo
enriches, that it is more than shadow and inert simulacrum. We are back at the
problem of the mirror which not only reflects but also generates light. The original
text gains from the orders of diverse relationship and distance established between
itself and the translations. The reciprocity is dialectic: new "formats" of significance
are initiated by distance and by contiguity. Some translations edge us away from
the canvas, others bring us up close.

This is so even where, perhaps especially where, the translation is only partly
adequate. The failings of the translator (I will give common examples) localize, they
project as on to a screen, the resistant vitalities, the opaque centres of specific genius
in the original. Hegel and Heidegger posit that being must engage other being in
order to achieve self-definition. This is true only in part of language which, at the
phonetic and grammatical levels, can function inside its own limits of diacritical
differentiation. But it is pragmatically true of all but the most rudimentary acts of
form and expression. Existence in history, the claim to recognizable identity (style),
are based on relations to other articulate constructs. Of such relations, translation
is the most graphic.

Nevertheless, there is unbalance. The translator has taken too much – he has
padded, embroidered, "read into" – or too little – he has skimped, elided, cut out

awkward corners. There has been an outflow of energy from the source and an inflow into the receptor altering both and altering the harmonics of the whole system. Péguy puts the matter of inevitable damage definitively in his critique of Leconte de Lisle's translations of Sophocles: "ce que la réalité nous enseigne impitoyablement et sans aucune exception, c'est que toute opération de cet ordre, toute opération de déplacement, sans aucune exception, entraîne impitoyablement et irrévocablement une déperdition, une altération, et que cette déperdition, cette altération est toujours considérable."[2] Genuine translation will, therefore, seek to equalize, though the mediating steps may be lengthy and oblique. Where it falls short of the original, the authentic translation makes the autonomous virtues of the original more precisely visible (Voss is weak at characteristic focal points in his Homer, but the lucid honesty of his momentary lack brings out the appropriate strengths of the Greek). Where it surpasses the original, the real translation infers that the source-text possesses potentialities, elemental reserves as yet unrealized by itself. This is Schleiermacher's notion of a hermeneutic which "knows better than the author did" (Paul Celan translating Apollinaire's *Salomé*). The ideal, never accomplished, is one of total counterpart or re-petition – an asking again – which is not, however, a tautology. No such perfect "double" exists. But the ideal makes explicit the demand for equity in the hermeneutic process.

Only in this way, I think, can we assign substantive meaning to the key notion of "fidelity". Fidelity is not literalism or any technical device for rendering "spirit". The whole formulation, as we have found it over and over again in discussions of translation, is hopelessly vague. The translator, the exegetist, the reader is *faithful to* his text, makes his response responsible, only when he endeavours to restore the balance of forces, of integral presence, which his appropriative comprehension has disrupted. Fidelity is ethical, but also, in the full sense, economic. By virtue of tact, and tact intensified is moral vision, the translator–interpreter creates a condition of significant exchange. The arrows of meaning, of cultural, psychological benefaction, move both ways. There is, ideally, exchange without loss. In this respect, translation can be pictured as a negation of entropy; order is preserved at both ends of the cycle, source and receptor. The general model here is that of Lévi-Strauss's *Anthropologie structurale* which regards social structures as attempts at dynamic equilibrium achieved through an exchange of words, women, and material goods. All capture calls for subsequent compensation; utterance solicits response, exogamy and endogamy are mechanisms of equalizing transfer. Within the class of semantic exchanges, translation is again the most graphic, the most radically equitable. A translator is accountable to the diachronic and synchronic mobility and conservation of the energies of meaning. A translation is, more than figuratively, an act of double-entry; both formally and morally the books must balance.

This view of translation as a hermeneutic of trust (*élancement*), of penetration, of embodiment, and of restitution, will allow us to overcome the sterile triadic model which has dominated the history and theory of the subject. The perennial distinction between literalism, paraphrase and free imitation, turns out to be wholly contingent. It has no precision or philosophic basis. It overlooks the key fact that a fourfold *hermeneia*, Aristotle's term for discourse which signifies because it interprets, is conceptually and practically inherent in even the rudiments of translation.

Notes

1   Cf. Paul Ricoeur, "Existence et herméneutique" in *Le Conflit des interprétations* (Paris, 1969).
2   Charles Péguy, "Les Suppliants parallèles" in *Œuvres en prose 1898–1908* (Paris, 1959), I, p. 890. This analysis of the art of poetic translation first appeared in December 1905. Cf. Simone Fraisse, *Péguy et le monde antique* (Paris, 1973), pp. 146–59.

Chapter 17

Itamar Even-Zohar

THE POSITION OF TRANSLATED LITERATURE WITHIN THE LITERARY POLYSYSTEM

Dedicated to the memory of James S. Holmes – a great student of translation and a dear friend.

1

IN SPITE OF THE BROAD RECOGNITION among historians of culture of the major role translation has played in the crystallization of national cultures, relatively little research has been carried out so far in this area. As a rule, histories of literatures mention translations when there is no way to avoid them, when dealing with the Middle Ages or the Renaissance, for instance. One might of course find sporadic references to individual literary translations in various other periods, but they are seldom incorporated into the historical account in any coherent way. As a consequence, one hardly gets any idea whatsoever of the function of translated literature for a literature as a whole or of its position within that literature. Moreover, there is no awareness of the possible existence of translated literature as a particular literary system. The prevailing concept is rather that of "translation" or just "translated works" treated on an individual basis. Is there any basis for a different assumption, that is for considering translated literature as a system? Is there the same sort of cultural and verbal network of relations within what seems to be an arbitrary group of translated texts as the one we willingly hypothesize for original literature? What kind of relations might there be among translated works, which are presented as completed facts, imported from other literatures, detached from their home contexts and consequently neutralized from the point of view of center-and-periphery struggles?

My argument is that translated works do correlate in at least two ways: (a) in the way their source texts are selected by the target literature, the principles of

1978/revised 1990

selection never being uncorrelatable with the home co-systems of the target literature (to put it in the most cautious way); and (b) in the way they adopt specific
norms, behaviors, and policies – in short, in their use of the literary repertoire –
which results from their relations with the other home co-systems. These are not
confined to the linguistic level only, but are manifest on any selection level as well.
Thus, translated literature may possess a repertoire of its own, which to a certain
extent could even be exclusive to it. (See Toury 1985 and 1985a.)

It seems that these points make it not only justifiable to talk about translated
literature, but rather imperative to do so. I cannot see how any scholarly effort
to describe and explain the behavior of the literary polysystem in synchrony
and diachrony can advance in an adequate way if that is not recognized. In other
words, I conceive of translated literature not only as an integral system within
any literary polysystem, but as a most active system within it. But what is its position
within the polysystem, and how is this position connected with the nature of its
overall repertoire? One would be tempted to deduce from the peripheral position
of translated literature in the study of literature that it also permanently occupies
a peripheral position in the literary polysystem, but this is by no means the
case. Whether translated literature becomes central or peripheral, and whether
this position is connected with innovatory ("primary") or conservatory ("secondary")
repertoires, depends on the specific constellation of the polysystem under
study.

2

To say that translated literature maintains a central position in the literary polysystem means that it participates actively in shaping the center of the polysystem.
In such a situation it is by and large an integral part of innovatory forces, and as
such likely to be identified with major events in literary history while these are
taking place. This implies that in this situation no clear-cut distinction is maintained
between "original" and "translated" writings, and that often it is the leading writers
(or members of the avant-garde who are about to become leading writers) who
produce the most conspicuous or appreciated translations. Moreover, in such a state
when new literary models are emerging, translation is likely to become one of the
means of elaborating the new repertoire. Through the foreign works, features (both
principles and elements) are introduced into the home literature which did not exist
there before. These include possibly not only new models of reality to replace the
old and established ones that are no longer effective, but a whole range of other
features as well, such as a new (poetic) language, or compositional patterns and
techniques. It is clear that the very principles of selecting the works to be translated are determined by the situation governing the (home) polysystem: the texts
are chosen according to their compatibility with the new approaches and the supposedly innovatory role they may assume within the target literature.

What then are the conditions which give rise to a situation of this kind? It seems
to me that three major cases can be discerned, which are basically various manifestations of the same law: (a) when a polysystem has not yet been crystallized, that
is to say, when a literature is "young," in the process of being established; (b) when

a literature is either "peripheral" (within a large group of correlated literatures) or "weak," or both; and (c) when there are turning points, crises, or literary vacuums in a literature.

In the first case translated literature simply fulfils the need of a younger literature to put into use its newly founded (or renovated) tongue for as many literary types as possible in order to make it serviceable as a literary language and useful for its emerging public. Since a young literature cannot immediately create texts in all types known to its producers, it benefits from the experience of other literatures, and translated literature becomes in this way one of its most important systems. The same holds true for the second instance, that of relatively established literatures whose resources are limited and whose position within a larger literary hierarchy is generally peripheral. As a consequence of this situation, such literatures often do not develop the same full range of literary activities (organized in a variety of systems) observable in adjacent larger literatures (which in consequence may create a feeling that they are indispensable). They may also "lack" a repertoire which is felt to be badly needed vis-à-vis, and in terms of the presence of, that adjacent literature. This lack may then be filled, wholly or partly, by translated literature. For instance, all sorts of peripheral literature may in such cases consist of translated literature. But far more important is the consequence that the ability of such "weak" literatures to initiate innovations is often less than that of the larger and central literatures, with the result that a relation of dependency may be established not only in peripheral systems, but in the very center of these "weak" literatures. (To avoid misunderstanding, I would like to point out that these literatures may rise to a central position in a way analogous to the way this is carried out by peripheral systems within a certain polysystem, but this cannot be discussed here.)

Since peripheral literatures in the Western Hemisphere tend more often than not to be identical with the literatures of smaller nations, as unpalatable as this idea may seem to us, we have no choice but to admit that within a group of relatable national literatures, such as the literatures of Europe, hierarchical relations have been established since the very beginnings of these literatures. Within this (macro-) polysystem some literatures have taken peripheral positions, which is only to say that they were often modelled to a large extent upon an exterior literature. For such literatures, translated literature is not only a major channel through which fashionable repertoire is brought home, but also a source of reshuffling and supplying alternatives. Thus, whereas richer or stronger literatures may have the option to adopt novelties from some periphery within their indigenous borders, "weak" literatures in such situations often depend on import alone.

The dynamics within the polysystem create turning points, that is to say, historical moments where established models are no longer tenable for a younger generation. At such moments, even in central literatures, translated literature may assume a central position. This is all the more true when at a turning point no item in the indigenous stock is taken to be acceptable, as a result of which a literary "vacuum" occurs. In such a vacuum, it is easy for foreign models to infiltrate, and translated literature may consequently assume a central position. Of course, in the case of "weak" literatures or literatures which are in a constant state of impoverishment (lack of literary items existing in a neighbor or accessible foreign literature), this situation is even more overwhelming.

3

Contending that translated literature may maintain a peripheral position means that it constitutes a peripheral system within the polysystem, generally employing secondary models. In such a situation it has no influence on major processes and is modelled according to norms already conventionally established by an already dominant type in the target literature. Translated literature in this case becomes a major factor of conservatism. While the contemporary original literature might go on developing new norms and models, translated literature adheres to norms which have been rejected either recently or long before by the (newly) established center. It no longer maintains positive correlations with original writing.

A highly interesting paradox manifests itself here: translation, by which new ideas, items, characteristics can be introduced into a literature, becomes a means to preserve traditional taste. This discrepancy between the original central literature and the translated literature may have evolved in a variety of ways, for instance, when translated literature, after having assumed a central position and inserted new items, soon lost contact with the original home literature which went on changing, and thereby became a factor of preservation of unchanged repertoire. Thus, a literature that might have emerged as a revolutionary type may go on existing as an ossified *système d'antan*, often fanatically guarded by the agents of secondary models against even minor changes.

The conditions which enable this second state are of course diametrically opposite to those which give rise to translated literature as a central system: either there are no major changes in the polysystem or these changes are not effected through the intervention of interliterary relations materialized in the form of translations.

4

The hypothesis that translated literature may be either a central or peripheral system does not imply that it is always wholly one or the other. As a system, translated literature is itself stratified, and from the point of view of polysystemic analysis it is often from the vantage point of the central stratum that all relations within the system are observed. This means that while one section of translated literature may assume a central position, another may remain quite peripheral. In the foregoing analysis I pointed out the close relationship between literary contacts and the status of translated literature. This seems to me the major clue to this issue. When there is intense interference, it is the portion of translated literature deriving from a major source literature which is likely to assume a central position. For instance, in the Hebrew literary polysystem between the two world wars literature translated from the Russian assumed an unmistakably central position, while works translated from English, German, Polish, and other languages assumed an obviously peripheral one. Moreover, since the major and most innovatory translational norms were produced by translations from the Russian, other translated literature adhered to the models and norms elaborated by those translations.

The historical material analyzed so far in terms of polysystemic operations is too limited to provide any far-reaching conclusions about the chances of translated literature to assume a particular position. But work carried out in this field by various other scholars, as well as my own research, indicates that the "normal" position assumed by translated literature tends to be the peripheral one. This should in principle be compatible with theoretical speculation. It may be assumed that in the long run no system can remain in a constant state of weakness, "turning point," or crisis, although the possibility should not be excluded that some polysystems may maintain such states for quite a long time. Moreover, not all polysystems are structured in the same way, and cultures do differ significantly. For instance, it is clear that the French cultural system, French literature naturally included, is much more rigid than most other systems. This, combined with the long traditional central position of French literature within the European context (or within the European macro-polysystem), has caused French translated literature to assume an extremely peripheral position. The state of Anglo-American literature is comparable, while Russian, German, or Scandinavian would seem to show different patterns of behavior in this respect.

5

What consequences may the position taken by translated literature have on translational norms, behaviours, and policies? As I stated above, the distinction between a translated work and an original work in terms of literary behavior is a function of the position assumed by the translated literature at a given time. When it takes a central position, the borderlines are *diffuse*, so that the very category of "translated works" must be extended to semi- and quasi-translations as well. From the point of view of translation theory I think this is a more adequate way of dealing with such phenomena than to reject them on the basis of a static and a-historical conception of translation. Since translational activity participates, when it assumes a central position, in the process of creating new, primary models, the translator's main concern here is not just to look for ready-made models in his home repertoire into which the source texts would be transferable. Instead, he is prepared in such cases to violate the home conventions. Under such conditions the chances that the translation will be close to the original in terms of adequacy (in other words, a reproduction of the dominant textual relations of the original) are greater than otherwise. Of course, from the point of view of the target literature the adopted translational norms might for a while be too foreign and revolutionary, and if the new trend is defeated in the literary struggle, the translation made according to its conceptions and tastes will never really gain ground. But if the new trend is victorious, the repertoire (code) of translated literature may be enriched and become more flexible. Periods of great change in the home system are in fact the only ones when a translator is prepared to go far beyond the options offered to him by his established home repertoire and is willing to attempt a different treatment of text making. Let us remember that under stable conditions items lacking in a target literature may remain untransferable if the state of the polysystem does not allow innovations. But the process of opening the system gradually brings certain literatures closer and in the longer run enables a situation where the postulates of (translational) adequacy and the realities of equivalence may overlap to a relatively high degree. This is the case of the European literatures, though in some of them the mechanism of rejection has been so strong that the changes I am talking about have occurred on a rather limited scale.

Naturally, when translated literature occupies a peripheral position, it behaves totally differently. Here, the translator's main effort is to concentrate upon finding the best ready-made secondary models for the foreign text, and the result often turns out to be a non-adequate translation or (as I would prefer to put it) a greater discrepancy between the equivalence achieved and the adequacy postulated.

In other words, not only is the socio-literary status of translation dependent upon its position within the polysystem, but the very practice of translation is also strongly subordinated to that position. And even the question of what is a translated work cannot be answered *a priori* in terms of an a-historical out-of-context idealized state; it must be determined on the grounds of the operations governing the polysystem. Seen from this point of view, translation is no longer a phenomenon whose nature and borders are given once and for all, but an activity dependent on the relations within a certain cultural system.

Chapter 18

Gideon Toury

THE NATURE AND ROLE OF
NORMS IN TRANSLATION

HOWEVER HIGHLY ONE MAY THINK of Linguistics, Text-Linguistics, Contrastive Textology or Pragmatics and of their explanatory power with respect to translational phenomena, being a translator cannot be reduced to the mere generation of utterances which would be considered "translations" within any of these disciplines. Translation activities should rather be regarded as having cultural significance. Consequently, "translatorship" amounts first and foremost to being able to *play a social role*, i.e., to fulfil a function allotted by a community – to the activity, its practitioners and/or their products – in a way which is deemed appropriate in its own terms of reference. The acquisition of a set of norms for determining the suitability of that kind of behaviour, and for manoeuvring between all the factors which may constrain it, is therefore a prerequisite for becoming a translator within a cultural environment.

The process by which a bilingual speaker may be said to gain recognition in his/her capacity as a translator has hardly been studied so far. [. . .] In the present chapter the nature of the acquired norms themselves will be addressed, along with their role in directing translation activity in socio-culturally relevant settings. This presentation will be followed by a brief discussion of translational norms as a second-order object of Translation Studies, to be reconstructed and studied within the kind of framework which we are now in the process of sketching. As strictly translational norms can only be applied at the *receiving* end, establishing them is not merely *justified* by a target-oriented approach but should be seen as its very *epitome*.

1978/revised 1995

1 Rules, norms, idiosyncrasies

In its socio-cultural dimension, translation can be described as subject to constraints of several types and varying degree. These extend far beyond the source text; the systemic differences between the languages and textual traditions involved in the act, or even the possibilities and limitations of the cognitive apparatus of the translator as a necessary mediator. In fact, cognition itself is influenced, probably even modified by socio-cultural factors. At any rate, translators performing under different conditions (e.g., translating texts of different kinds, and/or for different audiences) often adopt different strategies, and ultimately come up with markedly different products. Something has obviously changed here, and I very much doubt it that it is the cognitive apparatus as such.

In terms of their potency, socio-cultural constraints have been described along a scale anchored between two extremes: general, relatively absolute *rules*, on the one hand and pure *idiosyncrasies* on the other. Between these two poles lies a vast middle-ground occupied by intersubjective factors commonly designated *norms*. The norms themselves form a graded continuum along the scale: some are stronger, and hence more rule-like, others are weaker, and hence almost idiosyncratic. The borderlines between the various types of constraints are thus diffuse. Each of the concepts, including the grading itself, is relative too. Thus what is just a favoured mode of behaviour within a heterogeneous group may well acquire much more binding force within a certain (more homogeneous) section thereof, in terms of either human agents (e.g., translators among texters in general) or types of activity (e.g., interpreting, or legal translation, within translation at large).

Along the temporal axis, each type of constraint may, and often does move into its neighbouring domain(s) through processes of rise and decline. Thus, mere whims may catch on and become more and more normative, and norms can gain so much validity that, for all practical purposes, they become as binding as rules; or the other way around, of course. Shifts of validity and force often have to do with changes of *status* within a society. In fact, they can always be described in connection with the notion of norm, especially since, as the process goes on, they are likely to cross its realm, i.e., actually become norms. The other two types of constraints may even be redefined in terms of norms: rules as "[more] objective", idiosyncrasies as "[more] subjective [or: less intersubjective]" norms.

Sociologists and social psychologists have long regarded norms as the translation of general values or ideas shared by a community – as to what is right and wrong, adequate and inadequate – into performance instructions appropriate for and applicable to particular situations, specifying what is prescribed and forbidden as well as what is tolerated and permitted in a certain behavioural dimension (the famous "square of normativity", which has lately been elaborated on with regard to translation in De Geest 1992: 38–40). Norms are acquired by the individual during his/her socialization and always imply *sanctions* – actual or potential, negative as well as positive. Within the community, norms also serve as criteria according to which actual instances of behaviour are *evaluated*. Obviously, there is a point in assuming the existence of norms only in situations which allow for different kinds of behaviour, on the additional condition that selection among them be nonrandom.[1]

Inasmuch as a norm is really active and effective, one can therefore distinguish regularity of behaviour in recurrent situations of the same type, which would render regularities a main source for any *study* of norms as well.

The centrality of the norms is not only metaphorical, then, in terms of their relative position along a postulated continuum of constraints; rather, it is essential: Norms are the key concept and focal point in any attempt to account for the social relevance of activities, because their existence, and the wide range of situations they apply to (with the conformity this implies), are the main factors ensuring the establishment and retention of social order. This holds for cultures too, or for any of the systems constituting them, which are, after all, social institutions ipso facto. Of course, behaviour which does *not* conform to prevailing norms is always possible too. Moreover, "non-compliance with a norm in particular instances does not invalidate the norm" (Hermans 1991: 162). At the same time, there would normally be a price to pay for opting for any deviant kind of behaviour.

One thing to bear in mind, when setting out to study norm-governed behaviour, is that there is no necessary identity between the norms themselves and any formulation of them in language. Verbal formulations of course reflect *awareness* of the existence of norms as well as of their respective significance. However, they also imply other interests, particularly a desire to *control* behaviour i.e., to dictate norms rather than merely account for them. Normative formulations tend to be slanted, then, and should always be taken with a grain of salt.

2 Translation as a norm-governed activity

Translation is a kind of activity which inevitably involves at least two languages and two cultural traditions, i.e., at least two sets of norm-systems on each level. Thus, the "value" behind it may be described as consisting of two major elements:

1   being a text in a certain language, and hence occupying a position, or filling in a slot, in the appropriate culture, or in a certain section thereof;
2   constituting a representation in that language/culture of another, pre-existing text in some other language, belonging to some other culture and occupying a definite position within it.

These two types of requirement derive from two sources which – even though the distance between them may vary greatly – are nevertheless always different and therefore often incompatible. Were it not for the regulative capacity of norms, the tensions between the two sources of constraints would have to be resolved on an entirely *individual* basis, and with no clear yardstick to go by. Extreme free variation may well have been the result, which it certainly is not. Rather, translation behaviour within a culture tends to manifest certain *regularities*, one consequence being that even if they are unable to account for deviations in any explicit way, the persons-in-the-culture can often tell when a translator has failed to adhere to sanctioned practices.

It has proven useful and enlightening to regard the basic choice which can be made between requirements of the two different sources as constituting an **initial**

norm. Thus, a translator may subject him-/herself either to the original text, with the norms it has realized, or to the norms active in the target culture, or, in that section of it which would host the end product. If the first stance is adopted, the translation will tend to subscribe to the norms of the source text, and through them also to the norms of the source language and culture. This tendency; which has often been characterized as the pursuit of adequate translation,[2] may well entail certain incompatibilities with target norms and practices, especially those lying beyond the mere linguistic ones. If, on the other hand, the second stance is adopted, norms systems of the target culture are triggered and set into motion. Shifts from the source text would be an almost inevitable price. Thus, whereas adherence to source norms determines a translation's adequacy as compared to the source text, subscription to norms originating in the target culture determines its acceptability.

Obviously, even the most adequacy-oriented translation involves shifts from the source text. In fact, the occurrence of shifts has long been acknowledged as a true universal of translation. However, since the need itself to deviate from source-text patterns can always be realized in more than one way, the actual *realization* of so-called obligatory shifts, to the extent that it is non-random, and hence not idiosyncratic, is already truly norm-governed. So is everything that has to do with non-obligatory shifts, which are of course more than just possible in real-life translation: they occur everywhere and tend to constitute the majority of shifting in any single act of human translation, rendering the latter a contributing factor to, as well as the epitome of regularity.

The term "initial norm" should not be overinterpreted, however. Its initiality derives from its superordinance over particular norms which pertain to lower, and therefore more specific levels. The kind of priority postulated here is basically *logical*, and need not coincide with any "real", i.e., *chronological* order of application. The notion is thus designed to serve first and foremost as an *explanatory tool*. Even if no clear macro-level tendency can be shown, any micro-level decision can still be accounted for in terms of adequacy vs. acceptability. On the other hand, in cases where an overall choice has been made, it is not necessary that every single lower-level decision be made in full accord with it. We are still talking regularities, then, but not necessarily of any absolute type. It is unrealistic to expect absolute regularities anyway, in any behavioural domain.

Actual translation decisions (the results of which the researcher would confront) will necessarily involve some ad hoc combination of, or compromise between the two extremes implied by the initial norm. Still, for theoretical and methodological reasons, it seems wiser to retain the opposition and treat the two poles as distinct in principle: If they are not regarded as having distinct *theoretical* statuses, how would compromises differing in type or in extent be distinguished and accounted for?

Finally, the claim that it is basically a norm-governed type of behaviour applies to translation of all kinds, not only literary, philosophical or biblical translation, which is where most norm-oriented studies have been conducted so far. As has recently been claimed and demonstrated in an all too sketchy exchange of views in *Target* (M. Shlesinger 1989 and Harris 1990), similar things can even be said of *conference interpreting*. Needless to say, this does not mean that the exact same conditions apply to all kinds of translation. In fact, their application in different cultural sectors is precisely one of the aspects that should be submitted to study.

In principle, the claim is also valid for every society and historical period, thus offering a framework for historically oriented studies which would also allow for comparison.

3 Translation norms: an overview

Norms can be expected to operate not only in translation of all kinds, but also at every stage in the translating event, and hence to be reflected on every level of its product. It has proven convenient to first distinguish two larger groups of norms applicable to translation: preliminary vs. operational.

Preliminary norms have to do with two main sets of considerations which are often interconnected: those regarding the existence and actual nature of a definite translation policy, and those related to the directness of translation.

Translation policy refers to those factors that govern the choice of text types; or even of individual texts, to be imported through translation into a particular culture/language at a particular point in time. Such a policy will be said to exist inasmuch as the choice is found to be non-random. Different policies may of course apply to different subgroups, in terms of either text-types (e.g. literary vs. non-literary) or human agents and groups thereof (e.g., different publishing houses), and the interface between the two often offers very fertile grounds for policy hunting.

Considerations concerning *directness of translation* involve the threshold of tolerance for translating from languages other than the ultimate source language: is indirect translation permitted at all? In translating from what source languages/text-types/periods (etc.) is it permitted/prohibited/tolerated/preferred? What are the permitted/prohibited/tolerated/preferred mediating languages? Is there a tendency/obligation to mark a translated work as having been mediated or is this fact ignored/camouflaged/denied? If it is mentioned, is the identity of the mediating language supplied as well? And so on.

Operational norms, in turn, may be conceived of as directing the decisions made during the act of translation itself. They affect the matrix of the text – i.e. the modes of distributing linguistic material in it – as well as the textual make up and verbal formulation as such. They thus govern – directly or indirectly – the relationships as well that would obtain between the target and source texts, i.e., what is more likely to remain invariant under transformation and what will change.

So-called *matricial norms* may govern the very *existence* of target-language material intended as a substitute for the corresponding source-language material (and hence the degree of *fullness* of translation), its location in the text (or the form of actual *distribution*), as well as the textual *segmentation*.[3] The extent to which omissions, additions, changes of location and manipulations of segmentation are referred to in the translated texts (or around them) may also be determined by norms, even though the one can very well occur without the other.

Obviously, the borderlines between the various matricial phenomena are not clear-cut. For instance, large-scale omissions often entail changes of segmentation as well, especially if the omitted portions have no clear boundaries, or textual-linguistic standing, i.e., if they are not integral sentences, paragraphs or chapters. By the same token, a change of location may often be accounted for as an omission (in one place) compensated by an addition (elsewhere). The decision as to what may have "really" taken place is thus description-bound: What one is after is (more or less cogent) *explanatory hypotheses*, not necessarily "true-to-life" accounts, which one can never be sure of anyway.

Textual-linguistic norms, in turn, govern the selection of material to formulate the target text in, or replace the original textual and linguistic material with. Textual-linguistic norms may either be *general*, and hence apply to translation qua translation, or *particular*, in which case they would pertain to a particular text-type and/or mode of translation only. Some of them may be identical to the norms governing non-translational text-production, but such an identity should never be taken for granted. This is the methodological reason why no study of translation can, or should proceed from the assumption that the later is representative of the target language, or of any overall textual tradition thereof. (And see our discussion of "translation-specific lexical items".)

It is clear that preliminary norms have both logical and chronological precedence over the operational ones. This is not to say that between the two major groups there are no relationships whatsoever, including mutual influences or even two-way conditioning. However, these relations are by no means fixed and given, and their establishment forms an inseparable part of any study of translation as a norm-governed activity. Nevertheless, we can safely assume at least that the relations which do exist have to do with the initial norm. They might even be found to *intersect* it – another important reason to retain the opposition between "adequacy" and "acceptability" as a basic coordinate system for the formulation of explanatory hypotheses.[4]

Operational norms as such may be described as serving as a model, in accordance with which translations come into being, whether involving the norms realized by the source text (i.e., adequate translation) plus certain modifications or purely target norms, or a particular compromise between the two. Every model supplying performance instructions may be said to act as a *restricting* factor: it opens up certain options while closing others. Consequently, when the first position is fully adopted, the translation can hardly be said to have been made into the target language as a whole. Rather, it is made into a model language, which is at best some part of the former and at worst an artificial, and as such nonexistent variety.[5] In this last case, the translation is not really *introduced* into the target culture either, but is *imposed* on it, so to speak. Sure, it may eventually carve a niche for itself in the latter, but there is no initial attempt to accommodate it to any existing "slot". On the other hand, when the second position is adopted, what a translator is introducing into the target culture (which is indeed what s/he can be described as doing now) is a *version* of the original work, cut to the measure of a preexisting model. (And see our discussion of the opposition between the "translation of literary texts" and "literary translation" as well as the detailed presentation of the Hebrew translation of a German *Schlaraffenland* text.)

The apparent contradiction between any traditional concept of equivalence and the limited model into which a translation has just been claimed to be moulded can only be resolved by postulating that **it is norms that determine the (type and extent of) equivalence manifested by actual translations**. The study of norms thus constitutes a vital step towards establishing just how the functional–

relational postulate of equivalence has been realized – whether in one translated text, in the work of a single translator or "school" of translators, in a given historical period, or in any other justifiable selection.[6] What this approach entails is a clear wish to retain the notion of equivalence, which various contemporary approaches (e.g. Hönig and Kussmaul 1982; Holz-Mänttäri 1984; Snell-Hornby 1988) have tried to do without, while introducing one essential change into it: from an ahistorical, largely prescriptive concept to a historical one. Rather than being a single relationship, denoting a recurring type of invariant, it comes to refer to any relation which is found to have characterized translation under a specified set of circumstances.

At the end of a full-fledged study it will probably be found that translational norms, hence the realization of the equivalence postulate, are all, to a large extent, dependent on the position held by translation – the activity as well as its products – in the target culture. An interesting field for study is therefore comparative: the nature of translational norms as compared to those governing non-translational kinds of text-production. In fact, this kind of study is absolutely vital, if translating and translations are to be appropriately contextualized.

4 The multiplicity of translational norms

The difficulties involved in any attempt to account for translational norms should not be underestimated. These, however, lie first and foremost in two features inherent in the very notion of norm, and are therefore not unique to Translation Studies at all: the socio-cultural specificity of norms and their basic instability.

Thus, whatever its exact content, there is absolutely no need for a norm to apply – to the same extent, or at all – to all sectors within a society. Even less necessary, or indeed likely, is it for a norm to apply across cultures. In fact, "sameness" here is a mere coincidence – or else the result of continuous contacts between subsystems within a culture, or between entire cultural systems, and hence a manifestation of interference. (For some general rules of systemic interference see Even-Zohar 1990: 53–72.) Even then, it is often more a matter of apparent than of a genuine identity. After all, significance is only attributed to a norm by the *system* in which it is embedded, and the systems remain different even if instances of external behaviour appear the same.

In addition to their inherent specificity, norms are also unstable, changing entities; not because of any intrinsic flaw but by their very nature as norms. At times, norms change rather quickly; at other times, they are more enduring, and the process may take longer. Either way, substantial changes, in translational norms too, quite often occur within one's life-time.

Of course it is not as if all translators are *passive* in face of these changes. Rather, many of them, through their very activity, help in shaping the process, as do translation criticism, translation ideology (including the one emanating from contemporary academe, often in the guise of theory), and, of course, various norm-setting activities of institutes where, in many societies, translators are now being trained. Wittingly or unwittingly, they all try to interfere with the "natural" course of events and to divert it according to their own preferences. Yet the success of their endeavours is never fully foreseeable. In fact, the relative role of different agents in the overall dynamics of translational norms is still largely a matter of conjecture even for times past, and much more research is needed to clarify it.

Complying with social pressures to constantly adjust one's behaviour to norms that keep changing is of course far from simple, and most people – including translators, initiators of translation activities and the consumers of their products – do so only up to a point. Therefore, it is not all that rare to find side by side in a society three types of competing norms, each having its own followers and a position of its own in the culture at large: the ones that dominate the centre of the system, and hence direct translational behaviour of the so-called *mainstream*, alongside the remnants of *previous* sets of norms and the rudiments of *new* ones, hovering in the periphery. This is why it is possible to speak – and not derogatorily – of being "trendy", "old-fashioned" or "progressive" in translation (or in any single section thereof) as it is in any other behavioural domain.

One's status as a translator may of course be temporary, especially if one fails to adjust to the changing requirements, or does so to an extent which is deemed insufficient. Thus, as changes of norms occur, formerly "progressive" translators may soon find themselves just "trendy", or on occasion as even downright "*passé*". At the same time, regarding this process as involving a mere alternation of generations can be misleading, especially if generations are directly equated with age groups. While there often are correlations between one's position along the "dated" – "mainstream" – "avant-garde" axis and one's age, these cannot, and should not be taken as inevitable, much less as a starting point and framework for the study of norms in action. Most notably, young people who are in the early phases of their initiation as translators often behave in an extremely epigonic way: they tend to perform according to dated, but still existing norms, the more so if they receive reinforcement from agents holding to dated norms, be they language teachers, editors, or even teachers of translation.

Multiplicity and variation should not be taken to imply that there is no such thing as norms active in translation. They only mean that real-life situations tend to be complex; and this complexity had better be noted rather than ignored, if one is to draw any justifiable conclusions. As already argued, the only viable way out seems to be to contextualize every phenomenon, every item, every text, every act, on the way to allotting the different norms themselves their appropriate position and valence. This is why it is simply unthinkable, from the point of view of the study of translation as a norm-governed activity, for all items to be treated on a par, as if they were of the same systemic position, the same significance, the same level of representativeness of the target culture and its constraints. Unfortunately, such an indiscriminate approach has been all too common, and has often led to a complete blurring of the normative picture, sometimes even to the absurd claim that no norms could be detected at all. The only way to keep that picture in focus is to go beyond the establishment of mere "check-lists" of factors which may occur in a corpus and have the lists *ordered*, for instance with respect to the status of those factors as characterizing "mainstream", "dated" and "avant-garde" activities, respectively.

This immediately suggests a further axis of contextualization, whose necessity has so far only been implied; namely, the *historical* one. After all, a norm can only be marked as "dated" if it was active in a *previous* period, and if, at that time, it had a different, "non-dated" position. By the same token, norm-governed behaviour can prove to have been "avant-garde" only in view of *subsequent* attitudes towards it: an idiosyncrasy which never evolved into something more general can only be described as a norm by extension, so to speak (see Section 1 above). Finally, there is nothing inherently "mainstream" about mainstream behaviour, except when it happens to function as such, which means that it too is time-bound. What I am claiming here, in fact, is that historical contextualization is a must not only for a *diachronic* study, which nobody would contest, but also for *synchronic* studies, which still seems a lot less obvious unless one has accepted the principles of so-called "Dynamic Functionalism" (for which, see the Introduction to Even-Zohar 1990[7] and Sheffy 1992: passim).

Finally, in translation too, *non-normative behaviour* is always a possibility. The price for selecting this option may be as low as a (culturally determined) need to submit the end product to revision. However, it may also be far more severe to the point of taking away one's earned recognition as a translator; which is precisely why non-normative behaviour tends to be the exception, in actual practice. On the other hand, in retrospect, deviant instances of behaviour may be found to have effected *changes* in the very system. This is why they constitute an important field of study, as long as they are regarded as what they have really been and are not put indiscriminately into one basket with all the rest. Implied are intriguing questions such as who is "allowed" by a culture to introduce changes and under what circumstances such changes may be expected to occur and/or be accepted.

5 Studying translational norms

So far we have discussed norms mainly in terms of their activity during a translation event and their effectiveness in the act of translation itself. To be sure, this is precisely where and when translational norms are active. However, what is actually available for observation is not so much the norms themselves, but rather norm-governed instances of behaviour. To be even more precise, more often than not, it is the products of such behaviour. Thus, even when translating is claimed to be studied directly, as is the case with the use of "Thinking-Aloud Protocols", it is only *products* which are available, although products of a different kind and order. Norms are not directly observable, then, which is all the more reason why something should also be said about them in the context of an attempt to *account* for translational behaviour.

There are two major sources for a reconstruction of translational norms, textual and extratextual:[8]

1   **textual**: the translated texts themselves, for all kinds of norms, as well as analytical inventories of translations (i.e., "virtual" texts), for various preliminary norms;

2   **extratextual**: semi-theoretical or critical formulations, such as prescriptive "theories" of translation, statements made by translators, editors, publishers, and other persons involved in or connected with the activity, critical appraisals of individual translations, or the activity of a translator or "school" of translators, and so forth.

There is a fundamental difference between these two types of source: Texts are *primary* products of norm-regulated behaviour, and can therefore be taken as immediate representations thereof. Normative pronouncements, by contrast, are merely *by*-products of the existence and activity of norms. Like any attempt to formulate a norm, they are partial and biased, and should therefore be treated with every possible circumspection; all the more so since – emanating as they do from interested parties – they are likely to lean toward propaganda and persuasion. There may therefore be gaps, even contradictions, between explicit arguments and demands, on the one hand, and actual behaviour and its results, on the other, due either to subjectivity or naïveté, or even lack of sufficient knowledge on the part of those who produced the formulations. On occasion, a deliberate desire to mislead and deceive may also be involved. Even with respect to the translators themselves, intentions do not necessarily concur with any declaration of intent (which is often put down post factum anyway, when the act has already been completed); and the way those intentions are realized may well constitute a further, third category still.

Yet all these reservations – proper and serious though they may be – should not lead one to abandon semi-theoretical and critical formulations as legitimate sources for the study of norms. In spite of all its faults, this type of source still has its merits, both in itself and as a possible key to the analysis of actual behaviour. At the same time, if the pitfalls inherent in them are to be avoided, normative pronouncements should never be accepted at face value. They should rather be taken as *pre-systematic* and given an explication in such a way as to place them in a narrow and precise framework, lending the resulting explicata the coveted systematic status. While doing so, an attempt should be made to clarify the status of each formulation, however slanted and biased it may be, and uncover the sense in which it was not just accidental; in other words how, in the final analysis, it does reflect the cultural constellation within which, and for whose purposes it was produced. Apart from sheer speculation, such an explication should involve the comparison of various normative pronouncements to each other, as well as their repeated confrontation with the patterns revealed by [the results of] actual behaviour and the norms reconstructed from them – all this with full consideration for their contextualization. (See a representative case in Weissbrod 1989.)

It is natural, and very convenient, to commence one's research into translational behaviour by focussing on *isolated* norms pertaining to well-defined behavioural dimensions, be they – and the coupled pairs of replacing and replaced segments representing them – established from the source text's perspective (e.g., translational replacements of source metaphors) or from the target text's vantage, point (e.g., binomials of near-synonyms as translational replacements). However, translation is intrinsically *multi*-dimensional: the manifold phenomena it presents are tightly interwoven and do not allow for easy isolation, not even for methodical purposes. Therefore, research should never get stuck in the blind alley of the "paradigmatic" phase which would at best yield lists of "normemes", or discrete norms. Rather, it should always proceed to a "syntagmatic" phase, involving the *integration* of normemes pertaining to various problem areas. Accordingly, the student's task can be characterized as an attempt to establish what *relations* there are between norms pertaining to various domains by correlating his/her individual findings and weighing them against each other. Obviously, the thicker the network of relations thus established, the more justified one would be in speaking in terms of a norma-tive *structure* (cf. Jackson 1960: 149–60) or *model*.

This having been said, it should again be noted that a translator's behaviour cannot be expected to be fully systematic. Not only can his/her decision-making be differently motivated in different problem areas, but it can also be unevenly distributed throughout an assignment within a single problem area. Consistency in translational behaviour is thus a *graded* notion which is neither nil (i.e., total erratic-ness) nor 1 (i.e., absolute regularity); its extent should emerge at the end of a study as one of its conclusions, rather than being presupposed.

The American sociologist Jay Jackson suggested a "Return Potential Curve", showing the distribution of approval/disapproval among the members of a social group over a range of behaviour of a certain type as a model for the representation of norms. This model (reproduced as Figure 18.1) makes it possible to make a gradual distinction between norms in terms of *intensity* (indicated by the height of the curve, its distance from the horizontal axis), the *total range of tolerated behaviour* (that part of the behavioural dimension approved by the group), and the *ratio* of one of these properties of the norm to the others.

One convenient division that can be re-interpreted with the aid of this model is tripartite:[9]

a. **Basic (primary) norms**, more or less mandatory for *all* instances of a certain behaviour (and hence their minimal common denominator). Occupy the apex of the curve. Maximum intensity, minimum latitude of behaviour.

b. **Secondary norms**, or **tendencies**, determining favourable behaviour. May be predominant in certain *parts* of the group. Therefore common enough, but not mandatory, from the point of view of the group as a whole. Occupy that part of the curve nearest its apex and therefore less intensive than the basic norms but covering a greater range of behaviour.

c. **Tolerated (permitted) behaviour**. Occupies the rest of the "positive" part of the curve (i.e., that part which lies above the horizontal axis), and there-fore of minimal intensity.

"A special group," detachable from (c), seems to be of considerable interest and importance, at least in some behavioural domains:

c′. **Symptomatic devices**. Though these devices may be infrequently used, their occurrence is typical for narrowing segments of the group under study. On the other hand, their absolute *non*-occurrence can be typical of other segments.

We may, then, safely assume a *distributional* basis for the study of norms: the more frequent a target-text phenomenon, a shift from a (hypothetical) adequate reconstruction of a source text, or a translational relation, the more likely it is to reflect (in this order) a more permitted (tolerated) activity, a stronger tendency, a more basic (obligatory) norm. A second aspect of norms, their *discriminatory capacity*, is thus reciprocal to the first, so that the less frequent a behaviour, the smaller the group it may serve to define. At the same time, the group it does define is not just

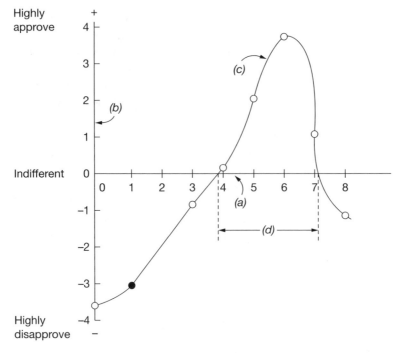

Figure 18.1 Schematic diagram showing the Return Potential Model for representing norms: (a)
a behaviour dimension; (b) an evaluation dimension; (c) a return potential curve,
showing the distribution of approval-disapproval among the members of a group over
the whole range of behaviour; (d) the range of tolerable or approved behaviour.

Source: Jackson 1960

any group; it is always a sub-group of the one constituted by higher-rank norms.
To be sure, even idiosyncrasies (which, in their extreme, constitute groups-of-one)
often manifest themselves as personal ways of realizing [more] general attitudes
rather than deviations in a completely unexpected direction.[10] Be that as it may, the
retrospective establishment of norms is always relative to the section under study,
and no automatic upward projection is possible. Any attempt to move in that direction and draw generalizations would require further study, which should be targeted
towards that particular end.

Finally, the curve model also enables us to redefine one additional concept: the
actual *degree of conformity* manifested by different members of a group to a norm
that has already been extracted from a corpus, and hence found relevant to it. This
aspect can be defined in terms of the distance from the point of maximum return
(in other words, from the curve's apex).

Notwithstanding the points made in the last few paragraphs, the argument for
the distributional aspect of the norms should not be pushed too far.

As is so well known, we are in no position to point to strict statistical methods
for dealing with translational norms, or even to supply sampling rules for actual
research (which, because of human limitations, will always be applied to samples

only). At this stage we must be content with our intuitions, which, being based on knowledge and previous experience, are "learned" ones, and use them as keys for selecting corpuses and for hitting upon ideas. This is not to say that we should abandon all hope for methodological improvements. On the contrary: much energy should still be directed toward the crystallization of systematic research methods, including statistical ones, especially if we wish to transcend the study of norms, which are always limited to one societal group at a time, and move on to the formulation of general laws of translational behaviour, which would inevitably be *probabilistic* in nature. To be sure, achievements of actual studies can themselves supply us with clues as to necessary and possible methodological improvements. Besides, if we hold up research until the most systematic methods have been found, we might never get any research done.

Notes

1   "The existence of norms is a sine qua non in instances of labelling and regulating; without a norm, all deviations are meaningless and become cases of free variation" (Wexler 1974: 4, n. 1).

2   "An adequate translation is a translation which realizes in the target language the textual relationships of a source text with no breach of its own [basic] linguistic system" (Even-Zohar 1975: 43; my translation).

3   The claim that principles of segmentation follow *universal* patterns is just a figment of the imagination of some discourse and text theoreticians intent on uncovering as many universal principles as possible. In actual fact, there have been various traditions (or "models") of segmentation, and the differences between them always have implications for translation, whether they are taken to bear on the formulation of the target text or ignored. Even the segmentation of sacred texts such as the Old Testament itself has often been tampered with by its translators, normally in order to bring it closer to *target* cultural habits, and by so doing enhance the translation's acceptability.

4   Thus, for instance, in sectors where the pursuit of adequate translation is marginal, it is highly probable that indirect translation would also become common, on occasion even preferred over direct translation. By contrast, a norm which prohibits mediated translation is likely to be connected with a growing proximity to the initial norm of adequacy. Under such circumstances, if indirect translation is still performed, the fact will at least be concealed, if not outright denied.

5   And see, in this connection, Izre'el's "Rationale for Translating Ancient Texts into a Modern Language" (1994). In an attempt to come up with a method for translating an Akkadian myth which would be presented to modern Israeli audiences in an oral performance, he purports to combine a "feeling-of-antiquity" with a "feeling-of-modernity" in a text which would be altogether simple and easily comprehensible by using a host of lexical items of *biblical* Hebrew in *Israeli* Hebrew grammatical and syntactic structures. Whereas "the lexicon . . . would serve to give an ancient flavor to the text, the grammar would serve to enable modern perception". It might be added that this is a

perfect mirror image of the way Hebrew translators started simulating spoken Hebrew in their texts: spoken lexical items were inserted in grammatical and syntactic structures which were marked for belonging to the written varieties (Ben-Shahar 1983), which also meant "new" into "old".

6   See also my discussion of "Equivalence and Non-Equivalence as a Function of Norms" (Toury 1980: 63–70).

7   "There is a clear difference between an attempt to account for some major principles which govern a system outside the realm of time, and one which intends to account for how a system operates both 'in principle' and 'in time.' Once the historical aspect is admitted into the functional approach, several implications must be drawn. First, it must be admitted that both synchrony and diachrony are historical, but the exclusive identification of the latter with history is untenable. As a result, synchrony cannot and should not be equated with statics, since at any given moment, more than one diachronic set is operating on the synchronic axis. Therefore, on the one hand a system consists of both synchrony and diachrony; on the other, each of these separately is obviously also a system. Second, if the idea of structuredness and systemicity need no longer be identified with homogeneity, a semiotic system can be conceived of as a heterogeneous, open structure. It is, therefore, very rarely a uni-system but is, necessarily, a polysystem" (Even-Zohar 1990: 11).

8   Cf. e.g., Vodička (1964: 74), on the possible sources for the study of literary norms, and Wexler (1974: 7–9), on the sources for the study of prescriptive intervention ("purism") in language.

9   Cf. e.g., Hrushovski's similar division (in Ben-Porat and Hrushovski 1974: 9–10) and its application to the description of the norms of Hebrew rhyme (in Hrushovski 1971).

10   And see the example of the seemingly idiosyncratic use of Hebrew *ki-xen* as a translational replacement of English "well" in a period when the norm dictates the use of *lu-vexen*.

1980s

THIS DECADE OPENS WITH the publication of Susan Bassnett's *Translation Studies*, a widely circulated book that consolidates various strands of translation research and, especially in English-speaking countries, fills the need for an introductory text in the translation classroom. It is a timely intervention that heralds the emergence of translation studies as a separate discipline, overlapping with linguistics, literary criticism, and philosophy, but exploring unique problems of cross-cultural communication. Bassnett takes a historical approach to theoretical concepts and understands practical strategies in relation to specific cultural and social situations. Even though she emphasizes literary translation, her book rests on what becomes the most common theoretical assumption during this period: the relative autonomy of the translated text.

Approaches informed by semiotics, discourse analysis, and poststructuralist textual theory display important conceptual and methodological differences, but they nonetheless agree that translation is an independent form of writing, distinct from the foreign text and from texts originally written in the translating language. Translating is seen as enacting its own processes of signification which answer to different linguistic and cultural contexts. This view recurs in translation traditions from antiquity onward, but now it is developed systematically, conceptualized according to the various discourses that characterize current academic disciplines. In some theorists, the autonomy of translation leads to a deeper functionalism, as theories and strategies are linked to specific cultural effects, commercial uses, and political agendas.

Defining equivalence inevitably comes to seem a less urgent problem. William Frawley questions the notion of equivalence as an identity between foreign text and translation, whether the identity is construed as empirical (absolute synonymy based on reference), biological (the same organs of perception and cognition), or linguistic (universals of language). Instead he reminds us that if translating is a form of communication, "there is information only in *difference*," so that a translation is actually a "code in its own right, setting its own standards and structural presuppositions and entailments, though they are necessarily derivative of the matrix information and target parameters" (Frawley 1984: 168, 169).

The concept of a "third code" enables Frawley to distinguish among translations according to their degree of semiotic "innovation" (ibid.: 173–174). He treats this distinction quantitatively, as a matter of how much "new knowledge" is produced, so he stops short of evaluating the translator's production of that knowledge or its impact on the cultural tradition within which the translation signifies. Although Frawley's examples are highly literary, taken from a poetic translation of a poem, his thinking assumes the claim of objectivity in theoretical linguistics, which excludes questions of literary value.

Shoshana Blum-Kulka's study of translation shifts further explores the third code by defining it as a type of discourse specific to translating: "explicitation." In the essay included below (1986), she speculates that translating always increases the semantic relations among the parts of the translated text, establishing a greater cohesion through explicitness, repetition, redundancy, explanation, and other discursive strategies. In contrast, shifts of coherence, deviations from an underlying semantic pattern in the foreign text, depend on reception, on reader and translator interpretations. To study them Blum-Kulka recommends empirical research in reading patterns, psycholinguistic studies of text processing.

Of course the very detection of a shift hinges on a crucial interpretive act, fixing a meaning or structure in the foreign text and then describing a deviation from it in the translation. No comparison between a foreign text and its translation can be unmediated, free of an interpretant, some third term that serves as the basis of the comparison, usually a standard of accuracy, but also a cultural and ideological code. To describe shifts, Kitty van Leuven-Zwart (1989, 1990) develops an elaborate analytical method based on the notion of an "architranseme," essentially a lexicographical equivalence between source and target languages, "identified with the help of a good descriptive dictionary in each of the two languages involved" (Leuven-Zwart 1989: 158).

Architransemes help to establish a relation between "microstructural" shifts of a semantic, stylistic or pragmatic variety and "macrostructural" shifts in narrative form and discourse. When applied to Dutch translations of Spanish and Spanish-American prose fiction between 1960 and 1985, the method reveals a tendency toward specification and explanation – precisely the finding that Blum-Kulka hypothesizes as a universal of translation.

Other theorists understand the autonomy of the translated text functionally, as a consequence of the social factors that direct the translator's activity. Instead of the term "translation" Justa Holz-Mänttäri (1984) prefers the broader neologism "translatorial action" (*translatorisches Handeln*) to signify various forms of cross-cultural communication, not just translating, paraphrasing or adapting, but editing and consulting. The translator is seen as an expert who designs a "product specification" in consultation with a client and then produces a "message trans-mitter" to serve a particular purpose in the receiving culture. Here translating does not seek an equivalence with the source text, but replaces it with a target text that fulfills the client's needs.

Holz-Mänttäri's abstract terminology may seem to reduce translation to an assembly-line process of text production, a Fordism that values mere efficiency. It was developed in translator training situations, where effective translation strate-gies and solutions are prized; and it does reflect actual practices among translators of technical, commercial, and official documents. It has the virtue of calling atten-tion to the professional role played the translator, his or her accountability, thus raising the issue of a translation ethics.

An action theory of translation surfaces independently in **Hans Vermeer**'s work. As the essay below (1989) indicates, Vermeer highlights the translator's *skopos* or aim as a decisive factor in a translation project. He conceives of the skopos as a complexly defined intention whose textual realization may diverge widely from the source text so as to reach a "set of addressees" in the target culture. The success of a translation depends on its coherence with the addressees' situation. Although the possible responses to a text can't be entirely predicted, a typology of potential audiences might guide the translator's labor and the historical study of translation.

Vermeer's approach bears a resemblance to contemporary trends in literary history and criticism, namely reader-response theory and the aesthetics of reception (*Rezeptionsästhetik*), where the meanings of literary texts are affiliated with particu-lar audiences or, in Stanley Fish's words, "interpretive communities" (Fish 1980). Within translation studies, *Skopostheorie* most resembles the target orientation associated with polysystem theory, which becomes increasingly influential during the 1980s.

André Lefevere takes up the seminal work of Even-Zohar and Toury and rede-fines their concepts of literary system and norm. Lefevere treats translation, criticism, editing, and historiography as forms of "refraction" or "rewriting." Refractions, he writes in the 1982 essay reprinted here, "carry a work of literature over from one system into another," and they are determined by such factors as "patronage," "poetics," and "ideology." This interpretive framework gives a new legitimacy to the study of literary translations by illuminating their creation of canons and traditions in the target culture. Lefevere sees that Romantic notions of authorial originality have marginalized translation studies, especially in the English-speaking world. And so he approaches the translated text with the sort of analytical sophistication that is usually reserved for original compositions.

The target orientation continues to guide large-scale research projects. At Göttingen University, a team of scholars studies German translations from the eight-eenth century to the present, exploring such topics as intermediate translation (German versions of French versions of English texts) and multiple translations of specific genres or an author's entire œuvre. They subsequently focus on anthologies of translated literature, which over two centuries reveal "representative historical patterns underlying German translation culture" (Kittel 1995: 277; see also Essman and Frank 1990).

For many theorists in this period, translation can never be an untroubled communication of a foreign text; it is rather manipulation, as announced in the title of Theo Hermans's 1985 anthology, a collection of current trends in polysystem research. Most scholarly work on translation still harbors an instrumental conception of language as primarily communicative, if not of a univocal meaning, then of a formalizable range of possibilities. It is only with the rise of poststructuralism that language becomes a site of uncontrollable polysemy, and translation is reconceived not simply as transformative of the foreign text, but interrogative or, as Jacques Derrida puts it, "deconstructive" (Derrida 1979: 93). If translation inescapably reduces source meanings, it also releases target potentialities which redound upon the foreign text in unsettling ways. This idea recurs in the poststructuralist essays collected in Joseph Graham's 1985 anthology.

Theorists like Derrida and Paul de Man are careful not to elevate translation into another original or the translator into another author. Instead they question the concepts of semantic unity, authorial originality, and copyright that continue to subordinate the translated to the foreign text. Both texts, they argue, are derivative and heterogeneous, consisting of diverse linguistic and cultural materials which destabilize the work of signification, making meaning plural and divided, exceeding and possibly conflicting with the intentions of the foreign writer and the translator. Translation is doomed to inadequacy because of irreducible differences, not just between languages and cultures, but also within them.

The skepticism in poststructuralist thinking revives the theme of untranslatability in translation theory, although in a more corrosive version than Quine's. Here the problem is not so much the incommensurability of cultures, the differences between conceptual schemes that complicate communication and reference, as the inherent indeterminacy of language, the unavoidable instability of the signifying process. Consequently, poststructuralism inspires literary experiments as theoretically inclined translators aim to release the play of the signifier in the translating language. At the same time, however, theorists give renewed attention to concepts of equivalence, now reformulated in linguistic terms that are at once cultural and historical, ethical and political.

Philip E. Lewis's contribution below (1985) addresses these issues through English versions of Derrida's inventive French texts. Setting out from the findings of comparative discourse analysis, Lewis submits translation to a poststructuralist critique of representation. Translating involves a "double interpretation" whereby the foreign text is rewritten in the "associative chains" and "structures of reference and enunciation" in the translating language. Because "English calls for more explicit, precise, concrete determinations [and] fuller, more cohesive delineations than does French," an early American translator of Derrida is inclined to "respect the use-values of English." He maintains immediate intelligibility through current English usage instead of trying to mimic the philosopher's conceptually dense wordplay.

To counter these tendencies, Lewis proposes a "new axiomatics of fidelity" which distinguishes between translating that "domesticates or familiarizes a message" and translating that "tampers with usage, seeks to match the polyvalencies or plurivocities or expressive stresses of the original." The latter kind of fidelity he calls "abusive": it both resists the constraints of the translating language and interrogates the structures of the foreign text.

Antoine Berman makes similar distinctions the basis of a translation ethics. He questions "ethnocentric" translating that "deforms" the foreign text by assimilating it to the target language and culture. Bad translation is not merely domesticating, but mystifying; "generally under the cloak of transmissibility, [it] performs a systematic negation of the foreignness of the foreign work" (Berman 1984: 17, my translation). Following German translators and theorists like Hölderlin and Schleiermacher, as well as French predecessors like Henri Meschonnic, Berman advocates literalism to register this foreignness. Good translation shows respect for the linguistic and cultural differences of the foreign text by developing a "correspondence" that "enlarges, amplifies and enriches the translating language" (Berman 1995: 94, my translation).

For Berman, every translation faces the "trial of the foreign" (*l'épreuve de l'étranger*), and textual analysis can gauge the degree to which the translating language admits into its own structures the foreign text. In the 1985 essay included below, he describes in detail the "deforming tendencies" by which translating preempts this trial, inviting comparison with Vinay and Darbelnet's influential methodology. The linguists view translation methods instrumentally, as effective in communicating the foreign text, regardless of how "oblique" or reductive they might be. In Berman's hermeneutic paradigm, such methods reconstitute the text, especially where the "polylogic" discourse of the novel is concerned, and so they raise ethical issues.

Berman is particularly effective in showing how the textual analysis of translations can be enriched through a psychoanalytic approach. The deforming tendencies at work in contemporary translation are "largely unconscious," he observes, "the internalized expression of a two-millennium-old tradition." Psychoanalysis illuminates the operation of these tendencies because the psyche performs and is analyzed through translating processes (see, for example, Mahony 1980).

The impact of poststructuralism on psychoanalysis, marxism and feminism makes theorists more aware of the hierarchies and exclusions in language use and thereby points to the ideological effects of translation, to the economic and political interests served by its representations of foreign texts. In the 1988 essay reprinted here, **Lori Chamberlain** focuses on the gender metaphors that have recurred in leading translation theorists since the seventeenth century, demonstrating the enormous extent to which a patriarchal model of authorship has underwritten the subordinate status of translation. Chamberlain suggests how a feminist concern with gender identities might be productive for translation studies, particularly in historical research that recovers forgotten translating women, but also in translation projects that are sensitive to ideologically coded foreign writing, whether feminist or masculinist. The experimental strategies devised by translators like Suzanne Jill Levine (1991) and Barbara Godard (1986) aim to challenge "the process by which translation complies with gender constructs."

The 1980s similarly witness the emergence of a postcolonial reflection on translation in anthropology, area studies and literary theory and criticism. Although translation figures among the ethnic and racial representations of the East demystified in Edward Said's *Orientalism* (1978), it is not until Vicente Rafael's 1988 study of Spanish colonialism in the Philippines that translation is compellingly revealed to be the agent (or subverter) of empire. Talal Asad (1986) questions the widespread use of "cultural translation" in ethnography by situating it amid the hierarchies that structure the global political economy. "The anthropological enterprise," he proposes, "may be vitiated by the fact that there are asymmetrical tendencies and pressures in the languages of dominated and dominant societies" (Asad 1986: 164).

Translation theory in this period is remarkably fertile and wide-ranging, taken up in a variety of discourses, fields, and disciplines. Yet the skeptical trends that are most characteristic of literary and cultural approaches to translation have little impact on the more technical and pragmatic projects informed by linguistics (and vice versa). Relying on a wealth of examples, including his own literary translations, Joseph Malone (1988) formulates a set of linguistic "tools" for analysis and practice which exceed Vinay and Darbelnet's in complexity, precision and abstraction. Here relations between the source and target texts might fall into categories like "zigzagging (divergence and convergence)," "recrescence (amplification and reduction)," and "repackaging (diffusion and condensation)." Malone's descriptive approach doesn't avoid value judgments entirely, since he occasionally explains his preference for a particular version by referring to an audience, "the average American reader," or to his own "sensibilities" (Malone 1988: 47, 49). These judgments are unsystematic, however, and far from the ethical politics of translation imagined by culturally oriented theorists like Berman or Chamberlain.

Further reading

Benjamin 1989, Davis 2001, Gentzler 1993, Hermans 1999, Lane-Mercier 1998, Massardier-Kenney 1997, Newmark 1991, Nord 1997, Pym 1995 and 1997, Robinson 1997 and 1997a, Simon 1996, Snell-Hornby 1988, Sturge 1997, Von Flotow 1997

Chapter 19

Hans J. Vermeer

SKOPOS AND COMMISSION IN TRANSLATIONAL ACTION

Translated by Andrew Chesterman

T**HIS PAPER IS A SHORT SKETCH** of my *skopos* theory (cf. Vermeer 1978, 1983; Reiss and Vermeer 1984; Vermeer 1986; and also Gardt 1989).

1 Synopsis

The skopos theory is part of a theory of translational action (*translatorisches Handeln* – cf. Holz-Mänttäri 1984; Vermeer 1986: 269–304 and also 197–246; for the historical background see e.g. Wilss 1988: 28). Translation is seen as the particular variety of translational action which is based on a source text (cf. Holz-Mänttäri 1984, especially p. 42f; and Nord 1988: 31). (Other varieties would involve e.g. a consultant's information on a regional economic or political situation, etc.)

Any form of translational action, including therefore translation itself, may be conceived as an action, as the name implies. Any action has an aim, a purpose. (This is part of the very definition of an action – see Vermeer 1986.) The word *skopos*, then, is a technical term for the aim or purpose of a translation (discussed in more detail below). Further: an action leads to a result, a new situation or event, and possibly to a "new" object. Translational action leads to a "target text" (not necessarily a verbal one); translation leads to a *translatum* (i.e. the resulting translated text), as a particular variety of target text.

The aim of any translational action, and the mode in which it is to be realized, are negotiated with the client who commissions the action. A precise specification of aim and mode is essential for the translator. – This is of course analogously true of translation proper: skopos and mode of realization must be adequately defined if the text-translator is to fulfil his task successfully.

The translator is "the" expert in translational action. He is responsible for the performance of the commissioned task, for the final *translatum*. Insofar as the duly specified skopos is defined from the translator's point of view, the source text is a constituent of the commission, and as such the basis for all the hierarchically ordered relevant factors which ultimately determine the *translatum*. (For the text as part of a complex action-in-a-situation see Holz-Mänttäri 1984; Vermeer 1986.)

One practical consequence of the skopos theory is a new concept of the status of the source text for a translation, and with it the necessity of working for an increasing awareness of this, both among translators and also the general public.

As regards the translator himself: experts are called upon in a given situation because they are needed and because they are regarded as experts. It is usually assumed, reasonably enough, that such people "know what it's all about"; they are thus consulted and their views listened to. Being experts, they are trusted to know more about their particular field than outsiders. In some circumstances one may debate with them over the best way of proceeding, until a consensus is reached, or occasionally one may also consult other experts or consider further alternative ways of reaching a given goal. An expert must be able to say – and this implies both knowledge and a duty to use it – what is what. His voice must therefore be respected, he must be "given a say". The translator is such an expert. It is thus up to him to decide, for instance, what role a source text plays in his translational action. The decisive factor here is the purpose, the skopos, of the communication in a given situation. (Cf. Nord 1988: 9.)

2 Skopos and translation

At this point it should be emphasized that the following considerations are not only intended to be valid for complete actions, such as whole texts, but also apply as far as possible to segments of actions, parts of a text (for the term "segment" (*Stück*) see Vermeer 1970). The skopos concept can also be used with respect to segments of a *translatum*, where this appears reasonable or necessary. This allows us to state that an action, and hence a text, need not be considered an indivisible whole. (Sub-skopoi are discussed below; cf. also Reiss 1971 on hybrid texts.)

A source text is usually composed originally for a situation in the source culture; hence its status as "source text", and hence the role of the translator in the process of intercultural communication. This remains true of a source text which has been composed specifically with transcultural communication in mind. In most cases the original author lacks the necessary knowledge of the target culture and its texts. If he did have the requisite knowledge, he would of course compose his text under the conditions of the target culture, in the target language! Language is part of a culture.

It is thus not to be expected that merely "trans-coding" a source text, merely "transposing" it into another language, will result in a serviceable *translatum*. (This view is also supported by recent research in neurophysiology – cf. Bergström 1989.)

As its name implies, the source text is oriented towards, and is in any case bound to, the source culture. The target text, the *translatum*, is oriented towards the target culture, and it is this which ultimately defines its adequacy. It therefore follows that source and target texts may diverge from each other quite considerably, not only in the formulation and distribution of the content but also as regards the goals which are set for each, and in terms of which the arrangement of the content is in fact determined. (There may naturally be other reasons for a reformulation, such as when the target culture verbalizes a given phenomenon in a different way, e.g. in jokes – cf. Broerman 1984; I return to this topic below.)

It goes without saying that a *translatum* may also have the same function (skopos) as its source text. Yet even in this case the translation process is not merely a "transcoding" (unless this translation variety is actually intended), since according to a uniform theory of translation a *translatum* of this kind is also primarily oriented, methodologically, towards a target culture situation or situations. Trans-coding, as a procedure which is retrospectively oriented towards the source text, not prospectively towards the target culture, is diametrically opposed to the theory of translational action. (This view does not, however, rule out the possibility that transcoding can be a legitimate translational skopos itself, oriented prospectively towards the target culture: the decisive criterion is always the skopos.)

To the extent that a translator judges the form and function of a source text to be basically adequate per se as regards the pretermined skopos in the target culture, we can speak of a degree of "intertextual coherence" between target and source text. This notion thus refers to a relation between *translatum* and source text, defined in terms of the skopos. For instance, one legitimate skopos might be an exact imitation of the source text syntax, perhaps to provide target culture readers with information about this syntax. Or an exact imitation of the source text structure, in a literary translation, might serve to create a literary text in the target culture. Why not? The point is that one must know what one is doing, and what the consequences of such action are, e.g. what the effect of a text created in this way will be in the target culture and how much the effect will differ from that of the source text in the source culture. (For a discussion of intertextual coherence and its various types, see Morgenthaler 1980: 138–140; for more on Morgenthaler's types of theme and rheme, cf. Gerzymisch-Arbogast 1987.)

Translating is doing something: "writing a translation", "putting a German text into English", i.e. a form of action. Following Brennenstuhl (1975), Rehbein (1977), Harras (1978; 1983), Lenk (edited volumes from 1977 on), Sager (1982) and others, Vermeer (1986) describes an action as a particular sort of behaviour: for an act of behaviour to be called an action, the person performing it must (potentially) be able to explain *why* he acts as he does although he could have acted otherwise. Furthermore, genuine reasons for actions can always be formulated in terms of aims or statements of goals (as an action "with a good reason", as Harras puts it). This illustrates a point made in another connection by Kaspar (1983: 139): "In this sense the notion of aim is in the first place the reverse of the notion of cause." (Cf. also Riedl 1983: 159f.) In his *De Inventione* (2.5.18.) Cicero also gives a definition of an action when he speaks of cases where "some disadvantage, or some advantage is neglected in order to gain a greater advantage or avoid a greater disadvantage" (Cicero 1949: 181–3).

3 Arguments against the skopos theory

Objections that have been raised against the skopos theory fall into two main types.

3.1 Objection (1) maintains that not all *actions* have an aim: some have "no aim". This is claimed to be the case with literary texts, or at least some of them. Unlike other texts (!), then, such texts are claimed to be "aimless". In fact, the argument is that in certain cases no aim *exists*, not merely that one might not be able explicitly to *state* an aim – the latter situation is sometimes inevitable, owing to human imperfection, but it is irrelevant here. As mentioned above, the point is that an aim must be at least potentially specifiable.

Let us clarify the imprecise expression of actions "having" an aim. It is more accurate to speak of an aim being *attributed* to an action, an author *believing* that he is writing to a given purpose, a reader similarly *believing* that an author has so written. (Clearly, it is possible that the performer of an action, a person affected by it, and an observer, may all have different concepts of the aim of the action. It is also important to distinguish between action, action chain, and action element – cf. Vermeer 1986.)

Objection (1) can be answered *prima facie* in terms of our very definition of an action: if no aim can be attributed to an action, it can no longer be regarded as an action. (The view that any act of speech is skopos-oriented was already a commonplace in ancient Greece – see Baumhauer 1986: 90f.) But it is also worth specifying the key concept of the skopos in more detail here, which we shall do in terms of translation proper as one variety of translational action.

The notion of skopos can in fact be applied in three ways, and thus have three senses: it may refer to

a. the translation process, and hence the goal of this process;
b. the translation result, and hence the function of the *translatum*;
c. the translation mode, and hence the intention of this mode.

Additionally, the skopos may of course also have sub-skopoi.

Objection (1), then, can be answered as follows: if a given act of behaviour has neither goal nor function nor intention, as regards its realization, result or manner, then it is not an action in the technical sense of the word.

If it is nevertheless claimed that literature "has no purpose", this presumably means that the creation of literature includes individual moments to which no goal, no function or intention can be attributed, in the sense sketched above.

For instance, assume that a neat rhyme suddenly comes into one's mind. (This is surely not an action, technically speaking.) One then writes it down. (Surely an action, since the rhyme could have been left unrecorded.) One continues writing until a sonnet is produced. (An action, since the writer could have chosen to do something else – unless the power of inspiration was simply irresistible, which I consider a mere myth.)

If we accept that the process of creating poetry also includes its publication (and maybe even negotiations for remuneration), then it becomes clear that such behaviour as a whole does indeed constitute an action. Schiller and Shakespeare undoubtedly took into account the possible reactions of their public as they wrote, as indeed anyone would; must we actually denounce such behaviour (conscious, and hence purposeful), because it was in part perhaps motivated by such base desires as fame and money?

Our basic argument must therefore remain intact: even the creation of literature involves purposeful action.

Furthermore, it need not necessarily be the case that the writer is actually conscious of his purpose at the moment of writing – hence the qualification (above) that it must be "potentially" possible to establish a purpose.

One recent variant of objection (1) is the claim that a text can only be called "literature" if it is art, and art has no purpose and no intention. So a work which did have a goal or intention would not be art. This seems a bit hard on literature, to say the least! In my view it would be simpler to concede that art, and hence also literature, can be assigned an intention (and without exception too). The objection seems to be based on a misunderstanding. Nowadays it is extremely questionable whether there is, or has even been, an art with no purpose. Cf. Busch (1987: 7):

> Every work of art establishes its meaning aesthetically [. . .] The aesthetic can of course serve many different functions, but it may also be in itself the function of the work of art.

Busch points out repeatedly that an object does not "have" a function, but that a function is attributed or assigned to an object, according to the situation.

And when Goethe acknowledges that he has to work hard to achieve the correct rhythm for a poem, this too shows that even for him the creation of poetry was not merely a matter of inspiration:

> Oftmals hab' ich auch schon in ihren Armen gedichtet,
> Und des Hexameters Mass leise mit fingernder Hand
> Ihr auf dem Rücken gezählt.
> (Römische Elegien 1.5.)

> [Often have I composed poems even in her arms,
> Counting the hexameter's beat softly with fingering hand
> There on the back of the beloved.]

Even the well-known "*l'art pour l'art*" movement ("art for art's sake") must be understood as implying an intention: namely, the intention to create art that exists for its own sake and *thereby* differs from other art. Intentionality in this sense is already apparent in the expression itself. (Cf. also Herding (1987: 689), who argues that the art-for-art's-sake movement was "a kind of defiant opposition" against idealism – i.e. it did indeed have a purpose.)

3.2 Objection (2) is a particular variant of the first objection. It maintains that not every *translation* can be assigned a purpose, an intention; i.e. there are translations that are not goal-oriented. (Here we are taking "translation" in its traditional sense, for "translation" with no skopos would by definition not be a translation at all, in the present theory. This does not rule out the possibility that a "translation" may be done retrospectively, treating the source text as the "measure of all things"; but this would only be a translation in the sense of the present theory if the skopos was explicitly to translate in this way.)

This objection too is usually made with reference to literature, and to this extent we have already dealt with it under objection (1): it can scarcely be claimed that literary translation takes place perforce, by the kiss of the muse. Yet there are three specifications of objection (2) that merit further discussion:

a.   The claim that the translator does not have any *specific* goal, function or intention in mind: he just translates "what is in the source text".
b.   The claim that a specific goal, function or intention would restrict the translation possibilities, and hence limit the range of interpretation of the target text in comparison to that of the source text.
c.   The claim that the translator has no specific addressee or set of addressees in mind.

Let us consider each of these in turn.

a.   Advertising texts are supposed to advertise; the more successful the advertisement is, the better the text evidently is. Instructions for use are supposed to describe how an apparatus is to be assembled, handled and maintained; the more smoothly this is done, the better the instructions evidently are. Newspaper reports and their translations also have a purpose: to inform the recipient, at least; the translation thus has to be comprehensible, in the right sense, to the expected readership, i.e. the set of addressees. There is no question that such "pragmatic texts" must be goal-oriented, and so are their translations.

It might be said that the postulate of "fidelity" to the source text requires that e.g. a news item should be translated "as it was in the original". But this too is a goal in itself. Indeed, it is by definition probably the goal that most literary translators traditionally set themselves. (On the ambiguity of the notion "fidelity", see Vermeer 1983: 89–130.)

It is sometimes even claimed that the very duty of a translator forbids him from doing anything else than stick to the source text; whether anyone might eventually be able to do anything with the translation or not is not the translator's business. The present theory of translational action has a much wider conception of the translator's task, including matters of ethics and the translator's accountability.

b.   The argument that assigning a skopos to every literary text restricts its possibilities of interpretation can be answered as follows. A given skopos may of course rule out certain interpretations because they are not part of the translation goal; but one possible goal (skopos) would certainly be precisely to preserve the breadth of interpretation of the source text. (Cf. also Vermeer 1983: a translation realizes something "different", not something "more" or "less"; for translation as the realization of *one* possible interpretation, see Vermeer 1986.) How far such a skopos is in fact realizable is not the point here.

c. It is true that in many cases a text-producer, and hence also a translator, is not thinking of a specific addressee (in the sense of: John Smith) or set of addressees (in the sense of: the members of the social democrat party). In other cases, however, the addressee(s) may indeed be precisely specified. Ultimately even a communication "to the world" has a set of addressees. As long as one believes that one is expressing oneself in a "comprehensible" way, and as long as one assumes, albeit unconsciously, that people have widely varying levels of intelligence and education, then one must in fact be orienting oneself towards a certain restricted group of addressees; not necessarily consciously – but unconsciously. One surely often uses one's own (self-evaluated) level as an implicit criterion (the addressees are (almost) as intelligent as one is oneself . . .). Recall also the discussions about the best way of formulating news items for radio and television, so that as many recipients as possible will understand.

The problem, then, is not that there is no set of addressees, but that it is an indeterminate, fuzzy set. But it certainly exists, vague in outline but clearly present. And the clarity or otherwise of the concept is not specified by the skopos theory. A fruitful line of research might be to explore the extent to which a group of recipients can be replaced by a "type" of recipient. In many cases such an addressee-type may be much more clearly envisaged, more or less consciously, than is assumed by advocates of the claim that translations lack specific addressees. (Cf. also Morgenthaler 1980: 94 on the possibility of determining a "diffuse public" more closely; on indeterminacy as a general cultural problem see Quine 1960.)

The set of addressees can also be determined indirectly: for example, if a publisher specializing in a particular range of publications commissions a translation, a knowledge of what this range is will give the translator a good idea of the intended addressee group (cf. Heinold *et al.* 1987: 33–6).

3.3 Objection (2) can also be interpreted in another way. In text linguistics and literary theory a distinction is often made between text as potential and text as realization. If the skopos theory maintains that every text has a given goal, function or intention, and also an assumed set of addressees, objection (2) can be understood as claiming that this applies to text as realization; for a text is also potential in the "supersummative" sense (Paepcke 1979: 97), in that it can be used in different situations with different addressees and different functions. Agreed; but when a text is actually composed, this is nevertheless done with respect to an assumed function (or small set of functions) etc. The skopos theory does not deny that the same text might be used later (also) in ways that had not been foreseen originally. It is well known that a *translatum* is a text "in its own right" (Holz-Mänttäri *et al.* 1986: 5), with its own potential of use: a point overlooked by Wilss (1988: 48). For this reason not even potential texts can be set up with no particular goal or addressee – at least not in any adequate, practical or significant way.

This brings us back again to the problem of the "functional constancy" between source and target text: Holz-Mänttäri (1988) rightly insists that functional constancy, properly understood, is the exception rather than the rule. Of relevance to the above objections in general is also her following comment (ibid.: 7):

Where is the neuralgic point at which translation practice and theory so often diverge? In my view it is precisely where texts are lifted out of their environment for comparative purposes, whereby their process aspect is ignored. A dead anatomical specimen does not evade the clutches of the dissecting knife, to be sure, but such a procedure only increases the risk that findings will be interpreted in a way that is translationally irrelevant.

3.4 I have agreed that *one* legitimate skopos is maximally faithful imitation of the original, as commonly in literary translation. True translation, with an adequate skopos, does not mean that the translator *must* adapt to the customs and usage of the target culture, only that he *can* so adapt. This aspect of the skopos theory has been repeatedly misunderstood. (Perhaps it is one of those insights which do not spread like wildfire but must first be hushed up and then fought over bitterly, before they become accepted as self-evident – cf. Riedl 1983: 147.)

What we have is in fact a "hare-and-tortoise" theory (Klaus Mudersbach, personal communication): the skopos is always (already) there, at once, whether the translation is an assimilating one or deliberately marked or whatever. What the skopos states is that one must translate, consciously and consistently, in accordance with some principle respecting the target text. The theory does not state what the principle is: this must be decided separately in each specific case. An optimally faithful rendering of a source text, in the sense of a trans-coding, is thus one perfectly legitimate goal. The skopos theory merely states that the translator should be aware that *some* goal exists, and that any given goal is only one among many possible ones. (How many goals are actually realizable is another matter. We might assume that in at least some cases the number of realizable goals is one only.) The important point is that a given source text does not have one correct or best translation only (Vermeer 1979 and 1983: 62–88).

We can maintain, then, that every reception or production of a text can at least retrospectively be assigned a skopos, as can every translation, by an observer or literary scholar etc.; and also that every action is guided by a skopos. If we now turn this argument around we can postulate *a priori* that translation – because it is an action – always presupposes a skopos and is directed by a skopos. It follows that every translation commission should explicitly or implicitly contain a statement of skopos in order to be carried out at all. Every translation presupposes a commission, even though it may be set by the translator to himself (*I will translate this keeping close to the original . . .*). "A" statement of skopos implies that it is not necessarily identical with the skopos attributed to the source text: there are cases where such identity is not possible.

4 The translation commission

Someone who translates undertakes to do so as a matter of deliberate choice (I exclude the possibility of translating under hypnosis), or because he is required to do so. One translates as a result of either one's own initiative or someone else's: in both cases, that is, one acts in accordance with a "commission" (*Auftrag*).

Let us define a commission as the instruction, given by oneself or by someone else, to carry out a given action – here: to translate. (Throughout the present article translation is taken to include interpretation.)

Nowadays, in practice, commissions are normally given explicitly (*Please translate the accompanying text*), although seldom with respect to the ultimate purpose of the text. In real life, the specification of purpose, addressees etc. is usually sufficiently apparent from the commission situation itself: unless otherwise indicated, it will be assumed in our culture that for instance a technical article about some astronomical discovery is to be translated as a technical article for astronomers, and the actual place of publication is regarded as irrelevant; or if a company wants a business letter translated, the natural assumption is that the letter will be used by the company in question (and in most cases the translator will already be sufficiently familiar with the company's own in-house style, etc.). To the extent that these assumptions are valid, it can be maintained that any translation is carried out according to a skopos. In the absence of a specification, we can still often speak of an implicit (or implied) skopos. It nevertheless seems appropriate to stress here the necessity for a change of attitude among many translators and clients: as far as possible, detailed information concerning the skopos should always be given.

With the exception of *forces majeures* – or indeed even including them, according to the conception of "commission" (cf. the role of so-called inspiration in the case of biblical texts) – the above definition, with the associated arguments, allows us to state that every translation is based on a commission.

A commission comprises (or should comprise) as much detailed information as possible on the following: (1) the goal, i.e. a specification of the aim of the commission (cf. the scheme of specification factors in Nord 1988: 170); (2) the conditions under which the intended goal should be attained (naturally including practical matters such as deadline and fee). The statement of goal and the conditions should be explicitly negotiated between the client (commissioner) and the translator, for the client may occasionally have an imprecise or even false picture of the way a text might be received in the target culture. Here the translator should be able to make argumentative suggestions. A commission can (and should) only be binding and conclusive, and accepted as such by the translator, if the conditions are clear enough. (I am aware that this requirement involves a degree of wishful thinking; yet it is something to strive for.) Cf. Holz-Mänttäri 1984: 91f and 113; Nord 1988: 9 and 284, note 4.

The translator is the expert in translational action (Holz-Mänttäri 1984 and 1985); as an expert he is therefore responsible for deciding whether, when, how, etc., a translation can be realized (the Lasswell formula is relevant here – see Lasswell 1964: 37; Vermeer 1986: 197 and references there).

The *realizability* of a commission depends on the circumstances of the target culture, not on those of the source culture. What is dependent on the source culture is the source text. A commission is only indirectly dependent on the source culture to the extent that a translation, by definition, must involve a source text. One might say that the realizability of a commission depends on the relation between the target culture and the source text; yet this would only be a special case of the general dependence on the target culture: a special case, that is, insofar as the commission is basically independent of the source text function. If the discrepancy is too great, however, no translation is possible – at most a rewritten text or the like. We shall not discuss this here. But it should be noted that a target culture generally offers a wide range of potential, including e.g. possible extension through the adoption of phenomena from other cultures. How far this is possible depends on the target culture. (For this kind of adoption see e.g. Toury 1980.)

I have been arguing – I hope plausibly – that every translation can and must be assigned a skopos. This idea can now be linked with the concept of commission: it is precisely by means of the commission that the skopos is assigned. (Recall that a translator may also set his own commission.)

If a commission cannot be realized, or at least not optimally, because the client is not familiar with the conditions of the target culture, or does not accept them, the competent translator (as an expert in intercultural action, since translational action is a particular kind of intercultural action) must enter into negotiations with the client in order to establish what kind of "optimal" translation can be guaranteed under the circumstances. We shall not attempt to define "optimal" here – it is presumably a supra-individual concept. We are simply using the term to designate one of the best translations possible in the given circumstances, one of those that best realize the goal in question. Besides, "optimal" is clearly also a relative term: "optimal under certain circumstances" may mean "as good as possible in view of the resources available" or "in view of the wishes of the client", etc. – and always only in the opinion of the translator, and/or of the recipient, etc. The translator, as the expert, decides in a given situation whether to accept a commission or not, under what circumstances, and whether it needs to be modified.

The skopos of a translation is therefore the goal or purpose, defined by the commission and if necessary adjusted by the translator. In order for the skopos to be defined precisely, the commission must thus be as specific as possible (Holz-Mänttäri 1984). If the commission is specific enough, after possible adjustment by the translator himself, the decision can then be taken about *how* to translate optimally, i.e. what kind of changes will be necessary in the *translatum* with respect to the source text.

This concept of the commission thus leads to the same result as the skopos theory outlined above: a *translatum* is primarily determined by its skopos or its commission, accepted by the translator as being adequate to the goal of the action. As we have argued, a *translatum* is not *ipso facto* a "faithful" imitation of the source text. "Fidelity" to the source text (whatever the interpretation or definition of fidelity) is one possible and legitimate skopos or commission. Formulated in this way, neither skopos nor commission are new concepts as such – both simply make explicit something which has always existed. Yet they do specify something that has hitherto either been implicitly put into practice more unconsciously than consciously, or else been neglected or even rejected altogether: that is, the fact that one translates according to a particular purpose, which implies translating in a certain manner, without giving way freely to every impulse; the fact that there must always be a clearly defined goal. The two concepts also serve to relativize a view-point that has often been seen as the only valid one: that a source text should be translated "as literally as possible".

Neglecting to specify the commission or the skopos has one fatal consequence: there has been little agreement to date about the best method of translating a given text. In the context of the skopos or the commission this must now be possible, at least as regards the macrostrategy. (As regards individual text elements we still know too little about the functioning of the brain, and hence of culture and language, to be able to rely on much more than intuition when choosing between different variants which may appear to the individual translator to be equally possible and appropriate in a given case, however specific the skopos.) The skopos can also help to determine whether the source text needs to be "translated", "paraphrased" or completely "re-edited". Such strategies lead to terminologically different varieties of translational action, each based on a defined skopos which is itself based on a specified commission.

The skopos theory thus in no way claims that a translated text should *ipso facto* conform to the target culture behaviour or expectations, that a translation must always "adapt" to the target culture. This is just one possibility: the theory equally well accommodates the opposite type of translation, deliberately marked, with the intention of expressing source-culture features by target-culture means. Everything between these two extremes is likewise possible, including hybrid cases. To know what the point of a translation is, to be conscious of the action – that is the goal of the skopos theory. The theory campaigns against the belief that there is no aim (in any sense whatever), that translation is a purposeless activity.

Are we not just making a lot of fuss about nothing, then? No, insofar as the following claims are justified: (1) the theory makes explicit and conscious something that is too often denied; (2) the skopos, which is (or should be) defined in the commission, expands the possibilities of translation, increases the range of possible translation strategies, and releases the translator from the corset of an enforced – and hence often meaningless – literalness; and (3) it incorporates and enlarges the accountability of the translator, in that his translation must function in such a way that the given goal is attained. This accountability in fact lies at the very heart of the theory: what we are talking about is no less than the ethos of the translator.

By way of conclusion, here is a final example illustrating the importance of the skopos or commission.

An old French textbook had a piece about a lawsuit concerning an inheritance of considerable value. Someone had bequeathed a certain sum to two nephews. The will had been folded when the ink was still wet, so that a number of small ink-blots had appeared in the text. In one place, the text could read either as *deux* "two" or *d'eux* "of them". The lawsuit was about whether the sentence in question read *à chacun deux cent mille francs* "to each, two hundred thousand francs," or *à chacun d'eux cent mille francs* "to each of them, one hundred thousand francs". Assume that the case was being heard in, say, a German court of law, and that a translation of the will was required. The skopos (and commission) would obviously be to translate in a "documentary" way, so that the judge would understand the ambiguity. The translator might for instance provide a note or comment to the effect that two readings were possible at the point in question, according to whether the apostrophe was interpreted as an inkblot or not, and explain them (rather as I have done here). – Now assume a different context, where the same story occurs as a minor incident in a novel. In this case a translator will surely not wish to interrupt the flow of the narrative with an explanatory comment, but rather try to find a target language solution with a similar kind of effect, e.g. perhaps introducing an ambiguity concerning the presence or absence of a crucial comma, so that 2000,00 francs might be interpreted either as 2000 or as 200000 francs. Here the story is being used "instrumentally"; the translation does not need to reproduce every detail, but aims at an equivalent effect. – The two different solutions are equally possible and attainable because each conforms to a different skopos. And this is precisely the point of the example: one does not translate a source text in a void, as it were, but always according to a given skopos or commission.

The above example also illustrates the fact that any change of skopos from source to target text, or between different translations, gives rise to a separate target text, e.g. as regards its text variety. (On text varieties (*Textsorten*), see Reiss and Vermeer 1984; but cf. also Gardt's (1987: 555) observation that translation strategies are bound to text varieties only "in a strictly limited way".) The source text does not determine the variety of the target text, nor does the text variety determine *ipso facto* the form of the target text (the text variety does not determine the skopos, either); rather, it is the skopos of the translation that also determines the appropriate text variety. A "text variety", in the sense of a classificatory sign of a *translatum*, is thus a consequence of the skopos, and thereby secondary to it. In a given culture it is the skopos that determines which text variety a *translatum* should conform to. For example:

An epic is usually defined as a long narrative poem telling of heroic deeds. But Homer's *Odyssey* has also been translated into a novel: its text variety has thus changed from epic to novel, because of a particular skopos. (Cf. Schadewaldt's (1958) translation into German, and the reasons he gives there for this change; also see Vermeer 1983: 89–130.)

Chapter 20

André Lefevere

MOTHER COURAGE'S CUCUMBERS: TEXT, SYSTEM AND REFRACTION IN A THEORY OF LITERATURE

T**RANSLATION STUDIES CAN** hardly be said to have occupied a central position in much theoretical thinking about literature. Indeed, the very possibility of their relevance to literary theory has often been denied since the heyday of the first generation of German Romantic theorists and translators. This article will try to show how a certain approach to translation studies can make a significant contribution to literary theory as a whole and how translations or, to use a more general term, refractions, play a very important part in the evolution of literatures.

H. R. Hays, the first American translator of Brecht's *Mutter Courage und ihre Kinder*, translates "Da ist ein ganzes Messbuch dabei, aus Altötting, zum Einschlagen von Gurken" as "There's a whole ledger from Altötting to the storming of Gurken" (B26/H5), in which the prayerbook Mother Courage uses to wrap her cucumbers becomes transformed into a ledger, and the innocent cucumbers themselves grow into an imaginary town, Gurken, supposedly the point at which the last transaction was entered into that particular ledger. Eric Bentley, whose translation of *Mother Courage* has been the most widely read so far, translates: "Jetzt kanns bis morgen abend dauern, bis ich irgendwo was Warmes in Magen krieg" as "May it last until tomorrow evening, so I can get something in my belly" (B128/B65), whereas Brecht means something like "I may have to wait until tomorrow evening before I get something hot to eat." Both Hays and Bentley painfully miss the point when they translate "wenn einer nicht hat frei werden wollen, hat der König keinen Spass gekannt" as "if there had been nobody who needed freeing, the king wouldn't have had any sport" (B58/H25) and "if no one had *wanted* to be free, the king wouldn't have had any fun" (B58/B25) respectively. The German means something bitterly ironical like "the king did not treat lightly any attempts to resist being liberated". Even the Manheim translation nods occasionally, as when "die Weiber reissen sich um dich" (the women fight over you) is translated as "the women tear each other's hair out over you" (B37/M143). This brief enumeration could easily be supplemented by a number of other howlers, some quite amusing, such as Hays' "if you sell your shot to buy rags" for "Ihr verkaufts die Kugeln, ihr Lumpen" (you are selling your bullets, you fools — in which Lumpen is also listed in the dictionary as rags (B51/H19). I have no desire, however, to write a traditional "Brecht in English" type of translation-studies paper, which would pursue this strategy to the bitter end. Such a strategy would inevitably lead to two stereotyped conclusions: either the writer decides that laughter cannot go on masking tears indefinitely, recoils in horror from so many misrepresentations, damns all translations and translators, and advocates reading literature in the original only, as if that were possible. Or he administers himself a few congratulatory pats on the back (after all, he has been able to spot the mistakes), regrets that even good translators are often caught napping in this way, and suggests that "we" must train "better and better" translators if we want to have "better and better" translations. And there an end.

Or a beginning, for translations can be used in other, more constructive ways. The situation changes dramatically if we stop lamenting the fact that "the Brechtian 'era' in England stood under the aegis not of Brecht himself but of various second-hand ideas and concepts *about* Brecht, an image of Brecht created from misunderstandings and misconceptions"[1] and, quite simply, accept it as a fact of literature — or even life. How many lives, after all, have been deeply affected by translations of the Bible and the *Capital*?

A writer's work gains exposure and achieves influence mainly through "misunderstandings and misconceptions," or, to use a more neutral term, refractions. Writers and their work are always understood and conceived against a certain background or, if you will, are refracted through a certain spectrum, just as their work itself can refract previous works through a certain spectrum.

An approach to literature which has its roots in the poetics of Romanticism, and which is still very much with us, will not be able to admit this rather obvious fact without undermining its own foundations. It rests on a number of assumptions, among them, the assumption of the genius and originality of the author who creates *ex nihilo* as opposed to an author like Brecht, who is described in the 1969 edition of the *Britannica* as "a restless piecer together of ideas not always his own."[2] As if Shakespeare didn't have "sources," and as if there had not been some writing on the Faust theme before Goethe. Also assumed is the sacred character of the text, which is not to be tampered with — hence the horror with which "bad" translations are rejected. Another widespread assumption is the belief in the possibility of recovering the author's true intentions, and the concomitant belief that works of literature should be judged on their intrinsic merit only: "Brecht's ultimate rank will fall to be reconsidered when the true quality of his plays can be assessed independently of political affiliations,"[3] as if that were possible.

A systemic approach to literature, on the other hand, tends not to suffer from such assumptions. Translations, texts produced on the borderline between two systems, provide an ideal introduction to a systems approach to literature.

First of all, let us accept that refractions – the adaptation of a work of literature to a different audience, with the intention of influencing the way in which that
audience reads the work – have always been with us in literature. Refractions are
to be found in the obvious form of translation, or in the less obvious forms of criticism (the wholesale allegorization of the literature of Antiquity by the Church
Fathers, e.g.), commentary, historiography (of the plot summary of famous works
cum evaluation type, in which the evaluation is unabashedly based on the current
concept of what "good" literature should be), teaching, the collection of works in
anthologies, the production of plays. These refractions have been extremely influential in establishing the reputation of a writer and his or her work. Brecht, e.g.
achieved his breakthrough in England posthumously with the 1965 Berliner
Ensemble's London production of *Arturo Ui*, when "the British critics began to rave
about the precision, the passion, acrobatic prowess and general excellence of it all.
Mercifully, as none of them understands German, they could not be put off by the
actual content of this play."[4]

It is a fact that the great majority of readers and theatre-goers in the Anglo-
Saxon world do not have access to the "original" Brecht (who has been rather
assiduously refracted in both Germanies anyway, and in German). They have to
approach him through refractions that run the whole gamut described above, a fact
occasionally pointed out within the Romanticism-based approaches to literature, but
hardly ever allowed to upset things: "a large measure of credit for the wider recognition of Brecht in the United States is due to the drama critic Eric Bentley, who
translated several of Brecht's plays and has written several sound critical apprecia-
tions of him."[5] It is admitted that Brecht has reached Anglo-Saxon audiences
vicariously, with all the misunderstandings and misconceptions this implies, and not
through some kind of osmosis which ensures that genius always triumphs in the end.
But no further questions are asked, such as: "how does refraction really operate?
and what implications could it have for a theory of literature, once its existence is
admitted?"

Refractions, then, exist, and they are influential, but they have not been much
studied. At best their existence has been lamented (after all, they are unfaithful to
the original), at worst it has been ignored within the Romanticism-based approaches,
on the very obvious grounds that what should not be cannot be, even though it is.
Refractions have certainly not been analysed in any way that does justice to the
immense part they play, not just in the dissemination of a certain author's work,
but also in the development of a certain literature. My contention is that they have
not been studied because there has not been a framework that could make analysis
of refractions relevant within the wider context of an alternative theory. That framework exists if refractions are thought of as part of a system, if the spectrum that
refracts them is described.

The heuristic model a systems approach to literature makes use of, rests on the
following assumptions: (a) literature is a system, embedded in the environment of
a culture or society. It is a contrived system, i.e. it consists of both objects (texts)
and people who write, refract, distribute, read those texts. It is a stochastic system,
i.e. one that is relatively indeterminate and only admits of predictions that have a
certain degree of probability, without being absolute. It is possible (and General
Systems Theory has done this, as have some others who have been trying to apply

a systems approach to literature) to present systems in an abstract, formalized way, but very little would be gained by such a strategy in the present state of literary studies, while much unnecessary aversion would be created, since Romanticism-based approaches to literature have always resolutely rejected any kind of notation that leaves natural language too far behind.

The literary system possesses a regulatory body: the person, persons, institutions (Maecenas, the Chinese and Indian Emperors, the Sultan, various prelates, noblemen, provincial governors, mandarins, the Church, the Court, the Fascist or Communist Party) who or which extend(s) patronage to it. Patronage consists of at least three components: an ideological one (literature should not be allowed to get too far out of step with the other systems in a given society), an economic one (the patron assures the writer's livelihood) and a status component (the writer achieves a certain position in society). Patrons rarely influence the literary system directly; critics will do that for them, as writers of essays, teachers, members of academies. Patronage can be undifferentiated – in situations in which it is extended by a single person, group, institution characterized by the same ideology – or differentiated, in a situation in which different patrons represent different, conflicting ideologies. Differentiation of patronage occurs in the type of society in which the ideological and the economic component of patronage are no longer necessarily linked (the Enlightenment State, e.g., as opposed to various absolutist monarchies, where the same institution dispensed "pensions" and kept writers more or less in step). In societies with differentiated patronage, economic factors such as the profit motive are liable to achieve the status of an ideology themselves, dominating all other considerations. Hence, *Variety*, reviewing the 1963 Broadway production of *Mother Courage* (in Bentley's translation), can ask without compunction: "Why should anyone think it might meet the popular requirements of Broadway – that is, be commercial?"[6]

The literary system also possesses a kind of code of behaviour, a poetics. This poetics consists of both an inventory component (genre, certain symbols, characters, prototypical situations) and a "functional" component, an idea of how literature has to, or may be allowed to, function in society. In systems with undifferentiated patronage the critical establishment will be able to enforce the poetics. In systems with differentiated patronage various poetics will compete, each trying to dominate the system as a whole, and each will have its own critical establishment, applauding work that has been produced on the basis of its own poetics and decrying what the competition has to offer, relegating it to the limbo of "low" literature, while claiming the high ground for itself. The gap between "high" and "low" widens as commercialization increases. Literature produced for obviously commercial reasons (the Harlequin series) will tend to be as conservative, in terms of poetics, as literature produced for obviously ideological reasons (propaganda). Yet economic success does not necessarily bring status in its wake: one can be highly successful as a commercial writer (Harold Robbins) and be held in contempt by the highbrows at the same time.

A final constraint operating within the system is that of the natural language in which a work of literature is written, both the formal side of that language (what is in grammars) and its pragmatic side, the way in which language reflects culture. This

latter aspect is often most troublesome to translators. Since different languages
reflect different cultures, translations will nearly always contain attempts to "naturalize" the different culture, to make it conform more to what the reader of the translation is used to. Bentley, e.g., translates "Käs aufs Weissbrot" as "Cheese on
pumpernickel" (B23/B3), rather than the more literal "cheese on white bread,"
on the assumption that an American audience would expect Germans to eat their
cheese on pumpernickel, since Germany is where pumpernickel came from.
Similarly "in dem schönen Flandern" becomes the much more familiar "in Flanders
fields" (B52/B22), linking the Thirty Years' War of the seventeenth century with
World War I, as does Bentley's use of "Kaiser," which he leaves untranslated
throughout. In the same way, Hays changes "Tillys Sieg bei Magdeburg" to "Tilly's
Victory at Leipsic" (B94/H44), on the assumption that the Anglo-American audience will be more familiar with Leipzig than with Magdeburg. It is obvious that these
changes have nothing at all to do with the translator's knowledge of the language he
is translating. The changes definitely point to the existence of another kind of constraint, and they also show that the translators are fully aware of its existence; there
would be no earthly reason to change the text otherwise. Translations are produced
under constraints that go far beyond those of natural language – in fact, other constraints are often much more influential in the shaping of the translation than are the
semantic or linguistic ones.

A refraction (whether it is translation, criticism, historiography) which tries to
carry a work of literature over from one system into another, represents a compromise between two systems and is, as such, the perfect indicator of the dominant
constraints in both systems. The gap between the two hierarchies of constraints
explains why certain works do not "take," or enjoy at best an ambiguous position
in the system they are imported into.

The degree of compromise in a refraction will depend on the reputation of the
writer being translated within the system from which the translation is made. When
Hays translated Brecht in 1941, Brecht was a little-known German immigrant,
certainly not among the canonized writers of the Germany of his time (which had
burnt his books eight years before). He did not enjoy the canonized status of a
Thomas Mann. By the time Bentley translates Brecht, the situation has changed:
Brecht is not yet canonized in the West, but at least he is talked about. When
Manheim and Willett start bringing out Brecht's collected works in English, they
are translating a canonized author, who is now translated more on his own terms
(according to his own poetics) than on those of the receiving system. A historio-
graphical refraction in the receiving system appearing in 1976 grants that Brecht
"unquestionably can be regarded, with justice, as one of the 'classic authors' of the
twentieth century."[7]

The degree to which the foreign writer is accepted into the native system will,
on the other hand, be determined by the need that native system has of him in a
certain phase of its evolution. The need for Brecht was greater in England than in
the US. The enthusiastic reception of the Berliner Ensemble by a large segment
of the British audience in 1956, should also be seen in terms of the impact it made
on the debate as to whether or not a state-subsidized National Theater should be
set up in England. The opposition to a National Theater could "at last be effectively

silenced by pointing to the Berliner Ensemble, led by a great artist, consisting of young, vigorous and anti-establishment actors and actresses, wholly experimental, overflowing with ideas – and state-subsidized to the hilt."[8] Where the "need" for the foreign writer is felt, the critical establishment will be seen to split more easily. That is, part of the establishment will become receptive to the foreign model, or even positively champion it: "Tynan became drama critic of the London *Observer* in 1954, and very soon made the name of Brecht his trademark, his yardstick of values."[9] In the US, that role was filled by Eric Bentley, but he did have to tread lightly for a while. His 1951 anthology, *The Play*, does not contain any work by Brecht; he also states in the introduction that "undue preoccupation with content, with theme, has been characteristic of Marxist critics."[10] In 1966, on the other hand, Series Three of *From the Modern Repertoire*, edited by Eric Bentley, is "dedicated to the memory of Bertolt Brecht."[11] All this is not to imply any moral judgment. It just serves to point out the very real existence of ideological constraints in the production and dissemination of refractions.

Refractions of Brecht's work available to the Anglo-Saxon reader who needs them are mainly of three kinds: translation, criticism, and historiography. I have looked at a representative sample of the last two kinds, and restricted translation analysis to *Mother Courage*. Brecht is not represented at all in thirteen of the introductory drama anthologies published between 1951 (which is not all that surprising) and 1975 (which is). These anthologies, used to introduce the student to drama, do play an important part in the American literary system. In effect, they determine which authors are to be canonized. The student entering the field, or the educated layman, will tend to accept the selections, offered in these anthologies as "classics," without questioning the ideological, economic, and aesthetic constraints which have influenced the selections. As a result, the plays frequently anthologized achieve a position of relative hegemony. The very notion of an alternative listing is no longer an option for the lay reader. Thus, formal education perpetuates the canonization of certain works of literature, and school and college anthologies play an immensely important part in this essentially conservative movement within the literary system.

When Brecht is represented in anthologies of the type just described, the play chosen is more likely to be either *The Good Woman of Sezuan* or *The Caucasian Chalk Circle*. From the prefaces to the anthologies it is obvious that a certain kind of poetics, which cannot be receptive to Brecht, can still command the allegiance of a substantial group of refractors within the American system. Here are a few samples, each of which is diametrically opposed to the poetics Brecht himself tried to elaborate: "the story must come to an inevitable end; it does not just stop, but it comes to a completion."[12] Open-ended plays, such as *Mother Courage*, will obviously not fit in. Soliloquy and aside are admitted to the inventory component of the drama's poetics, but with reservations: "both of these devices can be used very effectively in the theater, but they interrupt the action and must therefore be used sparingly"[13] – which does, of course, rule out the alienation effect. "The amount of story presented is foreshortened in a play: the action is initiated as close as possible to the final issue. The incidents are of high tension to start with, and the tension increases rapidly"[14] – which precludes the very possibility of epic drama. The important point here is that these statements are passed off as describing "the" drama as such, from a position of total authority. This poetics also pervades the 1969 *Britannica* entry on Brecht, which states quite logically and consistently that "he was often bad at creating living characters or at giving his plays tension and scope."[15]

Brecht "did not make refraction any easier," by insisting on his own poetics, which challenged traditional assumptions about drama. Refractors who do have a receptive attitude towards Brecht find themselves in the unenviable position of dealing with a poetics alien to the system they are operating in. There are a number of strategies for dealing with this. One can recognize the value of the plays themselves, while dismissing the poetics out of hand: "the theory of alienation was only so much nonsense, disproved by the sheer theatricality of all his better works."[16] One can also go in for the psychological cop-out, according to which Brecht's poetics can be dismissed as a rationalization of essentially irrational factors: "theory does not concern me. I am convinced that Brecht writes as he does, not so much from a predetermined calculation based on what he believes to be the correct goals for the present revolutionary age, as from the dictates of temperament."[17] A third strategy for adapting a refraction to the native system is to integrate the new poetics into the old one by translating its concepts into the more familiar terminology of the old poetics: "if there is *anagnorisis* (italics mine) in *Mother Courage*, it doesn't take place on stage, as in the Aristotelian tradition, but in the auditorium of Brecht's epic theatre."[18] The final strategy is to explain the new poetics and to show that the system can, in fact, accommodate it, and can allow it to enter into the inventory and functional components of its poetics, without necessarily going to pieces: "some critics have interpreted alienation to mean that the audience should be in a constant state of emotional detachment, but in actuality Brecht manipulated aesthetic distance to involve the spectator emotionally and then jar him out of his emphatic response so that he may judge critically what he has experienced."[19]

The same strategies surface again in interpretations of *Mother Courage* itself: (i) *Variety*'s review of the 1963 Broadway production: "sophomorically obvious, cynical, selfconsciously drab and tiresome (ii)."[20] "His imagination and his own love of life created a work that transcends any thesis . . . He could not take away Mother Courage's humanity; even rigidly Marxist critics still saw her as human (iii)."[21]

> The Zürich audience of 1941 may have come away with only sympathy for Courage the Mother who, like Niobe, sees her children destroyed by more powerful forces but struggles on regardless. But to see the play solely in these terms is to turn a blind eye to at least half the text, and involves complete disregard for Brecht's methods of characterization.[22]

"Mother Courage learns nothing and follows the troops. The theme, in lesser hands, might well have led to an idealisation of the poor and the ignorant. Brecht made no concessions, showing Mother Courage for nothing better than she is, cunning, stubborn, bawdy (iv)."[23]

Of the three translations, Manheim's is situated between iii and iv. Both Hays and Bentley weave in and out of ii and iii. The main problem seems to be to accommodate Brecht's directness of diction to the poetics of the Broadway stage. Hence the tendency in both Hays and Bentley to "make clear" to the spectator or reader what Brecht wanted that reader or spectator to piece together for himself. Brecht's stage direction: "Die stumme Kattrin springt vom Wagen und stösst rauhe Laute aus" is rendered by Hays as "Dumb Kattrin makes a hoarse outcry *because she notices the abduction*" (B37/H12 – Italics mine). Mother Courage's words to Kattrin: "Du bist selber ein Kreuz: du hast ein gutes Herz" are translated by Hays as "You're a cross yourself. *What sort of a help to me are you? And all the same* what a good heart you have" (B34/H11) and by Manheim as "you're a cross yourself *because* you have a good heart" (B34/M142) – what is italicized is not in the German. Bentley tries to solve the problem of making Brecht completely "lucid" by means of excessive use of hyphens and italics: "Wer seid ihr?" becomes "Who'd you think *you* are?" instead of plain "Who are you?" (B25/B4). "Aber zu fressen haben wir auch nix" is turned into "A fat lot of difference that makes, *we* haven't got anything to eat either" (B39/B13), instead of "we don't have anything to eat either" and "der Feldhauptmann wird Ihnen den Kopf abreissen, wenn nix aufm Tisch steht" is rendered as "I know your problem: if you don't find something to eat and quick, the Chief will-cut-your-fat-head-off" (B40/B14) instead of "the captain will tear your head off if there's nothing on the table."

Hays and Bentley also do their best to integrate the songs fully into the play, approximating the model of the musical. For example, Bentley adds "transitional lines" between the spoken text and the song in "Das Lied vom Weib und dem Soldaten," thus, also, giving the song more of a musical flavor:

> To a soldier lad comes an old fishwife
> and this old fishwife says she (B45/B18).

In the translation there is a tendency towards the vague, the abstract, the cliché. The need to rhyme, moreover, leads to excessive padding, where the original is jarring and concrete, as in

> Ihr Hauptleut, eure Leut marschieren
> Euch ohne Wurst nicht in den Tod
> Lasst die Courage sie erst kurieren
> Mit Wein von Leib und Geistesnot
>
> (Commanders, your men
> won't march to their death without sausage
> Let Courage heal them first
> with wine of the pains of body and soul),

which Hays translates as

> Bonebare this land and picked of meat
> The fame is yours but where's the bread?
> So here I bring you food to eat
> And wine to slake and soothe your dread (B25/4)

Bentley also makes the text of the songs themselves conform more to the style and the register of the musical. The lapidary, and therefore final

In einer trüben Früh
Begann mein Qual und Müh
Das Regiment stand im Geviert
Dann ward getrommelt, wies der Brauch
Dann ist der Feind, mein Liebster auch
Aus unsrer Stadt marschiert

(one drab morning
my pain and sorrow began
the regiment stood in the square
then they beat the drums, as is the custom
Then the enemy, my beloved too
marched out of our town)

is padded out with a string of clichés into

The springtime's soft amour
Through summer may endure
But swiftly comes the fall
And winter ends it all
December came. All of the men
Filed past the trees where once we hid
Then quickly marched away and did
Not come back again (B55/B23).

Little of Brecht is left, but the seasons and the sad reminiscence, so often *de rigueur* for Broadway, are certainly in evidence. The musical takes over completely when Bentley translates

ein Schnaps, Wirt, sei g'scheit
Ein Reiter hat keine Zeit
Muss für sein Kaiser streiten

(A schnapps, mine host, be quick
A soldier on horseback has no time
he has to fight for his emperor)

as

One schnapps, mine host, be quick, make haste!
A soldier's got no time to waste
He must be shooting, shooting, shooting
His Kaiser's enemies uprooting (B101/B49).

Other refrain lines in the song are treated with great consistency: "Er muss gen Mähren reiten" becomes

He must be hating, hating, hating
he cannot keep his Kaiser waiting

instead of the more prosaic "he has to go fight in Moravia," which is in the German text, while "Er muss fürn Kaiser sterben" is turned into

> He must be dying, dying, dying
> His Kaiser's greatness glorifying (B101/B50),

whereas the German merely means "he has to die for his emperor." The least that can charitably be said is that Bentley obviously works to a different poetics than Brecht; he must have believed that this difference would make Brecht more acceptable than a straight translation. These examples again make it clear that the problem lies not with the dictionary, that it is not one of semantic equivalence, but rather one of a compromise between two kinds of poetics, in which the poetics of the receiving system plays the dominant part.

The terse, episodic structure of Brecht's play and the stage directions designed to give some hint as to the way actors should act are two more features of the Brechtian poetics not seen as easily transferable from one system to another. Hays therefore redivides Brecht's text into acts and scenes, in accordance with the norms of receiving poetics. Bentley keeps Brecht's scenes, while giving each of them a title, which turns out to be the first line of Brecht's text. Both turn a lapidary stage direction like "Wenn der Koch kommt, sieht er verdutzt sein Zeug" (when the cook enters, he starts as he sees his things) into something more elaborate, more familiar to a generation of actors brought up on Stanislavsky: "Then the Cook returns, still eating. He stares in astonishment at his belongings" and "A gust of wind. Enter the Cook, still chewing. He sees his things" (B192/H72/B72). Even Manheim does not always trust Brecht on his own: when Kattrin is dead, Mother Courage says: "Vielleicht schlaft sie." The translation reads: "Maybe I can get her to sleep." Mother Courage then sings the lullaby and adds "Now she's asleep" (B153/M209) – the addition is not in the original. Similarly, when Mother Courage decides not to complain to the captain after all, but simply to get up and leave, thereby ending the scene, Bentley adds a stage direction: "The scrivener looks after her, shaking his head" (B90/B44).

Brechtian dialogue is another problem. It must be made to flow more if it is to fit in with the poetics of the receiving system. As a result, lines are redistributed: actors should obviously not be allowed to stand around for too long, without anything to say. Consequently:

> Yvette: Dann Können wir ja suchen gehn, ich geh gern herum und such mir was aus, ich geh gern mit dir herum, Poldi, das ist ein Vergnügen, nicht? Und wenns zwei wochen dauert?
>
> (Then we can go look, I love walking about and looking for things, I love walking about with you, Poldi, it's so nice, isn't it? Even if it takes two weeks?)

becomes

> Yvette: Yes, we can certainly look around for something. I love going around looking, I love going around with you, Poldy. . . .

> The Colonel: Really? Do you?
> Yvette: Oh, it's lovely. I could take two weeks of it!
> The Colonel: Really? Could you? (B76/B36).

In the same way a little emotion is added where emotion is too patently lacking, and never mind Brecht's poetics. Yvette's denunciation of the Cook: "das ist der schlimmste, wo an der ganzen flandrischen Küste herumgelaufen ist. An jedem Finger eine, die er ins Unglück gebracht hat" becomes "he's a bad lot. You won't find a worse on the whole coast of Flanders. He got more girls in trouble than . . . (*concentrating on the cook*) Miserable cur! Damnable whore hunter! Inveterate seducer!" (B125/B63). The stage direction and what follows it have been added.

Brecht's ideology is treated in the same way as his poetics in critical refractions produced in the receiving system. Sometimes it is dismissed in none too subtle ways: "Brecht made changes in the hope of suggesting that things might have been different had Mother Courage acted otherwise" (What could she have done? Established Socialism in seventeenth-century Germany?).[24] Sometimes it is engulfed in psychological speculation: "in a world without God, it was Marx's vision that saved Brecht from nihilistic despair"[25] and "Communist ideology provided Brecht with a rational form of salvation, for it indicated a clearly marked path leading out of social chaos and mass misery. At the same time, Communist discipline provided Brecht's inner life with the moral straitjacket he desperately needed at this time."[26]

Attempts to integrate Brecht into the American value system start by fairly acknowledging the problem: "Brecht's status as a culture hero of Communist East Germany further enhanced his appeal to the left and correspondingly diminished his chances of ever pleasing the artistic and political right wing,"[27] and end by stating the influence that the ideology Brecht subscribed to is supposed to have exerted on his artistic productions: "Nevertheless, Brecht maintains a neutral stance. That is, he pretends not to have any specific remedy in mind, although it is generally agreed that he favored a socialistic or communistic society. But he avoids saying so in his plays and instead declares that the audience must make up its own mind."[28] The multiplication of statements like this last one in recent years indicates a growing acceptance of Brecht in the receiving system. The Manheim translation, chronologically the latest, is easily the "best" of the three translations examined here, since it translates Brecht more on his own terms. But things are not that simple. It would be easy to say – as traditional translation studies have done time and again – that "Manheim is good; Hays and Bentley are both bad." It would be closer to the truth, however, to say that Manheim can afford to be good because Hays, and especially Bentley, translated Brecht before he did. They focused attention on Brecht and, in so doing, they got the debate going. If they had translated Brecht on his own terms to begin with, disregarding the poetics of the receiving system, chances are that the debate would never have got going in the first place – witness the disastrous performance of Brecht's *The Mother* in 1936. Hays and Bentley established a bridgehead for Brecht in another system; to do so, they had to compromise with the demands of the poetics and the patronage dominant in that system.

This is not to suggest that there is some kind of necessary progression ranging from the less acceptable all the way to the "definitive" translation – that Brecht, in other words, need now no longer be translated. Both the natural language and the politics of the receiving system keep changing; the spectrum through which refractions are made changes in the course of time. It is entirely possible, e.g., that Brecht can be used in the service of a poetics diametrically opposed to his own, as in the Living Theater's production of *Antigone*. To put this briefly in a somewhat wider context, it is good to remember that literary systems are stochastic, not mechanistic. Producers of both refracted and original literature do not operate as automatons under the constraints of their time and location. They devise various strategies to live with these constraints, ranging hypothetically from full acceptance to full defiance. The categories that a systems approach makes use of are formulated in some kind of "inertial frame," similar to the ideal world physicists postulate, in which all experiments take place under optimal conditions, and in which all laws operate unfailingly. Like the laws of physics, the categories of the systems approach have to be applied to individual cases in a flexible manner.

Hays and Bentley treat ideological elements in *Mother Courage* in ways roughly analogous to those used by their fellow refractors, the critics. Translating in 1941, Hays consistently plays down the aggressive pacifism of the play, omitting whole speeches like the bitterly ironical

> Wie alles Gute ist auch der Krieg am Anfang hält schwer zu machen. Wenn er dann erst floriert, ist er auch zäh: dann schrecken die Leute zurück vorm Frieden wie die Würfler vorn Aufhören, weil dann müssens zahlen, was sie verloren haben. Aber zuerst schreckens zurück vorm Krieg. Er ist ihnen was Neues.

> (Like all good things, war is not easy in the beginning. But once it gets going, it's hard to get rid of; people become afraid of peace like dice players who don't want to stop, because then they have to pay up. But in the beginning they are afraid of the war. It's new to them.)

Hays also weakens the obvious connection between war and commerce in the person of Mother Courage by omitting lines Brecht gives her, like, "Und jetzt fahren wir weiter, es ist nicht alle Tage Krieg, ich muss tummeln" (and now let's drive on; there isn't a war on every day, I have to get cracking). Bentley, translating after the Second World War, nevertheless follows partly the same course:

> Man merkts, hier ist zu lang kein Krieg gewesen. Wo soll da Moral herkommen, frag ich? Frieden, das ist nur Schlamperei, erst der Krieg schafft Ordnung. Die Menschheit schiesst ins Kraut im Frieden.

> (You can see there hasn't been a war here for too long. Where do you get your morals from, then, I ask you? Peace is a sloppy business, you need a war to get order. Mankind runs wild in peace.)

simply becomes "what they could do with here is a good war" (B22/B3). In addition, certain war-connected words and phrases are put into a nobler register in translation: "Wir zwei gehn dort ins Feld und tragen die Sach aus unter Männern" (the two of us will go out into that field and settle this business like men) becomes "the two of us will now go and settle the affair on the field of honor" (B30/B8) and "mit Spiessen und Kanonen" (with spears and guns) is rendered as "with fire and sword" (B145/B76). Not surprisingly, Manheim, translating later and in a more Brecht-friendly climate, takes the opposite direction and makes the pacifism more explicit, rendering

> So mancher wollt so manches haben
> Was es für manchen gar nicht gab
>
> (so many wanted so much
> that was not available for many)

as

> Some people think they'd like to ride out
> The war, leave danger to the brave (B113/M185).

Comprehension of the text in its semantic dimension is not the issue; the changes can be accounted for only in terms of ideology.

Finally, both Hays and Bentley eschew Brecht's profanities in their translations, submitting to the code of the US entertainment industry at the time the translations were written, albeit with sometimes rather droll results: "führt seine Leute in die Scheissgass," e.g., (leads his people up shit creek) becomes "leads his people into the smoke of battle" and "leads his soldiers into a trap" (B45/H17/B17); and "Du hast mich beschissen" is turned into "A stinking trick!" and "You've fouled me up!" (B33/H9/B9). Even Manheim, years later, goes easy on the swear words: "der gottverdammte Hund von einem Rittmeister" is toned down to "that stinking captain" (B83/M170).

The economic aspect of refraction is touched on in some of the prefaces to the anthologies in which Brecht is not represented, and in some of the reviews of American productions of *Mother Courage*. The economics of inclusion or exclusion obviously have something to do with copyright; it is not all that easy (or cheap) to get permission to reprint Brecht in English, and certain editors just give up – the economic factor in its purest form. Less obvious, but no less powerful, economic considerations are alluded to by Barnet in the introduction to *Classic Theatre*, a collection of plays designed to be the companion volume to the Public Broadcasting System's series of the same name, and therefore doubly under economic pressure. First, the order in which the plays are presented

> is nearly chronological: the few exceptions were made to serve the balance of television programming. Thus, because the producers wished the series to begin with a well-known play, Shakespeare's *Macbeth* (written about 1605–6) precedes Marlowe's *Edward II* (written in the early 1590s).[29]

It further turns out that two of the "classics" have never been written for the "theatre" at all, but that they were written more or less directly for the series, or certainly for television: "of the thirteen plays in this book, two were written for television, one of these is an adaptation of Voltaire's prose fiction, *Candide*, and the other is a play about the life of the English poet John Milton."[30] It is hard to see what these plays could possibly have to do with either "classic" or "theatre," and there would certainly have been room for Brecht if one or the other of them had been left out. The conclusion must be that Brecht was still, in 1975, considered commercially and poetically too unsafe (and maybe also too expensive) for inclusion in a series on "classic theatre." The same introduction claims that "the most vital theatre in the second half of the twentieth century is a fairly unified body of drama neatly labelled the "Theatre of the Absurd,"[31] hailing Artaud as the most pervasive influence on the modern stage.

The *Variety* review of the 1963 Broadway production of *Mother Courage* asks the million dollar question: "why should anyone think it might meet the popular requirements of Broadway – that is, be commercial," thus pointing with brutal honesty to an important element in American patronage Brecht never managed to get on his side. In 1963, Brecht's patrons could not guarantee a more or less complete production of his work under prevailing economic regulations:

> The original text contains nine songs. I have the impression that several of these have been cut – probably because, if they were retained, the time allowed to sing and play them might exceed twenty-four minutes and the Musicians' Union would list the production as a "musical." According to regulations, this classification would entail the employment of twenty-four musicians at heavy cost.[32]

And yet, to the Broadway goer with no German, or even to the Broadway goer with German, who prefers to watch plays rather than to read them, that was Brecht's *Mother Courage*. The refraction, in other words, is the original to the great majority of people who are only tangentially exposed to literature. Indeed, it would hardly be an exaggeration to say that this kind of reader is influenced by literature precisely through refractions, and little else. In the US, he or she will tell you that *Moby Dick* is a great novel, one of the masterpieces of American literature. He will tell you so because he has been told so in school, because she has read comic strips and extracts in anthologies, and because captain Ahab will forever look like Gregory Peck as far as he or she is concerned. It is through critical refractions that a text establishes itself inside a given system (from the article in learned magazines to that most avowedly commercial of all criticism, the blurb, which is usually much more effective in selling the book than the former). It is through translations combined with critical refractions (introductions, notes, commentary accompanying the translation, articles on it) that a work of literature produced outside a given system takes its place in that "new" system. It is through refractions in the social system's educational set-up that canonization is achieved and, more importantly, maintained. There is a direct link between college syllabi and paperback publishers' backlists of classics (Mann's *The Magic Mountain* and *Dr. Faustus* rather than *Joseph and His Brothers*).

All this is by no means intended to be moralistic; I am not lamenting an existing state of affairs, I am merely describing it and suggesting that it is eminently worthy of description, since refractions are what keeps a literary system going. They have been ignored by Romanticism-based approaches to literature, but they have been there all along. Their role should not be overestimated, but it should no longer be underestimated either.

Brecht defined his poetics against the dominant poetics of his time in Germany, and he managed to win a certain degree of acceptance for them by the time he died. He had achieved this through a combination of "original work" (the texts of the plays, the theoretical writings) and refractions: productions of his plays, reviews of those productions, translations, the ensuing critical industry. The functional component of his poetics (what the theater is for) was a fairly radical departure from the prevailing poetics of his time (though perhaps not so radical when compared to the poetics of a previous historical manifestation of the system he worked in, namely medieval morality plays), despite the fact that many of the devices he used existed in non-canonized forms of the theater of his time (Valentin's cabaret, e.g.) or in the theater of other cultures (Chinese opera, e.g.).

Small wonder, then, that a Romanticism-based approach to literature should ask the wretched question "in how far is all this new?" It is a wretched question because nothing is ever new; the new is a combination of various elements from the old, the non-canonized, imports from other systems (at about the same time Brecht was experimenting with adaptations from Chinese opera, the Chinese poet Feng Chi refracted the European sonnet into Chinese) rearranged to suit alternative functional views of literature. This holds true for both the implicit and the explicit concept of a poetics, *and* for individual works of literature which are, to a certain extent, recombinations of generic elements, plots, motifs, symbols, etc. – in fact, essentially the "piecing together of other people's ideas," but in such a way as to give them a novel impact.

The question of originality is also wretched because it prevents so many adherents of Romanticism-based approaches to literature from seeing so many things. Originality can only exist if texts are consistently isolated from the tradition and the environment in which (against which) they were produced. Their freshness and timelessness, their sacred and oracular status are achieved at a price: the loss of history, the continuum of which they are a part and which they help to (re)shape. Literature in general, and individual works, can, in the final analysis, be contemplated, commented on, identified with, applied to life, in a number of essentially subjective ways; and these activities are all refractions designed to influence the way in which the reader receives the work, concertizes it. Present-day refractions usually operate on underlying principles essentially alien to literature and imported into it, such as psychoanalysis and philosophy. In other words, the "natural" framework of investigation that was lost for literary studies when originality became the over-riding demand, has to be replaced by frameworks imported from other disciplines, a state of affairs rendered perhaps most glaringly obvious in the very way in which works of literature are presented to students who are beginning the task of studying literature: syllabi, reading lists, anthologies, more often than not offering disparate texts and pieces of texts, brought together in a more or less arbitrary manner to serve the demands of the imposed framework.

The word, then, can only be said to really create the world, as the Romanticism-based approaches would have it, if it is carefully isolated from the world in which it originates. And that is, in the end, impossible; the word does not create a world *ex nihilo*. Through the grid of tradition it creates a counterworld, one that is fashioned under the constraints of the world the creator lives and works in, and one that can be explained, understood better if these constraints are taken into account.

If not, all explanation becomes necessarily reductionistic in character, essentially subservient to the demands of imported frameworks.

A systems approach to literature, emphasizing the role played by refractions, or rather, integrating them, revalidates the concept of literature as something that is made, not in the vacuum of unfettered genius, for genius is never unfettered, but out of the tension between genius and the constraints that genius has to operate under, accepting them or subverting them. A science of literature, a type of activity that tries to devise an "imaginative picture" of the literary phenomenon in all its ramifications, to devise theories that make more sense of more phenomena than their predecessors (that are more or less useful, not more or less true), and that does so on the basis of the methodology that is currently accepted by the consensus of the scientific community, while developing its own specific methods suited to its own specific domain, will also have to study refractions. It will have to study the part they play in the evolution of a literary system, and in the evolution of literary systems as such. It will also have to study the laws governing that evolution: the constraints that help shape the poetics that succeed each other within a given system, and the poetics of different systems as well as individual works produced on the basis of a given poetics, or combination of poetics.

A systems approach does not try to influence the evolution of a given literary system, the way critical refractions and many translations avowedly written in the service of a certain poetics tend to do. It does not try to influence the reader's concretization of a given text in a certain direction. Instead, it aims at giving the reader the most complete set of materials that can help him or her in the concretization of the text, a set of materials he or she is free to accept or reject.

A systems approach to literary studies aims at making literary texts accessible to the reader, by means of description, analysis, historiography, translation, produced not on the basis of a given, transient poetics (which will, of course, take great pains to establish itself as absolute and eternal), but on the basis of that desire to know, which is itself subject to constraints not dissimilar to the ones operating in the literary system, a desire to know not as literature itself knows, but to know the ways in which literature offers its knowledge, which is so important that it should be shared to the greatest possible extent.

Notes

The text of Brecht's *Mutter Courage und ihre Kinder* referred to in this article is that published by Aufbau Verlag, Berlin in 1968. H.R. Hays' translation was published by New Directions, New York, in the anthology for the year 1941. It was obviously based on the first version of *Mother Courage*, and I have taken that into account in my analysis. The Bentley translation I refer to is the one published by Methuen in London in 1967. The Manheim translation is the one published in volume five of the collected plays of Bertolt Brecht, edited by Manheim and John Willet, and published by Vintage Books, New York in 1972.

1   Martin Esslin, *Reflections* (New York, 1969), p. 79.
2   *Encyclopedia Britannica* (Chicago, 1969), IV, 144a.

3   A. C. Ward, ed., *The Longman Companion to Twentieth Century Literature* (London, 1970), p. 88a.

4   Esslin, *Reflections*, p. 83.

5   S. Kunitz., ed., *Twentieth Century Authors, First Supplement* (New York, 1965), p. 116a.

6   Quoted in K. H. Schieps, *Bertolt Brecht* (New York, 1977), p. 265.

7   A. Nicoll, ed., *World Drama* (New York, 1976), p. 839.

8   Esslin, *Reflections*, p. 75–76.

9   Esslin, *Reflections*, p. 76.

10   E. Bentley, ed., *The Play* (Englewood Cliffs, 1951), p. 6.

11   E. Bentley, ed., *From the Modern Repertoire, Series Three*, (Bloomington, 1966), p. i.

12   S. Barnet, M. Berman and W. Burto, eds, *Classic Theatre: The Humanities in Drama* (Boston, 1975), p. v.

13   L. Perrine, ed., *Dimensions of Drama* (New York, 1970), p. 4.

14   L. Altenberg and L. L. Lewis, ed., *Introduction to Literature: Plays* (New York, 1969), p. 2.

15   *Encyclopedia Britannica*, IV, 144a.

16   M. Gottfried, *Opening Nights* (New York, 1969), p. 239.

17   H. Clurman, "Bertolt Brecht" in *Essays in Modern Drama*, ed. M. Freedman (Boston, 1974), p. 152.

18   K. A. Dickson, *Towards Utopia* (Oxford, 1978), p. 108.

19   O. G. Brockett, *Perspectives on Contemporary Theatre* (Baton Rouge, 1971), p. 216.

20   *Variety* review of the 1963 Broadway production, quoted in Schieps, *Bertolt Brecht*, p. 265.

21   M. Seymour-Smith, *Funk and Wagnall's Guide to World Literature* (New York, 1973), p. 642.

22   M. Morley, *Brecht* (London, 1977), p. 58.

23   K. Richardson, ed., *Twentieth Century Writings* (London, 1969), p. 89.

24   E. Bentley, ed., *The Great Playwrights* (New York, 1970), p. 2169.

25   J. A. Bédé and W.B. Edgerton, eds, *The Columbia Dictionary of Modern European Literature* (New York, 1980), p. 116a.

26   Bédé and Edgerton, *Columbia Dictionary*, p. 114b.

27   Esslin, *Reflections*, p. 77.

28   Brockett, *Perspectives*, p. 125.

29   Barnet, *Classic Theatre*, p. v.

30   Barnet, *Classic Theatre*, p. xvii.

31   Barnet, *Classic Theatre*, p. xviii.

32   H. Clurman, *The Naked Image* (New York, 1966), p. 62.

Chapter 21

Philip E. Lewis

THE MEASURE OF TRANSLATION EFFECTS

Difference in translation

C AN WE OR SHOULD WE be indifferent to the fact that this essay about the difference that translation makes is itself a kind of "free" translation? Does it matter that, under a quite different title,[1] the first version of these remarks was composed, presented, eventually revised, and published in French?[2] In what respect might it be significant that [this] piece for [the] book, *Difference in Translation*, enacts the process of translation, is a performance of translation?

We shall never really leave the terrain on which these somewhat embarrassed questions lie. For the moment, however, let us not pretend that we can tackle them head-on, or indeed that we can ever address them decisively. Let us be content with developing, in order to introduce the problem of translation with which we are trying to reckon, a single comment concerning the change in title. The original essay bore a resolutely tentative title, "Vers la traduction abusive," and had a somewhat programmatic cast; it sought to set forth in more or less theoretical terms a strategy that a translator of Derrida might well consider adopting. By contrast, the title "The Measure of Translation Effects" displaces the emphasis so as to take into account and reappropriate the ambivalence of the portentous heading "Difference in Translation." In the first place, "measure" refers to the means or process by which we can perceive the action of difference – the workings of a principle of fragmentation – in translation. In the second place, "effects" shifts the stress away from the program for strong translation toward a consideration of the results or consequences of translation. Putting these two references together, the preposition "of" discreetly

allows an alternative sense of measure – as a state of moderation, restraint, regulation – to come into play, just as the preposition "in" in "Difference in Translation,"
allows difference to signify either the active principle in translation or the product
of translation. "Of" and "in" are charges of discursive dynamite. In titles, where they
are parts of nominal phrases that initially appear underdetermined (since the titular
function is precisely to inaugurate the elaboration of a context as yet unset), these
stealthy little prepositors are versatile and indecisive; they readily enable a vacilla-
tion between two modes, active and passive, transitive and intransitive, on either
side of the relation they splice. "Of" and "in" are interpositional yokes allowing the
nominal forms – "difference," "translation," "measure," and even "effect" – to designate *indifferently* here a state or accomplished fact, there an activity or operative
principle. So the new title backs away from the lean into theoretical prescription
of the French "Vers la traduction abusive" (by contrast with "of" or "in," the preposition *vers* is unequivocally directional); it shifts the accent away from the tentative
program for translating Derrida and toward reflection on what translation actually
is and does, on how we might measure – understand and evaluate – its effects. But
in what sense does this shift entail translation? Is "The Measure of Translation
Effects" indeed a translation?

The literal rendering "Toward Abusive Translation" would doubtless be a
possible title in English. Yet that title fails to ring true. In part the reason is that
the English word "abusive" (meaning wrongful, injurious, insulting, and so forth)
does not immediately pick up another connotation of the French cognate: false,
deceptive, misleading, and so forth. Yet this is by no means the only consideration
underlying the recourse to a different title and with it an immediately altered slant.
The shift in question here has to do with the English language and concomitantly
with the Anglo-American intellectual environment that is circumscribed by the
language. In translating the French text, I want to achieve more than a stilted transfer
of meanings, to make it "work" in English, to endow it with the texture of a piece
written in English for an English-speaking audience. Now, my intuitive sense as a
native speaker of English who teaches in an American university is that a discussion
emphasizing the practical processes and concrete results of translation will work
better, fit in better, go down and over better, than a somewhat more theoretical
excursus on shall we say, "translativity" – on the conditions that make possible and
govern the work of translation.

This initially subjective hunch about what will sit well with an Anglophonic
audience – and how, therefore, the French original of this paper might best be
carried over (translate: from the Latin *trans* + *latus*, "carried across") into an English
version – is strongly reinforced by empirical research in contrastive linguistics. An
excellent case in point is a powerful book by the French linguist Jacqueline
Guillemin-Flescher, *Syntaxe comparée du français et de l'anglais: Problèmes de traduction*.[3]
In this work of applied discourse analysis, a comparative study of several translations of Flaubert's *Madame Bovary* serves as the principal basis for identifying a
number of important differences between French and English. Following the lead
of Antoine Culioli, Guillemin-Flescher sets her comparison of French and English
within a complex system of linguistic communication that includes the utterance,
the enunciation or act of utterance, the interlocutionary relations of an enunciator

and a coenunciator, and the dimension of reference. This allows for a number of levels of comparison and leads to remarks on syntax (for example, English tends to prefer fully formed, assertive clauses, whereas French is content with participial phrases or relatively elliptical expressions) and on aspect (English requires more, and more precise, aspectual markers) that analytically confirm tendencies long recognized by grammarians.

The big step forward in Guillemin-Flescher's work depends on the generalized scope of her analysis. Her achievement of a broadly inclusive comparison of the two languages is all the more impressive, since she carries it out while nonetheless pursuing exceedingly meticulous analysis of minute details. This interplay of microscopic analysis and large-scale comparison is one advantage that appears to derive directly from the purview of discourse analysis: the specific, often quite delicate operations it studies happen to be the ones that are responsible for cementing together large segments of discourse; when viewed collectively, those questions appear to constitute the structural orders or articulatory frames that allow extended textual constructs to develop cohesively. As Guillemin-Flescher's study proceeds, two such structural orders acquire over-arching importance: (1) "modes of enunciation," that is, besides the traditional grammatical modes, observation as distinct from commentary, direct discourse as distinct from indirect discourse; and also, in the last analysis, narrative as distinct from discourse; and (2) means or forms of *repérage*, that is, the frames of reference or processes of contextual binding internal to discourse, or, to put it a bit less abstrusely, the diverse relations – often made perceptible by deictics, sequence of tenses, iteratives, personal pronouns, positional adverbs, and so on – whereby terms refer to one another so as to mark the linkage between the enunciative situation and predication, between the subject and complement linked by predication, and between separate propositions or sentences. It is, of course, necessary to take stock of the detail and ordering of Guillemin-Flescher's analyses in order to appreciate their power and sophistication adequately. For our purposes here, however, we can derive the gain we need to make simply from weighing a handful of major points that her wide-sweeping comparison establishes demonstratively.

Here, then, are some of the characteristics of English that serve to contrast it with French:

1   A strong tendency to favor *actualization* (this word means roughly "concrete occurrence in a context"; actualization is thus defined in opposition to "abstract notion," so that, for example, the abstract term "heart" is actualized in the utterance "Frances' heart stopped beating at 10:47 this morning"; because it depends on the entire set of enunciative relations, actualization is a matter of degree, and its role is to be understood in relation to various forms of "disactualization," such as use of a term in conditional or hypothetical propositions, in statements that position it as having already occurred, and so forth).

2   A tendency to prefer direct or constative relations to the referent over commentary (this latter term is used in a technical sense to designate the operation whereby the discourse refers back to an element or set of elements or to a statement previously introduced in some manner; in other words, the constative/commentary distinction bears a certain resemblance to the

familiar opposition of narrative to description: the latter comments on elements posited by the former).

3   A strong tendency to tighten the network of internal linkages that bind the elements of discourse together and thereby to prefer a strict, precise, homogeneous set of relations to the looser, less forcefully determined relations that prevail in French.

4   As a corollary of point 3, a tendency to require consistency and compatibility of terms that are related in representations of reality (notable manifestations of this tendency surface in statements involving perception: (a) the tendency to orient the prevailing viewpoint around the category "alive/*human*"; and (b) the requirement of clear differentiation between observed and imagined reality).

What do contrastive observations such as these, arising from the comparison of original texts to translated texts, tell us about the problem of translating French into English? Clearly enough, there is a motif common to the four points summarized above. In both of the key domains – enunciative relations and referential operations – that Guillemin-Flescher highlights, English calls for more explicit, precise, concrete determinations, for fuller, more cohesive delineations than does French.

This difference, Guillemin-Flescher demonstrates massively, makes for innumerable problems in translation. The point is no longer merely the hackneyed though doubtless sensible claim that translation is "impossible" because the lexical correspondences between languages are imprecise (for example, because *la porte* in French does not have exactly the same meaning as "door" in English); nor, indeed, is the point the much more decisive one that translation is doomed to be inadequate because attempts to construct contrastive grammars powerful enough to support machine translation have revealed that a strong theory of translation, capable of prescribing correct choices, is not within reach. The point now is also that translation, when it occurs, has to move whatever meanings it captures from the original into a framework that tends to impose a different set of discursive relations and a different construction of reality. When English rearticulates a French utterance, it puts an interpretation on that utterance that is built into English; it simply cannot let the original say what it says in French, since it can neither allow the translated utterance to relate to previous utterances in the same chunk of discourse in the way the French statement does nor allow the English substitute to relate to the world it positions or describes in the way the French original does.

What comes into English from French will therefore be something different. This difference that depends on the dissimilarity of the languages is the difference always already in translation. As the very ground of translation – its raison d'être and its principle – it cannot be overcome. The difference that blocked or deferred communication in the mythical Babelian situation may be glossed over, but it never completely disappears; translation never suppresses it totally. The problem for the English-speaking interpreter of the French text might then be, initially, to specify in English what lost or modified enunciative and discursive relations are functioning in the French and what construction of reality is enacted by the French. For the translator, however, the problem is not the same; it is rather to reinscribe the

French message so as to make it comply with the discursive and referential structures of English, to put on the French text the particular interpretation inherent to English.

Or is it? For in fact the conventional view of translation puts the translator under pressure not simply to produce a version of the original that reads well or sounds right in the target language but also to understand and interpret the original masterfully so as to reproduce its messages faithfully. The very translation that imposes the interpretation attendant to its language should also offer an accurate interpretation, a re-presentation of the original. This contradictory exigency constitutes the classical translator's predicament: a good translation should be a double interpretation, faithful both to the language/message of the original and to the message-orienting cast of its own language. To say that translation is always already interpretation is therefore not enough: an adequate translation would be always already two interpretations, a double interpretation requiring, so to speak, a double writing; and it is the insurmountable fact that these two interpretations are mutually exclusive that consigns every translation to inadequacy.

The thrust of this comment on our question concerning the practice of translation being undertaken here, in this essay, should by now be fairly evident. Thanks to the opportunity to translate freely and expansively, a translator who is also the author of the original can undertake to do precisely what is not possible for the translator who works on the text of another author: in the present case, the author–translator can both interpret according to English and according to French, can shift at will between conventional translation that has to violate the original and commentary that attempts to compensate for the inadequacy of the translation. Such, it would seem, is the ready option of a translator determined not to allow the incidence of the translating language to assume a subtle priority, to do in the intricacies of the translated language. Even this option, we shall see, has insurmountable drawbacks. But by opening it up, perhaps we can appreciate better the lot of the translator who cannot have recourse to it, who is obliged, for example, simply to reproduce, for better or for worse, an English version of Derrida's ultra-refined French. The question for the translator deprived of the commentarial option is whether, and to what extent, anything can be done in translation to preserve the tenor or texture or tangents of the French that English would override. In the first instance, as I begin actually translating portions of the French version of this essay, I shall put the question to Derrida: what indicators might his writing offer us concerning the conduct of translation? Subsequently, I shall reapply the question, along with the answer, to the English translation of one of Derrida's most influential essays, "La mythologie blanche."

Abuse in translation

Translation could well, of course, be treated as a leitmotif in Derrida's work. Indeed, for initiates it is surely all too obvious that translation, as a concept and as a practice, falls within the larger framework of representation and mimesis, of analogy and metaphoricity, that Derrida has ushered through deconstructive analysis in his pursuit of a wide-ranging critical/historical account of metaphysics. Those same initiates will already have noticed a certain allusion to that analysis in my free introduction to this free translation: I have positioned translation as a form of representation that necessarily entails interpretation; and furthermore, I have observed that this re-presentation must seek futilely to mine two contradictory veins of interpretation. Such probing into representation and its derivatives could hardly fail to reflect, in its outlines, the project of deconstructive analysis that Derrida's early work persistently brought to bear on representation and that his recent work has often pursued specifically with respect to translation.

But I am not pretending to perform or reproduce Derridean deconstruction here in any serious or sustained way. For to attempt to repeat or resume or somehow reconstruct that analysis as it applies to translation would surely lead to precisely the form of failure – incompletion, distortion, infidelity – that is the inescapable lot of the translator. (We may reckon, then, that if the opportunity to disclaim makes the commentator's lot relatively more comfortable than the translator's, commentary is by no means an adequate solution: the only fidelity is exact repetition – of the original, in the original; and even that, it can well be argued, is finally a superficial fidelity.) As I have suggested, under normal circumstances the translator, confronted with the impossibility of importing signifiers and their associative chains from one language into another, and with the impossibility of transferring the original's structures of reference and enunciation, must try and fail to do the impossible, to elude infidelity. So granting this deplorable impasse occasioned by difference in translation, how, I am now asking, would Derrida deal with the risk and necessity of infidelity?

In "Le retrait de la métaphore," an essay translated into English under the daringly transliteral title of "The Retrait of Metaphor,"[4] Derrida has occasion to assert parenthetically, concerning the word *retrait*, with the adjective "good" in quotation marks, "une 'bonne' traduction doit toujours abuser" – "a 'good' translation must always commit abuses." Or perhaps "a good translation must always play tricks." Now, the point here is by no means to revalidate a superficial opposition of good to bad translation (to do so would be to fall prey to the kind of critical blows that are struck on the opposition of good and bad metaphor in "La mythologie blanche"); the point is rather to make clear the sense of a translation effect – the rendering, in Derrida's commentary, of the German *Entziehung* by the French term *retrait* – that, in relation to the text of Heidegger that Derrida is discussing, does not result from a simple concern for fidelity or adequacy but that, additionally, plays a strategic role in unveiling the possibility conditions that underlie Heidegger's statements on metaphor and doubtless underlie as well Derrida's extremely scrupulous criticism of Heidegger. In any case, the *retrait* functions not so much as a form of equivalence but as a factor in an *economy* of translation in a process of gain as well as loss that has to be conceived quantitatively rather than qualitatively, energetically rather than topically. The *retrait* will occasion a kind of controlled textual disruption: insofar as it is *abusive*, it exerts an unpacking and disseminating effect, and precisely that effect of the *retrait* as a textual operator makes it a "good" translation, justifies the translator's work on the original. The possibility that interests us here has to do with the use of abuse that is epitomized by this example: can we take it as a model? Can we reasonably extrapolate from it a kind of abuse principle? Can we proceed legitimately to use such a principle to measure effects wrought by the translation of Derrida's work?

Behind examples of capable translations such as the retrait or Derrida's celebrated rendering of Hegel's *Aufhebung* by a term, *la relève*, that can actually be incorporated into direct translations of Hegel's work, an inchoate axiology of translation can perhaps be glimpsed. On the one hand, the impossibility of a fully faithful translation points to a risk to be overcome, that of weak, servile translation, of a tendency to privilege what Derrida calls, in "La mythologie blanche," the *us*-system, that is, the chain of values linking the *usual*, the *useful*, and common linguistic *usage*. To accredit the use-values is inevitably to opt for what domesticates or familiarizes a message at the expense of whatever might upset or force or abuse language and thought, might seek after the unthought or unthinkable in the unsaid or unsayable. On the other hand, the real possibility of translation – the translatability that emerges in the movement of difference as a fundamental property of languages – points to a risk to be assumed: that of the strong, forceful translation that values experimentation, tampers with usage, seeks to match the polyvalencies or plurivocities or expressive stresses of the original by producing its own. But, it will quickly be asked, suppose we concede that the strength of translation lies in its abuses – in the productive difference consisting in that twist or skewing signaled by the prefix *ab* that is attached to the dominant c(h)ord of use: how far can the abuse be carried? does an abuse principle not risk sacrificing rigor to facility? sacrificing the faithful transmission of messages to playful tinkering with style and connotation?

No. The basic scruples of conventional translation – fidelity and intelligibility – remain intact and are indeed, in a sense, reinforced. Here is why. If the play of signifiers and the manipulation of enunciative and referential relations seem to make translation an activity of constant, inevitable compromise, this is not solely because the impossibility of transferring the linguistic substance of the original, as graphic or phonic elements on which both the higher-level relations and the effects of reception depend, makes for an inescapable difference in the translation. The translator's compromises also result from a tendency, specific to the translation of expository writing, to privilege the capture of signifieds, to give primacy to message, content, or concept over language texture. Now this means that the translating text works principally and principally by substitution and gives priority to re-presentational processes – to the identification of substitute signifiers, to metaphoricity – whereas it tends to subordinate or lose sight of the order of syntax or metonymy, in which the signifiers of the original are linked to one another and in which that more or less poetic activity that we might term "textual work" is carried on.

Now, on the horizon traced by Derrida, where the metaphoric concept of translation is thrown into question and where the clear-cut separability of signifier and signified, of force and meaning, is dismantled, what we face is never – never possibly – an utter collapse of distinctions or a withdrawal from the intelligible work of expression and translation; it is rather a new axiomatics of fidelity, one that requires attention to the chain of signifiers, to syntactic processes, to discursive structures, to the incidence of language mechanisms on thought and reality formation, and so forth. No less than in the translation of poetic texts, the demand is for fidelity to much more than semantic substance, fidelity also to the modalities of expression and to rhetorical strategies. A practice of abuse belongs, part and parcel, to this toughened exigency precisely because that abusiveness, in its multiple forms and functions, constitutes a modality in which this fidelity – we might call it an ab-imitative fidelity – to an analytic practice that is bound to a necessarily stratified, double-edged writing practice can be pursued. For the translator, the problem here can no longer be how to avoid the failures – the reductive and redirective interpretations – that disparity among natural languages assures; the problem is rather how to compensate for losses and to justify (in a graphological sense) the differences – how to renew the energy and signifying behaviour that a translation is likely to diffuse. In terms more germane to Derrida's move to displace the translation problem away from a logic of identity or equivalence, the question is how to supply for the inevitable lack.

So what is crucially at stake here is what the translation itself contributes, is that abuse, committed by the translator, whereby the translation goes beyond – fills in for – the original. But again, can this be just any abuse? The absurd question points up the salient features of the example we have used, the word *retrait*. In the first place, the abusive move in the translation cannot be directed at just any object, at just any element of the original; rather, it will bear upon a key operator or a decisive textual knot that will be recognized by dint of its own abusive features, by its resistance to the preponderant values of the "usual" and the "useful" that are placed under interrogation in "La mythologie blanche" and "Le retrait de la métaphore." Thus the abusive work of the translation will be oriented by specific nubs in the original, by points or passages that are in some sense forced, that stand out as clusters of textual energy – whether they are constituted by words, turns of phrase, or more elaborate formulations. In the second place, the abuse itself will take form in the translation in an ambivalent relation both with the text that it translates and with the language of the translation (the latter incorporates its own system of use-values to be resisted from within). No doubt the project we are envisaging here is ultimately impossible: the translator's aim is to rearticulate analogically the abuse that occurs in the original text, thus to take on the force, the resistance, the densification, that this abuse occasions in its own habitat, yet, at the same time, also to displace, remobilize, and extend this abuse in another milieu where, once again, it will have a dual function – on the one hand, that of forcing the linguistic and conceptual system of which it is a dependent, and on the other hand, of directing a critical thrust back toward the text that it translates and in relation to which it becomes a kind of unsettling aftermath (it is as if the translation sought to occupy the original's already unsettled home, and thereby, far from "domesticating" it, to turn it into a place still more foreign to itself).

Here again, given this strained relation between original and translation, an objection is sure to arise: does not the demand for reproduction of the original abuse, on the one hand, and for adaptive and reactive transformation of the abuse, on the other, simply constitute an untenable contradiction? Is this not just a radical version of, or reversion to, the irresolvable tension between French and English that we have already uncovered? Is not the practice of abuse doomed to give in to the preclusionary dominion of use in and under which it operates? If you can abuse only by respecting and thereby upholding the very usages that are contested, if the aggressive translator merely falls into a classic form of complicity, whereby, for example, deviation serves to ground and sustain the norm, then why all the fuss about abuse? Maybe this is just the same old trap, well known to the most conventional theories of translation, that Benjamin derides in "The Task of the Translator."

Precisely in this impasse, up against an apparent contradiction, one rediscovers the necessity of a double articulation, of that pluralized, dislocutory, paralogical writing practice that Derrida has so often cultivated and explained. In relation to the tensions within translation-as-representation that we have discerned, we might well situate Derrida's experiments with a double-edged writing as, precisely, a response to the pressure for two interpretations – the one in compliance with the target language, the other in realignment with the original text – that I have been underscoring. The response would consist in assuming the contradiction and attempting to make something of it. If such a response proves necessary in commentary on the problematics of representation, then a fortiori it would be necessary in the translation of that commentary. In terms of method, the question would, predictably, focus on a paradoxic imperative: how to say two things at once, how to enact two interpretations simultaneously? Or in the framework of our inquiry here, how to translate in acquiescence to English while nonetheless resurrecting a certain fidelity to the original French.

In principle, there would be a great deal to say here about the encounter with, or recourse to, or use and abuse of, operators of undecidability. Suffice it to refer to the interview entitled "Positions,"[5] and to add just one remark: the strategy, analytic as well as discursive, is grounded in the capacity of discourse to say and do many things at once and to make some of the relations among those things said and done indeterminate; recourse to such a strategy obviously makes certain texts of Derrida exceptionally resistant to translation. To deny that language has this capacity is demonstrably foolish, and to claim that philosophy or linguistic theory should not, or need not, reckon with the incidence of untranslatability seems hopelessly defensive. Far from arguing this point, however, let me stick with my quite limited project of delineating the elements of a translation practice that devolves from a disruptive or deconstructive writing practice, so as to suggest that, in translation, the difficulty of an already complex performance of language is aggravated, and with that heightened difficulty the very abusiveness that is made more difficult becomes that much more necessary.

Given two terms, original and translation, in a relation of thoroughgoing coimplication; and two registers, use and abuse, in simultaneous relations of contrariness and complementarity; and a translating operation that works in three zones, the language of the original, the language of the translation, and the space between the two; and two complicated aims, first to reproduce the use and abuse of the original in the translation and second to supply for what cannot in fact be reproduced with a remobilization of use and abuse that further qualifies the original as used and thus disabused. Now, after codification of these givens, we could construct logical and mathematical schemes to account for the modest number of combinations that come into play here; yet it is evident that, in the translator's experience, these combinations are elusive, that it is logistically impracticable to conduct the translational operations in a systematized or programmed fashion, and thus that, in the work of translation, the integration that is achieved escapes, in a vital way, from reflection and emerges in a experimental order, an order of discovery, where success is a function not only of the immense paraphrastic and paronomastic capacities of language but also of trial and error, of chance. The translation will be essayistic, in the strong sense of the word.

Use in translation

We now have in place, via some abusive use of snatches of Derrida, a modest scheme for measuring the effects of translating Derrida. In a nutshell, the proposal is (1) to concentrate evaluative attention on moments of density and intensity where the play of concepts and expression is affected by the disruptive, disseminatory power of language; (2) to insist on the transformations that the translation carries out, not just on the semantic, but also on syntactic and discursive levels; (3) to ask whether the translation articulates on its own textual effects that are consequentially and tellingly abusive with respect to the original. In order to see whether and how guidelines such as these might illuminate translation practice, it is of course necessary to examine a translation through the lenses they provide. The remarks that follow are based on a reading of a translation of "La mythologie blanche," selected for this purpose because it appears to have had, for circumstantial reasons, a considerable influence on the reception of Derrida's work in this country. The translation, "White Mythology," appeared in *New Literary History* in 1974.[6] The analytic work, which is extremely tedious, was concentrated on one portion of the essay, the final pages of its second section, "The Ellipsis of the Sun," where Derrida undertakes a commentary on Aristotle's discourse on metaphor. The very simple ad hoc procedure adopted was to compare the translation to the original, line by line and word by word, and to note diverse manifestions of difference. I shall now list some of the kinds of difference that are visible to a strictly amateur analyst.

1 *Punctuation and markers*. Derrida happens to be exceedingly and quite transparently careful about textual geography. It is therefore surprising to observe that the translation allows the italics that set off certain terms to be dropped; puts quotation marks around very important terms such as *métaphorologie* that do not have them in the French text; and goes so far as to insert in parentheses translator's notes that are not clearly identified as such. The effect of these alterations is subtractive: the translated version flattens or softens the original.

2 *Translation of translation*. "La mythologie blanche" has its own translation strategy, indicated not only in its elaborate explanations about terms in Aristotle and its explicit allusions to the difficulties of translation but also by its use of the well-established practice whereby a given Greek or German word that is being translated is given in brackets after the French term. At times, moreover, Derrida elects to refer only to the foreign word, set in italics. The text of "White Mythology" sometimes drops the words in brackets, making do with just the English word. One effect of this kind of omission is to reduce the attention to translation that is sustained in the original.

3 *Suffixes*. At the level of "semes," that is, elemental units of signification, we encounter – over and beyond a predictable "Anglo-Saxon" resistance on the part of the translator to forms ending in -*ist* and -*ism* (as in continuist, continuism, and so forth) – a curious hesitation with respect to the suffix -*ique* (-*ic* in English). Thus,

for example, the widely used French term *la métaphorique*, for which the English equivalent would be "metaphorics," sometimes becomes in "White Mythology" simply "metaphor." Or again, the coined term *l'anthropophysique*, carefully backgrounded by Derrida in analyses of *physis* and its antitheses before it is adopted, is simply rejected in favor of a paraphrase that refers to "l'homme physique" without suggesting that an abstract conceptualization that takes systemic outlines is at the nub of the argument. A still more disquieting and very frequent case is the suppression of the suffix -*ème*, as in the word *mimême* and especially in *philosophème*. The special conceptual value of this term, as a basic unit in a structured system, is trivialized in the translation, which resets it in common parlance as an "element of philosophy."

4 *Words*. There are innumerable examples in this category. Let us therefore note only a few terms that relate to important Derridean motifs, to begin with, the reflexive verb *se suppléer*. In the now-familiar logic of supplementarity so brilliantly analyzed and remobilized by Derrida, this verb is convenient for articulating the dual relations of "lack" and "supplement" precisely because it can convey a two-sided articulation, here meaning "to add to, to supplement," there meaning "to substitute for, to replace." The first time the term appears with this double function, the translation chooses the second of these meanings (rather than, for example, choosing to adopt the somewhat archaic English verb "supply," which can serve as a carrier of the two meanings). Among other important examples, let us note: (1) the crucial term "effect," although a key part of its connotational force clearly depends on the etiological context from which it is taken, is often translated by the word "phenomenon" (which is reserved for guarded use in Derrida's vocabulary); (2) the crucial term *valeur*, despite a very insistent discussion of the meaning it acquires in Saussurean linguistic theory, is often translated by "notion"; (3) the equally vital term *articulation*, even though it is pointedly coupled with the term *article* in a statement that alludes to the syntactic function of articles, is nonetheless translated by the word "joint." In the case that I mention here, where a relatively literal alternative is available in English, the selection of semantic neighbors does not necessarily modify the meaning of a statement in a radical way, but it does occasion an unnecessary loss of precision.

5 *Phrases*. In this zone of constructions still smaller than full sentences, there can of course be very difficult translation problems. The question is again, in the case of vitally important expressions, how far to deviate from a "literalist" rendering. Let us note two examples. First, the phrase "la métaphoricité par analogie," the process that is constitutive of the orders of similarity and proportionality, becomes "analogy producing metaphor." This conversion does not simply entail a slight displacement of meaning; it sets aside a key term designating the general status and operation of metaphor, both a state and an energetics; later on the general term will prove indispensable enough for the translation to deploy the word "metaphoricality" (a less satisfactory choice, since by analogy with words like "musicality" it would seem to designate a quality, than the more literal alternative, "metaphoricity"). Second, the somewhat tricky phrase "*la condition d'impossibilité* d'un tel projet" becomes "*the conditions which make it in principle impossible* to carry out such a project" (the project of constructing a future metaphorics). So Derrida is not looking for a set of conditions (it would be interesting to know why the plural

was adopted in the translation) that are constitutive of the operative principle; on the contrary, he is in fact proposing to search out the principle underlying a single impossibility condition that disables the project from the outset. Ultimately at stake in the slippage that this passage allows is the transmission, in translation, of Derrida's discourse on possibility conditions, which happens to be the veritable armature of a deconstructive analytic practice in general.

6 *Discourse.* This is of course the broad category on which we focused a good deal of attention in the first section of this essay thanks to the decisive investigations of Guillemin-Flescher. The range of phenomena encountered in this vast domain is so wide as to preclude a systematic accounting. Examples could be as discrete as the introduction of a single adverbial marker or as far-reaching as a series of syntactic adjustments extending over a full page or more. But here again, a handful of cases will suffice to give us a sense of the stakes.

a. French original: "C'est depuis l'au-delà de la différence entre le propre et le non-propre qu'il faudrait rendre compte des effets de propriété et de non-propriété" (p. 273). English version: "Account has to be given of the effects of that which is proper and that which is not by going beyond that difference itself" (p. 28). Here we can, of course, identify many changes: syntactic inversion, shift from the conditional verb (*il faudrait*) to the assertive "has to be" (an instance of English favoring actualization), deletion of the parallels between *propre/propriété* and *non-propre/non-propriété*, together with dilution of the conceptual specificity of these terms, and so forth. The shift at the start, however, involving the opening prepositional phrase of the French, "depuis l'au-delà de la différence," is perhaps most telling. The English adopts the present participial form (no doubt some purists would wish to protest that the participle, awkwardly appended to a passive construction and lacking a specified subject, dangles), which has two effects: it implies the presence of an agent who is absent in the French version, and it substitutes for the spatial positioning of "depuis l'au-delà" (indicating a locus from which the explanation would originate) a movement, an action of the agent or subject. We might then say that the resetting of Derrida's theoretical comment in the translation gives it a more immediate, practical tenor.

b. Consonant with the tendencies Guillemin-Flescher ascribes to English, the translator takes the liberty of adding conjunctions, concessives, and adversatives that tie sentences together much more tightly than does the French, which often leaves them crisply separated. There are also instances where the translation adds substantial phrases so as to transform elliptical utterances into well-formed sentences with subject and verbal complement. (This characteristic is more surprising than it might be in other French-to-English conversions because "La mythologie blanche," in its third major section "L'ellipse du soleil: l'énigme, l'incompréhensible, l'imprenable," contains forceful commentary on the effects of ellipsis. There can hardly be any doubt, therefore, that Derrida is making a deliberate, pointed use of ellipsis in his text.) Overall, the syntactic and programmatic adjustments that the translator allows himself to multiply rather freely do seem to conform to a bias openly stated in the translator's note, where we are told that natural, intelligible English renderings have been preferred except in a few cases where the argument required retention of more strained, literal forms. By and large, the tendency was then to respect the *use*-values of English.

c. In his studied writing practice, Derrida plays masterfully on the associative, poetic resources of French, generating articulatory structures that a reader of the French can hardly miss. He thus creates, to be sure, many a problem for the translator. To put it approximately, we might say that the global problem is to determine what to do about anaphoric structures (association of terms via parallel placement in sentences, paragraphs, and so forth) and anasemic formations (association of semes or terms in serial relations, often via word play), whether to stress retaining them or to let them lapse as English imposes its discursive order. A couple of examples follow.

1 In this passage, Derrida is weaving a commentary on the relation of *physis* and *mimesis* in Aristotle to which we have referred once before: "Le *mimesis* est le propre de l'homme. Seul l'homme imite proprement. Seul il prend plaisir à imiter, seul il apprend à imiter, seul il apprend par imitation. Le pouvoir de vérité, comme dévoilement de la nature (*physis*) par la *mimesis*, appartient congénitalement à la physique de l'homme, à l'anthropophysique" (p. 283). Now, the translation. "*Mimesis* is the property of man. Only man properly speaking imitates. He alone takes pleasure in imitating, learns to imitate, and learns by imitation. The power of truth, as an unveiling of nature (*physis*) by *mimesis*, is a congenital property of man as a physical being" (pp. 37–8). Attention to the anaphoric dimension here leads us at once to two remarks.

First, at the level of the passage's internal dynamics, a salient feature is the repetition, in the two middle sentences, of *seul* and of *imiter/imitation*. The English keeps the latter but drops the former, thereby diminishing the rhetorical effect of the series, which is by no means just a matter of elegance or sonority. Repeating the limitative adverbs "Seul . . . seul . . . seul" serves to set off the three members of the compound sentence as parallel propositions and thereby to confer on them a certain equivalence, to mark the three propositions of the second sentence as refinements that further specify the sense of the first sentence. The rhetoric is crucial to the placement of the two sentences in an interlocking definitional mode, and some of the vigor with which the two sentences and their four propositions are thus imbricated is drained off in the translation.

Second, at the level of the passage's connection with the motifs of the essay at large, a particularly decisive marker is the term *propre* and all its derivatives. With good cause the translator's note calls attention to *propre* and *propriété*, observing that in some cases the use of "proper" instead of "distinctive" or other equivalents seems strained, but that this literal rendering is nonetheless justified "so that the strategic role of 'the proper' in the argument may remain manifest" (p. 6). When the passage in question was translated, this sound remark was doubtless remembered. But how far is its application carried? In the context, it is clear that mimesis is the defining quality that distinguishes man from animals, and the shift in the translation from the adjectival noun *le propre* to the standard English noun "property" seems acceptable from this standpoint (an alternative, "mimesis is what is proper to man," would, however, be closer to the adjectival/definitional form and would cut back on the ambiguity of the assertion "mimesis is the property of man," which can also be read as meaning "mimesis is the possession of man"). The difficulty comes with the next proposition, "Seul l'homme imite proprement," and with its sense in relation to the preceding one and to the discourse on the *proper* in the essay at large. For the adverb *proprement*, the translation gives us "properly speaking," placed before the verb rather than after it, as in the French, so as to suggest that in the proper sense of the word "imitate," only man does it. The trouble is that the sentence with *proprement*, set up by *le propre* of the previous sentence, says poignantly "only man imitates *properly*." The sense of the adverb at this point depends on its function as a modifier of the verb "imitate": it specifies the manner of imitation. This certainly implies the meaning given by the proposition "only man properly speaking imitates," but it also says more in that it posits the actualization of the property, which the form "properly speaking" leaves in its notional guise, and it does something with the term *propre* that the English does not do, rearticulating it as an action-qualifying adverb (man's imitation is appropriative and self-defining). This capacity to signify literally and actively in the discourse on the proper could also be conferred upon the English "properly."

In all events, what is crucially at stake here is the sense, the meaning-capacity, the inferential resonance that the terms of an elaborate discourse can take on and draw upon as they are rearticulated.

2 The passage considered hereafter concerns the metaphor external to philosophy that presides over the system of metaphors within it, that is, in sum, the metaphor of metaphor.

> Cette métaphore en plus, restant hors du champ qu'elle permet de circonscrire, s'extrait ou s'abstrait encore ce champ, s'y soustrait donc comme métaphore en moins. En raison de ce que nous pourrions intituler, par économie, la supplementarité tropique, le tour de plus devenant le tour de moins, la taxinomie ou l'histoire des métaphores philosophiques n'y retrouverait jamais son compte. A l'interminable *déhiscence* du supplément (s'il est permis de jardiner encore un peu cette métaphore botanique) sera toujours refusé l'état ou le statut du complément. Le champ n'est jamais saturé. [p. 261]

> This extra metaphor, remaining outside the field which it enables us to circumscribe, also extracts or abstracts this field for itself, and therefore removes itself from that field as one metaphor the less. Because of what we might for convenience call metaphorical supplementation (the extra metaphor being at the same time a metaphor the less), no classification or account of philosophical metaphor can ever prosper. The supplement is always unfolding, but it can never attain the status of a complement. The field is never saturated.

Here we have a clear, straightforward instance of the logic of supplementarity, that of tropical supplementarity, which the translation actualizes as "metaphorical supplementation." For the moment, let us not quibble over this debatable choice of terms, over the omissions of Derrida's parenthesis pointing to the botanical metaphor in his own discourse, over the loose rendering of "la taxinomie ou l'histoire des métaphores philosophiques n'y retrouverait jamais son compte." Let us now consider only the anasemic play whereby tropical supplementarity is defined: "le tour de plus devenant le tour de moins," which the English moves into parentheses and renders "the extra metaphor being at the same time a metaphor the less."

The English transmits the main point about the operation of supplementarity well enough: from the standpoint of philosophy, the surplus trope on the outside is also a missing trope, it functions here as a plus but there as a minus, on this hand as a supplement but on the other one as a lack; whether added to the metaphorics of philosophy or subtracted from it, the unmanageable external metaphor assures its incompletion. Thus the set of philosophy's metaphors can never be the whole set. Now, since this point is made, why be concerned with a few little changes in the translation? Does it matter, for example, that le tour is translated as "metaphor," that devenant ("becoming") is translated as "being at the same time"?

It does matter if the anasemic play on the word tour matters. That it does indeed matter is easy enough to determine, since Derrida elects to re-mark the term by italicizing it and by distinguishing it from metaphor in the overture of the next section of the essay: "Chaque fois qu'une rhétorique définit la métaphore, elle implique non seulement une philosophie mais un réseau conceptuel dans lequel la philosophie s'est constituée. Chaque fil, dans ce réseau, forme de surcroît un tour, on dirait une métaphore si cette notion n'était ici trop dérivée" (p. 274). The translation: "In every rhetorical definition of metaphor is implied not just a philosophical position, but a conceptual network within which philosophy as such is constituted. Each thread of the net in addition forms a turn of speech (we might say a metaphor, but that the notion is too derivative in this case)."

From this, two points: there is clearly cause to refrain from simply substituting "metaphor" for tour, since the latter is, as it were, more primitive, less precisely fixed in a delineated system; there is also cause, as we consider the difference the translation makes by specifying the sense of tour as "turn of speech," to reflect on the considerable spectrum described by the word's many meanings. Among these: turn, revolution, circuit, circumference; twist, twisting; trick, feat, skill; shape, outline, course; sweep, lap; sprain. Hence a gamut quite as rich as that of the etymologically parallel English word "turn" and often corresponding to it, and one that is subject, moreover, to anasemic connections with retour and détour that prove to be critical in Derrida's writing. What, then, is the force of tour that we might wish to preserve in translation?

On the strength of these two points alone, having to do with the meaning-capacity of tour and with its relations to adjacent notions, it would seem important to reckon with the relatively abstract, conceptually imprecise and flexible nature of the term. More particularly, the semantic load borne by tour/"turn" prompts us to ask what seme makes for the amazing malleability that we grasp in its definition and multiple uses. Unsurprisingly the sense of "circular motion" that stands out in the etymology – the turning of the term "turn," we might say – is the key to its leverage: tour is one of those oscillatory nouns that can, depending on the context, designate a particular act, an ongoing activity, a fact, or a state – in other words, that can move across a continuum between active and passive poles or modes. Owing to its capacity as a conceptual shifter, the word can figure a wide range of representations that its semantic core, signifying an order of conversion and circumscription, enables it to hold in a state of potential relation or articulation. It is this articulatory power that a strong translation will seek to retain. In the case of the phrase we have under-scored here, "le tour de plus devenant le tour de moins," the anasemic opposition "tour de plus"/"tour de moins," obviously tends, via the repetition of *tour*, to set off the term "turn" as it is distinct from the term "metaphor"; but this is more telling here because the present participle *devenant* is an active form pointing to the very process of turning, the circular movement of perpetual shifting that the phrase attributes to tropical supplementarity. In this connection, moreover, the use of the term "tropical," rather than "metaphorical," to modify supplementarity also becomes significant because "trope" (from the Greek *tropos*) also means "turn" or "change." *Tour* instantiates the tropical.

So tropical supplementarity is not, or not just, the two-sidedness of the metaphor of metaphor; it is the turning in language – the very movement of differ-ence insofar as it is not the relation of same/inside to other/outside but the turning of the same away from yet necessarily back to itself – that is designated and also, by dint of the temporizing/temporalizing introduced by the present participle "becoming," exemplified or performed by the turning of this phrase that circum-scribes it. The linkage of the two turns, the extra one and the missing one, is not a simple identity but a ceaseless process of conversion in time. As the text bluntly asserts, the dehiscence of the supplement can never pass out of temporal process into the state of the complement. Thus the translation's suppression of the term "history" in the main clause of the sentence we have been worrying borders on the scandalous. The point is indeed that the extra/missing metaphor of metaphors cannot be the key to the taxonomy and history of philosophical metaphors, that for an account of metaphor in general it is rather necessary to appeal to tropical supplementarity.

After translation

From the foregoing observations and examples (they could be extended indefi-nitely), it is clear that "White Mythology" fails to measure up to the standard for abusive fidelity in translation that we have brought to bear on it. The abuses in the French text are commonly lost; the translation rarely produces any telling effects of its own; the special texture and tenor of Derrida's discourse get flattened out in an English that shies away from abnormal, odd-sounding constructions. Yet it is only fair to recognize that a negative evaluation is hardly appropriate here for two closely allied reasons. A comparative examination of original and translation shows that (1) the translation does comply with the expectations established by Guillemin-Flescher's contrastive characterization of French and English and also that, in so doing, (2) the translation complies with the aim to anglicize that is enunciated in the translator's introduction. The introduction states and comments on that aim as follows: "Intelligible English renderings have generally been preferred to direct transfers into English of M. Derrida's suggestive exploitation of nuances of French vocabulary. This results inevitably in some loss of the force of the original." Indeed, some force and also some sense get lost.

Yet the salient feature of the translator's introduction, which reaffirms the value of natural, intelligible, idiomatic English precisely by setting it off against Derrida's

tortuous, precious, language-straining French, is that the translator begins by pointing out quite explicitly that the essay, through its analyses and arguments, contests
the very criteria and suppositions that nonetheless govern his translation. The reader
of "White Mythology" does get a reasonably direct re-presentation of the Derridean
critique that challenges the originary status of nature, the priority of the intelligible,
the privileging of the semantic over the syntactic, the hegemony of use-values, and
so forth. Although with lesser clarity and incision, the reader also gets something
of the analytic strategy designed to pinpoint, in the play of mimetic particles, in
processes of articulation, anagrammatism, semantic displacement, in the aporias
occasioned by supplementarity, the work of heterogeneous factors that dislocate the
conception of metaphor, that undermine all attempts at theorizing metaphor, that
infest metaphoricity with the untameable energy of difference.

Integral to that analytic strategy are moves and moments, not simply inter-
rogatory, descriptive, or explanatory, that we might loosely term demonstrative
or even performative. These are moments at which the elements and processes of
rhetoric and syntax that Derrida points out analytically, or the theses that he articulates, are also put into play – are put on display, enacted, actualized – in his writing.
Such skids into performance are wrought in a practice that, for example, makes
visible the very incidence of syntactic formations upon meaning-generation that is
being argued. To miss that performative dimension is not to miss the message but,
just as the translator's note indicates, to miss or reduce its force by diminishing the energy devoted to tightening the link between message and discursive
practice. That is no small miss. What it leaves intact, by default, is a disparity – a
form of dissension or contradiction – between saying and doing, between telling
and showing, thesis and expression, program and performance, a disparity that
"La mythologie blanche" moves at discrete moments, with timely abuses, to override. The translation thus tends to sap the strength of the thesis it restates by blocking
off its enactment or enforcement by the statement and thereby allowing the
contested values to prevail unshaken in the fabric of the very discourse that purports
to contest them.

"La mythologie blanche" contains, in its discussion of the treatment of catachresis in Fontanier's rhetoric, a kind of tropical version of language-shaping abuse
– "le coup de force d'une torsion qui va *contre l'usage*" (p. 307) – that exemplifies
the practice we have envisioned for the translation of Derrida. The interest of
catachresis in Fontanier's theory, as Derrida's analysis shows, is its intermediate
status between irreducibly original inceptions of the signifying code and the standard taxinomy of usage. Exerting an abuse that estranges it from each order, the
trope can circulate between the two of them, exercising both an irruptive and an
integrative function. It exemplifies the double move that abusive translation has
to pursue: both to violate and to sustain the principles of usage. Like the *tour*, it
thus comes very close to metaphor, indeed more commonly taking a metaphoric
rather than metonymic turn, without, however, being reducible to it. But for translation the significance of the catachretic figure in "La mythologie" doubtless lies less
in the additional possibility it affords us for conceptualizing the work of translation
than in the critical questioning that Derrida introduces through his discussion of
Fontanier. At stake in the final section of the essay is the movement of domestication or recuperation by which rhetoric – and analogously, philosophy – bring the

abusive force of catachresis back under the control of a reigning interpretation, of meanings supposed to be already present in the storehouse of language. Derrida's forceful remarks about both rhetoric and philosophy stand as a warning, scarcely mistakable, against the very recuperation we have observed in the translation of his essay, in the passage from French to English – a warning against what amounts to recuperation by the "natural language," as we deem it, in which the original is, as we venture incautiously to claim, rendered. That recuperation is the obvious risk that a strong translation must run and overcome.

Despite its explicit disputation of and overt resistance to certain forms of re-cuperation that do not have to be accepted as simply inevitable, despite the manifest implications for translation of its treatment of analogy and processes of substitution or of its vigorous critique of the subordination of syntax in the metaphorology of metaphysics, "La mythologie blanche" could be, has been, translated in dissonance with its own program. This fact is a sobering commentary on the staying power of classical concepts of translation. No doubt their domination is so well built into our languages and thus into the thoughts we are able to articulate through them that even the most concerted efforts to translate abusively are doomed to suffer under their hegemony. Yet this is by no means to concede that resistance to recuperation in translation is therefore impossible or unwarranted, only that recuperation can never be completely thwarted and thus that the resistance has to be disabused. For the translator, the question is simply to what extent the recuperative effects of trans-lation can be controlled, to what extent the resistance the original puts up to the recuperations imposed by its own idiom can be remobilized in the language of the translation. In the case of Derrida, where that resistance is preeminently a matter of writing performance, the task of the translator is surely to work out a strategy that allows the most insistent and decisive effects of that performance to resurface in the translated text and to assume an importance sufficient to suggest the vital status of stratified or contrapuntal writing in the original.

The existence of weak, entropic translations surely depends in part on a time factor about which little can be done: the very possibility of translating strongly derives from that of reading insightfully, and the latter derives in turn from a famil-iarity that can only be gained over time. The closer a translation of a monumental text such as those of Derrida is to the original's date of publication, the more likely it is to be unduly deficient. Yet from the weak translation that is published and starts exerting influence well before the strong appreciation of the original has become possible, there remains an important lesson to be learned. That lesson concerns not translation but commentary. The history of deconstruction in North America during the past decade or so has included something of a debate among various partisans of the critical endeavor concerning the form in which Derrida's work should be disseminated. At one pole, a purist view, holding as uncompromisingly as possible to the integrity of Derrida's philosophical project; at the other pole, an adaptivist view, allowing for a domesticated version of deconstruction that could, for example, be sketched out as a method usable for literary criticism. Since some recuperation is inevitable in any derived text, be it translation or commentary, and since, indeed, both translation and commentary are initially caught up in the same struggle to transmit the force of the original, the issue can only be a question of degree: to what lengths should we go in order to minimize the recuperation?

As I suggested much earlier, the existence of weak, misleading translations does have an effect on the commentator's conception of her task. Insofar as an interpretation of Derrida in North America has to reckon with such translations, commentary must attempt not simply to explain the intricacies of the French text and to suggest how we might describe them and understand them in English but also to reject and explain away the translations and the misconceptions they spawn. The translation thus becomes a special problem for the commentary, intervening in the relation between original text and commentary so as to complicate the task of interpretation. At the risk of an excessively schematic account, let us lay out the problem in the following way.

1 Between the original French text and any commentary on it, there is a relation of supplementarity, that is, insofar as the commentary is an addition to the original text, saying something the original does not say, it implies something missing in the original that it seeks to supply, so that "paradoxically" what supplies (makes up for) the lack also supplies (furnishes) it; and once this process is under way, the lack is forever to be supplied, commentary will forever pursue a fundamentally productive course as the continuance of an interrogation undertaken in the original.

2 Between the translated French text and the commentary, there is a comparable relation of supplementarity, centered on the process of correction; the commentary strives to make up for what the translation states inadequately, recuperatively constituting the translation as a loss forever to be compensated in the ongoing history of that text's interpretations.

3 When relation (1) is complicated by relation (2), the effect is not to alter the supplemental relation between original and commentary in structure; it is simply to orient that relation toward an elemental task, that of a critical redress devoted rather more to describing the original – to pointing out what it really does and thereby says – than to saying what it does not say, to supplementing it in the strong sense.

Given this situation, the risk is then that the burden of lackluster translation will become an impedance to commentary, that it will interfere with the commentarial effort to respond strongly to the challenges of the original. The risk, we might say, is that commentary will be content to suggest what should come across in translation and will go no further. That would in fact be a failure to deal with the problem of recuperation as translation itself manifests it. For inadequate translation confronts the commentator with a dual necessity: on the one hand, it is clearly imperative to address critically the question of what the translation misses, to expose the crucial losses in the abusive and performative dimensions of the text; on the other hand, this very indictive/corrective operation makes it all the more essential for the commentary to supplement strongly with its own performance, to enact its own abuses, to regenerate the textual energy wasted in the translation. The increased difficulty of commentary stems from its having to dwell in the tension between these two responses, the one analytic, the other writerly, and somehow to program the former so that it will fecundate, rather than hold in check, the ploys of the latter.

As Derrida so clearly understands, commentary does not have the option of ignoring the effects of translation, of pretending to be separable from translation.

In the scheme we have outlined here, under the aegis of "free" translation, commentary is distinguished from translation above all by the former's opportunity to capture the abusive and performative dimensions of the original, not simply through reproduction, but also through invention. Relatively speaking, the translator's lot is an unhappy one because he plays an instrument more restrictively mimetic than that of the commentator. Translation imposes by default recuperations the commentator can reasonably seek to elude, entails limits on abuse and formulative discovery that she can studiously transgress. Yet the commentator's (pursuit of) translation still has to be valid, has to be rearticulable throughout the framework of her interpretation. The exigency of high fidelity never recedes. Thus, if commentary is to compensate in some measure for the recuperative losses occasioned by *usable* translations, it must meet the challenge of the original to supplement strongly, on a performative register, without forsaking the thankless task of the translator. Through the processes of supplementarity, the very demarcation of translation from commentary cannot help but become problematic. For commentary to supplement the translation is perhaps first to add to it, to correct it, simply to contest its recuperations by exposing them; but ultimately that move, if it is not to acquiesce to the very discursive order of the translation that it questions, *turns* into a replacement of the translation. So let us add, in all the senses of an elliptical phrase: commentary supplies the translation by doing other than translation. In the wake of translation, the mission of commentary is to translate in difference.

Notes

1 "Vers la traduction abusive," paper presented in the seminar "La Traduction" at the summer 1980 colloquium "Les Fins de l'Homme" at Cerisy-la-Salle, France.

2 "Vers la traduction abusive," in *Les fins de l'homme* (Paris: Galilée, 1981), pp. 253–61.

3 *Syntaxe comparée du français et de l'anglais: Problèmes de traduction* (Paris: Editions Ophrys, 1981).

4 "The Retrait of Metaphors," *Enclitic* 2 (Fall 1978), 5–33.

5 *Positions*, trans. Alan Bass (Chicago: University of Chicago Press, 1979).

6 "White Mythology," *New Literary History* 6: 1 (1974), 5–74. I refer to "La Mythologie blanche," in *Marges de la Philosophie* (Paris: Minuit, 1972), 247–324.

Chapter 22

Antoine Berman

TRANSLATION AND THE TRIALS
OF THE FOREIGN

Translated by Lawrence Venuti

THE GENERAL THEME of my essay will be *translation as the trial of the foreign (comme épreuve de l'étranger)*. "Trial of the foreign" is the expression that Heidegger uses to define one pole of poetic experience in Hölderlin (*Die Erfahrung des Fremden*). Now, in the poet, this trial is essentially enacted by translation, by his version of Sophocles, which is in fact the last "work" Hölderlin published before descending into madness. In its own time, this translation was considered a prime manifestation of his madness. Yet today we view it as one of the great moments of western translation: not only because it gives us rare access to the Greek tragic Word, but because while giving us access to this Word, it reveals the veiled essence of every translation.

Translation is the "trial of the foreign." But in a double sense. In the first place, it establishes a relationship between the Self-Same (*Propre*) and the Foreign by aiming to open up the foreign work to us in its utter foreignness. Hölderlin reveals the strangeness of the Greek tragic Word, whereas most "classic" translations tend to attenuate or cancel it. In the second place, translation is a trial *for the Foreign as well*, since the foreign work is uprooted from its own *language-ground (sol-de-langue)*. And this trial, often an exile, can also exhibit the most singular power of the translating act: to reveal the foreign work's most original kernel, its most deeply buried, most self-same, but equally the most "distant" from itself. Hölderlin discerns in Sophocles' work – in its language – two opposed principles: on the one hand, the immediate violence of the tragic Word, what he calls the "fire of heaven," and on the other, "holy sobriety," i.e., the rationality that comes to contain and mask this violence. For Hölderlin, translating first and foremost means liberating the violence repressed in the work through a series of *intensifications* in the translating language – in other words, accentuating its strangeness. Paradoxically, this accentuation is the only way of giving us access to it. Alain addressed the topic of translation in one of his remarks on literature:

> I have this idea that one can always translate a poet – English, Latin, or Greek – exactly word for word, without adding anything, preserving the very order of the words, until at last you find the meter, even the rhymes. I have rarely pushed the experiment that far; it takes time, I mean, a few months, plus uncommon patience. The first draft resembles a mosaic of barbarisms; the bits are badly joined; they are cemented together, but not in harmony. A forcefulness, a flash, a certain violence remains, no doubt more than necessary. It's more English than the English text, more Greek than the Greek, more Latin than the Latin [. . .]
>
> (Alain 1934: 56–7)

Thanks to such translation, the language of the original shakes with all its liberated might the translating language. In an article devoted to Pierre Klossowski's translation of the *Aeneid*, Michel Foucault distinguishes between two methods of translation:

> It is quite necessary to admit that two kinds of translations exist; they do not have the same function or the same nature. In one, something (meaning, aesthetic value) must remain identical, and it is given passage into another language; these translations are good when they go "from like to same" [. . .] And then there are translations that hurl one language against another [. . .] taking the original text for a projectile and treating the translating language like a target. Their task is not to lead a meaning back to itself or anywhere else; but to use the translated language to derail the translating language.
>
> (Foucault 1964: 21)

Doesn't this distinction simply correspond to the great split that divides the entire field of translation, separating so-called "literary" translations (in the broad sense) from "non-literary" translations (technical, scientific, advertising, etc.)? Whereas the latter perform only a semantic transfer and deal with texts that entertain a relation of exteriority or instrumentality to their language, the former are concerned with *works*, that is to say texts so bound to their language that the translating act inevitably becomes a manipulation of signifiers, where two languages enter into various forms of collision and somehow *couple*. This is undeniable, but not taken seriously. A superficial glance at the history of translation suffices to show that, in the literary domain, everything transpires as if the second type of translation came to usurp and conceal the first type. As if it were suddenly driven to the margins of exception and heresy. As if translation, far from being the trials of the Foreign, were rather its negation, its acclimation, its "naturalization." As if its most individual essence were radically repressed. Hence, the necessity for reflection on the properly *ethical* aim of the translating act (receiving the Foreign as Foreign). Hence, the necessity for an analysis that shows how (and why) this aim has, from time immemorial (although not always), been skewed, perverted and assimilated to something other than itself, such as the play of hypertextual transformations.

The analytic of translation

I propose to examine briefly the system of textual deformation that operates in every translation and prevents it from being a "trial of the foreign." I shall call this examination the *analytic of translation*. Analytic in two senses of the term: a detailed analysis of the deforming system, and therefore an analysis in the Cartesian sense, but also in the psychoanalytic sense, insofar as the system is largely unconscious, present as a series of tendencies or *forces* that cause translation to deviate from its essential aim. The analytic of translation is consequently designed to discover these forces and to show where in the text they are practiced – somewhat as Bachelard, with his "psychoanalysis" of the scientific spirit, wanted to show how the materialist imagination confused and derailed the objective aim of the natural sciences.

Before presenting the detailed examination of the deforming forces, I shall make several remarks. First, the analysis proposed here is provisional: it is formulated on the basis of my experience as a translator (primarily of Latin American literature into French). To be systematic, it requires the input of translators from other domains (other languages and works), as well as linguists, "poeticians" and . . . psychoanalysts, since the deforming forces constitute so many censures and resistances.

This *negative* analytic should be extended by a *positive* counterpart, an analysis of operations which have always limited the deformation, although in an intuitive and unsystematic way. These operations constitute a sort of counter-system destined to neutralize, or attenuate, the negative tendencies. The negative and positive analytics will in turn enable a *critique of translations* that is neither simply descriptive nor simply normative.

The negative analytic is primarily concerned with ethnocentric, annexationist translations and hypertextual translations (pastiche, imitation, adaptation, free rewriting), where the play of deforming forces is freely exercised. Every translator is inescapably exposed to this play of forces, even if he (or she) is animated by another aim. More: these unconscious forces form part of the translator's *being*, determining the *desire* to translate. It is illusory to think that the translator can be freed merely by becoming aware of them. The translator's practice must submit to analysis if the unconscious is to be neutralized. It is by yielding to the "controls" (in the psychoanalytic sense) that translators can hope to free themselves from the system of deformation that burdens their practice. This system is the internalized expression of a two-millennia-old tradition, as well as the ethnocentric structure of every culture, every language; it is less a crude system than a "cultivated language." Only languages that are "cultivated" translate, but they are also the ones that put up the strongest resistance to the ruckus of translation. They censor. You see what a psychoanalytic approach to language and linguistic systems can contribute to a "translatology." This approach must also be the work of analysts themselves, since they experience translation as an essential dimension of psychoanalysis.

A final point: the focus below will be the deforming tendencies that intervene in the domain of literary prose – the novel and the essay.

Literary prose collects, reassembles, and intermingles the polylingual space of a community. It mobilizes and activates the totality of "languages" that coexist in any language. This can be seen in Balzac, Proust, Joyce, Faulkner, Augusto Antonio Roa Bastos, Joao Guimarães Rosa, Carlo Emilio Gadda, etc. Hence, from a *formal* point of view, the language-based cosmos that is prose, especially the novel, is characterized by a certain *shapelessness*, which results from the enormous brew of languages and linguistic systems that operate in the work. This is also characteristic of canonical works, *la grande prose*.

Traditionally, this shapelessness has been described negatively, that is, within the horizon of poetry. Herman Broch, for example, remarks of the novel that

> in contrast to poetry, it is not a producer, but a consumer of style. [. . .] It applies itself with much less intensity to the duty of looking like a work of art. Balzac is of greater weight than Flaubert, the form-less Thomas Wolfe more than the artistic Thornton Wilder. The novel does not submit, like proper poetry, to the criteria of art.
>
> (Broch 1966: 68)

In effect, the masterworks of prose are characterized by a kind of "bad writing," a certain "lack of control" in their texture. This can be seen in Rabelais, Cervantes, Montaigne, Saint-Simon, Sterne, Jean Paul Richter, Balzac, Zola, Tolstoy, Dostoevsky.

The lack of control derives from the enormous linguistic mass that the prose writer must squeeze into the work – at the risk of making it formally explode. The more totalizing the writer's aim, the more obvious the loss of control, whether in the proliferation, the swelling of the text, or in works where the most scrupulous attention is paid to form, as in Joyce, Broch, or Proust. Prose, in its multiplicity and rhythmic flow, can never be entirely mastered. And this "bad writing" is rich. This is the consequence of its polylingualism. *Don Quixote*, for example, gathers into itself the plurality of Spanish "languages" during its epoch, from popular proverbial speech (Sancho) to the conventions of chivalric and pastoral romances. Here the languages are intertwined and mutually ironized.

The Babelian proliferation of languages in novels pose specific difficulties for translation. If one of the principal problems of poetic translation is to respect the polysemy of the poem (cf. Shakespeare's *Sonnets*), then the principal problem of translating the novel is to respect its *shapeless polylogic* and avoid an arbitrary homogenization.

Insofar as the novel is considered a lower form of literature than poetry, the deformations of translation are more accepted in prose, when they do not pass unperceived. For they operate on points that do not immediately reveal themselves. It is easy to detect how a poem by Hölderlin has been massacred. It isn't so easy to see what was done to a novel by Kafka or Faulkner, especially if the translation seems "good." The deforming system functions here in complete tranquillity. This is why it is urgent to elaborate an analytic for the translation of novels.

This analytic sets out to locate several deforming tendencies. They form a systematic whole. I shall mention twelve here. There may be more; some combine with or derive from others; some are well known. And some may appear relevant only to French "classicizing" translation. But in fact they bear on all translating, at least in the western tradition. They can be found just as often in English translators as in Spanish or German, although certain tendencies may be more accentuated in one linguistic–cultural space than in others. Here are the twelve tendencies in question:

1   rationalization
2   clarification
3   expansion
4   ennoblement and popularization
5   qualitative impoverishment
6   quantitative impoverishment
7   the destruction of rhythms
8   the destruction of underlying networks of signification
9   the destruction of linguistic patternings
10   the destruction of vernacular networks or their exoticization
11   the destruction of expressions and idioms
12   the effacement of the superimposition of languages

Rationalization

This bears primarily on the syntactical structures of the original, starting with that most meaningful and changeable element in a prose text: *punctuation*. Rationalization recomposes sentences and the sequence of sentences, rearranging them according to a certain idea of discursive *order*. Wherever the sentence structure is relatively free (i.e., wherever it doesn't answer to a specific idea of order), it risks a rationalizing contraction. This is visible, for instance, in the fundamental hostility with which the French greet repetition, the proliferation of relative clauses and participles, long sentences or sentences without verbs – all elements essential to prose.

Thus, Marc Chapiro, the French translator of the *Brothers Karamazov*, writes:

> The original heaviness of Dostoevsky's style poses an almost insoluble problem to the translator. It was impossible to reproduce the bushy undergrowth of his sentences, despite the richness of their content.
> (cited by Meschonnic 1973: 317)

This signifies, quite openly, that the cause of rationalization has been adopted. As we have seen, the essence of prose includes a "bushy undergrowth." Moreover, every formal excess curdles novelistic prose, whose "imperfection" is a condition of its existence. The signifying shapelessness indicates that prose plunges into the depths, the strata, the polylogism of language. Rationalization destroys all that.

It annihilates another element of prose: *its drive toward concreteness*. Rationalization means abstraction. Prose is centered on the concrete and even tends to render concrete the numerous abstract elements bobbing in its flood (Proust, Montaigne). Rationalization makes the original pass from concrete to abstract, not only by reordering the sentence structure, but – for example – by translating verbs into substantives, by choosing the more general of two substantives, etc. Yves Bonnefoy revealed this process with Shakespeare's work.

This rationalization/abstraction is all the more pernicious in that it is not *total*. It doesn't mean to be. It is content to *reverse* the relations which prevail in the original between formal and informal, ordered and disorderly, abstract and concrete. This conversion is typical of ethnocentric translation: it causes the work to undergo a change of *sign*, of *status* – and seemingly without changing form and meaning.

To sum up: rationalization deforms the original by *reversing* its basic tendency.

Clarification

This is a corollary of rationalization which particularly concerns the level of "clarity" perceptible in words and their meanings. Where the original has no problem moving in the *indefinite*, our literary language tends to impose the definite. When the Argentine novelist Roberto Arlt writes: "y los excesos eran desplazados por desmedimientos de esperanza" (the excesses were displaced by the excessiveness of hope; Arlt 1981: 37), French does not tolerate a literal rendering because everywhere, in this passage from *Los Siete Locos*, excess is *still* in question. French asks: an excess of what?

The same goes for Dostoevsky. Chapiro writes: "To render the suggestions of a Russian sentence, it is often necessary to complete it" (cited by Meschonnic 1973: 317–18).

Clarification seems to be an obvious principle to many translators and authors. Thus, the American poet Galway Kinnell writes: "The translation should be a little clearer than the original" (cited by Gresset 1983: 519).

Of course, clarification is inherent in translation, to the extent that every translation comprises some degree of explicitation. But that can signify two very different things:

(1) the explicitation can be the manifestation of something that is not apparent, but concealed or repressed, in the original. Translation, by virtue of its own movement, puts into play this element. Heidegger alludes to the point for philosophy: "In translation, the work of thinking is transposed into the spirit of another language and so undergoes an inevitable transformation. But this transformation can be fecund, because it shines a new light on the fundamental position of the question" (Heidegger 1968: 10).

The power of illumination, of *manifestation*, (1) as I indicated apropos Hölderlin, is the supreme power of translation. But in a negative sense, (2) explicitation aims to render "clear" what does not wish to be clear in the original. The movement from polysemy to monosemy is a mode of clarification. Paraphrastic or explicative translation is another. And that leads us to the third tendency.

Expansion

Every translation tends to be longer than the original. George Steiner said that translation is "inflationist." This is the consequence, in part, of the two previous
tendencies. Rationalizing and clarifying require expansion, an *unfolding* of what, in
the original, is "folded." Now, from the viewpoint of the text, this expansion can
be qualified as "empty." It can coexist quite well with diverse quantitative forms of
impoverishment. I mean that *the addition adds nothing*, that it augments only the
gross mass of text, without augmenting its way of speaking or signifying. The addition is no more than babble designed to muffle the work's own voice. Explicitations
may render the text more "clear," but they actually obscure *its own mode of clarity*.
The expansion is, moreover, a stretching, a slackening, which impairs the rhythmic
flow of the work. It is often called "overtranslation," a typical case of which is Armel
Guerne's translation of *Moby Dick* (1954). Expanded, the majestic, oceanic novel
becomes bloated and uselessly titanic. In this case, expansion aggravates the initial
shapelessness of the work, causing it to change from a shapeless plenitude to a shapeless void or hollow. In German, the *Fragments* of Novalis possess a very special
brevity, a brevity that contains an infinity of meanings and somehow renders them
"long," but vertically, like wells. Translated by the same Guerne (1973), they are
lengthened immoderately and simultaneously flattened. Expansion flattens, hori-
zontalizing what is essentially deep and vertical in Novalis.

Ennoblement

This marks the culminating point of "classic" translation. In poetry, it is "poetization." In prose, it is rather a "rhetorization." Alain alludes to this process (with
English poetry):

> If a translator attempts a poem by Shelley into French, he will first spread
> it out, following the practice of our poets who are mostly a bit too
> oratorical. Setting up the rules of public declamation as his standard, he
> will insert their thats and whichs, syntactical barriers that weigh upon
> and prevent – if I can put it this way – the substantial words from biting
> each other. I don't disdain this art of articulation. . . . But in the end it
> isn't the English art of speaking, so clenched and compact, brilliant,
> precise and strongly enigmatic.
>
> (Alain 1934: 56)

Rhetorization consists in producing "elegant" sentences, while utilizing the
source text, so to speak, as *raw material*. Thus the ennoblement is only a rewriting,
a "stylistic exercise" based on – and at the expense of – the original. This procedure
is active in the literary field, but also in the human sciences, where it produces texts
that are "readable," "brilliant," rid of their original clumsiness and complexity so as
to enhance the "meaning." This type of rewriting thinks itself justified in recovering
the rhetorical elements inherent in all prose – but in order to banalize them and
assign them a predominant place. These elements – in Rousseau, Balzac, Hugo,

Melville, Proust, etc. – restore a certain "orality," and this orality effectively possesses its own norms of nobility – those of "good speaking," which may be popular or "cultivated." But good speaking in the original has nothing to do with the "rhetorical elegance" extolled by the *rewriting* that ennobles. In fact, the latter simultaneously annihilates both oral rhetoric and formless polylogic (see above).

The logical opposite of ennoblement – or its counterpart – occurs in passages judged too "popular": blind recourse to a pseudo-slang which *popularizes* the original, or to a "spoken" language which reflects only a *confusion between oral and spoken.* The degenerate coarseness of pseudo-slang betrays rural fluency as well as the strict code of urban dialects.

Qualitative impoverishment

This refers to the replacement of terms, expressions and figures in the original with terms, expressions and figures that lack their sonorous richness or, correspondingly, their signifying or "iconic" richness. A term is iconic when, in relation to its referent, it "creates an image," enabling a perception of resemblance. Spitzer alludes to this iconicity: "A word that denotes facetiousness, or the play of words, easily behaves in a whimsical manner – just as in every language worldwide, the terms that denote the butterfly change in a kaleidoscopic manner" (Spitzer 1970: 51).

This does not mean that the word "butterfly" objectively resembles "a butterfly," but that in its sonorous, physical substance, in its density as a word, we feel that it possesses something of the butterfly's butterfly existence. Prose and poetry produce, in their own peculiar ways, what can be called *surfaces of iconicity*.

When translating the Peruvian *chuchumeca* with *pute* (whore), the meaning can certainly be rendered, but none of the word's phonetic-signifying truth. The same goes for every term that is commonly qualified with *savoureux* (spicy), *dru* (robust), *vif* (vivid), *coloré* (colorful), etc., epithets that all refer to the iconic physicality of the sign. And when this practice of replacement, which is most often unconscious, is applied to an entire work, to the whole of its iconic surface, it decisively effaces a good portion of its signifying process and mode of expression – what makes a work *speak* to us.

Quantitative impoverishment

This refers to a lexical loss. Every work in prose presents a certain *proliferation* of signifiers and signifying chains. Great novelistic prose is "abundant." These signifiers can be described as *unfixed*, especially as a signified may have a multiplicity of signifiers. For the signified *visage* (face) Arlt employs *semblante*, *rostro* and *cara* without justifying a particular choice in a particular sentence. The essential thing is that *visage* is marked as an important *reality* in his work by the use of three signifiers. The translation that does not respect this multiplicity renders the "visage" of an unrecognizable work. There is a loss, then, since the translation contains *fewer* signifiers than the original. The translation that attends to the lexical texture of the work, to its mode of lexicality – enlarges it. This loss perfectly coexists with an increase of the gross quantity or mass of the text with expansion. For expansion consists in adding articles and relatives (*le*, *la*, *les*, *qui*, *que*), explicative and decorative signifiers that have nothing to do with the lexical texture of the original. The translating results in a text that is at once *poorer* and *longer*. Moreover, the expansion often works to mask the quantitative loss.

The destruction of rhythms

I shall pass rapidly over this aspect, however fundamental it may be. The novel is not less rhythmic than poetry. It even comprises a multiplicity of rhythms. Since the entire bulk of the novel is thus in movement, it is fortunately difficult for translation to destroy this rhythmic movement. This explains why even a great but badly translated novel continues to transport us. Poetry and theater are more fragile. Yet the deforming translation can considerably affect the rhythm – for example, through an arbitrary revision of the punctuation. Michel Gresset (1983) shows how a translation of Faulkner destroys his distinctive rhythm: where the original included only *four* marks of punctuation, the translation uses *twenty-two*, eighteen of which are commas!

The destruction of underlying networks of signification

The literary work contains a hidden dimension, an "underlying" text, where certain signifiers correspond and link up, forming all sorts of networks beneath the "surface" of the text itself – the manifest text, presented for reading. It is this *subtext* that carries the network of word-obsessions. These underlying chains constitute one aspect of the rhythm and signifying process of the text. After long intervals certain words may recur, certain kinds of substantives that constitute a particular network, whether through their resemblance or their aim, their "aspect." In Arlt you find words that witness the presence of an obsession, an intimacy, a particular perception, although distributed rather far from each other – sometimes in different chapters – and without a context that justifies or calls for their use. Hence, the following series of *augmentatives*:

| *portalón* | *alón* | *jaulón* | *portón* | *gigantón* | *callejón* |
| gate | wing | cage | door/entrance | giant | lane/alley |

which establishes a network:

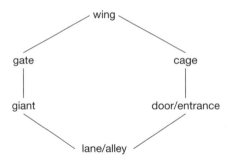

This simple network shows that the signifiers in themselves have no particular value, that what *makes sense* is their linkage, which in fact signals a most important dimension of the work. Now, all of these signifers are *augmentatives*, appropriately enough, as Arlt's novel *Los Siete Locos* contains a certain *dimension of augmentation*: gates, wings, cages, entrances, giants, alleys acquire the inordinate size they have in nocturnal dreams. If such networks are not transmitted, a signifying process in the text is destroyed.

The misreading of these networks corresponds to the treatment given to *groupings of major signifiers* in a work, such as those that organize its mode of expression. To sketch out a visual domain, for example, an author might employ certain verbs, adjectives and substantives, and *not others*. V. A. Goldsmidt studies the words that Freud did *not use* or *avoided* where they might be expected. Needless to say, translators have often inserted them.

The destruction of linguistic patternings

The systematic nature of the text goes beyond the level of signifiers, metaphors, etc.; it extends to the type of sentences, the sentence constructions employed. Such patternings may include the use of time or the recourse to a certain kind of subordination (Gresset cites Faulkner's "because"). Spitzer studies the patterning system in Racine and Proust, although he still calls it "style". Rationalization, clarification, expansion, etc. destroy the systematic nature of the text by introducing elements that are excluded by its essential system. Hence, a curious consequence: when the translated text is more "homogeneous" than the original (possessing more "style" in the ordinary sense), it is equally more *incoherent* and, in a certain way, more heterogeneous, more *inconsistent*. It is a *patchwork* of the different kinds of writing employed by the translator (like combining ennoblement with popularization where the original cultivates an orality). This applies as well to the position of the translator, who basically resorts to every reading possible in translating the original. Thus, a translation always risks appearing *homogeneous and incoherent* at the same time, as Meschonnic has shown with the translation of Paul Celan. A carefully conducted textual analysis of an original and its translation demonstrates that the writing-of-the-translation, the-discourse-of-the-translation is *asystematic*, like the work of a neophyte which is rejected by readers at publishing houses from the very first page. Except that, in the case of translation, this asystematic nature is not apparent and in fact is concealed by what still remains of the linguistic patternings in the original. Readers, however, perceive this inconsistency in the translated text, since they rarely bestow their trust on it and do not see it as the or a "true" text. Barring any prejudices, the readers are right: it is not a "true" text; it lacks the distinguishing features of a text, starting with its systematic nature. *Homogenization can no more conceal asystematicity than expansion can conceal quantitative impoverishment.*

The destruction of vernacular networks or their exoticization

This domain is essential because all great prose is rooted in the vernacular language. "If French doesn't work," wrote Montaigne, "Gascon will!" (cited by Mounin 1955: 38).

In the first place, the polylogic aim of prose inevitably includes a plurality of vernacular elements.

In the second place, the tendency toward concreteness in prose necessarily includes these elements, because the vernacular language is by its very nature more physical, more iconic than "cultivated" language. The Picard "bibloteux" is more expressive than the French "livresque" (bookish). The Old French "sorcelage" is richer than "sorcellerie" (sorcery), the Antillais "dérespecter" more expressive than "manquer de respect" (to lack respect).

In the third place, prose often aims explicitly to recapture the orality of vernacular. In the twentieth century, this is the case with a good part – with *the* good part – of such literatures as Latin American, Italian, Russian, and North American.

The effacement of vernaculars is thus a very serious injury to the textuality of prose works. It may be a question of effacing diminutives in Spanish, Portuguese, German or Russian; or it may involve replacing verbs by nominal constructions, verbs of action by verbs with substantives (the Peruvian "alagunarse," s'enlaguner, becomes the flat-footed "se transformer en lagune," "to be transformed into a lagoon"). Vernacular signifiers may be transposed, like "porteño," which becomes "inhabitant of Buenos Aires."

The traditional method of preserving vernaculars is to *exoticize* them. Exoticization can take two forms. First, a typographical procedure (italics) is used to isolate what does not exist in the original. Then, more insidiously, it is "added" to be "more authentic," emphasizing the vernacular according to a certain stereotype of it (as in the popular woodcut illustrations published by Épinal). Such are Mardrus's over-Arabizing translations of the *Thousand and One Nights* and the *Song of Songs*.

Exoticization may join up again with popularization by striving to render a foreign vernacular with a local one, using Parisian slang to translate the *lunfardo* of Buenos Aires, the Normandy dialect to translate the language of the Andes or Abruzzese. Unfortunately, a vernacular clings tightly to its soil and completely resists any direct translating into another vernacular. *Translation can occur only between "cultivated" languages.* An exoticization that turns the foreign from abroad into the foreign at home winds up merely ridiculing the original.

The destruction of expressions and idioms

Prose abounds in images, expressions, figures, proverbs, etc. which derive in part from the vernacular. Most convey a meaning or experience that readily finds a parallel image, expression, figure, or proverb in other languages.

Here are two idioms from Conrad's novel *Typhoon*:

> He did not care a tinker's curse
> Damme, if this ship isn't worse than Bedlam!

Compare these two idioms with Gide's amazingly literal version:

> Il s'en fichait comme du juron d'un étameur
> (He didn't give a tinker's curse)

Que diable m'emporte si l'on ne se croirait pas à Bedlam!
(The Devil take me if I didn't think I was in Bedlam!)

(cited by Meerschen 1982: 80)

The first can easily be rendered into comparable French idioms, like "il s'en fichait comme de l'an quarante, comme d'une guigne, etc.," and the second invites the replacement of "Bedlam," which is incomprehensible to the French reader, by "Charenton" (Bedlam being a famous English insane asylum). Now it is evident that even if the meaning is identical, replacing an idiom by its "equivalent" is an ethnocentrism. Repeated on a large scale (this is always the case with a novel), the practice will result in the absurdity whereby the characters in *Typhoon* express themselves with a network of French images. The points I signal here with one or two examples must always be multiplied by five or six thousand. To play with "equivalence" is to attack the discourse of the foreign work. Of course, a proverb may have its equivalents in other languages, but . . . these equivalents do not *translate* it. To translate is not to search for equivalences. The desire to replace ignores, furthermore, the existence in us of a *proverb consciousness* which immediately detects, in a new proverb, the brother of an authentic one: the world of our proverbs is thus augmented and enriched (Larbaud 1946).

The effacement of the superimposition of languages

The superimposition of languages in a novel involves the relation between dialect and a common language, a koine, or the coexistence, in the heart of a text, of two or more koine. The first case is illustrated by the novels of Gadda and Günter Grass, by Valle-Inclan's *Tirano Banderas*, where his Spanish from Spain is decked out with diverse Latin American Spanishes, by the work of Guimarães Rosa, where classic Portuguese interpenetrates with the dialects of the Brazilian interior. The second case is illustrated by José Maria Arguedas and Roa Bastos, where Spanish is modified profoundly (syntactically) by two other languages from oral cultures: Quechua and Guarani. And there is finally – the limit case – Joyce's *Finnegans Wake* and its sixteen agglutinated languages.

In these two cases, the superimposition of languages is threatened by translation. The relation of tension and integration that exists in the original between the vernacular language and the koine, between the underlying language and the surface language, etc. tends to be effaced. How to preserve the Guarani–Spanish tension in Roa Bastos? Or the relation between Spanish from Spain and the Latin American Spanishes in *Tirano Banderas*? The French translator of this work has not confronted the problem; the French text is completely homogeneous. The same goes for the translation of Mario de Andrade's *Macumaïma*, where the deep vernacular roots of the work are suppressed (which does not happen in the Spanish version of this Brazilian text).

This is the central problem posed by translating novels – a problem that demands maximum reflection from the translator. Every novelistic work is characterized by linguistic superimpositions, even if they include sociolects, idiolects, etc. The novel, said Bakhtin, assembles a *heterology* or diversity of discursive types, a *heteroglossia* or diversity of languages, and a *heterophony* or diversity of voices (Bakhtin 1982: 89). Thomas Mann's novel *The Magic Mountain* offers a fascinating example of heteroglossia, which the translator, Maurice Betz, was able to preserve: the dialogues between the "heroes," Hans Castorp and Madame Chauchat. In the original, both communicate in French, and the fascinating thing is that the young German's French is not *the same* as the young Russian woman's. In the translation, these two varieties of French are in turn framed by the translator's French. Maurice Betz let Thomas Mann's German resonate in his translation to such an extent that the three kinds of French can be distinguished, and each possesses its specific foreignness. This is the sort of success – not quite impossible, certainly difficult – to which every translator of a novel ought to aspire.

The analytic of translation broadly sketched here must be carefully distinguished from the study of "norms" – literary, social, cultural, etc. – which partly govern the translating act in every society. These "norms," which vary historically, never specifically concern translation; they apply, in fact, to any writing practice whatsoever. The analytic, in contrast, focuses on the universals of deformation inherent in translating as such. It is obvious that in specific periods and cultures these universals overlap with the system of norms that govern writing: think only of the neoclassical period and its "belles infidèles." Yet this coincidence is fleeting. In the twentieth century, we no longer submit to neoclassical norms, but the universals of deformation are not any less in force. They even enter into conflict with the new norms governing writing and translation.

At the same time, however, the deforming tendencies analyzed above are not ahistorical. They are rather historical in an original sense. They refer back to the figure of translation based on Greek thought in the West or more precisely, Platonism. The "figure of translation" is understood here as the form in which translation is deployed and appears to itself, before any explicit theory. From its very beginnings, western translation has been an embellishing restitution of meaning, based on the typically Platonic separation between spirit and letter, sense and word, content and form, the sensible and the non-sensible. When it is affirmed today that translation (including non-literary translation) must produce a "clear" and "elegant" text (even if the original does not possess these qualities), the affirmation assumes the Platonic figure of translating, even if unconsciously. All the tendencies noted in the analytic lead to the same result: the production of a text that is more "clear," more "elegant," more "fluent," more "pure" than the original. They are the destruction of the letter in favor of meaning.

Nevertheless, this Platonic figure of translation is not something "false" that can be criticized theoretically or ideologically. For it sets up as an absolute only one essential possibility of translating, which is precisely the restitution of meaning. All translation is, and must be, the restitution of meaning.

The problem is knowing whether this is the unique and ultimate task of translation or whether its task is something else again. The analytic of translation, insofar as the analysis of properly deforming tendencies bears on the translator, does in fact presuppose another figure of translating, which must necessarily be called literal translation. Here "literal" means: attached to the letter (of works). Labor on the letter in translation is more originary than restitution of meaning. It is through this labor that translation, on the one hand, restores the particular signifying process of works (which is more than their meaning) and, on the other hand, transforms the translating language. Translation stimulated the fashioning and refashioning of the great western languages only because it labored on the letter and profoundly modified the translating language. As simple restitution of meaning, translation could never have played this formative role.

Consequently, the essential aim of the analytic of translation is to highlight this other essence of translating, which, although never recognized, endowed it with historical effectiveness in every domain where it was practiced.

Chapter 23

Shoshana Blum-Kulka

SHIFTS OF COHESION AND COHERENCE IN TRANSLATION

THE NEGOTIATION OF MEANING between interactants in natural discourse is based on the assumption that subsequent turns of talk are related to each other in coherent ways. This expectation does not necessarily entail that utterances have to be linked to each other in textually overt ways. Consider for example the following alternative replies to a "how are you" query:

1   How are you?
1a. I'm fine.
1b. I've failed the test.
1c. Johnny is leaving for the States tomorrow.
1d. Those are pearls that were his eyes.

The listener presumably has no difficulty to accept 1b as an alternative response instead of 1a; though there is no overt response to the "how" question, shared knowledge of the world will suffice to interpret 1b as meaning "not so well". In both 1a and 1b responses are overtly linked to the question, at least by the "I – you" relationship. In 1c there is no such linking, yet the answer may be perfectly acceptable. Its interpretation would presumably need some specific shared knowledge between interactants, the nature of which would tell whether the speaker is announcing "good news" or "bad news". With a stretch of the imagination, we can even possibly imagine a context in which 1d would be heard as coherent. For example, had we interrupted T. S. Eliot while pondering over "The Wasteland", he might well have responded by uttering these words aloud.

1986

Thus we can see that the search for coherence is a general principle in discourse interpretation. Coherence can be viewed *as a covert potential meaning relationship among parts of a text, made overt by the reader or listener through processes of interpretation.* For this process to be realized, the reader or listener must be able to relate the text to relevant and familiar worlds, either real or fictional. Cohesion, on the other hand, will be considered as *an overt relationship holding between parts of the text, expressed by language specific markers.*

In the following, I shall address the issue of possible shifts of cohesion and coherence in the translation of written texts. The main argument postulated is that the process of translation necessarily entails shifts both in textual and discoursal relationships. The argument is developed by adopting a discoursal and communicative approach to the study of translation. It is assumed that translation should be viewed as an *act of communication*; as in the study of all acts of communication, considerations of both the process and the product of the communicative act necessarily relate to at least the linguistic, discoursal and social systems holding for the two languages and cultures involved.

1 Shifts in cohesion

On the level of cohesion, shifts in types of cohesive markers used in translation seem to affect translations in one or both of the following directions:

a. Shifts in levels of explicitness; i.e. the general level of the target texts' textual explicitness is higher or lower than that of the source text.
b. Shifts in text meaning(s); i.e. the explicit and implicit meaning potential of the source text changes through translations.

1.1 Shifts in levels of explicitness

The overt cohesive relationships between parts of the texts are necessarily linked to a language's grammatical system (Halliday and Hasan 1976). Thus, grammatical differences between languages will be expressed by changes in the types of ties used to mark cohesion in source and target texts. Such transformations might carry with them a shift in the text's overall level of explicitness. Consider 2a and 2b:

2a. *Source language (SL) (English)*	2b. *Target language (TL) (French)*
Marie was helping Jimmy climb the biggest *branch* of the tree in the front yard, to start work on their tree house. The *branch* looked very strong but when Jimmy grabbed hold, *it* started to crack. He might really get hurt!	Marie était en train d'aider Jimmy à grimper sur la plus haute branche de l'arbre du jardin pour commencer à construire leur cabane. *La branche* avait l'air tres solide, mais quand Jimmy *l'attrapa, elle* commença à craquer. Il pourrait vraiment se faire mal.

(Harvard Language and Literary Skills Project;
provided by courtesy of Catherine Snow).

As required by the French grammatical system, in the French version, the anaphoric reference to the "branch" is marked twice for gender ("La branche, elle commença") and repeated once more than in English ("l'attrapa"). The result is a slightly higher level of redundancy in the French as compared to the English version, a trend that would be reversed had the translation used French as the source language.

On a higher, textual level, such shifts in levels of explicitness through translations have been claimed to be linked to differences in stylistic preferences for types of cohesive markers in the two languages involved in translation. Levenston (1976) and Berman (1978) have contrasted English with Hebrew, and noted the preference of Hebrew for lexical repetition or pronominalization. Levenston claims that given the choice between lexical repetition and pronominalization, Hebrew writers tend to prefer the former while English writers tend to choose the latter. Berman modifies this claim by arguing that both in Hebrew and in English, pronominalization is preferred whenever possible, but since a choice is often not grammatically possible in Hebrew, in fact lexical repetition is far more frequent in Hebrew than in English. A similar claim has recently been made for Portuguese and English (Vieira 1984), namely that cohesive features in Portuguese reflect a stronger need for clarity and a higher degree of specification than English.

The phenomenon depicted in these studies might indeed indicate different norms governing the use of particular cohesive devices in the source and target languages. Such differences may also, however, be ascribed to constraints imposed by the translation process itself.

The process of translation, particularly if successful, necessitates a complex text and discourse processing. The process of interpretation performed by the translator on the source text might lead to a TL text which is more redundant than the SL text. This redundancy can be expressed by a rise in the level of cohesive explicitness in the TL text. This argument may be stated as "*the explicitation hypothesis*", which postulates an observed cohesive explicitness from SL to TL texts regardless of the increase traceable to differences between the two linguistic and textual systems involved. It follows that explicitation is viewed here as inherent in the process of translation.

For lack of large-scale empirical studies that might validate either or both the "stylistic preference" and the "explicitation" hypothesis, more evidence for the latter might be sought by examining different types of interlanguages, from those produced by language learners to the products of both non-professional and professional translators.

The first indication of this trend is thus to be sought in the written work of language learners. Stemmer (1981) analyzed the use of cohesive devices in German learners' English, and found that of the five types of cohesive devices she investigated (substitution, ellipsis, reference, lexical cohesion and conjunction), it was *lexical cohesion* (e.g. lexical repetition) as well as conjunctions which were markedly overrepresented in the learner data, with a non-comitant underrepresentation of *reference linkage* (e.g. pronominalization). The use of cohesive devices was different with English native speakers who tended to prefer referential linkage over lexical cohesion, substitution, ellipsis and conjunction. In Berman's (1978) study, a similar overrepresentation of *lexical cohesion* was depicted in the English written work of native speakers of Hebrew.

Moving from the domain of language learning to that of translation, we can expect to find a trend for explicitation especially marked in the work of "non-professional" translators. In many contexts, bilingual speakers are called upon to mediate between monolingual interactants (Knapp-Potthoff and Knapp 1986) orally, or to render texts from one language to another for some specific practical ends. The less experienced the translator, the more his or her process of interpretation of the SL might be reflected in the TL.

Thus, it is not surprising that in translations done by (bilingual) graduate research assistants working on the Harvard Literacy Skills project the trend is for the TL texts to be longer than the SL ones; for example in three short texts the differences in length were as follows:

	English, SL (graphemic words)	French TL (graphemic words)
3	64	85
4	54	69
5	127	149

The difference in length reflects the trend toward explicitation evident on closer examination. The following are examples of how SL text has been expanded in TL:

	SL (English)		TL (French)
3a	. . . Halfway up he realized that the ladder was swaying	3b	. . . Il n'était pas encore en haut de l'échelle, *lorsque'il* a *senti que celle-ci etait en train de basculer*
4a	Ruth was just carrying the garbage out through the front door	4b	Isabelle était justement *en train de sortir* de la maison *pour mettre les poubelles dehors*
4c	Harvey ran in from playing and dropped his roller skates on the front steps on his way to the kitchen for a cookie	4d	Herve rentra chez lui en courant et jeta ses patins à roulettes sur les escaliers devant la porte d'entrée *parce qu'il etait pressé d'aller prendre un gâteau dans la cuisine*
5a	She told them not to help each other	5b	Elle leur dit de ne pas s'aider et *de travailler tout seul*
5c	The teacher began, "g", "l", "o", "n"	5d	La maîtresse dit, "Écrivez "g", "l", "o", "n"

In all of these examples, explicitation goes beyond changes in cohesive forms; in 3a and 3b the expression "halfway up" is decomposed in the translation to read "he wasn't yet on top of the ladder when". In 4a and 4b as well as 4c and 4d, similar syntactic transformations take place, which lead to the addition of explicit connectives ("parce que" and "pour") in both. While in texts 3 and 4 the process of explicitation might be connected to syntactic or lexical language differences, no such argument can be used to explain the examples in 5. The translator simply expands the TL text, building into it a semantic redundancy absent in the original.

The net result in all cases is a rise in the target text's level of explicitness. Example 6 shows that this phenomenon is not absent from professional translations:

6a.   J'ai montré mon chef d'œuvre aux grandes personnes et je leur ai demandé si mon dessin leur faisait peur.
Elles m'ont repondu "Pourquoi un chapeau ferait-il peur?"

(Saint-Exupéry, *Le Petit Prince*, p. 11)

6b.   I showed my masterpiece to the grown-ups and asked them whether the drawings frightened them.
But they answered, *"Frightened?* Why should anyone be frightened by a hat?"

(English version, 1962 by K. Woods)

Thus, it might be the case that explicitation is a universal strategy inherent in the process of language mediation, as practiced by language learners, non-professional translators and professional translators alike.

1.2 Meaning and cohesion

As pointed out by Halliday and Hasan (1976) cohesion ties do much more than provide continuity and thus create the semantic unity of the text. The choice involved in the types of cohesive markers used in a particular text can affect the texture (as being "loose" or "dense") as well as the style and meaning of that text. Particularly in literature, the choice of cohesive markers can serve central functions in the text. It follows that shifts in types of cohesive ties through translation may alter these functions.

In Pinter's play, *Old Times*, (Pinter 1971) the stage directions call for "dim light", in which three figures can be discerned: Deeley, slumped in an armchair, still, Kate curled on a sofa, still, and Anna standing at the window, looking out. Following a Pinteresque silence, the lights go up on Deeley and Kate, smoking, while Anna's figure remains still in dim light at the window. As is often the case in modern plays, the first sentences spoken give the impression that the conversation has been going on for some time:

7

	SL (English)	TL (Hebrew)
1	Kate: Dark. (pause)	kehah (dark)
2	Deeley: Fat or thin?	šmena or raza? (fat or thin)
3	Kate: Fuller than me, I think. (pause)	yoter mlea mimeni, ani xoševet (more full than me, I think)
4	Deeley: She was then?	kax hayta az? (so she was then?)
5	Kate: I think so.	kax ani xoševet (so I think)
6	Deeley: She may not be now.	yitaxen sıena kax kaet (perhaps she is not so now)

(Pinter, 1971, Hebrew version by R. Kislev)

By the end of these six turns (and three pauses) we know that the dialogue concerns one female person and two time frames (then and now). But this information is deliberately unfolded to us in stages, disambiguating each line by the subsequent one. The first line, "dark", is ambiguous in regard to referent: is Kate referring to the dim light on the stage/off stage or to a person? The second line establishes by semantic means that the referent is probably human. It is only by the fourth turn that gender is established ("she was then") too. Retrospectively, the first three lines thus create a lexical cohesive network (dark, fat, thin, full) not apparent on first reading or listening.

The Hebrew translator is faced with two problems from the very first line. First, Hebrew requires the adjective to be marked for gender. Thus, regardless of the lexical item used, the gender of the referent is established immediately. Second, there is no equivalent polysemic lexical item for "dark". The word chosen "kehah", can only apply to "human" referents. Consequently, in the next lines, the Hebrew text is at no point ambiguous in regard to the kind of entity or person Kate and Deeley are talking about. The result is that whereas in the original the turns relate to each other by subtle means of lexical cohesion, in Hebrew they are connected explicitly, lexically and grammatically, giving the text a dense, close texture instead of the looser one Pinter probably intended.

For the first four turns, this effect is partly unavoidable since it's due to differences in the grammatical systems between the two languages. By the fourth turn, it becomes apparent that unavoidable changes in cohesive markers made by the translator play an important part in creating this dense texture.

The Hebrew translator added twice the word "so": once in turn 4 and again in turn 6, and postposed the word "so" in turn 5. These seemingly trivial changes actually affect the indirect speech acts transmitted by the original, a phenomenon often detectable in literary translations (Blum-Kulka 1981). Kate's hesitant replies to Deeley's queries (the repetition of "I think", "I think so" in 3 and 5) are met by a comment (6) that casts doubt on Kate's expertise on the topic discussed. In interactional terms, if we classify moves as either "supportive" or "challenging" in regard to each other (Burton 1980; Blum-Kulka 1983), the challenging moves in this exchange belong to Deeley, while Kate's moves are supportive, thus showing Deeley at some advantage over his wife. In the Hebrew version, move 4, which in English might still be interpreted as a simple request for clarification, implies wonder or doubt, thus suggesting that it is meant as a challenge. In 5 (in Hebrew "so I think") the challenge is met by Kate by an emphatic counter-challenge, countered again in move 6. Thus, the power struggle between the couple, at this stage of the play still only hinted at, seems to turn in translation into an ordinary argument between married people, of which neither comes out with an advantage over the other.

I would like to suggest that the functional shifts caused by changes in types of cohesion markers apparent in the translation of *Old Times* are by no means unusual. They fit in with the trend for explicitation discussed earlier. Except that in literary texts, especially in modern plays where the short lines of seemingly ordinary talk are so heavy with implied meanings, each shift in cohesion has far-reaching consequences for the interpretation of those meanings.

2 Shift of coherence

As we have seen, cohesion is an overt textual relationship, objectively detectable. The study of cohesion lends itself to quantitative analysis. Hence it should be possible to ascertain by empirical research to what extent explicitation is indeed a norm that cuts across translations from various languages and to what extent it is a language pair-specific phenomenon.

Coherence, on the other hand, defies quantitative methods of analysis, unless approached from the reader's point of view. I understand coherence as *the realization(s) of the text's meaning potential*; this realization can be approached either theoretically, by postulating an "ideal reader" (as suggested by Fillmore 1981) or empirically, by investigating the ways a given text has been remembered or interpreted by various readers, as done in text-processing psycholinguistic research (Van Dijk and Kintsch 1983).

Thus, I agree with Edmondson (1981) who equates coherence with the text's interpretability. In considering "shifts in coherence" through translation, I will be concerned, on the most general level, with examining the possibility that texts may change or lose their meaning potential through translation.

The following points will be argued:

a. That there is a need to distinguish between *reader-focused* and *text-focused* shifts of coherence, and that probably, the former are less avoidable than the latter.
b. That text-focused shifts of coherence are linked to the process of translation per se, while reader-focused shifts are linked to a change in reader audiences through translation.
c. That both types of shifts can be studied to a certain extent by psycholinguistic methods of text processing.

2.1 Reader-focused shifts of coherence

Texts may cohere with respect to subject matter (e.g. mathematics), to genre conventions (literature) or with respect to any possible world evoked and/or presupposed by the text. For the reader, the text becomes a coherent discourse if he can apply relevant schemas (e.g. based on world knowledge, subject matter knowledge, familiarity with genre conventions) to draw the necessary inferences for understanding both the letter and the spirit of the text. In Fillmore's (1981) terms, this process leads to an envisionment of the text in the reader's mind. Envisionments can, of course, vary with individual readers and with different types of audiences. Thus, *King Lear* would not "mean the same" to the British reader and to the French bilingual reader who can read and understand the original. Needless to say, the differences in envisionments between these two readers might increase considerably if the French speaker has to read *King Lear* in translation.

As pointed out by Eugene K. Bristow, in his introduction to his translation of Chekhov's plays, "Even within the skin of his own language, every person translates what he sees or reads, from his own experience" (Bristow 1977: XV). To illustrate this point he tells the story of how *The Cherry Orchard* was not the same in the minds of the directors of the Moscow Art Theatre as in Chekhov's mind. To the directors the play was a tragedy, to its author, "a comedy, in places even a farce". Though the directors eventually had their way, Chekhov insisted that "not once had either one read through my play carefully" (Bristow 1977: ibid.).

In examining the final translation product, the question then is: can we distinguish between shifts of coherence due to the necessary shift between audience types as distinct from those shifts that are traceable to the process of translation per se? I would like to suggest that it is important to attempt to draw this distinction, so that we can have a better understanding of what translation can and can *not* do, or, in other words, to better understand the true limits of translatability.

It follows that if bridging across cultures and languages, as is always the case in translation, is indeed different from switching primarily between audiences (even if a language shift is involved), then we should see evidence for reader-based shifts in texts originally aimed at two audiences and written in two languages as 8:

8

Vous seriez prêt à parier qu'ils sont en voyage de noces?	They look like they're on their honeymoon, don't they?
N'en faites rien, vous perdriez votre pari.	But they're not.
M. et Mme. Gauthier sont mariés depuis douze ans.	The Jacksons have been married twelve years.
Ils se rendent à New York, lui pour affaires, elle pour faire des emplettes de Noël dans Fifth Avenue. Elle est heureuse de cette diversion dans le train-train quotidien, heureuse de partir avec lui – et ça se voit.	Mr. Jackson's on his way to close an important deal in New York. Mrs. Jackson's going to do some Christmas shopping on Fifth Avenue. No wonder she's smiling, Mr. Jackson didn't leave her behind this trip.

(Air Canada, no date)

The two versions of the Air Canada advertisement illustrate the copy writer's awareness of the difference in the cultural assumptions of the audience they were catering for. The emphasis on the importance of Mr. Jackson's business in New York caters to Canadian Anglopohones, while for the French Canadian community the mention of Mr. Gauthier's business alone seems to suffice; the wives in both versions only accompany their husbands, but while in the English version the woman's so-called happiness comes from not being left behind, the French version plays both on the woman's breaking away from daily chores and on the romantic notion of being happy to travel with Mr. Gauthier.

Obviously these texts might have been translated from either of the two languages to the other. The fact that apparently they were written as two versions to serve the same purpose testifies to the fact that the Air Canada public relations people are aware of the different needs of the two language communities.

As shown by Toury (1977) translations "proper" operate with respect to two opposing sets of norms: on the one hand, that of showing concern for the contemporary reader (thus being licensed to restructure the SL text in the TL); and on the other hand that of remaining as faithful as possible to the SL. Reader-based shifts of coherence are hence linked, to a certain extent, to the prevailing normative system within which the translator operates.

The prevailing norm in the 20th century has been, on the most general level, to expect translations to live up to some expectation of "faithfulness" or "dynamic equivalence" (Nida 1964). In other words, most published translations are regarded as attempts to render a given text in another language, and *not* as attempts to convey a given message to a new audience. Hence, since TL audiences are by definition almost always "new" to some, if not all, of SL audiences, and writers' shared worlds, reader-focused shifts of coherence in translation are, to a large extent, unavoidable.

The clearest examples of shifts of coherence that result from the change in audience and *not* language come from the area of reference. Whether real world or literary, allusions to persons, places or other texts may play a central role in building up the coherence of a given story. Writers themselves may be aware of the fact that their reference network is not shared by their readers and take pains to explain it in footnotes or otherwise. In translation the translator becomes the judge as to the extent to which he or she finds it necessary to explain the source text's reference network to the target-language audience.

For example, Camus, in *L'Homme revolté* (Camus 1951), evokes Heathcliff's passion for Cathy in *Wuthering Heights* to illustrate his point for discriminating between crimes of passion and crimes of logic. The German translator felt a need to add a footnote explaining that the reference is to a novel by Emily Brontë, while neither the English translator (Bower 1953) (understandably) nor the Hebrew one (Arad 1951) judged this necessary.

While in reading Camus, following the allusion to *Wuthering Heights* is not necessary for understanding the main argument, in another text a similar allusion might be central.

In literary as well as non-literary texts, the issue of shared or non-shared reference networks is not an absolute one. For complex literary works perhaps only literary critics come to or claim to decipher all of the writer's references and allusions. Through the process of translation (as well as in the teaching of literature) the problem is to delimit those central allusions without the understanding of which the reader might have difficulty in even following the main argument or plot. Even more complex are cases where reference networks and presuppositions of the original text are a necessary condition for drawing the *relevant implications* from the text.

The opening passage of Hemingway's story "The Killers" (Hemingway 1938) provides a good example for two reasons: first, because its analysis highlights the different significance cohesion and coherence markers might carry in the translation of one particular text, and second, because the coherence of this text hinges on familiarity with a seemingly almost trivial reference network.

9 "The Killers"

SL (English)	TL (Hebrew)
The door of Henry's lunch room opened and *two men came in*. They sat down at the counter.	sne anašim nixnsu (two men entered)

1 "What's yours?" George asked them.

2 "I don't know," *one of the men said,*
   "What do you want to eat Al?" Outside
   it was getting dark. The street-light
   came on outside the window. *The two
   men* at the counter read the menu.
   From the other end of the counter
   Nick Adams watched them. He had
   been talking to George when they
   came in.

amar axad haanašim
(said one of the men)

šnei haanašim (the two
men)

3 "I'll have a roast pork tenderloin with
   apple sauce and mashed potatoes,"
   the first man said.

amar haiš harišon (said the
first man)

4 "It isn't ready yet."

5 "What the hell do you put it on the
   card for?"

6 "That's the dinner," George explained.
   "You can get that at six o'clock."

7 "The clock says twenty minutes past
   five," *the second man said.*

amar haiš ha šeni (the
second man said)

8 "It's twenty minutes fast."

9 "Oh, the hell with the clock," *the first
   man said.* "What have you got to eat?"

amar haiš harišon (the first
man said)

10 "I can give you any kind of sandwiches,"
    George said.

11 "You can have ham and eggs, bacon
    and eggs, liver and bacon or a steak."

12 "Give me chicken croquettes with
    green peas and cream sauce and mashed
    potato."

13 "That's the dinner."

(Hemingway 1938, Hebrew version
by R. Nof and Y. Swarts)

The cohesive device consists of two separate sets of identification and co-reference networks in the text: one for "the two men" who are not identified by name (unless mentioned by each other) and the second for the people present in the lunchroom, who are named and referred to by name. This obvious difference in co-reference networks helps to set up "the two men" as "the strangers" and establishes the story's point of view as that of the people within the lunchroom. The perspective established already in the first sentence – "two men came in" causes a problem for translation into Hebrew only in this key sentence. The verb used "enter", (lehikanes), otherwise an appropriate choice, is neutral to the presupposition of perspective.

For the rest of the passage, the simplicity of the co-referential device lends itself easily to translation. The reference network is translated almost word for word to Hebrew and thus compensates for the loss in perspective in the first sentence of the story.

On the other hand, deriving the relevant implications from this text, i.e. building a coherent interpretation, necessitates familiarity with certain presuppositions which have to do with simple, everyday knowledge of the physical outlay and behavioral norms of American lunchrooms. In the exchange taking place between the owner of the lunchroom, George, and the two men who enter, the accelerating tension and threat embedded in the men's appearance, to be revealed as a real threat later on, is transmitted through a dialogue centered on the ordering of food.

To understand the interactional balance and indirect speech acts of this exchange, the reader has to be able to draw the appropriate inferences from a conversation overtly concerned with food, and covertly centering on the issue of power. Through this exchange, the two men display an aggressive attitude which is met by a "correct", even appeasing, behavior on the part of George. By the end of the exchange, the inequality between participants becomes clear, with "the men" as aggressors, possessing threatening power over all other participants.

To follow the process by which the interaction unfolds, it is important to realize which moves in the dialogue constitute a challenge and which are attempts at cooperative behavior. I would like to suggest that in part such understanding hinges on familiarity with the cultural presuppositions of the story, the lack of which might lead to inappropriate inferences.

The systematic challenging inherent in the two men's moves is transmitted by their violations of conversational rules, i.e. by violations of Gricean (Grice 1975) maxims of relevance, manner, quantity and quality. A close examination of the passage, turn by turn, unfolds this process.

In turn 3 there is a subtle violation of manner: instead of naming the order ("I'll have the . . .") as customary, the first man reads out from the menu the full description of the dish ordered. To the non-American ear, this description might suggest an elaborate dish to be associated with fancy restaurants. The American reader, accustomed to the embellished style in which food is listed in the simplest of American restaurants, recognizes the order as something quite common. Thus, the rejection of the order by George in turn 4 might be interpreted in two different ways, depending on shared or non-shared background knowledge. The reader who is impressed by the name of the dish might wonder at the food not being available upon order at a presumably fancy restaurant, thus perhaps finding the overtly challenging question of turn 5 justifiable. Actually, George is acting perfectly within his rights (i.e. being cooperative) by relying on the accepted custom of having "dinner" and "non-dinner" foods. Since this division is also probably listed on the menu, his customers' deliberate refusal to accept this norm becomes a threatening challenge. Thus, turn 12 violates the maxim of relevance by openly ignoring the "dinner order" constraint.

Thus, knowledge of two cultural schemes seems to be important for this exchange – the relative "fancyness" or "non-fancyness" of the dishes mentioned and the cultural norm of having a time limit for dinner and non-dinner orders. The lack of both might transform the interactional balance depicted in the story from one in which one party represents the aggressors and the other the potential victims, to one in which the two parties are more or less on an equal footing and both are challenging each other.

Obviously, the last possibility is exaggerated, since there are further overt indicators in the dialogue for the customer's refusal to abide by the rule. (See turns 7–9 on the discussion of the time.) Yet, the grasping of the full scope of indirect meanings conveyed in this exchange is only available to the reader who shares the text's cultural presuppositions.

There is not much the translator can do to remedy this situation. Contrary to occasional references to specific referents, which can be provided by different techniques, the nature of cultural institutions, as is the case in this story, is not easily explained in a footnote. It follows that reader-focused shifts of coherence in translation are to some extent unavoidable, unless the translator is normatively free to "transplant" the text from one cultural environment to another.

2.2 Text-focused shifts of coherence

The difference in the translator's role in regard to reader-based versus text-based shifts of coherence can be seen as that of two types of medical practice. For reader-based shifts, the translator is in the position of the practitioners of preventive medicine: his role is to foresee the possibilities of "damage" to interpretation in the TL and to apply means to minimize them. With regard to text-based shifts, the translator is in the position of the physician administering treatment: in this area, accurate diagnosis is the necessary first condition to successful treatment. In other words, text-based shifts of coherence often occur as a result of particular choices made by a specific translator, choices that indicate a lack of awareness on the translator's part of the SL text's meaning potential.

In part, text-based shifts of coherence are linked to well-known differences between linguistic systems. Yet I would like to suggest that the most serious shifts occur not due to the differences as such, but because the translator failed to realize the functions a particular linguistic system, or a particular form, plays in conveying indirect meanings in a given text. The following example illustrates this point:

10

	SL (English)	(TL Hebrew)
1	A: Do you want to come in?	
2	B: No thanks, really I can't.	
3	A: Oh, come on. You've been to church, have a reward. Have some coffee.	
4	B: No, look (. . .) You're a doll but I got this wife now.	
5	A. I beg your pardon.	avekeš et slixatxa (I'm (I' . . .) ask your pardon).
6	But thanks, anyway.	

(John Updike 1960: 223, Hebrew version by E. Kaspi)

In the dialogue between a man and a woman in Updike's *Rabbit Run*, the major messages are being transmitted indirectly. The coherence of the dialogue hinges on relating a set of implications to each other: first, that the woman's (A) invitation must have been interpreted by the man (B) as referring to something else beyond coffee, and second, that it is the implied rather than the stated invitation which he declines by mentioning his wife. The woman's reaction in turn 5 – "I beg your pardon" – might be conveying a number of different indirect speech acts. She might be showing indignation at being, presumably, misinterpreted; she might be apologizing for having made the offer, or she might be simply signalling non-comprehension. As the story continues, the woman angrily slams the door in the man's face. Thus context rules out the last two interpretations and the reader is left to puzzle with the hero: "was she mad because he had turned down a proposition, or because he had shown that he had thought she had made one?" (Updike 1960: 224). The Hebrew translation for "I beg your pardon" means literally, "I'm asking (or I'll ask) for your pardon". This phrase is habitually used for apologizing in a slightly formal way. Thus, in Hebrew, the woman is heard as apologizing for having made the offer. Hence the translation is shown to limit the dialogue's interpretative options. Furthermore it should be noted that given the context of the dialogue, this mistranslation causes a shift in the text's structure of coherence, leaving the hero's puzzle over the woman's anger a real puzzle for the TL reader too.

Three further passages from the Hebrew translation of Pinter's *Old Times* considered earlier provide a further example.

11

	SL (English)	TL (Hebrew)
A		
1	Deeley: Any idea what she drinks?	
2	Kate: None.	
3	Deeley: She may be a vegetarian.	
4	Kate: Ask her.	
5	Deeley: It's too late. You've already cooked your casserole. Pause	meuxar miday. at kvar bišalt ettavsil sil hakaserol šelax. Yes baze gam basar vegam yerakot. (It's too late. You've already cooked your casserole dish. It contains both vegetables and meat.)
	Why isn't she married? I mean, why isn't she bringing her husband?	
6	Kate: Ask her.	
B		
1	Deeley: You haven't seen her for twenty years.	
2	Kate: You've never seen her. There's a difference. Pause	
3	Deeley: At least the casserole is big enough for four.	lefaxot sir hakaserol maspik learba'a (at least the casserole dish is big enough for four).
4	Kate: You said she was a vegetarian. Pause	

C

1   Deeley: My work takes me away
    quite often, of course. But Kate stays
    here.

2   Anna: You have a wonderful   yeš lexa kasserol nifla (you
    casserole.   have a wonderful casserole).

3   Deeley: What?

4   Anna: I mean wife. A wonderful wife.
    So sorry.

(Pinter 1971, Hebrew version by R. Kislev)

The first time Deeley mentions "casserole" he and Kate are still talking about a third, presumably non-present person. On one level, the phrase "you've cooked your casserole" is a perfectly relevant comment in the discussion about appropriate food for a possibly vegetarian guest, assuming, of course, that the dish contains meat. The translator, apparently worried that her Hebrew readers will not have available the relevant "meat casserole" schema, took pains to expand the text by way of explanation. But, though the specific ingredients of the dish thus become crystal clear, the more important indirect message conveyed by this line is completely lost. The fact that Deeley is not solely concerned with cooking is hinted at by the apparent change of topic in his next line ("Why isn't she married, etc.") and reinforced with further references to "casseroles" in text B and C. The real issue discussed seems to be Kate's preference for marriage over life with her woman friend, Anna. Basically, the play concerns a triangle, where husband and friend, Anna, are involved in a struggle over wife. Viewed in this context, Deeley's change of topic from food to marriage is quite coherent, as well as his reference to a casserole "big enough for four" in turn B3. At some point during the first act, Anna turns from the window, speaking, and moves down to Kate and Deeley joining in the conversation. Following comments about the house and the silence, she says, "You have a wonderful casserole" (turn C2). Quite obviously, by this third reference to "casserole" the reader or listener is not even permitted a literal interpretation. Since the translator opted for literal meaning only on two previous occasions, the overall shift of coherence in the play is inevitable.

It has often been noted (Goffman 1976; Grice 1975) that natural conversations have a residual ambiguity, whereby what *is said* can, on closer analysis, seem obscure, while what is *meant* is usually obvious and clear. The main point I tried to argue in respect to shifts of cohesion and coherence in translation can be summarized by contrasting the process of translation with that of natural discourse: contrary to natural discourse, translation is a process by which what is *said* might become obvious and clear, while what is *meant* might become vague and obscure.

3 The need for empirical studies

The discussion of shifts of cohesion and coherence presented above has been derived from two basic assumptions: first, that translation is a process that operates on *texts* (rather than words or sentences) and hence its products need to be studied within the framework of discourse analysis; and second, that translation is an act of communication, and hence both its processes, products and effects can and need to be studied empirically within the methodological framework of studies in communication.

I have attempted to develop this approach theoretically by suggesting the distinction between shifts of cohesion and shifts of coherence and the types of shifts that might occur within each of these major categories. I would like to conclude by re-examining the distinctions offered from an empirical standpoint, i.e., to consider the ways in which empirical validation might be sought for all or some of the translation shifts postulated.

As concerns shifts of cohesion in translation, I have argued for a need to examine the effect of the use of cohesive features in translation on the TL text's level of explicitness and on the TL text's overt meaning(s), as compared to the SL text. Possible changes in levels of explicitness through translation were postulated to occur either as a result of differences in stylistic preferences between two languages (i.e., one language showing a tendency for higher levels of redundancy through cohesion) or as a result of an explicitation process suggested to be inherent to translation. To establish the relative validity of these hypotheses it would be necessary to first carry out a large-scale contrastive stylistic study (in a given register) to establish cohesive patterns in SL and TL, and then to examine translations to and from both languages to investigate shifts in cohesive levels that occur through translation.

Such studies will need to establish independently: (1) the preferences in choice of cohesive ties in a given register in language A; (2) the preferences in the parallel register in language B; (3) the shifts in cohesive ties in translated texts of the same register from language A to B, and vice versa.

In considering texts in languages A and B independently, such studies will have to differentiate clearly between *obligatory* and *optional* choices of cohesive ties: i.e., between choices dictated by the grammatical systems of the two languages as compared to those attributable to stylistic preferences. In considering translated texts from A to B and vice versa, only the *optional* choices should be taken into account, since only these can be legitimately used as evidence for showing certain trends in shifts of cohesion through translation.

Granted that the study would reveal differences in patterns of cohesion *across* the two languages examined, the examination of the translations could then reveal any of the following:

1   that cohesive patterns in TL texts tend to *approximate* the norms of TL texts of the same register.
2   that cohesive patterns in TL texts tend to reflect norms of SL texts in the same register, which may be due to processes of *transfer* operating on the translation.
3   that cohesive patterns in TL texts are neither TL nor SL norms oriented, but form a system of their own, possibly indicating a process of explicitation.

Between languages that do not differ substantially in their cohesive patterns either grammatically or stylistically, shifts in cohesive patterns through translation from either TL or SL norms could be considered evidence for hypothesis 3, possibly

indicating processes of explicitation. For languages that seem to differ both grammatically and stylistically, as in the case of Hebrew and English, and where one is
probably more explicit cohesively than the other, a trend towards explicitation in
translations into Hebrew could be considered as evidence for both hypotheses 2
(i.e. transfer) and 3 (i.e., explicitation). However, if the same shifts involving
preferences of lexical cohesion over grammatical cohesion are also found in the
reverse direction, i.e., in translations from Hebrew to English, this would mean
that a process of explicitation is indeed taking place in translation.

As concerns shifts of coherence in translation, I have argued for a need to distinguish between *reader-based* shifts, which occur as a result of a text being read by
culturally different audiences, and *text-based* shifts, which occur as a result of the
translation process per se. In both cases, such shifts are thought of as affecting the
text's meaning potential.

Hence, in the study of such shifts, the analysis of texts should be followed by
an investigation of text effects. In other words, I advocate a psycholinguistic
approach to the study of translation effects. Only such an approach, following
general discourse-oriented psycholinguistic studies of text processing (such as van
Dijk and Kintsch 1983) can validate or refute claims pertaining to shifts of meaning
through translation. For example, a study of possible shifts in indirect meanings in
translation should establish: (a) the interpretations agreed on in regard to a particular text by a homogenous group of readers in the SL; (b) the interpretations agreed
on by a parallel group of readers in the TL. Should the results indicate a "mismatch"
between the two sets of interpretations, these in turn might indicate either reader-
based or text-based shifts of coherence.

With the exception of some preliminary attempts in this direction (Sarig 1979),
translation studies to date – this paper being no exception – tend to base their claims
mostly on contrastive textual analysis. Yet, further advances in the field of translation seem to depend on a clearer conceptualization, through empirical research, of
the process of interaction between texts and readers in both the source and target
languages.

Chapter 24

Lori Chamberlain

GENDER AND THE METAPHORICS OF TRANSLATION

IN A LETTER TO the nineteenth-century violinist Joseph Joachim, Clara Schumann declares, "Bin ich auch nicht producierend, so doch reproducierend" (Even if I am not a creative artist, still I am recreating).[1] While she played an enormously important role reproducing her husband's works, both in concert and later in preparing editions of his work, she was also a composer in her own right; yet until recently, historians have focused on only one composer in this family. Indeed, as feminist scholarship has amply demonstrated, conventional representations of women – whether artistic, social, economic, or political – have been guided by a cultural ambivalence about the possibility of a woman artist and about the status of woman's "work." In the case of Clara Schumann, it is ironic that one of the reasons she could not be a more productive composer is that she was kept busy with the eight children she and Robert Schumann produced together.

From our vantage point, we recognize claims that "there are no great women artists" as expressions of a gender-based paradigm concerning the disposition of power in the family and the state. As feminist research from a variety of disciplines has shown, the opposition between productive and reproductive work organizes the way a culture values work: this paradigm depicts originality or creativity in terms of paternity and authority, relegating the figure of the female to a variety of secondary roles. I am interested in this opposition specifically as it is used to mark the distinction between writing and translating – marking, that is, the one to be original and "masculine," the other to be derivative and "feminine." The distinction is only superficially a problem of aesthetics, for there are important consequences in the areas of publishing, royalties, curriculum, and academic tenure. What I propose here is to examine what is at stake for gender in the *representation* of translation: the struggle for authority and the politics of originality informing this struggle.

"At best an echo,"[2] translation has been figured literally and metaphorically in secondary terms. Just as Clara Schumann's performance of a musical composition is seen as qualitatively different from the original act of composing that piece, so the act of translating is viewed as something qualitatively different from the original act of writing. Indeed, under current American copyright law, both translations and musical performances are treated under the same rubric of "derivative works."[3] The cultural elaboration of this view suggests that in the original abides what is natural, truthful, and lawful, in the copy, what is artificial, false, and treasonous. Translations can be, for example, echoes (in musical terms), copies or portraits (in painterly terms), or borrowed or ill-fitting clothing (in sartorial terms).

The sexualization of translation appears perhaps most familiarly in the tag *les belles infidèles* – like women, the adage goes, translations should be either beautiful or faithful. The tag is made possible both by the rhyme in French and by the fact that the word *traduction* is a feminine one, thus making *les beaux infidèles* impossible. This tag owes its longevity – it was coined in the seventeenth century[4] – to more than phonetic similarity: what gives it the appearance of truth is that it has captured a cultural complicity between the issues of fidelity in translation and in marriage. For *les belles infidèles*, fidelity is defined by an implicit contract between translation (as woman) and original (as husband, father, or author). However, the infamous "double standard" operates here as it might have in traditional marriages: the "unfaithful" wife/translation is publicly tried for crimes the husband/original is by law incapable of committing. This contract, in short, makes it impossible for the original to be guilty of infidelity. Such an attitude betrays real anxiety about the problem of paternity and translation; it mimics the patrilineal kinship system where paternity – not maternity – legitimizes an offspring.

It is the struggle for the right of paternity, regulating the fidelity of translation, which we see articulated by the earl of Roscommon in his seventeenth-century treatise on translation. In order to guarantee the originality of the translator's work, surely necessary in a paternity case, the translator must usurp the author's role. Roscommon begins benignly enough, advising the translator to "Chuse an author as you chuse a friend," but this intimacy serves a potentially subversive purpose:

> United by this Sympathetick Bond,
> You grow Familiar, Intimate, and Fond;
> Your thoughts, your Words, your Stiles, your Souls agree,
> No longer his Interpreter, but He.[5]

It is an almost silent deposition: through familiarity (friendship), the translator becomes, as it were, part of the family and finally the father himself: whatever struggle there might be between author and translator is veiled by the language of friendship. While the translator is figured as a male, the text itself is figured as a female whose chastity must be protected:

With how much ease is a young Muse Betray'd
How nice the Reputation of the Maid!
Your early, kind, paternal care appears,
By chast Instruction of her Tender Years.
The first Impression in her Infant Breast
Will be the deepest and should be the best.
Let no Austerity breed servile Fear
No wanton Sound offend her Virgin Ear.[6]

As the translator becomes the author, he incurs certain paternal duties in relation
to the text, to protect and instruct – or perhaps structure – it. The language used
echoes the language of conduct books and reflects attitudes about the proper differences in educating males and females; "chast Instruction" is proper for the female,
whose virginity is an essential prerequisite to marriage. The text, that blank page
bearing the author's imprint ("The first Impression . . . Will be the deepest"), is
impossibly twice virgin – once for the original author, and again for the translator
who has taken his place. It is this "chastity" which resolves – or represses – the
struggle for paternity.[7]

The gendering of translation by this language of paternalism is made more
explicit in the eighteenth-century treatise on translation by Thomas Francklin:

Unless an author like a mistress warms,
How shall we hide his faults or taste his charms,
How all his modest latent beauties find,
How trace each lovelier feature of the mind,
Soften each blemish, and each grace improve,
And treat him with the dignity of Love?[8]

Like the earl of Roscommon, Francklin represents the translator as a male who
usurps the role of the author, a usurpation which takes place at the level of grammatical gender and is resolved through a sex change. The translator is figured as a
male seducer; the author, conflated with the conventionally "feminine" features of
his text, is then the "mistress," and the masculine pronoun is forced to refer to the
feminine attributes of the text ("*his* modest latent beauties"). In confusing the gender
of the author with the ascribed gender of the text, Francklin "translates" the creative
role of the author into the passive role of the text, rendering the author relatively
powerless in relation to the translator. The author-text, now a mistress, is flattered
and seduced by the translator's attentions, becoming a willing collaborator in the
project to make herself beautiful – and, no doubt, unfaithful.

This *belle infidèle*, whose blemishes have been softened and whose beauties have
therefore been improved, is depicted both as mistress and as a portrait model. In
using the popular painting analogy, Francklin also reveals the gender coding of that
mimetic convention: the translator/painter must seduce the text in order to "trace"
(translate) the features of his subject. We see a more elaborate version of this
convention, though one arguing a different position on the subject of improvement
through translation, in William Cowper's "Preface" to Homer's *Iliad*: "Should a
painter, professing to draw the likeness of a beautiful woman, give her more or

fewer features than belong to her, and a general cast of countenance of his own invention, he might be said to have produced a *jeu d'esprit*, a curiosity perhaps in its way, but by no means the lady in question."[9] Cowper argues for fidelity to the beautiful model, lest the translation demean her, reducing her to a mere "*jeu d'esprit*," or, to follow the text yet further, make her monstrous ("give her more or fewer features"). Yet lurking behind the phrase "the lady in question" is the suggestion that she is the *other* woman – the beautiful, and potentially unfaithful, mistress. In any case, like the earl of Roscommon and Francklin, Cowper feminizes the text and makes her reputation – that is, her fidelity – the responsibility of the male translator/author.

Just as texts are conventionally figured in feminine terms, so too is language: our "mother tongue." And when aesthetic debates shifted the focus in the late eighteenth century from problems of mimesis to those of expression – in M. H. Abrams's famous terms, from the mirror to the lamp – discussions of translation followed suit. The translator's relationship to this mother figure is outlined in some of the same terms that we have already seen – fidelity and chastity – and the fundamental problem remains the same: how to regulate legitimate sexual (authorial) relationships and their progeny.

A representative example depicting translation as a problem of fidelity to the "mother tongue" occurs in the work of Schleiermacher, whose twin interests in translation and hermeneutics have been influential in shaping translation theory in this century. In discussing the issue of maintaining the essential foreignness of a text in translation, Schleiermacher outlines what is at stake as follows:

> Who would not like to permit his mother tongue to stand forth every-where in the most universally appealing beauty each genre is capable of? Who would not rather sire children who are their parents' pure effigy, and not bastards? . . . Who would suffer being accused, like those parents who abandon their children to acrobats, of bending his mother tongue to foreign and unnatural dislocations instead of skillfully exercising it in its own natural gymnastics?[10]

The translator, as father, must be true to the mother/language in order to produce legitimate offspring; if he attempts to sire children otherwise, he will produce bastards fit only for the circus. Because the mother tongue is conceived of as natural, any tampering with it – any infidelity – is seen as unnatural, impure, monstrous, and immoral. Thus, it is "natural" law which requires monogamous relations in order to maintain the "beauty" of the language and in order to insure that the works be genuine or original. Though his reference to bastard children makes clear that he is concerned over the purity of the mother tongue, he is also concerned with the paternity of the text. "Legitimacy" has little to do with motherhood and more to do with the institutional acknowledgment of fatherhood. The question, "Who is the real father of the text?" seems to motivate these concerns about both the fidelity of the translation and the purity of the language.

In the metaphorics of translation, the struggle for authorial rights takes place both in the realm of the family, as we have seen, and in the state, for translation has also been figured as the literary equivalent of colonization, a means of enriching both the language and the literature appropriate to the political needs of expanding nations. A typical translator's preface from the English eighteenth century makes this explicit:

> You, my Lord, know how the works of genius lift up the head of a nation above her neighbors, and give as much honor as success in arms; among these we must reckon our translations of the classics; by which when we have naturalized all Greece and Rome, we shall be so much richer than they by so many original productions as we have of our own.[11]

Because literary success is equated with military success, translation can expand both literary and political borders. A similar attitude toward the enterprise of translation may be found in the German Romantics, who used *Übersetzen* (to translate) and *verdeutschen* (to Germanize) interchangeably: translation was literally a strategy of linguistic incorporation. The great model for this use of translation is, of course, the Roman Empire, which so dramatically incorporated Greek culture into its own. For the Romans, Nietzsche asserts, "translation was a form of conquest."[12]

Then, too, the politics of colonialism overlap significantly with the politics of gender we have seen so far. Flora Amos shows, for example, that during the sixteenth century in England, translation is seen as "public duty." The most stunning example of what is construed as "public duty" is articulated by a sixteenth-century English translator of Horace named Thomas Drant, who, in the preface to his translation of the Roman author, boldly announces,

> First I have now done as the people of God were commanded to do with their captive women that were handsome and beautiful: I have shaved off his hair and pared off his nails, that is, I have wiped away all his vanity and superfluity of matter. . . . I have Englished things not according to the vein of the Latin propriety, but of his own vulgar tongue. . . . I have pieced his reason, eked and mended his similitudes, mollified his hardness, prolonged his cortall kind of speeches, changed and much altered his words, but not his sentence, or at least (I dare say) not his purpose.[13]

Drant is free to take the liberties he here describes, for, as a clergyman translating a secular author, he must make Horace morally suitable: he must transform him from the foreign or alien into, significantly, a member of the family. For the passage from the Bible to which Drant alludes (Deut. 21:12–14) concerns the proper way to make a captive woman a wife: "Then you shall bring her home to your house; and she shall shave her head and pare her nails" (Deut. 21:12, Revised Standard Version). After giving her a month in which to mourn, the captor can then take her as a wife; but if he finds in her no "delight," the passage forbids him subsequently to sell her because he has already humiliated her. In making Horace suitable to become a wife, Drant must transform him into a woman, the uneasy effects of which remain in the tension of pronominal reference, where "his" seems to refer to "women." In addition, Drant's paraphrase makes it the husband–

translator's duty to shave and pare rather than the duty of the captive Horace. Unfortunately, captors often did much more than shave the heads of captive women (see Num. 31:17–18); the sexual violence alluded to in this description of translation provides an analogue to the political and economic rapes implicit in a colonizing metaphor.

Clearly, the meaning of the word "fidelity" in the context of translation changes according to the purpose translation is seen to serve in a larger aesthetic or cultural context. In its gendered version, fidelity sometimes defines the (female) translation's relation to the original, particularly to the original's author (male), deposed and replaced by the author (male) of the translation. In this case, the text, if it is a good and beautiful one, must be regulated against its propensity for infidelity in order to authorize the originality of this *production*. Or, fidelity might also define a (male) author–translator's relation to his (female) mother-tongue, the language into which something is being translated. In this case, the (female) language must be protected against vilification. It is, paradoxically, this sort of fidelity that can justify the rape and pillage of another language and text, as we have seen in Drant. But again, this sort of fidelity is designed to enrich the "host" language by certifying the originality of translation; the conquests, made captive, are incorporated into the "works of genius" of a particular language.

It should by now be obvious that this metaphorics of translation reveals both an anxiety about the myths of paternity (or authorship and authority) and a profound ambivalence about the role of maternity – ranging from the condemnation of *les belles infidèles* to the adulation accorded to the "mother tongue." In one of the few attempts to deal with both the practice and the metaphorics of translation, Serge Gavronsky argues that the source of this anxiety and ambivalence lies in the oedipal structure which informs the translator's options. Gavronsky divides the world of translation metaphors into two camps. The first group he labels pietistic: metaphors based on the coincidence of courtly and Christian traditions, wherein the conventional knight pledges fidelity to the unravished lady, as the Christian to the Virgin. In this case, the translator (as knight or Christian) takes vows of humility, poverty – and chastity. In secular terms, this is called "positional" translation, for it depends on a well-known hierarchization of the participants. The vertical relation (author/translator) has thus been overlaid with both metaphysical and ethical implications, and in this missionary position, submissiveness is next to godliness.

Gavronsky argues that the master/slave schema underlying this metaphoric model of translation is precisely the foundation of the oedipal triangle:

> Here, in typically euphemistic terms, the slave is a willing one (a hyperbolic servant, a faithful): the translator considers himself as the child of the father-creator, his rival, while the text becomes the object of desire, that which has been completely defined by the paternal figure, the phallus-pen. Traditions (taboos) impose upon the translator a highly restricted ritual role. He is forced to curtail himself (strictly speaking) in order to respect the interdictions on incest. To tamper with the text would be tantamount to eliminating, in part or totally, the father-author(ity), the dominant present.[14]

Thus, the "paternal care" of which the earl of Roscommon speaks is one manifestation of this repressed incestuous relation with the text, a second being the concern for the purity of "mother" (madonna) tongues.

The other side of the oedipal triangle may be seen in a desire to kill the symbolic father text/author. According to Gavronsky, the alternative to the pietistic translator is the cannibalistic, "aggressive translator who seizes possession of the 'original,' who savors the text, that is, who truly feeds upon the words, who ingurgitates them, and who, thereafter, enunciates them in his own tongue, thereby having explicitly rid himself of the 'original' creator."[15] Whereas the "pietistic" model represents translators as completely secondary to what is pure and original, the "cannibalistic" model, Gavronsky claims, liberates translators from servility to "cultural and ideological restrictions." What Gavronsky desires is to free the translator/translation from the signs of cultural secondariness, but his model is unfortunately inscribed within the same set of binary terms and either/or logic that we have seen in the metaphorics of translation. Indeed, we can see the extent to which Gavronsky's metaphors are still inscribed within that ideology in the following description: "The original has been captured, raped, and incest performed. Here, once again, the son is father of the man. The original is mutilated beyond recognition; the slave–master dialectic reversed."[16] In repeating the sort of violence we have already seen so remarkably in Drant, Gavronsky betrays the dynamics of power in this "paternal" system. Whether the translator quietly usurps the role of the author, the way the earl of Roscommon advocates, or takes authority through more violent means, power is still figured as a male privilege exercised in family and state political arenas. The translator, for Gavronsky, is a male who repeats on the sexual level the kinds of crimes any colonizing country commits on its colonies.

As Gavronsky himself acknowledges, the cannibalistic translator is based on the hermeneuticist model of George Steiner, the most prominent contemporary theorist of translation; Steiner's influential model illustrates the persistence of what I have called the politics of originality and its logic of violence in contemporary translation theory. In his *After Babel*, Steiner proposes a four-part process of translation. The first step, that of "initiative trust," describes the translator's willingness to take a gamble on the text, trusting that the text will yield something. As a second step, the translator takes an overtly aggressive step, "penetrating" and "capturing" the text (Steiner calls this "appropriative penetration"), an act explicitly compared to erotic possession. During the third step, the imprisoned text must be "naturalized," must become part of the translator's language, literally incorporated or embodied. Finally, to compensate for this "appropriative 'rapture,'" the translator must restore the balance, attempt some act of reciprocity to make amends for the act of aggression. His model for this act of restitution is, he says, "that of Lévi-Strauss's *Anthropologie structurale* which regards social structures as attempts at dynamic equilibrium achieved through an exchange of words, women, and material goods." Steiner thereby makes the connection explicit between the exchange of women, for example, and the exchange of words in one language for words in another.[17]

Steiner makes the sexual politics of his argument quite clear in the opening chapter of his book, where he outlines the model for "total reading." Translation, as an act of interpretation, is a special case of communication, and communication is a sexual act: "Eros and language mesh at every point. Intercourse and discourse, copula and copulation, are sub-classes of the dominant fact of communication. . . . Sex is a profoundly semantic act."[18] Steiner makes note of a cultural tendency to see this act of communication from the male point of view and thus to valorize the position of the father/author/original, but at the same time, he himself repeats this male focus in, for example, the following description of the relation between sexual intercourse and communication:

> There is evidence that the sexual discharge in male onanism is greater than it is in intercourse. I suspect that the determining factor is articulateness, the ability to conceptualize with especial vividness . . . Ejaculation is at once a physiological and a linguistic concept. Impotence and speech-blocks, premature emission and stuttering, involuntary ejaculation and the word-river of dreams are phenomena whose interrelations seem to lead back to the central knot of our humanity. Semen, excreta, and words are communicative products.[19]

The allusion here to Lévi-Strauss, echoed later in the book in the passage we have already noted ("an exchange of words, women, and material goods"), provides the narrative connecting discourse, intercourse, and translation, and it does so from the point of view of a male translator. Indeed, we note that when communication is at issue, that which can be exchanged is depicted at least partially in male terms ("semen, excreta, and words"), while when "restitution" is at issue, that which can be exchanged is depicted in female terms.

Writing within the hierarchy of gender, Steiner seems to argue further that the paradigm is universal and that the male and female roles he describes are *essential* rather than *accidental*. On the other hand, he notes that the rules for discourse (and, presumably, for intercourse) are social, and he outlines some of the consequent differences between male and female language use:

> At a rough guess, women's speech is richer than men's in those shadings of desire and futurity known in Greek and Sanskrit as optative; women seem to verbalize a wider range of qualified resolve and masked promise. . . . I do not say they lie about the obtuse, resistant fabric of the world: they multiply the facets of reality, they strengthen the adjective to allow it an alternative nominal status, in a way which men often find unnerving. There is a strain of ultimatum, a separatist stance, in the masculine intonation of the first-person pronoun; the "I" of women intimates a more patient bearing, or did until Women's Liberation. The two language models follow on Robert Graves's dictum that men do but women are.[20]

But, while acknowledging the social and economic forces which prescribe differences, he wants to believe as well in a basic biological cause: "Certain linguistic differences do point towards a physiological basis or, to be exact, towards the intermediary zone between the biological and the social."[21] Steiner is careful not to insist on the biological premises, but there is in his own rhetoric a tendency to treat even the socialized differences between male and female language use as immutable. If the sexual basis of communication *as* the basis for translation is to be taken as a universal, then Steiner would seem to be arguing firmly in the tradition we have here been examining, one in which "men do" but "women are." This tradition is not, of course, confined to the area of translation studies, and, given the influence of both Steiner and Lévi-Strauss, it is not surprising to see gender as the framing concept of communication in adjacent fields such as semiotics or literary criticism.[22]

The metaphorics of translation, as the preceding discussion suggests, is a symptom of larger issues of western culture: of the power relations as they divide in terms of gender; of a persistent (though not always hegemonic) desire to equate language or language use with morality; of a quest for originality or unity, and a consequent intolerance of duplicity, of what cannot be decided. The fundamental question is, why have the two realms of translation and gender been metaphorically linked? What, in Eco's terms, is the metonymic code or narrative underlying these two realms?[23]

This survey of the metaphors of translation would suggest that the implied narrative concerns the relation between the value of production versus the value of reproduction. What proclaims itself to be an aesthetic problem is represented in terms of sex, family, and the state, and what is consistently at issue is power. We have already seen the way the concept of fidelity is used to regulate sex and/in the family, to guarantee that the child is the production of the father, reproduced by the mother. This regulation is a sign of the father's authority and power; it is a way of making visible the paternity of the child — otherwise a fiction of sorts — and thereby claiming the child as legitimate progeny. It is also, therefore, related to the owning and bequeathal of property. As in marriage, so in translation, there is a legal dimension to the concept of fidelity. It is not legal (shall I say, legitimate) to publish a translation of works not in the public domain, for example, without the author's (or appropriate proxy's) consent; one must, in short, enter the proper *contract* before announcing the birth of the translation, so that the parentage will be clear. The coding of production and reproduction marks the former as a more valuable activity by reference to the division of labor established for the marketplace, which privileges male activity and pays accordingly. The transformation of translation from a reproductive activity into a productive one, from a secondary work into an original work, indicates the coding of translation rights as property rights — signs of riches, signs of power.

I would further argue that the reason translation is so overcoded, so overregulated, is that it threatens to erase the difference between production and reproduction which is essential to the establishment of power. Translations can, in short, masquerade as originals, thereby short-circuiting the system. That the *difference* is essential to maintain is argued in terms of life and death: "Every saddened reader knows that what a poem is most in danger of losing in translation is its life."[24] The danger posed by infidelity is here represented in terms of mortality; in a comment on the Loeb Library translations of the classics, Rolfe Humphries articulates the risk in more specific terms: "They emasculate their originals."[25] The sexual violence implicit in Drant's figuration of translation, then, can be seen as directed not simply against the female material of the text ("captive women") but against the sign of male authority as well; for, as we know from the story of Samson and Delilah,

Drant's cutting of hair ("I have shaved off his hair and pared off his nails, that is, I have wiped away all his vanity and superfluity of matter") can signify loss of male power, a symbolic castration. This, then, is what one critic calls the *manque inévitable*: what the original risks losing, in short, is its phallus, the sign of paternity, authority, and originality.[26]

In the metaphoric system examined here, what the translator claims for "himself" is precisely the right of paternity; he claims a phallus because this is the only way, in a patriarchal code, to claim legitimacy for the text. To claim that translating is like writing, then, is to make it a creative – rather than merely re-creative – activity. But the claims for originality and authority, made in reference to acts of artistic and biological creation, exist in sharp contrast to the place of translation in a literary or economic hierarchy. For, while writing and translating may share the same figures of gender division and power – a concern with the rights of authorship or authority – translating does not share the redemptive myths of nobility or triumph we associate with writing. Thus, despite metaphoric claims for equality with writers, translators are often reviled or ignored: it is not uncommon to find a review of a translation in a major periodical that fails to mention the translator or the process of translation. Translation projects in today's universities are generally considered only marginally appropriate as topics for doctoral dissertations or as support for tenure, unless the original author's stature is sufficient to authorize the project. While organizations such as PEN and ALTA (American Literary Translators Association) are working to improve the translator's economic status, organizing translators and advising them of their legal rights and responsibilities, even the best translators are still poorly paid. The academy's general scorn for translation contrasts sharply with its reliance on translation in the study of the "classics" of world literature, of major philosophical and critical texts, and of previously unread masterpieces of the "third" world. While the metaphors we have looked at attempted to cloak the secondary status of translation in the language of the phallus, western culture enforces this secondariness with a vengeance, insisting on the feminized status of translation. Thus, though obviously both men and women engage in translation, the binary logic which encourages us to define nurses as female and doctors as male, teachers as female and professors as male, secretaries as female and corporate executives as male also defines translation as, in many ways, an archetypal feminine activity.

What is also interesting is that, even when the terms of comparison are reversed – when writing is said to be like translating – in order to stress the re-creative aspects of both activities, the gender bias does not disappear. For example, in a short essay by Terry Eagleton discussing the relation between translation and some strands of current critical theory, Eagleton argues as follows:

> It may be, then, that translation from one language into another may lay bare for us something of the very productive mechanisms of textuality itself . . . The eccentric yet suggestive critical theories of Harold Bloom . . . contend that every poetic producer is locked in Oedipal rivalry with a "strong" patriarchal precursor – that literary "creation" . . . is in reality a matter of struggle, anxiety, aggression, envy and repression. The

> "creator" cannot abolish the unwelcome fact that . . . his poem lurks in the shadows of a previous poem or poetic tradition, against the authority of which it must labour into its own "autonomy." On Bloom's reading, all poems are translations, or "creative misreadings," of others; and it is perhaps only the literal translator who knows most keenly the psychic cost and enthrallment which all writing involves.[27]

Eagleton's point, through Bloom, is that the productive or creative mechanism of writing is not *original*, that is, texts do not emerge *ex nihilo*; rather, both writing and translating depend on previous texts. Reversing the conventional hierarchy, he invokes the secondary status of translation as a model for writing. In equating translation and "misreading," however, Eagleton (through Bloom) finds their common denominator to be the struggle with a "'strong' patriarchal precursor"; the productive or creative mechanism is, again, entirely male. The attempt by either Eagleton or Bloom to replace the concept of originality with the concept of creative misreading or translation is a sleight of hand, a change in name only with respect to gender and the metaphorics of translation, for the concept of translation has here been defined in the same patriarchal terms we have seen used to define originality and production.

At the same time, however, much of recent critical theory has called into question the myths of authority and originality which engender this privileging of writing over translating and make writing a male activity. Theories of intertextuality, for example, make it difficult to determine the precise boundaries of a text and, as a consequence, disperse the notion of "origins"; no longer simply the product of an autonomous (male?) individual, the text rather finds its *sources* in history, that is, within social and literary codes, as articulated by an author. Feminist scholarship has drawn attention to the considerable body of writing by women, writing previously marginalized or repressed in the academic canon; thus this scholarship brings to focus the conflict between theories of writing coded in male terms and the reality of the female writer. Such scholarship, in articulating the role gender has played in our concepts of writing and production, forces us to reexamine the hierarchies that have subordinated translation to a concept of originality. The resultant revisioning of translation has consequences, of course, for meaning-making activities of all kinds, for translation has itself served as a conventional metaphor or model for a variety of acts of reading, writing, and interpretation; indeed, the analogy between translation and interpretation might profitably be examined in terms of gender, for its use in these discourses surely belies similar issues concerning authority, violence, and power.

The most influential revisionist theory of translation is offered by Jacques Derrida, whose project has been to subvert the very concept of *difference* which produces the binary opposition between an original and its reproduction – and finally to make this difference undecidable. By drawing many of his terms from the lexicon of sexual difference – dissemination, invagination, hymen – Derrida exposes gender as a conceptual framework for definitions of mimesis and fidelity, definitions central to the "classical" way of viewing translation. The problem of translation, implicit in all of his work, has become increasingly explicit since his essay "Living On/Border Lines," the pretexts for which are Shelley's "Triumph of Life" and

Blanchot's *L'Arrêt de mort*.[28] In suggesting the "intertranslatability" of these texts, he violates conventional attitudes not only toward translation, but also toward influence and authoring.

The essay is on translation in many senses: appearing first in English — that is, in translation — it contains a running footnote on the problems of translating his own ambiguous terms as well as those of Shelley and Blanchot. In the process, he exposes the impossibility of the "dream of translation without remnants"; there is, he argues, always something left over which blurs the distinctions between original and translation. There is no "silent" translation. For example, he notes the import-ance of the words *écrit, récit*, and *série* in Blanchot's text and asks:

> Note to the translators: How are you going to translate that, *récit*, for example? Not as *nouvelle*, "novella," nor as "short story." Perhaps it will be better to leave the "French" word *récit*. It is already hard enough to understand, in Blanchot's text, in French.[29]

The impossibility of translating a word such as *récit* is, according to Derrida, a function of the law of translation, not a matter of the translation's infidelity or secon-dariness. Translation is governed by a double bind typified by the command, "Do not read me": the text both requires and forbids its translation. Derrida refers to this double bind of translation as a *hymen*, the sign of both virginity and consum-mation of a marriage. Thus, in attempting to overthrow the binary oppositions we have seen in other discussions of the problem, Derrida implies that translation is both original and secondary, uncontaminated and transgressed or transgressive. Recognizing too that the translator *is* frequently a woman — so that sex and the gender-ascribed secondariness of the task frequently coincide — Derrida goes on to argue in *The Ear of the Other* that

> the woman translator in this case is not simply subordinated, she is not the author's secretary. She is also the one who is loved by the author and on whose basis alone writing is possible. Translation is writing; that is, it is not translation only in the sense of transcription. It is a produc-tive writing called forth by the original text.[30]

By arguing the interdependence of writing and translating, Derrida subverts the autonomy and privilege of the "original" text, binding it to an impossible but neces-sary contract with the translation and making each the debtor of the other.

In emphasizing both the reproductive and productive aspects of translation, Derrida's project — and, ironically, the translation of his works — provides a basis for a necessary exploration of the contradictions of translation and gender. Already his work has generated a collection of essays focusing on translation as a way of talking about philosophy, interpretation, and literary history.[31] These essays, while not explicitly addressing questions of gender, build on his ideas about the double-ness of translation without either idealizing or subordinating translation to conventionally privileged terms. Derrida's own work, however, does not attend closely to the historical or cultural circumstances of specific texts, circumstances that cannot be ignored in investigating the problematics of translation.[32] For example, in some historical periods women were allowed to translate precisely *because* it was defined as a secondary activity.[33] Our task as scholars, then, is to learn to listen to the "silent" discourse – of women, as translators – in order to better articulate the relationship between what has been coded as "authoritative" discourse and what is silenced in the fear of disruption or subversion.

Beyond this kind of scholarship, what is required for a feminist theory of translation is a practice governed by what Derrida calls the double bind – not the double standard. Such a theory might rely, not on the family model of oedipal struggle, but on the double-edged razor of translation as collaboration, where author and translator are seen as working together, both in the cooperative and the subversive sense. This is a model that responds to the concerns voiced by an increasingly audible number of women translators who are beginning to ask, as Suzanne Jill Levine does, what it means to be a woman translator in and of a male tradition. Speaking specifically of her translation of Cabrera Infante's *La Habana para un infante difunto*, a text that "mocks women and their words," she asks,

> Where does this leave a woman as translator of such a book? Is she not a double betrayer, to play Echo to this Narcissus, repeating the archetype once again? All who use the mother's father tongue, who echo the ideas and discourse of great men are, in a sense, betrayers: this is the contradiction and compromise of dissidence.
>
> [Levine 1983: 92]

The very choice of texts to work with, then, poses an initial dilemma for the feminist translator: while a text such as Cabrera Infante's may be ideologically offensive, not to translate it would capitulate to that logic which ascribes all power to the original. Levine chooses instead to subvert the text, to play infidelity against infidelity, and to follow out the text's parodic logic. Carol Maier, in discussing the contradictions of her relationship to the Cuban poet Octavio Armand, makes a similar point, arguing that "the translator's quest is not to silence but to give voice, to make available texts that raise difficult questions and open perspectives. It is essential that as translators women get under the skin of both antagonistic and sympathetic works. They must become independent, 'resisting' interpreters who do not only let antagonistic works speak . . . but also speak with them and place them in a larger context by discussing them and the process of their translation."[34] Her essay recounts her struggle to translate the silencing of the mother in Armand's poetry and how, by "resisting" her own silencing as a translator, she is able to give voice to the contradictions in Armand's work. By refusing to repress her own voice while speaking *for* the voice of the "master," Maier, like Levine, speaks through and against translation. Both of these translators' work illustrates the importance not only of translating but of writing about it, making the principles of a practice part of the dialogue about revising translation. It is only when women translators begin to discuss their work – and when enough historical scholarship on previously silenced women translators has been done – that we will be able to delineate alternatives to the oedipal struggles for the rights of production.

For feminists working on translation, much or even most of the terrain is still uncharted. We can, for example, examine the historical role of translation in women's writing in different periods and cultures; the special problems of translating explicitly feminist texts, as, for example, in Myriam Diaz-Diocaretz's discussion of the problems of translating Adrienne Rich into Spanish;[35] the effects of the canon and the market-place on decisions concerning which texts are translated, by whom, and how these translations are marketed; the effects of translations on canon and genre; the role of "silent" forms of writing such as translation in articulating woman's speech and subverting hegemonic forms of expression. Feminist and poststructuralist theory has encouraged us to read between or outside the lines of the dominant discourse for information about cultural formation and authority; translation can provide a wealth of such information about practices of domination and subversion. In addition, as both Levine's and Maier's comments indicate, one of the challenges for feminist translators is to move beyond questions of the sex of the author or translator. Working within the conventional hierarchies we have already seen, the female translator of a female author's text and the male translator of a male author's text will be bound by the same power relations: what must be subverted is the process by which translation complies with gender constructs. In this sense, a feminist theory of translation will finally be utopic. As women write their own metaphors of cultural production, it may be possible to consider the acts of authoring, creating, or legitimizing a text outside of the gender binaries that have made women, like translations, mistresses of the sort of work that kept Clara Schumann from her composing.

Notes

I want to acknowledge and thank the many friends whose conversations with me have helped me clarify my thinking on the subject of this essay: Nancy Armstrong, Michael Davidson, Page duBois, Julie Hemker, Stephanie Jed, Susan Kirkpatrick, and Kathryn Shevelow.

1   Joseph Joachim, *Briefe von und an Joseph Joachim*, ed. Johannes Joachim and Andreas Moser, 3 vols. (Berlin: Julius Bard, 1911–13), 2: 86; cited in Nancy B. Reich, *Clara Schumann: The Artist and the Woman* (Ithaca: Cornell University Press, 1985), p. 320; the translation is Reich's. See the chapter entitled "Clara Schumann as Composer and Editor," pp. 225–57.

2   This is the title of an essay by Armando S. Pires, *Américas* 4: 9 (1952): 13–15, cited in *On Translation*, ed. Reuben A. Brower (Cambridge: Harvard University Press, 1959), p. 289.

3   United States Code Annotated, Title 17, section 101 (St. Paul, Minnesota: West Publishing Co., 1977).

4   Roger Zuber, *Les "Belles Infidèles" et la formation du goût classique* (Paris: Libraire Armand Colin, 1968), p. 195.

5   Earl of Roscommon, "An Essay on Translated Verse," in *English Translation Theory, 1650–1800*, ed. T. R. Steiner (Assen: Van Gorcum, 1975), p. 77.

6   Ibid., p. 78.

7   On the woman as blank page, see Susan Gubar, "'The Blank Page' and Issues of Female Creativity," in *Writing and Sexual Difference*, ed. Elizabeth Abel (Chicago: University of Chicago Press, 1982), pp. 73–91; see also Stephanie

Jed, *Chaste Thinking: The Rape of Lucretia and the Birth of Humanism* (Bloomington: Indiana University Press, 1989).

8   Thomas Francklin, "Translation: A Poem," in *English Translation Theory*, pp. 113–14.

9   William Cowper, "Preface" to *The Iliad of Homer*," in *English Translation Theory*, pp. 13–56.

10 Friedrich Schleiermacher, "Über die verschiedenen Methoden des Übersetzen," trans. André Lefevere, in *Translating Literature: The German Tradition from Luther to Rosenzweig*, ed. André Lefevere (Assen: Van Gorcum, 1977), p. 79.

11 Cited in Flora Ross Amos, *Early Theories of Translation* (1920; rpt. New York: Octagon, 1973), pp. 138–9.

12 Friedrich Nietzsche, *The Gay Science*, trans. Walter Kaufmann (New York: Random House, 1974), p. 90.

13 Cited in Amos, *Early Theories of Translation*, pp. 112–13.

14 Serge Gavronsky, "The Translation: From Piety to Cannibalism," *SubStance*, 16 (1977): 53–62, especially 55.

15 Ibid., p. 60.

16 Ibid.

17 George Steiner, *After Babel* (London and New York: Oxford University Press, 1975), pp. 296, 298, 300, 302.

18 Ibid., p. 38.

19 Ibid., pp. 44, 39.

20 Ibid., p. 41.

21 Ibid., p. 43.

22 In her incisive critique of semiotics argued along these lines, Christine Brooke-Rose makes a similar point about Steiner's use of Lévi-Strauss; see "Woman as Semiotic Object," *Poetics Today*, 6 (1985): 9–20; reprinted in *The Female Body in Western Culture: Contemporary Perspectives*, ed. Susan Rubin Suleiman (Cambridge, Mass.: Harvard University Press, 1986), pp. 305–16.

23 Umberto Eco, *The Role of the Reader: Explorations in the Semiotics of Texts* (Bloomington: Indiana University Press, 1979), p. 68.

24 Jackson Matthews, "Third Thoughts on Translating Poetry," in *On Translation*, p. 69.

25 Rolfe Humphries, "Latin and English Verse – Some Practical Considerations," in *On Translation*, p. 65.

26 Philip Lewis, "Vers la traduction abusive," in *Les fins de l'homme: A partir du travail de Jacques Derrida*, ed. Philippe Lacoue-Labarthe and Jean-Luc Nancy (Paris: Editions Galilée, 1981), pp. 253–61, especially p. 255.

27 Terry Eagleton, "Translation and Transformation," *Stand*, 19: 3 (1977): 72–7, especially 73–4.

28 Jacques Derrida, 'Living On/Border Lines," trans. James Hulbert, in *Deconstruction and Criticism* (New York: Continuum, 1979), pp. 75–176.

29 Ibid., pp. 119, 86.

30 Ibid., p. 145; Jacques Derrida, *The Ear of the Other: Otobiography, Transference, Translation*, ed. Christie V. McDonald, trans. Peggy Kamuf (New York: Schocken, 1985), p. 153.

31   *Difference in Translation* ed. Joseph F. Graham (Ithaca: Cornell University Press, 1985).

32   For a critique of Derrida's "Living On/Border Lines" along these lines, see Jeffrey Mehlman's essays, "Deconstruction, Literature, History: The Case of *L'Arrêt de mort*," in *Literary History: Theory and Practice*, ed. Herbert L. Sussman, Proceedings of the Northeastern University Center for Literary Studies (Boston, 1984), and "Writing and Deference: The Politics of Literary Adulation," in *Representations*, 15 (1986): 1–14.

33   *Silent But for the Word: Tudor Women as Patrons, Translators, and Writers of Religious Works*, ed. Margaret P. Hannay (Kent, Ohio: Kent State University Press, 1985).

34   Carol Maier, "A Woman in Translation, Reflecting," *Translation Review*, 17 (1985): 4–8, especially 4.

35   Myriam Diaz-Diocaretz, *Translating Poetic Discourse: Questions on Feminist Strategies in Adrienne Rich* (Amsterdam/Philadelphia: John Benjamins Publishing Co., 1985). For other work that begins to address the specific problem of gender and translation, see also the special issue of *Translation Review* on women in translation, 17 (1985); and Ronald Christ, "The Translator's Voice: An Interview with Helen R. Lane," *Translation Review*, 5 (1980): 6–17.

1990s and beyond

IN THE LAST DECADE of the twentieth century, translation studies achieves a certain institutional authority, manifested most tangibly by a worldwide proliferation of translator training programs and a flood of scholarly publishing. The publications, issued by commercial as well as university presses, are academic in the strict sense: training manuals, encyclopedias, journals, conference proceedings, collections of research articles, monographs, and readers that gather a variety of theoretical statements – such as the present one (see also Lefevere 1992a, Schulte and Biguenet 1992, Robinson 1997b). A new kind of textbook also begins to appear: the primer of theory that presents research methodologies to students (see Pym 1998, Hatim 2001, Munday 2001, Williams and Chesterman 2002).

The conceptual paradigms that animate translation research are a diverse mix of the theories and methodologies that characterized the previous decade, continuing trends within the discipline (polysystem, skopos, poststructuralism, feminism), but also reflecting developments in linguistics (pragmatics, critical discourse analysis, computerized corpora) and in literary and cultural theory (postcolonialism, sexuality, globalization). Theoretical approaches to translation multiply, and research, which for much of the century was shaped by traditional academic specializations, now fragments into subspecialties within the growing discipline of translation studies.

At virtually the same time, another interdiscipline emerges, cultural studies, cross-fertilizing such fields as literary theory and criticism, film and anthropology. And this brings a renewed functionalism to translation theory, a concern with the social effects of translation and their ethical and political consequences. Culturally oriented research tends to be philosophically critical and politically engaged, so it inevitably questions the claim of scientific objectivity in empirically oriented work which focuses on forms of description and classification, whether linguistic, experimental, or historical. The decade sees provocative assessments of the competing paradigms. It also sees productive syntheses where theoretical and methodological differences are shown to be complementary, and precise descriptions of translated text and translation processes are linked to cultural and political issues. At the start of the new millennium, translation studies is an international network of scholarly communities who conduct research and debate across conceptual and disciplinary divisions.

Varieties of linguistics continue to dominate the field because of their usefulness in training translators of technical, commercial and other kinds of nonfiction texts. Theoretical projects typically reflect the training situation by applying the findings of linguistics to articulate and solve translation problems. Leading theorists draw on text linguistics, discourse analysis, and pragmatics to conceptualize translation on the model of Gricean conversation (see Hatim and Mason 1990; Baker 1992; Neubert and Shreve 1992; cf. Robinson 2003). In these terms, translating means communicating the foreign text by cooperating with the target reader according to four conversational "maxims": "quantity" of information, "quality" or truthfulness, "relevance" or consistency of context, and "manner" or clarity (Grice 1975). A translation is seen as conveying a foreign message with its "implicatures" by exploiting the maxims of the target linguistic community. Pragmatics-based translation theories assume a communicative intention and a relation of equivalence, based on textual analysis. They also recognize that these factors are further constrained by the function of the translated text.

Ernst-August Gutt (1991) takes a cognitive approach by modelling translation on another area of linguistics: relevance theory. Here ostensive or "deliberate" communication depends on the interplay between the psychological "context" or "cognitive environment" of an utterance – construed broadly as an individual's store of knowledge, values and beliefs – and the processing effort required to derive contextual effects (see Sperber and Wilson 1986: 13–14). Gutt extrapolates from this basic theory by arguing that "faithfulness" in translation is a matter of communicating an "intended interpretation" of the foreign text through "adequate contextual effects" that avoid "unnecessary processing effort" (Gutt 1991: 101–102). The degree to which the interpretation resembles the foreign text and the means of expressing that interpretation are determined by their relevance to a target readership, their accessibility and ease of processing.

Gutt boldly claims that relevance ultimately does away with the need for an independent theory of translation by subsuming it under the more abstract category of verbal communication. He asserts that the many "principles, rules and guidelines of translation" handed down by centuries of commentators are in fact "applications of the principle of relevance" (ibid.: 188). His stress on cognition is admittedly reductive: it effectively elides the specificity of translation as a linguistic and cultural practice, its specific textual forms, situations, and audiences. Relevance theory assumes "a universal principle believed to represent a psychological characteristic of our human nature" (ibid.) and therefore offers an extremely complex yet abstract formalization that highlights individual psychology without figuring in social factors.

When applied to translation by Gutt, this seems to mean a universal reader, one characterized by an overwhelming desire for minimal processing effort, if not for immediate intelligibility. Thus, in his exposition, relevance privileges a particular kind of translation, "clear and natural in expression in the sense that it should not be unnecessarily difficult to understand" (ibid.: 102).

Other linguistics-oriented theorists do not aim to explain the success or failure of a translation, like Gutt, but rather to describe translated texts in finely discriminating analyses. The work of Basil Hatim and Ian Mason, alone and in collaboration, brings together an ambitious array of analytical concepts from different areas of linguistics. And their examples embrace a wide variety of text types, literary and religious, journalistic and political, legal and commercial. Their work shows how far linguistic approaches have advanced over the past three decades: Catford applied Hallidayan linguistic theory to translation problems, mostly at the level of word and sentence, and he used manufactured examples; Hatim and Mason perform nuanced analyses of actual translations in terms of style, genre, discourse, pragmatics, and ideology. Their unit of analysis is the whole text, and their analytical method takes into account – but finally transcends – the differences between "literary" and "non-literary" translation (see Hatim and Mason 1990 and 1997).

Large corpora of translated texts began to be studied in the 1970s, despite the onerous task of examining translations against the foreign texts they translate. In the 1990s, corpus linguistics, the study of language through vast computer-stored collections of texts, provides translation studies with powerful analytical tools. The first computerized corpora of translations are created, and theorists such as Mona Baker and Sara Laviosa formulate concepts to analyze them. One of their goals has been to isolate the distinctive features of the language used in translations, features that are not the result of interference from the source language or simple lack of competence in the target language. This continues the interest in the autonomy of the translated text that so occupied previous decades, especially the 1980s. Thus far the analytical concepts have included Shoshana Blum-Kulka's "explicitation" hypothesis, "normalization" or "the tendency to conform to patterns and practices which are typical of the target language," "lexical density" or "the proportion of lexical as opposed to grammatical words" that facilitate text processing, and "sanitization" or "the adaptation of a source text reality to make it more palatable for target audiences" (Baker 1997: 17–67, 183; Kenny 1998: 515; see also Baker 1993 and 1995).

Scholars engaged in corpus-based studies have pointed to theoretical problems raised by the search for universals of translated language. Because the computerized analysis is governed by "abstract, global notions," it may emphasize norms over innovative translation strategies; and since these notions are constructions derived from "various manifestations on the surface" of a text, they exclude the various interpretations a text may have in different contexts (Baker 1997: 179, 185). Computerized translation analysis is focused on text production to the exclusion of reception – except by the computer programmed to identify and quantify the abstract textual categories.

Nonetheless, computer analysis can elucidate significant translation patterns in a parallel corpus of foreign texts and their translations, especially if the patterns are evaluated against large "reference" corpora in the source and target languages. For example, unusual collocations of words can be uncovered in a foreign text so as to evaluate their handling in a translation. And this kind of description might be brought to bear on cultural and social considerations. Dorothy Kenny interestingly suggests that "a careful study of collocational patterns in translated text can shed light on the cultural forces at play in the literary marketplace, and vice versa" (Kenny 1998: 519; see also Kenny 2001). Computer-discovered regularities in translation strategies can support historical studies, confirming or questioning hypotheses about translation in specific periods and locales.

In the 1990s increasing attention is given to "process-oriented" research, as James Holmes termed it, where the mental activity of translating is studied. Empirical data are collected through "think-aloud protocols," where translators are asked to verbalize their thinking during or immediately after the translation process (see, for example, Lörscher 1991 and 1996; Fraser 1996). These studies have observed translators at various levels of expertise, both trainees and professionals. Some research emphasizes psycholinguistic procedures; some aims to improve training, especially by giving it a stronger vocational slant, approximating current trends in the profession.

Think-aloud protocols are beset by a number of theoretical problems that must be figured into any use made of their data. Verbalization won't register unconscious factors and automatic processes, and it can change a mental activity instead of simply reporting it. Similarly, subjects are sometimes instructed to provide specific kinds of information: description, for instance, without any justification. And obviously the data will be affected by how articulate and self-conscious a subject may be.

Still, think-aloud protocols, as well as interviews and questionnaires, can document the practices that translators currently perform. The quality of the data inevitably depends on the theoretical and methodological sophistication of the experimental design. Some studies can give a glimpse of the translator's intellectual labor over linguistic and cultural differences, shifting through problems of terminology to encompass questions of culture and politics. Janet Fraser has observed community translators rendering an English public information leaflet into several minority languages in the UK (see Fraser 1993). "If observational studies produce too few regularities to construct a model of the translation process," writes Candace Séguinot, "they are nonetheless useful to test theories in the light of concrete data" (Séguinot 1996: 77). These theories can include not just abstract mental processes, but the specific intercultural dimensions of translating.

Culturally oriented research suspects regularities and universals and emphasizes the social and historical differences of translation. This approach stems partly from the decisive influence of poststructuralism, the doubt it casts on abstract formalizations, metaphysical concepts, timeless and universal essences, which might have been emancipatory in the Enlightenment, but now appear totalizing and repressive of local differences. Poststructuralist translation theory, in turn, calls attention to the exclusions and hierarchies that are masked by the realist illusion of transparent language, the fluent translating that seems untranslated. And this enables an incisive interrogation of cultural and political effects, the role played by translation in the creation and functioning of social movements and institutions.

In an exemplary project that combines theoretical sophistication and political awareness, linguistic analysis and historical detail, **Annie Brisset** (1990/1996) studies recent Québécois drama translations that were designed to form a cultural identity in the service of a nationalist agenda. The extract included here relies on Henri Gobard's concept of linguistic functions to describe the ideological force of Québécois French as a translating language. In the politicized post-1968 era, as Brisset demonstrates, nationalist writers fashioned Québécois French into what Gobard calls a "vernacular," a native or mother tongue, a language of community. Between 1968 and 1988 Québécois translators worked to turn this vernacular into a "referential" language, the support of a national literature, by using it to render canonical world dramatists, notably Shakespeare, Strindberg, Chekhov, and Brecht. In these translations, Québécois French acquired cultural authority and challenged its subordination to North American English and Parisian French.

Yet a struggle against one set of linguistic and cultural hierarchies might install others that are equally exclusionary. Sharing Antoine Berman's concern with ethnocentrism in translation, Brisset points out that the Québécois versions, even when they used a heterogeneous language like the working-class dialect *joual*, ultimately cultivated a sameness, a homogeneous identity, in the mirror of foreign texts and cultures whose differences were thereby reduced. "Doing away with any 'ambiguity' of identity," as she puts it, "means getting rid of the Other." Brisset's work illuminates the cultural and political risks taken by minor languages and cultures who resort to translation for self-preservation and development.

The 1990s witness a series of historical studies that explore the identity-forming power of translation, the ways in which it creates representations of foreign texts that answer to what is intelligible and interesting in the translating culture. Resting on a synthesis of various theoretical and political discourses, including Marxism and feminism, poststructuralism and postcolonial theory, this work shows how the identities constructed by translation are variously determined by ethnicity and race, gender and sexuality, class and nation. Here translating goes beyond the communication of foreign meanings to encompass a political inscription.

Eric Cheyfitz (1991) argues that strongly ethnocentric translating has underwritten Anglo-American imperialism, from the English colonization of the New World in the early modern period to US expansion into Indian lands during the nineteenth and twentieth centuries to current US foreign policy in the Third World and elsewhere. In the case of American Indians, native social relations based on kinship and communal ownership were routinely translated into the "European identity of *property*" (Cheyfitz 1991: 43, his emphasis). Tejaswini Niranjana (1992) argues that the British colonial project in India was strengthened by translations inscribed with the colonizer's image of the colonized, an ethnic or racial stereotype that rationalized domination. After the introduction of English education in

India, Indians came to study Orientalist translations of Indian-language texts, and many acceded both to the cultural authority of those translations and to their discriminatory images of Indian cultures.

The question of ideology in translation had been anticipated by the concept of "norms" in polysystem theory, which is now further refined by Even-Zohar and Toury. They consolidate their influence by revising their key essays into cogent statements that avoid the tentative and somewhat polemical cast of the earlier versions. Yet in line with other trends in culturally oriented research, the polysystem approach also addresses the role of translation in "discursive self-definition." Viewing translation as an "explicit confrontation with 'alien' discourses," Clem Robyns argues that "the intrusion of alien, convention-violating elements is a potential threat" to the "common norms" that define the identity of the target community (Robyns 1994: 405, 407). He presents a taxonomy of the relationships between the translating and foreign cultures that might be embodied in the translated text: "imperialist," "defensive," "trans-discursive," and "defective." The defective stance, for instance, is taken by the translating culture that turns to the foreign to supply some discursive lack at home.

Translation is frequently theorized as a cultural political practice that might be strategic in bringing about social change. The 1992 essay by **Gayatri Spivak** reprinted below constitutes a feminist intervention into postcolonial translation issues. But it is also a working translator's manifesto, a record of the complex intentions that motivated her versions of the Bengali fiction writer Mahasweta Devi.

Spivak outlines a poststructuralist conception of language use, where, following Derrida and de Man, "rhetoric" continually subverts meanings constructed by "logic" and "grammar," a subversion that is also social in effect, "a relationship between social logic, social reasonableness and the disruptiveness of figuration in social practice." Spivak argues that translators of Third World literatures need this linguistic model because "without a sense of the rhetoricity of language, a species of neocolonialist construction of the non-western scene is afoot." She criticizes western translation strategies that render Third World literatures "into a sort of with-it translatese," immediately accessible, enacting a realistic representation of those literatures, but devoid of the linguistic, cultural, and geopolitical differences that mark them. She advocates literalism, an "in-between discourse," that disrupts the effect of "social realism" in translation and gives the reader "a tough sense of the specific terrain of the original."

Spivak is aware of the contingency of cultural political agendas, whether couched in theoretical statements like her essay or in translation strategies. Different social situations can change the political valence of a translation. The metropolitan feminist, she observes, "translates a too quickly shared feminist notion of accessibility," when the fact is that a politically laden term like "gendering" can't be easily translated into Bengali. The ideologically motivated translator of Third World writing must be mindful that "what seems resistant in the space of English may be reactionary in the space of the original language."

Kwame Anthony Appiah also imagines a "frankly political" role for literary translation. In the 1993 essay reprinted here, however, his point of departure is different: a critique of analytical philosophy of language. Appiah restates the argument against translatability by questioning the use of the "Gricean mechanism," wherein communicative intentions are realized through inferential meanings derived from conventions. A literary translation, Appiah argues, doesn't communicate the foreign author's intentions, but tries to create a relationship to the linguistic and literary conventions of the translating culture that matches the relationship between the foreign text and its own culture. The match is never perfect and might be "unfaithful to the literal intentions" of the foreign text so as "to preserve formal features." Perhaps most importantly, "why texts matter" to a community "is not a question that convention settles" because "there can always be new readings, new things that matter about a text." A literary translation, like any interpretation, can proliferate meanings and values, which, however, remain indeterminate in their relation to the foreign text.

Appiah indicates that the indeterminacy is usually resolved in academic institutions, in pedagogical contexts. There "what counts as a fine translation of a literary text [. . .] is that it should preserve for us the features that make it worth teaching." Appiah cites a translation project that evokes the asymmetries in the global cultural and political economy: an English version of an African oral literature, proverbs in the Twi language. He acknowledges that the political significance of this translation would not be the same in the American academy as in the English-speaking academy in Africa. Whatever the location, however, a political pedagogy is best served by what Appiah calls a "thick" translation, which "seeks with its annotations and its accompanying glosses to locate the text in a rich cultural and linguistic context." This translating uses an ethnographic approach to the foreign text (Appiah's term is taken from anthropologist Clifford Geertz's notion of "thick description"). Yet it is ultimately designed to perform an ideological function in the target culture, combating racism, for instance, or challenging Western cultural superiority.

Jacques Derrida's wide-ranging contribution to this volume, a 1998 lecture delivered to a French translators association, addresses the potential social effects of translation strategies by examining the concept of relevance. For Derrida, the relevant translation is mystifying: it "presents itself as the transfer of an intact signified through the inconsequential vehicle of any signifier whatsoever," whereas in fact the translator replaces the signifiers of the foreign text with another signifying chain, trying to fix a signified that is no more than an interpretation oriented towards the receiving culture. Although critical of this mystification, Derrida sees it as inevitable insofar as every translation participates in an "economy of in-betweenness," positioned somewhere between "absolute relevance, the most appropriate, adequate, univocal transparency, and the most aberrant and opaque irrelevance."

His lecture presents two practical applications of this thinking, both involving the French word *relève*. One is Derrida's own use of the word to render the Hegelian term *Aufhebung*, a translation that served his interpretive interests thirty years ago, but that ultimately underwent "institutional accreditation and canonization in the public sphere," achieving widespread use in philosophical circles and becoming "known as the most relevant translation possible." The other application hinges on his interpretation of Shakespeare's play *The Merchant of Venice* according to the code of translation: in Portia's line, "when mercy seasons justice," Derrida uses *relève* to render "seasons." In his philosophical lexicon, *relève* highlights the contradictions in Hegel's dialectics. By rendering Portia's line with this word, Derrida suggests that in her legal translating of Shylock's demands for justice she seeks an optimal – yet contradictory – relevance to the Christian doctrine of mercy, since her translation leads to his total expropriation as well as his forced conversion to Christianity. When relevant translation occurs within an institution like the state, then, it can become the instrument of legal interdiction, economic sanction, and political repression, motivated here by racism.

Film translation has received some scholarly attention, theoretical accounts that map areas of research, as well as case studies that attend to cultural and political issues like censorship and nationalism (see Delabastita 1989; Lambert 1990; Danan 1991; Gambier 1996). But much of the literature remains oriented towards practical issues, despite the insights that this kind of translation might yield for various fields. Subtitling must preserve coherence under narrow temporal and spatial constraints (audiovisual synchronization, number of characters), so it necessarily offers a partial communication of foreign meanings, which are not simply incomplete, but re-established according to target concepts of coherence.

This is precisely the area that **Abé Mark Nornes** explores in his 1999 essay (included below). He shows how a synthesis of translation theory with film history might illuminate the cultural and social implications of subtitling and suggest innovative translation practices. A professional subtitler himself, Nornes draws on Japanese film translation to illustrate what he calls "corrupt" subtitles: "in the process of converting speech into writing within the time and space limits of the subtitle they conform the original to the rules, regulations, idioms, and frame of reference of the target language and its culture." Such subtitles are corrupt because they conceal their own "textual violence" and pre-empt any "experience of the foreign" for the audience.

Nornes uses Goethe's account of the different "epochs" of translation not only to trace subtitling practices from the development of sound film production, but to propose a theory of "abusive" film translation that relies as much on Antoine Berman's ethics as on Philip Lewis's poststructuralist approach. For Nornes, "the abusive subtitler assumes a respectful stance vis-à-vis the original text, tampering with both language and the subtitling apparatus itself" so as to signal the linguistic and cultural differences of the foreign film. He imagines a range of experimental procedures that include different styles of the translating language to match the stylistic peculiarities of the screenplay, as well as changes in the font, color, and positioning of the subtitles to complement the visual and aural qualities of the film.

Some of the most compelling translation research during the 1990s seeks to combine a linguist's attention to textual detail with a cultural historian's awareness of social and political trends. Taking English-language translations of Russian literature, Rachel May (1994) analyzes such textual features as deictic expressions, register shifts, and implicatures to expose the revisionary impact of translating on narrative form. She presents a history of the British and American reception of this literature and shows that English translations tend to omit the rich textual play that complicates narrative point of view in Russian fiction. She explains this tendency by situating it in the Anglo-American translation tradition. There the dominance of fluent strategies leads to "clashing attitudes toward narrative and style in the original and target languages"; and this clash is manifested in the translation as a "struggle between translator and narrator for control of the text's language" (May 1994: 59).

In the 1998 article reprinted here, **Keith Harvey** calls on the explanatory power of linguistics to analyze a particular literary discourse, "camp," and its homosexual coding in recent French and Anglo-American fiction. He then considers the various issues raised by translating this discourse into English and French, shedding light on the interrelationships between translation, cultural difference, and sexual identity. A French translator, for instance, omitted the camp in an American novel about gay men for French cultural reasons: the existence of a sexual minority signalled by this discourse runs counter to Enlightenment notions of universal humanity that have prevailed in France since the Revolution. An American translator, in contrast, not only reproduced the camp assigned to a character in a French novel, but also recast a seduction scene in homosexual terms. The English translation reflects the more militant approach to sexual identity in Anglo-American culture, where a discourse like camp functions as a "semiotic resource of gay men in their critique of straight society and in their attempt to carve out a space for their difference."

Harvey takes a tool-kit approach to analytical concepts, using what might prove useful in describing a specific translation strategy regardless of whether a concept originated in linguistics or literary criticism or cultural studies. Interestingly, his very stress on specific languages and discourses, cultures and sexualities forces a revision of the universalizing impulse in certain types of linguistics. Thus, he draws on politeness theory, a formalization of speech acts by which a speaker maintains or threatens an addressee's "face," where "face" is defined as "the want to be unimpeded and the want to be approved of in certain respects" (Brown and Levinson 1987: 58). This theory assumes a "Model Person" motivated by "rationality" (i.e., means-to-ends reasoning) and the desire to satisfy "face-wants" (ibid.). Yet Harvey's use of politeness theory reveals how gay fictional characters might deviate from the model, since they occasionally address face-threatening acts to themselves: camp includes a strong element of self-mockery. Harvey advances linguistic approaches to translation because he makes textual effects intelligible by referring to specific cultural and political differences (between France and two English-speaking countries, Britain and the United States). His essay implicitly questions any universalist assumptions in those approaches by suggesting that they undergo redefinition when applied to specific social situations and communities, like sexual minorities.

In a 2003 essay reprinted here in a revised version, **Ian Mason** demonstrates, in effect, that Michael Halliday's systemic grammar might make a more significant contribution to translation studies if a grammatical category is studied in relation to a particular social issue, such as the institutional sites of translating. Taking translations of documents from the European Union and UNESCO, Mason examines shifts in "transitivity," the linguistic representation of reality through such factors as agent, action, and circumstances. He finds "little uniformity of practice or evidence of influence of institutional guidelines on translator behaviour"; instead he observes "translators either adhering as closely as possible to their source text or, in departing from it, displaying traces of other discourses, faint echoes of ideological stances which are present in the environment."

Because Mason takes an empirical approach, he is guarded about the generalizability of his conclusions and regards his analyses as "descriptive" rather than critical. Yet since the documents he analyzes involve extremely controversial problems like Mad Cow Disease, the examination of transitivity factors actually enables a critique of the ideologies that inform the translations. Perhaps his essay reveals not so much that more empirical data is needed before the analyst can generalize about institutional translations, as that the linguistic analysis of such translations can expose ideological determinations towards which the analyst necessarily, even if unintentionally, takes a stand. To expose an ideology in translations designed to communicate impartially is not to accept it as true or right, but to treat it with critical detachment.

Lawrence Venuti's work typifies main trends in culturally oriented research during the 1990s. It theorizes translation according to poststructuralist concepts of language, discourse, and subjectivity so as to articulate their relations to cultural difference, ideological contradiction, and social change. The point of departure is the current situation of English-language translating: on the one hand, marginality and exploitation; on the other, the prevalence of fluent strategies that make for easy readability and produce the illusion of transparency, enabling a translated text to pass for the original and thereby rendering the translator invisible. Fluency masks a domestication of the foreign text that is appropriative and potentially imperialistic, putting the foreign to domestic uses which, in British and American cultures, extend the global hegemony of English. It can be countered by "foreignizing" translation that registers the irreducible differences of the foreign text – yet only in domestic terms, by deviating from the values, beliefs, and representations that currently hold sway in the target language. This line of thinking revives Schleiermacher and Berman, German Romantic translation and one of its late twentieth-century avatars. But following poststructuralist Philip Lewis and modernist poet-theorist Ezra Pound, it goes beyond literalism to advocate an experimentalism: innovative translating that samples the dialects, registers, and styles already available in the translating language to create a discursive heterogeneity which is defamiliarizing, but intelligible in different ways to different constituencies in the translating culture.

The final contribution below addresses a question that haunts translation theory informed by Continental philosophical traditions like poststructuralism and their contemporary political ramifications in feminism, postcolonialism, and queer studies. If translating doesn't so much communicate the foreign text as inscribe it with the intelligibilities and interests of the translating culture, how can a translated text reach the ethical and political goal of building a community with foreign cultures, a shared understanding with and of them? This question prompts a return to basic issues in twentieth-century translation theory: equivalence and shifts, audience and function, identity and ideology. The autonomy of the translated text is redefined as the target-language "remainder" that the translator releases in the hope of bridging the linguistic and cultural boundaries among readerships. Translating always encounters incommensurabilities, different ways of comprehending and evaluating the translated text and indeed the world. But these encounters do not so much negate the communicative function of a translation as splinter it into potentialities that can only be realized in reception.

Further reading

Arrojo 1998, Baker 1996, Bassnett and Lefevere 1990, Davis 2001, Fawcett 1997, Hermans 1999, Lane-Mercier 1997, Laviosa 1998, Pym 1996 and 1997, Robinson 1997 and 1997a, Simon 1996 and 1999, Simon and St-Pierre 2000, Tirkkonen-Condit 1992, Tymoczko 2000, Venuti 1996 and 2003

Chapter 25

Annie Brisset

THE SEARCH FOR A NATIVE LANGUAGE: TRANSLATION AND CULTURAL IDENTITY

Translated by Rosalind Gill and Roger Gannon

> . . . we need more than a mother tongue to come into our own, we also need a native language.
>
> Gaston Miron, *L'Homme rapaillé*

Issues of language in the theory of translation

LANGUAGE IS AN INDISPENSABLE element in the realization of the verbal act. It is a necessary precondition for communication. As Jakobson observes, "the message requires . . . a Code fully, or at least partially, common to the addresser and addressee (or in other words, to the encoder and the decoder of the message)."[1] Translation is a dual act of communication. It presupposes the existence, not of a single code, but of two distinct codes, the "source language" and the "target language." The fact that the two codes are not isomorphic creates obstacles for the translative operation. This explains why linguistic questions are the starting-point for all thinking about translation. A basic premise of translation theory is the famous "prejudicial objection" dismantled by Mounin, piece by piece, in one of the first works to elevate translation to the status of a quasi-scientific area of scholarship.[2] Translation is a unidirectional operation between two given languages. The target language is thus, every bit as much as the source language, a *sine qua non* of the translative operation. If the target language remains elusive, the act of translation becomes impossible. This is true even in the hypothetical case in which a text must be translated into a language that has no writing system. Throughout history, translators have had to contend with the fact that the target language is deficient when it comes to translating the source text into that language. Such deficiencies can be clearly identified as, for example, lexical or morpho-syntactic deficiencies or as problems of polysemy. More often, however, the deficiency in the receiving code has to do with the relation between signs and their users, a relation that reflects such things as individuality, social position, and geographical origin of the speakers: "thus the relatively simple question arises, should one translate or not translate argot by argot, a patois by a patois, etc. . . ."[3] Here, the difficulty of translation does not arise from the lack of a specific translation language. It arises, rather, from the absence in the target language of a subcode equivalent to the one used by the source text in its reproduction of the source language. How should the cockney dialogue in *Pygmalion* be translated? What French-language dialect equivalent should be used to render the lunfardo of Buenos Aires in translations of Roberto Arlt's novels? What variety of French would correspond to the Roman dialect of the Via Merulana in a translation of Carlo Emilio Gadda's *Quer pasticciaccio brutto de via Merulana*? What is the French equivalent of the English of the American South in Faulkner's novels? Such are the questions ritually posed by the translator, torn between the source text and the target language. These problems become more complex when historical time is factored in. Should the translator re-create the feeling of the time period of the text for the contemporary reader? Or, conversely, should the archaic form of the language be modernized to make the text more accessible to the contemporary reader? Should Dante, Shakespeare, Cervantes, or Chaucer be translated into archaic language? Should Cicero's style be rendered by the style of a well-known politician of modern times?[4] The choice of a target language becomes even more difficult when the text to be translated is a parody of a variety of the source language. *Gaweda*, a "museum language" of Great Poland, reproduced and parodied by Gombrowicz in his *Trans-Atlantyk*,[5] is a case in point. Translation problems can arise not only from deficiencies in the receiving society but also from a surfeit of linguistic options. For example, in certain societies, the language of men is different from that of women, and these differences are governed by particularly strict constraints. Charles Taber and Eugene Nida have discussed the problem of whether the Scriptures should be translated into the language of men or of women.[6] Writings on the translative operation abound with such questions. Translators address these issues in prefaces to their work, outlining the deficiencies of the target language, deficiencies arising from sociological, geographical, or historical variation in the source language.

Although the target language cannot always provide equivalents of the source language, the absence of a target language, the language into which one translates, is not usually cited as a formal translation problem. One could object that there have been instances in which translation has indeed created languages. But then there would have to be some agreement on the meaning of the word "create," because it would be wrong to assume that these languages had no prior existence and that translation created them from whole cloth. A case in point is the translation of the Bible by Luther, a translation that gave rise to the German language. In this case, the difficulty of translation arose from the fact that the target language was not a single unified language but a number of dialects:

Good German is the German of the people. But the people speak an infinite number of Germans. One must then translate into a German that somehow rises above the multiplicity of *Mundarten* without rejecting them or suppressing them. Thus Luther attempted to do two things: translate into a German that a priori can only be local, his own German, *Hochdeutsch*, but at the same time elevate, by the very process of translation, this local German to the status of a common German, a *lingua franca*. So that the German he used did not become itself a language cut off from the people, he had to preserve in it something of the *Mundarten*, of the general modes of expression and of the popular dialects. Thus, we find at the same time a consistent and deliberate use of a very oral language, full of images, expressions, turns of phrase, together with a subtle purification, de-dialectalization of this language . . . Luther's translation constitutes a first decisive self-affirmation of literary German. Luther, the great "reformer," was henceforth considered as a writer and as a creator of a language . . . [7]

Another example is the replacement of Latin by French after the edict of Villers-Cotterêts in the sixteenth century. By requiring that all civil acts be "pronounced, registered and delivered to the parties in the French mother tongue,"[8] François I set into motion a translation movement that helped "elevate our vulgar [tongue] to the equal of and as a model for the other more famous languages."[9] As a result of this and ensuing decrees, vernacular French was to become the language of law, science, and literature. It acquired the status of national language, the founding language of the French state.

Strictly speaking, translation does not fill a linguistic void, no more so in the France of Du Bellay than in the Germany of Luther. Translation can, however, change the relation of linguistic forces, at the institutional and symbolic levels, by making it possible for the *vernacular language* to take the place of the *referential language*, to use distinctions from Henri Gobard's tetraglossic analysis. According to his analysis, a cultural field, or a linguistic community, has at its disposal four types of language or subcode:

I   A *vernacular language*, which is local, spoken spontaneously, less appropriate for communicating than for *communing*, and the only language that can be considered to be the mother tongue (or native language).

II A *vehicular language*, which is national or regional, learned out of necessity, to be used for communication in the city.

III A *referential language*, which is tied to cultural, oral, and written traditions and ensures continuity in values by systematic reference to classic works of the past.

IV A *mythical language*, which functions as the ultimate recourse, verbal magic, whose incomprehensibility is considered to be irrefutable proof of the sacred . . . [10]

In "renascent" France as well as in "reformist" Germany, the referential language was a *foreign* language. In the corpus under review, the goal of translation is to supplant such foreign forms of expression, which are viewed as alienating, literally dispossessing. The task of translation is thus to replace the language of the Other by a native language. Not surprisingly, the native language chosen is usually the vernacular, "the linguistic birthright, the indelible mark of belonging."[11] Translation becomes an act of reclaiming, of recentering of the identity, a re-territorializing operation. It does not create a new language, but it elevates a dialect to the status of a national and cultural language.

'Translated into Québécois'

The inclusion of the annotation "traduit en québécois" (translated into Québécois) on the cover of Michel Garneau's translation of *Macbeth* can be explained by the translation's role as a re-territorializing operation. This reference to the language of translation is a reversal of usual procedure, which is to inform the reader of the language from which the work has been translated. Normally, the language of translation is a given; for readers, it is implicit, understood, that the language of translation will be the language of their own literature. A French publisher would never preface a book by Claude Simon, Marguerite Duras, or Michel Tournier with the annotation "written in French." The reader of a translation does not need to be told what language has been used to translate the foreign text. However, in cases where the reader is unlikely to be aware of the language of the original text, information about the language of origin is normally provided with the expression "Translated from." But when, against all normal usage, there is a perceived need to indicate that the translation is "into Québécois," it is precisely because it cannot be taken for granted that a work will be translated into Québécois. Similarly, would one not write the annotation "translated into Occitan" on a literary work in France? The annotation underscores the marginality of the language. But there is a considerable difference between the linguistic status of Occitan and that of Québécois. Occitan is a different sign system from French, as Catalan is from Spanish. Québécois is not a different sign system from French: "*Phenomenology of the Mind* would never be translated into Québécois."[12] Thus, the expression "traduit en Québécois" forms part of the ideological construction of the presumed difference between "Québécois" and French. Clearly, this annotation heralds the birth of a language that translation will have to bring to the fore, or at least, *expose*, in the photographic sense of the word. This function of translation, to give more exposure to the language, is reinforced by the proliferation of lexicographical studies of Québécois. New dictionaries of Québécois appear almost yearly. Of these, Léandre Bergeron's was the best-known during the period under study.[13] The dictionary aims less to codify usage than to demonstrate, if not to construct, the difference between Québécois and the French of France. The following examples, taken from the *Practical Handbook of Canadian French – Manuel pratique du français canadien* by Sinclair Robinson and Donald Smith are a good illustration of such a lexicographical endeavour. The handbook, whose very title is a serious misnomer, sets out to prove to anglophone students that Canadian French is a separate language. "It has the same capacity to express the whole range of human concerns as any other tongue."[14] Using a more ideologically motivated than naïve categorization, the authors divide French and Québécois lexical items into three pseudo-contrastive groups:

Canada	France	Translation
beurre d'arachides	pâté de cacahouètes	peanut butter
lait écrémé	–	skim milk
colline parlementaire	emplacement en pente du gouvern-ment canadien	Parliament Hill
électorat	corps électoral	electorate
relevé de notes	copie des notes au niveau universitaire	transcript[15]

Mystified by the alleged difference between the two types of French, the reader of the handbook will be left with the impression that the French of France is a limited language, and that it is fundamentally incapable of expressing "Québécois reality." On the other hand, Léandre Bergeron defines "Québécois," as opposed to French, as "a sign system, mainly spoken but sometimes written by the Québécois people."[16] The existence of a Québécois language is also tangible proof of the existence of a "Québécois people," in the restrictive sense of the expression "a people" as compared with "a population." Bergeron's Québécois is a language "rich with all the tension of a small people who are still wet from their birth on the eve of the twenty-first century, still shy in the presence of grown-ups, reluctant to walk among all those big people."[17] This explains why so much importance is placed on translation, because it proves irrefutably that the Québécois language exists. "We have even started to be translated into other languages for those who want to hear our distinctness, to talk about Melville to the Americans, make the 'matantes' heard in Tokyo, and make the citizens of Berlin dream of our forests."[18] Conversely, translating canonical works or literary masterpieces such as *Macbeth* into Québécois is an attempt to legitimize Québécois by elevating it from its status as a dialect. It proves that it is the language of a people and that it can replace French as the language of literature for its people. Here, the roles are reversed: the goal of a translation is not to provide an introduction to the Other or to mediate the foreign work. It is the foreign work that is given a mission – to vouch for the existence of the language of translation and, by so doing, vouch for the existence of a Québécois "people." Thus, when Shakespeare, Chekhov, and Brecht are given the task of establishing Québécois as a literary language in its own right, and ultimately as a national language, they are also given the task of reflecting the reality of the society that speaks that language, of literally speaking for it, or of being its mirror. Thus, when a foreign text is adapted or "culturally translated," it stands to reason that it will be translated into "Québécois."[19]

The annotation "traduit en québécois" and, at a different level, the proliferation of lexicographical works are both signs of institutional conflict in Quebec. The battle has begun against the language that hitherto served as a referential vehicle. This language is, of course, French. French is not a foreign language in Quebec, as Latin or Italian were in Du Bellay's time; yet it has suddenly been rejected as foreign, that is, incomprehensible. Consider, for example, this extract from *Défense et illustration de la langue québécoise* by Michèle Lalonde:

> Thus, even for the most educated people in the country, there is still a wide gap between spoken and written language and a kind of conflict that could cause great anguish and terrible feelings of dichotomy when a whole chagrin tries to express itself. And it is true that, in that light, the French language of France is like a second language to us, an almost foreign language because it does not have a strong emotional content and immediate allusions to our affects and experiences.[20]

Rejecting French is tantamount to eliminating internal bilingualism, a bilingualism that puts the vernacular language in conflict with the referential; a language without constraints is set against a highly regulated, "polished" language from overseas, a language thus not suitable for translating local experience. The "chagrin" that is inexpressible in the French of France is the "Conquest," the "colonization," the socio-economic "oppression," the very foundation of the nationalist interpretation of history, both real and ideologically constructed.[21] The language conflict was one expression of nationalist aspirations at the time. Another, in the political arena, was the nationalist movement that led to the birth of the Parti Québécois and the emergence of the Front de Libération du Québec. The demand for territorial and political autonomy was logically extended to a demand for a distinct native language. Suddenly, the French of France became unsuitable for communication among Québécois. The nationalist *doxa* used a solipsistic concept of language to explain why French was suddenly incapable of expressing the "affects and experiences" of the Québécois people, who, it would appear, do not share the affects and experiences of other peoples and other nations. After being in contact with a new reality, French had undergone a transformation, with the following result: "even when the words are the same, they express another reality, another experience."[22] It may appear to be the same language, but this is deceptive – Quebec French is no longer the same language as the French of France. This argument is generally supported by allegedly irrefutable proof – a vocabulary list. The manuals and dictionaries mentioned above are a development of this trend. They also lend "scientific" support[23] to the argument for the difference between the two languages. A case in point being the list of Québécois words produced by Michèle Lalonde, which includes such un-French words as "savane," "raquette," and "feu-follet"![24]

The year 1968 marked the beginning of changes in Quebec's relation to the French of France. To satisfy the needs of the nationalist cause, French was held up as an ideological fiction – a socially and geographically homogeneous language, homogeneous to the point of being totalitarian. Was it not continuously subjected to normalization by a small group of academicians, and to censorship by a handful of intellectuals in Paris? This portrayal of the French language as a frigid and withered language, as opposed to a vigorous, natural Québécois, has been widely debated and denounced by many.[25] We will, thus, not pursue the matter here. Suffice it to say that the language conflict that developed around 1968 is clearly symptomatic of a change in relations with the Foreigner.

Québécois in the market of symbolic commodities

A linguistic community is a market. Its vernacular and referential languages are its symbolic commodities, each with its own use value and its own exchange value. The circulation of these commodities is governed by power relations.

> A linguistic community appears to be a sort of *huge market in which words, expressions and messages circulate as commodities*. We may ask ourselves what rules govern the circulation of words, expressions and messages, beginning with the values according to which they are *consumed* and *exchanged*.[26]

As nationalist Quebec began asserting itself at the end of the 1960s, its vernacular and referential languages suddenly started competing with each other. Thus, in the market economy of symbolic commodities, there was competition between the exchange values of the two languages. On the cultural level, the Québécois product had to take precedence over the imported product. This gave rise to a form of protectionism, the aim of which was to limit importation and circulation of non-Québécois symbolic commodities in cultural institutions such as theatrical publishing and production, criticism, and literary awards and grants. The language conflict mirrored the newly engaged battle to conquer the symbolic-commodities market, that is, the battle to become institutionally dominant.

In the theatre, foreign symbolic commodities were dominant, but they remained so by default. Statistics [. . .] reveal, however, that as the number of Québécois productions increased, the exchange value of artistic creations such as foreign translations was more and more seriously eroded. If they were to replace French productions, which were clearly dominant, and if they were to appropriate the symbolic capital held by these productions, Québécois productions had to be different. This was the first condition for the emergence of a distinctly Québécois theatrical institution. Here is how Jacques Dubois explains the "law of distinctness" as it applies to the literary institution:

> . . . at the time when an institution is being founded, we see the development of legitimacy within the literary sphere, and this legitimacy defines the activity of this sphere as autonomous and distinctive . . . Thus, writers find themselves engaged in the logic of distinctness. If distinctness becomes the issue for them, and that is indeed how one gains the recognition of one's peers and competitors, the only way to achieve recognition is to make one's writing culturally marked in a way that is pertinent in a given literary field.[27]

In the dramatic arts, language would fulfil the distinctive function that was needed for Québécois productions to become institutionally recognized and autonomous vis-à-vis French and French-Canadian productions.

The distinctive function of Québécois

This breaking away into a separate aesthetic particularity closely paralleled contemporary political demands, with all their ramifications. We have seen that, in Quebec, the quest for a native language is tied to the need to be different, not to be mixed in with the others in the North American melting pot:

> nous distincts
> différents
> à ne point confondre

> [we [are]
> distinct
> different
> not to be confused with anyone].[28]

'*Québécité*' (Quebecness) defines itself as the search for absolute distinctness, a distinctness that will counteract the danger of assimilation. The threat of assimilation looms on a number of fronts. First, a battle must be waged against the assimilation inherent in the position of a francophone community hemmed in by anglophones. But, of course, the danger of anglicization comes not only from the geopolitical structures of Quebec within the Canadian federation; it also comes from the proximity of the United States, which exerts a strong sociocultural fascination. Economically and politically all-powerful, the United States provides Quebec with its new cultural models and can be viewed, therefore, as a second assimilating front. A third threatening front is immigration. The foreigner, who is called "immigrant," "ethnic," and "allophone" or "neo-Québécois," is seen as the enemy within:

> Mais au contraire, à peine peuvent-ils [les Québécois] s'aventurer hors de leur demeure sans être cernés de toutes parts par des puissances estrangières tantôt Anglaise, tantôt Américaine, voire, récemment, Italienne, qui les repoussent à leur bon plaisir et les soumettent à leurs lois, privilèges ou droits acquis de plus ou moins longue date sur ce territoire . . .

> [But on the contrary, they (the Québécois) can hardly step outside their doors without being surrounded on all sides by foreign powers, sometimes English, sometimes American, and more recently, Italian, who feel free to push them aside and subject them to their laws, privileges, or rights that were acquired a more or less long time ago on this land . . .][29]

This way of thinking attributes to the Italian, the symbol of all immigrants, the assimilating characteristics of the anglophone. The assimilation of francophones is an undeniable threat, if only by virtue of the law of numbers. Moreover, immigrants were quick enough to decide which group to model themselves after, the minority group or the dominant prestigious group. Imbued with the American dream, immigrants had not left everything behind only to end up in the camp of a group that insists on depicting itself as the colonized, the loser, and the victim.

It is easy to understand why their allegiances go spontaneously to the anglophones, who, in fact, have traditionally extended a warm welcome to immigrants, excluded, as they themselves were, from francophone institutions on linguistic or religious grounds. The immigrant thus becomes an agent of assimilation. But this negative portrayal of the immigrant goes even further. It characterizes the newly arrived as the conqueror, the usurper, who receives special treatment. We know how the English got where they are; they have history on their side. But where does an Italian (a Portuguese, a Greek, a Pole, a Haitian, a Vietnamese, a Chilean, a Turk), that bare-foot peasant who just arrived yesterday on "our" soil, get such rights? There is an interesting transfer of blame in this depiction of the immigrant, for it is clear that, in reality, the immigrant does not exactly occupy the upper social, economic, cultural, and political echelons of Quebec society. Is this depiction not, in fact, an indictment specifically designed to justify keeping immigrants on the margin of society, outside all spheres of authority in Quebec? In a province "under siege," the Italian symbolizes internal alterity, a sort of fifth column, a true incarnation of the fear of the Other. No one has been more forthright than Jean Êthier-Blais in expressing the idea of the "foreign peril," a peril that had only become more threatening with the arrival of the Vietnamese, the Chileans, and the Tamils:

> [. . .] le Québec est déjà divisé contre lui-même. D'une part, Montréal, qui se veut *multiculturel, donc objectivement anti-québécois, viscéralement, dans ses néocomposantes*; d'autre part le grand Québec, qui joue la politique de l'autruche et sombre dans l'optimisme tactique. [. . .] Nos gouvernements sont prêts à sacrifier tout ce qui nous est cher, langue, histoire, pour ne pas décevoir *ces "réfugiés politiques"*.

> [. . . Quebec is already divided against itself. On the one hand, Montreal, which likes to see itself as *multicultural, thus objectively anti-Québécois, viscerally, in its neo-composition*; on the other, Quebec as a whole, which plays the politics of the ostrich, drowning in tactical optimism . . . Our governments are ready to sacrifice everything we hold dear, language, history, so as not to disappoint these "political refugees."][30]

Clearly, here, group membership is not fortuitous or a natural state of affairs. It is guided by nationalist interests, and by definition does not allow for inclusion of neo-Québécois. They have the misfortune of being what they are: foreigners. This argument, which is designed to prevent the dissolution of the Québécois identity, tacitly reproduces the dominant/subordinate schema that is so vigorously denounced when the group is speaking of itself. Any relationship with the Other seems inconceivable outside this framework of domination. This is because the Other is at fault and wears a mask, as insinuated by Êthier-Blais's use of quotation marks, which make the official status of "political refugee" suspect – no doubt, illegitimate. Only the Québécois are tragic figures, exiles in their own country. Foreigners use a false identity to pass themselves off as victims and abuse the generosity of an overly hospitable country. The poetry of Michel Garneau opposes the fascist undertones of such rhetoric. His apologia for cross-breeding uses poetic language to reveal and acclaim the mixed background of the Québécois identity: "J'ai tout le sang mêlé /

les ancêtres sont mes étrangers / un peu d'hurabénaquois / un peu d'irlancossais
[. . .]" ["My blood is all mixed up / my ancestors are foreigners / Hurabénaquois
/ a little Irishscotch . . ."] In another poem, "L'avenir câllé" (Calling to the Future)
he even writes:

> qu'on réalise québécois combien nous sommes
> écœuremment racistes
> baie-james-réserves-rythme de nègres-
> maudits-anglais-français-italiens-juifs
> poloks-chicken flied lice-sauvages
> pis qu'on arrête ça tout d'suite.

> [that we Québécois realize how sickeningly racist
> we are
> James-Bay-reservations-nigger rhythm-
> cursed-English-French-Italians-Jews
> Polaks-chicken flied lice-savages
> now let's stop that right now.][31]

The foreigner poses a problem precisely because he introduces heterogeneity,
impurity into the Québécois community.

> Nous autres
> dit couramment ce peuple
> à propos de lui-même
> marquant ainsi d'un mot
> l'intime ambiguïté
> de son identité.

> ["Nous autres"
> says frequently this people
> about itself
> underlining thus with a single word
> the intimate ambiguity
> of its identity.][32]

Ideally, no foreign presence should ever stain the Québécois identity. Doing away
with any "ambiguity" of identity means getting rid of the Other. In the name of
distinctness, the salvation of the Québécois identity, all forms of alterity must be automatically ejected from the group, confined to their own differences. The first-person
plural, "nous," is used to justify various kinds of difference – ethnicity, language, identity, and separation. Close association between "nous" and "les autres" is dangerous,
harmful, and therefore to be deplored. The "Québécois language" is entrusted with
establishing this separation and constitutes, in effect, the *differentia specifica* of the
Québécois. If the French language is no longer sufficient, it is because the stakes are
no longer simply linguistic; they have become topological. Language must be co-
extensive with a territory. There can be no sharing of language or territory.

The enigmatic Québécois language[33]

Gaston Miron makes a distinction between "mother tongue" and "native language," a distinction, he says, the Québécois need to make.[34] How does he explain the relevance of this distinction between two concepts that, in actual usage, are one and the same? He does not define what he means by "native language," but he holds it up as the symbol of political liberation. Miron's native language is still French, but it is not spoken in the same cultural and sociopolitical circumstances as French. In fact, Miron uses the notion of a native language as an antithesis to a series of axioms on which his whole argument is built: if a native language is to emerge, Quebec must rid itself of its colonial status; once Quebec is freed of its colonial socio-economic constraints, its newly emerged native language can be used to justify the rejection of French culture. The existence of a native language presupposes that its speakers are "in the world according to a culture, that is according to an ontology" which is *unique* to that language, and to that language only. In other words, the emergence of a native language implies the elimination of alterity.[35] To acquire a native language is to be reborn in a free country, to have a country entirely to oneself. Reclaiming one's native language naturally leads to the idea of a pure nation that exists in "the consciousness of the world."[36] Their own native language or national language is a sign of the unity and purity of the Québécois "people." It is the distinctive feature of what Gaston Miron calls the "*Québécanthrope*," the *homo quebecensis*, who sees himself, to use Weinmann's rejoinder, "as a new man" who comes from a *separate* branch of the development of humanity.[37] Miron's native language does not exist. It is a political postulate founded on an identity fetish and on the rejection of the Other: "only political action can restore him [the Québécois] to his homogeneity, the basis for exchange between cultures."[38] The call for a return to homogeneity is not exactly a subtle one. There seems to be no awareness of the fact that there is no such thing as a homogeneous culture, no more than there is homogeneous literature. Indeed, the ideology of homogeneity rejects all dialogism and is, thus, a form of totalitarianism.[39]

Creating a distinction between a native language and a mother tongue entails more than the reappropriation of the native language, a language deformed and alienated by interference from English. The distinction also implies rejection of the mother tongue, which, in this case, is the language of a "foreign" culture, the French culture. Pierre Gobin points out what this distinction specifically means to the playwright "living in a society that bears the marks of colonial experience." The author "experiences even more profoundly the distance between 'indigenous' language and 'foreign' writing, especially if both have the same linguistic heritage, that is to say, if there is *diglossia* rather than *bilingualism*."[40] Furthermore, sharing a language with French does not sit well with a solipsistic and ontological concept of culture. According to this line of thinking, the mother tongue of the Québécois is someone else's language, in the same way that their native country, which has been despoiled by the English, has become someone else's country. Therefore, claiming one's native language means rejecting one's mother, severing a tie that, in any case, was never nourishing:

Ya-t-il doncques une Langue Québecquoyse, ou Québécouayse, ou kébékouaze distincte de la Française comme celle-ci l'était naguère du latin dans laquelle je puisse m'exprimer? D'aucuns aussi prompts à trancher cette question que lents à trancher le cordon ombilical qui les relie à la Mère-patrie, soutiennent péremptoirement que *non* et qualifient de barbare & impure la Parlure de nostre "vulgaire" qu'il faudrait châtier sans pitié comme une façon tout au plus de parler ineptement français.

[Is there indeed a Québecquoyse, or Québecouayse or kébékouaze language distinct from French, in the way French used to be distinct from Latin, in which I can express myself? Some are as quick to answer this question as they are slow to cut the umbilical cord that connects them to the Mother Country; they maintain that the answer is simply no, and say that the language of our "vulgar" is a barbarous and impure way of speaking that should be punished mercilessly for being an inept way of speaking French.][41]

Mother tongue is not the same notion for Michèle Lalonde as it is for Gaston Miron. Lalonde's concept of mother tongue corresponds more to what Miron terms a "native" language. For Lalonde, the mother tongue is not the language of the mother country, a borrowed language, with "a French superior lineage, devoid of all our turpitude, thus of a less vulgar Culture."[42] The mother tongue is truly the language-of-my-mother [la langue-à-ma-mère]. It is the language of one's roots, full of "lovely words . . . invented to describe, for example, *les bordages* (in-shore ice), *les bordillons* (piles of in-shore ice), *les fardoches* (undergrowth), and *les cédrières* (cedar groves), and other common things in our wild surroundings."[43] The mother tongue is an Edenic, native, natural language, dating from the idyllic era of colonization (when "we" were the colonizers). In those days, it was a free language, a language in perfect harmony with the territory of the Québécois, a language nothing could resist, "neither the blue spruce, nor the white cedar, nor the plains, nor the hemlock spruce, that so awed our ancestors but did not leave them speechless and unable to name them."[44] Lalonde's definition of mother tongue is full of nostalgia for a paradise lost, a time when the Québécois could invent their own names for things, when the Québécois language was "Cratylean" and in complete harmony with nature. The deterioration of the language followed the loss of the country to the venal hands of a foreign power:

À la claire fontaine du Toronto Stock Exchange il en
coule des dollars sous nos doigts comme billets
d'amour pour la belle dame des maîtres

brrou goudourou xouliminimini crrah vrrah khmè strix
j'attendais un vrai language là où il n'y avait que des
pieuvres pour me bouffer tout cru tout vivant

crisse de câlice de tabarnaque
le jour où j'ai pensé hors des fantômes admis pensé de
ce qu'est vivre ici je n'ai su que sacrer profaner.

[In the clear fountain of the Toronto Stock Exchange
dollars flow through our fingers like love
notes for the beautiful lady of the masters

brrou goudourou xouliminimini crrah vrrah khmè strix
I was expecting a real language in the place where there was
only octopus to eat me completely raw and totally alive

crisse de câlice de tabarnaque
the day I thought outside of the acceptable ghosts thought about
what it is to live here I could only swear profanities.][45]

In a lyrical, humorous register, Paul Chamberland's poem "L'afficheur hurle"
also takes up the theme of nostalgia for a pure language unspoiled by the Other.
He expresses his anguish that a "true language" is impossible and sings the praises
of a paradise lost:

l'amour m'a mis entre les dents les clés de la vengeance
[. . .]
pourtant j'aurais pu être tendre comme de la dentelle
mais il aurait fallu depuis toujours voler rouler sur
le muscle d'une terre forte cascader sur les hanches
d'une mère ouverte aux razzias du plaisir Mère
Liberté Mère Amour Mère debout dans le création du monde.

[love put the keys of vengeance in my mouth
. . .
but I could have been tender like lace
but it would have been necessary to fly roll
over the muscle of a strong land cascade onto the hips
of a mother open to the plunders of pleasure. Mother
Liberty Mother Love Mother standing in the creation of the world.][46]

It would be possible to return to the mother on two conditions: she must be
a lover and she must incarnate liberty. The metaphor of incest sits well with the
metaphor of the family that is often used to describe Québécois society ("this little
society that comes together like a family").[47] Implicit in the metaphor of incest is a
longing for an unreal past, a past that can be re-created by staying among one's own
people. Thus, we see the formation of a vicious circle of nostalgia which, exclusive
and inward-turning, rejects the Other and its culture. In this nostalgia for a return
to nature, there is also a call for a return to a language which, if not lost, has yet
to re-emerge.

How does one choose between the language of a paradise lost and the futile
search for a native language; futile because the language is contaminated by the
"contemporary landscape in which *le Workshop, le Warehouse* and *le Shopping-centre*
already have a name before they even sprout and there are many more of them than
the *blé d'Inde* [corn on the cob] and the *arbre à sucre* [maple tree]"?[48] This is the
very dilemma that led Michèle Lalonde, in her defence of the Québécois language,
to adopt the sixteenth-century French of Joachim Du Bellay just as Du Bellay had

vindicated French by using an Italian text as a model. And we know how highly he thought of Italy! Returning to this archaic form of French represents an attempt to pay "homage to the very rich and original Langue Québécoyse, to the time when it was spoken freely and without so many unhappy complications on the free Canadian soil."[49] In other words, the Québécois language is a nostalgic language, a myth, a fiction, a fantasy of a lost object. Justification for its existence is found in nationalist rhetoric, which equates a language with a people and with a specific territory. None the less, when Michèle Lalonde is not writing manifestos, she switches to standard contemporary educated French to explain what the relationship between the Québécois writer and the language of Québécois society should be:

> The role of writers is simply to take as much interest as possible in the Québécois collectivity and to ADDRESS THIS COLLECTIVITY IN ITS LANGUAGE. By this I mean: we must regenerate the language, rediscover it, reinvent it, we must give it new significance, fill in the gaps with the help of international French, shake it up, refine it, make love to it with abandon, and do with it what we will but adopt it as the language of the six million who speak Québécois.[50]

Here, once again, we encounter the view that language must be homogeneous and unified, as should the people who speak it in their daily lives. But these people have never used this language in their literature. Oh, Guilty Literature! You must be removed from your place at the centre of the institution! The Québécois writer who is deserving of the title should "renounce literary egocentrism" and "for the time being pull out of the Prix Goncourt," and adopt the language of the Québécois, the true speech of "real people." The duty of writers is in fact to "give the power of speech back to the collectivity from which they come . . . to the point where they should try to have more contact with students, workers, in other words, with ordinary Québécois, even if it means going to write among them."[51] And, of course, Québécois workers, like their French counterparts, are avid readers of *Change*, the avant-garde journal in which this exhortation appeared! But the contradiction is even more profound: Québécois writers, who themselves do not speak the language of the collectivity, are asked to return to their linguistic roots. What is truly paradoxical here is that writers are expected to use the language of the people while playing the role of demiurge. Are they not expected to restore the language, consolidate it, give it back the vigour it had at the time of its origins, the time of liberty? To rediscover freedom of language is to regain liberty itself. To give the power of speech back to a people is, in both senses of the word, to allow them to speak and to provide them with a language. More to the point, it is, in fact, to give them what the Other took away with the injunction "Speak White!"[52] But does this not constitute a change in ideological direction? The nationalist goal, anchored in the notion of "difference," does, in fact, need to be reinforced by distinctive characteristics, and language is the most important of these. Yet, this form of Québécois distinctness really exists only in the lower classes. In other words, the desire to give a language back to the "people," a conveniently ambiguous term, masks the ideological reappropriation of the language by the élite, as they attempt to prove the absoluteness of the Québécois "difference," and thereby justify the demand for political autonomy. Perhaps more than anything else, such a difference guarantees recognition to a new group of writers and sets them apart institutionally from other writers. This, of course, ensures that they have no competition from those who continue to compete for the "Prix Goncourt."

Michèle Lalonde's suggestion that writers should live and write among the working class – which V. L. Beaulieu does for several months of the year – brings to mind Luther's dilemma as he pondered the state of the German language at a time when it was not yet unified. What variety of German would be appropriate for translation? Luther proposed the following:

> . . . We must seek out the mother in her home, the children in the streets, the common man in the market-place and examine what they are saying to discover how they speak; so that we may translate according to that. Then they will understand and notice that we speak German just like them.[53]

In pre-referendum nationalist Quebec as well as in reformist Germany, the success or failure of an ideology depended on a willingness to communicate with the people. To achieve hegemony, a group needs grassroots support. This was the case in the creation of a new religious institution in Germany and remains so for the creation of a literary institution in Quebec. The emergence of a truly Québécois literary institution is dependent upon the existence of a public. The Québécois language, which has been entrusted with this mission, is to "international French" what the dialects of Germany were to Latin. But there is a difference. Whereas Latin was truly a foreign language to the "mother in her home" and to "the common man in the market-place," international French in Quebec is found on the radio, in the newspapers, on television, and in the theatre. Nationalist ideology rejects the notion of Quebec French being "international." In this context, the word "international" has a negative connotation and reveals a desire to exclude; the "multicultural" and the "transcultural" are negative values, to be fought at all costs. Suddenly characterized as "international," French has been defined as, and deliberately made into, a foreign language. Such an ideology emphasizes the illegitimacy of French, claiming that it is neither heard nor understood in Quebec. And proof of this assertion is to be found in the speech of ordinary Québécois.

More than any other literary genre, the theatre lends itself to the differentiating role entrusted to language. More than any other, the theatre, which gives primacy to the oral, makes it possible to hear the difference between referential French and vernacular French, a difference that is mainly a phonetic one.

The myths of "Québécois" as a language of translation

The phrase "traduit en québécois" contains a paradox. It indicates, in French, that the language in which the work will be read is not French. This contradiction clearly illustrates the confusion surrounding the meaning of "Québécois." Native language? Mother tongue? Lost language or the true speech of the Québécois? But which Québécois, and under which circumstances? Characterizations of Québécois range from the myth of its Edenic origins via the standard French of Gaston Miron or Michèle Lalonde, all the way to the sociolectal reality of a "decimated" language called "joual." What does "traduit en québécois" then mean? Theatre translation illustrates the elusive nature of the Québécois language. Inconsistencies in the target language from one translator to another reflect the paradoxes and the incoherence of definitions of Québécois, as well as the diglossia of those who speak it. As definitions of Québécois itself fluctuate, so translations assume various forms.

Michel Garneau, the translator of *Macbeth*, appears to have given himself the task of rebuilding the original language of Quebec, the language of a distant past when Quebec was still free. With this goal, translation becomes a philological endeavour. To return to the birth of the spoken tongue in Quebec, Garneau undertook a veritable archaeological exploration of the language: "I dug deep (as if digging a well) into the Québécois language until I reached its ancestral source, I rummaged through the glossaries like crazy."[54] Garneau also states that he reproduced the phonetics of the Gaspésie dialect. But why not the dialect of the Beauce or the Saguenay? His choice was apparently based on a concern for greater authenticity: "Beginning with lexical and syntactic archaisms, from the rural poetry of old laments and Gaspésien pronunciation (that Garneau, like Jacques Ferron, finds more authentic), he creates a sort of ideal Quebec language."[55]

The primacy Garneau accords to the speech of the Gaspé Peninsula clearly smacks of ideology. It so happens that the Gaspésie was the original site of Quebec, since it was here that Jacques Cartier landed in 1534 and planted a cross to claim the new land. The motivation for choosing the Gaspésie dialect is perhaps unconscious. The choice, none the less, is a functional one, since its purpose is to restore the Quebec language to its original truth and purity. The resulting language is an "ideal" language – in other words, a perfect, nostalgic, mythical language. It is, indeed, the same language as the native tongue called for by Miron; it represents, literally, the language of the country at its birth. It is the language of the "savage that I was," according to Garneau, "in the infancy of the tall grass."[56] Moreover, nostalgia for this lost innocence suffuses the whole of the "naïve" poetry of the author of *Petits chevals amoureux* (Little Amorous Horses) or *L'élégie au massacre des nasopodes* (Elegy for the Massacre of the Nasopodes). The language in Garneau's *Macbeth* allows us to hear the words of the mother tongue that Michèle Lalonde calls the "language-of-my-mother," in a world inhabited by *chats sovages*, *engoul'vents*, *éparviers*, where people *criaillent*, *s'époérinent*, *rôdaillent*, and *s'acagnardissent*. Listen to Lady Macbeth convince her husband of the necessity of the crime:

> Toute est organisé pis tu sais pus d'quel côté avoér peur?
> Écoute, j'ai déjà nourri à mon lait, j'sais c'que c'est
> D'aimer le p'tit qui tète après toé, ben si j'ava's juré
> De l'fére comme t'as juré, même pendant qu'y m'ara't
>   gazouillé
> Su'a falle, j'y a'ra's arraché l'teton des gencives
> Pis j'y'a'ra's craqué 'a tête en deux![57]

The language in Michel Garneau's *Macbeth* harks back to the early days of Quebec. It is a language both innocent and ancestral, a "natural" language imbued with a primitive force. It is the language of the pioneers who had to hold their own against a hostile nature. It ties the search for identity to the myth of origins, a myth that the language itself helps to create. The Shakespearian world, and, in particular, that of *Macbeth*, a sacrificial tragedy of primitive violence, provides a perfect backdrop for a prehistorical exploration of the Quebec language. It is a perfect vehicle for reconstructing a past and for bringing to light a time when the language and those who spoke it owed nothing to anybody. The archaeology of the Quebec language reduces "alienation" to degree zero and returns the language to its point of origin, where all forms of dependence on the Other are abolished.

Literary classics such as *Macbeth* are chosen as vehicles for the Quebec language in an attempt to remove the language from its dialect status and to prove that it is capable of fulfilling a referential function. At least, this is the view of critics: "Shakespeare, through his work, gave poetic status to a language which hitherto had none; Garneau wants to demonstrate the richness of the Quebec language and to place it on an equal footing with other languages."[58] Based on an inaccurate idea of the state of the English language in pre-Elizabethan times, this view makes Garneau the equal of Shakespeare and elevates Québécois to the status of a language at the height of its poetic maturity. The Québécois in Garneau's *Macbeth* is an anachronistic language, just as Shakespeare's language is today. In this sense, we can say that Michel Garneau's translation aims to provide contemporary Quebec speakers, not with a language they can actually speak, but rather with a feeling for their history and their ancestral ties. In any case, the creation of this ancestral language, "native language" according to Miron, or "mother tongue" according to Michèle Lalonde, brings to a successful conclusion the search for a language of one's own, a necessary condition for establishing the Québécois identity.

Michel Garneau's philological endeavors are unique. Generally speaking, what is termed "Québécois" translation attempts to establish a difference between the contemporary French of Quebec and the "French of France." In this way, it falls in line with the programme of the new Quebec theatre, which, according to Jean-Claude Germain, must "restore our national language to the full vigour of its true expression."[59] But this language, which is theoretically the language of the Québécois "nation," displays astonishing diversity when used as a language of translation. Let us look, for example, at several extracts from the stage directions of Québécois translations:

Chekhov, *Les Trois Sœurs* (*The Three Sisters*), translated by Robert Lalonde

LA MAISON DES COTÉ. UN SALON MODESTE; BEAUCOUP DE MEAUBLES ET DE BIBELOTS. ATMOSPHERE TRES "FAMILIALE" ET ORDINAIRE. LA SALLE À MANGER EST CONTIGUË AU SALON. C'EST UN DIMANCHE ENSOLEILLÉ DE PRINTEMPS.

GISÈLE EST EN UNIFORME D'INSTITUTRICE POUR JEUNES FILLES ET CORRIGE SES DEVOIRS. ANGÉLE EST ASSISE; SON CHÂLE SUR LES GENOUX ET LIT. ISABELLE EST OCCUPÉE À METTRE LA TABLE. ON VA DÎNER.

Gisèle (EN CORRIGEANT SES DEVOIRS): – Ça fait un an aujourd'hui que papa est mort. Le jour de ta fête Isabelle. On gelait. J'pensais virer folle. Toi Isabelle, t'étais étendue sur le divan, blanche comme une morte . . . Ça fait rien qu'un an pis on peut déjà en parler comme de n'importe quoi d'autre . . . Tu vois, t'es-t-en robe blanche Isabelle, pis t'as l'air tellement en santé! T'es si belle dans c'te robe là. C'est avec la robe de maman que tu l'as faite?[60]

Theoretically, the translator has reproduced authentic North American rural French. The dialogue uses oral contractions such as "j'pensais," "pis," "t'as," and "c'te robe là." Expressions like "virer folle" and "être en santé" immediately identify the speaker as French Canadian. She is a teacher and a doctor's daughter, but her speech, full of expressions like "t'es-t-en robe," is not the speech of a cultivated person and is in marked contrast to the "Québécois" used by the translator in his stage directions. These language choices can be explained by the fact that translators of plays into Québécois always begin by transposing the original setting into a lower register. Brigadier-General Prosorov's house becomes the house of a village notable. The "salon" (complete with columns) "behind which there is a large room"[61] is transformed into "a modest living-room" with a "very domestic and ordinary" atmosphere. We have already noted that Garneau has a tendency to remove from the original text any indicators that place the characters in a dominant social position. It could be said that, in the interests of representing *québécité* on the stage, the characters of the original work undergo a social lowering in the translation. We may well ask, then, to what extent the choice of foreign plays translated in Quebec is a function of the social position of their characters. This social lowering has a direct effect on the language used by the characters in the translation, allowing them to speak a type of language marked by phonetic, lexical, and syntactic features characteristic of speech in Quebec, and particularly characteristic of the lower classes. And it is the lower classes who must be portrayed, since portrayal of the lower classes reinforces the sovereigntist credo, based, as it is, on the concept of the alienation of the people. This ideology of difference does not allow for the neutrality of the French spoken by the educated classes in Quebec. The difference between Quebec French and the French of France is, in point of fact, a sociolectal one. This is evident in written stage directions, which carry no specific linguistic markers of Québécois speech.

Brecht, *La Bonne Âme de Se-Tchouan* (*The Good Person of Sechuan*), translated by Gilbert Turp

LE SOIR – LE VENDEUR D'EAU S'ADRESSE AU PUBLIC

Wang – Chu vendeur d'eau dans capitale du Setchouan: ici.
mon travail? c'est pénible
pendant les sécheresses – faut que je cours à l'autre bout du monde pour trouver de l'eau
pis pendant les pluies ben . . . j'en vends pas
ce qui règne surtout dans notre belle province c'est la misère
en fin de compte – ya à peu près rien que sués Dieux

qu'on peut compter pour se faire aider
ben à ma plus grande . . . grande joie
j'ai appris par un marchand de bétail comme yen passe souvent dans le
coin que des Dieux – pis des hauts placés – sont en route pour icite pis
qu'on serait en droit de s'attendre à les recevoir
je suppose que le ciel s'est tanné de nous entendre nous plaindre vers
lui dins airs.[62]

The central ideological matrix of the discourse on Québécois alienation mirrors the
theme of Brecht's *Good Person of Sechuan*, a fable set in the province of Sechuan,
"which represented all those places where men exploit other men."[63] And Quebec
is one of those places where men . . . By sheer chance, the first line of the play sets
the tone for the theme of Québécois identity. Wang is the very symbol of the
Québécois. The "marchand d'eau" (water merchant) of the French version becomes
in Quebec the "vendeur d'eau" (water-seller). This change may appear insignificant,
but the phonetic significance of the expressions chosen by the Québécois translator
should not be overlooked. The "vendeur d'eau" captures much better the sense of
the "porteur d'eau," a term traditionally employed by Québécois to describe the
inferiority of their social condition and their exploitation since the English Conquest.
Elsewhere in the play, the expression "notre province" acquires a modifier,
becoming "notre belle province," thereby changing the referent of the discourse:
Sechuan becomes an allegory for Quebec, just as Scotland does in the Québécois
translation of *Macbeth*: ("les drapeaux des étranges insultent not' beau ciel" – "foreign
flags are an insult to our beautiful sky"). This new referent echoes one of the main
themes of the discourse of Québécois alienation: "Quebec is a despoiled nation," a
theme that clearly informs Garneau's idiosyncratic translation: "O nation miserable"
/ "J'appartiens à eune nation ben misérabe" and corresponds exactly to "Chu
vendeur d'eau" (I'm a water-seller). We now begin to see why translation into
Québécois almost always involves proletarization of the language.[64] The pauperiza-
tion of the signifier reflects the alienation of the Québécois public for whom the
text is intended. The procedure used to achieve this is graphemization. By graphemization we mean the graphic realization of the difference between the phonetics of
the Québécois language and those of an unmarked French: "chu" / "je suis," "sués"
/ "sur les," "dins airs" / "dans les airs." But this transcription is not always functional. Consider, for example, Jean-Claude Germain's retranslation of Brecht's
A Respectable Wedding:

> *La mariée*: Ah oui . . . çé lui qu'y a eu l'idée pour toute han? . . . Ya tiré
> les plans, y a achté le bois, y l'a scié, y l'a sablé pis y l'a collé . . . parsque
> toute est embouffeté pis collé han . . . a parre les pantures, y a pas un
> clou . . . çé faitte rustique![65]

Here, the written form is tampered with to give the illusion that there is an irreconcilable difference between "Québécois" and French. But how does the French
pronunciation of words such as "acheter," "embouveté," "parce que," or "à part"
differ from the Québécois pronunciation, a pronunciation that is supposedly
reflected in Germain's spelling? On the same page and in the mouth of the same

character we find the following: "votre oncque Hubert" and "votte oncque Huberre."[66] There are similar inconsistencies throughout the text. As we mentioned earlier, these inconsistencies form part of an ideological pattern: the deformed spelling, invented by Germain and presented as what he calls "our national language," is in fact an "in" code that functions primarily as a form of differentiation and, consequently, a form of exclusion.

In many cases, the language used for translation resembles that used in dramatic writing, in which an alienated speech variety is realistically transposed and takes on a cathartic function. This is what Michel Tremblay set out to achieve. His plays paved the way for implementation of Michèle Lalonde's program for the Québécois language:

> . . . the subject of *joual* as a language for the theatre has received a great deal of attention . . . Many accepted it immediately, while others categorically rejected it; however, both groups spent too much time and effort on the subject, in my opinion, to the detriment of its intended use in the theatre . . . As I have often said . . . it is all well and good to speak of my audacity in writing in "true" *joual*, but we must not forget what lies behind this outcast of a language, this ugly, poor, anaemic "disgraceful" etc., etc., etc. . . . It is not only the élite who have "profoundly human problems" and it is possible to say "I am unhappy" without a glass of Martini in one's hand . . . Rose Ouimet's "Maudit cul!" is the strongest expression of despair that a Québécoise can utter. Did the audience understand this in *Les Belles-Soeurs* or was it enough for them to be shocked because it was vulgar?[67]

The sociolect chosen by Tremblay is functional. It plays a role in the renewal of the theatrical aesthetic by modifying those norms that produce the effect of reality. The naturalistic reproduction of the language jolts people into a new awareness. But Tremblay does not claim to be supplanting what previously functioned as a referential language. *Joual* is for him simply one of those registers available in the written language:

> My role is to continue to describe the working-class world, while from time to time allowing myself the luxury of a "Lysistrata" and a "Cité dans l'Oeuf." But those whose role is to continue to produce such plays as "Lysistrata" and "Cité dans l'Oeuf," they, too, ought to allow themselves the luxury of a "Belles-Soeurs" occasionally . . . I cannot accept people looking down their noses at *Les Belles-Soeurs* just because it is vulgar . . . they should read Edward Albee, Tennessee Williams, and John Arden in English! Were the Americans and the English ashamed of coming to grips with *their* "joual"?[68]

Michel Tremblay's *joual* plays created an opening in the literary system in Quebec. No such opening existed in the literary system of France. This new theatrical form had an important consequence; it broadened the translatability of the sociolects of Anglo-American plays, which now had a "natural equivalent" in

Quebec culture, though not in French culture: "It is time for us to begin translating American plays ourselves! The French, whom I much admire incidentally, have the gift of 'disfiguring' American theatre."[69] The inadequacy Tremblay addresses here is systemic and was a feature of French theatre of the time, as opposed to Québécois theatre, where the translation of works by Tennessee Williams, Edward Albee, or Eugene O'Neill was no longer faced with a linguistic void. Let us look at two Québécois translations of the following extract from *Desire under the Elms*:

> *Cabot*: I couldn't work today. I couldn't take no interest. T'hell with the farm! I'm leavin' it! I've turned the cows an' other stock loose! I've druv 'em into the woods whar they kin be free! By freein' 'em, I'm freein' myself! I'm quittin' here today! I'll set fire t'house an' barn an' watch 'em burn, an' I'll leave Yer Maw t'haunt the ashes, an' I'll will the fields back t'God, so that nothin' human kin never touch 'em! I'll be a-goin' to Californi-a.[70]

Translation by Robert Ripps and Yves Sauvageau

> *Cabot*: J'pourrais pas travailler aujourd'hui . . . m'y sens pas l'coeur. Au diable la terre! J'la lâche là! J'viens d'lâcher les vaches pis l'reste du bétail! J'les ai poussés de par le bois où c'est qu'y vont ête libes! Leu rendant la liberté, j'me la donne aussi. C't'aujourd'hui que j'pars d'ici. J'vas sacrer l'feu à maison pis à grange, m'a r'garder brûler les bâtiments . . . m'a laisser ta mére s'promener dins cendres . . . pis m'a r'mette mes champs au bon yeu comme ça y aura jamais rien d'un humain qui y toucheront. M'a m'embarquer pour la California.[71]

Translation by Michel Dumont and Marc Grégoire

> *Cabot*: J'ai pas été capable de m'mette à l'ouvrage aujourd'hui. Ça m'tentà pas. Au yâbe la farme! J'en veux pus. Les vaches, j'les ai lâchées lousses, pis toute le resse du bétail itou! J'les ai amenées dans l'bois pour qu'y soyent libes! J'les ai libérées pis en faisant ça, J'me sus libéré moé-même! J'm'en va d'icitte pas plus tard qu'aujourd'hui! J'va sacrer l'feu à maison pis aux bâtiments; j'va les r'gârder brûler, pis toute c'que j'va laisser au fantôme de ta mére, c'est des cendres; c'est l'bon Yeu qui m'a denné la térre, j'va y r'denner à mon tour, pis y arra pus jamà rien d'humain qui va pouvouère y toucher! J'va partir pour la Califournie.[72]

The diversity of social and regional lects of vernacular French in Quebec provides the translator with a broad range of language possibilities. This "co-linguism" exists to the same extent in France. There is no reason why a French translator should not translate O'Neill into the sociolect of farmers of any region in the country. Such a translation, however, would be considered as artificial as a translation into "neutral" French, as Michel Tremblay is all too well aware. The target text would not meet the criteria of acceptability set by the literary institution.

To translate sociolects into French, the translator has to contend, not with an intrinsic deficiency in the linguistic system of France, but rather with *a linguistic void in the normative system of its literature*. Ideology can be detected behind the void, as

Renée Balibar has shown in her study of language use and its social effect in the nineteenth-century French novel.[73] A Québécois writer managed to use language to establish a new and distinctive dramatic form. No French writer has ever managed to defy the normalizing linguistic ideology of the Republic to this end. Two social currents in Quebec made this possible – the glorification of difference and the recognition of an American component in the affirmation of the Québécois identity. Since Michel Tremblay began writing in *joual*, abundant use has been made of all the social registers of spoken French in Quebec, both on the stage and on television. Yet, it would not be unreasonable to suggest that *joualization* of the French-Canadian theatre has been influenced by the sociolectal character of the Anglo-American theatre, the most popular foreign-language theatre in Quebec. One thing is clear, the use of the vernacular, an innovation in Quebec, has led to the emergence and institutionalization of a national theatre that does not use French models. Use of the vernacular has also reinforced sovereigntist aspirations by turning the theatre into an ideological springboard. The vernacular is thus an effective vehicle for the central theme of the sovereigntist discourse – the alienation of Quebec society.

Why translate into Québécois?

The search for a language of one's own offers one explanation for the phenomenon of retranslation. The rejection of the French of France, deemed inadequate for translating foreign plays into Québécois reality, provides another. The search for a native language also explains the phenomenon of retranslation. The "repatriation" to Quebec of the translation of foreign works hitherto available only in French translation is seen as essential. Quebec is able to provide its own translations of foreign plays, but they will be retranslations. Retranslation is a particularly interesting phenomenon from the point of view of comments that are made in relation to it.

As it is deemed important to avoid using imported translations, Québécois translators have been known to translate from languages they are not familiar with. In such cases, the translator has to work from intermediate translations. For example, Gilles Marsolais translated Strindberg and Chekhov without knowing Swedish or Russian. The same is true of Michel Tremblay's translation of *Uncle Vanya*. Both used word-for-word translations provided by speakers familiar with the language of the original text. They then produced the definitive version by working with existing French or English translations. On occasion, the influence of these earlier translations is so pronounced that the origins of the Québécois version are hardly in doubt. A comparison of two translations of *Uncle Vanya* speaks for itself:

Michel Tremblay	**Elsa Triolet**
SÉRÉBRIAKOV	SÉRÉBRIAKOV
Donner toute sa vie	Donner toute sa vie
à la science,	à la science,
s'habituer à son cabinet	être habitué à son cabinet
de travail,	de travail,

à son auditoire, à des camarades vénérés	à son auditoire, à des camarades vénérables
et, tout d'un coup, de but en blanc,	et, soudain, on ne sait pourquoi,
se retrouver dans ce sépulcre	se retrouver dans ce caveau,
côtoyer tous les jours des gens stupides	voir tous les jours des gens idiots,
écouter des propos insignifiants . . .	écouter des conversations qui ne présentent pas le moindre intérêt . . .
je veux vivre, j'aime le succès	je veux vivre, j'aime le succès
j'aime la célébrité, le bruit et, ici,	j'aime la célébrité, le bruit, et, ici,
j'ai l'impression d'être en exil.	c'est l'exil.
Pleurer sans arrêt le passé,	Pleurer sans arrêt le passé
épier le succès des autres,	épier le succès des autres,
craindre la mort . . .	craindre la mort . . .
Je n'en peux plus!	Je n'en peux plus
Je n'en ai pas la force!	Je n'en ai pas la force!
Et là, en plus,	Et si avec ça,
on ne veut pas me pardonner	on ne veut pas me pardonner
ma vieillesse!	ma vieillesse![74]

The two extracts are remarkably similar. Compared with Elsa Triolet's translation, Michel Tremblay's translation contains occasional paradigmatic differences (caveau/ sépulcre), but his syntax follows Triolet's almost exactly. The similarity makes one wonder what the real role of retranslation is in Quebec. In some countries, inter- mediate translations play an essential role. They provide access to foreign works that would remain otherwise unknown for want of a translator capable not only of reading them in the original but of translating them directly into the language of the country.[75] There are a number of explanations for the phenomenon of indirect translation in Quebec, that is to say, translation based on earlier translations. Works translated in this manner *already* exist in the target language. There can even be several contemporary translations of a single work. A number of French translations of classics from other languages have achieved canonical status – translations of Strindberg by Boris Vian, Pirandello by Benjamin Crémieux, or Chekhov by Elsa Triolet. Given the similarity between Québécois translations and their French "models," it is difficult to sustain the notion that a Québécois audience would find the French version hard to understand. Moreover, when the translations are by Adamov, Pitoeff, or Vitez, one can hardly claim that they do not measure up because they were not translated by theatre specialists. We may therefore conclude that, in the Quebec theatre, translations imported from France are seen to play an anti- mediating role. This is Gilbert Turp's argument: "When I read the French translation of *Mother Courage*, no image came immediately to mind . . . what was lacking in the French translation was not reflection or emotion; rather, it was evoca- tion. The French translation of *Mother Courage* said nothing to me."[76] This same argument is used by Michel Tremblay and Gilles Marsolais to justify their own translations, which were mediated, paradoxically, through the very French translations they wished to replace:

> When he read Elsa Triolet's translation, Tremblay was struck by its relatively rigid, literary character . . . He therefore invited Kim Yaroshevskaya, whose native language is Russian, to translate for him, word by word, the language of Chekhov. The result was significant and revealing. Tremblay noticed that Chekhov's language is *more natural than literary* and that Chekhovian dialogue is full of understatement. It was in this spirit that he produced his translation . . . The result, and you will be able to judge for yourself, is a *direct idiom*. It is certainly closer to Chekhov than Elsa Triolet's translation, precise but not *too literary*.[77]

Director Gilles Marsolais used the same procedure in his translation of *Miss Julie*:

> As I didn't know Swedish, I would not have dared to produce a French translation of *Miss Julie* except that I was fortunate to meet Ulla Ryghe, a Swedish cinematographer living in Quebec . . . I was then able, thanks to her collaboration (and to her dictionaries!), to go directly to the Swedish text and to correct certain mistakes which had been carried over from translation to translation . . . I compared this text to existing translations and was then able to produce the first draft of the present translation.[78]

After reworking the first translation, which he felt to be too literal, Gilles Marsolais arrived at the same conclusion as Michel Tremblay:

> The result was a second, more direct, more "spoken" translation, a translation more immediately accessible to the public and, finally, I believe, closer to the spirit of Strindberg.[79]

The similarity of argumentation is striking. Paradoxically, ignorance of the source language led the two translators to discover the "truth" of the original text that previous translations, and especially French translations, had concealed. According to Tremblay, the two English translations of *Uncle Vanya* are more "natural, simpler and closer to us."[80] The literariness, or artificiality that the Québécois translator criticizes in French translations can be seen as proof that the distance between the vernacular and the literary language is no longer the same in France as it is in Quebec. This is especially true for the theatre. The new Québécois theatre has achieved its own singularity, by doing away with this linguistic distinction. It has given the *koine*, the language of the home and the street, its status as a literary language. To conform to the criteria of acceptability in the new Québécois theatre system, the translation of a work like *Mademoiselle Julie* by Boris Vian must be shorn of its French literariness. This is precisely what G. Marsolais did in his translation:

Boris Vian

Jean: Je rêve d'ordinaire
que je suis couché sous un
grand arbre dans une forêt
obscure. Je veux monter,
monter au sommet, pour voir
le clair paysage tout brillant
de soleil, et dénicher le nid
où dorment les oeufs d'or.[81]

Gilles Marsolais

Jean: Moi, Je rêve
d'ordinaire que je suis
couché sous un grand arbre
dans une forêt sombre. Et
j'ai envie de monter,
monter jusqu'au sommet,
pour regarder le clair paysage
où brille le soleil et dérober les oeufs
d'or de cette nichée.[82]

Marsolais's retranslation has removed the poetic scansion that reinforces the expression of the dream, but, aside from that, in what other ways is his translation particularly Québécois? We are dangerously close to the ideology of "the language of one's own" and of solipsism when a work written in or translated into the French of France is rejected on the grounds that it would be inaccessible to the Québécois public. Monique Mercure, who played Mother Courage in Gilbert Turp's Québécois translation, has this to say:

> In the French translation there are occasional expressions that I didn't understand and a different syntax; these have become patently clear in this translation. If, for example, I had had to act in the French translation of the play, I would have had to read the English translation to grasp all the subtleties and all the nuances. This is often the case for French translations of foreign writers.[83]

The French translation, understood by the Québécois public for decades, suddenly becomes opaque and inaccessible to this very same public. To understand the French text, the francophone reader in Quebec must henceforth make a detour by way of English, that is to say, via a foreign language. Granted, what the actress is really objecting to in French translations is the "polished" language that detracts from the original text.

According to Gilles Marsolais, it would be abnormal if a foreign-language play were not "translated or adapted by a Québécois before being staged."[84] Given the desire to reterritorialize, the nationality of the translator becomes, apparently, a major criterion for legitimizing translations of plays staged in Quebec and for ensuring their acceptance. Yet Marsolais echoes Boris Vian, who himself foresaw the necessity for a "new Francicization of *Julie* . . . as part of the evolution of the language of the French theatre."[85]

In 1968, the language of the theatre in Quebec underwent a revolution of truly Copernican proportions. Québécois translators had good reason for trying to bridge the gap between the language of the French theatre and the language of the new theatre. For Tremblay and for many others, Québécois translations are more effective on the stage than French translations because they make use of an oralcy that echoes everyday speech. And indeed, parts of the dialogue in Michel Tremblay's translation of *Uncle Vanya* are markedly different from those of Elsa Triolet's version:

Tremblay

Marina: On est touttes
des pique-assiette chez le
bon Dieu. Toi, comme Sonia,
comme Ivan Pétrovitch,
personne reste à rien faire,
on travaille toutes!
Toutes . . . Ousqu'est Sonia

Téléguyine: Au jardin.
Avec le docteur, ils
cherchent Ivan Pétrovitch
partout. Ils ont peur qu'il
se fasse du mal.

Marina: Pis ousqu'i est
son fusil?

Elsa Triolet

Marina: Nous sommes tous
des parasites chez le bon Dieu.
Toi, comme Sonia, comme Ivan
Pétrovitch, personne ici ne reste
à ne rien faire, tous nous
travaillons! Tous . . . Où est
Sonia?

Téléguyine: Au jardin. Elle
est avec le docteur, ils
cherchent partout Ivan
Pétrovitch. Ils ont peur qu'il
n'attente à sa vie.

Marina: Et où est son
pistolet?

The difference between these two translations reflects the difference between French and Québécois literary codes for the theatre. In the Québécois theatre, the "naturalist" code is the equivalent of the French literary code. This is clearly exemplified in Tremblay's plays. But in his translation of *Uncle Vanya*, the naturalist code is found only in the language employed by Marina. If we compare Tremblay's and Triolet's translations of the play, it becomes clear that there is only a fine line between the theatrical language of the two countries. It is even finer in Gilles Marsolais's translation of *Mademoiselle Julie*. His Québécois translation of the play belies what, as a translator, he says of his work: "our approach to international French is far removed from that of our French cousins. We have a vocabulary, a spirit, which are all our own." He has hidden this irreconcilable difference extremely well:

> *Julie*: Assez pour commencer! Viens avec moi! Je ne puis voyager seule aujourd'hui, le jour de la Saint-Jean, entassée dans un train étouffant, au milieu d'une foule de gens qui vous dévisagent! Et le train qui s'arrête à chaque station, quand on voudrait voler! Non, je ne peux pas. Je ne peux pas![86]

Is this not the language of an aristocrat? The cook expresses herself in an international Québécois as refined as that of her mistress, even if occasionally she uses a local turn of phrase emphasizing her status as a woman of the "people":

> *Christine*: Écoutez Jean, voulez-vous venir danser avec moi quand j'aurai fini? [. . .]
>
> Oh, ses mauvais jours approchent et elle est toujours à l'envers *dans ce temps-là*. Venez-vous danser avec moi maintenant?[87]

There is, however, a difference between the language used to translate and the language used by translators to discuss their translations, especially when the translators are playwrights or directors, and therefore belong to the theatre. Quite clearly, they are trying to dissociate themselves from their French cultural and linguistic heritage. They are trying to place a *cordon sanitaire* around their burgeoning theatre, but they have failed to create a distinctive language for the theatre, a language that could be used as a systematic and coherent language of translation. When the chosen target language is a sociolect that is distinctively Québécois, we are immediately struck by the diglossia between the translation, on the one hand, and the preface and instructions to the directors or actors, on the other. The justification for the "Quebecization" of foreign texts is written in a language that no longer bears any trace of its *québécité*. We have already observed that the language translators use to translate is not the same as the language they use to explain to their Québécois readers that the play was translated for the express purpose of putting it within their reach. Gilles Marsolais and Jean-Claude Germain are, each in his own way, the most obvious examples of this tendency. Québécois translators are inconsistent, in that they employ both the vernacular and the referential language. However, the role of the languages is reversed: the vernacular is used to translate the foreign text, while the referential language is used to comment on the text. Translations into Québécois therefore play an ideological rather than a mediating role. The diglossia between the dialogue and the commentary or stage directions in these translations demonstrates to what extent the audience is being manipulated. The discourse on language used by translators, who often double as playwrights, enables them to introduce an ideology of *québécité* to the public, a public from which they exclude themselves.

Notes

1   Jakobson, 1969, 353.
2   Mounin, 1963. See also Ladmiral's synthesis (1979, 85–114).
3   Mounin, 1963, 165.
4   These very questions were raised by T. Savory:

> Cervantes published *Don Quixote* in 1605; should that story be translated into contemporary English, such as he would have used at the time had he been an Englishman, or into the English of today? There can be, as a rule, very little doubt as to the answer, for, in most cases, a reader is justified in expecting to find the kind of English that he is accustomed to. If a function of translation is to produce in the minds of its readers the same emotions as those produced by the original in the minds of the readers, the answer is clear. Yet there is need to notice in passing the possibility of exceptions whenever the original author is read more for his manner than for his matter. We may read the speeches of Cicero, for example, chiefly that we may have an opportunity to appreciate his eloquence. Of recent years the most eloquent speaker of English has been Sir Winston Churchill, and Churchill's style was not Cicero's style. Should a speech by Cicero be so translated as to sound as if it had been delivered by Churchill? No.
>
> (1968, 56–7)

5   "Gaweda" is a synthesis of several registers, the styles of nineteenth-century
    Polish story-tellers and of seventeenth-century Sarmatian Baroque. In his novel
    Trans-Atlantyk, Gombrowicz re-creates "the sound of a stylized way of speaking
    . . . , deliberately rustic (an affection comparable to the language Proust gave
    to the Guermantes) . . . a mixture that conjures up a 'Polishness' of former
    times." After explaining how an invented language is used to expose the
    archaeological layers of this nostalgic Polishness, C. Jelenski demonstrates how
    translators of the novel managed to deal with what appeared to be deficien-
    cies in the target language:

> It seemed futile to look for . . . a coherent French model. In cases
> where there was an archaically colourful word in the Polish text,
> we turned to writers such as Madame de Sévigné, Saint-Simon, or
> even La Fontaine, and simply borrowed expressions similar to the
> ones in the original. These expressions played the same role in the
> French text (contrast between contemporary and past time
> periods, witty allusion to quaint former times) as their equivalent
> in the Polish text. On occasion, a dated syntactic device enabled
> us to render the fin-de-siècle colour of certain passages, that kind
> of mocking, humorous distinction used to describe particularly
> superficial characters in the novel.
>
> (Gombrowicz, 1976, 20; our translation)

6   E. Nida has found a practical answer to this difficult question: the speech of
    women should have priority because it is women, not men, who are respon-
    sible for educating the children. The proselytizing objective that motivates
    Nida's translation of the Bible explains this "pragmatic" solution to a funda-
    mentally linguistic problem (Nida and Taber 1982, 32). In more common
    cases of bilingualism or diglossia, Nida and Taber's choice of priorities is
    similarly motivated:

> . . . priority is given to the larger of two languages, or to a
> language designated as national or official, or to a language spoken
> by an appreciable number of people who cannot communicate
> effectively in any other language . . . With respect to the level of
> language to be used in the translation, priority is given to common
> language or popular language translations over translations made
> in literary language.
>
> (ibid., 176–7)

7   Berman, 1984, 46–7; our translation.
8   Quoted by C. Bruneau, 1955, 126.
9   Du Bellay, *Deffense et illustration de la langue françoyse*, Book I, Ch.V (quoted
    by Mounin, 1955, 14). We should not forget, however, that Du Bellay
    rejected and impugned translation as an agent of this transformation.
10   Gobard, 1976, 34; our translation.
11   Ibid.
12   Trudeau, 1982, 122.
13   Bergeron, 1980.

14   S. Robinson and D. Smith, *Practical Handbook of Canadian French* (Toronto: Macmillan 1973), i.

15   Ibid., 1, 6, 102, 72, 74.

16   Bergeron, 1981, 11; our translation.

17   Ibid., 9.

18   Ibid., 8.

19   This is how Nida defines adaptation (1982, 134).

20   Lalonde, 1979, 21; our translation.

21   On the construction of "memory-screens" and reinterpretations made by nationalist historiographers of the Conquest, which is portrayed as "the initial catastrophe of French Canada, the *Apocalypse Now* that plunged a country happy under the French, into subjection and humiliation," see Weinmann, 1987, 277–88.

22   Rioux, 1974, 17; our translation.

23   Here is how the authors, both university professors, describe the goal of the *Practical Handbook of Canadian French*: "It is the authors' hope that it will aid communication and understanding between the two main language groups and also demonstrate the richness of expression of French-Canadian speech, a language attuned to our Canadian reality", 1973, back cover.

24   Lalonde, 1979, 53.

25   See, in particular, Marcel, 1982 and Trudeau, 1982.

26   Rossi-Landi, 1983, 87; emphasis in the original.

27   Dubois, 1978, 44–5; our translation.

28   Lalonde, 1979, 53; our translation.

29   Ibid., 15.

30   J. Éthier-Blais, "Sept auteurs en proie au mal québécois," in *Le Devoir*, 20 Feb. 1988, D-8; our translation, emphasis added.

31   Garneau, 1974; our translation.

32   Lalonde, 1979, 53. In an article by J. Godbout, entitled "Ma langue, ma maison," we find the same theme of the impurity introduced by the immigrant:

> In the villages and towns of Quebec, there are particularly ugly neighbourhoods where buildings, besides being covered in multicoloured neon lights, are decorated in an astonishing variety of styles . . . The passer-by sees in these places the delirious expression of a shattered culture where styles, inspired by the traditional Canadian house, the Spanish castle, or by Victorian turrets, remind us that here, in our country, people can reconstruct their universe as they wish . . . Why has Montreal been disfigured? To build American sky-scrapers. To build Italian white-brick buildings in red-brick streets. Could the Greeks have been forbidden to put blue paint on the grey stones and could the Portuguese have been told not to transform slate roofs into rainbows? . . . We should perhaps perceive bilingualism in this way. A single language is harmony, more than one language is war . . . But since language is the architecture of emotions and

thought, there are places on the verge of madness. We are living in one.

(*L'Actualité*, July 1987, 104)

33 J.-P. Faye uses the expression "cette inconnue énigmatique" in his preface to Lalonde, 1979 (p. 6).

34 Miron, 1970, 118.

35 Ibid., 118, 124.

36 Ibid., 118.

37 Weinmann, 1987, 315.

38 Miron, 1970, 118.

39 The desire for a State, to be constituted in a Nation-State, thus corresponds necessarily to the desire that motivates certain individuals or certain groups within a society to impose their interpretation of the national interest on all members of the society . . . When the former take over the power of the State, you may expect the national interest they invoke to be represented as all the more urgent and at the same time all the more objective, so great will be the desire for power that motivates them, and so imperious their determination to impose on all of society a conception of itself that is destructive of its habitual way of living and thinking.

(Morin and Bertrand, 1979, 138–9)

40 Gobin, 1978, 107; our translation, emphasis in the original.

41 Lalonde, 1979, 12.

42 Ibid., 13.

43 Ibid.

44 Ibid., 15.

45 Chamberland, 1969, 69; our translation.

46 Ibid.

47 Lalonde, 1979, 20. The incest theme is also found, interestingly, in Michel Tremblay's *Bonjour là, bonjour* (1974). The theme appears in a number of plays, but Tremblay uses it as a metaphor and not just to evoke a social problem.

48 Lalonde, 1979, 13.

49 Ibid., 18.

50 Ibid., 164.

51 Ibid., 166.

52 Lalonde, 1974, "poème-affiche" (protest-poem).

53 Luther, quoted in Berman, 1984, 45; our translation.

54 M. Garneau, production notes for *Macbeth* at Le Théâtre de la Manufacture; quoted by Andrès and Lefebvre, 1979, 84.

55 Ibid.

56 M. Garneau, "AG, aile gauche," in 1974.

57 Shakespeare, 1978, 41. The original text is as follows:

I have given suck, and know / How tender 'tis to love the babe that milks me. / I would, while it was smiling at my face, / Have

plucked my nipple from his boneless gums / And dashed the brains
out, had I sworn as you / Have done to this.

(Shakespeare, 1962, 851)

58 Andrès and Lefebvre, 1979, 84; our translation.

59 The following appears on the back cover of the play by J.-C. Germain, 1972:
Diguidi, diguidi, ha! ha! ha! followed by *Si les Sansoucis s'en soucient, ces
Sansoucisci s'en soucieront-ils? Bien parler, c'est se respecter!*

60 Chekhov, n.d., 2.

61 "V dome Prozorovyx. *Gostinnaja s kolonnami, za kotoroj viden bol'šoj zal.* Polden;
na dvore solnečno, veselo. V zale nakry-vajut stol dlja zavtraka": Chekhov,
1984, 307; emphasis added.

62 Brecht, "La Bonne Âme de Se-Tchouan," unpublished, trans. Gilbert Turp.
The extract is quoted directly from the manuscript, deposited with the
National Theatre School library. The following is the original text (p. 1).

> *EST IST ABEND, WANG, DER WASSERVERKAÜFER, STELLT SICH
> DEM PUBLIKUM VOR. Wang: Ich bin Wasserverkaüfer* hier in der
> Haupstadt von Sezuan. Mein Geschäft ist mühselig. Wenn es wenig
> Wasser gibt, muss ich weit danach laufen. Und gibt es viel, bin ich
> ohne Verdienst. Aber in *unserer Provinz* herrscht überhaupt grosse
> Armut. Es heisst allgemein, dass uns nur noch die Götter helfen
> können. Zu meiner unaussprechlichen Freude erfahre ich von
> einem Vieheinkaüfer, der viel herumkommt dass einiger der höch-
> sten Götter schon unterwegs sind und auch hier in Sezuan erwartet
> werden dürfen. Der Himmel soll sehr beunruhigt sein wegen der
> vielen Klagen, die zu ihm aufsteigen.
>
> (Brecht, "Der gute Mensch von Sezuan," in *Die
> Stücke von Bertolt Brecht*, 595; emphasis added)

63 Editor's note in Brecht, 1975, 11.

64 French translations use the reverse procedure. The "marchand d'eau"
expresses himself as if he were a member of high society:

> WANG – Je suis marchand d'eau, ici, dans la capitale du Se-
> Tchouan. Mon commerce est pénible. Quand il n'y a pas beaucoup
> d'eau, je dois aller loin pour en trouver. Et quand il y en a beau-
> coup, je suis sans ressources. Mais dans notre province règne
> généralement une grande pauvreté. Tout le monde dit que seuls
> les dieux peuvent encore nous aider. Joie ineffable, j'apprends
> d'un maquignon qui circule beaucoup que quelques-uns des dieux
> les plus grands sont déjà en route et qu'on peut aussi compter sur
> eux au Se-Tchouan. Le ciel serait très inquiet du fait des nom-
> breuses plaintes qui montent vers lui.
>
> (ibid., 7)

65 Brecht, 1976, 30.

66 Ibid., 31.

67 Tremblay, 1969, 3.

68 Ibid.

69   Tremblay, program for *L'Effet des rayons gamma sur les vieux garçons*, quoted in *Cahiers de la Nouvelle Compagnie Théâtrale* 1 (October 1974), 10.

70   O'Neill, *Desire under the Elms*, in 1959, 57.

71   O'Neill, n.d., 81.

72   Ibid., 100.

73   R. Balibar (1985, 280–98) has analysed the procedures used by French novelists to create local colour. She notes in particular that textual elements employed to create a rural effect often appear in italics and must be read in a different tone and treated differently from the main body of the text. A novel like *Jeanne* by G. Sand, in which there is an attempt to defend a dialect, the old French of Berri, was a failure. Balibar points out that the use of the dialect in the same context as the national language had no influence on French thought of the time. She attributes this failure to the contemporary ideological atmosphere, the Republican ideal being to promote communication among citizens with different mother tongues. The legitimate language was the language of the state, and every effort had to be made to eradicate differences.

74   Chekhov, 1967, 373; 1983, 44–5.

75   This situation can be applied to a country like Israel. In this respect, see G. Toury, 1980.

76   Turp, 1984, 3; our translation.

77   Krysinski, 1983, 10–11; our translation, emphasis added. This observation is similar to M. Bataillon's analysis of the translation of *Platonov* by E. Triolet; the analysis ends with the following observation: "The translation trap in Elsa's work is that she is splendidly fluid." This "polished" translation, adds Bataillon, "corresponded exactly to what was happening in the theatre of the fifties": *Sixièmes assises de la traduction littéraire* (Arles: Actes Sud 1989), 82–5.

78   Marsolais, 1977, 11; our translation.

79   Ibid.

80   Krysinski, 1983, 11.

81   Strindberg, 1985, 13.

82   Ibid., 14.

83   MacDuff, 1984, 14.

84   Marsolais, 1977, 12.

85   Ibid.

86   Strindberg, n.d., 52.

87   Ibid., 5, 8.

Chapter 26

Gayatri Chakravorty Spivak

THE POLITICS OF TRANSLATION

T HE IDEA FOR THIS TITLE comes from Michèle Barrett's feeling that
the politics of translation takes on a massive life of its own if you see language
as the process of meaning construction.[1]

In my view, language may be one of many elements that allow us to make sense
of things, of ourselves. I am thinking, of course, of gestures, pauses, but also of
chance, of the sub-individual force-fields of being which click into place in different
situations, swerve from the straight or true line of language-in-thought. Making
sense of ourselves is what produces identity. If one feels that the production of
identity as self-meaning, not just meaning, is as pluralized as a drop of water under
a microscope, one is not always satisfied, outside of the ethico-political arena as
such, with "generating" thoughts on one's own. (Assuming identity as origin may
be unsatisfactory in the ethico-political arena as well, but consideration of that
now would take us too far afield.) One of the ways to get around the confines of
one's "identity" as one produces expository prose is to work at someone else's title,
as one works with a language that belongs to many others. This, after all, is one of
the seductions of translating. It is a simple miming of the responsibility to the trace
of the other in the self.

Responding, therefore, to Michèle with that freeing sense of responsibility, I
can agree that it is not bodies of meaning that are transferred in translation. And
from the ground of that agreement I want to consider the role played by language
for the *agent*, the person who acts, even though intention is not fully present to
itself. The task of the feminist translator is to consider language as a clue to the
workings of gendered agency. The writer is written by her language, of course. But

the writing of the writer writes agency in a way that might be different from that of the British woman/citizen with the history of British feminism, focused on the task of freeing herself from Britain's imperial past, its often racist present, as well as its "made in Britain" history of male domination.

Translation as reading

How does the translator attend to the specificity of the language she translates? There is a way in which the rhetorical nature of every language disrupts its logical systematicity. If we emphasize the logical at the expense of these rhetorical inter-ferences, we remain safe. "Safety" *is* the appropriate term here, because we are talking of risks, of violence to the translating medium.

I felt that I was taking those risks when I recently translated some late eighteenth-century Bengali poetry. I quote a bit from my "Translator's Preface":

> I must overcome what I was taught in school: the highest mark for the most accurate collection of synonyms, strung together in the most prox-imate syntax. I must resist both the solemnity of chaste Victorian poetic prose and the forced simplicity of "plain English", that have imposed themselves as the norm . . . Translation is the most intimate act of reading. I surrender to the text when I translate. These songs, sung day after day in family chorus before clear memory began, have a peculiar intimacy for me. Reading and surrendering take on new meanings in such a case. The translator earns permission to transgress from the trace of the other – before memory – in the closest places of the self.[2]

Language is not everything. It is only a vital clue to where the self loses its boundaries. The ways in which rhetoric or figuration disrupt logic themselves point at the possibility of random contingency, beside language, around language. Such a *diss*emination cannot be under our control. Yet in translation, where meaning hops into the spacy emptiness between two named historical languages, we get perilously close to it. By juggling the disruptive rhetoricity that breaks the surface in not neces-sarily connected ways, we feel the selvedges of the language-textile give way, fray into *frayages* or facilitations.[3] Although every act of reading or communication is a bit of this risky fraying which scrambles together somehow, our stake in agency keeps the fraying down to a minimum except in the communication and reading of and in love. (What is the place of "love" in the ethical?) The task of the translator is to facilitate this love between the original and its shadow, a love that permits fraying, holds the agency of the translator and the demands of her imagined or actual audience at bay. The politics of translation from a non-European woman's text too often suppresses this possibility because the translator cannot engage with, or cares insufficiently for, the rhetoricity of the original.

The simple possibility that something might not be meaningful is contained by the rhetorical system as the always possible menace of a space outside language. This is most eerily staged (and challenged) in the effort to communicate with other possible intelligent beings in space. (Absolute alterity or otherness is thus differed-deferred into an other self who resembles us, however minimally, and with whom we can communicate.) But a more homely staging of it occurs across two earthly languages. The experience of contained alterity in an unknown language spoken in a different cultural milieu is uncanny.

Let us now think that, in that other language, rhetoric may be disrupting logic in the matter of the production of an agent, and indicating the founding violence of the silence at work within rhetoric. Logic allows us to jump from word to word by means of clearly indicated connections. Rhetoric must work in the silence between and around words in order to see what works and how much. The jagged relationship between rhetoric and logic, condition and effect of knowing, is a relationship by which a world is made for the agent, so that the agent can act in an ethical way, a political way, a day-to-day way; so that the agent can be alive, in a human way, in the world. Unless one can at least construct a model of this for the other language, there is no real translation.

Unfortunately it is only too easy to produce translations if this task is completely ignored. I myself see no choice between the quick and easy and slapdash way, and translating well and with difficulty. There is no reason why a responsible translation should take more time in the doing. The translator's preparation might take more time, and her love for the text might be a matter of a reading skill that takes patience. But the sheer material production of the text need not be slow.

Without a sense of the rhetoricity of language, a species of neo-colonialist construction of the non-western scene is afoot. No argument for convenience can be persuasive here. That is always the argument, it seems. This is where I travel from Michèle Barrett's enabling notion of the question of language in post-structuralism. Post-structuralism has shown some of us a staging of the agent within a three-tiered notion of language (as rhetoric, logic, silence). We must attempt to enter or direct that staging, as one directs a play, as an actor interprets a script. That takes a different kind of effort from taking translation to be a matter of synonym, syntax and local colour.

To be only critical, to defer action until the production of the utopian translator, is impractical. Yet, when I hear Derrida, quite justifiably, point out the difficulties between French and English, even when he agrees to speak in English – "I must speak in a language that is not my own because that will be more just" – I want to claim the right to the same dignified complaint for a woman's text in Arabic or Vietnamese.[4]

It is more just to give access to the largest number of feminists. Therefore these texts must be made to speak English. It is more just to speak the language of the majority when through hospitality a large number of feminists give the foreign feminists the right to speak, in English. In the case of the Third World foreigner, is the law of the majority that of decorum, the equitable law of democracy, or the "law" of the strongest? We might focus on this confusion. There is nothing necessarily meretricious about the western feminist gaze. (The "naturalizing" of Jacques Lacan's sketching out of the psychic structure of the gaze in terms of group political behaviour has always seemed to me a bit shaky.) On the other hand, there is nothing essentially noble about the law of the majority either. It is merely the easiest way of being "democratic" with minorities. In the act of wholesale translation into English there can be a betrayal of the democratic ideal into the law of the strongest. This happens when all the literature of the Third World gets translated into a sort of with-it translatese, so that the literature by a woman in Palestine begins to resemble, in the feel of its prose, something by a man in Taiwan. The rhetoricity of Chinese and Arabic! The cultural politics of high-growth, capitalist Asia-Pacific, and devastated West Asia! Gender difference inscribed and inscribing in these differences!

For the student, this tedious translatese cannot compete with the spectacular stylistic experiments of a Monique Wittig or an Alice Walker.

Let us consider an example where attending to the author's stylistic experiments can produce a different text. Mahasweta Devi's "Stanadāyini" is available in two versions.[5] Devi has expressed approval for the attention to her signature style in the version entitled "Breast-giver". The alternative translation gives the title as "The Wet-nurse", and thus neutralizes the author's irony in constructing an uncanny word; enough like "wet-nurse" to make that sense, and enough unlike to shock. It is as if the translator should decide to translate Dylan Thomas's famous title and opening line as "Do not go gently into that good night". The theme of treating the breast as organ of labour-power-as-commodity and the breast as metonymic part-object standing in for other-as-object – the way in which the story plays with Marx and Freud on the occasion of the woman's body – is lost even before you enter the story. In the text Mahasweta uses proverbs that are startling even in the Bengali. The translator of "The Wet-nurse" leaves them out. She decides not to try to translate these hard bits of earthy wisdom, contrasting with class-specific access to modernity, also represented in the story. In fact, if the two translations are read side by side, the loss of the rhetorical silences of the original can be felt from one to the other.

First, then, the translator must surrender to the text. She must solicit the text to show the limits of its language, because that rhetorical aspect will point at the silence of the absolute fraying of language that the text wards off, in its special manner. Some think this is just an ethereal way of talking about literature or philosophy. But no amount of tough talk can get around the fact that translation is the most intimate act of reading. Unless the translator has earned the right to become the intimate reader, she cannot surrender to the text, cannot respond to the special call of the text.

The presupposition that women have a natural or narrative-historical solidarity, that there is something in a woman or an undifferentiated women's story that speaks to another woman without benefit of language-learning, might stand against the translator's task of surrender. Paradoxically, it is not possible for us as ethical agents to imagine otherness or alterity maximally. We have to turn the other into something like the self in order to be ethical. To surrender in translation is more erotic than ethical.[6] In that situation the good-willing attitude "she is just like me" is not very helpful. In so far as Michèle Barrett is not like Gayatri Spivak, their friendship is more effective as a translation. In order to earn that right of friendship or surrender of identity, of knowing that the rhetoric of the text indicates the limits of language for you as long as you are with the text, you have to be in a different relationship with the language, not even only with the specific text.

Learning about translation on the job, I came to think that it would be a practical help if one's relationship with the language being translated was such that sometimes one preferred to speak in it about intimate things. This is no more than a practical suggestion, not a theoretical requirement, useful especially because a woman writer who is wittingly or unwittingly a "feminist" – and of course all woman writers are not "feminist" even in this broad sense – will relate to the three-part staging of (agency in) language in ways defined out as "private", since they might question the more public linguistic manoeuvres.

Let us consider an example of lack of intimacy with the medium. In Sudhir Kakar's *The Inner World*, a song about Kālī written by the late nineteenth-century monk Vivekananda is cited as part of the proof of the "archaic narcissism" of the Indian [sic] male.[7] (Devi makes the same point with a light touch, with reference to Krsna and Siva, tying it to sexism rather than narcissim and without psycho-analytic patter.)

From Kakar's description, it would not be possible to glimpse that "the disciple" who gives the account of the singular circumstances of Vivekananda's composition of the song was an Irishwoman who became a Ramakrishna nun, a white woman among male Indian monks and devotees. In the account Kakar reads, the song is translated by this woman, whose training in intimacy with the original language is as painstaking as one can hope for. There is a strong identification between Indian and Irish nationalists at this period; and Nivedita, as she was called, also embraced what she understood to be the Indian philosophical way of life as explained by Vivekananda, itself a peculiar, resistant consequence of the culture of imperialism, as has been pointed out by many. For a psychoanalyst like Kakar, this historical, philosophical and indeed sexual text of translation should be the textile to weave with. Instead, the English version, "given" by the anonymous "disciple", serves as no more than the opaque exhibit providing evidence of the alien fact of narcissism. It is not the site of the exchange of language.

At the beginning of the passage quoted by Kakar, there is a reference to Ram Prasad (or Ram Proshad). Kakar provides a footnote: "Eighteenth century singer and poet whose songs of longing for the Mother are very popular in Bengal". I believe this footnote is also an indication of what I am calling the absence of intimacy.

Vivekananda is, among other things, an example of the peculiar reactive construction of a glorious "India" under the provocation of imperialism. The rejection of "patriotism" in favour of "Kālī" reported in Kakar's passage is played out in this historical theatre, as a choice of the cultural female sphere rather than the colonial male sphere.[8] It is undoubtedly "true" that for such a figure, Ram Proshad Sen provides a kind of ideal self. Sen had travelled back from a clerk's job in colonial Calcutta before the Permanent Settlement of land in 1793 to be the court poet of one of the great rural landowners whose social type, and whose connection to native culture, would be transformed by the Settlement. In other words, Vivekananda and Ram Proshad are two moments of colonial discursivity translating the figure of Kālī. The dynamic intricacy of that discursive textile is mocked by the useless footnote.

It would be idle here to enter the debate about the "identity" of Kālī or indeed other goddesses in Hindu "polytheism". But simply to contextualize, let me add that it is Ram Proshad about whose poetry I wrote the "Translator's Preface" quoted earlier. He is by no means simply an archaic stage-prop in the disciple's account of Vivekananda's "crisis". Some more lines from my "Preface": "Ram Proshad played with his mother tongue, transvaluing the words that are heaviest with Sanskrit meaning. I have been unable to catch the utterly new but utterly gendered tone of affectionate banter" – not only, not even largely, "longing" – "between the poet and Kāli." Unless Nivedita mistranslated, it is the difference in tone between Ram Proshad's innovating playfulness and Vivekananda's high nationalist solemnity that, in spite of the turn from nationalism to the Mother, is historically significant. The politics of the translation of the culture of imperialism by the colonial subject has changed noticeably. And that change is expressed in the gendering of the poet's voice.

How do women in contemporary polytheism relate to this peculiar mother, certainly not the psychoanalytic bad mother whom Kakar derives from Max Weber's misreading, not even an organized punishing mother, but a child-mother who punishes with astringent violence and is also a moral and affective monitor?[9] Ordinary women, not saintly women. Why take it for granted that the invocation of goddesses in a historically masculist polytheist sphere is necessarily feminist? I think it is a western and male-gendered suggestion that powerful women in the Sākta (Sakti or Kāli-worshipping) tradition take Kāli as a role model.[10]

Mahasweta's Jashoda tells me more about the relationship between goddesses and strong ordinary women than the psychoanalyst. And here too the example of an intimate translation that goes respectfully "wrong" can be offered. The French wife of a Bengali artist translated some of Ram Proshad Sen's songs in the twenties to accompany her husband's paintings based on the songs. Her translations are marred by the pervasive orientalism ready at hand as a discursive system. Compare two passages, both translating the "same" Bengali. I have at least tried, if failed, to catch the unrelenting mockery of self and Kāli in the original:

> Mind, why footloose from Mother?
> Mind mine, think power, for freedom's dower, bind bower with love-
>   rope
> In time, mind, you minded not your blasted lot.
> And Mother, daughter-like, bound up house-fence to dupe her dense
>   and devoted fellow.
> Oh you'll see at death how much Mum loves you
> A couple minutes' tears, and lashings of water, cowdung-pure.

Here is the French, translated by me into an English comparable in tone and vocabulary:

> Pourquoi as-tu, mon âme, délaissé les pieds de Mâ?
> O esprit, médite Shokti, tu obtiendras la délivrance.
> Attache-les ces pieds saints avec la corde de la dévotion.
> Au bon moment tu n'as rien vu, c'est bien là ton malheur.
> Pour se jouer de son fidèle, Elle m'est apparue
> Sous la forme de ma fille et m'a aidé à réparer ma clôture.
> C'est à la mort que tu comprendras l'amour de Mâ.
> Ici, on versera quelques larmes, puis on purifiera le lieu.

Why have you, my soul [*mon âme* is, admittedly, less heavy in French],
    left Ma's feet?
O mind, meditate upon Shokti, you will obtain deliverance.
Bind those holy feet with the rope of devotion.
In good time you saw nothing, that is indeed your sorrow.
To play with her faithful one, She appeared to me
In the form of my daughter and helped me to repair my enclosure.
It is at death that you will understand Ma's love.
Here, they will shed a few tears, then purify the place.

And here the Bengali:

মন কেন মার চরণ-ছাড়া ।
ও মন, তার শক্তি, পায়ে ভুক্তি, বাঁধ দিয়ে ভক্তি-ডোরা ॥
সময় থাকতে, না দেখলে মন, কেমন তোমার কান্নেগোড়া ।
খেলা তরে ছলিতে, তনয়া রূপেতে আমায় আসি ধারের বেড়া ॥
মায়ে মত ভানাবাসে, মরা যাবে ছেড়ে শেষ,
রোদন দিও-দুচার কন্নাবর্ষাই, শেষে দিবে গোররুড়া ।

I hope these examples demonstrate that depth of commitment to correct cultural
politics, felt in the details of personal life, is sometimes not enough. The history of
the language, the history of the author's moment, the history of the language-in-
and-as-translation, must figure in the weaving as well.

By logical analysis, we don't just mean what the philosopher does, but also
reasonableness – that which will allow rhetoricity to be appropriated, put in its
place, situated, seen as only nice. Rhetoricity is put in its place that way because it
disrupts. Women within male-dominated society, when they internalize sexism as
normality, act out a scenario against feminism that is formally analogical to this.
The relationship between logic and rhetoric, between grammar and rhetoric, is also
a relationship between social logic, social reasonableness and the disruptiveness of
figuration in social practice. These are the first two parts of our three-part model.
But then, rhetoric points at the possibility of randomness, of contingency as such,
dissemination, the falling apart of language, the possibility that things might not
always be semiotically organized. (My problem with Kristeva and the "pre-
semiotic" is that she seems to want to expand the empire of the meaning-ful by
grasping at what language can only point at.) Cultures that might not have this
specific three-part model will still have a dominant sphere in its traffic with language
and contingency. Writers like Ifi Amadiume show us that, without thinking of this
sphere as biologically determined, one still has to think in terms of a sphere determined by definitions of secondary and primary sexual characteristics in such a way
that the inhabitants of the other sphere are para-subjective, not fully subject.[11] The
dominant groups' way of handling the three-part ontology of language has to be
learnt as well – if the subordinate ways of rusing with rhetoric are to be disclosed.

To decide whether you are prepared enough to start translating, then, it might
help if you have graduated into speaking, by choice or preference, of intimate

matters in the language of the original. I have worked my way back to my earlier point: I cannot see why the publishers' convenience or classroom convenience or time convenience for people who do not have the time to learn should organize the construction of the rest of the world for western feminism. Five years ago, berated as unsisterly, I would think, "Well, you know one ought to be a bit more giving etc.", but then I asked myself again, "What am I giving, or giving up? To whom am I giving by assuring that you don't have to work that hard, just come and get it? What am I trying to promote?" People would say, you who have succeeded should not pretend to be a marginal. But surely by demanding higher standards of translation, I am not marginalizing myself or the language of the original?

I have learnt through translating Devi how this three-part structure works differently from English in my native language. And here another historical irony has become personally apparent to me. In the old days, it was most important for a colonial or post-colonial student of English to be as "indistinguishable" as possible from the native speaker of English. I think it is necessary for people in the Third World translation trade now to accept that the wheel has come around, that the genuinely bilingual post-colonial now has a bit of an advantage. But she does not have a real advantage as a translator if she is not strictly bilingual, if she merely speaks her native language. Her own native space is, after all, also class organized. And that organization still often carries the traces of access to imperialism, often relates inversely to access to the vernacular as a public language. So here the requirement for intimacy brings a recognition of the public sphere as well. If we were thinking of translating Marianne Moore or Emily Dickinson, the standard for the translator could not be "anyone who can conduct a conversation in the language of the original (in this case English)". When applied to a Third World language, the position is inherently ethnocentric. And then to present these translations to our unprepared students so that they can learn about women writing!

In my view, the translator from a Third World language should be sufficiently in touch with what is going on in literary production in that language to be capable of distinguishing between good and bad writing by women, resistant and conformist writing by women.

She must be able to confront the idea that what seems resistant in the space of English may be reactionary in the space of the original language. Farida Akhter has argued that, in Bangladesh, the real work of the women's movement and of feminism is being undermined by talk of "gendering", mostly deployed by the women's development wings of transnational non-government organizations, in conjunction with some local academic feminist theorists.[12] One of her intuitions was that "gendering" could not be translated into Bengali. "Gendering" is an awkward new word in English as well. Akhter is profoundly involved in international feminism. And her base is Third World. I could not translate "gender" into the US feminist context for her. This misfiring of translation, between a superlative reader of the social text such as Akhter, and a careful translator like myself, speaking as friends, has added to my sense of the task of the translator.

Good and bad is a flexible standard, like all standards. Here another lesson of post-structuralism helps: these decisions of standards are made anyway. It is the attempt to justify them adequately that polices. That is why disciplinary preparation in school requires that you write examinations to prove these standards.

Publishing houses routinely engage in materialist confusion of those standards. The translator must be able to fight that metropolitan materialism with a special kind of specialist's knowledge, not mere philosophical convictions.

In other words, the person who is translating must have a tough sense of the specific terrain of the original, so that she can fight the racist assumption that all Third World women's writing is good. I am often approached by women who would like to put Devi in with just Indian women writers. I am troubled by this, because "Indian women" is not a feminist category. (Elsewhere I have argued that "epistemes" – ways of constructing objects of knowledge – should not have national names either.)[13] Sometimes Indian women writing means American women writing or British women writing, except for national *origin*. There is an ethno-cultural agenda, an obliteration of Third World specificity as well as a denial of cultural citizenship, in calling them merely "Indian".

My initial point was that the task of the translator is to surrender herself to the linguistic rhetoricity of the original text. Although this point has larger political implications, we can say that the not unimportant minimal consequence of ignoring this task is the loss of "the literarity and textuality and sensuality of the writing" (Michèle's words). I have worked my way to a second point, that the translator must be able to discriminate on the terrain of the original. Let us dwell on it a bit longer.

I choose Devi because she is unlike her scene. I have heard an English Shakespearean suggest that every bit of Shakespeare criticism coming from the subcontinent was by that virtue resistant. By such a judgement, we are also denied the right to be critical. It was of course bad to have put the place under subjugation, to have tried to make the place over with calculated restrictions. But that does not mean that everything that is coming out of that place after a negotiated independence nearly fifty years ago is necessarily right. The old anthropological supposition (and that is bad anthropology) that every person from a culture is nothing but a whole example of that culture is acted out in my colleague's suggestion. I remain interested in writers who are against the current, against the mainstream. I remain convinced that the interesting literary text might be precisely the text where you do not learn what the majority view of majority cultural representation or self-representation of a nation state might be. The translator has to make herself, in the case of Third World women writing, almost better equipped than the translator who is dealing with the western European languages, because of the fact that there is so much of the old colonial attitude, slightly displaced, at work in the translation racket. Post-structuralism *can* radicalize the field of preparation so that simply boning up on the language is not enough; there is also that special relationship to the staging of language as the production of agency that one must attend to. But the agenda of post-structuralism is mostly elsewhere, and the resistance to theory among metropolitan feminists would lead us into yet another narrative.

The understanding of the task of the translator and the practice of the craft are related but different. Let me summarize how I work. At first, I translate at speed. If I stop to think about what is happening to the English, if I assume an audience, if I take the intending subject as more than a springboard, I cannot jump in, I cannot surrender. My relationship with Devi is easygoing. I am able to say to her: I surrender to you in your writing, not you as intending subject. There, in friendship, is another kind of surrender. Surrendering to the text in this way means, most of the time, being literal. When I have produced a version this way, I revise. I revise not in terms of a possible audience, but by the protocols of the thing in front of me, in a sort of English. And I keep hoping that the student in the classroom will not be able to think that the text is just a purveyor of social realism if it is translated with an eye toward the dynamic staging of language mimed in the revision by the rules of the in-between discourse produced by a literalist surrender.

Vain hope, perhaps, for the accountability is different. When I translated Jacques Derrida's *De la grammatologie*, I was reviewed in a major journal for the first and last time. In the case of my translations of Devi, I have almost no fear of being accurately judged by my readership here. It makes the task more dangerous and more risky. And that for me is the real difference between translating Derrida and translating Mahasweta Devi, not merely the rather more artificial difference between deconstructive philosophy and political fiction.

The opposite argument is not neatly true. There is a large number of people in the Third World who read the old imperial languages. People reading current feminist fiction in the European languages would probably read it in the appropriate imperial language. And the same goes for European philosophy. The act of translating into the Third World language is often a political exercise of a different sort. I am looking forward, as of this writing, to lecturing in Bengali on deconstruction in front of a highly sophisticated audience, knowledgeable both in Bengali and in deconstruction (which they read in English and French and sometimes write about in Bengali), at Jadavpur University in Calcutta. It will be a kind of testing of the post-colonial translator, I think.

Democracy changes into the law of force in the case of translation from the Third World and women even more because of their peculiar relationship to whatever you call the public/private divide. A neatly reversible argument would be possible if the particular Third World country had cornered the Industrial Revolution first and embarked on monopoly imperialist territorial capitalism as one of its consequences, and thus been able to impose a language as international norm. Something like that idiotic joke: if the Second World War had gone differently, the United States would be speaking Japanese. Such egalitarian reversible judgements are appropriate to counter-factual fantasy. Translation remains dependent upon the language skill of the majority. A prominent Belgian translation theorist solves the problem by suggesting that, rather than talk about the Third World, where a lot of passion is involved, one should speak about the European Renaissance, since a great deal of wholesale cross-cultural translation from Graeco-Roman antiquity was undertaken then. What one overlooks is the sheer authority ascribed to the originals in that historical phenomenon. The status of a language in the world is what one must consider when teasing out the politics of translation. Translatese in Bengali can be derided and criticized by large groups of anglophone and anglograph Bengalis. It is only in the hegemonic languages that the benevolent do not take the limits of their own often uninstructed good will into account. That phenomenon becomes hardest to fight because the individuals involved in it are genuinely benevolent and you are identified as a trouble-maker. This becomes particularly difficult when the metropolitan feminist, who is sometimes the assimilated post-colonial, invokes, indeed translates, a too quickly shared feminist notion of accessibility.

If you want to make the translated text accessible, try doing it for the person who wrote it. The problem comes clear then, for she is not within the same history of style. What is it that you are making accessible? The accessible level is the level of abstraction where the individual is already formed, where one can speak individual rights. When you hang out and with a language away from your own (*Mitwegsein*) so that you want to use that language by preference, sometimes, when you discuss something complicated, then you are on the way to making a dimension of the text accessible to the reader, with a light and easy touch, to which she does not accede in her everyday. If you are making anything else accessible, through a language quickly learnt with an idea that you transfer content, then you are betraying the text and showing rather dubious politics.

How will women's solidarity be measured here? How will their common experience be reckoned if one cannot imagine the traffic in accessibility going both ways? I think that idea should be given a decent burial as ground of knowledge, together with the idea of humanist universality. It is good to think that women have something in common, when one is approaching women with whom a relationship would not otherwise be possible. It is a great first step. But, if your interest is in learning if there *is* women's solidarity, how about leaving this assumption, appropriate as a means to an end like local or global social work, and trying a second step? Rather than imagining that women automatically have something identifiable in common, why not say, humbly and practically, my first obligation in understanding solidarity is to learn her mother-tongue. You will see immediately what the differences are. You will also feel the solidarity every day as you make the attempt to learn the language in which the other woman learnt to recognize reality at her mother's knee. This is preparation for the intimacy of cultural translation. If you are going to bludgeon someone else by insisting on your version of solidarity, you have the obligation to try out this experiment and see how far your solidarity goes.

In other words, if you are interested in talking about the other, and/or in making a claim to be the other, it is crucial to learn other languages. This should be distinguished from the learned tradition of language acquisition for academic work. I am talking about the importance of language acquisition for the woman from a hegemonic monolinguist culture who makes everybody's life miserable by insisting on women's solidarity at her price. I am uncomfortable with notions of feminist solidarity which are celebrated when everybody involved is similarly produced. There are countless languages in which women all over the world have grown up and been female or feminist, and yet the languages we keep on learning by rote are the powerful European ones, sometimes the powerful Asian ones, least often the chief African ones. The "other" languages are learnt only by anthropologists who *must* produce knowledge across an epistemic divide. They are generally (though not invariably) not interested in the three-part structure we are discussing.

If we are discussing solidarity as a theoretical position, we must also remember that not all the world's women are literate. There are traditions and situations that remain obscure because we cannot share their linguistic constitution. It is from this angle that I have felt that learning languages might sharpen our own presuppositions about what it means to use the sign "woman". If we say that things should be accessible to us, who is this "us"? What does that sign mean?

Although I have used the examples of women all along, the arguments apply across the board. It is just that women's rhetoricity may be doubly obscured. I do not see the advantage of being completely focused on a single issue, although one must establish practical priorities. In this book, we are concerned with post-structuralism and its effect on feminist theory. Where some post-structuralist thinking can be applied to the constitution of the agent in terms of the literary operations of language, women's texts might be operating differently because of the social differentiation between the sexes. Of course the point applies generally to the colonial context as well. When Ngugi decided to write in Kikuyu, some thought he was bringing a private language into the public sphere. But what makes a language shared by many people in a community private? I was thinking about those so-called private languages when I was talking about language learning. But even within those private languages it is my conviction that there is a difference in the way in which the staging of language produces not only the sexed subject but the gendered agent, by a version of centring, persistently disrupted by rhetoricity, indicating contingency. Unless demonstrated otherwise, this for me remains the condition and effect of dominant and subordinate gendering. If that is so, then we have some reason to focus on women's texts. Let us use the word "woman" to name that space of para-subjects defined as such by the social inscription of primary and secondary sexual characteristics. Then we can cautiously begin to track a sort of commonality in being set apart, within the different rhetorical strategies of different languages. But even here, historical superiorities of class must be kept in mind. Bharati Mukherjee, Anita Desai and Gayatri Spivak do not have the same rhetorical figuration of agency as an illiterate domestic servant.

Tracking commonality through responsible translation can lead us into areas of difference and different differentiations. This may also be important because, in the heritage of imperialism, the female legal subject bears the mark of a failure of Europeanization, by contrast with the female anthropological or literary subject from the area. For example, the division between the French and Islamic codes in modern Algeria is in terms of family, marriage, inheritance, legitimacy and female social agency. These are differences that we must keep in mind. And we must honour the difference between ethnic minorities in the First World and majority populations of the Third.

In conversation, Barrett had asked me if I now inclined more toward Foucault. This is indeed the case. In "Can the Subaltern Speak?", I took a rather strong critical line on Foucault's work, as part of a general critique of imperialism.[14] I do, however, find, his concept of *pouvoir-savoir* immensely useful. Foucault has contributed to French this ordinary-language doublet (the ability to know [as]) to take its place quietly beside *vouloir-dire* (the wish to say – meaning to mean).

On the most mundane level, *pouvoir-savoir* is the shared skill which allows us to make (common) sense of things. It is certainly not only power/knowledge in the sense of *puissance/connaissance*. Those are aggregative institutions. The common way in which one makes sense of things, on the other hand, loses itself in the sub-individual.

Looking at *pouvoir-savoir* in terms of women, one of my focuses has been new immigrants and the change of mother-tongue and *pouvoir-savoir* between mother and daughter. When the daughter talks reproductive rights and the mother talks protecting honour, is this the birth or death of translation?

Foucault is also interesting in his new notion of the ethics of the care for the self. In order to be able to get to the subject of ethics it may be necessary to look at the ways in which an individual in that culture is instructed to care for the self rather than the imperialism-specific secularist notion that the ethical subject is given as human. In a secularism which is structurally identical with Christianity laundered in the bleach of moral philosophy, the subject of ethics is faceless. Breaking out, Foucault was investigating other ways of making sense of how the subject becomes ethical. This is of interest because, given the connection between imperialism and secularism, there is almost no way of getting to alternative general voices except through religion. And if one does not look at religion as mechanisms of producing the ethical subject, one gets various kinds of "fundamentalism". Workers in cultural politics and its connections to a new ethical philosophy have to be interested in religion in the production of ethical subjects. There is much room for feminist work here because western feminists have not so far been aware of religion as a cultural instrument rather than a mark of cultural difference. I am currently working on Hindu performative ethics with Professor B. K. Matilal. He is an enlightened male feminist. I am an active feminist. Helped by his learning and his openness I am learning to distinguish between ethical catalysts and ethical motors even as I learn to translate bits of the Sanskrit epic in a way different from all the accepted translations, because I rely not only on learning, not only on "good English", but on that three-part scheme of which I have so lengthily spoken. I hope the results will please readers. If we are going to look at an ethics that emerges from something other than the historically secularist ideal – at an ethics of sexual differences, at an ethics that can confront the emergence of fundamentalisms without apology or dismissal in the name of the Enlightenment – then *pouvoir-savoir* and the care for the self in Foucault can be illuminating. And these "other ways" bring us back to translation, in the general sense.

Translation in general

I want now to add two sections to what was generated from the initial conversation with Barrett. I will dwell on the politics of translation in a general sense, by way of three examples of "cultural translation" in English. I want to make the point that the lessons of translation in the narrow sense can reach much further.

First, J. M. Coetzee's *Foe*.[15] This book represents the impropriety of the dominant's desire to give voice to the native. When Susan Barton, the eighteenth-century Englishwoman from *Roxana*, attempts to teach a muted Friday (from *Robinson Crusoe*) to read and write English, he draws an incomprehensible rebus on his slate and wipes it out, withholds it. You cannot translate from a position of monolinguist superiority. Coetzee as white creole translates *Robinson Crusoe* by representing Friday as the agent of a withholding.

Second, Toni Morrison's *Beloved*.[16] Let us look at the scene of the change of the mother-tongue from mother to daughter. Strictly speaking, it is not a change, but a loss, for the narrative is not of immigration but of slavery. Sethe, the central character of the novel, remembers: "What Nan" – her mother's fellow-slave and friend – "told her she had forgotten, along with the language she told it in. The same language her ma'am spoke, and which would never come back. But the message – that was – that was and had been there all along" (p. 62). The representation of this message, as it passes through the forgetfulness of death to Sethe's ghostly daughter Beloved, is of a withholding: "This is not a story to pass on" (p. 275).

Between mother and daughter, a certain historical withholding intervenes. If the situation between the new immigrant mother and daughter provokes the question as to whether it is the birth or death of translation (see above, p.381), here the author represents with violence a certain birth-in-death, a death-in-birth of a story that is not to translate or pass on, strictly speaking, therefore, an aporia, and yet it is passed on, with the mark of *un*translatability on it, in the bound book, *Beloved*, that we hold in our hands. Contrast this to the confidence in accessibility in the house of power, where history is waiting to be restored.

The scene of violence between mother and daughter (reported and passed on by the daughter Sethe to her daughter Denver, who carries the name of a white trash girl, in partial acknowledgement of women's solidarity in birthing) is, then, the condition of (im)possibility of *Beloved*:[17]

> She picked me up and carried me behind the smokehouse. Back there she opened up her dress front and lifted her breast and pointed under it. Right on her rib was a circle and a cross burnt right in the skin. She said, "This is your ma'am. This," and she pointed . . . "Yes, Ma'am," I said . . . "But how will you know me? . . . Mark me, too," I said . . . "Did she?" asked Denver. "She slapped my face." "What for?" "I didn't understand it then. Not till I had a mark of my own." (p. 61)

This scene, of claiming the brand of the owner as "my own", to create, in this broken chain of marks owned by separate white male agents of property, an unbroken chain of re-memory in (enslaved) daughters as agents of a history not to be passed on, is of necessity more poignant than Friday's scene of withheld writing from the white woman wanting to create history by giving her "own" language. And the lesson is the (im)possibility of translation in the general sense. Rhetoric points at absolute contingency, not the sequentiality of time, not even the cycle of seasons, but only "weather". "By and by all trace is gone, and what is forgotten is not only the footprints but the water and what it is down there. The rest is weather. Not the breath of the disremembered and unaccounted for" – after the effacement of the trace, no project for restoring (women's?) history – "but wind in the eaves, or spring ice thawing too quickly. Just weather" (p. 275).

With this invocation of contingency, where nature may be "the great body without organs of woman", we can align ourselves with Wilson Harris, the author of *The Guyana Quartet*, for whom trees are "the lungs of the globe".[18] Harris hails the (re)birth of the native imagination as not merely the trans-lation but the trans-substantiation of the species. What in more workaday language I have called the obligation of the translator to be able to juggle the rhetorical silences in the two languages, Harris puts this way, pointing at the need for translating the Carib's English:

> The Caribbean bone flute, made of human bone, is a seed in the soul of the Caribbean. It is a primitive technology that we can turn around [trans-version?]. Consuming our biases and prejudices in ourselves we can let the bone flute help us open ourselves rather than read it the other way – as a metonymic devouring of a bit of flesh.[19] The link of music with cannibalism is a sublime paradox. When the music of the bone flute opens the doors, absences flow in, and the native imagination puts together the ingredients for quantum immediacy out of unpredictable resources.

The bone flute has been neglected by Caribbean writers, says Wilson Harris, because progressive realism is a charismatic way of writing prize-winning fiction. Progressive realism measures the bone. Progressive realism is the too-easy accessibility of translation as transfer of substance.

The progressive realism of the west dismissed the native imagination as the place of the fetish. Hegel was perhaps the greatest systematizer of this dismissal. And psychoanalytic cultural criticism in its present charismatic incarnation sometimes measures the bone with uncanny precision. It is perhaps not fortuitous that the passage below gives us an account of Hegel that is the exact opposite of Harris's vision. The paradox of the sublime and the bone here lead to non-language seen as inertia, where the structure of passage is mere logic. The authority of the supreme language makes translation impossible:

> The Sublime is therefore the paradox of an object which, in the very field of representation, provides a view, in a negative way, of the dimension of what is unpresentable . . . The bone, the skull, is thus an object which, by means of its *presence*, fills out the void, the impossibility of the signifying *representation* of the subject . . . The proposition "Wealth is the Self" repeats at this level the proposition "The Spirit is a bone" [both propositions are Hegel's]: in both cases we are dealing with a proposition which is at first sight absurd, nonsensical, with an equation the terms of which are incompatible; in both cases we encounter the same logical structure of passage: the subject, totally lost in the medium of language (language of gesture and grimaces; language of flattery), finds its objective counterpart in the inertia of a non-language object (skull, money).[20]

Wilson Harris's vision is abstract, translating Morrison's "weather" into an oceanic version of quantum physics. But all three cultural translators cited in this section ask us to attend to the rhetoric which points to the limits of translation, in the creole's, the slave-daughter's, the Carib's use of "English". Let us learn the lesson of translation from these brilliant inside/outsiders and translate it into the situation of other languages.

Reading as translation

In conclusion, I want to show how the post-colonial as the outside/insider translates white theory as she reads, so that she can discriminate on the terrain of the original. She wants to use what is useful. Again, I hope this can pass on a lesson to the translator in the narrow sense.

"The link of music with cannibalism is a sublime paradox." I believe Wilson Harris is using "sublime" here with some degree of precision, indicating the undoing of the progressive western subject as realist interpreter of history. Can a theoretical account of the aesthetic sublime in English discourse, ostensibly far from the bone flute, be of use? By way of answer, I will use my reading of Peter de Bolla's superb scholarly account of *The Discourse of the Sublime* as an example of sympathetic reading as translation, precisely not a surrender but a friendly learning by taking a distance.[21]

P. 4: "What was it to be a subject in the eighteenth century?" The reader-as-translator (RAT) is excited. The long eighteenth century in Britain is the account of the constitution and transformation of nation into empire. Shall we read that story? The book will least touch on that issue, if only to swerve. And women will not be seen as touched in their agency formation by that change. The book's strong feminist sympathies relate to the Englishwoman only as gender victim. But the erudition of the text allows us to think that this sort of rhetorical reading might be the method to open up the question "What is it to be a post-colonial reader of English in the twentieth century?" The representative reader of *The Discourse of the Sublime* will be post-colonial. Has that law of the majority been observed, or the law of the strong?

On p. 72 RAT comes to a discussion of Burke on the sublime:

> The internal resistance of Burke's text . . . restricts the full play of this trope [power . . . as a trope articulating the technologies of the sublime], thereby defeating a description of the sublime experience uniquely in terms of the enpowered [sic] subject. Put briefly, Burke, for a number of reasons, among which we must include political aims and ends, stops short of a discourse on the sublime, and in so doing he reinstates the ultimate power of an adjacent discourse, theology, which locates its own self-authenticating power grimly within the boundaries of godhead.

Was it also because Burke was deeply implicated in searching out the recesses of the mental theatre of the English master in the colonies that he had some notion of different kinds of subject and therefore, like some Kurtz before Conrad, recoiled in horror before the sublimely empowered subject? Was it because, like some Kristeva before *Chinese Women*, Burke had tried to imagine the Begums of Oudh as legal subjects that he had put self-authentication elsewhere?[22] *The Discourse of the Sublime*, in noticing Burke's difference from the other discoursers on the sublime, opens doors for other RATs to engage in such scholarly speculations and thus exceed and expand the book.

Pp. 106, 111–12, 131: RAT comes to the English National Debt. British colonialism was a violent deconstruction of the hyphen between nation and state.[23] In imperialism the nation was subl(im)ated into empire. Of this, no clue in *The*

Discourse. The Bank of England is discussed. Its founding in 1696, and the transformation of letters of credit to the ancestor of the modern cheque, had something like a relationship with the fortunes of the East India Company and the founding of Calcutta in 1690. The *national* debt is in fact the site of a crisis-management, where the nation, sublime object as miraculating subject of ideology, changes the sign "debtor" into a catachresis or false metaphor by way of "an acceptance of a permanent discrepancy between the total circulating specie and the debt". The French War, certainly the immediate efficient cause, is soon woven into the vaster textile of crisis. *The Discourse* cannot see the nation covering for the colonial economy. As on the occasion of the race-specificity of gendering, so on the discourse of multi-national capital, the argument is kept domestic, within England, European.[24] RAT snuffles off, disgruntled. She finds a kind of comfort in Mahasweta's livid figuration of the woman's body as body rather than attend to this history of the English body "as a disfigurative device in order to return to [it] its lost literality". Reading as translation has misfired here.

On p. 140 RAT comes to the elder Pitt. Although his functionality is initially seen as "demanded . . . by the incorporation of nation", it is not possible not at least to mention empire when speaking of Pitt's voice:

> the voice of Pitt . . . works its doubled intervention into the spirit and character of the times; at once the supreme example of the private individual in the service of the state, and the private individual eradicated by the needs of a public, nationalist, commercial empire. In this sense the voice of Pitt becomes the most extreme example of the textualization of the body for the rest of the century. (p. 182)

We have seen a literal case of the textualization of the surface of the body between slave mother and slave daughter in *Beloved*, where mother hits daughter to stop her thinking that the signs of that text can be passed on, a lesson learnt *après-coup*, literally after the blow of the daughter's own branding. Should RAT expect an account of the passing on of the textualization of the interior of the body through the voice, a metonym for consciousness, from master father to master son? The younger Pitt took the first step to change the nationalist empire to the imperial nation with the India Act of 1784. Can *The Discourse of the Sublime* plot that sublime relay? Not yet. But here, too, an exceeding and expanding translation is possible.

Predictably, RAT finds a foothold in the rhetoricity of *The Discourse*. Chapter 10 begins: "The second part of this study has steadily examined how 'theory' sets out to legislate and control a practice, how it produces the excess which it cannot legislate, and removes from the centre to the boundary its limit, limiting case" (p. 230). This passage reads to a deconstructive RAT as an enabling self-description of the text, although within the limits of the book, it describes, not itself but the object of its investigation. By the time the end of the book is reached, RAT feels that she has been written into the text:

> As a history of that refusal and resistance [this book] presents a record of its own coming into being as history, the history of the thought it wants to think differently, over there. It is therefore, only appropriate

that its conclusion should gesture towards the limit, risk the reinversion of the boundary by speaking from the other, refusing silence to what is unsaid.

Beyond this "clamour for a kiss" of the other space, it is "just weather".

Under the figure of RAT (reader-as-translator), I have tried to limn the politics of a certain kind of clandestine post-colonial reading, using the master marks to put together a history. Thus we find out what books we can forage, and what we must set aside. I can use Peter de Bolla's *The Discourse on the Sublime* to open up dull histories of the colonial eighteenth century. Was Toni Morrison, a writer well-versed in contemporary literary theory, obliged to set aside Paul de Man's "The Purloined Ribbon"?[25]

> Eighteen seventy-four and white folks were still on the loose . . . Human blood cooked in a lynch fire was a whole other thing . . . But none of that had worn out his marrow . . . It was the ribbon . . . He thought it was a cardinal feather stuck to his boat. He tugged and what came loose in his hand was a red ribbon knotted around a curl of wet woolly hair, clinging still to its bit of scalp . . . He kept the ribbon; the skin smell nagged him.
>
> (pp. 180–1)

Morrison next invokes a language whose selvedge is so frayed that no *frayage* can facilitate full passage: "This time, although he couldn't cipher but one word, he believed he knew who spoke them. The people of the broken necks, of fire-cooked blood and black girls who had lost their ribbons" (p. 181). Did the explanation of promises and excuses in eighteenth-century Geneva not make it across into this "roar"? I will not check it out and measure the bone flute. I will simply dedicate these pages to the author of *Beloved*, in the name of translation.

Notes

1   The first part of this essay is based on a conversation with Michèle Barrett in the summer of 1990.
2   Forthcoming [2002] from Seagull Press, Calcutta.
3   "Facilitation" is the English translation of a Freudian term which is translated *frayage* in French. The dictionary meaning is:

> Term used by Freud at a time when he was putting forward a neurological model of the functioning of the psychical apparatus (1895): the excitation, in passing from one neurone to another, runs into a certain resistance; where its passage results in a permanent reduction in this resistance, there is said to be facilitation; excitation will opt for a facilitated pathway in preference to one where no facilitation has occurred.
>
> (J. Laplanche and J.-B. Pontalis, *The Language of Psycho-Analysis* [Hogarth Press, London, 1973], p. 157)

4   Jacques Derrida, "Force of Law: The 'Mystical Foundation of Authority'", tr. Mary Quaintance, *Deconstruction and the Possibility of Justice: Cardozo Law Review*, XI (July–Aug. 1990); p. 923.

5   "The Wet-nurse", in Kali for Women (eds), *Truth Tales: Stories by Indian Women* (The Women's Press, London, 1987), pp. 1–50 (first published by Kali for Women, Delhi, 1986), and "Breast-giver", in Gayatri Chakravorty Spivak, *In Other Worlds: Essays in Cultural Politics* (Methuen/Routledge, New York, 1987), pp. 222–40.

6   Luce Irigaray argues persuasively that, Emmanuel Levinas to the contrary, within the ethics of sexual difference the erotic is ethical ("The Fecundity of the Caress", in her *Ethics of Sexual Difference*, tr. Carolyn Burke and G. C. Gill (Cornell University Press, Ithaca, N.Y. [1993]).

7   Sudhir Kakar, *The Inner World: A Psycho-analytic Study of Childhood and Society in India*, 2nd edn (Oxford University Press, Delhi, 1981), pp. 171ff. Part of this discussion in a slightly different form is included in my "Psychoanalysis in Left Field; and Fieldworking: Examples to fit the Title", in Michael Munchow and Sonu Shamdasani (eds), *Psychoanalyis, Philosophy and Culture* (Routledge, London, 1994), pp. 41–75.

8   See Partha Chatterjee, "Nationalism and the Woman Question", in Kumkum Sangari and Sudesh Vaid (eds), *Re-Casting Women* (Rutgers University Press, New Brunswick, NJ, 1990), pp. 233–53, for a detailed discussion of this gendering of Indian nationalism.

9   Max Weber, *The Religion of India: The Sociology of Hinduism and Buddhism*, tr. Hans H. Gerth and Don Martindale (Free Press, Glencoe, Ill., 1958).

10   More on this in a more personal context in Spivak, "Stagings of the Origin", in *Third Text*.

11   Ifi Amadiume, *Male Daughters Female Husbands* (Zed Books, London, 1987).

12   For background on Akhter, already somewhat dated for this interventionist in the history of the present, see Yayori Matsui (ed.), *Women's Asia* (Zed Books, London, 1989), ch. 1.

13   "More on Power/Knowledge", in Thomas E. Wartenberg (ed.), *Re-Thinking Power* (State University of New York Press, Albany, NY, 1992).

14   Spivak, "Can the Subaltern Speak?", in Cary Nelson and Lawrence Grossberg (eds), *Marxism and the Interpretation of Culture* (University of Illinois Press, Urbana, Ill., 1988), pp. 271–313.

15   For an extended consideration of these and related points, see my "Versions of the Margin: Coetzee's *Foe* reading Defoe's *Crusoe/Roxana*", in Jonathan Arac (ed.), *Theory and Its Consequences* (Johns Hopkins University Press, Baltimore, 1990).

16   Toni Morrison, *Beloved* (Plume Books, New York, 1987). Page numbers are included in my text.

17   For (im)possibility, see my "Literary Representation of the Subaltern", in my *In Other Worlds*, pp. 241–68.

18   Karl Marx, "Economic and Philosophical Manuscripts", in Rodney Livingstone and George Benton tr., *Early Writings* (Vintage, New York, 1975), pp. 279–400; Wilson Harris, *The Guyana Quartet* (Faber, London, 1985). These quotations are from Wilson Harris, "Cross-cultural Crisis: Imagery, Language,

and the Intuitive Imagination", Commonwealth Lectures, 1990, Lecture no. 2, 31 Oct. 1990, University of Cambridge.

19   Derrida traces the trajectory of the Hegelian and pre-Hegelian discourse of the fetish (Jacques Derrida, *Glas*, tr. Richard Rand and John P. Leavey, Jr. [University of Nebraska Press, Lincoln, Nebr., 1986]). The worshipper of the fetish eats human flesh. The worshipper of God feasts on the Eucharist. Harris transverses the fetish here through the native imagination.

20   Slavoj Zizek, *The Sublime Object of Ideology*, tr. Jon Barnes (Verso, London, 1989), pp. 203, 208, 212.

21   Peter de Bolla, *The Discourse of the Sublime: Readings in History, Aesthetics and the Subject* (Blackwell, Oxford, 1989). Page numbers are given in my text.

22   References and discussion of "The Begums of Oudh", and "The Impeachment of Warren Hastings" are to be found in *The Writings and Speeches of Edmund Burke*, ed. P. J. Marshall (Clarendon Press, Oxford, 1981), vol. 5: *India: Madras and Bengal*, pp. 410–12, pp. 465–6, p. 470; and in vol. 6: *India: Launching of The Hastings Impeachment* respectively.

23   See my "Reading the Archives: the Rani of Sirmur", in Francis Barker (ed.), *Europe and Its Others* (University of Essex, Colchester, 1985), pp. 128–51.

24   Ibid.

25   Paul de Man, "The Purloined Ribbon", reprinted as "Excuses (*Confessions*)" in de Man, *Allegories of Reading* (Yale University Press, New Haven, 1979), pp. 278–301.

Chapter 27

Kwame Anthony Appiah

THICK TRANSLATION

Asém a éhia Akanfoö no na Ntafoö de goro brékété.
[A matter which troubles the Akan people, the people of Gonja take to play the brékété drum.[1]]

Kaka ne éka ne ayafunka fanyinam éka.
[Toothache and indebtedness and stomach ache, debt is preferable.[2]]

Kamesékwakye se: sé önim sé abé rebébere a, anka wanköware adöbé nkonto.
[The drongo says: if he had known that the palm nuts were going to ripen, then he would not have married the raffia palm with a twisted leg.]

I

THESE PROVERBS ARE in (one dialect of) the Twi-language – now, for reasons too intricate to discuss quickly here, often called "Akan" – which is the major language spoken in and around my hometown of Kumasi in Ghana. They are but three of the 7000-odd proverbs that my mother has collected over roughly the period of my lifetime, and she and some friends have been trying to understand them for the last decade or so; latterly I have joined them in setting out to prepare a manuscript that (as we say) reduces many of these sayings for the first time to writing, that glosses them in English, and that offers also, in each case, what I have offered you: what we call a literal translation.

1993

Coincidentally (or, perhaps, not so coincidentally) I have spent much of the same decade working in what analytic philosophers call the theory of meaning or philosophical semantics: in the activity of trying to say what an adequate theoretical account of the meanings of words and phrases and sentences should look like.

It would seem natural enough, *prima facie*, to bring these two activities – of translating and theorizing about meaning – together, because of the simplest of beginning thoughts about translation: namely that it is an attempt to find ways of saying in one language something that means the same as what has been said in another. What I would like to do in this essay is to explore some of the reasons why it is that this *prima facie* thought should be resisted: I shall argue that most of what interests us in the translations that interest us most is not meaning, in the sense that philosophy of language uses the term: in many cases, as the proverbs surely show and for reasons they exemplify, getting the meaning, in this sense, right is hardly even a first step towards understanding.

II

Let me start again with a simple thought: what we translate are utterances, things made with words by men and women, with voice or pen or keyboard; and those utterances are the products of actions, which like all actions are undertaken for reasons. Since reasons can be complex and extensive, grasping an agent's reasons can be a difficult business; and we can easily feel that we have not dug deeply enough, when we have told the best story we can. Utterances – ordinary everyday remarks – are in this respect somewhat unusual for while it may not be easy to give a *full* account of why someone has, for example, uttered the words "It's a lovely, sunny day," in the ordinary course of things English speakers will be inclined to suppose that anyone who says this to them has, as one reason for uttering, the intention to express the thought that it is a lovely, sunny day.

I say "in the ordinary course of things" because, in odd enough circumstances, we might suppose no such thing; and that is because in odd enough circumstances it might not be true. Perhaps – to impose on you one of those bizarre fantasies that mark the style of the philosopher – this is a speaker who has been told this is an English sentence without being told what it means; perhaps, she is uttering it not to express that thought – which she does not know it expresses – but to mislead us into thinking she is anglophone. Perhaps we know all this. Perhaps. Still assertoric utterances do ordinarily propose themselves as motivated, at least in part, by a desire to express a certain specific thought.

This is easy enough, of course, to explain: part of what is distinctive about utterance as a kind of action, with distinctive sorts of reasons, is that it is *conventional*; and the thought we normally take someone to be intending to express in uttering a sentence is the thought[3] that the conventions of language associate with it.

Grice famously suggested that we could say what an (assertoric) utterance meant by identifying the (content of) the belief[4] that it was conventionally intended to produce; and he identified, correctly in my view, the heart of the mechanism by which these beliefs are supposed to be produced. Roughly, he suggested that when a speaker communicates a belief by way of the utterance of a sentence, she does so by getting her hearers to recognize *both* that this is the belief she intends them to have *and* that she intends them to have that belief in part *because* they recognize that primary intention. This is the heart of utterance – meaning; the conventions of language associate words with roles in determining *which* belief is to be communicated by an utterance, but it is by way of the Gricean mechanism that this communication occurs, when it does.

This Gricean mechanism – the act that achieves its purpose because its purpose is recognized – is central to meaning just because it occurs both in the cases where meaning is conventional and in those cases where it is not. If I say that "John is in the kitchen or the den," in ordinary circumstances. I get you to believe, by way of the Gricean mechanism, something I have not literally *said* – namely that I don't know which.

To explain why you believe this, we should begin with the fact that in ordinary contexts our exchanges are governed by what Grice called conversational maxims: by understandings to the effect that we are trying to be helpful, trying to be, for example, both maximally and relevantly informative.

Since I know you know this, I can assume you will infer that I do not know more precisely where John is. In uttering the sentence I will have your recognizing this as one of its intended effects. But you know I know you know this, and so you can infer that I intended that you should believe that I was being helpful and, thus, infer that I intended you to believe that I did not know more precisely where John was. That this is a case of the Gricean mechanism follows from that fact that, because I know you know I know you know this, I expect you to recognize that I had this intention and to come to believe that I did not know more precisely where John was in part because you recognized the intention. It is no surprise that Grice, who discovered this mechanism, also discovered such so-called conversational implicatures: these thoughts we communicate by encouraging others to draw inferences that go beyond the meaning of the words we utter. (It will be useful later to have a name for the case where you and I both know P, each knows the other knows it, and also knows the other knows that each knows the other knows it, and so on . . . I shall use a standard shorthand for this and say that in this case we "mutually know" that P.)

Characteristically for a philosopher, I have focused on language that is assertoric; but similar lines of thought can be applied to optatives which express preferences – wishes or wants – rather than beliefs. They differ from simple assertions in expressing different sorts of states of the speaker. To deal with questions and orders, we must give a different account of the intended response from the hearer, since questions and commands are aimed at something more active than mere belief.[5]

For performatives, more yet is required: for I can pronounce you man and wife only when there exists a social practice of marrying, in which my utterances are conventionally given a certain role.

Despite these differences, the general theoretical point here applies across the board: it is possible to have the reasons we ordinarily have for uttering only because

there exists within any community of speakers of a single language a specific structure of mutual expectations about reasons for uttering. Learning the grammar and
the lexicon of a language is learning a complex set of instructions for generating
acts that are standardly intended to achieve their effects in others who know the
same instructions . . . and precisely by way of a recognition of those intentions.

When somebody speaks, therefore, in the ordinary course of things and in the
absence of contrary evidence, she will be taken and will expect to be taken by participants in the conventions of her language to have the intentions that those
conventions associate, by way of grammar and lexicon, with her utterance.[6] To be
able to identify *those* intentions is to know the literal meaning of what she has said;
and the literal meanings of words and phrases are determined by the way in which
they contribute to fixing the intentions associated with the speech-acts in which they
can occur. Let me call these the *literal* intentions. While each utterance of a sentence
will be surrounded and motivated by more than its literal intentions, will have (in
other words) more reasons than these, and while *some* utterances will not even have
these intentions – because, for example, they are clearly ironically intended – it
remains true that explanations of what a speaker is doing in uttering a sentence will
almost always involve reference to the standard intentions, even in the cases where
they are absent.

III

If, as I originally suggested, translation is an attempt to find ways of saying in one
language something that means the same as what has been said in another; and if,
as I have recently suggested, the literal meaning of an utterance is a matter of what
intentions a speaker would ordinarily be taken to have in uttering it; then a literal
translation ought to be a sentence of, for example, English, that would ordinarily
be taken to be uttered with the intention that the original, for example, Twi,
sentence, was conventionally associated with.[7]

This thought has been rejected more often than it has been affirmed in recent
philosophy of language because, for a variety of reasons, it has been thought that
the literal intention that goes with some or perhaps all sentences is one that you
can have only if you speak the language to which those sentences belong. If you do
not recognize the Sapir–Whorf hypothesis when dressed up this way, it is because
the hypothesis is normally expressed as the view that what language you speak affects
what thoughts you can have: but then, if that were true, it would affect what
thoughts you could intend to express also. If what language you speak determines
what thoughts or intentions you can have, translation, thus conceived, will always
be impossible.

Perhaps because I was brought up between several languages, not all of them
varieties of English, I have never quite believed that this could be right. Of course
there are some thoughts that it is hard to imagine someone having without *some*
language – the thought that a particle is a neutral boson, for example – and others
that require linguistic knowledge constitutively: the thought that Ronald Reagan is
smarter than my dog surely requires that I know – which means know how to use

in sentences — Ronald Reagan's name. But surely there are thoughts — "It's a cat," say — that you can have without speaking English; have, uncontroversially, no questions begged. And if that is so, can we not see how you could have the thought that this is a neutral boson, not because you know the words "neutral boson" but because you know some other words that refer, in some other language, to the same thing? So, at least, I think, though I shall not argue it here; because what I want to notice now is that even if this is right, we need only consider the case of proper names to see that it will often be a matter of luck whether the relevant intentions are possible for both of two communities, between which we are translating. To make the point at its least complicated, it is no surprise that you cannot exactly say in Twi that the wall is, well, burnt sienna.

This impossibility, though of the first importance in translation, is not theoretically puzzling; explanations of why Twi does not have the concept of burnt sienna or of a neutral boson are too obvious to be worth giving. What I am inclined to deny is the more exciting claim — which follows from any view that involves holism about meanings — that we cannot translate any talk at all, because, for example, every sentence in which it can occur subtly shades the meaning of every word, so that "table" and "Tisch" do not mean the same, because nothing adequately gets the sense of "Der Tisch ist gemütlich." In standard circumstances the literal intentions with which I utter "It's a table" and Hans says "Es ist ein Tisch" are, for all the arguments I know, the same.

On this topic I am only saying where I stand, not making arguments: if I am right, there are barriers to translation to be noted here, but, as I say, while they are important to an understanding of why translation is so difficult, they do not seem theoretically puzzling. If you cannot conventionally communicate a certain literal intention in language A and you can in language B, then the translator cannot produce a literal translation; that is all it amounts to.

IV

But literal intentions as we have seen are not the only ones that can operate by the Gricean mechanism. Searle makes a distinction between direct and indirect speech-acts, the key to which is whether the main point of the utterance is accounted for by the literal intentions: if not, then what is primarily being communicated is being communicated indirectly. Notice, in passing, that the distinction between indirect and direct is not the same as the distinction between literal and non-literal uses: I may say "There's an ant on your shoulder" with the primary intention of getting you to recognize by the Gricean mechanism that I care about you, an effect which will depend on what I say being taken literally as well and being seen to be true; or I may say "Juliet is the sun" non-literally (that is, with the intention that you not ascribe to me the literal intentions) but in order to communicate indirectly that Juliet is the central fact of my little universe. In other words, sometimes indirect communication proceeds by way of the literal intentions and sometimes it doesn't. All of this can be captured in translation, provided the relevant literal intentions are available.

V

Let us look back at the proverbs with which I began, and explore them for a moment with some of these distinctions in mind. What you need now, along with all this apparatus, is a little richer – or to advert to the Geertzean vocabulary of my title, thicker – contextualization. These sayings belong to a *genre* – what I have called the proverb, which in Twi is called *ébé* (pl. *mmé*) – that is well-known to speakers of that language. In the case of the last proverb – the drongo says: if he had known that the palm nuts were going to ripen, then he would not have married the raffia palm with a twisted leg – it is recognizable by its *form* as a proverb; speaker and hearers of such a proverb mutually know (in the technical sense introduced above) that drongos don't speak and that one kind of *ébé* begins "The such-and-such says: . . ." and thus have mutual knowledge, in the ordinary course of things, that this is, indeed, *mmébuo*, proverb-making.[8]

The first immediate consequence of this mutual recognition is that the literal intentions are, so to speak, cancelled. Just as, when I begin a narration with the words "Once upon a time . . ." I withdraw the usual licence to suppose that I believe what I am saying to be, as we say, literally true, so recognition that I am uttering an *ébé* cancels the implication that what I am saying is literally true. (It does not carry the implication that what I say is literally *false*, however. Precisely, mutual recognition that I am uttering a proverb, which says that P, has the consequence that we mutually know that my intention is not to indicate that I believe that P.) What makes this case different from the fairy-tale "Once upon a time . . ." is that a different intention is now conventionally implied: an implication to the effect that, starting with the literal meaning – starting from the very literal intentions I have "cancelled" – and building on mutually known fact (some of it, perhaps, extremely context-bound), you can work out a truth that I *do* intend to express.

Thus, in a typical use of the first proverb, for example – Asém a éthia Akanfoö no na Ntafoö de goro brékété [A matter which troubles the Akan people, the people of Gonja take to play the brékété drum] – I might utter it in the midst of an argument with my father about whether it matters that I do not want to go to church with him one Sunday; our contrasting attitudes, he will infer, are being likened to the contrasting attitudes of Dagomba and Akan peoples – for the brékété drum is one they play for entertainment at dances, and represents fun. "Different peoples have different attitudes" is the generalization that seems to cover both cases, the one we may suppose he will grasp, by the Gricean mechanism, as my target thought. In this inference the literal intentions of the proverb-sentence have to be identified to go through the reasoning – the literal meaning is there and is what the sentence means; but it is not what I mean by it, not the indirect burden of the speech-act, which marks itself by its form as non-literally intended.

But now I want to point out that I am only saying about the proverb what Davidson, I think, meant to say about metaphors: namely that in so far as the sentences used in them literally mean anything, they literally mean exactly what they say. They have utterance meanings, and those utterance meanings are the ones that convention associates with those words in that order. But in the broader sense of meaning, in the sense of meaning which has to do with understanding adequately why someone has spoken as she has – where that means, minimally, understanding what she intends us to understand by way of the Gricean mechanism – it is plain that neither metaphors nor proverbs mean only what they say.

VI

I have been essentially accepting the thought that meaning in the broadest sense is what is communicated by the Gricean mechanism. Literal intentions work in the Gricean way; I have suggested that the proverbs do, too, though I have not said much about how. It is clear I think that metaphor works like this, however the details go. On one sort of contemporary view, "Juliet is the sun" is a literal false-hood which invites us to think of Juliet as standing to the speaker as the sun stands to the world; on another, resurrected by Bob Fogelin, it is elliptical for a simile whose rough meaning is that "Juliet has a significant number of the (contextually) salient features of the sun."[9] So she is central, a source of warmth and nourishment, enlivening, important and – one must add prosaically – . . . and so on. But on either view the metaphor is supposed to work by getting you to see how it is supposed to work and getting you to recognize that that is how I want you to understand it. And here both convention (*metaphor*, however it works in detail, is mutually known to all of us) and specific features of the mutual knowledge of speaker and hearer that derives from context interact to produce meaning.

What philosophers of language have largely attended to in thinking about meaning are these Gricean aspects of meaning – they include both what are normally thought of as semantical and as pragmatic phenomena, and they broadly, as I say, exhaust the range of philosophical interest in language. Having identified this interest and its scope, my argument from now is directed towards examining the ways in which the point of much translation transcends what I am calling the Gricean aspects of meaning.

VII

And to begin to see why, let us observe that the sorts of things I have been saying about meaning are not much favored by those who spend their time in literary studies, in part, I think, because faced with a real live text, it seems bizarrely in-appropriate to spend one's time speculating about the author's intentions: the author may be long dead, unknown to us, uninteresting, and surely, it will seem, her inten-tions have nothing to do with what we are interested in. Nor do I disagree with any of this: whether a work is fictional or not, our literary interest in it has usually very little to do with psychological facts about its historical author. But it remains true that in order to begin to have a literary understanding of many texts, we must usually first know its language well enough to be able to identify what the inten-tions conventionally associated with each of its sentences are: that we must begin with the literal meanings of words, phrases, sentences. More than this, in under-standing many of the texts that we address as literary, we must grasp not merely the literal intentions but the whole message that would be communicated by the utterance of the sentence in more ordinary settings: metaphor and implicature, as they occur in fiction, occur also outside it. These more complex elements of the Gricean message of the utterance in its context also occur with the usual intentions suspended: we do not have to believe that Jane Austen tells us that "it is a truth universally acknowledged, that a single man in possession of a good fortune, must be in want of a wife" in order to express her own ironic attitude to the relations of marriage, gender and property, but we *are* plainly meant to rely on our understanding of the fact that an utterance of this sentence would convey that ironic attitude outside the fiction.

Many, perhaps most texts, in other words, require us to grasp the Gricean burden that the words would bear in ordinary uses. But only "most"; for with some texts – symbolist poems, late James Joyce, the productions of the dada "poets" – it seems that, while we often need to understand the roles that the words in those texts play in their more normal habitats, there is no intention at all that our language associates with the strings of words that fall between periods. And sometimes, as in Joyce (and "Jabberwocky"), we do not even have word-meanings to rely on: the words themselves often have no established meaning – no rules for how they should contribute to determining literal intentions; and what we then do is either to see them as made from existing words, invoking those meanings, or to rely on associations of sound and thought that are based on other things than meanings, or, perhaps, to give up altogether!

But even in the case of narrative fiction, where the sentences do not raise these problems of identifying the literal intentions, I agree, as I say, that the literal intentions can hardly be the point of the matter, since to be packaged as a fiction is to be offered with the literal intentions cancelled.

It is a serious question, I think, why on earth we should have the practice of producing language whose understanding requires us both to grasp what would have been its literal intentions and to accept that these are not the writer's intentions in the present case. It is a question about whether we can *justify* the practice of fiction externally. It is plain, I think, that we *can*, though the story is complicated and has many elements, but that is not an issue to pursue now. What *is* important now is that literary practice, like linguistic practice, is conventional – which is to say it is governed by a specific structure of mutual expectations – but that these literary conventions – unlike linguistic conventions – do not usually invoke the Gricean mechanism.

Akan uses of proverbs are, in this respect, quite atypical. To use a proverb *as such* is, as I said, to imply that, starting with the literal meaning – starting from the very literal intentions I have "cancelled" – and building on mutually known fact (some of it, perhaps, extremely context-bound), you can work out a truth that I *do* intend to express, even though it is not the truth associated with the literal intentions. This is a feature that proverbs share with two genres of fiction – the parable and the fable – but not with most others. While the form of the novel is constrained by historically developing conventions, those conventions do not carry a message: are not, that is, supposed to operate in such a way as to allow us to read off the governing intentions of the author, to answer the question, "why did she write this?" And it is for this reason, I think, that attention to intentions – in the novel and in many other genres – is likely to strike us as a mistake.

Literary conventions, simply put, make possible acts that can be defined by reference not only to the meanings – both literal and non-literal, direct and indirect – of utterances, but also to features that are broadly formal – alliteration, meter, rhyme, plot-structure. What they do not usually do – and here, as I say, proverbs are an exception – is determine how we should construct a meaning – in the sense of a set of intentions operating through the Gricean mechanism – for the work.

Because the novel and the sonnet are not conventionally constituted by a process of meaning-generation, there is no set of conventions to which we can refer, analogous to the conventions of literal meaning, for deciding what the work means; there are no literary intentions, conventional and Gricean, to correspond to literal intentions. Because there are literal intentions we can say what a literal assertoric utterance is for – it is to communicate such-and-such information; it may be possible, then, in literal translation, to find a sentence in a target language that has more or less the same literal intentions as the utterance in the object-language. If it is not possible, it may be clear enough why: there is no way of expressing that thought in the target language, perhaps because the referent of some term is unknown there, or because a social practice in which the utterance is embedded – the curse, say – is absent. Success and failure at this level are well-enough defined.

But for literary translation our object is not to produce a text that reproduces the literal intentions of the author – not even the one's she is cancelling – but to produce something that shares the central literary properties of the object-text; and, as is obvious, these are very much under-determined by its literal meaning, even in the cases where it has one. A literary translation, so it seems to me, aims at producing a text whose relation both to the literary and to the linguistic conventions of the culture of the translation is relevantly like the relations of the object-text to its culture's conventions. A precise set of parallels is likely to be impossible, just because the chances that metrical and other formal features of a work can be reproduced while preserving the identity of literal and non-literal, direct and indirect, meaning are vanishingly small.

And, in fact, we may choose, rightly, to translate a term in a way that is unfaithful to the literal intentions, because we are trying to preserve formal features that seem more crucial. But even if we did not have to make such choices, even if we could, *per impossibile*, meet all the constraints of the Gricean meaning and all the literary conventions, we would not have produced the perfect translation: we could do better, we could aim to reproduce literary qualities of the object-text that are not a matter of the conventions.

So that the reason why we cannot speak of the perfect translation here is not that there is a definite set of desiderata and we know they cannot all be met; it is rather that there is no definite set of desiderata. A translation aims to produce a new text that matters to one community the way another text matters to another: but it is part of our understanding of why texts matter that this is not a question that convention settles; indeed, it is part of our understanding of literary judgment, that there can always be new readings, new things that matter about a text, new reasons for caring about new properties.

VIII

It is a feature, simply put, of the written text that we do not have settled and definite ideas about what matters about it. What is also clear is that in our culture we have settled on a particular set of institutional mechanisms for addressing the question of what matters. As my friend John Guillory argued recently in a paper on the "Canonical and Non-Canonical: A Critique of the Current Debate," in *English Literary History*,[10] the role of literature, indeed, the formation of the concept, the institution of "literature" – which is to say *our* concept of it – is indissoluble from pedagogy. Roland Barthes expressed the point in a characteristic – and justly oft-cited – apothegm:

> "l'enseignement de la littérature" est pour moi presque tautologique. La littérature, c'est ce qui s'enseigne, un point c'est tout.[11]

Abstracted from its context, this formulation no doubt requires some qualifying glosses. But let me express the point only slightly hyperbolically: what counts as a fine translation of a literary text – which is to say a taught text – is that it should preserve for us the features that make it worth teaching.

Questions of adequacy of translation thus inherit the indeterminacy of questions about the adequacy of the understanding displayed in the process we now call "reading" – which is to say that process of writing about texts which is engaged in by people who teach them. If I may be excused the solecism of quoting what I myself have written elsewhere.

> To focus on the issue of whether a reading is *correct* is to invite the question, "What is it that a reading is supposed to give a correct account *of*?" The quick answer – one that, as we shall immediately see, tells us less than it pretends to – is, of course, "the text." But the text exists as linguistic, as historical, as commercial, as political event; and while each of these ways of conceiving the very same object provides opportunities for pedagogy, each provides different opportunities: opportunities between which we must choose. We are inclined at the moment to talk about this choice as if the purposes by which it is guided were, in some sense, given. But were that true, we would have long agreed on the nature of a literary reading: and there is surely little doubt that the concept of a "literary reading," like the concept of "literature" is what W. B. Gallie used to call an "essentially contested concept." To understand what a reading is, is to understand that what counts as a reading is always up for grabs.[12]

In the same place I argued that we should give up language that implies an epistemology in which the work has already a meaning that is waiting for us to find and ask instead what modes of reading are productive. Since reading in this sense is, as I have suggested, so strongly bound up with questions about teaching, answers to the question "What modes of reading are productive?" will derive from an ethics and politics of literary pedagogy: from a sense about why we should teach texts, *which* we should teach, what this teaching is worth to our students, and so on. And what this notion suggests, of course, for the concerns of this talk is that we might seek to operate with a correlative notion of productive modes of translation.

Such an approach to translation – like the approach I have elsewhere suggested in the same pragmatist spirit to what literary scholars call "reading" – will depend on our having some sense of what our practice – of teaching or translating – is for. I have surreptitiously introduced assumptions about the kind of translation I am discussing by inventing what may have struck some of you as the artificial category of the literary translation. Actually this term might be used equally well to denote two rather different kinds of activity. I might have meant by it – though I did not – a translation that aims itself to be a literary work, a work worth teaching, a work whose value as an object of study depends very little on what it tells us about the culture from which the object-text it translates has come. Such translations – Fitzgerald's *Ruáiyát* as opposed to that of Peter Avery and John Heath-Stubbs – can be read as rewardingly as any literary works.

But I had in mind a different notion of a literary translation; that, namely, of a translation that aims to be of use in literary teaching; and here it seems to me that such "academic" translation, translation that seeks with its annotations and its accompanying glosses to locate the text in a rich cultural and linguistic context, is eminently worth doing. I have called this "thick translation"; and I shall say in a moment why. But before I do say *why*, I should like to say something about the purposes that I would urge for this sort of activity, the purposes by which its productivity may be judged.

Remember what I said at the start: utterances are the products of actions, which like all actions, are undertaken for reasons. Understanding the reasons characteristic of other cultures and (as an instance of this) other times is part of what our teaching is about: this is especially important because in the easy atmosphere of relativism – in the world of "that's just your opinion" that pervades the high schools that produce our students – one thing that can get entirely lost is the rich differences of human life in culture. One thing that needs to be challenged by our teaching is the confusion of relativism and tolerance so scandalously perpetuated by Allan Bloom, in his, the latest in a long succession of American jeremiad. And that, of course, is a task for my sort of teaching – philosophical teaching – and it is one I am happy to accept. But there is a role here for literary teaching also, in challenging this easy tolerance, which amounts not to a celebration of human variousness but to a refusal to attend to how various other people really are or were. A thick description of the context of literary production, a translation that draws on and creates that sort of understanding, meets the need to challenge ourselves and our students to go further, to undertake the harder project of a genuinely informed respect for others. Until we face up to difference, we cannot see what price tolerance is demanding of us.

In the American academy, therefore, the translation of African texts seems to me to need to be directed at least by such purposes as these: the urge to continue the repudiation of racism (and, at the same time, through explorations of feminist issues and women's writing, of sexism); the need to extend the American imagination – an imagination that regulates much of the world system economically and politically – beyond the narrow scope of the United States; the desire to develop views of the world elsewhere that respect more deeply the autonomy of the Other, views that are not generated solely by the legitimate but local political needs of America's multiple diasporas.

To stress such purposes in translation is to argue that, from the standpoint of an analysis of the current cultural situation — an analysis that is frankly political — certain purposes are productively served by the literary, the text-teaching, institutions of the academy. To offer our proverbs to American students is to invite them, by showing how sayings can be used within an oral culture to communicate in ways that are complex and subtle, to a deeper respect for the people of pre-industrial societies.

Let me end by saying that such a way of understanding reading and translating will make the question of how we should do it highly context-dependent; so that, to teach these proverbs in the English-speaking academy in Africa is a different matter yet again. If one believes that the kinds of cultural inferiority complexes represented in the attitudes of many African students need to be exorcised, then the teaching of "oral" literature in the Westernized academy in Africa will require an approach that does two crucial things: first, stress that the continuities between pre-colonial forms of cultural production and contemporary ones are genuine (and thus provide a modality through which students can value and incorporate the African past); second, challenge directly the assumption of the cultural superiority of the West, both by undermining the aestheticized conceptions of value that it presupposes, and by distinguishing sharply between a domain of technological skill in which — once goals are granted — comparisons of efficiency are possible, and a domain of value, in which such comparisons are by no means so unproblematic.[13] This final challenge — to the assumption of Western cultural superiority — requires us, in the last analysis, to expose the ways in which the systematic character of literary (and, more broadly, aesthetic) judgments of value is the product of certain institutional practices and not something that exists independently of those practices and institutions. But it requires, at the start, a thick and situated understanding of oral literatures of the sort for which I have, I am sure, provided only the barest hint of a sketch; the sort of understanding that will leave you able both to understand and understand the truth in the words with which I began:

Asém a éhia Akanfoö no na Ntafoö de goro brékété.

A matter which troubles the Akan people, the people of Gonja take to play the brékété drum.

Notes

1 Brékété is the (Akan) name of one of the main Dagomba drums, which accompanies dancing.
2 The most obvious thought suggested by this proverb is that if one has to choose among evils one should choose the least of them. (The proverb is typical of a whole class of proverbs that depend on playing with the similar-sounding names of dissimilar objects.)

3   Or one of the thoughts. The conventions allow for all kinds of ambiguity.

4   Putting it this way avoids taking sides on questions about whether or not our semantics should be one that assigns content in a broadly direct realist manner. I think that for many terms direct realism about contents is correct: but that is a separate issue here.

5   And, since epistemic authority in respect of one's own beliefs is normal, while the authority to command others assumes certain relations of power, the range of intentions one can intelligibly be held to have depends, in the case of commands, in part on what speaker and hearer know about their power-relations.

6   Of course the conventions may make the intentions depend on features of the context – what is perceptually salient, what has just been said, what time it is, and a whole host of more such features.

7   Philosophers will probably want at this point to suggest that the right way to proceed here is to insist on differences I have been blurring: between utterance-meaning and speaker-meaning; or between what is directly communicated and what indirectly; or between properties of the token-sentence and of the type. For them, let me say that in the ordinary cases these notions connect with those I have been using in the following way: the meaning of the token-utterance is the speaker-meaning conventionally associated with a standard unadorned utterance of the token when the contextual features conventionally determined as relevant are those of the actual context of utterance; the meaning of the type-utterance is the function from contexts to token-utterance meanings; the speaker-meaning conventionally associated with an utterance is fixed by the literal intentions associated with it, the intentions an utterer of the token unadorned and in standard circumstances is conventionally recognized as having.

8   This proverb would naturally be used in a context where someone has expressed vain regrets. The thought is something like this: that if you (the drongo) had known that one person (the palm-nuts) would prosper, you would not have relied on a person who was less successful (the crippled raffia-palm.)

9   Robert J. Fogelin, *Figuratively Speaking* (New Haven: Yale University Press, 1988).

10   John Guillory, "Canonical and Non-Canonical: A Critique of the Current Debate," *ELH* 54 (1987).

11   " 'The Teaching of Literature' is for me almost tautological. Literature is what is taught, that is all." "Reflections sur un manuel" in Tzvetan Todorov and Serge Doubrovsky, *Enseignement de la littérature* (Paris: Plon, 1971), 170.

12   "Out of Africa: Topologies of Nativism," *The Yale Journal of Criticism* 2.1 (1988): 153–78.

13   These are, in essence, the prescriptions of "Topologies of Nativism" (see above).

Chapter 28

Keith Harvey

TRANSLATING CAMP TALK: GAY IDENTITIES AND CULTURAL TRANSFER

CAMP IS REGULARLY ATTESTED in fictional representations of homosexual men's speech in French- and English-language texts from the 1940s to the present. What is more, camp talk is associated with a whole range of homosexual identities in French and English fiction, from the marginalized transvestite (Genet 1948), through to middle class "arty" types (Vidal 1948/65, Wilson 1952, Bory 1969), the post-Stonewall hedonistic "faggot" (Navarre 1976, Kramer 1978) and the politicized AIDS-aware "queer" (Kushner 1992). It could be assumed from this that when translating such fiction translators need merely to be aware of the comparable resources of camp in source and target language cultures. However, while the formal aspects of camp might appear constant, the functions that camp performs in its diverse contexts are far from uniform. I will argue later that one of the chief variables determining these functional differences is the conception of homosexuality as a defining property of identity. For the moment it is important to note that the functions of camp are intimately bound up with the question of its *evaluation*.

1 Formal and functional dimensions of camp

In order to open up the factor of evaluation to scrutiny, the functions of camp talk can usefully be broken down into two distinct (micro and macro) dimensions. First, the immediate fictional context of camp talk will often suggest whether it is to be given a positive or negative evaluative load. For example, a character such as

1998

Clarence in Jean-Louis Bory's novel *La Peau des Zèbres* (1969) is presented to the reader as a cynical, self-absorbed, emotionally stunted individual. His camp talk (he is the only homosexual character in the book to employ camp) is read in the novel as a key symptom of his limited affective potential. In contrast, Belize in Tony Kushner's play *Angels in America, Part One: Millennium Approaches* (1992) is presented as the main source of emotional and practical support for Prior, a young gay man dying of an AIDS-related illness. His camp is positively viewed in the play as a source of strength and much-needed humour. In both of these cases, the evaluation is located at a micro-functional fictional level. The macro-functional dimension taps into the wider (sub)cultural values that homosexual/gay identity has established for itself and within which the fictional text operates and develops its meanings. Bory's novel works hard to promote the notion of homosexual ordinariness. His characters love, suffer and live their lives just as heterosexual characters do in countless other love stories. They just happen to love people of the same sex. In this context, Clarence's camp talk is a macro-cultural trace of difference and marginality which it is deemed desirable to overcome. In contrast, Kushner's representations of camp at the micro level are instrumental in the elaboration of subcultural difference as a desirable goal. *Angels in America* presents camp as a sign of gay resistance and solidarity in the face of a whole array of threats to the gay individual and his community, from AIDS to the discriminations and hypocrises of the dominant culture. In Kushner's text, camp is invested with a political charge predicated upon an irreducible and subversive gay difference. Camp here, then, receives a positive evaluative load in both functional dimensions.

It is with this recognition of the double-layered nature of the evaluation of camp that the work of a translator reaches a key point of difficulty. For, while the micro-functional dimension of evaluation in a given source text might arguably be apparent to a translator, as to any attentive reader, recognition of the macro-functional dimension of camp will depend on a cluster of factors that go beyond close attention to the source text and involve cultural and even autobiographical issues for the translator. These issues include: (a) the existence, nature and visibility of *identities* and *communities* predicated upon same-sex object choice in the target culture; (b) the existence or absence of an established *gay literature* in the target culture; (c) the stated *gay objectives* (if retrievable) inherent in the undertaking of the translation and publication of the translation (for example, whether the text is to be part of a gay list of novels); (d) the *sexual identity* of the translator and his or her relation to a gay subcultural group, its identities, codes and political project. In what follows I wish above all to focus on the questions of homosexual/gay identities, communities and writing in source and target cultures and to attempt to link the existence of such pressures with the translated textual product.

I will begin by analysing an example of verbal camp in a contemporary English-language text, relating this to a general description of verbal camp. I will then outline some major accounts of camp as a cultural phenomenon by straight and gay-identified commentators before discussing two specific examples of camp and its translation, one from English to French and the other from French to English.

2 Verbal camp

A couple of related points need to be made briefly before looking at the example. The first concerns the specificity to the repertoire of camp talk of the features I identify. The second relates to the nature of the evidence I am considering. Rusty Barrett's (1995, 1997) enquiries into gay men's language practice are valuable in order to think through these issues. His use of Pratt's (1987) linguistics of contact is particularly useful.

In a contact model of language use, speakers "constitute each other relationally and in difference" (Pratt 1987: 60). This model contrasts with the more familiar "linguistics of community" present in dialectology, according to which essentially homogeneous language practices result from a consensual process of socialization of the individual by a community. As Barrett notes wryly, "Generally, people do not raise their children to talk like homosexuals" (1997: 191). A linguistics of contact would recognize the fact that gay men and lesbians work within and appropriate prevailing straight (and homophobic) discourses. Specifically, it would be able to account for gay speakers' frequent use of language practices associated with a whole range of communities "defined in terms of ethnicity, class, age, or regional background" (ibid.). For example, Barrett suggests that while white middle-class gay men may draw upon lexis identified with African-American vernacular speech (for example *girlfriend* and *Miss Thang*, often employed as vocatives) and upon the ritual insults associated with black speech events (see also Murray 1979, Leap 1996: 5–10), African American gay men might make use of those features of white woman's English that Lakoff (1975) suggested were typical, for example the careful discrimination of colour terms and the use of tag questions. This account points to a powerful citational fluidity in language styles that is consonant with Pratt's contact model. As Pratt herself notes: "A linguistics of contact will be deeply interested in processes of appropriation, penetration or co-optation of one group's language by another" (1987: 61).

This notion of "contact" in language practice is also useful in addressing the question of the status of the evidence in my description of camp talk. I am chiefly interested in literary representations, but occasionally reference is also made to work done in the sociolinguistics of actual language practice. There seems, however, to be little justification for mixing the two types of language. The evidence from each field of study appears, strictly speaking, to be inadmissible in the other. This conclusion itself turns out to rest upon an assumption that can be challenged, namely that whereas fictional representations of talk are *constructed* deliberately by an author for the purposes of character development and narrative advancement, real language use is a *reflection* of the sociolinguistic group(s) to which speakers belong. Barrett's account of the inherently citational nature of gay camp talk undermines the clear distinction between fictional representations of talk and real talk. Both, in this account, draw on a stock of language features that are invested with cultural (and stereotypical) values in order to achieve the *effect* of a specific communal identity: "For speakers who wish to use language in a way that will index a gay identity . . . the form of language often reflects a stereotype of gay men's speech" (Barrett 1997: 192). What counts, then, is not the empirically verifiable truth of the relation between a language feature and a speaker's identity, but the fact that these language features have come to stand for certain gendered and subcultural differences. Camp talk enlists these stereotypical differences in order to index a distinct sexual identity.

2.1 On the surface of camp

Tony Kushner's *Angels in America, Part One: Millennium Approaches* (1992; Act Two, Scene Five: 44) features a verbal exchange between two gay male characters, Belize and Prior. Belize is black and Prior white. They were once lovers. Belize used to be a drag queen. He is visiting Prior in hospital, where the latter is receiving care for an AIDS-related illness. Prior is referring to the fact that the drug he is being given causes him to hear "a voice". Belize has threatened to tell the doctor unless Prior does so himself:

> *Prior*: . . . You know what happens? When I hear it, I get hard.
> *Belize*: Oh my.
> *Prior*: Comme ça. (*He uses his arm to demonstrate.*) And you know I am
>   slow to rise.
> *Belize*: My jaw aches at the memory.
> *Prior*: And would you deny me this little solace – betray my concupis-
>   cence to Florence Nightingale's stormtroopers?
> *Belize*: Perish the thought, ma bébé.
> *Prior*: They'd change the drug just to spoil the fun.
> *Belize*: You and your boner can depend on me.
> *Prior*: Je t'adore, ma belle Nègre.
> *Belize*: All this girl-talk shit is politically incorrect, you know. We should
>   have dropped it back when we gave up drag.
> *Prior*: I'm sick, I get to be politically incorrect if it makes me feel better.

We can begin by noting that in this passage there are certain propositional features that are typical of gay camp talk. The preoccupation with sexual activity (the erection, fellatio) is often associated, as here, with references to extinct passion and a tragi-comic awareness of the ephemeral nature of sexual desire. Furthermore, in camp the talk of sex contrasts with an attentiveness to conventional moral codes of behaviour, with speakers often alluding to the principles of decency and rectitude to which they feign to adhere (for example Prior's suggestion that Belize could not possibly "betray" him). The incongruity inherent in the juxtaposition of a detailed interest in the mechanics of sex with a trumpeted adherence to traditional moral codes is one of the chief sources of irony in camp.

Turning to the formal level, this passage is rich with camp traits. The most obvious is the inversion of gender-specific terms, the "girl-talk" that Belize refers to. The practice of girl-talk overlaps with the camp strategy of renaming that includes the adoption of male names marked as "queer" – Quentin Crisp's name was *Denis* before he "dyed" it (Crisp 1968: 15) – and the disturbance of the arbitrary practice of attributing proper names – for example, Rechy's *Whorina* (Rechy 1963: 304) and *Miss Ogynist* (ibid.: 336). Lucas (1994: 132) gives evidence of how such queer renaming has a history that dates back at least to the eighteenth century in

Britain, while Pastre (1997: 372) shows how similar practices are at work in contemporary queer France. In the Kushner extract, the female terms combine with the use of French and are realized by feminine adjectives in vocative expressions (*ma bébé, ma belle* Nègre). The effect of such renaming is to signal the speaker's critical distance from the processes that produce and naturalize categories of identity. Because this opens up disjunctures between appearance and reality, the effect is also to undermine the schemata with which the addressee is operating. Thus, even a gay man has his perception of the world disturbed by a man who introduces himself as *Vicky* (Navarre 1976), or *Miss Rollarette* (Kramer 1978).

However, femininity is not only signalled in the text by such obvious lexical devices as names. The exclamative sentence *Oh my* is multiply determined as camp style and constitutes an example of what I would call the emphatics of camp, all of which contributes to camp's construction of the theatricalized woman. Alongside exclamations, these emphatics include a taste for hyperbole as well as the use of the "uninvolved" or "out of power" adjectives (*marvellous, adorable*) that Lakoff (1975: 11–14) claimed were typical of women's language. The imitative nature of emphatics is made clear by Crisp when describing a Mrs Longhurst he knew as a child: "This woman did not fly to extremes: she lived there. I also became an adept at this mode of talk and, with the passing of the years, came to speak in this way unconsciously" (Crisp 1968: 24). In this connection King (1994), citing the polemical book *The Phoenix of Sodom* (1813), notes how "talking like a woman" has been a feature of homosexual camp at least since London's eighteenth-century Molly Houses (where homosexual men met in secret to have sex). Once arrived in a Molly House, men affected "to speak, walk, talk, tattle, curtsy, cry, scold, & mimick all manner of effeminacy" (quoted in King 1994: 42). Furthermore, "every one was to talk of their Husbands & Children, one estolling [sic] the Virtues of her Husband, another the genius & wit of their Children: whilst a Third would express himself sorrowfully under the character of a Widow" (ibid.). The construction of a "woman" is clearly achieved through the parodic accumulation of stereotypical language features, such as those I term "emphatics".

However, the form of the exclamation "Oh my" in the Kushner extract does more than just suggest a generalized femininity. For a gay reader, it evokes a specific culturally situated and theatricalized type of femininity, namely the "Southern Belle" made famous by Vivien Leigh in *Gone With the Wind* – see also John Rechy's queens in *City of Night* (1963: 48, 287, 328), who often affect Southern accents. As such, the phrase builds into the text the type of intertextual reference to a major example of popular culture that is typical of gay talk. Leap (1996: 15), for example, traces a reference to film star Mae West's famous line "Why don't ya come up and see me some time" in an overheard discussion between a maitre d' and a potential customer, both of whom Leap assumes to be gay. In another reference to a famous film heroine, Maupin's (1980) novel *Tales of the City* includes this exchange between lovers Michael and Jon (Maupin 1980: 119):

> Michael shrugged. "I want to deceive him just long enough to make him want me."
>
> "What's that from?"
>
> "Blanche Dubois. In *Streetcar*."

Such intertextualities have at least two effects. First, they create ironic distance around all semiotic practice, constituting devices of "defamiliarization" (Fowler 1986: 40–52) and, in particular, signal a suspicion of all encodings of sincerity. Second, they reinforce gay solidarity between interlocutors. To understand the slang or catch on to the allusion is also to feel that one belongs to the community. (Note how Jon immediately identifies Michael's sentence as a quote in the extract above.)

Prior's lines "Comme ça" and "Je t'adore ma belle Nègre" draw on another of verbal camp's most consistent devices in English, the use of French. Clearly, this accomplishes a humorous nod to sophistication and cosmopolitanism, French language and culture being saturated for the Anglo-Saxon world with the qualities of style and urbanity. What is more, France is popularly known first and foremost for its consummate skills in the arts of *surface* refinement (fashion, perfume). The use of French, then, does not just decorate the text linguistically. Rather, it alludes to a complex of cultural values and stereotypes that carry decorativeness as an attribute. It is interesting to note that French camp, in a parallel gesture, resorts to the use of English words and phrases: "*Well, thank you very much, kind Sir* . . ." (Camus 1988: 64, italics in original); "C'est exciting!" (Navarre 1976: 177). While the English use of French signalled a kind of tongue-in-cheek sophistication, the French use of English here points (perhaps with equal ironic distance) to the spread of English-language popular culture across the world in the late twentieth century. Indeed, a phrase like "*Well, thank you very much, kind Sir*" suggests the intertextual reference to Hollywood heroines already noted. In other words. English in French camp also functions principally as a cultural, rather than merely linguistic sign.

Language games such as these may be characteristic of a type of critical semiotic awareness that is especially heightened in gay people, resulting from a long exclusion from mainstream signifying practices. But they may also signal a more defiant attitude to cultural norms, as Sullivan has suggested when noting that gay people show "in their ironic games with the dominant culture that something in them is ultimately immune to its control" (Sullivan 1996: 71–72). Comparable in its effect is the formal aspect of register-mixing that verbal gay camp typically delights in. Camp likes to expose the mechanisms at work in the choices speakers make with regard to appropriateness. Camp speakers, for example, will typically use levels of formality/informality that are incongruous in a particular context, or juxtapose different levels of formality in a way that creates linguistic incongruity. In Kramer's *Faggots*, a character (re-)named *Yootha* juxtaposes mock-literary and low registers to describe a sexual encounter with another man in a toilet: "He immediately inquires, 'how much?' I, *not expecting such bountiful tidings*, because I would have *done him for free* . . . I am saying 'My pleasure'" (Kramer 1978: 179: my italics). And Prior's rhetorical flourish ("And would you deny me this little solace – betray my concupiscence to Florence Nightingale's stormtroopers?") contrasts with his next utterance, an informal and unadorned expression of potential displeasure ("They'd change the drug just to spoil the fun"). Indeed, the whole exchange, based around sexual innuendo and wordplay, could be construed as highly inappropriate given Prior's rapidly declining health. However, as the last lines suggest, this inappropriateness also accomplishes an act of critical resistance.

2.2 Ambivalent solidarity and politeness theory

It is important to add to our description of this passage a consideration of a micro-functional feature that I would term *ambivalent solidarity*. This is a crucial interactive aspect of gay camp that can be obscured by an exclusively formal and taxonomic approach. Broadly, ambivalent solidarity revolves around the mechanisms of attack and support, either of which can be covert or on-record. Thus, two characters might feign support for each other by surface propositional and formal means while in fact attacking the other's sexual prowess or probity through innuendo and double-entendre, as in the conversation between the transvestites Divine and Mimosa in *Notre-Dame des Fleurs* (Genet 1948: 177–8). Crisp describes the stylized cattiness that was characteristic of gay get-togethers when he was younger as "a formal game of innuendoes about other people being older than they said, about their teeth being false and their hair being a wig. Such conversation was thought to be smart and very feminine" (Crisp 1968: 29). In the Kushner passage, there are elements of covert attack (e.g. Belize's mock complaint at Prior's slowness at getting an erection) alongside numerous on-record assurances of support and trustworthiness (e.g. Belize's "Perish the thought"). In contrast, gay characters might deploy the put-down as an on-record attack. White (1988: 42) gives the following example:

> We were all smiling. I was mute and ponderous beside my new compan-
> ions. I assumed each bit of repartee had been coined on the spot. Only
> later did I recognise that the routines made up a repertory, a sort of folk
> wisdom common to "queens", for hadn't Morris recklessly announced,
> "Grab your tiaras, girls, we're all royalty tonight, why I haven't seen so
> many crowned heads since Westminster Abbey –"
> 'I know you *give* head, Abbie, but the only crowns you've seen are
> on those few molars you've got left."

Here, the parting shot, though vicious, is in fact part of an elaborate game used to hone the tools of queer verbal self-defence and to reassert, albeit paradoxically, a communal belonging (see the pioneering work on gay insults by Murray 1979).

The pragmatic theory of politeness (Brown and Levinson 1987), with its key notion of the "face-threatening act", could usefully be brought to bear on this aspect of camp talk. According to politeness theory, all speakers have both negative and positive face-wants which they strive mutually to respect. Negative face-wants are based upon a desire not to be restricted in one's freedom of action. As a result, a speaker will mitigate the imposition implicit in the formulation of a request (the "face threat") by the encoding of an utterance that fronts deference. Camp talk threatens an addressee's negative face-wants with its on-record requests for soli-darity and support. Positive face-wants, in contrast, are based upon the desire to be appreciated and approved of. In Brown and Levinson's terms, camp can often be seen to involve threats to an addressee's positive face-wants by indicating that the speaker does not care about the addressee's positive self-image, hence, the insults, ridicule, put-downs etc. One small example will suffice to show the poten-tial of this approach to the analysis and its usefulness in describing translations. After a nocturnal sexual encounter in a public garden, the narrator of Camus' *Tricks* (1988: 70) meets an acquaintance on the cruising ground. This man comments:

– Tiens, Renaud, mais vous vous dévergondez! Qu'est-ce que vous faites là?

[Hey, Renaud, but you are getting into bad ways! What are you doing here?]

This remark constitutes a clear threat to the addressee's positive face-wants by casting aspersions on his behaviour. Yet it is overloaded with the ironies of ambivalent solidarity: first, the speaker could just as easily address the remark to himself (he, too, is on the cruising ground): second, the notion of "getting into bad ways" is one which both addressor and addressee know belongs to the moral code of the dominant culture. Through such a comment, this code is thus being mocked for the benefit of both addressor and addressee. It is interesting that the English translation (Howard 1996: 30) exaggerates the threat to the positive face-wants of the addressee:

"Hey, Renaud, you whore! What are you doing here?"

Here the face-threatening act is intensified by several means: whereas the source text encoded a comment on the moral behaviour of the addressee, the speech act here is a clear (grammatically moodless) insult: in the French, the speaker ironically affects moral superiority through the use of a term (se dévergonder) more usually associated with formal registers, while in the English the vulgarity of whore diminishes the speaker's claims to a superior moral stance: further, the use of whore exemplifies the typical camp move of employing a term usually reserved for women. The target text, then, amplifies the camp in several ways, but in doing so arguably loses some of the irony present in the source text's (feigned) encoding of moral censure. Politeness theory can be used to help identify exactly how shifts of this type might occur.

3 Camp, gay sensibility and queer radicalism

From Sontag (1964) to queer theorists of the 1990s, much of the work on camp has taken place within cultural studies, film studies and gay and lesbian studies. It has not, therefore, paid much attention to the detailed mechanisms of language. However, its insights are relevant to our purposes.

In "Notes on Camp", Sontag conceives of camp as a type of aesthetic sensibility that is characterized by a delight in "failed seriousness" and the "theatricalization of experience" (1964: 287). In order to explain the link between camp and homosexuals. Sontag suggests that the camp sensibility serves a propagandistic agenda for the homosexual cause: "Homosexuals have *pinned their integration* into society on promoting the aesthetic sense. Camp is a *solvent* of morality. It *neutralizes* moral indignation, sponsors playfulness" (ibid.: my emphases). It would seem reasonable to suggest that a bid for social integration by a minority group was political by nature. However, by insisting that camp is first and foremost "an aesthetic phenomenon" (ibid.), Sontag makes her view of it as "disengaged, depoliticized or at least apolitical" (ibid.) prevail to the detriment of any political potential. While also downplaying its political potential, Booth (1983: 17) nonetheless breaks with Sontag by asserting that "Camp is primarily a matter of self-presentation." He is thereby able to include a characterization of the verbal style of camp people in his account, noting characteristics that extend from the level of topic (marriage, "manly" sporting activities, etc.) to a specific manner of vocal delivery (ibid.: 67):

> A camp quality of voice may also express lassitude: the typical diction is slow almost to the point of expiration, with heavy emphasis on inappropriate words (lots of capital letters and italics) rising painfully to a climax, to be followed by a series of swift cadences – a sort of rollercoaster effect, which in Regency times was known as the "drawing room drawl".

The reference to "capital letters and italics" is interesting here. Booth is ostensibly talking about non-written camp "performance", yet the literary quality of this style suggests the presence of written-textual devices of emphasis. This confusion of different linguistic channels is in itself a testimony to the success of camp's deconstruction of the binarism "spoken/written" as an analogy of "natural/constructed".

As far back as the 1970s, gay-identified commentators argued that there were limitations to an exclusively aesthetic and depoliticized reading of camp practice (Dyer 1977, Babuscio 1977/1993). Babuscio, a historian, suggests that camp emerged as a gay response to contemporary society's penchant for "a method of labeling [that] ensures that individual types become polarized" (Babuscio, 1977/1993: 20–1). Thus, camp's critical mechanisms are specifically developed to mock, dodge and deconstruct the multiple binarisms in our society that stem from the postulation of the categories natural/unnatural. Using film texts for his examples, Babuscio suggests that gay camp deploys four linked strategies: irony; aestheticism; theatricality; humour. Irony is based upon the principle of "incongruous contrast between an individual or thing and its context or association". Babuscio suggests various examples of gender crossing through masquerade (e.g. Garbo in *Queen Christina*). In order to be effective, irony must be shaped. This is where the strategy of aestheticism comes into play. The camp emphasis on style deliberately "signifies performance rather than existence" (ibid.: 23). What is more, it leads typically to a deliberately exaggerated reliance on questions of (self-) presentation: "the emphasis shifts from what a thing or person *is* to what it *looks* like; from *what* is being done to *how* it is being done" (ibid.: 24). Theatricality in camp develops inevitably from its aestheticism. Babuscio's explanation for the gay deployment of theatricality takes its place in a long line of feminist critiques of the constructedness of gender roles (e.g. Millet 1971, Butler 1990):

> If "role" is defined as the appropriate behaviour associated with a given position in society, then gays do not conform to socially expected ways of behaving as men and women. Camp, by focusing on the outward appearances of role, implies that roles, and, in particular, sex roles, are superficial – a matter of style.
>
> (Babuscio 1977/1993: 24)

Humour, born of the ironic appreciation of incongruity, is the fourth of the features Babuscio mentions. Interestingly, it is with humour that Babuscio explicitly points up the political potential of camp. He writes of camp humour "undercutting rage by its derision of concentrated bitterness" (ibid.: 28). Calling camp a "protopolitical phenomenon", he notes moreover that it "steadfastly refuses to repudiate our long heritage of gay ghetto life" (ibid.). This gives rise to the typical inversion of values that camp revels in "even when this takes the form of finding beauty in the seemingly bizarre and outrageous, or discovering the worthiness in a thing or person that is supposedly without value" (ibid.).

If Babuscio recognized camp's political potential, then 1990s' queer Camp – written with an upper-case "C" when "conceptualized as a politicized, solely queer discourse" (Meyer 1994: 21, n. 2) – has gone much further. Not only has queer criticism redefined Camp as a central strategy in its exposure of the functioning of "straight" institutions and values, queer thinkers have used it to found the wider "ontological challenge" (ibid.: 2) of queer: "Queerness can be seen as an oppositional stance not simply to essentialist formations of gay and lesbian identities, but to a much wider application of the depth model of identity" (ibid.: 3). Queer's radical indeterminacy resides in its conception of identity as a pure effect of performance: 'at some time, the actor must *do* something in order to produce the social visibility by which the identity is manifested" (ibid.: 4). Language contributes actively to this elaboration of the effect of identity. Furthermore, the "performance paradigm" that Meyer inherits from Judith Butler's theory of gender means that contemporary sexual identities ultimately depend on "*extrasexual* performative gestures" (ibid.: 4, my emphasis). This is an important insight for understanding the way "gay" functions semiotically in contemporary culture. For, if the fact of sexual activity itself between people of the same gender appears to be the *sine qua non* for the (self-) attribution of the labels "gay" or "lesbian", it is also true that such activity is actually absent from view and only present through the work of other extrasexual signifying practices which thereby become linked to it metonymically.

In this play of surfaces feigning substance, it is hardly surprising that Camp should occupy a central place as the total body of performative practices and strategies used to enact a queer identity. Meyer's reading of Camp and its political potency is achieved through a deployment of Hutcheon's conception of parody as "an extended repetition with critical difference" (Hutcheon 1985: 7). Thus, parody (and, for Meyer, Camp) emerges as an essentially intertextual operation on the value that is invested in an original text. The traditional denigration of parody stems from an ideological position that endows the original with supreme cultural importance and suppresses any suggestion that the source is itself the outcome of an intertextual process. A re-evaluation of parody as a primary and pervasive cultural operation entails a reconsideration of the hierarchy of values that have hitherto marginalized it. Meyer suggests that Hutcheon's work is particularly useful for theorists of Camp if the factor of process rather than form is highlighted: "By employing a performance-oriented methodology that privileges process, we can restore a knowledgeable *queer* social agent to the discourse of Camp parody" (Meyer 1994: 10). In other words, a focus on the doer and the doing, and not the finished textual product, allows the queer theorist to highlight the neglected potential for cultural agency in the parodic moment: "the relationship between texts becomes simply an indicator of the power relationships between social agents who wield those texts, one who possesses the 'original', the other who possesses the parodic alternative" (ibid.).

Meyer's Camp is thus a kind of Trojan Horse penetrating the otherwise un-breachable preserve of straight semiotic practice, a necessarily parasitic enterprise that manages nonetheless to endow the voiceless queer with cultural agency. The required link to dominant practices is also helpful in explaining how different evaluations of Camp can be adhered to within the gay community: "Camp appears, on the one hand, to offer a transgressive vehicle yet, on the other, simultaneously invokes the specter of a dominant ideology" (ibid.). For some, the "specter of dominant ideology" embedded in Camp blocks its potential as an instrument of cultural critique and political action. Penelope and Wolfe (1979: 10, cited in Jacobs 1996: 62), for example, castigate the use of derogatory terms for women in the camp put-down because it endorses "the politics of patriarchy". In contrast, for Meyer himself the transgression inherent in Camp founds queer's suspicion of identity categories and constitutes the necessary backdrop for queer cultural agency.

4 Translations, transformations

I will now examine two extracts from novels that contain fictionalized camp talk and set them alongside their published translations. The first novel is Gore Vidal's *The City and the Pillar* (1948/1965), translated into French as *Un Garçon près de la Rivière* (1981) by Philippe Mikriammos. The second is Tony Duvert's *Paysage de Fantaisie* (1973), translated into English as *Strange Landscape* (1975) by Sam Flores. I will seek to show that in the first translation the camp is either minimized or deprived of its gay communal values. In contrast, the second translation fronts the gay camp elements and transforms the passage into one with a clear homosexual message. These textual facts will be related to the cultural contexts in which they were produced.

4.1 Vidal and Mikriammos: coming out in New York and Paris

In Vidal's 1965 Afterword to *The City and the Pillar* we are told that homosexual behaviour is entirely natural since "All human beings are bisexual" (Vidal 1948/1965: 157). However, Vidal insists that "of course there is no such thing as a homosexual"; the word is "not a noun describing a recognizable type" (ibid.). He thus deprives homosexuality of its claim to constitute a key element of identity in the same gesture as he legitimizes it. In one sense. Vidal's view is consistent with the description of the hero, Jim, an ordinary American male who can, and often does, pass as heterosexual. Nonetheless, the novel contains a portrait of well-established communities of men who certainly do identify as homosexuals. While it is true that the picture of these communities that emerges is far from positive (the men Jim meets at gay parties are often bitchy, jealous and small-minded), they do exist as a distinct social group. And their use of verbal camp is presented as one of their defining traits: Vidal notes that "their conversation was often cryptic", a "suggestive ritual" (ibid.: 46). Jim, the hero, does not contribute to camp, and is sometimes bored or made to feel uneasy by it. On the microcontextual level, then, camp receives a negative evaluation. However, one of the key features of camp is that it has irony at its own expense built into it. Through this irony, camp is often able to subvert the negative evaluation that might be loaded on to it. As a result, I contend, camp emerges in Vidal's novel – and despite its author's avowed intentions – as a macro-contextual sign of an established homosexual identity and community.

The extract I wish to examine is from a passage describing a party held in New York by Nicholas J. Rolloson (Rolly), a minor character. Jim has been taken to the party by his ex-lover, a film star called Shaw. By this time in the novel, Jim has had two important homosexual affairs and gay social life is not unfamiliar to him. Mikriammos's translation of the passage is reproduced immediately after Vidal's text.

> "You know, I loathe these screaming pansies," said Rolly, twisting an emerald and ruby ring. "I have a perfect weakness for men who are butch. I mean, after all, why be a queen if you like other queens, if you follow me? Luckily, nowadays everybody's *gay*, if you know what I mean . . . *literally* everybody! So different when I was a girl. Why, just a few days ago a friend of mine . . . well, I wouldn't go so far as to say a *friend*, actually I think he's rather *sinister*, but anyway this acquaintance was actually keeping Will Jepson, the *boxer*! Now, I mean, really, when things get that far, things have really gone far!"
>
> Jim agreed that things had indeed gone far. Rolly rather revolted him but he recognized that he meant to be kind and that was a good deal.
>
> "My, isn't it crowded in here? I love for people to enjoy themselves! I mean the right kind of people who appreciate this sort of thing. You see, I've become a Catholic."
>
> (Vidal 1948/65: 120)

> – Je déteste ces tantes si voyantes, s'exclama Rolloson en tournant la grosse bague de rubis et d'émeraudes qu'il portait à son doigt. J'ai un faible pour les garçons qui sont costauds. Je ne vois pas l'intérêt qu'il y a, pour nous autres tantes, à aimer les tantes! Vous me suivez? Heureusement, aujourd'hui, tout le monde en est: absolument tout le monde . . . Tellement différent du temps où j'étais une fille! Mon cher, il y a quleques jours un de mes amis, je ne devais pas dire un ami car je le trouve assez sinistre, mais enfin . . . cet ami m'a appris donc qu'il entretenait Will Jepson le boxeur! Quand les choses en sont là, c'est qu'elles sont déjà avancées!
>
> Jim dit qu'en effet la situation avait évolué. Rolloson le révoltait un peu mais il se disait que le bonhomme avait de bonnes intentions et que c'était très bien comme ça.
>
> – Quelle foule j'ai ce soir! J'adore voir les gens qui s'amusent . . . Enfin, je veux dire les gens qui vibrent comme nous . . . Vous savez que je viens de me convertir au catholicisme?
>
> (Mikriammos 1981: 152–3)

I will examine two groups of features in these texts: first, lexical and prosodic; second, textual and pragmatic.

In the English text, the lexis of Rolly's camp is rich with subcultural value, both at the level of individual items and that of collocation. For example, Rolly (he remains the more formal "Rolloson" throughout the translation) employs *pansies* with a pejorative meaning to describe other homosexuals and *queen* as an elected (albeit ironic) term to describe himself. Such uses concord with the values that gay men would still invest in these items today. The distinction, however, is flattened in the translation, where both terms are translated by *tante/s* (literally "aunt/s"), a pejorative term, even amongst French homosexuals. Rolly's ironic reflection on the vogue for *gay* is historically intriguing. Vidal could not have known in 1948 that this term was to play a crucial role as a definer of a distinct identity. However, *gay* in the translation (published, let us remind ourselves, in 1981) becomes the largely pejorative *en être* (literally, "to be of it/them"), a term which also effectively erases the sense of an emerging identity by employing a phrase that is void of lexical content, functioning entirely through implication. For French readers, *en être* is also likely to carry a Proustian resonance, being employed in *La recherche du temps perdu* to designate homosexual characters (e.g. Proust 1924: 17–18). This literary echo, far from reinforcing the idea of an identity/community across time, brings with it Proust's fundamental ambivalence with regard to homosexuality: in *La recherche* homosexual characters might be increasingly omnipresent, but they are nonetheless judged to be unfortunate victims of a moral flaw. Rolly's stock of subcultural signs is further impoverished by the translation of *butch* as *costauds* (literally, "stocky, well-built"). *Butch* is a long-standing member of the gay lexicon, usually employed (ironically) to designate the surface features of desirable masculinity, either of another gay man (who is not a "queen") or of a heterosexual male. In contrast, *costauds* is a mainstream French term that fails to connote the irony accruing to the gay awareness of gender performativity.

The source text also features collocations that are gay-marked. For example, *screaming pansies* is gay camp not primarily because of the noun (which could be employed as abuse by heterosexuals), but because of its collocation with *screaming*, an ironic/pejorative term indicating how out and flamboyant a particular gay man is. Despite its potential force as criticism, *screaming* also contains an element of approval when used by a gay man, suggesting as it does unmistakable gay visibility. The translation, *ces tantes si voyantes* (literally, "these (such) showy aunts") uses a term, *voyantes* ("showy"), that, again, is mainstream French and unambiguously pejorative. Another collocation, *perfect weakness*, also functions as camp in Rolly's talk. The use of *perfect* with *weakness* is marked hyperbole in general English, its quasi-oxymoronic quality suggesting the self-conscious intensity of the feeling being expressed. The translator makes no attempt to capture this and translates it simply as *faible* ("weakness"). Five other lexical items in this passage are realized in italics (*gay, literally, friend, sinister, boxer*), thereby contributing to the emphatics in which the collocation *perfect weakness* plays a part. This typographical feature is typical of representations of verbal camp in English. It exaggerates (and thereby renders susceptible to irony) the speaker's own investment in the propositional content of his speech. and helps to take the addressee – willingly or not – into his confidence. It thus binds together speaker and addressee in discoursal and subcultural solidarity. The stress patterns of French, as a syllable-timed language, do not allow this prosodic feature (and its written encoding) to the same degree.

The translator, therefore, has not used italics in this passage; neither does he attempt to compensate for the loss of this stylistic feature. As a result, Rolly's camp is diminished, as is the passage's construction of a clear type of homosexual identity.

It is also important to note the textual and pragmatic functions that the many co-operative discourse markers have in the text: for example: *You know; if you know what I mean; actually; Now, I mean, really* . . . As well as furthering the speaker's propositional stream, such terms act as a constant "involving" mechanism directed at the addressee. They are devices that crucially contribute to the gossipy tone of Rolly's talk. None of those co-operative markers just cited is translated in Mikriammos's text. With one notable exception, the French text downplays the verbal links that Rolly attempts to make with his fellow homosexual Jim. The exception is the translation of Rolly's exclamatory use of *Why* by *Mon cher* (literally, "My dear"), which might constitute an attempt at compensation. A final important example of the way a discourse marker such as *You see* can function is in Rolly's last comment: "I love for people to enjoy themselves! I mean the right kind of people who appreciate this sort of thing. You see, I've become a Catholic". The joke is excellent, Rolly suggesting that there is a causal link between his conversion to Catholicism and his desire for people to enjoy themselves at parties. The latter becomes thereby transformed into an act of Christian charity, with *You see* making the link. As is typical with camp, we cannot be entirely sure whether the speaker is intentionally sending himself up or whether the joke is at his expense. At any rate, it manages to ridicule and trivialize piety and the Church, a frequent butt of gay jokes. Mikriammos changes *You see* to "You know" and precedes it with suspension marks. The combined effect is not to suggest a causal link between Rolly's propositions, but rather to mark a topic change. The camp joke is thus missed.

How can the changes noted in the translation be explained? I would like to suggest that the translator has (inevitably, one might say) produced a text that harmonizes with the prevailing view of human subjectivity that obtains in his – the target – culture. Edmund White's (1997) suggestion that gayness – construed as a defining property of a distinct group of human beings – conflicts in France with the philosophy of the universal subject inherited from the Enlightenment can be useful here. Thus, in France there is a suspicion (even amongst those who practise "homosexual activity") of the validity of a subcultural label such as "gay". Indeed, the very imported nature of the term makes its use unstable, as is clear from a comment such as the following: "We can use the English spelling 'gay' *to stress its cultural meaning imported from the USA*, or the French spelling 'gai', with the same meaning" (Gais et Lesbiennes Branchés, Website 1995, English-language version; my italics). We are reminded here of Mikriammos' suppression of the item *gay* from his translation. This lack of a comfortable, home-grown label for the category reflects a more general reluctance in France to recognize the usefulness of identity categories as the springboard for political action. In his Preface to Camus' *Tricks* (1988), Barthes critiques the self-categorizing speech act predicated on "I am" for its implicit submission to the demands of the Other.

> Yet to proclaim yourself something is always to speak at the behest of a vengeful Other, to enter into his discourse, to argue with him, to seek from him a scrap of identity: "You are . . ." "Yes, I am . . ." Ultimately,

the attribute is of no importance; what society should not tolerate is that
I should be . . . *nothing*, or to be more exact, that the *something* that I
am should be openly expressed as provisional, revocable, insignificant,
inessential, in a word: irrelevant. Just say "I am", and you will be socially
saved.

(Barthes, in Howard 1996: vii)

Advocates of Anglo-American attempts to theorize and promote gay and lesbian
visibility would no doubt respond that *nothing* precisely identifies the dominant
culture's goal with regard to homosexual self-articulation; "nothing" and "irrelevance" have long been the nullifying conditions against which we struggle. The
relative reluctance of French homosexuals to self-identify according to the variable
of sexuality has direct implications for the construction of a subcultural community
based on sexual difference. It leads to scepticism of "la tentation communautaire"
("the temptation of the community", Martel 1996: 404), a symptom of the fear that
the construction of a distinct gay community would constitute a regrettable retreat
into separatism.

   Edmund White attributes a view such as Martel's to a specific Gallic conception of the relationship between the individual and the collective:

   The French believe that a society is not a federation of special interest
   groups but rather an impartial state that treats each citizen regardless of
   his or her gender, sexual orientation, religion or colour as an abstract,
   universal individual.

(White 1997: 343)

Thus, although some early French theoretical work in the field (e.g. Hocquenghem
1972) may still strike a chord today in Anglo-American queer thinking, there is
relative absence of radical gay (male) theorizing in contemporary France. Merrick
and Ragan (1996: 4) have noted the consequences this has had for research within
the French academy:

   [L]ess work has been done on the history of homosexuality in France
   than in some other Western countries . . . The emphasis on national
   identity has led to the downplaying of differences in race, sex, and sexual
   orientation . . . Figures like Gide and Yourcenar have been treated more
   as French writers, who happened to have sex with people of the same
   sex, than as homosexual writers per se.

The resulting consensus appears grounded in the view that, even if one were to
construe homosexuality as a key factor of identity, homosexuals would be well
advised to lay their hopes in the general progress of human rights that find their
origin in the universalizing Republican texts and events of 1789. This has led to an
attitude to issues of gay identity, history and community that appears conservative from the perspective of Britain and the USA. Camp, I have argued throughout
this paper, can be seen as a typical (indeed, perhaps as the key) semiotic resource
of gay men in their critique of straight society and in their attempt to carve out a

space for their difference. I would like to suggest that we see a significant textual consequence/realization of the French resistance to this view in Mikriammos' decision to avoid reproducing the gay verbal camp in Vidal's text.

4.2 Duvert and Flores: polymorphous perversity or gay sex?

If the identity category "gay" is problematic in France, it follows that the notions of gay writing and gay literature are also disabled in the French cultural polysystem by a universalizing tendency in the Gallic conception of subjectivity. White recalls an interview he gave in the early 1980s to a French gay magazine during which he "astonished" the journalist by telling him that "of course" he considered himself a "gay writer". He also remembers how in the mid-1980s all the male French writers who had been invited to an international gay literary conference in London "indignantly refused" to attend (White 1994: 277–8). This is put down to a resistance on the part of French writers to the perceived limitation that would be imposed upon their subjectivity, as well as their literary activity, by such a label. Instructive in this respect is Renaud Camus' rejection of the term "homosexual writer" in *Notes Achriennes* (1982; translated and quoted in Vercier 1996: 7):

> Nothing is so ridiculous as this concept of "homosexual writer", unless it's "Catholic writer", "Breton writer", "avant-garde writer". I already have trouble being a "writer". I'd rather be two or three of them or more than agree to being a "homosexual writer".

As a consequence, it could be argued that there is indeed no gay fiction in France: the immediate cultural and political identity necessary to give it momentum (both in terms of production and reception) is undermined by the resistance inherent in larger social and cultural factors. French fiction that treats aspects of homosexuality and "the homosexual condition" exists, of course. Of this, twentieth-century French literature has many examples (see Robinson 1995). However, this literature tends not to contribute to the articulation of a culture, identity and sensibility that is differently gay. In this context, it is not surprising that the figures, say, of the transvestite and the queen continue to be marginalized or downplayed in contemporary French writing and that their characteristic linguistic register, camp, fails to accrue the positive values it has gained in much Anglo-American work.

The work of Tony Duvert, though little commented upon in France (and barely read or translated outside France), gives us an insight into the vision of non-mainstream sexualities that has long existed amongst French "homosexual" writers such as Gide and Peyrefitte. No one could dispute that homosexuality is one of Duvert's chief preoccupations. However, in Duvert's novels and theoretical works (1974, 1980), homosexual activity takes place in the context of a larger interest in pre-pubescent and adolescent sexualities. Ultimately, Duvert's texts seek to explore and extend the human experience of sex and sexuality *per se*. He repeatedly returns to the theme of sexual relations between children and between children and adults. Although much of this activity is same-sex based, there is a clear sense in which it is the openness, polymorphousness and (to use a Duvertian word) "innocence" of children's interest in physical and sexual activity that is his central theme.

It is important when considering Duvert that the distinct universe of modern French writing on sexual diversity is attended to. Thus, so-called "pederastic literature" (Robinson 1995: 144–73) in French letters should not be conflated with the existence of a gay literature as this is understood in both British and American literary polysystems. Indeed, many Anglo-American writers would probably resist having their work on adult same-sex relations conflated with explorations of pederasty.

The passage from Duvert's work that I have chosen to comment upon here comes from *Paysage de Fantaisie* (1973), a strange visionary text which employs many of the techniques of the high *nouveau roman* to suggest fragmentary consciousness, shifting narrative points of view, and problematized identity. The action, such as it is, appears to take place in and around a boarding school/correction centre/hideaway for children and adolescents. Sexual games and activity are a central concern. In the following passage, a group of boys are role-playing the visit to a heterosexual brothel by several adult men who first have to negotiate with the Madam of the establishment before they can enjoy one of the girls for sale. This scene is interesting for its role-playing of sexual commerce, and also because it gives us a literary representation of male parody of women's talk, one of the key aspects of camp. (I have edited the source and target texts, reproduced here one after the other, so as to concentrate on the representations of direct speech. I have also italicized the speech of the Madam to facilitate readability. The lack of standard punctuation and the use of space between portions of text is, however, an original feature of source and target texts.)

> . . . la maquerelle un petit bavard comme une pie a chapeau de paille défoncé leur dit
>> *hélas mes beaux messieurs avez-vous quelque argent?*
>> c'est combien? demandent les garçons
>> *oh là là c'est cher cher!* . . .
>
> . . .
>
>> He la p'tite dame z'avez une putain qui met les bouts!
>> *oh la garce eh Jacky pourquoi tu joues plus?*
>> c'est la merde avec vos conneries j'vais dehors moi
>
> . . .
>
>> c'fille-là elle a des couilles madame dit un client . . .
>> *nos demoiselles des couilles pas du tout!* proteste la gérante et elle courait de gamin en gamin soulevant les jupes
>
> . . .
>
>> *baisez celle du milieu seulement hein* il me montrait . . .
>
> (Duvert 1973: 102–3)

> . . . the madam one of the smaller kids as gossipy as a magpie pinned to some old dame's bashed in gay nineties straw boater says
>> *alas my good sirs have you enough money?*
>> how much is it? asks one of the boys
>> *dearie dearie me it's not cheap oh no not for any of my darling girls!* . . .
>
> . . .
>
>> Hey madame you've a whore here who's cutting out!

oh that bitch hey there Simon why aren't you playing with us anymore?

you're all full of shit that's what you are with all your stupid asshole fairy games I'm going out for a walk

. . .

hey this floozy here has got balls says one of the clients to the twittering madam

one of my young lovelies sporting balls really sir you must cease this vulgarity instantly! the madam gives a toss to her head then runs from lady to lady lifting skirts

. . .

then I'll fuck that one lying there in the middle   he pointed at me

(Flores 1975: 111–12)

There is evident camp here in the source text Madam's utterances. Three main camp features can be mentioned: (a) a readiness with feigned outrage, expressed through exclamations (*oh*) and the presence of exclamation marks; (b) a playfulness with archaic linguistic register, as in *hélas mes beaux messieurs* (literally, "alas my handsome sirs"), the interrogative inversion of *avez-vous* and the use of *quelque*, instead of the partitive article, to modify *argent* ("money"). This contrasts with the coarseness of *la garce* ("the bitch") and the sexual explicitness of *des couilles* ("balls"); (c) the self-conscious teasing and seductiveness of the dispreferred response to the boys' direct question *c'est combien* ("how much is it?"): *oh là là c'est cher cher!* (literally, "oh la la it's expensive expensive"). This response only in fact replies to the question by pre-empting the outraged response that the men will probably have when told how expensive it is. It is an acute comment on the differential power factor at work in a dialogue that is part business deal, part sexual politics.

Flores's translation transfers much of the camp. It also significantly transforms Duvert's text in two ways: first, the Madam's camp is intensified and made still more theatrical; second, the scene becomes one of homosexual seduction and less a playing out of childish curiosity with sexual roles and boundaries. In short, Flores's text is "gayed". How is this achieved textually? The main strategy is that of additions to source text material. For example, the Madam is introduced in the French text as wearing *un chapeau de paille défoncé* (literally, "a bashed-in straw hat"). The translation carries out a transformation here by suggesting that the source text's "pie" ("magpie") is itself "pinned to . . . [a] straw boater". More significant is the presence in this sentence of two added details, neither of which appears motivated by the source text: (a) *some old dame* (modifying *straw boater*) functions metonymically to reinforce the element of gender parody; (b) *gay nineties*, through the presence of the dangerously homonymic *gay*, sets off a subtheme that becomes explicit by the end of the passage. The gender roles parody is further reinforced by the addition of *oh no not for any of my darling girls* to the Madam's *dearie dearie me it's not cheap*. Later additions include, *really sir you must cease this vulgarity instantly*, further developing the feigned outrage of the "woman", and *the madam gives a toss of her head* (for *proteste la gérante*: literally "protests the manageress") before *then runs from lady to lady* (for *elle courait de gamin en gamin*: literally, "she ran from boy to boy"). The cumulative effect of these additions is to heighten the factor of performance in the gender roles and to intensify the theatricality of the Madam.

The other trend I mentioned is that of the fronting of homosexual seduction. This is contextualized and facilitated by the intensified theatricalization of the Madam's drag. Indeed, in this connection the addition to the target text of the adjective *twittering* to describe the Madam is significant, as the metaphor of bird (and other animal) noises is often applied to the speech of homosexual men – especially camp ones – in both source and target cultures (cf. Crisp 1968: 84, Duvert 1969: 52, Green 1974: 45). The presence of *twittering*, like that of *gay*, sets off suggestive resonances of homosexual identity that are not present in the source text. The manifestation of this identity becomes explicit when one of the boys refuses to play, complaining: *you're all full of shit that's what you are with your stupid asshole fairy games* (for *c'est la merde avec vos conneries*: literally, "it's shit with your cunt-stupidities"). The addition of *stupid asshole fairy games* makes clear Flores's homosexual reading of the source text. The references to anality and to sexual deviance suddenly transform the scene into an elaborate excuse for male–male intercourse, and thereby deflect from a reading that prioritizes the polymorphous explorations of children. This gaying of the text culminates in a decisive transformation:

> then I'll fuck that one lying there in the middle   he pointed at me.

Here, a crucial element of agency is attributed to the boy who utters the phrase (beginning "I") and then points at the narrator (another boy). This rewrites the source text's:

> baisez celle du milieu seulement hein il me montrait
> (lit.: just fuck the one [female] in the middle hey? he pointed at me)

In the source text it is the Madam who gives an imperative and maintains the fiction of the heterosexual role-playing with *celle* ("the one" [female]). Later in this scene, when two boys actually do sneak off for gay sex, their activity appears in the source text to be yet another experiment in pre-adult sexual activity. In the target text, their same-sex activity is already contextualized and prepared for by the homoeroticism in Flores's reading of the role-playing.

In the light of the transformations in Flores's text, it may be considered unlikely that Duvert himself played any role in producing the translation. However, in a Translator's Note at the front of the book. Flores writes: "I would like to thank the author, Tony Duvert, for his Job-like patience in dealing with my many queries concerning his text, and also for replying so lengthily to them." Although this does not prove that Duvert read (or understood) the whole of the translation, it certainly puts us on our guard against concluding that Flores was able to take unwarranted and unsanctioned liberties with the text. We are permitted then to surmise that perhaps Duvert both understood and approved of the English version. One might suggest that this is because Duvert, as a relatively marginalized and untranslated author, would be pleased with any translation into another language of his work, whatever the quality. Perhaps a more serious suggestion would be that Duvert was aware of the emerging movement of homosexual liberation in the USA in the mid-1970s, and also of the contribution that a gay literature could make to such a movement. Through gay liberation Duvert may have hoped that the message in his books with regard to child sexuality would receive a better reception in the USA by becoming caught up in the general sweep of a sexual revolution that was led by adult homosexuals. In this context, it may be argued that he was willing for his work to undergo the textual interventions deemed suitable in order for it to join this incipient social, cultural and literary movement (to be "gayed", in short). It is also worth noting that Grove Press, who published *Strange Landscape*, has consistently championed gay writing over the years (Pulsifer 1994: 216). By 1975 their gay list may already have been taking shape. A gay text, in the American sense, would have been just what they were looking for from Duvert's writing. Flores, in short, was responding to these combined (sub)cultural and commercial pressures.

5 Concluding remarks: texts and contexts in translation studies

I have sought to establish how a verbal style, camp, is linked with the delineation of homosexual male characters in French- and English-language fiction and, further, how the translation of this style in its fictional settings reveals the effects of constraints and priorities of differing cultural settings. Specifically, I have suggested that the changes, omissions and additions present in two translated texts can be illuminated by recourse to debates on sexual identity and to the literary systems operational in French and Anglo-American contexts.

It would be disingenuous of me to say at this point that any uncertainty discernible in my conclusions (the hedges, *mights* and *maybes* of the preceding paragraphs) is due primarily to the "work-in-progress" nature of this paper. The problems this uncertainty raises are much more fundamental and threaten to disable attempts to *explain* (as opposed to merely *describe*) the data offered. They are a consequence, I believe, of crucial theoretical and methodological issues currently confronting translation studies, namely the need to make explicit the imbrication of texts and contexts. Translation is not just about texts: nor is it only about cultures and power. It is about the relation of the one to the other. In this respect, translation studies is not unlike critical linguistics, the branch of contemporary language study that has grown out of the fusion of functional-systemic linguistics and critical theory. Critical linguistics is also struggling to produce paradigms that will allow it to relate the minutiae of textual analysis to the interactional, social and political contexts that produce language forms and upon which those language forms operate. As Fowler has recently put it, it is now time for the critical linguist "to take a professionally responsible attitude towards the analysis of context" in order to avoid an overreliance on "intersubjective intuitions" and on "informal accounts of relevant contexts and institutions" (Fowler 1996: 10; see also Fairclough 1992: 62–100). Much the same could be said to the scholar of translation.

What is required, then, in translation studies is a methodology that neither prioritizes broad concerns with power, ideology and patronage to the detriment of the need to examine representative examples of text, nor contents itself with detailed text-linguistic analysis while making do with sketchy and generalized notions of context. Specifically with regard to my work, many more instances of camp talk call for description in order to bring out the trends not only between

French, British and American texts, but also between texts from different periods (e.g. pre- and post- the AIDS crisis), between texts that fictionally represent different social strata, and also texts that demonstrate different literary aspirations. It is important, in other words, to maintain the notion of camp as a potentially plural one, remaining alert to its textual inflections and variations. This is the close text-linguistic branch of the work. However, macro-cultural trends also crucially need to be kept in view and related to the textual descriptions in a heuristically satisfying manner. Ultimately, these trends alone are able to offer us convincing explanations of how a text comes to mean in its context, of what value a text accrues as a sign, be it of a postulated universal subjectivity or an irreducible subcultural difference. The challenge is to find a way not just to *situate* discourse in its inter-actional and cultural settings, but to give the relationship between setting and discourse the force of causality.

Acknowledgements

I am very grateful to the following people for their encouragement and criticism during the writing of this paper, as well as for opportunities to discuss the material in workshops and seminars: Mona Baker, Jean Boase-Beier, Peter Bush, Roger Fowler, Lawrence Venuti. I would like to thank Christopher Robinson for pointing out the Proustian resonance of *en être*, discussed on page 414.

Chapter 29

Jacques Derrida

WHAT IS A "RELEVANT" TRANSLATION?

Translated by Lawrence Venuti

Then must the Jew be merciful.
(I leave untranslated this sentence from Portia in *The Merchant of Venice*.)
Portia will also say, *When mercy seasons justice*, which I shall later propose
to translate as *Quand le pardon relève la justice* . . .

HOW DARE ONE SPEAK of translation before you who, in your vigi-
lant awareness of the immense stakes – and not only of the fate of literature
– make this sublime and impossible task your desire, your anxiety, your travail,
your knowledge, and your knowing skill?[1]

How dare I proceed before you, knowing myself to be at once rude and inex-
perienced in this domain, as someone who, from the very first moment, from his
very first attempts (which I could recount to you, as the English saying goes, *off the
record*), shunned the translator's métier, his beautiful and terrifying responsibility,
his insolvent duty and debt, without ceasing to tell himself "never ever again":
"no, precisely, I would *never* dare, I should *never*, could *never*, would *never* manage
to pull it off"?

If I dare approach this subject before you, it is because this very discourage-
ment, this premature renunciation of which I speak and from which I set out, this
declaration of insolvency before translation was always, in me, the other face of a
jealous and admiring love, a passion for what summons, loves, provokes and defies
translation while running up an infinite debt in its service, an admiration for those
men and women who, to my mind, are the only ones who know how to read

and write – translators. Which is another way of recognizing a summons to translation at the very threshold of all reading–writing. Hence the infinity of the loss,
the insolvent debt. Much like what is owed to Shylock, insolvency itself. Speaking,
teaching, writing (which I also consider my profession and which, after all, like
many here among you, engages me body and soul almost constantly) – I know that
these activities are meaningful in my eyes only in the proof of translation, through
an experience that I will never distinguish from experimentation. As for the word
(for the word will be my theme) – neither grammar nor lexicon hold an interest
for me – I believe I can say that if I love the word, it is only in the body of its
idiomatic singularity, that is, where a passion for translation comes to lick it as a
flame or an amorous tongue might: approaching as closely as possible while refusing
at the last moment to threaten or to reduce, to consume or to consummate, leaving
the other body intact but not without causing the other to appear – on the very
brink of this refusal or withdrawal – and after having aroused or excited a desire
for the idiom, for the unique body of the other, in the flame's flicker or through a
tongue's caress. I don't know how, or in how many languages, you can translate
this word *lécher* when you wish to say that one language licks another, like a flame
or a caress.

But I won't put off any longer saying "merci" to you, in a word, addressing this
mercy to you in more than (and no longer) one language.

For no sooner will I have thanked you for the hospitality with which you honor
me than I will need to ask your forgiveness and, in expressing my gratitude [*grâce*]
to you, beg your pardon [*grâce*], ask you to be *merciful* to me. For your part, forgive
me from the outset for availing myself of this word *merciful* as if it were a citation.
I'm *mentioning* it as much as I'm *using* it, as a speech act theorist might say, a bit
too confident in the now canonical distinction between *mention* and *use*.

In other words, I certainly won't delay in thanking you for the signal honor
you have accorded me, but also, via this word of gratitude and *mercy*, in asking your
forgiveness for all the limits, starting with my own inadequacies, which hinder me
from measuring up to it. As for my inadequacies, I will no doubt make a vain effort
to dissemble them with contrivances more or less naively perverse.

Before these thanks rendered, this pardon begged, I must first acknowledge a
defect of language that could well be a breach in the laws of hospitality. In effect,
is it not the first duty of the *guest* [*hôte*] that I am to speak a language that is intelligible and transparent, hence without equivocation? And therefore to speak a single
language, namely that of the addressee, here of the *host* [*hôte*], a language especially
designed for whoever must and can understand it, a language that is shared, like
the very language of the other, that of the other to whom one addresses it, or at
the very least a language that the listener or reader can make his or her own?
A language that is, in a word, translatable?

Now, here is one of the admissions that I owe you on several scores. First, on
the score of my title and on the score of speaking, as I shall do in a moment, about
my title in an entirely untranslatable manner. Admitting more than one failure, I
confess this double inadequacy that is all the more impossible to avoid because it
bears a self-contradiction: if I need to address you in a single language, French
(thereby recognizing that every so-called discourse *on* translation, every metalanguage or meta-theorem on the topic of translation is fated to inscribe itself within

the limits and possibilities of a single idiom), I am nevertheless always already inclined to leap over this language, my own, and I shall do it again, thus leaving undecided the question of a simple choice between language and metalanguage, between one language and another. At the word go we are within the multiplicity of languages and the impurity of the limit.

Why would my title remain forever untranslatable? In the first place, because one can't decide the source language to which it is answerable [*relève*]; nor, therefore, in what sense it travails, *travels*, between *hôte* and *hôte*, *guest* and *host*.

It is impossible to decide the source language to which, for example, the word "relevante" answers [*relève*], a word that I leave within quotation marks for now. Nor the language to which it belongs at the moment when I use it, in the syntagms or the phrases where I move to reinscribe it. Does this word speak one and the same language, *in* one and the same language? At the same time, we don't even know if it is really one word, a single word with a single meaning, or if, homonym or homophone of itself, it constitutes more than one word in one.

What I shall propose to you under this title ("What is a 'relevant' translation?"), undoubtedly short of any reflection worthy of this word about the word, about the unity of the word in general, will perhaps be a more modest and *laborious* approach, on the basis of a single word, the word "relevant." I underline *laborious* to announce several words in *tr.* and to indicate that the motif of *labour* [*travail*], the *tr*avail of childbirth, but also the *transferential* and *transformational tr*avail, in all possible codes and not only those of psychoanalysis, will enter into competition with the apparently more neutral motif of translation, as *transaction* and as *transfer*. We shall then wind up revolving around a single example, a punning example, if there is such a thing, and if the word "relevant" may be one, unique, solitary, at once an adjectival and verbal form, a sort of present participle that becomes an epithet or predicate.

What of this vocable "relevant"? It possesses all the traits of the linguistic unity that one familiarly calls a word, a verbal body. We often forget, in this same familiarity, how the unity or identity, the independence of the word remains a mysterious thing, precarious, not quite natural, that is to say historical, institutional, and conventional. There is no such thing as a word in nature. Well, this word "relevant" carries in its body an on-going process of translation, as I will try to show; as a translative body, it endures or exhibits translation as the memory or stigmata of suffering [*passion*] or, hovering above it, as an aura or halo. This translative body is in the process of being imported into the French language, in the act of crossing borders and being checked at several intra-European customs points that are not only Franco-English, as one might infer from the fact that this word of Latin origin is now rather English (*relevant/irrelevant*) in its current usage, in its use-value, in its circulation or its *currency*, even though it is also in the process of Frenchification. This acculturation, this Frenchification is not *strictu senso* a translation. The word is not only *in* translation, as one would say in the works or in transit, *traveling*, *travailing*, in *labor*. In my proposed title, it serves, through a supplementary fold, to qualify translation, as well as what a translation might be *obliged* to be, namely *relevant*.

Those of you who are familiar with English perhaps already understand the word as a domestication, an implicit Frenchification [*francisation*] or – dare I say? – a more or less tacit and clandestine enfranchisement [*l'affranchissement*] of the English adjective *relevant*, which would have thus passed into our language with bag and baggage, with its predicates of denotation and connotation. The French feminine of this word ("une traduction *relevante*") sounds even more English and takes us back to the signature and the sexual difference at stake wherever translation or translators (in the masculine or feminine) are involved.

What is most often called "relevant"? Well, whatever feels right, whatever seems pertinent, apropos, welcome, appropriate, opportune, justified, well-suited or adjusted, coming right at the moment when you expect it – or corresponding as is necessary to the object to which the so-called relevant action relates: the relevant discourse, the relevant proposition, the relevant decision, the relevant translation. A relevant translation would therefore be, quite simply, a "good" translation, a translation that does what one expects of it, in short, a version that performs its mission, honors its debt and does its job or its duty while inscribing in the receiving language the most *relevant* equivalent for an original, the language that is *the most* right, appropriate, pertinent, adequate, opportune, pointed, univocal, idiomatic, and so on. *The most* possible, and this superlative puts us on the trail of an "economy" with which we shall have to reckon.

The verb *relever* brings me back to a modest but effective experiment in translation in which I have found myself engaged for more than thirty years, almost continuously, first between German and French, then more recently between English and French. That this same French word (the very same word, assuming that it is the very same word, and that henceforth it is French through and through), that this same word could have thus operated, in a single language, between three languages, so as to "translate," or in any case to put to *work* different words belonging to apparently different contexts in at least two other source languages (German and English) – this fact seems an incalculable stroke of luck, an invention or necessity for which I wonder who can bear the responsibility, even if it was apparently mine at first and mine to sign. I harbor no illusion or pretension in this respect: if I took the initiative in these quasi-translations, I could do so only to hear, in order to record, various possibilities or laws – semantic and formal – already inscribed in this family of languages and, first and foremost, in "my" language. In any case, because the happy coincidence in question has since then become somewhat more familiar to me, because I feel less exposed – in my incompetence – to the risk of saying highly irrelevant things about translation in general before the expert scholars and accomplished professionals that you are, I have therefore preferred to suggest that we prowl around a small word and follow it like a "go-between" rather than engage anew, on the level of generality, in theoretical or more obviously philosophical or speculative reflections which I have elsewhere ventured on various universal problems of Translation, in the wake of Walter Benjamin, James Joyce, and several others.

And perhaps I should then confess under this very heading, thus pleading guilty without extenuating circumstances, that I chose my title precisely because of its untranslatability, premeditating my crime in this way, conspiring to insure the apparent untranslatability of my title through a single word, a word wherein I sign, in an idiom that is something like my signature, the theme of this lecture, which will therefore resemble a seal that, cowardice or arrogance, would abridge itself into my initials.

What remains is that – trust me – I don't transgress a code of decency or modesty through a provocative challenge, but through a trial: by submitting the experience of translation to the trial of the untranslatable.

As a matter of fact, I don't believe that anything can ever be untranslatable – or, moreover, translatable.

How can one dare say that nothing is translatable and, by the same token, that nothing is untranslatable? To what concept of translation must one appeal to prevent this axiom from seeming simply unintelligible and contradictory: "nothing is translatable; nothing is untranslatable"? To the condition of a certain *economy* that relates the translatable to the untranslatable, not as the same to the other, but as same to same or other to other. Here "economy" signifies two things, *property* and *quantity*: *on the one hand*, what concerns the law of *property* (*oikonomia*, the law – *nomos* – of the *oikos*, of what is proper, appropriate to itself, at home – and translation is always an attempt at appropriation that aims to transport home, in its language, in the most appropriate way possible, in the most relevant way possible, the most proper meaning of the original text, even if this is the proper meaning of a figure, metaphor, metonymy, catachresis or undecidable impropriety) and, *on the other hand*, a law of *quantity* – when one speaks of economy, one always speaks of calculable quantity. *On compte et on rend compte*, one counts and accounts for. A relevant translation is a translation whose economy, in these two senses, is the best possible, the most appropriating and the most appropriate possible.

How does a *principle of economy* permit one to say two apparently contradictory things at the same time (1. "Nothing is translatable"; 2. "Everything is translatable") while confirming the experience that I suppose is so common to us as to be beyond any possible dispute, namely, that any given translation, whether the best or the worst, actually stands between the two, between absolute relevance, the most appropriate, adequate, univocal transparency, and the most aberrant and opaque irrelevance? To understand what this economy of in-betweenness signifies, it is necessary to imagine two extreme hypotheses, the following two hyperboles: if to a translator who is fully competent in at least two languages and two cultures, two cultural memories with the sociohistorical knowledge embodied in them, you give all the time in the world, as well as the words needed to explicate, clarify, and teach the semantic content and forms of the text to be translated, there is no reason for him to encounter the untranslatable or a remainder in his work. If you give someone who is competent an entire book, filled with *translator's notes*, in order to explain everything that a phrase of two or three words can mean in its particular form (for example, the *he war* from *Finnegans Wake*, which has occupied me in another place,[2] or else *mercy seasons justice* from *The Merchant of Venice*, which we shall discuss below), there is really no reason, in principle, for him to fail to render – without any remainder – the intentions, meaning, denotations, connotations and semantic overdeterminations, the formal effects of what is called the original. Of course, this operation, which occurs daily in the university and in literary criticism, is not what is called a translation, a translation worthy of the name, translation in the strict sense, the translation of a *work*. To make legitimate use of the word "translation" (*traduction*, *Übersetzung*, *traducción*, *translaciôn*, and so forth), in the rigorous sense conferred on it over several centuries by a long and complex history in a given cultural situation (more precisely, more narrowly, in Abrahamic and post-Lutheran Europe), the translation must be *quantitatively* equivalent to the original, apart from any paraphrase, explication, explicitation, analysis, and the like. Here I am not speaking of quantity in general or of quantity in the prosodic sense (meter, rhythm, cæsura, rhyme – all the classic constraints and limits that are in principle and in fact insurmountable by translation). I also deliberately set aside all sorts of phenomena – quite interesting, as a matter of fact – due to which this form of quantitative equivalence is never rigorously approachable. It has been recognized that certain languages with a tendency toward excessively long constructions take them much farther in translation. No translation will ever reduce this quantitative or, in a Kantian sense, this aesthetic difference, since it concerns the spatial and temporal forms of sensibility. But this will not be my point. No, what matters to me more and today in particular, in this quantitative law, in this economy, is the unit of measurement that governs at once the classic concept of translation and the calculus that informs it. This quantitative unit of measurement is not in itself quantitative; it is rather qualitative in a certain sense. It is not a question of measuring a homogeneous space or the weight of a book, nor even of yielding to an arithmetic of signs and letters; it is not a question of counting the number of signs, signifiers or signifieds, but of counting the *number of words*, of lexical units called "words." The unit of measurement is the unit of the word. The philosophy of translation, the ethics of translation – if translation does in fact have these things – *today* aspires to be a philosophy of the word, a linguistics or ethics of the word. At the beginning of translation is the word. Nothing is less innocent, pleonastic and natural, nothing is more historical than this proposition, even if it seems too obvious. This has not always been the case, as you well know. As it was formulated, among others, by Cicero, I believe, to watch impassively over subsequent developments, to watch over a turbulent and differentiated history of translation, of its practices and its norms, the first imperative of translation was most certainly not the command of "word to word." In *De optimo genere oratorum*, Cicero freed translation from its obligation to the *verbum*, its debt to word-for-word. The operation that consists of converting, turning (*convertere, vertere, transvertere*) doesn't have to take a text at its word or to take the word literally. It suffices to transmit the idea, the figure, the force. And the slogan of St. Jerome, who with Luther was one of the fathers of a certain translation ethics, an ethics that survives even if it is contested in our modernity, is *non verbum e verbo, sed sensum exprimere de sensu* [to express not word by word, but sense by sense]. He was speaking just as much of translating the Greeks as of translating the Holy Scriptures, even if he had been tempted to make an exception for the "mysterious order of words" (*verborum ordo mysterium*)[3] in the Bible. In recent times, for scarcely a few centuries, a so-called literal translation that aims to attain the greatest possible relevance hasn't been a translation that renders letters or even only what is placidly termed the sense, but rather a translation that, while rendering the so-called proper meaning of a word, its literal meaning (which is to say a meaning that is determinable and not figural), establishes as the law or ideal – even if it remains inaccessible – a kind of translating that is not *word-to-word*, certainly, or *word-for-word*, but nonetheless stays as close as possible to the equivalence of "one word *by* one word" and thereby respects verbal quantity as a quantity of words, each of which is an irreducible body, the indivisible unity of an acoustic form incorporating or signifying the indivisible unity of a meaning or concept. This is why, whenever several words occur in one or the same acoustic or graphic form, whenever a *homophonic* or *homonymic effect* occurs, translation in the strict, traditional and dominant sense of the term encounters an insurmountable limit – and the beginning of its end, the figure of its ruin (but perhaps a translation is devoted to ruin, to that form of memory or commemoration that is called a ruin; ruin is perhaps its vocation and a destiny that it accepts from the very outset). A homonym or homophone is never translatable word-to-word. It is necessary either to resign oneself to losing the effect, the economy, the strategy (and this loss can be enormous) or to add a gloss, of the translator's note sort, which always, even in the best of cases, the case of the greatest relevance, confesses the impotence or failure of the translation. While indicating that the meaning and formal effects of the text haven't escaped the translator and can therefore be brought to the reader's attention, the translator's note breaks with what I call the economic law of the word, which defines the essence of translation in the strict sense, the normal, normalized, pertinent, or relevant translation. Wherever the unity of the word is threatened or put into question, it is not only the operation of translation which finds itself compromised; it is also the concept, the definition, and the very axiomatics, the idea of translation that must be reconsidered.

In saying these things, I have gotten ahead of myself, formalized too quickly, proceeded to an unintelligible economy. What I have just said undoubtedly still remains untranslatable. I shall slow down, then, and start over.

You might ask to what language the word *relevante* belongs. It is one of those English words that, in a confused and irregular way, is in the process of winning both use-value and exchange-value in French without ever having been, to my knowledge, officially sanctioned through the institutional channels of any academy. On this score, it represents one of those words whose use floats between several languages (there are more and more examples of them) and that merits an analysis that is at once linguistic and sociological, political and especially historical, wherever the phenomena of hegemony thus come to inscribe their signature on the body of a kind of idiom that is European or indeed universal in character (that it may in the first place be European, moreover, far from excludes the fact that it is spreading universally, and that it involves a vast question of translation without translators, if I can put it this way, although I must set it aside, like so many previous questions, for want of time).

This word "relevant," this present participle that functions as a predicate, is here entrusted with an exorbitant task. Not the task of the translator, but the task of defining – nothing less – the essence of translation. This word, whose relation to French or English is not very certain or decidable and which – I hope to show shortly – also retains an obscure Germanic filiation, thus comes to occupy a position that is *doubly* eminent and exposed.

On the one hand, it extends and announces the accomplishment of an ambitious response to the question of the essence of translation. (What is a translation?) To know what a relevant translation can mean and be, it is necessary to know what the essence of translation, its mission, its ultimate goal, its vocation is.

On the other hand, a relevant translation is assumed, rightly or wrongly, to be better than a translation that is not relevant. A relevant translation is held, rightly or wrongly, to be the best translation possible. The teleological definition of translation, the definition of the essence that is realized in translation, is there-fore implicated in the definition of a relevant translation. The question, What is a relevant translation? would return to the question, What is translation? or, What should a translation be? And the question, What should a translation be? implies, as if synonymously, What should the best possible translation be?

Put another way (and put another way, the expression "put another way," "in other terms," "in other words," "en d'autres mots" is the phrase that silently announces every translation, at least when it designates itself as a translation and tells you, in an autodeictic manner, look, I am a translation, you are reading a trans-lation, not an interlinguistic translation, to make use of Roman Jakobson's distinction, but an intralinguistic[4] one – and I am not sure whether or not this autodeixis accompanies the word "relevante" in my title), put another way, if the question, What is a relevant translation? signifies nothing other than the question, What is a translation? or What should the best possible translation be? then one should jettison the word "relevant" and forget it, dropping it without delay.

And yet I have kept it. Why? Perhaps to try to convince you of two things: on the one hand, this word of Latin origin, even though I no longer know to what language it belongs, whether French or English, has become indispensable to me, in its uniqueness, to translate several words originating in several languages, starting with German (as if it in turn contained more than one word in a single one); on the other hand, this translative word has become in turn untranslatable for the same reason. And when I say that this has happened to me, as I try to relate it, I don't mean at all that it is empirically personal, because what has happened to me, or what has passed through me coming from languages and returning to them, was also a project of institutional accreditation and canonization in the public sphere. My first concern, then, has never been to appropriate this translation for myself, but to legitimate it, to make it known as the most relevant translation possible and therefore, on the contrary, to expropriate it from myself, to dispossess myself of it, while putting it on the market – even if I could still dream of leaving my like-ness on this common currency and, like Shylock, expect an IOU for it.

How can I try to justify, or in any case submit for your discussion, the reasons for which, several times over the space of thirty years, I have judged relevant my use of one and the same verb, *relever*, to translate first a German word, then an English one?

The English word – let us start at the end – can be found in *The Merchant of Venice*. The privilege that I assign here to Shakespeare's play does not only depend on the presence of this word to be translated. In addition, by virtue of connotation, everything in the play can be retranslated into the code of translation and as a problem of translation; and this can be done according to the three senses that Jakobson distinguishes: interlinguistic, intralinguistic, intersemiotic – as, for example, between a pound of flesh and a sum of money. At every moment, trans-lation is as necessary as it is impossible. It is the law; it even speaks the language of the law beyond the law, the language of the impossible law, represented by a woman who is disguised, transfigured, converted, travestied, read *translated*, into a man of law. As if the subject of this play were, in short, the task of the translator, his impos-sible task, his duty, his debt, as inflexible as it is unpayable. At least for three or four reasons:

1. First there is an *oath*, an untenable promise, with the risk of perjury, a debt and an obligation that constitute the very impetus for the intrigue, for the *plot*, for the conspiracy [*complot*]. Now it would be easy to show (and I have tried to do so elsewhere)[5] that all translation implies an insolvent indebtedness and an oath of fidelity to a given original – with all the paradoxes of such a law and such a promise, of a *bond* and a contract, of a promise that is, moreover, impossible and asymmetrical, transferential and countertransferential, like an oath doomed to treason or perjury.

2. Then there is the theme of economy, calculation, capital, and interest, the unpayable debt to Shylock: what I said above about the unit of the word clearly set up a certain economy as the law of translation.

3. In *The Merchant of Venice*, as in every translation, there is also, at the very heart of the obligation and the debt, an incalculable equivalence, an impossible but incessantly alleged correspondence between the pound of flesh and money, a required but impractical translation between the unique literalness of a proper body and the arbitrariness of a general, monetary, or fiduciary sign.

4. This impossible translation, this conversion (and all translation is a conversion: *vertere, transvertere, convertere,* as Cicero said) between the original, literal flesh and the monetary sign is not unrelated to the Jew Shylock's forced conversion to Christianity, since the traditional figure of the Jew is often and conventionally situated on the side of the body and the letter (from bodily circumcision or Pharisaism, from ritual compliance to literal exteriority), whereas after St. Paul the Christian is on the side of the spirit or sense, of interiority, of spiritual circumcision. This relation of the letter to the spirit, of the body of literalness to the ideal interiority of sense is also the site of the passage of translation, of this conversion that is called translation. As if the business of translation were first of all an Abrahamic matter between the Jew, the Christian, and the Muslim. And the *relève*, like the relevance I am prepared to discuss with you, will be precisely what happens to the flesh of the text, the body, the spoken body and the translated body – when the letter is mourned to save the sense.

Shylock recalls that he promised *under oath* to respect the original text of the contract, the IOU. What is owed to him refers, literally, to the pound of flesh. This oath binds him to heaven, he recalls, he can't break it without perjuring himself, that is to say, without betraying it by translating its terms into monetary signs. In the name of the letter of the contract, Shylock refuses the translation or transaction (translation is a transaction). Portia proceeds to offer him three times the sum of money he is owed in exchange for the pound of flesh. If you translate the pound of flesh into money, she essentially proposes to him, you will have three times the sum owed. Shylock then exclaims:

> An oath, an oath, I have an oath in heaven,–
> Shall I lay perjury upon my soul?
> No not for Venice.[6]

Portia pretends to take note of this refusal and to recognize that "this bond is forfeit." With the contract, the bond, the IOU falling due, the Jew has the right to claim a pound of flesh that he must literally cut out very close to the merchant's heart:

Why this bond is forfeit,
And lawfully by this the Jew may claim
A pound of flesh, to be by him cut off
Nearest the merchant's heart.

[*MV*, 4.1.226–29]

Portia will press Shylock one last time to pardon while cancelling the debt, remitting it, forgiving it. "Be merciful," she asks, "Take thrice the money, bid me tear the bond," the promissory note, the contract. Shylock again refuses; he swears truly on his soul that he cannot perjure himself and retract his oath. Countersigning his act of faith, swearing on what he has already sworn, he refers to language, to a tongue of man incapable of being measured, in its relative economy, in the proposed translation or transaction, against the absolute oath that binds his soul, unconditionally, before God:

by my soul I swear,
There is no power in the tongue of man
To alter me, – I stay here on my bond.

[*MV*, 4.1.236–38]

Thus the oath is, *in* the human tongue, a promise that human language, however, cannot itself undo, control, obliterate, subject by loosening it. An oath is a bond *in* human language that the human tongue, as such, insofar as it is human, cannot loosen. *In* human language is a *bond* stronger than human language. More than man in man. In human language (the element of translation) is an inflexible law that at once prohibits the translation of the transaction but commands respect for the original literalness or the given word. It is a law that presides over translation while commanding absolute respect, without any transaction, for the word given in its original letter. The oath, the sworn faith, the act of swearing is transcendence itself, the experience of passing beyond man, the origin of the divine or, if one prefers, the divine origin of the oath. This seems true of the law of translation in general. No sin is more serious than perjury, and Shylock repeats, while swearing, that he cannot perjure himself; he therefore confirms the first oath by a second oath, in the time of a repetition. This is called fidelity, which is the very essence and vocation of an oath: when I swear, I swear in a language that no human language has the power to make me abjure, to disrupt, that is to say, to make me perjure myself. The oath passes *through* language, but it passes beyond human language. This would be the truth of translation.

In this fabulous tale of the oath, of the contractual *bond*, at issue is an indebtedness in which the exchange-values are incommensurable and thus each is untranslatable into the other (money/pound of flesh). In 4.1 Portia, disguised as a lawyer, first addresses herself to Antonio to ask him to acknowledge, to confess his unpaid or unpayable debt: "Do you confess the bond?" Do you confess, do you recognize the contract, the promise, the bond? "Reconnais-tu le billet?" ["Do you recognize the note?"] is the flat rendering by François-Victor Hugo, whose translation I have followed, at times modifying it.[7] Do you acknowledge the acknowledgement of the debt, the IOU? Do you confirm the signed pledge, the bond, that which you owe, that because of which you are in debt or in default, indeed at fault (hence the word "confess")? Antonio's response: "I do" (a performative). Yes, I confess, I acknowledge, I recognize, I confirm and sign or countersign. *I do*. A sentence as extraordinary as a "yes." The economy and brevity of the response: as simple and bare as possible, the utterance implies not only an "I," an "I" who *does* what it says while saying it, confirming that he himself is the very person who has already heard, understood, memorized in its entirety the meaning of the question posed and integrated in turn into the response that signs the identity between the *I* who has heard and the *I* who utters the "yes" or the "I do." But it is also, given this understanding and the memory of the question, the same person as the one posing the question: I say *yes, I do*, precisely in response to what you mean by asking me this or posing this question to me. We think and mean the same thing (intralinguistic translation), we are the same person in the mirror of this measure. This mirrored or transparent univocity, this ideal translation, is supposed to be at work in all performative utterances of the type "I pardon."

After Antonio's confession, the response falls like a verdict. "Then must the Jew be merciful." Six brief words name *the Jew* and *mercy* in the same breath. This short sentence simultaneously signs both the economy and the incomparable genius of Shakespeare. It deserves to rise above this text as an immense allegory; it perhaps recapitulates the entire history of forgiveness, the entire history between the Jew and the Christian, the entire history of economics (*merces*, market, merchandise, *merci*, mercenary, wage, reward, literal or sublime) as a history of translation: "Then must the Jew be merciful."

Then (hence, consequently, *igitur*) the Jew must be *merciful*. He must be *clément*, *indulgent*, say certain French translations. Obviously, this means *here*: therefore, *igitur*, *then*, since you acknowledge the debt or the fault, the Jew (*this* Jew, Shylock, in this precise context) must free you from it. But the elliptical force of the verdict tends to take on a colossal symbolic and metonymic value, on the scale of every historical period: "the Jew" also represents every Jew, the Jew in general in his *différend* with his Christian counterpart, Christian power, the Christian State. The Jew must forgive.

(Permit me a parenthesis here: while rereading this extraordinary verdict whose ruse we shall analyze in a moment – namely, the phrase that says "then the Jew must forgive," implying that "it is the Jew who must forgive," "it is up to the Jew in general to forgive" – I can't avoid recalling the Pope's extraordinary sigh at the end of the second millennium. Several months ago, as he was about to board a plane for one of his transcontinental journeys, he was asked what he thought of the French episcopate's declaration of repentance, and after sighing, after feeling a bit sorry for himself, after feeling a bit sorry for Christianity and Catholicism, he said: "I notice that it is always we who are asking for forgiveness." Well! The implication: forgiveness from the Jews [even if some people legitimately think of certain American Indians too, as well as various other victims of the Inquisition whom the Pope has since put on the list as an another duty of commemoration, as it is called – or of repentance]. It is always we, Christians or Catholics, who are asking for forgiveness, but why? Yes, why? Is it that forgiveness is a Christian thing and

Christians should set an example because Christ's Passion consisted of assuming sin on the cross? Or indeed because, under the circumstances, a certain Church, if not Christianity, will always have reproached itself a great deal, while asking for forgiveness, and first of all from the Jew, whom it has asked for forgiveness – and to be *merciful*? "Then must the Jew be merciful.")

Portia thus addresses herself to Antonio, her accomplice, and while referring to the Jew as a third party, she hears what the Jew hears: faced with your recognition, your acknowledgement, your confession, the Jew must be *merciful*, compassionate, forbearing, capable of forgiving, of remitting your pain or your payment, of erasing the debt, and so on. But the Jew doesn't understand Portia's deductive reasoning, he entirely refuses to understand this logic. She would like him to grant forgiveness and absolve the debt simply because it is recognized. The Jew then grows indignant:

"In virtue of what obligation, what constraint, what law must I be *merciful*?" The word that is translated by "obligation" or "constraint" or "law" is an interesting one: it is *compulsion*, which signifies an irresistable impulse or constraining power. "In virtue of what compulsion should I show myself *merciful*?"

> On what compulsion must I? Tell me that.
>
> [*MV*, 4.1.179]

In response to the Jew's question, Portia launches into a grand panegyric of the power of forgiveness. This superb speech defines *mercy*, forgiveness, as the supreme power. Without constraint, without obligation, gratuitous, an act of grace, a power above power, a sovereignty above sovereignty, a superlative might, mightier than might since it is a might without might, a respite within might, this transcendent might of *mercy* rises above might, above the economy of might and therefore above sanction as well as transaction. This is why mercy is the king's attribute, the right of grace, the absolute privilege of the monarch (or, in this case, of the doge). Yet it is also an infinite extravagance, another tread or trade in an infinite ascent, and just as this power is above power, a might mightier than might, so the monarch's attribute is at the same time above him and his sceptre. This might passes beyond humanity even as it passes through humanity, just as language does (as we mentioned earlier): it is only in God's keeping. Grace is divine, in earthly power it recalls what most resembles divine power, it is the superhuman within the human. The two discourses here echo or mirror one another, that of Shylock the Jew and Portia the Christian or the Christian in the guise of the law. Both place something (the oath, forgiveness) above human language *in* human language, beyond the human order *in* the human order, beyond human rights and duties *in* human law.

The strength of forgiveness, if you listen to Portia, is *more than* just, more just than justice or the law. It rises above the law or above what in justice is only law; it is, beyond human law, the very thing that invokes prayer. And what is, finally, a discourse on translation (possible/impossible) is also a discourse of *prayer on prayer*. Forgiveness is prayer; it belongs to the order of benediction and prayer, on two sides, that of the person who requests it and that of the person who grants it. The essence of prayer has to do with forgiveness, not with power and law. Between the elevation of prayer or benediction – above human power, above even royal

power insofar as it is human, above the law, above the penal code – and the elevation of forgiveness above human power, royal power and the law, there exists a
sort of essential affinity. Prayer and forgiveness have the same provenance and the
same essence, the same eminence that is more eminent than eminence, the eminence
of the Most High.

Shylock is frightened by this exorbitant exhortation to forgive beyond the law,
to renounce his right and his due. He is being asked to do more than he can and
more than he even has the right to grant, given the *bond* (one is tempted to say the
Bund) that obliges him beyond every human link. Shylock also senses that it is an
attempt to steer his ship in circles, if I can speak this way about a story that involves
a ship and a shipwreck. He who is presented as a diabolical figure ("the devil . . .
in the likeness of a Jew" [*MV*, 3.1.20]) senses that he is in the process of being had,
of being diabolically possessed in the name of the sublime transcendence of grace.
There is a pretense of elevating him above everything, with this tale of divine and
sublime forgiveness, but it is a ruse to empty his pockets while distracting him,
to make him forget what he is owed and to punish him cruelly. So he protests, he
grumbles, he complains, he clamors for the law, his right, his penalty. In any case,
he is not deceived. In the name of this sublime panegyric of forgiveness, an economic
ruse, a calculation, a stratagem is being plotted, the upshot of which (you know it
well: the challenge to cut flesh without shedding one drop of blood) will be that
Shylock loses everything in this translation of transaction, the monetary signs of his
money as well as the literal pound of flesh – and even his religion, since when the
situation takes a bad turn at his expense he will have to convert to Christianity, to
translate himself (*convertere*) into a Christian, into a Christian language, after having
been in turn forced, through a scandalous reversal – he who was entreated to be
merciful – to implore the doge for mercy on his knees ("Down therefore," Portia
will tell him, "and beg mercy from the duke"). The doge of Venice pretends to
grant him this pardon so as to show how superior his generosity as a Christian and
a monarch is to that of the Jew:

> That thou shalt see the difference of our spirit
> I pardon thee thy life before thou ask it:
> For half thy wealth, it is Antonio's,
> The other half comes to the general state,
> Which humbleness may drive unto a fine.
>
> [*MV*, 4.1.364–69]

The sovereignty of the doge, in its crafty manifestation, mimics absolute forgiveness, the pardon that is granted even where it is not requested, yet it is the pardon
of a life. As for the rest, Shylock is totally expropriated, half of his fortune going
to a private subject, Antonio, half to the State. And then – another economic ruse
– in order to receive a reduction of the penalty and avoid total confiscation, the
doge adds a condition, which is that Shylock repent ("repentir" is François-Victor
Hugo's translation for "humbleness"): if you give proof of humility while repenting,
your penalty will be reduced and you will have only a fine to pay instead of total
expropriation. As for the absolute pardon, the doge wields such sovereign power
over it that he threatens to withdraw it:

> He shall do this, or else I do recant
> The pardon that I late pronounced here.
>
> [*MV*, 4.1.387–88]

Portia had protested against the offer to reduce the total confiscation to a fine on the condition of repentance. She says, "Ay for the state, not for Antonio" (which means that the penalty of confiscation is reduced for what Shylock owes the State, but not for what he owes Antonio). Then Shylock rebels and refuses the pardon. He refuses to pardon, for sure, to be *merciful*, but he also refuses, reciprocally, to be pardoned at this price. He therefore refuses both to grant and to ask for forgiveness. He calls himself a foreigner, in short, to this entire phantasmic tale of forgiveness, to this entire unsavory plot of forgiveness, to all the Christian and theologico-political preaching that tries to pass off the moon as green cheese. He prefers to die than to be pardoned at this price because he understands or in any case senses that he would actually have to pay very dearly for the absolute and merciful pardon, and that an economy always hides behind this theatre of absolute forgiveness. Shylock then says, in a sort of counter-calculation: Well, keep your pardon, take my life, kill me, for in taking from me everything that I have and all that I am, you in effect kill me.

> Nay, take my life and all, pardon not that, –
> You take my house, when you do take the prop
> That doth sustain my house: you take my life
> When you do take the means whereby I live.
>
> [*MV*, 4.1.370–73]

You know how things turn out: the extraordinary economy of rings and oaths. Regardless of whether Shylock is implicated in it, he finally loses everything. Once the doge has threatened to withdraw his pardon, he must agree to sign a complete remission of the debt and to undergo a forced conversion to Christianity.

> Gratiano tells him:
> In christ'ning shalt thou have two godfathers, –
> Had I been judge, thou shouldst have had ten more,
> To bring thee to the gallows, not to the font.
>
> [*MV*, 4.1.394–96]

Exit Shylock.

Immediately after the scene I have just evoked, when Shylock has lost everything and left the stage (no more Jew on stage, no more Jew in the story), the profits are split, and the doge beseeches, implores, entreats (which is rendered into French as *conjure*) Portia to dine with him. She refuses, humbly begging his pardon: "I humbly do desire your grace of pardon" (the fact that great people are often called Your Grace or Your Gracious Majesty clearly underscores the power we are discussing here). She begs His Grace's pardon because she must travel out of town. The doge orders that *she*, or *he*, be remunerated ("gratify"), that she/he be paid or rewarded for her/his services:

Antonio, gratify this gentleman,
For in my mind you are much bound to him.

[*MV*, 4.1.402–3]

This gratuity, this reward is a wage. Portia knows it, she recognizes it, she knows and says that she has been paid for performing well in a scene of forgiveness and pardon as an able and cunning man of law; she admits, this woman in the guise of a man, that she has in some way been paid as a mercenary of gratitude [*le merci*], or mercy [*la merci*]:

He is well paid that is well satisfied,
And I delivering you, am satisfied,
And therein do account myself well paid, –
My mind was never yet more mercenary.

[*MV*, 4.1.411–14]

No one could better express the "mercenary" dimension of "merci" in every sense of this word. And no one could ever express it better than Shakespeare, who has been charged with anti-Semitism for a work that stages with an unequalled power all the great motives of Christian anti-Judaism.

Finally, again in the same scene, Bassanio's response to Portia passes once more through a logic of forgiveness:

Take some remembrance of us as a tribute,
Not as a fee: grant me two things I pray you, –
Not to deny me, and to pardon me.

[*MV*, 4.1.418–20]

Such is the context in which Portia displays the eloquence for which she is paid as a mercenary man of law.

Now here is the main dish, the plat de résistance. I have left the spiciest [*relevé*] taste for the end. Just after saying, "Then must the Jew be merciful," and after Shylock protests by asking, "On what compulsion must I?" Portia begins to speak again. I cite her speech in English, then translate or rather paraphrase it, step by step. It raises the stakes in admirable rhythms:

First movement:
The quality of mercy is not strain'd,
It droppeth as the gentle rain from heaven
Upon the place beneath: it is twice blest,
It blesseth him that gives, and him that takes,

[*MV*, 4.1.180–83]

The quality of mercy is not forced, constrained: mercy is not commanded, it is free, gratuitous; grace is gratuitous. Mercy falls from heaven like a gentle shower. It can't be scheduled, calculated; it arrives or doesn't, no one decides on it, nor does any human law; like rain, it happens or it doesn't, but it's a good rain, a gentle rain; forgiveness isn't ordered up, it isn't calculated, it is foreign to calculation, to economics, to the transaction and the law, but it is good, like a gift, because mercy gives by forgiving, and it fecundates; it is good, it is *beneficient, benevolent* like a *benefit* as opposed to a *male*faction, a good deed as opposed to a misdeed. It falls, like rain, from above to below ("it droppeth . . . upon the place beneath"): the person who forgives is, like forgiveness itself, on high, very high, above the person who asks for or obtains forgiveness. There is a hierarchy, and this is why the metaphor of rain is not only that of a phenomenon that is not ordered up, but also that of a vertical descending movement: forgiveness is given from above to below. "It is twice blest;/It blesseth him that gives, and him that takes": thus there is already a sharing of the good, of the good deed, a sharing of the benediction, a performative event and a mirroring between two benefits of the benediction, a mutual exchange, a translation between giving and taking.

> Second movement:
> 'Tis the mightiest in the mightiest, it becomes
> The throned monarch better than his crown.
> His sceptre shows the force of temporal power,
> The attribute to awe and majesty,
> Wherein doth sit the dread and fear of kings:
> But mercy is above this sceptred sway,
> It is enthroned in the hearts of kings,
> It is an attribute to God himself;
> And earthly power doth then show likest God's
> When mercy seasons justice.
>
> [*MV*, 4.1.184–93]

Forgiving mercy is the mightiest or the almighty *in* the almighty: "'Tis the mightiest in the mightiest," the omnipotence of omnipotence, the omnipotence in omnipotence or the almighty among all the almighty, absolute greatness, absolute eminence, absolute might in absolute might, the hyperbolic superlative of might. The omnipotence of omnipotence is at once the essence of power, the essence of might, the essence of the possible, but also what, like the essence and superlative of might, is at once the mightiest *of* might and more *than* might, *beyond* omnipotence. This limit of power, of might and of the possible obliges us to ask ourselves if the experience of forgiveness is an experience of "power," of the "power-to-forgive," the affirmation of power through forgiveness at the conjunction of all the orders of "I can," and not only of political power, or even the beyond of all power. What is always at issue here – another problem of translation – is the status of *more* as *the most* and as *more than*, of the mightiest as *more mighty than* – and as *more than* mighty, and therefore as another order than might, power, or the possible: the impossible that is *more than impossible and therefore possible*.[8]

In the same way, if forgiveness, if "mercy" or "the quality of mercy" is "the mightiest in the mightiest," this situates both the apex of omnipotence and something more and other than absolute power in "the mightiest in the mightiest." We should be able to follow, accordingly, the wavering of this limit between power and absolute powerlessness, powerlessness or the absolute impossible as unlimited power – which is not unrelated to the im-possible possible of translation.

Mercy becomes the throned monarch, Portia says, but even better than his crown. It is higher than the crown on a head; it *suits* the monarch, it becomes him, but it *suits* higher than his head and the head [*la tête et le chef*], than the attribute or sign of power that is the royal crown. Like the sceptre, the crown manifests temporal power, whereas forgiveness is a supratemporal, spiritual power. Above the authority of the sceptre, it is enthroned in the heart of kings. This omnipotence is different from temporal might, and to be different from might that is temporal and therefore earthly and political, it must be interior, spiritual, ideal, situated in the king's heart and not in his exterior attributes. The passage across the limit clearly follows the trajectory of an interiorization that passes from the visible to the invisible by becoming a thing of the heart: forgiveness as *pity* [*miséricorde*], if you wish, pity being the sensitivity of the heart to the misfortune of the guilty, which motivates forgiveness. This interior pity is divine in essence, but it also says something about the essence of translation. Portia obviously speaks as a Christian, she is already trying to convert or to pretend that she is preaching to a convert. In her effort to persuade Shylock to forgive, she is already attempting to convert him to Christianity; by feigning the supposition that he is already a Christian so that he will listen to what she has to say, she turns him toward Christianity by means of her logic and her rhetoric; she predisposes him to Christianity, as Pascal said, she preconverts him, she converts him inwardly, something that he will soon be forced to do physically, under constraint. She tries to convert him to Christianity by persuading him of the supposedly Christian interpretation that consists of interiorizing, spiritualizing, idealizing what among Jews (it is often said, at least, that this is a very powerful stereotype) will remain physical, external, literal, devoted to a respect for the letter. As with the difference between the circumcision of the flesh and the Pauline circumcision of the heart — there will certainly be a need to look for a translation, in the broad sense, with regard to this problematic of circumcision (literal circumcision of the flesh versus ideal and interior circumcision of the heart, Jewish circumcision versus Christian circumcision, the whole debate surrounding Paul). What happens between the Jew Shylock and the legislation of the Christian State in this wager of a pound of flesh before the law, the oath, the sworn faith, the question of literalness, and so on? If forgiveness dwells within the king's heart and not in his throne, his sceptre, or his crown, that is, in the temporal, earthly, visible, and political attributes of his power, a leap has been made toward God. The power to pardon interiorized in mankind, in human power, in royal power as human power, is what Portia calls divine: it will be God-*like*. This "like," this analogy or resemblance supports a logic, or analogic, of theologico-political translation, of the translation of the theological into political.

> It is enthroned in the hearts of kings,
> It is an attribute to God himself;
> And earthly power doth then show likest God's
> When mercy seasons justice.

The earthly power that most resembles God is that which "seasons justice," which "tempers" justice with forgiveness.

"Tempère" [tempers] is Hugo's translation for "seasons." It isn't an erroneous choice; it in fact means "to season" [*assaisonner*], to mix, to cause to change, to modify, to temper, to dress food or to affect a climate, a sense of taste or quality. Let's not forget that this speech began by trying to describe "the quality of mercy."

Yet I am tempted to replace Hugo's translation, "tempère," which is not bad, with another. It will not be a true translation, above all not a relevant translation. It will not respond to the name *translation*. It will not *render*, it will not pay its dues, it will not make a full restitution, it will not pay off all its debt, first and foremost its debt to an assumed concept, that is, to the self-identity of meaning alleged by the word *translation*. It will not be answerable to [*relever de*] what is currently called a translation, a *relevant* translation. But apart from the fact that the most relevant translation (that which presents itself as the transfer of an intact signified through the inconsequential vehicle of any signifier whatsoever) is the least relevant possible, the one I offer will allow me to attempt at least *three gestures* at once, to tie together, in the same economy, three necessities that will all be linked to the history of a translation that I took the somewhat rash initiative in proposing, over thirty years ago, and which is now publicly canonized in French – all the while naturally remaining untranslatable into any other language. I shall therefore translate "seasons" as "relève": "when mercy seasons justice," "quand le pardon relève la justice (ou le droit)" [*when mercy elevates and interiorizes, thereby preserving and negating, justice (or the law)*].

1. *First justification*: an immediate guarantee in the play of the idiom. *Relever* first conveys the sense of cooking suggested here, like *assaisonner*. It is a question of giving taste, a different taste that is blended with the first taste, now dulled, remaining the same while altering it, while changing it, while undoubtedly removing something of its native, original, idiomatic taste, but also while adding to it, and in the very process, *more* taste, while cultivating its natural taste, while giving it *still more of its own taste*, its own, natural flavor – this is what we call "relever" in French cooking. And this is precisely what Portia says: mercy seasons [*relève*] justice, the quality of mercy seasons the taste of justice. Mercy keeps the taste of justice while affecting it, refining it, cultivating it; mercy resembles justice, but it comes from somewhere else, it belongs to a different order, at the same time it modifies justice, it at once tempers and strengthens justice, changes it without changing it, converts it without converting it, yet while improving it, while exalting it. Here is the first reason to translate *seasons* with "relève," which effectively preserves the gustatory code and the culinary reference of *to season*, "assaisonner": *to season with spice*, to spice. *A seasoned dish* is, according to the translation in the *Robert* dictionary, "un plat relevé."[9] Justice preserves its own taste, its own meaning, but this very taste is better when it is *seasoned* or "relevé" by mercy. Without considering that *mercy* can redeem, deliver, ease, indemnify, indeed cure (this is the chain *heal, heilen, holy, heilig*) justice which, thus eased, lightened, delivered (*relieved*), redeems itself with a view to sacrosanct salvation.

2. *Second justification*: "relever" effectively expresses elevation. Mercy elevates justice, it pulls and inspires justice toward highness, toward a height higher than the crown, the sceptre, and power that is royal, human, earthly, and so on. Sublimation, elevation, exaltation, ascension toward a celestial height, the highest or the most high, higher than height. Thanks to forgiveness, thanks to mercy, justice is even

more just, it transcends itself, it is spiritualized by rising and thus lifting itself [*se relevant*] above itself. Mercy sublimates justice.

3. There is, finally, a *third justification* for the verb *relever*. I use this word *justification* to reconcile what would render this translation relevant to the conjoined motif of justice ("Mercy seasons justice") and justness or appropriateness [*justesse*], to what must be the appropriate word, the most appropriate possible, more appropriate than appropriate. This last justification would then give a philosophical meaning and coherence to the economy, accumulation, capitalization of good grounds. In 1967, to translate a crucial German word with a double meaning (*Aufheben, Aufhebung*), a word that signifies at once to suppress and to elevate, a word that Hegel says represents the speculative risk of the German language, and that the entire world had until then agreed was untranslatable – or, if you prefer, a word for which no one had agreed with anyone on a stable, satisfying translation into any language – for this word, I had proposed the noun *relève* and the verb *relever*. This allowed me to retain, joining them in a single word, the double motif of the elevation and the replacement that preserves what it denies or destroys, preserving what it causes to disappear, quite like – in a perfect example – what is called in the armed forces, in the navy, say, the relief [*relève*] of the guard. This usage is also possible in English, to relieve.[10] Was my operation a translation?[11] I am not sure that it deserves this term. The fact is that it has become irreplaceable and nearly canonized, even in the university, occasionally in other languages where the French word is used as if it were quoted from a translation, even where its origin is no longer known, or when its place of origin – I mean "me" – or its taste is disliked. Without plunging us very deeply into the issues, I must at least recall that the movement of *Aufhebung*, the process of establishing relevance, is always in Hegel a dialectical movement of interiorization, interiorizing memory (*Erinnerung*) and sublimating spiritualization. It is also a translation. Such a *relève* is precisely at issue here, in Portia's mouth (mercy *relève*, it elevates, replaces and interiorizes the justice that it seasons). Above all, we find the same need for the *Aufhebung*, the *relève*, at the very heart of the Hegelian interpretation of mercy, particularly in *The Phenomenology of Mind*: the movement toward philosophy and absolute knowledge as the truth of the Christian religion passes through the experience of mercy.[12] Mercy is a *relève*, it is in its essence an *Aufhebung*. It is translation as well. In the horizon of expiation, redemption, reconciliation, and salvation.

When Portia says that mercy, above the sceptre, seated on the interior throne in the king's heart, is an attribute of God himself, and that therefore, as an earthly power, mercy *resembles* a divine power at the moment when it elevates, preserves, and negates [*relève*] justice (that is, the law), what counts is the resemblance, the analogy, the figuration, the maximal analogy, a sort of human translation of divinity: in human power mercy is what most resembles, what most is and reveals itself *as* a divine power ("then show likest God's"):

> But mercy is above the sceptred sway,
> It is enthroned in the hearts of kings,
> It is an attribute to God himself;
> And earthly power doth then show likest God's
> When mercy seasons justice.

Which doesn't mean, necessarily, that mercy comes only from one person, up there, who is called God, from a pitying Father who lets his mercy descend upon us. No, that can also mean that as soon as there is mercy, if in fact there is any, the so-called human experience reaches a zone of divinity: mercy is the genesis of the divine, of the holy or the sacred, but also the site of pure translation. (A risky interpretation. It could, let us note too quickly, efface the need for the singular person, for the pardoning or pardoned person, the "who" irreducible to the essential quality of a divinity, and so forth.)

This *analogy* is the very site of the theologico-political, the hyphen or translation between the theological and the political; it is also what underwrites political sovereignty, the Christian incarnation of the body of God (or Christ) in the king's body, the king's two bodies. This analogical – and Christian – articulation between two powers (divine and royal, heavenly and earthly), insofar as it passes here through the sovereignty of mercy and the right of grace, is also the sublime greatness that authorizes or enables the authorization of every ruse and vile action that permit the lawyer Portia, mouthpiece of all Shylock's Christian adversaries from the merchant Antonio to the doge, to get the better of the Jew, to cause him to lose everything, his pound of flesh, his money, even his religion. In expressing all the evil that can be thought of the Christian ruse as a discourse of mercy, I am not about to praise Shylock when he raises a hue and cry for his pound of flesh and insists on the literalness of the *bond*. I analyze only the historical and allegorical cards that have been dealt in this situation and all the discursive, logical, theological, political, and economic resources of the concept of mercy, the legacy (our legacy) of this semantics of mercy – precisely inasmuch as it is indissociable from a certain European interpretation of translation.

After thus proposing three justifications for my translation of *seasons* and *Aufhebung* as *relève* (verb and noun), I have gathered too many reasons to dissemble the fact that my choice aimed for the best transaction possible, the most economic, since it allows me to use a single word to translate so many other words, even languages, with their denotations and connotations. I am not sure that this transaction, even if it is the most economic possible, merits the name of *translation*, in the strict and pure sense of this word. It rather seems one of those other things in *tr.*, a transaction, transformation, travail, *travel* – and a treasure trove [*trouvaille*] (since this invention, if it also seemed to take up [*relever*] a challenge, as another saying goes, consisted only in discovering what was waiting, or in waking what was sleeping, in the language). The treasure trove amounts to a travail; it puts to work the languages, first of all, without adequation or transparency, here assuming the shape of a new writing or rewriting that is performative or poetic, not only in French, where a new use for the word emerges, but also in German and English. Perhaps this operation still participates in the travail of the negative in which Hegel saw a *relève* (*Aufhebung*). If I supposed, then, that the quasi-translation, the transaction of the word *relève* is indeed "relevant" (an English word in the process of Frenchification), that would perhaps qualify the effectiveness of this travail and its supposed right to be legitimated, accredited, quoted at an official market price. But its principal interest, if I can evaluate it in terms of usury and the market, lies in what it might say about the economy of every interlinguistic translation, this time in the strict and pure sense of the word. Undoubtedly, in taking up a challenge [*en relevant un défi*], a word is added to the French language, a word in a word. The use that I have just made of the word *relever*, "en relevant un défi," also becomes a challenge, a challenge, moreover, to every translation that would like to welcome into another language all the connotations that have accumulated in this word. These remain innumerable in themselves, perhaps unnameable: more than one word in a word, more than one language in a single language, beyond every possible compatibility of homonyms. What the translation with the word "relevant" also demonstrates, in an exemplary fashion, is that every translation should be relevant by vocation. It would thus guarantee the *survival* of the body of the original (*survival* in the double sense that Benjamin gives it in "The Task of the Translator," *fortleben* and *überleben*: prolonged life, continuous life, *living on*, but also life after death).

Isn't this what a translation does? Doesn't it guarantee these *two* survivals by losing the flesh during a process of conversion [*change*]? By elevating the signifier to its meaning or value, all the while preserving the mournful and debt-laden memory of the singular body, the first body, the unique body that the translation thus elevates, preserves, and negates [*relève*]? Since it is a question of a travail – indeed, as we noted, a travail of the negative – this relevance is a travail of mourning, in the most enigmatic sense of this word, which merits a re-elaboration that I have attempted elsewhere but cannot undertake here.[13] The measure of the *relève* or relevance, the price of a translation, is always what is called meaning, that is, value, preservation, truth as preservation (*Wahrheit, bewahren*) or the value of meaning, namely, what, in being freed from the body, is elevated above it, interiorizes it, spiritualizes it, preserves it in memory. A faithful and mournful memory. One doesn't even have to say that translation preserves the value of meaning or must raise [*relever*] the body to it: the very concept, the value of meaning, the meaning of meaning, the value of the preserved value originates in the mournful experience of translation, of its very possibility. By resisting this transcription, this transaction which is a translation, this *relève*, Shylock delivers himself into the grasp of the Christian strategy, bound hand and foot. (The cost of a wager between Judaism and Christianity, blow for blow: they translate themselves, although not into one another.)

I insist on the Christian dimension. Apart from all the traces that Christianity has left on the history of translation and the normative concept of translation, apart from the fact that the *relève*, Hegel's *Aufhebung* (one must never forget that he was a very Lutheran thinker, undoubtedly like Heidegger), is explicitly a speculative *relève* of the Passion and Good Friday into absolute knowledge, the travail of mourning also describes, through the Passion, through a memory haunted by the body lost yet preserved in its grave, the resurrection of the ghost or of the glorious body which rises, rises again [*se relève*] – and walks.

Without wishing to cause any grief to Hegel's ghost, I leave aside the third movement that I had announced in Portia's speech (which would have dealt with translation as prayer and benediction).[14]

Merci for the time you have given me, pardon, *mercy*, forgive the time I have taken from you.

Notes

1   [Derrida's text is a lecture that he delivered in 1998 at the annual seminar of the Assises de la Traduction Littéraire à Arles (ATLAS). A French organization with approximately eight hundred members, ATLAS works to promote literary translation and to protect the status of the literary translator. Derrida's mention of his "very first attempts" in the next sentence glances at his first book, which was a translation of Edmund Husserl's *L'origine de la géométrie* (Paris: Presses Universitaires de France, 1962). Trans.]

2   *Ulysse Gramophone, deux mots pour Joyce* (Paris: Galilée, 1987) [An English translation of Derrida's text is available in *Post-structuralist Joyce: Essays from the French*, ed. Derek Attridge and Daniel Ferrer (Cambridge: Cambridge University Press, 1984). Trans.]

3   See St. Jerome, *Liber de optimo genere interpretendi* (*Epistula* 57). [A translation of St. Jerome's letter is included in this volume. Trans.] For this reference I am indebted to the admirable recent work (still unpublished) of Andrès Claro, *Les Vases brisés: Quatre variations sur la tâche du traducteur*.

4   If one reflects on Jakobson's classification, only *interlinguistic* translation (the operation that transfers from one language to another and to which one most often refers as translation in the proper or strict sense) is governed by the economy I have described and, within it, by the unit of the word. Neither *intralinguistic* translation nor *intersemiotic* translation is governed by a principle of economy or above all by the unit of the word. [Derrida is referring to the essay by Roman Jakobson reprinted in this volume. Trans.]

5   [See Derrida's essay, "Des Tours de Babel" (1985). Trans.]

6   This abstract arithmetic, this apparently arbitrary economy of multiplication by three – three times more than the monetary signs – points us to the scene of Portia's three suitors at the end of the play and the entire problematic of the three caskets, from *The Merchant of Venice* to *King Lear*. Read through a Freud who has been mobilized and interrogated, this will also be a great scene of transfer, metaphor, and translation. [See William Shakespeare, *The Merchant of Venice*, ed. John Russell Brown, vol. 23 of *The Arden Edition of the Works of William Shakespeare*, ed. Una Ellis-Fermor (London: Methuen, 1951), 4.1.224-26; hereafter abbreviated *MV*. Trans.]

7   [François-Victor Hugo (1828-1873), the son of the poet, novelist and dramatist Victor Hugo, published his French version of Shakespeare's works between 1863 and 1873. Trans.]

8   This structure is analogous to what Angelus Silesius, in *The Cherubic Pilgrim* (which I cite and analyze in *Sauf le nom* [Paris: Galilée, 1993], p.33), calls *Überunmöglichste* and describes as possible - this is God: *das Überunmöglichste ist möglich* - which can be translated, depending on how *über* is understood, as "*the most* impossible, the absolute impossible, the impossible par excellence is possible" or as "the more *than* impossible, the beyond of impossible is possible." These renderings are very different yet amount to the same thing, because in the two cases (the one comparative, the other superlative) they wind up saying that the tip of the summit (the peak) belongs to another order than that of the summit; the highest is therefore contrary to or other than

what it surpasses; it is higher than the height of the most high: the most impossible and the more *than* impossible belong to another order than the impossible in general and can therefore be possible. The meaning of "possible," the significance of the concept of possibility, meanwhile, has undergone a mutation, at the point and limit of the im-possible - if I can put it this way — and this mutation indicates what is at stake in our reflection on the impossible possibility of translation: there is no longer any possible contradiction between possible and impossible since they belong to two heterogeneous orders. [An English version of Derrida's commentary on Angelus Silesius appears in *On the Name*, trans. David Wood and John P. Leavey Jr., ed. Thomas Dutoit (Stanford, Calif.: Stanford University Press, 1995). Trans.]

9   The rich entry in the *Oxford English Dictionary* gives some splendid uses for such diverse meanings as "to render more palatable by the addition of some savoury ingredient," "to adapt," "to accommodate to a particular taste," "to moderate, to alleviate, to temper, to embalm; to ripen, to fortify." A more rare and more archaic (sixteenth century) use: "to impregnate, to copulate," as in "when a male hath once seasoned the female, he never after touches her."

10 I have just alluded to the navy. Well, then, Joseph Conrad, for example, writes in "The Secret Sharer": I would get the second mate to relieve me at that hour"; then "I ... returned on deck for my relief."

11 Curiously, the first time that the word *relève* seemed to me indispensable for translating (without translating) the word *Aufhebung* was on the occasion of an analysis of the sign. See *Le Puits et la pyramide: Introduction à la semiologie de Hegel*, a lecture delivered at the Collège de France in Jean Hyppolite's seminar during January 1968, reprinted in *Marges de la philosophie* (Paris: Éditions de Minuit, 1972), p. 102 [See Derrida, "The Pit and the Pyramid: An Introduction to Hegel's Semiology," *Margins of Philosophy*, trans. Alan Bass (Chicago: University of Chicago Press, 1982). Trans.].) Most of the so-called undecidable words that have interested me ever since are also, by no means accidentally, untranslatable into a single word (*pharmakon*, supplément, différance, hymen, and so on). This list cannot, by definition, be given any closure.

12 In *The Phenomenology of Mind*, at the end of *Die offenbare Religion*, just before *Das absolute Wissen*, therefore at the transition between absolute religion and absolute knowledge - as the truth of religion.

13 [See Derrida, *Spectres de Marx: l'état de la dette, le travail du deuil et la nouvelle internationale* (Paris: Galilée, 1993); *Specters of Marx: The State of the Debt, the Work of Mourning, and the New International*, trans. Peggy Kamuf (London and New York: Routledge, 1994). Trans.]

14 This would be a matter, without speaking further about the doge and the State, of examining and weighing justice on one side (and justice here must be understood as the law, the justice that is calculable and *enforced*, applied, applicable, and not the justice that I distinguish elsewhere from the law; here justice means: the juridical, the judiciary, positive, indeed penal law). To examine and weigh justice on one side with salvation on the other, it seems necessary to choose between them and to renounce law so as to attain salvation. This would be like giving an essential dignity simultaneously to the word and the

value of *prayer*; prayer would be that which allows one to go beyond the law toward salvation or the hope of salvation; it would belong to the order of forgiveness, like benediction, which was considered at the beginning (forgiveness is a *double benediction*: for the person who grants it and for the person who receives it, for whoever gives and for whoever takes). Now if prayer belongs to the order of forgiveness (whether requested or granted), it has no place at all in the law. Nor in philosophy (in onto-theology, says Heidegger). But before suggesting that a calculation is an economy again lurking in this logic, I read these lines from Portia's speech. Just after saying "when mercy seasons justice," she (or he) continues:

> Therefore, Jew
> Though justice be thy plea, consider this,
> That in the course of justice, none of us
> Should see salvation: we do pray for mercy,
> And that same prayer, doth teach us all to render
> The deeds of mercy. I have spoken thus much
> To mitigate the justice of thy plea,
> Which if thou follow, this strict court of Venice
> Must needs give sentence 'gainst the merchant there.
>
> [*MV*, 4.1.193-210]

Paraphase: "Thus, Jew, although justice (the good law) may be your argument (*plea*: your allegation, what you plead, that in the name of which you plead, your cause but also your plea), consider this: that with the simple process of the law (the simple juridical procedure) none of us would attain salvation: we pray, in truth, for forgiveness (mercy) (*we do pray for mercy*), and this is the prayer, this prayer, this very prayer (*that same prayer*) that teaches us to do merciful acts (to forgive) to everyone. Everything I have just said is to mitigate the justice of your cause; if you persist, if you continue to pursue this cause, the strict tribunal of Venice will necessarily have to order the arrest of the merchant present here."

Chapter 30

Abé Mark Nornes

FOR AN ABUSIVE SUBTITLING

> Translators are like busy matchmakers who praise a half-veiled beauty
> as being very lovely: they arouse an irrepressible desire for the original.
> Goethe, *Maxims and Reflections* (trans. S. Heyvaert)

A LL OF US HAVE, at one time or another, left a movie theater wanting
to kill the translator. Our motive: the movie's murder by incompetent
subtitle. The death of a text through translation is an age-old trope, but it takes on
new meaning with its transposition into cinema. The very possibility of that death
implies a state of animation, a state that is, after all, essential to the moving image.
As in the case of literature, that death is a discursive condition, but with film it also
constitutes a perceptual category. Spectators often find cinema's powerful sense of
mimesis muddied by subtitles, even by skillful ones. The original, foreign, object
– its sights and its sounds – is available to all, but it is easily obscured by the graphic
text through which we necessarily approach it. Thus, the opacity or awkwardness
of subtitles easily inspires rage.

I began thinking about the vagaries of the subtitle when I translated my first
subtitles for Ogawa Shinsuke and Iizuka Toshio's *A Movie Capital* (*Eiga no miyako,*
1991). It was an experience filled with surprises. Here was an extraordinarily close
form of textual analysis where every element of verbal and visual language is read
off the image, repeatedly, line by line, even frame by frame. I was fascinated by the
way this particular field of film analysis naturally raised theoretical problems in the
course of working out practical solutions to seemingly simple problems. But nothing

1999/revised 2004

is simple when it comes to subtitles; every turn of phrase, every punctuation mark, every decision the translator makes holds implications for the viewing experience of foreign spectators. However, despite the rich complexity of the subtitler's task and its singular role in mediating the foreign in cinema, it has been virtually ignored in film studies. In translation studies, in contrast, there has been a proliferation of work, but it has almost exclusively concentrated on practical issues for translators or the physiology of the peculiar brand of speed reading demanded by subtitles. Scholars in either discipline have yet to explore in depth the cultural and ideological issues I will attend to here.[1] As for cinema's global audience, it is likely that no one has ever come away from a foreign film admiring the translation. If the subtitles attract comment, it is only a desire for reciprocal violence, a revenge for the text in the face of its corruption. For, as we shall see, all subtitles are corrupt.

It is particularly curious that considering today's celebration of other cultures, this corruption has gone unconsidered, unchecked. I suspect the explanation lies in subtitling's ancillary, even hidden, position in the film's journey from production to exhibition. Fighting this corruption will require pushing the fact of translation out of the darkness. We must understand the limits of the subtitle in order to explore new methods. The violence of the subtitle is unavoidable, but there is no reason that it should necessarily lead to death – or that that violence should not be valuable, even enjoyable. In the 1990s we are witnessing the emergence of a new form of subtitling which is by nature positively abusive. With all the attention directed toward multiculturalism and diversity, now is the time to reconsider the mode of translation through which our cinematic experiences with the foreign are mediated. Looking closely at translations between English and Japanese, and moving between practical and theoretical poles, this paper will identify some of the dilemmas subtitlers face as well as their responses to them over the past 70 years. Only then can we move towards creative solutions through strategic abusiveness.

I have elaborated the notion of an abusive translation originally proposed by Philip E. Lewis in "The Measure of Translation Effects," an essay he originally wrote in French and translated into English himself (see Lewis in this volume). To analyze another critic's translation of Derrida's essay, "La mythologie blanche," Lewis delineates the differences between the French and English languages, arguing that "translation, when it occurs, has to move whatever meanings it captures from the original into a framework that tends to impose a different set of discursive relations and a different construction of reality" (p. 259). The dissimilarity between languages creates differences that simply cannot be overcome, inevitably compromising the activity of translation. This is further compounded by the tendency for translation of essayistic texts to concentrate on meaning to the exclusion of texture and materiality. As both writer and translator of his essay, Lewis discovers a freedom to diverge from the original text unavailable to the typical translator. It is from this position that he proposes a new approach, "that of the strong, forceful translation that values experimentation, tampers with usage, seeks to match the polyvalencies or plurivocities or expressive stresses of the original by producing its own" (p.262). This is to locate the strength of a translation in its abuses. Where an original text strains language through textual knots dense with signification, the translation performs analogous violence against the target language. Corrupt subtitlers disavow the violence of the subtitle while abusive translators revel in it.

Put more concretely, the abusive subtitler uses textual and graphic abuse – that is, experimentation with language and its grammatical, morphological, and visual qualities – to bring the fact of translation from its position of obscurity, to critique the imperial politics that ground corrupt practices while ultimately leading the viewer to the foreign original being reproduced in the darkness of the theater. This original is not an origin threatened by contamination, but a locus of the individual and the international which can potentially turn the film into an *experience of translation*.

A corrupt practice

Facing the violent reduction demanded by the apparatus, subtitlers have developed a method of translation that conspires to hide its work – along with its ideological assumptions – from its own reader-spectators. In this sense we may think of them as *corrupt*. They accept a vision of translation that violently appropriates the source text, and in the process of converting speech into writing within the time and space limits of the subtitle they conform the original to the rules, regulations, idioms, and frame of reference of the target language and its culture. It is a practice of translation that smooths over its textual violence and domesticates all otherness while it pretends to bring the audience to an experience of the foreign. The peculiar challenges posed by subtitling and the violence they necessitate are a matter of course; they are variations of the difficulties in any translation and in this sense are analogous to the problems confronted by the translator of poetry. It is the subtitler's response to those challenges which are corrupt. Subtitlers say they promote learning and facilitate enjoyable meetings with other cultures, bringing the sense behind actors' speech acts to viewers through their skillful rendering at the edges of the screen. In fact, they conspire to hide their repeated acts of violence through codified rules and a tradition of suppression. It is this practice that is corrupt – feigning completeness in their own violent world. One of the few attempts at theorizing the subtitle touches on these issues, although it is ultimately unsatisfying. Trinh T. Minh-ha writes,

> The duration of the subtitles, for example, is very ideological. I think that if, in most translated films, the subtitles usually stay on as long as they technically can – often much longer than the time needed even for a slow reader – it's because translation is conceived here as part of the operation of suture that defines the classical cinematic apparatus and the technological effort it deploys to naturalize a dominant, hierarchically unified worldview. The success of the mainstream film relies precisely on how well it can hide [its articulated artifices] in what it wishes to show. Therefore, the attempt is always to protect the unity of the subject; here to collapse, in subtitling, the activities of reading, hearing, and seeing into one single activity, as if they were all the same. What you read is what you hear, and what you hear is more often than not, what you see.

> (Trinh 1992: 102)

We can accept Trinh's gloss to the extent that we recognize how, in this mode of translation, all forms of difference are suppressed and troublesome texts are fitted into the most conservative of frameworks.

Take the example of sexual difference. In Japanese gender is clearly marked linguistically, and subtitles dramatize difference through stereotypes of the way men or women *should* speak. In subtitles this is accomplished primarily through sentence-final particles. For example, the male ending *zo* has a hard, assertive sound, while female speech is softened by particles like *wa* and *no*. As with any corruption, habits are hard to break and behavior is ruled by convention. At the beginning of the Japanese subtitled version of *Robocop*, for instance, the female and male cops meet each other just after the female officer beats a rowdy criminal into submission. After this display of no-nonsense brutality the new partners are introduced to each other, they get into a squad car, and drive away. The action is innocuous enough, but the dialogue involves an intense play for power that's entirely linguistic:

> *Female Officer*: I better drive until you know your way around.
> *Male Officer*: I usually drive when I'm breaking in a new partner.

In Japan this was subtitled in the following manner:

> *Female*: *Watashi ga unten suru wa.* / I will drive.
> *Male*: *Kimi ni wa makaseraren.* / I can't leave it to you.

Not only is this conversation reduced to its barest, literal meaning, but the power dynamic is changed from a struggle over knowledge to a simple domination. The woman's soft sentence-final particle *wa* contrasts with the male officer's curt verb ending; the difference strongly suggests he occupies a superior position (a position cemented by deployment of the second-person pronoun *kimi,* which one uses only with subordinates). The woman's subtitle would have been much stronger with a different particle, such as *yo*. This particle is associated with patriarchal power and is typically used by middle-aged women when they want to speak forcefully. Indeed, it is difficult to imagine this aggressive female cop actually using *wa* in any context. Without their accompanying image, the lines read like a gangster talking to his moll. The translator took great liberties, matching the substance of the target language with the image but evacuating the power play.[2]

We may be able to understand the basic, underlying logic of corruption by turning to its most extreme manifestation: dubbing. The journal *The Velvet Light Trap* recently published what amounts to an apology for the practice of dubbing. Its author, Antje Ascheid, argues for dubbing as an exchange of one voice for another which produces a new text free of the constraints on the translator because there is no debt to an original. This allows the translator to bring the reader (read *consumer*) a readily digestible package that easily supplants any ideological baggage carried by the original film. While subtitles are described as purist and elitist, the author argues the dubbed soundtrack is liberating: mass audiences will not resist the foreign film because the dubber can resist the ideological underpinnings that link film to geopolitical struggles. Strange, then, that this is the essay's conclusion:

Dubbing [. . .] mostly succeeds in effacing the fact of the film text's foreign origin; or, rather, it gives its new audience the chance to disavow what they really know, hence opening an avenue for cultural ventriloquism through voice postsynchronization. In doing so, the dubbed film appears as a radically new product rather than a transformed old one, a single text rather than a double one. Like a Japanese game computer, a Taiwanese shirt, or a German car, products that have been constructed to fit consumer desires in an international marketplace through the reduction of their cultural specificities, the to-be-dubbed film original initially fulfills an important criterion with which most other international commodities also comply: it foregrounds its function, ceasing to be a "foreign" film in order to become just a film. [. . .] In the international marketplace the film original thus functions as a transnational decultured product; it becomes the raw material that is to be reinscribed into the different cultural contexts of the consumer nations through the use of dubbing.

(Ascheid 1997: 40)

Just a film indeed. Aside from an insufficient theorization of translation itself, this suspicious essay reduces the foreign tongue to nothing more than a "cultural disadvantage" where dubbing is perceived as "a strategy of empowerment." This is a fine example of a valorization of postmodern play being coopted by capital. The "exchange" facilitated by the "to-be-dubbed film" is simply of the capitalist variety: money for pleasure. This is the logic of corruption in its dubbed version, the one practiced by distributors for whom translation serves little more than surplus value. Today's subtitles participate in it to an unfortunate degree; any translator who wishes to think otherwise is blind.

These forms of corruption could be critiqued from the ideology of fidelity, which invokes the authority of the original and portrays it as an endangered purity or origin. This would reveal how subtitlers are reluctant to discuss the issue of fidelity, as it would expose their violence and make them appear incompetent. We could also extend the domain of this purity under siege to the terrain of the screen itself, like the Japanese cinematographer who decries ugly, superimposed subtitles for despoiling the image and separating spectators from the beauty of the original (Fujinami 1977: 81–84). Indeed, any measure of fidelity is a standard the apparatus itself will not permit. However, even though the term "corrupt" threatens to pose the original as territory unspoiled by subjectivity, there are theoretical reasons that the abusive translator steers clear of such easy binaries to take a quite different tack. The first step is to simply expose the act of translation, release it from its space of suppression, and understand what subtitling actually is and how it came to its corrupt condition.

The apparatus of translation

The practice of subtitling has been even more obscured than the translation of written, printed texts. Indeed, most people probably have never thought of subtitling *as translation*. There is no question that English-language film criticism about foreign cinema has taken the mediation of subtitles entirely for granted. Outside of the writing aimed at professional translators and the academic audiences of translation studies, virtually nothing has been written about them. Indeed, the translators themselves, along with their technicians, film-makers, writers, censors, and the producers that hire them all, go to great lengths to suppress any acknowledgment of their conspiracy. It has been noted more than once that the unlucky translator is an author but not The Author, that her translation is a work but not The Work. But even this dynamic is absent from both popular and scholarly discourses on the cinema. This absence speaks doubly of the dominance of the image and the utter suppression of the subtitler's central role in enabling a film's border crossing.

To transport the subtitle from its space of obscurity and uncover the root of its corruption, we must consider what is specific to it as a particular mode of translation. This includes its material conditions and its historical contingency. In the cinema a massive apparatus necessitates a violent translation of the source text. The film's utterances are segmented by time; natural breaks in speech are marked for the temporal borders of the subtitle. The translator determines the length of each unit of translation down to the frame, that is, down to a 24th of a second. As the translation proceeds, the translator strives to match the timing of the subtitle with the sound and motion of the source text. A humorous line, for example, must be arranged to meet its audio-visual punctuation. Once accomplished, the translation moves through the hands of countless technicians, some of whom think nothing of "adjusting" a subtitle here or there for their own capricious, technical reasons. As we will see, this can lead to the kind of embarrassing mistakes that make translators cringe.

Finally, the translation is grafted onto the original text in one of three ways (in the case of film). The subtitles are photographed optically and sandwiched together with the sound and image as a third film strip, literally a third track. Or they are cut into the emulsion itself, incised, scratched onto the very tissue of the image. Or, more recently, they come to be burned into the tissue of the celluloid with a computer-driven laser.

Beyond the difficulties posed by this complicated process, the translator confronts an array of challenges that seem to lead down the path of corruption. The space and time available for translation are decided by the apparatus itself; this may be analogous to the challenge posed by poetry, but is actually a different problem. In film the machine runs at a constant speed and mindlessly unspools its translation at an unchanging rate. The translator must condense his translation in the physical space of the frame and the temporal length of the utterance. The reader cannot stop and dwell on an interesting line; as the reader scans the text, the machine instantly obliterates it. There are protocols for this condensation, but they differ depending on the translator and the apparatus. The number of spaces available for text depends on the format of the film (16mm, 35mm), the lens (1:33, 1:85, CinemaScope), the script of the language, and the subtitling method itself. The translator then determines how many letters or characters are legible in the second or two or three available to each title. It is often said that actors talk twice as fast as spectators can read, but this is hardly a useful starting point for the work of translation. Donald Richie, for example, allows for about one word per foot, or a two-line title per 12 feet (Richie 1991: 16). Japanese subtitlers are fond of citing the rule, "Four characters per second."[3] Toda Natsuko explains how this rule was arrived at: the first subtitlers had to determine how fast the typical Japanese could read, so they showed a film to a Shinbashi *geisha* (!) and came up with three to four characters per second with a 13-character line.[4] Over the years the Japanese subtitlers reduced the line to ten to prevent sloppy projectionists from cutting off the characters at the edges, but soon the four-characters-per-second rule was clad in iron. (By way of contrast, subtitles in other languages can be two to three times as long, depending on the format, aperture, and a number of other factors.) Actually, this history is far more nuanced than their representation of it. In any case, against this matrix of time and space, the translator submits the original text to a violent reduction that most readers consider inept – if they dodge the translator's feints and pause to think about it at all.

The Japanese language seems ready-made for subtitling: for one thing, Japanese does not waste precious space on gaps between words and can even break a line in mid-word. *Kanji* (Chinese characters) express the maximum amount of meaning in a minimum of syllables; neologisms and abbreviations are easily accomplished through the creative combination of *kanji*. Even better, Japanese often leaves out the subject, direct object, or other parts of speech, saving much needed space. Because this forces speakers to be aware of context, the language itself prepares its readers to seek out what subtitles leave unsaid. Finally, in addition to italics, Japanese has the enviable ability to be inscribed both horizontally and vertically, a resource whose abusive potential is provocative. Finding the source language a richer linguistic world than one's own target language is probably a universal – and frustrating – experience for translators, but we must not let this impression lead toward an essentialist relationship to translation and its tools. A far more powerful ground for developing a translation attuned to its time is a thorough historicization, especially one that takes into account multiple national contexts. To avoid this is to flirt with the dangers demonstrated by the nationalist chauvinism of postwar Japanese subtitlers.

The subtitle has never been entirely ignored in Japan. Since at least the 1930s, *en-face* scenarios of foreign films have been published on a routine basis. However, the bulk of these contain complete translations of the films, and this speaks more for the Japanese film world's appreciation of the art of scenario writing than of subtitling per se. At the same time, there are currently schools devoted to training translators, and the name of the subtitler is always included as a credit in the Japanese prints of foreign films (at least in much of the postwar era). In fact, a number of these translators have achieved reputations among general audiences. Some subtitlers even have fans! The most famous – Shimizu Shunji, Okaeda Shinji, Kamishima Kimi, and Toda Natsuko – have published autobiographies, how-to books, and textbooks that use subtitles to teach English conversation.[5]

While many of history's most famous essays on translation have emerged in the course of practice, these authors' writings on "the art of subtitling" are deeply disappointing. Their conception of translation is regrettably simplistic. For example, the Russian cinematic adaptation and subsequent Japanese translation of *Hamlet* naturally raise the issue of the authority of the original text; oblivious to this kind of issue, Toda Natsuko – by far the most popular subtitler in Japan – uses the film only to suggest what a pity it would have been if dubbing had erased the main actor's beautiful, velvety voice (Toda 1994: 10). Similarly, her mentor Shimizu Shunji describes his subtitles for Olivier's *Othello*. Noting that the great actor's performance was more theatrical than cinematic, he made much of his going to the unusual length of listening to a tape recording of the soundtrack while translating (Shimizu 1992: 61–62). Now for most translators, Shakespeare's words provide their most daunting task, a test case for the most basic, pressing theoretical issues in translation. This does not occur to Shimizu or Toda. In both cases, the actor and his voice replace Shakespeare as the sources to which the translator owes a debt.

These authors' understanding of film history is just as impoverished; they have done little or no research into the past or present conditions of their field, but they never hesitate to explain or analyze it. In his "Philosophy of Subtitling," Okaeda Shinji bases his aesthetics of cinema on a naïve equation of silent and sound film narration. He unproblematically compares the narrative function of silent era intertitles to that of sound subtitles in the 1980s to support his aesthetics of cinema: the less words a film has the better.[6] He does not begin to consider the vast ontological and semiotic differences between silent and sound cinema. For example, he does not even mention the crucial role of the *benshi,* the famous screen-side narrator of Japanese silent film who offered both narrative commentary and mimicked the voices of the characters. This is a typical example of how simplistic is the conception of cinema with which corrupt subtitlers operate.

Furthermore, their understanding of the relationship of subtitlers to the world film industry and its politics is particularly inadequate. Toda reduces "America's standard practice of dubbing" to the fact that it is a nation of immigrants, a comment that feels uncannily similar to statements over which a number of ministers have resigned in recent years. Certainly an adequate explanation would have to deal with a complex overdetermination of forces: the emergence of English as a lingua franca of international business and politics; the world domination of Hollywood, its location within US borders, and its near total domination of the home market; and an education system that places no value on foreign language study. Furthermore, while mass-market films may be dubbed, it is incorrect to say this is standard practice. The actual market for foreign films has historically demanded subtitles, and this has also become true of mainstream releases for foreign films as of the 1980s.

Toda's brand of radical reduction is complemented by tedious gloating over the Japanese language, the sensitivity of Japanese spectators, and the special skills required of the translator of films. Toda: "Japanese people's special tendency to want to see the original created a unique subtitle nation [*yuniiku najimakukoku*]; here, we are happy that every Japanese can read, an extremely special condition anywhere in the world" (Toda 1994: 11). Okaeda: "Japanese people's intention [*shikō*] towards the original is strong [and one of the reasons] subtitles are the mainstream. [. . .] Considering this, subtitles are immortal. We could say, 'Japan: Nation of the Subtitle Culture'" (Okaeda 1989: 6). Subtitling is not in a repressed condition in Japan; rather, it is overvalued through the idealization of Japanese language and its own practice of translation of the foreign. Common sense might dictate that dubbing would be the translation method of choice for fervent nationalists (see, for example, the work of Martine Danan 1991); however, the Japanese case suggests how subtitling may also find itself subject to cultural and national chauvinism. In Japan, both the usual methods of repressing the subtitler and Japan's unusual fetishization of the subtitle achieve an identical effect in the end. They deflect or disavow the erasure of difference and the inequality of languages which the act of translation always threatens to expose.

A submerged history

There is a pressing need to update our approach to film translation and perhaps even to undertake new translations of old film texts. To provide some context for this project – and to further push subtitling from its obscured position – we must uncover its history. Like the workings of the apparatus, this history has been ignored (or, in the case of Japanese authors, reduced to anecdote and gossip). This should not be surprising when we note that subtitles were invented shortly after the coming of sound – the moment when text was globally suppressed from the cinema.

Much has been made of Hollywood's innovative attempts to overcome the obstacles sound posed to business in non-English speaking countries. However, current histories concentrate exclusively on the early solutions: teaching stars new languages and making identical foreign-language versions with different actors on the same set (for example, Vincendeau 1988, Andrew 1980, Danan 1999, Gomery 1980). Surprisingly enough, the invention of subtitles – the greatest innovation and ultimate solution to the problem – is a gap in our history. There were interesting precursors to the subtitle as translators attempted a number of strategies to transport the unwieldy apparatus across the language barrier. In Japan and other parts of the world on the cusp of the sound era, a typical work-around involved silent-film-style intertitles explaining each section of the plot. Rudolf Arnheim, that obstinate critic of the talking film, discussed his frustration with these early attempts at translation in a 1929 essay entitled, "Sound Film Confusion":

> But we are already caught in the midst of a babel of tongues. Erich Pommer wants to mix languages when he makes his next UFA [Universal Filmaktiengesellschaft] film. This will also force him to judge his actors not only by way of artistic measures, but also those of the Berlitz school [. . .] Those with no linguistic geniuses among their actors must either sell talking films as silent abroad, in which case the dialogue scenes are shortened and replaced with laborious inter-titles (a process which is already beginning to raise general protest), or they must shoot the same film twice, as a talkie and as a silent. Both processes are only possible when the film is a piece of industrial waste for the masses and not art. For a work of art is not a shirt with removable sleeves.
>
> (Arnheim 1997: 33–34)

Arnheim hoped that such frustration would repel spectators from the talkie and turn them back to the silent film. However, translators were searching for new methods. Luckily, the people that subtitled the first films (and in so doing wrote the rules and conventions of subtitling) have committed their memories to print. Herman Weinberg was the first translator in the world to use subtitles; he is probably their inventor. In the course of his career, he claimed to have titled over 400 films in Sicilian, Japanese, Swedish, Hindustani, Spanish, Brazilian, Greek, Finnish, Czech, Hungarian, and Yugoslavian (sic!) . . . obviously, a believer in knowing the target language better than the source language. (Surprisingly enough, this is not so unusual. In his 1989 profile, Okaeda Shinji claims over 1,000 titles to his credit, including *Citizen Kane*, *Star Wars*, and films in French, German, Italian, Russian and Spanish (Okaeda 1989: 229). Needless to say, one must wonder about quality in the face of such enthusiastic boasting over quantity.) Here Weinberg explains, in his own way, the experimentation that led to the codification of the practice:

> Someone with nothing better to do one day discovered the principle of the photo-electric cell which made it possible to transmit soundwaves into light waves and vice-versa, and which now made it possible for movies to talk. But when the films I was working with talked it was in French and German. What do we do now? Full screen titles was the first answer, stopping the action and giving the audience a brief synopsis of what they were going to see in the next ten minutes. Ten minutes later, another full-screen synopsis. This was not only silly but annoying as those in the audience who could understand the language could laugh at the jokes in between the full screen titles while those who couldn't (and they constituted the majority, by far) sat there glum, doubly irritated by the laughter of the linguists in the house. Obviously something had to be done to placate the customers before they started asking for their money back. Then someone discovered the existence of a mechanism called a "moviola." [. . .] It had a counter which enabled you to measure every piece of dialogue because it, too, was now equipped with that magical photo-electric cell so that you could now measure not only the length of every scene but that of every line of dialogue. And from these measurements we were able, by the trial and error method [. . .] to determine what we were doing and why. Whew! And when I say "we" I mean *me*, as no one knew any more than anyone else did about it and I seemed to be the only one willing to go ahead with the actual writing and make something out of it. At the beginning, I was very cautious and superimposed hardly more than 25 or 30 titles to a ten-minute reel. [. . .] Then I'd go into the theatre during a showing to watch the audiences' faces, to see how they reacted to the titles. I'd wondered if they were going to drop their heads slightly to read the titles at the bottom of the screen and then raise them again after they read the titles (like watching a tennis match and moving your head from left to right and back again) but I needn't have worried on this score; they didn't drop their heads, they merely dropped their eyes, I noticed. This emboldened me to insert more titles, when warranted, of course, and bit by bit more and more of the original dialogue got translated until at the end of my work in this field I was putting in anywhere from 100 to 150 titles a reel [. . .] tho', I must repeat, only when the dialogue was good enough to warrant it.
>
> (Weinberg 1985: 107–108)

This new technology of translation is what enabled Hollywood to avoid any inter-ruption in its dominance of the international film market. In Japan, new technology adding canned sound to image caused debates on many fronts, from the *benshi* who saw their livelihoods threatened to thoughtful critics theorizing a new practice for scenarios to leftist critics with industrial critiques. Most relevant to the discussion at hand, Marxist critic Iwasaki Akira argued the talkie was "anti-internationalistic" (*hikokusaiteki*) for the way sound emphasized the national character of films, particu-larly in the narrative drama (Iwasaki 1930: 74–75). Although not his main point, this unexpected awareness of the source culture through the insertion of the source language/sound is precisely the quality that subtitlers came to suppress. There were alternatives in the very early period. Tokyo's Teigeki and Horakuza theaters experimented with titles projected to the side of the screen and a number of Hollywood films used Japanese Americans for dubbing soundtracks. More often than not, the *benshi* would call translations over the soundtrack, which was turned down to facilitate the narrator's competition with the new sound technology.[7] Theaters adopted differing conceptions of translation. The famous *benshi* Matsui Suisei represented one approach, which restricted the translation to bare-bones plot summaries throughout the film; however, in other Asakusa theaters, *benshi* attended to each individually spoken line. Once every week, Matsui's Shibazonokan Theater held "no explanation talkie days" (*tōkii musetsumei dē*) for those who disliked the *benshi*'s interference with the pleasurable sounds of the original (Tachibana 1930: 118–119).

However, the method that became standard operating procedure was the super-imposed (sub)title – in parentheses because they were not always at the bottom of the frame. Within a year or two of the talkie's public appearance, the major studios brought translators to New York to subtitle the latest films. This included Shimizu Shunji and Tamura Yukihiko, who conducted the first translation with film subtitles in Japanese. The film was von Sternberg's *Morocco*, and this is Tamura's description of the process:

> First of all, the first problem we encountered was whether to use vertical or horizontal lines. For this, I performed various experiments. In the case of vertical lines, three-and-a-half feet of film were required to read one line with 12 characters. However, we found that if we printed the same line horizontally it would be impossible to read without five or more feet. Besides the decision to print vertically, we had to decide to put the subtitle on the right or left side. It was impossible to settle on a position. We'd put them on the right to avoid covering something on the left and vice versa. So we watched previews and investigated the problem scene by scene. [. . .] About 30 cards per reel was the limit. We were careful to avoid showing the embarrassing sight of titles from one scene running over into the next.
>
> (Tanaka 1980: 207)

After reading these first-person accounts by the pioneers of film translation, it would appear that the conventions of subtitling have changed little since their invention. This is to say that the rules and regulations that govern the production of subtitles (exclusive of those related to the apparatus itself) were set during the age of the Hollywood studio system. One might think this explains why subtitles look and function the way they do. However, it must also be stressed that while the subtitling apparatus itself has changed little, the practice of subtitlers has, and the changes themselves are closely tied to the ideological context at the moment of translation. Likewise, any theorization of subtitles must be considered against its historical moment, which points us to the weakness of Trinh's analysis of subtitling. Her understanding of a subtitling buttressing a unified subject position and the implicit call for an oppositional avant-garde is anchored too deeply in 1970s suture theory (see Creed 1998, Silverman 1983 and Rodowick 1988 for good historiographies of this theory). While I share her concerns over the ideological dimension of subtitling, I steer away from such essentialized arguments and toward a theorization grounded in a strong historical contextualization.

Let us focus on the example of Japanese subtitling and its historical development. A closer consideration of Tamura's description suggests there are crucial differences between prewar and present subtitling conventions. Unfortunately, most of the foreign films distributed in Japan before World War II were destroyed in the Film Center fire in the 1970s. (According to Shimizu Shunji, Films Inc. in Tokyo holds a 35mm print of Tamura's *Morocco*.) Other prewar prints of foreign films are extremely rare, and should they exist they would be equally difficult to view. There is, however, a way around this problem.

When a film was imported into Japan, the Home Ministry required the submission of a *ken'etsu daihon* (censorship scenario).[8] *Ken'etsu daihon* typically included a complete translation of every utterance and a description of nearly every sound effect. They also included an *en-face* listing of the film's subtitles. Only 3 copies were made, the official copy that received the Home Ministry seal, one for studio use, and one for preservation at the Ministry (with the establishment of the Film Law of 1939, two more copies were created for the Home Ministry's Information Bureau and the Ministry of Education). In any case, it should not be surprising that only a handful of these precious scenarios are extant.

Shimizu Shunji recently acquired the *ken'etsu daihon* of *Morocco*. His analysis is predictably superficial, but provides a useful starting point for exploring the real history of Japanese subtitles. Shimizu counts 297 subtitles in Tamura's version. Tamura's original translation used only 234, but after seeing a test print he felt the extra 63 titles were necessary.[9] Throughout his books, Shimizu often notes that before the war subtitlers used somewhere between a half and a third of the subtitles used today. With the *ken'etsu daihon* for *Morocco* in hand, he attempts to find the difference. First, he parses the scenario according to today's standards and decides his own count would come to 492. Then he counts Kikuji Hiroshi's postwar subbing of the film, which uses 491. Finally, he compares Kikuji's and Tamura's actual translations, concluding that outside of a few old *kanji*, excessively long subtitles, and Tamura's choice not to translate Dietrich's songs, there is no significant difference.

I find this a rather startling conclusion. Putting the actual translation of words aside for the moment, the difference between 297 and 492 strongly suggests we are dealing with two very dissimilar conceptions of translation. Shimizu was pursuing the wrong questions. Rather than wondering about the phrasing of individual titles, he should have been asking, "If Tamura chose to subtitle only half of the utterances, then what exactly was he translating? *What was the object of translation?*"

I have found the *ken'etsu daihon* for King Vidor's *The Champ* (1931), which contains Shimizu Chiyota's subtitles.[10] Consistent with Shimizu Shunji's writing, roughly half of the film's utterances went untranslated. Only 328 of the film's 869 lines received titles.[11] Upon closer examination, the first thing one notices is that the translation pares down the film primarily to narrative movement. This means certain characters which the translator deemed insignificant are virtually (or even completely) written out of the film because their lines go unsubtitled. For example, not only are the lines of Jackie Coogan's half-sister mostly untranslated, Shimizu ignored all references to her. The film never firmly establishes their relationship, so for viewers of the subtitled version she is simply a cute little girl who shows up every once in a while, says something incomprehensible, and then disappears. Her excision from the film via subtitles marks the film with a patriarchal reading placed *between* text and reader/spectator.

Another crucial criterion for selection appears to be thematic. *The Champ* is well known as an early response to the social effects of the Great Depression. The film's characterization revolves around a woman who divorced her poor husband (the boxer) for a rich man; the mother wants to remove their son from the Champ's custody to save the child from the "poor environment." However, Shimizu's translation tends to leave out verbal references to the class discourse of the film. Virtually the only subtitles that retain it point to visual markers of class which the audiences would not have missed, such as the difference between the Champ's flop-house apartment and the mother's luxurious hotel. Significantly, even class differences in speech itself – inflection, vocabulary, grammar, and the like – are largely unreflected in the style of the subtitles. We can find the real effects of Shimizu's selective translation in a special section devoted to Ozu's *Passing Fancy* (*Dekigokoro*, 1933) in *STS*, one of Japan's earliest film theory journals. At the time, this film was often compared to *The Champ* for its narrative centered on an intense father–son relationship, and apparently Ozu based the script on Vidor's film. In his *STS* article, Mura Chio attempts a structural comparison of the two films' scripts to investigate the differences between sound and silent film scenario writing. One of his conclusions: "In terms of story telling, [Frances] Marion's firm, text-heavy scenario style and Vidor's direct, solid directorial method precisely show us the instinctual love of father and child. However, they do not in any way describe the world that lower-middle-class people inhabit" (Mura 1933: 25). This suggests that the translator regards speech primarily as a vehicle for narrative propulsion, and that many of the choices regarding what to retain as relevant have quite serious ideological implications. However, the most important criterion is also the least obvious.

The Champ has (at least) three moments of melodramatic excess which are fascinating for their translation. By "excess" I mean elements such as mise-en-scène, sound, acting, and writing which are heightened to complement emotional distress. These scenes are the horse race where Jackie Coogan's horse stumbles just as it is about to win, the jail scene where Wallace Beery rejects Jackie and tells him to go to his mother, and the prize fight at the end. Shimizu's translation sets up each scene – and then simply stops. For example, the narrative tension of the horse race comes primarily from the announcer's call. Without his description of Coogan's come-from-behind bid for first place, it is impossible to tell which horse is in which position. There are no subtitles providing this information. The heartbreaking jail scene – by far the most memorable moment of the film – begins with a quiet dialogue between the Champ and his trainer Sponge. Of their nine lines, all but two are translated (and these were easy to guess by context). When the Champ's son Dink arrives, the melodrama gradually intensifies while the subtitle count drops steeply. From here until the moment Dink leaves the jail crushed by his father's explosive rejection, only nine of 24 lines are translated! Near the end, when the two scream at each other and the Champ violently strikes his son through the prison bars, the subtitles stop. This breaks the most cherished rules of today's corrupt subtitlers who – in a seemingly natural way – assign meaning to every utterance as a matter of course.

This returns us to our original question: "If not the meaning of every line, what exactly was the object of translation?" On the one hand, Shimizu was ignoring linguistic aspects that contribute to expression and simply translating the narrative meaning behind the words. He generally uses a translation strategy that strips the lines of dialogue to their barest, most basic function of moving the plot (granted, as he interprets it). On the other hand, for moments when the speech act itself was contributing to the overall expression of the film's emotional impact, *he chose not to translate*. Implicit in this decision was the assumption that the grain of the voice was more important than the meaning it articulated.

The example of *The Champ* is not an isolated fluke. In fact, other reports concerning prewar subtitling practices suggest a variety of graphic tactics that also exhibit a translation strategy focused on the materiality of language. For example, in *M* there is a scene in which a boy hawks newspapers; as the camera nears the boy, his voice gets louder on the soundtrack. At the same time, the Japanese subtitles translating the boy's voice grow correspondingly larger and larger, providing a graphic representation of the increasing volume.[12] Furthermore, Japanese subtitlers routinely placed their titles in different areas of the scene depending on the cinematographer's composition. It was thought that the position of the words should complement mise-en-scène and movement. At the same time, there are indications that subtitle positioning depended upon narrative as well. One story from critic Yodogawa Nagaharu describes a dreamy Hollywood love scene where the subtitles appeared between the two lovers (Toda 1994: 26–27). Of course!

The conception of translation in the talkie period circulated between two poles, between a hermeneutic search for, and transmission of, meaning, and a curious foregrounding of the material qualities of language (or a choice not to translate underpinned by the same values). The reason for this indeterminacy lies in the historical moment. We can detect as much from an article about the subtitling of *Morocco* which Tamura published ten days before the film's public release: "This time, there was the fear that with too few subtitles, the meaning would not come through. At least, I thought that it was necessary to use the same number of titles as silent movies. Spanish and Portuguese subtitles used far too many subtitles, more than 400 subtitles for one film. However, because Japanese audiences are sensitive to the feelings of films, I believed it was unnecessary to attach more than 30 subtitles per reel" (Tamura 1931). This is an approach to translation that relies on a conception of cinema grounded in the silent era. In the jail scene of *The Champ*, the subtitles initially correspond to the narrative mode of the talkie as it set up the premise for the confrontation between father and son; then it shifted back to silent cinema for the melodramatic finish.

While this seems to be a likely explanation, we must return to the silent era to adequately understand the specificities of this national cinema context and its historical moment. One might say that the *benshi* was the first form of dubbing in the pre-history of the talkie. These screen-side narrators would describe the action on the screen and supply voices for all the actors, eliminating the need for the translation of silent film intertitles. Aaron Gerow's research into the critical discourses surrounding the figure of the *benshi* reveals that reformers of the Pure Film Movement sought to modernize Japanese cinema by renovating the role of the *benshi* and revising the standard use of intertitles (Gerow 1996: 33). The *benshi*, they felt, should avoid flowery elocution for everyday speech and stick closely to the film-maker's plotting instead of their independent elaborations of the narrative. In other words, they hoped the *benshi* would become invisible, much like the corrupt subtitles of later decades. In the end, the *benshi* proved more powerful and popular, setting the stage for the unusual subtitles of the talkie era in Japan. We can attribute the two styles of pre-subtitle *benshi* translation – paraphrase vs. line-by-line – to these very discursive tensions designed by the Pure Film Movement. Second, the same reformers called for the elimination of intertitles, since film was essentially a visual medium. This could also help explain why so few subtitles were used in the 1930s compared to today. These are probably precedents contributing to an over-determination of forces bearing down on Japan's first subtitles.

By the end of the decade the shift to the postwar emphasis on narrative meaning becomes detectable. In a 1939 article entitled "The Impoverished Japanese of Spoken Titles," Ota Tatsuo criticizes contemporary subtitles and calls on translators to work towards a new Japanese language for film translation. He uses tropes for translation strategies which have circulated throughout the history of translation theory:

> Understanding [a film] means not intellectually, but perfectly matching the feelings, as if one with the same atmosphere, and soaking through to the inside of the hearts of the Japanese masses. Thus we must stop the spoken titles that are messengers brought from a foreign language; spoken titles should be messengers from a meeting with Japanese language. In other words, they are not translations of foreign language, but they must create in Japanese the things that are trying to be expressed in the foreign language.
>
> (Ota 1939: 51)

To this end, Ota calls for the end of direct translation of foreign words and the creation of a new Japanese language specifically for film translation. Subtitlers must stop relying on the advice of experts hired from university literature departments and write subtitles that speak directly to the soul of the masses. To this end, subtitlers must recognize the limits of *kanji* and restrict their usage of characters to a level attuned to the masses, which he determines is somewhere at or below the elementary school graduate's level. Subtitlers must strive to be like the *benshi*, which is to say become one with the fabric of the film so they may speak directly to their audience in the deepest sense (again a conception of the *benshi* consistent with the reformers of the Pure Film Movement). Above all, their subtitles should not be direct translations of foreign words, but strive for a perfect match with the Japanese soul.

This last assertion is crucial because it expresses the shift, and its historical moment, most clearly. Ota is calling for a subtitling practice that completely dominates the foreign. As with the Roman poets' relationship to Greek literature and Early Christian translators' relationship to the Hebrew and Greek Bibles, he hopes to enrich his own language in the process of appropriation. St. Jerome stated the premise of this kind of translation most directly: "The translator did not attend to the drowsy letter [. . .], but by right of victory carried the sense captive into his own language" (see Jerome in this volume). The issue of translation cuts straight through to the relationship of self and other. Ota's essay, written at a time when Japan was penetrating deep into China and contemplating a colonization of Asia, reveals a totalitarian wish for a subtitle that erases difference and incorporates foreign meaning into a perfected, harmonized mass readership. It is a theory of translation tailored to Japan's geopolitical aspirations. Ota's vision of a meaning-oriented translation would evolve into the codes of corruption in the postwar period, a style of translation that effaces its violent, mediating presence by hiding in the margins of the frame and discreetly translating every utterance on the soundtrack.

While Ota calls for a new writing and a new language, he still defends most of the prewar conventions, such as the number and placement of titles. However, an example from the other side of the globe may teach us that conventions themselves can be changed most easily at particular moments in history when the rules governing practices are in flux. Jean Eustache's *The Mother and the Whore* (*La Maman et la putain*, 1973) is a central post-1968 film made in the wake of the French New Wave. This film movement was centered on breaking cinematic conventions and indulging in those things only cinema is capable of – it was essentially abusive film-making. This liberated Eustache's translator to deal with the problem of the subtitle's violence with the kind of experimentation that works only at that kind of moment in film history. Throughout this clever film, the transparency of the subtitles would be interrupted with the bracketed note: *[Untranslatable French Pun]*. This provides a cogent example of the flexibility of subtitling that is engaged in the cinematic practice of its time. The very conception of this subtitle was possible only because the French New Wave film-makers were systematically attacking every convention of cinema. The freedom to experiment with textual knots of impossibility, however, can make the untranslatable French pun translatable. We must not reject impossibility, but embrace it. Moments of untranslatability – a nearly constant condition for the subtitler – are times for *celebration*, for not only are they privileged encounters with the foreign, but they are also opportunities for translators to ply the highest skills of their craft. They are moments crying for abuse.

The abusive turn

There is a potential and emerging subtitling practice that accounts for the unavoidable limits in time and space of the subtitle, a practice that does not feign completeness, that does not hide its presence through restrictive rules. We must reconsider our own historical moment and work toward a subtitling that engages today's sensibilities with a violence which is not corrupt, but abusive.

To sketch out the character of abusive subtitling and establish some sense for how it fits into the context of its own history, I propose we divide sound film history into three epochs of translation, the last of which is only just emerging. The history of translation discourse is full of tripartite formulas to describe different modes of translation, from Dryden to Novalis and Goethe to Jakobson. The epochs I suggest may be seen as historical phases through which cinema has passed, but they also surpass this diachronic structure and appear simultaneously. The potential for this simultaneity will be particularly important for our understanding of abusive subtitling. Roughly sketched, the three epochs of translation may be described in the following manner.

The first kind of translation occurs in the talkie era. It uses a straightforward prose to introduce the pleasures of foreign texts. The language of the subtitles themselves exhibits a functionality clearly designed to communicate the power of the foreign original as efficiently as possible. In this respect the first era of subtitles brings the foreign text to the spectators on their own domestic terms. At the same time, the translator remains fully cognizant of the material dimensions of language – both its graphic and aural qualities. It may be that this is a conception of cinematic translation anchored firmly to that transition into amplified aurality. However, while there can be no question of its historical specificity in this instance, we still must resist restricting a given mode of translation *as a possibility* in any period of cinema.

In the second epoch of cinematic translation, the translator pretends to move toward the foreign, dwell there, and bring its wonders to the waiting crowds. This era is replete with rules designed to guarantee a translation's quality, but what this regulation actually accomplishes is an appropriation of the source text and its thorough domestication. The rules also enforce a territorialization and professionalization of translation, producing stars and experts and excluding all alternatives. This mode of translation, which I have contemptuously called corrupt, conforms the foreign to the framework of the target language and its cultural codes. All that cannot be explained within the severe limits of the regulation subtitle gets excised or reduced to domestic meanings which are often irrelevant or inappropriate. These subtitlers claim to bring their readers/spectators to a pleasurable experience of the foreign, but in fact their impoverished translations keep audiences ignorant of the conspiracy and the riches that remain hidden from the cinematic experience.

The final part of this triptych brings us to the abusive. For this epoch of translation, I wish to borrow another phrase from Goethe, both for the power of its image and to specify what abusive subtitling is not. In the third stage of Goethe's own periodization of translation, "the goal of the translation is to achieve perfect identity with the original, so that the one does not exist instead of the other but in the other's place" (see Goethe in this volume). Here the translator identifies strongly with the source text and the culture in which it was produced, so much so that he cedes the particular powers of his own culture to accomplish a translation that invites the reader/spectator to a novel and rich experience of the foreign. Of course, Goethe's conception of translation is deeply tied to Romantic notions that seek to define the self through its various others – another form of domestication. However, abusive subtitling avoids this kind of erasure of difference, seeking to intensify the interaction between the reader and the foreign. This translation does not present a foreign divested of its otherness, but strives to translate from and within the place of the other by an inventive approach to language use and a willingness to bend the rules, both linguistic and cinematic.

As we have seen, the key differences between the translation of printed texts and the subtitling of moving image media are that the cinema adds the human voice to the equation and is propped up by an apparatus that *requires* a violent translation which in turn exhibits many of the traits Philip Lewis calls abusive. Even the subtitles for the most nondescript, realist film tamper with language usage and freely ignore or change much of the source text; however, corrupt subtitlers suppress the fact of this violence necessitated by the apparatus, while the abusive translator enjoys foregrounding it, heightening its impact and testing its limits and possibilities. To the extent that Lewis's abusive translation demonstrates a new articulation of fidelity in its will to play with convention, his model is attractive to the subtitler of the emergent third epoch. This theorization will prove particularly attractive in an age where the experience of the foreign is valued, and where abuse helps inject a palpable sense of the foreign.

In the Derridian approach to translation theorized by Lewis, abuse is directed at both language and its metaphysical assumptions. While this is a component of the abusive subtitle, the objects and ends of abuse do not amount to a mere resurrection of 1970s film theory and its valorization of experimentation in combating the evils of Hollywood realism with a deconstructive or Brechtian avant-garde.[13] The problems with such a position have since been argued on many fronts: its Eurocentrism, its elitism, and its inability to account for popular reading modes. Still, we may consider the critiques of poststructuralist film theory the segue between the second and third epochs of subtitling.

Because we are interested in the domesticating tendencies of the conventional subtitling practices of the second epoch, we may position abusive subtitling as a critique of dominant ideology. However, it does not amount to a simple experimentation designed to block ideological interpellation through distanciation techniques. Faced with the losses inevitable in all translation, the abusive subtitler assumes a respectful stance vis-à-vis the original text, tampering with both language and the subtitling apparatus itself in order to release what Lawrence Venuti has called the "remainder," textual and cinematic effects that exceed the creation of a narrative-focused equivalence and work only in the receiving culture (see Venuti in this volume). It is a new notion of fidelity attentive to the various aural and visual qualities of language in motion pictures, this in addition to the linguistic and literary styles of screenwriting.

Let us look at a number of concrete examples that suggest that corrupt subtitling practices are obsolete and the time for abuse is ripe. Donald Richie, who has subtitled some of the most famous Japanese films, is the translator of Kurosawa's *Ran*, one of the most abusive translations ever undertaken (with the possible exception of the Situationist René Viénet's appropriations of kung-fu films in post-1968 France or the dubbing of Woody Allen's *What's Up, Tiger Lily?*).[14] With the coming of talkies, Japanese samurai films found it necessary to codify a version of what pre-Meiji Japanese language should sound like. They ended up with a samurai version of Jacobean English, which has remained a central feature of the genre up to the present. This poses an interesting dilemma for the subtitler, who is well aware of the generic importance of this specialized language – one can hardly imagine a period film without it (indeed, to replace it with "standard Japanese" would probably be perceived as daringly experimental). However, there is no way to bring this important element of the genre to a foreign spectator without breaking the laws of corruption, which is exactly what Richie attempted. He writes, "Carried away by all the pageantry I relaxed my guard and thought to intrude a bit of period color of my own. [. . .] I left out the occasional prepositions in a way common to formal court English. Something like 'I want you to go,' I foolishly rendered as 'I would with you go.' Not incorrect but, in dialogue titles, completely inappropriate" (Richie 1991: 16). Obviously regretting his experiment, Richie finally exemplifies the sensibility of corruption when he calls for a "scrupulously anonymous kind of English." He continues, "I feel that the translation should be invisible. [. . .] Any oddity, any term too heightened, as well as any mistake, calls attention to this written dialogue. I won't even use exclamation points. The language should enter the ear as the image enters the eye" (Ibid.). I couldn't disagree more. Actually, these subtitles were quite wonderful for the way they released certain effects into English that correspond to the generically tortured Japanese of the film itself, but subsequent video versions have substituted Richie's subtitles with an extremely anonymous translation. Richie self-censors his smart impulse to abuse the text.

Rob Young confronted similar issues with Yamamoto Masashi's *Tenamonya Connection* (*Tenamonya konekushon*, 1991), which celebrates Osaka's culture and dialect. This film is subtitled "Fools Cross Borders" (*Aho wa kyokai o koeru*) and in the course of its 90-odd minutes it criss-crosses between Tokyo, Hong Kong, and Osaka, blurring the boundaries between Hong Kong/Tokyo, fiction/documentary, Hong Kong comedy/Japanese comedy, male/female, and even inside movie/outside theater. Young takes this rowdy playfulness as license to experiment ever so slightly. He manipulates his English in a manner analogous to Richie, filling his text with excessive contractions, slang, and nonstandard dialects of English where the scenario deploys an analogous fast-and-loose approach to speech, or where it celebrates linguistic markers of class and regional difference. Another tactic he uses comes far closer to the spirit of abusiveness. Obscene expressions like *konchikusho!* and *konoyarō!* are translated *!%&$#!@!!*

We can learn several things from Young's example. First, this is not the kind of censorship we expect of corrupt subtitles, which often leave obscene language untranslated. Granted, it would have been far more abusive to actually use obscenities in English, but to do so would risk damaging the film's chances at international distribution. As we've seen, the censors lurk at every stage of film production and distribution. So Young runs the gauntlet of censors by experimenting with language in ways that are analogous to the linguistic playfulness of the original scenario and its verbalization. Second, faced with the seemingly untranslatable, the abusive subtitler may seek to produce polyvalencies and knots of signification that may not coincide precisely with the problem in the source text. Not all of Young's subtitles using nonstandard grammar have a one-to-one correspondence with similar utterances on the soundtrack. Nevertheless, his approach cues the spectator to the elaborate playfulness of the dialogue that would have been completely erased by corrupt titles. Third, despite his instinctual abusiveness, Young, like Richie before him, also restricts himself to the time/space/graphic limits of the standard subtitle. Attuned to his historical moment in the third epoch, Young hints at the possibilities; but a truly abusive subtitling would have been as wild as the original film. It would have brought the spectator exceedingly close to the film. This would appear radical from the perspective of the second era, but surely you, who live in the emerging third era, can feel the problems with convention.

There are more daring and thrilling examples of the emerging abusive subtitle elsewhere, places where capital does not enforce the rules and regulations of corruption. In the spring of 1993, Professor Laurel Rodd of the University of Colorado assigned her Japanese translation class the task of translating subtitles for the opening of Itami Jūzo's *A Taxing Woman Returns* (*Marusa no onna 2*, 1987). This short sequence includes strings of *kango* (Chinese words) and snatches of classical Japanese. The class quickly learned to appreciate the difficulties facing the translator of films, but their intuitive solutions to confronting the practical issues had little to do with the corrupt rules of the second epoch's subtitlers. They regretted their "inability" to experiment by putting subtitles in different colors and in different parts of the frame. In fact, their exercise was hypothetical and nothing was preventing them from indulging in the most outrageous innovation (the new technologies of video which link the apparatus with computers can easily manipulate the material aspects of the subtitle through colors, fonts, sizes, and animation). The tools are in place, but the professionals, like the students above, check themselves, held back as they are by the inertia of convention and the ideology of corruption.

Actually, this has not restrained one group of translators from whom we may learn much. In fact, this article was inspired by their work. In the past few years, a massive fandom has developed around Japanese animation (*anime*) throughout the world. A substantial portion of the fan activity concentrates on translation. Scripts are posted on internet newsgroups and circulated among clubs and individuals. Fan hackers write software for the Amiga and other computer platforms, software that enables them to take the subtitling apparatus into their own hands. Groups collaborate on not-for-profit subtitled versions of their favorite *anime*. Working outside of the mainstream translation industry, lacking any formal training, these fans have produced abusive subtitles *quite by instinct*. In scenes with overlapping dialogue, they use different colored subtitles. Confronted with untranslatable words, they introduce the foreign word into the English language with a definition that sometimes fills the screen. Footnotes! Some tapes include small-type definitions and cultural explanations which are illegible on the fly (here we find a completely new viewing protocol made possible by video where the viewer halts the apparatus's mindless march and reads subtitles at leisure). They use different fonts, sizes, and colors to correspond to material aspects of language, from voice to dialect to written text within the frame. And they freely insert their titles all over the screen. It is as if history folds back on itself and we find a resurgence of the subtitling practice of the talkie era, but the underlying differences put the two worlds apart.

The example of *anime* fandom reveals the distance between the often elitist valorizations of anti-Hollywood experimentation and the abusive subtitle. Both may be canny on ideological problems, both may innovatively break convention, but the latter attempts to engage readers' sensibilities with the same sensibilities with which the readers engage their texts. Just as the spectator approaches films from faraway places to enjoy an experience of the foreign, the abusive translator attempts to locate his or her subtitles in the place of the other. Rather than smothering the film under the regulations of the corrupt subtitle, rather than smoothing the rough edges of foreignness, rather than convening everything into easily consumable meaning, the abusive subtitles always direct spectators back to the original text. Abusive subtitles circulate between the foreign and the familiar, the known and the unknown. Were we speaking of the translation of printed texts, the third epoch would most likely be filled with interlinear books (among other, more stylistically innovative tactics). And is this not a characteristic of the foreign film's structure? The subtitled moving image is a constellated figure; both the original and the translation are simultane-ously available, as if they were *en face*. Most important, viewers work off the original text whether they understand its language or not. Although corrupt subtitles work strongly against this reading practice, abusive subtitles encourage it.

The time is ripe for abuse, if only because we are in an age where moving image literacy includes the ability to manage complex text/image relations. Audiences bring those talents to the foreign film, but they go entirely unused. Indeed, what once was radical experimentation is now the stuff of Hollywood cinema, MTV and pop-up video, commercials, sitcoms, and the nightly news. Complex image/text relationships are a normalized textuality from everyday experience (exceedingly so in Japan). From this perspective, corrupt subtitling is actually archaic. Thus, abuse is directed at convention, even at spectators and their expectations. And when abusive subtitling becomes normalized, we will think of other terms – or simply drop the adjective. It is likely that abusive translations will begin with animation, comedies, the art film, and the documentary – texts that are themselves transgres-sive or essayistic – but there is nothing holding us back from subjecting the most non-violent films to abuse. The only other choice is corruption.

Notes

1 For excellent bibliographies collecting this work, see Gambier 1994 and de Linde and Kay 1999. I would like to extend my thanks to Darrell Davis, David Desser, and particularly to Lawrence Venuti, Makino Mamoru and Aaron Gerow for their help and comments while writing this essay. Gerow in particular helped me flesh out the section on the Pure Cinema Movement. His dissertation on the movement is groundbreaking work (Gerow 1996).

2 An analogous reversal of power may be found in the translation of *The X-Files* for Japanese television, in this case through the apparatus of dubbing. Mulder is dubbed by a man with a husky, deep, tough-man voice, while Sculley's rela-tively low, business-like tone is replaced with the high-pitched voice one usually associates with soap operas and weather report announcers. This manipulation of the material qualities of language – in this case the grain of the voice – reverses the sexual play and politics of the show. While less dramatic, the *Robocop* example displays the same dynamic. As I will argue below, standard subtitles ignore the material aspects of language.

3 See for example, Toda 1994: 27, Okaeda 1988: 18, Kamijima 1995: 22.

4   Toda (1994: 27) is reporting hearsay; it appears she has done no real research for her history.

5   Biographies include Toda 1994, Kamijima 1995, and Shimizu 1985. The latter is the most famous, but Kamijima's is the most interesting of the bunch. How-to books are popular among translators looking to add variety to their usual slate of boring business translations; a few of them are apparently used as text-books in classes offered by some of the more high-profile subtitlers: see Kamijima 1995, Okaeda 1988 and 1989, Shimizu 1988 and 1992.

6   Okaeda 1989: 194–195. Far more disturbing is his ignorant homophobia when he prefaces a section on homosexuality and subtitling with a bizarre aside implying America has "homos" and Japan does not, and explicitly blaming AIDS on American homosexuals.

7   This strategy continued well into the postwar period in many parts of Asia that used narrators throughout the silent period.

8   The subtitler's collaboration with structures of censorship is an important form of corruption I do not have time to explore in this context. In Japan, subtitles were strictly censored in both prewar and postwar eras. More recently, censorship has largely been directed at the image exclusive of the soundtrack. Shimizu served for many years on the board of Eirin, one of the primary censorship authorities in Japan. Okaeda has a curious passage in his lectures about subtitling pornography. For example, he warns his students not to translate "Oh, that feels so good" directly over the utterance/sex act because the translation would never pass censorship proceedings; however, if the subtitle appears before or after, as in "I'll make you feel good," there should be no problem. How this practice affects the translation of mainstream texts is left unexplained (Okaeda 1989: 201–202).

9   Shimizu 1988: 350. While Shimizu's account says this version never reached public theaters, a contemporary article suggests otherwise. In "A Quick Note on the Talkie," Hayashi Chitose went to the trouble of counting lines of dialogue and subtitles. Hayashi's count: 387 spoken lines/229 subtitles with 4 "inserted subtitles," for an average of 32 lines/19 subtitles per reel. While he notes that the most dialogue-heavy scene of the film uses more subtitles (41 for 52 lines), Hayashi stops his analysis with the basic argument that less is better. I argue below this is nothing other than a silent era-specific concep-tion of cinema carded over the sound barrier (Hayashi 1931: 39).

10   These and other ken'etsu daihon are preserved in the Makino Mamoru Collection and the Kawakita Institute. Shimizu Chiyota was, along with Tamura, one of the founding members of Kinema Junpo, the premier film maga-zine from the early twentieth century to the present.

11   Longer lines required multiple subtitles, making the total number of subtitles 360. The other ken'etsu daihon I inspected appeared to have similar subtitle counts. They may be found in the Makino Mamoru Collection.

12   This was related to me by Komatsu Hiroshi, who saw the print while working at the National Film Center of Japan.

13   Antje Ascheid's article on dubbing attempts to avoid these traps, but falls into others because of an inadequate theorization of translation itself.

14 In 1973 René Viénet created incendiary subtitles for a Hong Kong kung fu film called *The Crush* (dir. Doo Kwang Gee and Lam Nin Tung, 1972). The credit for the translation went to "Association pour le développement de la lutte des classes et la propagation du matérialisme dialectique," and the release title was *La Dialectique peut-elle casser les briques? (Can the Dialectic Break Bricks?)*. Robert Stam and Ella Shohat report that "A sequence of devastating karate blows would be subtitled: 'Down with the bourgeoisie!'" (Stam and Shohat 1985: 35–59). For a contemporary review of this curious translation, see S. 1973: 110–111. *What's Up, Tiger Lily?* is actually a low-budget Japanese detective film with Allen's parodic dubbing on the soundtrack. One could also imagine an abusive dubbing, although ultimately dubbing is mired in corruption because it completely erases the experience of foreign sound, one of the most crucial material aspects of language. These examples are also curious for their parody, which indulges in the abusive translator's pleasure in experiencing the foreign, while sharing the corrupt translator's domination of the source text.

Chapter 31

Ian Mason

TEXT PARAMETERS IN TRANSLATION: TRANSITIVITY AND INSTITUTIONAL CULTURES

1 Introduction

IT IS AT LEAST PLAUSIBLE to suggest that large institutions may develop translational cultures of their own. This might happen because guidelines are issued to all translators working for the institution, in the form of glossaries, style guides, codes of practice and so on; or it might simply be a development which grows over a period of years out of shared experience, the need to find common approaches to recurring problems or through advice and training offered to new employees. Relatively little has been written about such phenomena and the issue of institutional approaches to translating might be considered to be a neglected factor within the field of translation studies. There are of course some exceptions. Mossop (1988, 1990) looks at the assumptions underlying advice to translators issued by the Federal Government of Canada and the implications of the policy. Koskinen (2000) asks similar questions of the translation doctrine of the European Union (EU) institutions, noting on the way that the EU tends to develop a culture of its own and thus 'develops its own idiom in 11 dialects'. She thus sees the translations produced by EU institutions as 'intra-cultural' (Koskinen 2000: 58). But the primary value of these studies is that they open up a field of enquiry and point to the need for further research into such matters. An appropriate question will be: do the guidelines issued by institutions affect actual translational practice in any uniform way? Within the scope of this article, it will not be possible to reach a valid and reliable answer to such a broad question. The evidence adduced, however, may be sufficient to cast doubt on some views about the control of translators by the institutions which employ them.

2003/revised 2004

For Mossop, it is the goals of the institution that determine the general approach taken by translators:

> Customers may well ask for literal renderings, but whether or not literal renderings get produced will depend on whether the institution's doctrine of translation allows for this approach.
>
> (Mossop 1988: 66)

What we have here are the makings of a testable hypothesis. It should be possible to track, in some systematic way, the transfer of stated policy into practice, to gauge the extent to which translator behaviour is influenced by the institution's goals or policy on translation.

Now, one way of measuring this would be to match actual lexical choice by translators to the advice to be found in the in-house glossaries, style guides and other guidelines issued to them. But this, of course is the more conscious and deliberate end of the implementation of policy. If a given item of terminology calls for a particular rendering, then that is the way it will be treated, irrespective of the translator's own preferred style and inclinations. But there are other text parameters worth exploring, for what they can reveal about underlying attitudes towards text and translating. Prominent among these is **transitivity**, a key site for exploring basic strategies since it pertains to the way processes are viewed and presented. In Systemic Grammar (e.g. Halliday 1985), transitivity is located within the ideational function, pertaining to the representation of experiential meaning in the clause. It shows 'how speakers encode in language their mental picture of reality and how they account for their experience of the world around them' (Simpson 1993: 88). For Fowler (1996: 74), 'agency, state, process and so on', the elements of transitivity, 'seem to be the basic categories in terms of which human beings present the world to themselves through language'. It follows that any text, including a translation, embodies a representation of experience, signalled through the transitivity system, and that shifts in transitivity may consequently involve shifts in representation. In this way, transitivity is closely bound up with **point of view.** The latter is of course not restricted to transitivity but also involves such parameters as deixis, modality and thematicity. But shifts of transitivity may involve shifts of point of view. For although individual choices of process type pertain at clause level, they concatenate at text level to form an overall pattern of representation.

Returning now to the starting hypothesis about institutional doctrines affecting individual translator styles, it would seem that translator behaviour within the parameter of transitivity could usefully be compared to whatever institutional advice is available at the time of translating. Broadly, one might expect, within the general variety of language in use and making allowance for grammatical or idiomatic preferences of particular languages, some evidence of **consistent translation practice** within an institution. Specifically, then, in what follows, we shall be interested in seeking to address two questions:

1   What evidence is there, if any, of a uniformity of approach across different language sections, consistent with the professed aims of the institution?

2   To what extent do actual shifts of transitivity contribute to signalling significantly different values at the level of text and discourse in translated
documents?

As suggested above, there can, for the time being, be no definitive answers to
such questions. The investigation reported here is simply on too small a scale to be
able to yield reliable and generalisable findings. At most, we shall be able to put
forward some tentative hypotheses, to be tested against longer and broader
data sets.

2 Translating for institutions

There is scope for a much more detailed investigation of the guidance offered within
institutions to translators, be they full-time in-house staff or regular or occasional
freelancers. So far, we have no more than a patchwork of insights from a variety of
sources, together with discussions in Mossop (1988, 1990), Koskinen (2000),
Munday (2001), Wagner, Bech and Martinez (2002). It is interesting to compare
some of the institutional policies reported by these scholars. According to Mossop
(1990: 346n.), 'the [Canadian] federal government's "translation doctrine" states
that one should render "not the **words** or the **structures** of the source-text but
rather the message or, in other words, the author's intention"' (Translation Bureau
1984: 3; emphasis mine). In similar vein, a later document (*Revisers' Handbook* 1985)
from the same source advises against 'keeping slavishly to the expressions and structures chosen by the author'. Implied here is a view that structures belong to the
formal make-up of texts and are entirely separable from the 'message' to be relayed
in translation. This would, in practice, entail wholesale changes to source-text (ST)
transitivity structures in the interests of relaying 'intention'. There are, of course,
many questionable assumptions here. For the moment, let us leave these aside and
compare other institutional attitudes and policies.
    A further aspect of the Canadian Translation Bureau's policy is the requirement
of 'authenticity':

> Authenticity is the impression conveyed by a translation that it is not,
> in fact, a translation, that it was composed in the target language from
> the outset, that it is an original piece of writing.
>   (Translation Bureau 1984: 6, cited in Mossop 1990: 347n.)

It is, to say the least, an interesting twist to our understanding of the notion of
'authenticity' to extend it to a process whereby something which is, in fact, a translation is presented as something which is not! What is being proposed here is, of
course, an illusion; but it is a widespread one. The supposed invisibility of the translator is well ingrained in Western (and especially Anglo-American) culture, as amply
documented by Venuti (1995). It is also worth noting that the notion of authenticity is inscribed in the Treaty of Rome (1957) and underlies translation policy in
EU institutions.

The two institutions selected for this study of institutional translator behaviour are the European Parliament and UNESCO, using evidence from translations of the debates in Parliament and of articles in the UNESCO *Courier*, which during its existence (1948–2001) was a monthly publication that appeared in many different language editions. Both sets of translator output are available on the internet, at **www3.europarl.eu.int/omk/omnsapir.so/debats** and **www.unesco. org/courier** respectively. Evidence of official guidance on translation policy is available in a number of publications and some salient points are worth recording here. Koskinen (2000: 54) writes of the EU Commission's Translation Service that 'there is a clear, albeit unwritten, preference for surface-level similarity, which is assumed to guarantee that readers of the various translations all get the same message'. Equivalence, she claims, 'is often taken to mean linguistic correspondence, or literal rerendering' (2000: 55). In line with this and with the notion of 'authenticity' as discussed above, it is official policy in all EU institutions that translations are not referred to as such but rather as 'language versions'. That is, the translations are presented as if texts were drafted in all languages simultaneously, as if no source text existed (Wagner, Bech and Martinez 2002: 8–9). This ensures that no text can be taken to be more authoritative than any other and that there is, consequently, complete equality between all official languages. In the particular case of the debates of the European Parliament, the interventions of successive members, all speaking in their own native tongue, can be read all in one language, as if the debate itself had been monolingual. These presentational features are important indicators of institutional policy and of the way translations are expected to be viewed by their users.

Munday (2001: 31) reports that UNESCO has issued a set of Guidelines for its translators (Kidd 1997), in which it is said that accuracy is 'the very first requirement' for all translations. The organisation's translating activities, of course, span a range of fields and genres, including documents for meetings and conferences, in which discrepancies between different language versions can be a source of trouble and are therefore shunned as far as possible. In the case of periodicals – the focus of this study – it is said (Kidd 1997: 3) that 'while accuracy is still of the greatest importance', journal editors will insist on receiving a 'readable text'. As Munday observes, some of the terms used here to offer advice to translators are of the most traditional kind, a point which applies more generally to policy statements on translation. They are also usually under-specified: 'accurate', 'idiomatic', 'equivalent', 'literal', 'message' are all terms which beg more questions than they resolve, as is now more or less universally recognised in the field of translation studies. Finally, some of the requirements may be seen to conflict with each other, the final judgement being left to the translator.

3 Transitivity: the evidence

In the light of all this, we return to the initial question: what evidence is there of uniformity of practice within institutions? For the purposes of analysis, a basic model of transitivity was used, based on those advanced by Halliday (1985), Simpson

Table 31.1 Process, participants and circumstances

Process	Participants	Circumstances
Material (doing)	Actor/Goal	
	Prices fell	in August
	He made the coffee	
Verbal (saying)	Sayer/Target/Verbiage	
	She asked him a question	
	The forecast warns of rain	
Mental (sensing)	Senser/Phenomenon	
	Her head ached	
	She forgot his name	
Relational (being, having)	Carrier/Attribute	
	Jill was talkative	at breakfast
	Jill has millions	in the bank
	Jill got drunk	on vodka

(1993) and Martin, Matthiessen and Painter (1997). Schematically, this can be represented and exemplified as in Table 31.1.

Using a small corpus of randomly selected texts in English, French and Spanish and their translations into each other language, shifts of transitivity were tracked in the translations of speeches delivered in the European Parliament and of articles that appeared in the UNESCO *Courier*. Attempts at quantification of the findings proved to be fraught with difficulty. The first problem is that, given structural/systemic differences between languages, a number of shifts are obligatory (Calzada Pérez 1997: 130) and will be introduced automatically by any competent translator. These then give no indication at all of translators' strategies or spontaneous behaviour since there is no choice but to shift. Consequently, they have to be filtered out of any analysis which seeks to count shifts introduced by the translator as a deliberate action on their part. An example is the pronominal verbal construction in Spanish, whereby a process can be presented in an agentless way and the translator has to find an alternative structure in English (often the passive). Thus, the sequence,

> De no hacerse así – y no se ha hecho así – el riesgo que se corre [. . .]
> (Calzada Pérez 1997: 153),

might become 'if it is not done in this way – and it has not in fact been done in this way – the risk that is run [. . .]'. But even in these cases, there is choice and the translator opted here for 'if he fails to do this – and he has not done it – he runs the risk', identifying the agent of the material action process. The shift then becomes a significant one but if all shifts of Spanish pronominal processes are counted, the resulting figures would undoubtedly obscure the relative incidence on translations of translator choice.

A second problem is the boundary between disallowed structures and those which are (more or less strongly) dispreferred. It would for example be possible to translate

> Cela permet d'évacuer rapidement le personnel
>
> (Mossop 1990)

as 'This allows rapid evacuation of staff' or even 'This facilitates evacuating the staff quickly'. But neither of these is a preferred option in English: 'In this way staff can be evacuated quickly' (Mossop 1990: 343) is a far more likely option. The dividing line between this category and the previous one is fuzzy, leading to endless problems of classification. Those shifts which are properly the focus of attention in this study are the ones which result from the independent exercise of choice by the translator: more-or-less automatic shifts obscure the true picture. Finally, there is the issue of the relative significance of shifts. Many alter the sense in which a process may be viewed by the text receiver in a significant way, particularly when they combine with other shifts in their textual environment. Others, however, may appear relatively insignificant. For example, a French Member of the European Parliament (MEP), commenting on an industrial accident, offers,

> Ma pensée va aux victimes,

which is translated as: 'My thoughts are with the victims'. Technically, the two utterances receive a different transitivity analysis, as Material Action Process and Relational Process respectively. Including such shifts in a quantification of total shifts, however, would tell us very little about translator behaviour and would overwhelm any figures representing significant shifts. Yet it is difficult to define a reliable – i.e. replicable – boundary between the insignificant and the rest.

For reasons such as these, quantitative analysis was abandoned at this stage in the research. Nevertheless, there is scope for a quantitative study of more limited features, such as the treatment in translation of participants in processes represented by personal pronouns, where there would seem to be great variation within the corpus. What follows is a qualitative analysis of the overall patterns of treatment of transitivity in the texts studied. Before presenting these trends, two final observations are in order. First, the analysis is in no way intended to be normative. No judgements or criticisms of translators' actions are intended. Rather, the study is intended as a contribution to Descriptive Translation Studies, in the interests of learning more of regularities of translator behaviour. Second, the singling out of instances of shifts is not intended to be taken as a plea for literalism in translation. On the contrary, the translator's creativity and the limits which translators themselves impose on this are the focus of our attention.

4 Uniformity of approach

We now return to the first of the two questions posed at the outset. The first broad and general finding is a predictable one. Overall, the translations of the speeches to the European Parliament stay relatively close to the transitivity patterns observable in the source texts (STs). The sensitivity of pronouncements by prominent politicians and the need to avoid misrepresenting not only intended meanings but the words actually spoken by them could conceivably be a motivating factor here. Conversely, the UNESCO *Courier* translators display greater latitude, as befits the field of journalism where ease of processing by the reader of the translations may be seen as a high priority (cf. the Guidelines reviewed above).

In the case of the Parliament translations, many shifts appear to have been effected for the sake of idiomatic preference. For example, English material processes frequently become French nominalisations; French active processes become English passives; Spanish 'se hace', etc. becomes French 'on fait', and so on; in English, there is often personalisation of actors in material processes, where in French and Spanish the actor is not made explicit. These are, of course, familiar contrastive regularities of natural expression in the languages concerned and a seasoned translator may well regard such shifts as routine tactics. Yet the reverse processes are also evinced in the data with significant regularity. Personalisation may be added in translations from English into French and English nominalisations become French material action processes:

English nominalisations	French material processes
adoption	l'adopte
the separation	maintenir à l'écart
implementation	mettre en œuvre
co-operation	coopérer

Above all, it is apparent that a heterodox range of approaches to the task co-exist in both institutions. In some cases, there is a high incidence of calques of ST transitivity.

That such cases are common is in no way surprising since there is often no need to alter ST transitivity in any way. A process may best be represented in the target-language text (TT) by the same process type. Examples 1–4 below, however, seem to go beyond this and are characteristic of a widespread strategy – evinced in both institutions – of adhering as closely as possible to the formal arrangement of the ST.

> **1 ST** By destroying accumulated wealth and the sources of future production, total war has sharply increased the pressure of existing populations upon their resources and has thereby sharply curtailed the liberties of vast numbers of men and women, belonging not only to the vanquished nations, but also to those which were supposed to be victorious.
>
> **TT** Al destruir la riqueza acumulada y las fuentes de la producción futura, la guerra mundial ha aumentado intensamente la presión de la [sic] poblaciones existentes sobre sus recursos, y, por lo mismo, ha mutilado gravemente las libertades de un vasto número de hombres y mujeres pertenecientes no sólo a las naciones vencidas, sino también a aquellas que se suponían victoriosas.
>
> (*Courier*, December 2001)

> **2 ST** It [the accident] rendered a large number of houses uninhabitable and affected the electricity distribution system.
>
> **TT** Il a par ailleurs rendu inhabitables de nombreuses maisons et affecté le système de distribution électrique.
>
> (Wallström, 1 October 2001)

3 ST [. . .] parce que l'Etat et la mairie n'ont pas voulu imposer les mesures nécessaires

TT [. . .] because the government and the town hall did not want to impose the necessary measures

(Laguiller, 1 October 2001)

4 ST La orientación de la PAC ha favorecido la aparición de ciertos problemas. La búsqueda de la competitividad a cualquier precio favorece la introducción de métodos y técnicas cuyas consecuencias a largo plazo se desconocen.

TT L'orientation de la PAC a favorisé l'apparition de certains problèmes. La recherche de la compétitivité à tout prix favorise l'introduction de méthodes et de techniques dont les conséquences à long terme ne sont pas connues.

(Jové Peres, 6 June 1996)

Certainly, the highest incidence of such calques is to be found in translations between French and Spanish, as might be expected given the syntactic similarities of the two languages. The calque is the lowest common denominator, as it were, of translating and may, for some translators, be a default mechanism, to be over-ridden only where necessary. But calques are also frequent in translations in both directions between English and French or Spanish. Moreover, this is true of both institutional settings – despite the institutional preferences referred to above.

Co-existing with these calques, however, there is striking ST/TT variation in translations to be found in the immediate environment of those just reviewed. In the *Courier*, a frequent, if not constant, trend is attenuation of agency (in all translation pairs). This may be effected by agent deletion, displacement to a less salient position or re-lexicalisation of participants from more to less specific designations.

In the case of French-to-English translations of one parliamentary debate, there are instances of a move towards increased directness affecting process, participants or circumstances. In examples 5–9, highlighting has been added to draw attention to modifications which serve to intensify some aspect of the overall process.

5 ST Mais peut-on voir se succéder les catastrophes qui ont frappé mon pays [. . .] sans que la solidarité puisse se manifester?
[But can one watch follow each other the catastrophes which have struck my country . . . without solidarity being able to manifest itself?]
TT But can we **just sit back and** watch the disasters that have struck France [. . .] without demonstrating some European solidarity?

(Berès, 1 October 2001)

6 ST c'est un homicide
[It is a homicide]
TT It is **murder**

(Laguiller, 1 October 2001)

7 ST La responsabilité du trust TotalFinaElf [. . .] est entière.
[The responsibility of the TotalFinaElf trust . . . is complete.]
TT The TotalFinaElf corporation [. . .] **is** fully responsible.

(Laguiller, 1 October 2001)

8 ST Le groupe TotalFinaElf récidive, de manière tragique
[The TotalFinaElf group is committing another offence, in a tragic way]
TT The TotalFinaElf group [. . .] has acted **criminally**, once again

(Krivine, 1 October 2001)

9 ST pour que l'on accepte de poser la question de [. . .]
[in order that one accepts to ask the question]
TT before we **agree to discuss**

(Isler Béguin, 1 October 2001)

The intensification occurs through various moves: re-lexicalisations, affecting process (9) or attribute (6), added material process (5), shift of circumstantial from expression of attitude to accusation (8) and shift from presupposition to direct allegation (7). (It is interesting that at same time there is some evidence of a move towards conventionalised *indirectness* where routine courtesies are concerned. Thus, 'j'évoquerai la solidarité avec les victimes [I shall evoke solidarity with . . .]' becomes 'I *would like to* express my solidarity with the victims'.) What is most striking, however, is a general tendency in these translations to move further in the direction of perceived intended meanings. That is, there are plenty of discoursal signals in the co-text of the examples cited, which point to a discourse of blame (following a serious industrial accident) and can be seen to offer justification for the moves highlighted in 5–9, which serve to intensify the blame or signal dissent. In the context of this particular debate, then, signs of a coherent translator strategy emerge in the French-to-English pair. But this approach is not generalised and widely varying approaches are apparent in the translations of different speeches. Thus, in the Spanish-to-French pair, calques such as example 4 above co-exist with translations showing a large number and variety of significant transitivity shifts. The same is true of the *Courier* translations, where extreme literalness in the transfer of process types from French to Spanish co-exists with considerable latitude elsewhere. In short, the treatment of transitivity patterns varies widely within each institution and within each language pair.

5 Discoursal shifts

Individual shifts may be individually significant and provide some clues to translators' approaches to their task. They are, nevertheless, generally unlikely to have a significant impact on their own on the reception of the whole translated text. Where, on the other hand, shifts concatenate and establish a trend within a text, a whole discourse may be shifted, such that a different impression may be received of the ST producer's attitude or intentions. In the case of the *Courier*, a single example will serve to illustrate the point. The final edition of the periodical

(December 2001) carried the text of a speech delivered by the French writer and statesman André Malraux at UNESCO in 1960. In it, he hailed the launch of an international campaign to preserve the monuments of ancient Egypt. We noted earlier a general tendency for French active material processes to become English passives and suggested that this might be a standard French-to-English translator procedure. However, the move is rarely systematic and would not normally draw attention to itself. But when, within a 1500-word article, there are no fewer than 16 instances of active processes becoming passive ones, an overall trend is established in which processes may be viewed as happening independently of agents or at least the dynamism of actors in processes is reduced. In the English translation of the Malraux speech, this trend is accompanied by two instances of Relational Processes (of being – 'être') becoming Mental Processes (of seeming) and of a general reduction of the role of Egypt from Actor to Acted upon, as in 10 and 11.

10 ST L'Egypte conquit [. . .] son autonomie.
[Egypt won . . . her autonomy.]
TT Egypt came into her own.

11 ST la mystérieuse présence par laquelle les œuvres de l'Egypte s'unissent aux statues de nos cathédrales
[the mysterious presence whereby the works of Egypt unite with the statues of our cathedrals]
TT the inexplicable quality which brings the Egyptian masterpieces into communion with the statues of our own cathedrals

In the ST of both 10 and 11, not only does 'l'Egypte' feature within the subject noun phrase but the verbal process itself is a material action one. A semantic shift in the TT of 10 turns this action intention process into what Simpson (1993: 89) calls an action supervention process, that is where the process may occur independently of the volition of the actor. Meanwhile, in 11, the Egyptian masterpieces have turned from actor to goal and are thus seen as acted upon rather than as acting.

The European Parliament translations are not immune from these discoursal shifts (for supporting evidence, see the excellent analysis in Calzada Pérez 2001). A good example is provided by the French and English translations of a speech delivered by a Spanish MEP, critical of the British government's handling of the crisis over BSE (Bovine Spongiform Encephalopathy or, more popularly, Mad Cow Disease) and the European Commission's alleged lack of firmness in dealing with the matter. Whereas the English translation of the speech displays a number of cases of attenuation affecting the transitivity of processes, the French translation exhibits a certain amount of intensification. The examples are presented as 12–17 below.

12 ST La supeditación de las decisiones políticas a las presiones económicas en el Reino Unido está en el origen de la problemática inherente a la EEB.
[The subordination of political decisions to economic pressures in the UK is at the root of the inherent problem of BSE.]

TT The underlying problem with BSE is that political decisions have been subordinated to economic pressures in the United Kingdom.

13 ST No se ha llevado a cabo la erradicación de la enfermedad.
[The eradication of the disease has not been carried out (literally, has not carried itself out).]
TT The disease has not been eradicated.

14 ST No habrá otra solución que pensar que la Comisión ha adoptado decisiones que pueden presentar riesgos.
[There will not be another solution than to believe that the Commission has adopted decisions which can present risks.]
TT The impression will inevitably be given that the Commission has adopted decisions which may present risks.

15 ST La enfermedad se originó con la introducción de harinas de carne.
[The disease began with the introduction of bone meal.]
TT Cette maladie est due à l'introduction de farines de viande...
[This disease is due to the introduction of bone meal.]

16 ST [el gobierno británico . . .] forzando la adopción de decisiones
[the British Government . . . forcing the adoption of decisions]
TT [le gouvernement britannique . . .] contraignant l'Union à adopter des décisions
[the British Government . . . forcing the Union to adopt decisions]

17 ST preguntarnos si no es el momento de que la PAC deje de centrarse sólo en [. . .]
[ask ourselves if it is not the moment for the CAP (Common Agricultural Policy) to stop concentrating solely on . . .]
TT nous demander si le moment n'est pas venu de cesser d'axer uniquement la PAC sur [. . .]
[ask ourselves if the time has not come to stop basing the CAP solely on . . .]

As previously observed, the shifts may occur in a number of different ways and may, individually, be of little significance. But they are mutually reinforcing in that, within a text, they all go in the same direction: towards attenuation in English and intensification in French. In the ST of 12, the 'subordination' of politicians to economic pressure in the UK is presupposed (i.e. taken for granted) and then declared to be at the root of the BSE problem. The speech act thus concentrates on the *results* of this subordination. The English TT merely *claims* the subordination and relegates the UK from being (part of) the Actor to a Circumstantial. In 13, the ST presents an action intention process (with an implied human agent held responsible for the goal not being attained). In the TT, it simply alleged that the goal has not been attained. In 14, the English translation deletes the goal of the process (to whom is the 'impression' given?) and allows the inference that the 'impression' may be unfortunate and even false; in the ST, however, the verb 'pensar' (believe) is accompanied by deontic modality (the notion of being obliged to reach the conclusion) and associated with an implied human senser – 'us'.

Conversely, the French translation in 15 introduces direct causation (est due à/is due to) and thus enhances the accusatory illocutionary force, its force as a speech act that performs the action of accusation, by making it explicit. The translation of 16 adds a goal (l'Union) to the action intention process of 'forcing', thus explicitly identifying the European Union as the victim of UK government action. Finally, in example 17, whereas the ST presents the CAP (Common Agricultural Policy) as actor in a mental process, the TT makes the CAP the goal of a material action process with an implied human actor. In this way, the call for action by the EU institutions becomes more direct (i.e. it is time for us to stop basing policy solely on . . .). The combined effect of these various shifts is a subtle change to the ostension (Sperber and Wilson 1986) in the translated text, making the criticisms more or less direct than in the corresponding ST.

6 Conclusions

In general, the limited evidence on which this study is based suggests that, overall, the European Parliament translations stay fairly close to their STs. The UNESCO *Courier* translations exhibit more latitude, with a more frequent incidence of shifts in transitivity. Within this general trend, however, there is a surprising degree of variation. Close calques of ST transitivity co-exist in both sets of data with radical shifts, involving increased directness, attenuation, personalisation and so on. Occasionally, a set of shifts with similar intensifying or attenuating effects serves to construct a discoursal shift at the level of the whole text. There is, then, little uniformity of practice or evidence of influence of institutional guidelines on translator behaviour. The overriding impression is one of translators either adhering as closely as possible to their source text or, in departing from it, displaying traces of other discourses, faint echoes of ideological stances which are present in the environment (and which, by their very nature, are transindividual). Given the heavy use made of freelance translators by both institutions, this may not seem surprising. Yet the Parliament exerts close control over the recruitment of freelancers and remains responsible for quality control of all translations. UNESCO, meanwhile, issues practical guidelines to those it employs on a freelance basis. A further consideration is the vagueness of the guidelines issued, their inherent contradictions and the questionable assumptions on which some concepts ('authentic', 'accurate', 'message', etc.) are based. The evidence adduced here suggests that the whole issue of institutional cultures of translating, in comparison to the treatment of transitivity by translators, is worthy of more systematic exploration, across a range of institutions and language pairs.

Chapter 32

Lawrence Venuti

TRANSLATION, COMMUNITY, UTOPIA

> Language is a repository of ancient errors and a treasury of potential truths.
>
> Jean-Jacques Lecercle

An antinomy in theory

EVEN THOUGH NO ONE seems likely to deny that communication is the primary aim and function of a translated text, today we are far from thinking that translating is a simple communicative act. In contemporary translation theory informed by Continental philosophical traditions such as existential phenomenology and poststructuralism, language is constitutive of thought, and meaning a site of multiple determinations, so that translation is readily seen as investing the foreign-language text with a domestic significance (see, for example, Heidegger 1975, Lewis this volume, Benjamin 1989). Translation never communicates in an untroubled fashion because the translator negotiates the linguistic and cultural differences of the foreign text by reducing them and supplying another set of differences, basically domestic, drawn from the receiving language and culture to enable the foreign to be received there. The foreign text, then, is not so much communicated as inscribed with domestic intelligibilities and interests. The inscription begins with the very choice of a text for translation, always a very selective, densely motivated choice, and continues in the development of discursive strategies to translate it, always a choice of certain domestic discourses over others. Hence, the domesticating process is totalizing, even if never total, never seamless or final. It can be said to operate in every word of the translation long before the translated text is further processed by readers, made to bear other domestic meanings and to serve other domestic interests.

Seen as domestic inscription, never quite cross-cultural communication, translation has moved theorists towards an ethical reflection wherein remedies are formulated to restore or preserve the foreignness of the foreign text (see, for example, Berman, this volume, and Venuti 1995, 1998). Yet an ethics that counters the domesticating effects of the inscription can only be formulated and practiced primarily in *domestic* terms, in domestic dialects, registers, discourses, and styles. And this means that the linguistic and cultural differences of the foreign text can only be signalled indirectly, by their displacement in the translation, through a domestic difference introduced into values and institutions at home. This ethical attitude is therefore simultaneous with a political agenda: the domestic terms of the inscription become the focus of rewriting in the translation, discursive strategies where the hierarchies that rank the values in the domestic culture are disarranged to set going processes of defamiliarization, canon reformation, ideological critique, and institutional change. A translator may find that the very concept of the domestic merits interrogation for its concealment of heterogeneity and hybridity which can complicate existing stereotypes, canons, and standards applied in translation.

When motivated by this ethical politics of difference, the translator seeks to build a community with foreign cultures, to share an understanding with and of them and to collaborate on projects founded on that understanding, going so far as to allow it to revise and develop domestic values and institutions. The very impulse to seek a community abroad suggests that the translator wishes to extend or complete a particular domestic situation, to compensate for a defect in the translating language and literature, in the translating culture. As Maurice Blanchot argues, the very notion of community arises when an insufficiency puts individual agency into question (Blanchot 1988: 56). The ethically and politically motivated translator cannot fail to see the lack of an equal footing in the translation process, stimulated by an interest in the foreign, but inescapably leaning towards the receptor. This translator knows that translations never simply communicate foreign texts because they make possible only a domesticated understanding, however much defamiliarized, however much subversive or supportive of the domestic.

In the absence of cross-cultural communication unaffected by domestic intelligibilities and interests, what kinds of communities can translation possibly foster? What communities can be based on the domestic inscription of the foreign that limits and redirects the communicative aim of translation?

Communication in translation

In the 1970s, the formalist theorist Gideon Toury tried to define translation as a communicative act while acknowledging the domestic values that come into play, the target norms that constrain communication. Translation, he wrote,

> is *communication in translated messages* within a certain cultural-linguistic system, with all relevant consequences for the decomposition of the

source message, the establishment of the invariant, its transfer across the
cultural-linguistic border and the recomposition of the target message.
(Toury 1980: 17; his emphasis)

"The establishment of the invariant": if communication in translation is defined as
the transmission of an invariant, doesn't the very need to establish the invariant
mean that translating does something more and perhaps other than communicate?
The source message is always interpreted and reinvented, especially in cultural
forms open to interpretation, such as literary texts, philosophical treatises, film
subtitling, advertising copy, conference papers, legal testimony. How can the source
message ever be invariant if it undergoes a process of "establishment" in a "certain"
target language and culture? It is always reconstructed according to a different set
of values and always variable according to different languages and cultures. Toury
ultimately reckoned with the problem of communication by sidestepping it altogether: he shifted the emphasis away from exploring an equivalence between the
translation and the foreign text and instead focused on the acceptability of the translation in the target culture. Thinking about the foreign is thus preempted in favor
of research that describes domestic cultural norms.

But let's pursue this preempted line of enquiry. What formal and thematic
features of a foreign novel, for instance, can be described as invariant in the translation process? Since canons of accuracy vary according to culture and historical
moment, definitions of what constitutes the invariant will likewise vary. Let's ask
the question of current translation practices. Today, translators of novels into most
languages seek to maintain unchanged the basic elements of narrative form. The
plot isn't rewritten to alter events or their sequence. And none of the characters'
actions is deleted or revised. Dates, historical and geographical markers, the characters' names – even when the names are rather complicated and foreign-sounding
– these are generally not altered or only in rare cases (e.g. Russian names).
Contemporary canons of accuracy are based on an adequacy to the foreign text: an
accurate translation of a novel must not only reproduce the basic elements of narrative form, but should do so in roughly the same number of pages.

In 1760, however, Abbé Prévost claimed that accuracy governed his French
version of Samuel Richardson's *Pamela* even though he reduced the seven English
volumes to four in French. "I have not changed anything pertaining to the author's
intention," the Abbé asserted, "nor have I changed much in the manner in which he
put that intention into words" (Lefevere 1992a: 39). To us, such statements don't
merely substitute a different canon of accuracy (founded on notions of authorial
intention and style); they also seem to exceed the very genre of translation.
Prévost's text involved abridgement and adaptation as well.

In current practices, a translation of a novel can and must communicate the
basic elements of narrative form that structure the foreign-language text. But it is
still not true that these elements are free from variation. Any language use is likely
to vary the standard dialect by sampling a diversity of substandard or minor formations: regional or group dialects, jargons, clichés and slogans, stylistic innovations,
archaisms, neologisms. Jean-Jacques Lecercle calls these variations the "remainder"
because they exceed communication of a univocal meaning and instead draw attention to the conditions of the communicative act, conditions that are in the first

instance linguistic and cultural, but that ultimately embrace social and political factors (Lecercle 1990). The remainder in literary texts is much more complicated, of course, usually a sedimentation of formal elements and generic discourses, past as well as present (Jameson 1981: 140–1).

Any communication through translating, then, will involve the release of a domestic remainder, especially in the case of literature. The foreign text is rewritten in domestic dialects and discourses, registers and styles, and this results in the production of textual effects that signify only in the history of the receiving language and culture. The translator may produce these effects to communicate the foreign text, trying to invent domestic analogues for foreign forms and themes. But the result will always go beyond any communication to release target-oriented possibilities of meaning.

Consider a recent English translation of an Italian novel, *Declares Pereira*, Patrick Creagh's 1995 version of Antonio Tabucchi's *Sostiene Pereira* (1994). Creagh's English consists mostly of the current standard dialect. But he cultivated a noticeable strain of colloquialism that sometimes veers into underworld argot. He rendered "taceva" ("silent") as "gagged," "quattro uomini dall'aria sinistra" ("four men with a sinister air") as "four shady-looking characters," "stare con gli occhi aperti" ("stay with your eyes open") as "keep your eyes peeled," "un personaggio del regime" ("a figure in the regime") as "bigwig," "senza pigiama" ("without pyjamas") as "in his birthday-suit," and "va a dormire" ("go to sleep") as "beddy-byes" (Tabucchi 1994: 13, 19, 43, 73, 108, 196; Creagh 1995: 5, 9, 25, 45, 67, 127). Creagh also mixed in some distinctively British words and phrases. He rendered "orrendo" ("horrible") as "bloody awful," "una critica molto negativa" ("a very negative criticism") as "slating," "pensioncina" ("little boarding house") as "little doss-house," "sono nei guai" ("I'm in trouble") as "I'm in a pickle," "parlano" ("they talk") as "natter," and "a vedere" ("to look") as "to take a dekko" (Tabucchi 1994: 80, 81, 84, 104, 176; Creagh 1995: 50, 51, 54, 64, 115).

Within parentheses I have inserted alternative renderings to highlight the range and inventiveness of Creagh's translating. The alternatives should not be regarded as somehow more accurate than his choices. In each case, both renderings establish a lexicographical equivalence, a similarity to the Italian text consistent with dictionary definitions. Creagh's choices communicate meanings that can be called "invariant" only insofar as they are reduced to a basic meaning shared by both the Italian and the English.

Creagh's translation, however, varies this meaning. The variation might be called a "shift" as that concept has been developed in translation studies since the 1960s (see, for example, Catford 1965; Blum-Kulka this volume; Toury 1995). If Creagh's English is juxtaposed to Tabucchi's Italian, lexical shifts can indeed be detected, shifts in register from the current standard dialect of Italian to various colloquial dialects in British and American English. In response to my queries, Creagh admitted that "some phrases are more colloquial in English than in Italian," making clear that his shifts are not required by structural differences between the two languages, but rather motivated by literary and cultural aims: "I even tried," Creagh stated, "to use only idioms that would have been current in 1938," the period of the novel, "and to hand them to the right speaker, to make slight linguistic differences between the characters" (personal correspondence: 8 December 1998).

Yet the notion of a shift does not entirely describe the textual effects set going by Creagh's choices. His translation signifies beyond his literary and cultural intentions by releasing a peculiarly English remainder: the different dialects and registers establish a relation to English literary styles, genres, and traditions. In terms of generic distinctions, Tabucchi's novel is a political thriller. Set under the Portuguese dictator António de Oliveira Salazar, it recounts how one Pereira, the aging cultural editor of a Lisbon newspaper, is slowly radicalized over a few weeks which climax when he prints an attack on the fascist regime. Creagh's polylingual mixture of standard and colloquial, British and American, gives his prose an extremely conversational quality that is consistent with Tabucchi's presentation of the thriller plot: Pereira's narrative takes an oral form, an official testimony to an unnamed authority (hence the curious title). Yet the slangy English also alters the characterization of Pereira by suggesting that he is less staid and perhaps younger than the elderly journalist presented in the Italian text.

At the same time, the British and American slang refers to moments in the history of English-language fiction. It recalls thrillers that address similar political themes, notably such novels of Graham Greene as *The Confidential Agent* (1939), which, like Tabucchi's, is set during the Spanish Civil War and involves an attempt to aid the Republican side against Franco. By virtue of this literary reference, Creagh's translation in effect invites the reader to distinguish between Tabucchi's leftwing opposition to fascism and Greene's more cautious liberalism (Diemert 1996: 180–1). Greene saw his thrillers as "entertainments" engaged in social and political issues, designed "not to change things but to give them expression" (Allain 1983: 81). The linguistic resemblances between Creagh's translation and Greene's novel highlight the ideological differences that distinguish Tabucchi's and Greene's treatments of the same historical event.

Thus, although Creagh's translation can be said to communicate the form and theme of Tabucchi's novel, neither of these features escapes the variations introduced by the inscription of an English-language remainder. The remainder does not just inscribe a domestic set of linguistic and cultural differences in the foreign text, but supplies the loss of the foreign-language differences which constituted that text. The loss occurs, as Alasdair MacIntyre has observed, because in any "tradition-bearing community" the "language-in-use is closely tied to the expression of the shared beliefs of that tradition," and this gives a "historical dimension" to languages which often fails to survive the translating process (MacIntyre 1988: 384). MacIntyre argued that this problem of untranslatability is most acute with "the internationalized languages-in-use in late twentieth-century modernity," like English, which "have minimal presuppositions in respect of possibly rival belief systems" and so will "neutralize" the historical dimension of the foreign text (ibid.). In English translation, therefore,

> a kind of text which cannot be read as *the text it is* out of context is nevertheless rendered contextless. But in so rendering it, it is turned into a text which is no longer the author's, nor such as would be recognized by the audience to whom it was addressed.
>
> (ibid.: 385, MacIntyre's emphasis)

Creagh's translation at once inscribed an English-language cultural history in Tabucchi's novel and displaced the historical dimension of the Italian text. This text occupies a place in a narrative tradition that includes resistance novels during and after the Second World War, as well as novels about life under fascism, Alberto Moravia's *Il conformista* (1951; *The Conformist*), for instance, and Giorgio Bassani's *Il giardino dei Finzi-Contini* (1962; *The Garden of the Finzi-Continis*). The very fact that Italian history contains a fascist tradition ensured that Tabucchi's readers would understand the Salazarist regime in distinctively Italian terms, not merely as an allusion to Mussolini's dictatorship, but as an allegory of current events. *Sostiene Pereira* was written in 1993 and published the following year, when a center-right coalition gained power in Italy with the election victory of Silvio Berlusconi's Forza Italia movement. As Tabucchi himself said of his novel, "those who didn't love the Italian political situation took it as a symbol of resistance from within" (Cotroneo 1995: 105, my translation). Invested with this peculiarly Italian significance, *Sostiene Pereira* sold 300,000 copies within a year of publication.

Although favorably received by British and American reviewers, Creagh's translation hardly became a bestseller. Within two years of publication the American edition published by New Directions sold 5,000 copies. Creagh maintained a lexicographical equivalence, but the remainder in his translation was insufficient to restore the cultural and political history that made the novel so resonant for Italian readers, as well as readers in other European countries with similar histories, such as Spain.

Communication through inscription

Can a translation ever communicate to its readers the understanding of the foreign text that foreign readers have? Yes, I want to argue, but this communication will always be partial, both incomplete and inevitably slanted towards the domestic scene. It occurs only when the domestic remainder released by the translation includes an inscription of the foreign context in which the text first emerged.

The form of communication at work here is second-order, built upon but signifying beyond a lexicographical equivalence, encompassing but exceeding what Walter Benjamin called "information" or "subject matter" (Benjamin this volume). "Translations that are more than transmissions of subject matter," Benjamin wrote, "come into being when in the course of its survival a work has reached the age of its fame." I understand the term "fame" to mean the overall reception of a literary text, not only in its own language and culture, but in the languages of the cultures that have translated it, and not only the judgments of reviewers at home and abroad, but the interpretations of literary historians and critics and the images that an internationally famous text may come to bear in other cultural forms and practices, both elite and mass. A translation of a foreign novel can communicate, not simply dictionary meanings, not simply the basic elements of narrative form, but an interpretation that participates in its "potentially eternal afterlife in succeeding generations." And this interpretation can be one that is shared by the foreign-language readers for whom the text was written. The translation will then foster a common understanding with and of the foreign culture, an understanding that in part restores the historical context of the foreign text – although for domestic readers.

Take, for example, Camus's novel *L'Étranger* (1942). As Camus himself acknowledged, the peculiarities of style, plot, and characterization that distinguish the French text were derived from American fiction during the early twentieth century, especially the writing of Ernest Hemingway, but more generally the hard-boiled or tough-guy prose of writers like James M. Cain. The stylistic features of Matthew Ward's 1988 translation, *The Stranger*, make this intertextual connection for the English-language reader much more effectively than Stuart Gilbert's 1946 version. The differences are apparent on the opening page:

> Aujourd'hui, maman est morte. Ou peut-être hier, je ne sais pas. J'ai reçu un télégramme de l'asile: "Mère décédée. Enterrement demain. Sentiments distingués." Cela ne veut rien dire. C'était peut-être hier.
>
> L'asile de vieillards est à Marengo, à quatre-vingts kilomètres d'Alger. Je prendrai l'autobus à deux heures et j'arriverai dans l'après-midi. Ainsi, je pourrai veiller et je rentrerai demain soir. J'ai demandé deux jours de congé à mon patron et il ne pouvait pas me les refuser avec une excuse pareille. Mais il n'avait pas l'air content. Je lui ai même dit: "Ce n'est pas de ma faute." Il n'a pas répondu. J'ai pensé alors que je n'aurais pas dû lui dire cela. En somme, je n'avais pas à m'excuser. C'était plutôt à lui de présenter ses condoléances. Mais il le fera sans doute après-demain, quand il me verra en deuil. Pour le moment, c'est un peu comme si maman n'était pas morte. Après l'enterrement, au contraire, ce sera une affaire classé et tout aura revêtu une allure plus officielle.
>
> (Camus 1942: 1)

> Mother died today. Or, maybe, yesterday; I can't be sure. The telegram from the Home says: YOUR MOTHER PASSED AWAY. FUNERAL TOMORROW. DEEP SYMPATHY. Which leaves the matter doubtful; it could have been yesterday.
>
> The Home for Aged Persons is at Marengo, some fifty miles from Algiers. With the two o'clock bus I should get there well before night-fall. Then I can spend the night there, keeping the usual vigil beside the body, and be back here tomorrow evening.
>
> I have fixed up with my employer for two days' leave; obviously, under the circumstances, he couldn't refuse. Still, I had an idea he looked annoyed, and I said, without thinking: "Sorry, sir, but it's not my fault, you know."
>
> Afterwards it struck me I needn't have said that. I had no reason to excuse myself; it was up to him to express his sympathy and so forth. Probably he will do so the day after tomorrow, when he sees me in black. For the present, it's almost as if Mother weren't really dead. The funeral will bring it home to me, put an official seal on it, so to speak.
>
> (Gilbert 1946: 1–2)

Maman died today. Or yesterday maybe, I don't know. I got a telegram from the home: "Mother deceased. Funeral tomorrow. Faithfully yours." That doesn't mean anything. Maybe it was yesterday.

The old people's home is at Marengo, about eighty kilometers from Algiers. I'll take the two o'clock bus and get there in the afternoon. That way I can be there for the vigil and come back tomorrow night. I asked my boss for two days off and there was no way he was going to refuse me with an excuse like that. But he wasn't too happy about it. I even said, "It's not my fault." He didn't say anything. Then I thought I shouldn't have said that. After all, I didn't have anything to apologize for. He's the one who should have offered his condolences. But he probably will day after tomorrow, when he sees I'm in mourning. For now, it's almost as if Maman weren't dead. After the funeral, though, the case will be closed, and everything will have a more official feel to it.

(Ward 1988: 3)

The English in both versions is cast in a fairly colloquial register, but once they are juxtaposed, the differences begin to proliferate. Gilbert translated freely. He added words for clarification, expanding "je pourrai veiller" ("I shall be able to keep vigil") into "I can spend the night there, keeping the usual vigil beside the body." He revised and softened the abruptness of the French phrasing, turning "Cela ne veut rien dire" ("That does not mean anything") into "Which leaves the matter doubtful." And he endowed his prose with a formality and politeness, rendering "maman" as "Mother," "patron" as "employer," and "Ce n'est pas de ma faute" as "Sorry, sir, but it's not my fault, you know." Ward, in sharp contrast, translated closely. He reproduced the lexical and syntactical peculiarities of the French, departing from Gilbert not only by making choices like "Maman" and "boss," but also by adhering to Camus's brief, precise sentences: "That doesn't mean anything," "It's not my fault." As a result, Ward endowed his prose with a familiarity and directness. Where Gilbert resorted to phrases like "two days' leave" ("deux jours de congé"), "Home for Aged Persons" ("l'asile de vieillards"), and "I had no reason to excuse myself" ("je n'avais pas à m'excuser"), Ward used "two days off," "old people's home," and "I didn't have anything to apologize for." Ward himself described the difference between the two versions as dialectal: he called Gilbert's a "'Britannic' rendering," and saw his own as "giving the text a more 'American' quality" (Ward 1988: v–vi). And Ward knew that he was drawing a cultural difference as well, releasing a literary remainder that leads the English-language reader to an American narrative tradition, to "Hemingway, Dos Passos, Faulkner, Cain" (ibid.).

Gilbert's version, even though free in places, established a lexicographical equivalence that does in fact transmit the distinctive plot and characterization of Camus's novel. Hence, his translation can also enable English-language readers to perceive the American literary origins of the French text even when they don't know its larger French context. The leading American critic Edmund Wilson reviewed Gilbert's version for the *New Yorker* the year it was published, offering a remarkable account of his response. He knew that Camus was "one of the principal exponents in literature of what is called the Existentialist philosophy," but he immediately added a confession of ignorance: "I have read very little of Sartre and

nothing by Camus but this novel, and I am entirely unfamiliar with the philosophical background of their writing" (Wilson 1946: 99). Because of his limited knowledge Wilson headed straight for what was familiar and emphasized the domestic
reference in Gilbert's translation: "One feels sure," he wrote, "that M. Camus must
have been reading such American novels as 'The Postman Always Rings Twice'."
And this reference ultimately prompted an unfavorable comparison. Wilson judged
The Stranger as a failed imitation of Cain's novel, not as a French narrative that used
American forms to explore European philosophical themes. The absence of the
foreign context was supplied by the realism that has long dominated the American
narrative tradition, so that Camus's main character was dismissed as "incredible; his
behavior is never explained or made plausible" (ibid.).

Ward was fortunate in having a better-informed readership: he could rely
on some four decades of literary criticism and history during which *L'Étranger*
was studied, taught, and admitted to the canon of contemporary world literature
– in the United States as well as in many countries worldwide. Gilbert's version
undoubtedly helped the novel to achieve this status for English-language readers,
but not until Ward's was there a translation that produced a stylistic analogue
for Camus's experiment, a heterogeneous mix of linguistic and cultural forms,
both American and French. In this way, Ward's version communicated an understanding of the French text that is available to French readers. This understanding
motivated his decision, for example, to retain the French "Maman" in the opening
sentence:

> In his notebooks Camus recorded the observation that "the curious
> feeling the son has for his mother constitutes *all* his sensibility." And
> Sartre, in his "Explication de *L'Étranger*," goes out of his way to point
> out Meursault's use of the child's word "Maman" when speaking of his
> mother. To use the more removed, adult "Mother" is, I believe, to
> change the nature of Meursault's curious feeling for her.
>
> (Ward 1988: vii)

Ward's writing released a remainder inscribed with American and French references, and for the English-language reader the result was truly defamiliarizing. Not
only did American narrative forms acquire a philosophical density they did not
possess in the American writers who used them, but Gilbert's version was deprived
of its authority as an interpretation of the French text. This was evident in a brief
but appreciative notice that appeared, appropriately enough, in the *New Yorker*:

> The effect of the closer, simpler rendering is to make Meursault seem
> even stranger – more alien and diffident – than the explanatory confider
> of the British version. He becomes not so much an exponent of illu-
> sionless hedonism as a psychological study who is brought, through a
> gratuitous, sun-dazzled act and its merciless social consequences, to a
> rapport with his dead mother and a recognition of his fraternity with
> "the gentle indifference of the world"–a palpable improvement upon
> Gilbert's grander phrase "the benign indifference of the universe."
>
> (*New Yorker* 1988: 119)

The "improvement," judging from this anonymous reviewer's response, involved an increased plausibility. Ward gave Camus's character the psychological realism that Wilson found lacking in Gilbert, although for a later American readership. Ward's translation was more acceptable to his readers, partly because they knew more about French literature and philosophy, but also because of his writing: his style was more evocative of American and French cultural forms and therefore more communicative of the French text.

Heterogeneous communities

The domestic inscription in translating constitutes a unique communicative act, however indirect or wayward. It creates a domestic community of interest around the translated text, an audience to whom it is intelligible and who put it to various uses. This shared interest may arise spontaneously when the translation is published, attracting readers from different cultural constituencies that already exist in the translating language. It may also be housed in an institution where the translation is made to perform different functions, academic or religious, cultural or political, commercial or municipal. Any community that arises around a translation is far from homogeneous in language, identity, or social position. Its heterogeneity might best be understood in terms of what Mary Louise Pratt calls a "linguistics of contact," in which language-based communities are seen as decentered across "lines of social differentiation" (Pratt 1987: 60). A translation is a linguistic "zone of contact" between the foreign and translating cultures, but also within the latter.

The interests that bind the community through a translation are not simply focused on the foreign text, but reflected in the domestic values, beliefs, and representations that the translator inscribes in it. And these interests are further determined by the ways the translation is used. In the case of foreign texts that have achieved canonical status in an institution, a translation becomes the site of interpretive communities that may support or challenge current canons and interpretations, prevailing standards and ideologies (cf. Fish 1980 and the criticisms in Pratt 1986: 46–52). In the case of foreign texts that have achieved mass circulation, a translation becomes the site of unexpected groupings, fostering communities of readers who would otherwise be separated by cultural differences and social divisions yet are now joined by a common fascination. A translation can answer to the interests of a diverse range of domestic audiences, so that the forms of reception will not be entirely commensurable. Because translating traffics in the foreign, in the introduction of linguistic and cultural differences, it is equally capable of crossing or reinforcing the boundaries between domestic audiences and the hierarchies in which they are positioned. If the domestic inscription includes part of the social or historical context in which the foreign text first emerged, then a translation can also create a community that includes foreign intelligibilities and interests, an understanding in common with another culture, another tradition.

Consider the readerships that gather around a poetry translation. In 1958 the American translator Allen Mandelbaum published the first book-length English version of the modern Italian poet Giuseppe Ungaretti. It was warmly welcomed by Italian academic specialists at American universities, some of whom were themselves Italian natives. The reviewer for the journal *Comparative Literature*, Giovanni Cecchetti, wrote his review in Italian and concluded that Mandelbaum's translation "does honor to Italian studies in America and can be recommended to anyone who wishes to familiarize himself with the work of one of the major poets of our time" (Cecchetti 1959: 268, my translation). The "our" suggests the extent of Cecchetti's esteem for Ungaretti's poetry, an assertion of universal value. But since he was reviewing in Italian the first English translation of that poetry, the "our" couldn't be universal because it didn't yet include British and American readers lacking Italian. Cecchetti imagined a community that was partly actual, professional, and partly potential.

The Ungaretti project also applied a standard of accuracy consistent with the interpretation that prevailed in the Italian academic community. Mandelbaum maintained a fairly strict lexicographical equivalence and even imitated Ungaretti's syntax and line breaks. He read Ungaretti's achievement, like the Italian scholars, as an effort "to bury the cadaver of literary Italian" by developing a spare, precise poetic language devoid of "all that was but ornament" (Mandelbaum 1958: xi). It was in these terms that the reviewers judged Mandelbaum's versions successful. "If one is tempted to observe that in many places the translation is too literal," wrote Carlo Golino, "further reflection will show that it would have been impossible to do otherwise and still retain the rich allusiveness of Ungaretti's words" (Golino 1959: 76).

Mandelbaum's translation was thus the site of an academic community's interest in Ungaretti's poetry, an American readership that nonetheless shared an Italian understanding of the text and in fact included Italian natives. In this context the translation ultimately achieved canonical status. In 1975, almost two decades after its first publication, it was reissued in a revised and expanded edition from Cornell University Press.

All the same, it is possible to perceive an appeal to another community in Mandelbaum's translation, a domestic readership that is incommensurable with the interests of the Italian academics and the prevailing interpretation of Ungaretti. While Mandelbaum adhered closely to the terse fragmentation of Ungaretti's Italian texts, he also introduced a poetical register, a noticeable strain of Victorian poeticism. Mandelbaum rendered "morire" ("die") as "perish," "buttato" ("thrown") as "cast," "ti basta un'illusione" ("an illusion is enough for you") as "you need but an illusion," "sonno" ("sleep") as "slumber," "riposato" ("rested") as "reposed," "potrò guardarla" ("I can watch her") as "I can gaze upon her" (Mandelbaum 1958: 7, 13, 25, 37, 145). He used syntactical inversions: some were added, while others were the results of literal translating, calques of the Italian. Both kinds amounted to poetical archaisms in English:

> *Lontano*
> Lontano lontano
> come un cieco
> m'hanno portato per mano.

> *Distantly*
> Distantly distantly
> like a blind man
> by the hand they led me.

Una Colomba
D'altri diluvi una colomba ascolto.

A Dove
Of other floods I hear a dove.

(Mandelbaum 1958: 35, 53)

Sometimes the poeticism deviated from the otherwise simple language of the context, as in the last six lines of "Giugno" ("June"):

Ho perso il sonno

Oscillo
al canto d'una strada
come una lucciola

Mi morirò
questa notte?

I have lost slumber
Sway
at a street-corner
like a firefly

Will this night die
from me?

(Mandelbaum 1958: 39)

On other occasions the poetical register swells with a lush Romanticism, usually to match a more expansive poetic line in Ungaretti. Compare Mandelbaum's version of the Virgilian sestina, "Recitativo di Palinurno," with Tennyson's "Ulysses." Both English texts were written in an Elizabethan pentameter (Shakespearean, Marlovian) pitched at an epic height:

Per l'uragano all'apice di furia
Vicino non intesi farsi il sonno;
Olio fu dilagante a smanie d'onde,
Aperto campo a libertà di pace,
Di effusione infinita il finto emblema
Dalla nuca prostrandomi mortale.

I could not, for the hurricane at fury's
Summit, sense the coming-on of slumber;
An oil that overspread the raving breakers,
Field open to the freedom that is peace,
Of infinite outpouring the feigned emblem
Thrusting at the nape downdashed me mortal.

(Mandelbaum 1958: 145)

> I cannot rest from travel: I will drink
> Life to the lees: all times I have enjoyed
> Greatly, have suffered greatly, both with those
> That loved me, and alone; on shore, and when
> Through scudding drifts the rainy Hyades
> Vex the dim sea: I am become a name [. . .]

(Tennyson 1972: 562)

What made Ungaretti's poetry seem so innovative in Italy was the hard-edged language, a modernist precision that turned away from the ornate, rhetorical styles developed by decadent writers like Gabriele D'Annunzio. Mandelbaum's version reinscribed these styles in Ungaretti, restoring what the translator himself called the "cadaver of literary Italian" – although now transmogrified into archaic English poetries.

In releasing this domestic remainder, Mandelbaum's translation not only positioned Ungaretti in English-language poetic traditions, but affiliated him with the dominant trends in contemporary poetry translation. For the fact is that during the 1950s a mixture of current standard English with poetical archaisms constituted the discourse for translating poetry favored by leading American translators. Richmond Lattimore's 1951 version of the *Iliad*, which became the most widely read translation in the United States, claimed to have avoided any "poetical dialect of English" because "in 1951, we do not have a poetic dialect," and "the language of Spenser or the King James Version" seemed inappropriate to Homer's "plainness" (Lattimore 1951: 55). Yet Lattimore's text is dotted with Victorian poeticisms: "as when rivers in winter spate," "So he spoke, vaunting," "he strides into battle," "his beloved son," "that accursed night" (ibid.: 125, 131, 279, 438). John Ciardi's 1954 version of Dante's *Inferno*, which for over four decades has been continuously available in a mass-market paperback, aimed for "something like idiomatic English" to evoke the anti-rhetorical character of the Italian; "sparse, direct, and idiomatic," wrote Ciardi, Dante's language "seeks to avoid elegance simply for the sake of elegance" (Ciardi 1954: ix–x). Yet this paradoxical understanding of Dante's Italian also describes Ciardi's text, which, although mostly in a plain register of current usage, is strewn with poetical words and phrases: "drear," "piteous," "fleers," "beset," "perils," "sorely pressed," "thy," "anew," "it seemed to scorn all pause," "bite back your spleen" (for "non ti crucciare": "don't be distressed"), "his woolly jowls" (ibid.: 28, 30, 36, 38, 39, 43, 44, 45).

Mandelbaum's version bridged the cultural gap between Ungaretti's actual Italian readership and his potential American audience. Translating a modern Italian poet into the discourse that dominated American poetry translation was effectively a canonizing gesture, a poetic way of linking him – for American readers – to canonical poets like Homer and Dante (not to mention the echoes of Tennyson, Shakespeare, Marlowe). Yet this domestic inscription deviated from Ungaretti's significance in the Italian poetic tradition, the view, as Mandelbaum put it, that "Ungaretti purged the language of all ornament" (Mandelbaum 1958: xi). The ornate English version was addressing another audience, distinctly American, poetry readers familiar with British and American poetic traditions as well as recent translations that were immensely popular.

Indeed, Mandelbaum's translation discourse was so familiar as to be invisible to the reviewer for *Poetry* magazine, Ned O'Gorman, an American poet who published his first collection of poems in the same year. O'Gorman found Ungaretti's poetry "truly magnificent," while quoting and commenting on the translation as if it were the Italian text (O'Gorman 1959a: 330). What O'Gorman liked about (Mandelbaum's) Ungaretti was the fact that it was poetical: he praised the Italian poet for writing "of a world transformed into poetry" and proclaimed "the *Recitative*" as "his finest poem" (ibid.: 331). The poems in O'Gorman's first book reflected this judgment. They included "An Art of Poetry," where he wrote: "Poetry begins where rhetoric does" (O'Gorman 1959b: 26).

Mandelbaum's readerships were fundamentally incommensurable. Even though written in English, the translation was intelligible to each of them in different linguistic and cultural terms. The Italian academic community also did not recognize the Victorian poeticism. For them, however, this stylistic feature was invisible because English was not their native language and because, as foreign-language academics, they were most concerned with the relation between the English version and the Italian text: lexicographical equivalence. Cecchetti noticed one of Mandelbaum's poetical turns, his rendering of "smemora" ("to lose one's memory," "to forget") with the archaism "disremembers" (ibid.: 51; cf. *OED*). Yet this choice was seen as appropriate to "the rare and suggestive flavor" of the Italian and indicative of the translator's "poetic sensibility" (Cecchetti 1959: 267).

The fact that in English this sensibility might be alien to Ungaretti's modernist poetics seems to have been recognized – in print – only by a British reader, interestingly enough. A reviewer for the London *Times*, who agreed with Cecchetti that Ungaretti was "one of the most distinguished poets alive," felt that "Mr. Mandelbaum translates with a quite exceptional insensitivity" (*The Times* 1958: 13C). There can be no doubt that the reviewer had Mandelbaum's poeticisms in mind, since he preferred to recommend a "good crib," the very close French version that Jean Lescure published in 1953 (where "D'altri diluvi una colomba ascolto" was turned into "J'écoute une colombe venue d'autres déluges" (Lescure 1953: 159)). Only a native reader of English poetry who also knew the Italian texts and their position in the Italian poetic tradition was able to perceive the English-language remainder in Mandelbaum's version.

The readerships that gathered around this poetry translation were limited, professionally or institutionally defined, and determined by their cultural knowledge, whether of the foreign language and literature or the literary traditions in the translating language. The translation became the focus of divergent communities, foreign and domestic, scholarly and literary. And in its ability to support their linguistic and cultural differences, to be intelligible and interesting to them in their own terms, the translation fostered its own community, one that was *imagined* in Benedict Anderson's sense: the members "will never know most of their fellow-members, meet them, or even hear of them, yet in the minds of each lives the image of their communion" (Anderson 1991: 6). In the case of a translation, this image is derived from the representation of the foreign text constructed by the translator, a communication domestically inscribed. To translate is to invent for the foreign text new readerships who are aware that their interest in the translation is shared by other readers, foreign and domestic – even when those interests are incommensurable.

The imagined communities that concerned Anderson were nationalistic, based on the sense of belonging to a particular nation. Translations have undoubtedly formed such communities by importing foreign ideas that stimulated the rise of large-scale political movements at home. At the turn of the twentieth century, the Chinese translator Yan Fu chose works on evolutionary theory by T. H. Huxley and Herbert Spencer precisely to build a national Chinese culture. He translated the Western concepts of aggression embodied in social Darwinism to form an aggressive Chinese identity that would withstand Western colonial projects, notably British (Schwartz 1964; Pusey 1983). Hu Shih, a contemporary observer, later recalled the impact of Huxley's *Evolution and Ethics* in Yan Fu's version: "after China's frequent military reversals, particularly after the humiliation of the Boxer years, the slogan 'Survival of the Fittest' (lit., 'superior victorious, inferior defeated, the fit survive') became a kind of clarion call" (translated and quoted in Schwartz 1964: 259, n. 14).

The imagined communities fostered by translation produce effects that are commercial, as well as cultural and political. Consider, for example, the mass audience that gathers around a translated bestseller. Because of its sheer size, this community is an ensemble of the most diverse domestic constituencies, defined by their specific interests in the foreign text, yet aware of belonging to a collective movement, a national market for a foreign literary fascination. These constituencies will inevitably read the translation differently, and in some cases the differences will be incommensurable. Yet the greatest communication gap here may be between the foreign and domestic cultures. The domestic inscription in the translation extends the appeal of the foreign text to a mass audience in another culture. But widening the domestic range of that appeal means that the inscription cannot include much of the foreign context. A translated bestseller risks reducing the foreign text to what domestic constituencies have in common, a dialect, a cultural discourse, an ideology.

This can be seen in the reception that greeted Irene Ash's English version of *Bonjour Tristesse* (1955), Françoise Sagan's bestselling novel. In France, the French text had been acclaimed as an accomplished work of art: it won the Prix des Critiques and sold 200,000 copies. In England and the United States, the translation drew favorable comments on its style and likewise stayed on the bestseller lists for many months. But no reviewer failed to abandon considerations of aesthetic form for more functional standards, expressing amazement at the youthful age of the author (19) and distaste for the amorality of its theme: a 17-year-old girl schemes to prevent her widowed father from remarrying, so that he can continue to engage in a succession of affairs. The *Chicago Tribune* was typical: "I admired the craftsmanship, but I was repelled by the carnality" (Hass 1955: 6).

This general response varied according to the values of the particular constituency addressed by the reviewer. The Catholic weekly *Commonweal* sternly pronounced the novel "childish and tiresome in its single-minded dedication to decadence" (Nagid 1955: 164), whereas the sophisticated *New Yorker* referred simply to the "father's hedonistic image," subtly suggesting that at 40 he deserves "pity" (Gill 1955: 114–15). In post-Second World War America, where the patriarchal family assumed new importance and "husbands, especially fathers, wore the badge of 'family man' as a sign of virility and patriotism" (May 1988: 98), Sagan's pleasure-seeking father and daughter were certain to make her novel an object of both moral panic and titillation. The reviewer for the *New Statesman and Nation* was unique in trying to understand it in distinctively French terms, describing the youthful heroine as "a child of the *bebop*, the night clubs, the existentialist cafés," comparing her and her father to "M. Camus's amoral Outsider" (Raymond 1955: 727–8).

Ash's English version was of course the decisive factor that enabled Sagan's novel to support a spectrum of very different responses in Anglo-American cultures. The translation was immediately intelligible to a wide English-language readership: it was cast in the most familiar dialect of current English, the standard, but it also contained some lively colloquialisms that matched similar forms in the French text. Ash rendered "le dernier des salauds" ("the last of the sluts") as "the most awful cad," "loupé" ("failed") as "flunked," and "ce fut la fin" ("that was the end") as "things came to a head" (Sagan 1954: 32, 34, 45; Ash 1955: 25, 27, 35). She aimed for a high degree of fluency by translating freely, making deletions and additions to the French to create more precise formulations in English:

> Au café, Elsa se leva et, arrivée à la porte, se retourna vers nous d'un air langoureux, très inspiré, à ce qu'il me sembla, du cinéma américain et mettant dans son intonation dix ans de galanterie française: "Vous venez, Raymond?"

> (After coffee, Elsa stood up and, on reaching the door, turned back towards us with a languorous air, very inspired – so it seemed to me – by American cinema, and investing her tone with ten years of French flirtation: "Are you coming, Raymond?")
>
> (Sagan 1954: 38, my translation)

> After coffee, Elsa walked over to the door, turned around, and struck a languorous, movie-star pose. In her voice was ten years of French coquetry:
>   "Are you coming, Raymond?"
>
> (Ash 1955: 30)

Here the translator cut down forty words of French to twenty-nine in English. The use of the popular "movie-star pose" (for "du cinéma américain") is symptomatic of the drive toward readability.

By increasing the readability of the English text, such freedoms endowed the narrative with verisimilitude, producing the illusion of transparency that permitted the English-language reader to take the translation for the foreign text (Venuti 1995: 12). The reviewer for the *Atlantic*, impressed that "the novel has such a solid air of reality about it," commented on Ash's writing as if it were Sagan's: "Simple, crystalline, and concise, her prose flows along swiftly, creating scene and character with striking immediacy and assurance" (Rolo 1955: 84, 85).

Ash's freedoms may have been invisible, but they inevitably released a domestic remainder, textual effects that varied according to the specific passage where they occurred, but that were generally engaging, even provocative. The reviewer for the *New Statesman and Nation* was also unique in noticing her freedoms ("she has not been afraid to pare and clip the text to suit the English reader"), and he discussed an example where the "distinct gain in English" consisted of "an added, elegiac dimension" (Raymond 1955: 728). With a different passage, Ash's rewriting might be not just sentimental or melodramatic, but steamy, exaggerating the erotic overtones of the French:

> il avait pour elle des regards, des gestes qui s'adressaient à la femme qu'on ne connaît pas et que l'on désire connaître – dans le plaisir.

> (for her he had looks [and] gestures that are addressed to the woman whom one does not know yet desires to know – in pleasure.)
> (Sagan 1954: 378, my translation)

> I noticed that his every look and gesture betrayed a secret desire for her, a woman whom he had not possessed and whom he longed to enjoy.
> (Ash 1955: 29)

Ash's translation, however free in places, maintained a sufficient degree of lexicographical equivalence to communicate the basic narrative elements of the French text. Yet the addition of words like "betrayed" and "secret" in this passage shows that she made the narrative available to an English-language audience with rather different moral values from its French counterpart, a morality that would restrict sexuality to marriage or otherwise conceal it. This is a rather odd effect in a novel where a father does not conceal his sexual promiscuity from his adolescent daughter. Ash inscribed Sagan's novel with a domestic intelligibility and interest, addressing a community that shared little of the foreign context where the novel first emerged.

The utopian dimension in translation

The communities fostered by translating are initially potential, signalled in the text, in the discursive strategy deployed by the translator, but not yet possessing a social existence. They depend for their realization on the ensemble of domestic cultural constituencies among which the translation will circulate. To engage these constituencies, however, the translator involves the foreign text in an asymmetrical act of communication, weighted ideologically towards the translating culture. Translating is always ideological because it releases a domestic remainder, an inscription of values, beliefs, and representations linked to historical moments and social positions in the receiving culture. In serving domestic interests, a translation provides an ideological resolution for the linguistic and cultural differences of the foreign text.

Yet translating is also utopian. The domestic inscription is made with the very intention to communicate the foreign text, and so it is filled with the anticipation that a community will be created around that text – although in translation. In the remainder lies the hope that the translation will establish a domestic readership, an imagined community that shares an interest in the foreign, possibly a market from the publisher's point of view. And it is only through the remainder, when inscribed with part of the foreign context, that the translation can establish a

common understanding between domestic and foreign readers. In supplying an ideological resolution, a translation projects a utopian community that is not yet realized.

Behind this line of thinking lies Ernst Bloch's theory of the utopian function of
culture, although revised to fit an application to translation. Bloch's is a Marxist
utopia. He saw cultural forms and practices releasing a "surplus" that not only
exceeds the ideologies of the dominant classes, the "status quo," but anticipates a
future "consensus," a classless society, usually by transforming the "cultural heritage"
of a particular class, whether dominant or dominated (Bloch 1988: 46–50).

I construe Bloch's utopian surplus as the domestic remainder inscribed in
the foreign text during the translation process. Translating releases a surplus of
meanings which refer to domestic cultural traditions through deviations from the
current standard dialect or otherwise standardized languages – through archaisms,
for example, or colloquialisms. Implicit in any translation is the hope for a
consensus, a communication and recognition of the foreign text through a domestic
inscription.

Yet the inscription can never be so comprehensive, so total in relation to
domestic constituencies, as to create a community of interest without exclusion or
hierarchy. It is unlikely that a foreign text in translation will be intelligible or interesting (or both simultaneously) to every readership in the receiving situation.
And the asymmetry between the foreign and domestic cultures persists, even
when the foreign context is partly inscribed in the translation. Utopias are based on
ideologies, Bloch argued, on interested representations of social divisions, representations that take sides in those divisions. In the case of translating, the interests
are ineradicably domestic, always the interests of certain domestic constituencies
over others.

Bloch also pointed out that the various social groups at any historical moment
are non-contemporaneous or non-synchronous in their cultural and ideological
development, with some containing a "remnant of earlier times in the present"
(Bloch 1991: 108). Cultural forms and practices are heterogeneous, composed of
different elements with different temporalities and affiliated with different groups.
In language, the dialects and discourses, registers and styles that coexist in a particular period can be glimpsed in the remainder released by every communicative act.
The remainder is a "diachrony-within-synchrony" that stages "the return within
language of the contradictions and struggles that make up the social; it is the persistence within language of past contradictions and struggles, and the anticipation of
future ones" (Lecercle 1990: 182, 215). Hence, the domestic inscription in any
translation is what Bloch calls an "anticipatory illumination" (*Vor-Schein*), a way of
imagining a future reconciliation of linguistic and cultural differences, whether those
that exist among domestic groups or those that divide the foreign and domestic
cultures.

In Mandelbaum's version of Ungaretti's poetry, the utopian surplus is the
Victorian poeticism. This English-language remainder didn't just exceed the
communication of the Italian texts; it also ran counter to the modernist experiment
they cultivated in the context of Italian poetic traditions. During the 1950s,
however, Mandelbaum's poeticism projected an ideal community of interest in
Ungaretti by reconciling the differences between two readerships, Italian and
American, scholarly and literary. Today, we may be more inclined to notice, not

the ideal, but the ideologies of this community: Mandelbaum's translation was an asymmetrical act of communication that at once admitted and excluded the Italian context, while supporting incommensurable responses among American constituencies. Yet the ideological force of the translation made it utopian in its own time, hopeful of communicating the foreign significance of the foreign text through a domestic inscription. And this utopian projection eventually produced real effects. The American readership latent in Mandelbaum's poetical remainder reflected a dominant tendency in American poetry translation, helping his version acquire cultural authority in and out of the academy.

Translating that harbors the utopian dream of a common understanding between foreign and domestic cultures may involve literary texts, whether elite or mass. But usually it takes much more mundane forms, serving technical or pragmatic purposes. Consider community or liaison interpreting, the oral, two-way translating done for refugees and immigrants who must deal with the social agencies and institutions of the host country. Community interpreters perform in a variety of legal, medical, and educational situations, including requests for political asylum, court appearances, hospital admissions, and applications for welfare. Codes of ethics, whether formulated by professional associations or by the agencies and institutions themselves, tend to insist that interpreters be "panes of glass" which "allow for the communication of ideas, once again, without modification, adjustment or misrepresentation" (Schweda Nicholson 1994: 82; see also Gentile, Ozolins and Vasilakakos 1996). But such codes don't take into account the cultural and political hierarchies in the interpreting situation, the fact that – in the words of a British interpreting manual – "the client is part of a powerless ethnic minority group whose needs and wishes are often ignored or regarded as not legitimate by the majority group" (Shackman 1984: 18; see also Sanders 1992). And of course the "pane of glass" analogy represses the domestic inscription in any translating, the remainder that prevents the interpreting from being transparent communication even when the interpreter is limited to exact renderings of foreign words.

In practice, many community interpreters seem to recognize the asymmetries in the interpreting situation and make an effort to compensate for them through various strategies (Wadensjö 1998: 36). Robert Barsky's study of refugee hearings in Canada demonstrates that the interpreter can put the refugee on a equal footing with the adjudicating body only by releasing a distinctively domestic remainder. The foreign-language testimony must be inscribed with Canadian values, beliefs, and representations, producing textual effects that work only in English or French. Legal institutions value linear, transparent discourse, but the experiences that refugees must describe – exile, financial hardship, imprisonment, torture – are more than likely to shake their expressive abilities, even in their own languages. "Restricting the interpreter's role to rendering an 'accurate' translation of the refugee's utterances – which may contain hesitations, grammatical errors and various infelicities – inevitably jeopardizes the claimant's chances of obtaining refugee status, irrespective of the validity of the claim" (Barsky 1996: 52). Similarly, the interpreter must reconcile the cultural differences between Canada and the refugee's country by adding information about the foreign context, historical, geographical, political, or sociological details that may be omitted in testimony and unknown to Canadian judges and lawyers. "Insisting upon an interpretation limited exclusively to words uttered evacuates the cultural data which could be essential to the refugee's claim" (Barsky 1994: 49).

Barksy provides a telling example of a Pakistani claimant who spoke French during the hearing, apparently in an effort to lend weight to his case with the Québec authorities. But his French was weak, and his claim was previously denied because of interpreting problems, as he tried to explain:

> Moi demander, moi demander Madame, s'il vous plaît, cette translation lui parle français. Vous demander, parle français. Parce qu'elle m'a compris, vous qu'est ce qu'elle a dit. Moi compris. Madame m'a dit, désolé Monsieur, seul anglais.
>
> (Literally: Me ask, me ask Madame, please this translation speak to him French. You ask, speak French. Because she understood me, you that is what she said. Me understand. Madam said to me, sorry sir, only English.)
>
> (Barsky 1996: 53, his translation)

The claimant was testifying with a Pakistani interpreter who rendered the broken French into intelligible and compelling English:

> He has a complaint with the interpreter there. He speaks better French than English, but the interpreter was interpreting from Urdu to English. He is not too good in English, better in French, which he could understand. An interpreter was provided to interpret the hearing into English, which he did not agree to. So he was having a hard time expressing himself or understanding the CPO, lawyers, himself, and the interpreter. There is no satisfaction in the hearing. And that is one reason why I lost the case.

When effective, community interpreting provides a complicated ideological resolution for the linguistic and cultural differences of the refugee's or immigrant's speech. The interpreting inevitably communicates the foreign text in domestic terms, in the terms of the host country, but the domestic inscription also needs to include a significant part of the foreign context that gives meaning to the claim. This sort of interpreting, although seemingly partial to the client, is not in fact ideologically one-sided: it serves both foreign and domestic interests. The ideology of the resolution is fundamentally democratic insofar as the aim is to overcome the asymmetries that exist between the client and the representatives of the social agency within and outside of the interpreting situation. According to the British manual, the community interpreter permits "professional and client, with very different backgrounds and perceptions and in an unequal relationship of power and knowledge, to communicate to their mutual satisfaction" (Shackman 1984: 18). An important requirement for this mutual satisfaction, clearly, is the idea that a consensus as to the validity of the claim, shared by the two parties, has emerged in rational communication. Yet the communication can be seen as rational only when the interpreter so intervenes as to enable both the client to participate fully and the agency representatives to arrive at an informed understanding of the claim.

Community interpreting that takes an interventionist approach thus presupposes what Jürgen Habermas calls an "ideal speech situation," distinguished by conditions that are normally "counterfactual" because "improbable": they include "openness to the public, inclusiveness, equal rights to participation, immunization against external or internal compulsion, as well as the participants' orientation toward reaching understanding (that is, the sincere expression of utterances)" (Habermas 1998: 367). In presupposing such conditions, the community interpreter works ultimately to foster a domestic community that is receptive to foreign constituencies, but that is not yet realized – or at least its realization will not be advanced until the client is given political asylum, due process, medical care, or welfare benefits, as the case may be. Even then, of course, the receptive domestic community is primarily a utopian projection that does not eliminate the social hierarchies in which the refugee or immigrant is actually positioned. Still, it does express the hope that linguistic and cultural differences will not result in the exclusion of foreign constituencies from the domestic scene. Translating might be motivated by much more questionable things.

BIBLIOGRAPHY

Alain (1934) *Propos de littérature*, Paris: Gonthier.

Allain, M.-F. (1983) *The Other Man: Conversations with Graham Greene*, trans. G. Waldman, London: Bodley Head.

Amos, F. R. (1920) *Early Theories of Translation*, New York: Columbia University Press.

Anderson, B. (1991) *Imagined Communities: Reflections on the Origin and Spread of Nationalism*, revised edition, London and New York: Verso.

Anderson, D. (1983) *Pound's Cavalcanti: An Edition of the Translations, Notes, and Essays*, Princeton, NJ: Princeton University Press.

Andrès, B., and P. Lefebvre (1979) "'Macbeth,' Théâtre de la Manufacture," *Jeu* 11: 80–8.

Andrew, D. (1980) "Sound in France: the Origins of a Native School," *Yale French Studies* 60: 94–114.

Arnheim, R. (1997) *Film Essays and Criticism*, Madison, WI: University of Wisconsin Press.

Arrojo, R. (1998) "The Revision of the Traditional Gap between Theory and Practice and the Empowerment of Translation in Postmodern Times," *The Translator* 4: 25–48.

Asad, T. (1986) "The Concept of Cultural Translation in British Social Anthropology," in J. Clifford and G. E. Marcus (eds) *Writing Culture: The Poetics and Politics of Ethnography*, Berkeley and Los Angeles: University of California Press, pp. 141–64.

Ascheid, A. (1997) "Speaking Tongues: Voice Dubbing in the Cinema as Cultural Ventriloquism," *The Velvet Light Trap* 40 (Fall): 32–41.

Ash, I. (trans.) (1955) F. Sagan, *Bonjour Tristesse*, New York: Dutton.

Augustine. (1958) *On Christian Doctrine*, trans. D. W. Robertson Jr, Indianapolis: Bobbs-Merrill.

Babuscio, J. (1977/1993) "Camp and Gay Sensibility," in D. Bergman (ed.) *Camp Grounds: Style and Homosexuality*, Amherst: University of Massachusetts Press, pp. 19–38.

Bacardí, M., J. Fontcuberta, and F. Parcerisas (eds) (1998) *Cent anys de traducció al català (1891–1990): Antologia*, Vic and Barcelona: Eumo.

Baker, M. (1992) *In Other Words: A Coursebook on Translation*, London and New York: Routledge.

—— (1993) "Corpus Linguistics and Translations: Implications and Applications," in M. Baker, G. Francis, and E. Tognini-Bonelli (eds) *Text and Technology: In Honour of John Sinclair*, Amsterdam: Benjamins, pp. 233–50.

—— (1995) "Corpora in Translation Studies: An Overview and Some Suggestions for Future Research," *Target* 7: 223–43.

—— (1996) "Linguistics and Cultural Studies: Complementary or Competing Paradigms?" in A. Lauer, H. Gerzymisch-Arbogast, J. Haller and E. Steiner (eds) *Übersetzungswissenschaft im Umbruch*, Tübingen: Narr, pp. 9–19.

—— (1997) "Corpus-based Translation Studies: The Challenges that Lie Ahead," in H. Somers (ed.) *Technology, LSP and Translation: Studies in Language Engineering in Honour of Juan C. Sager*, Amsterdam: Benjamins, pp. 175–86.

—— (ed.) (1998) *Encyclopedia of Translation Studies*, London and New York: Routledge.

—— (2000) "Towards a Methodology for Investigating the Style of a Literary Translation," *Target* 12: 241–66.

Bakhtin, M. (1982) *Le Principe dialogique: suivi d'écrits du Cercle de Bakhtin*, Paris: Seuil.

Balibar, R. (1985) *L'Institution du français*, Paris: Presses Universitaires de France.

Ballard, M. (1992) *De Cicéron à Benjamin: Traducteurs, traductions, réflexions*, Lille: Presses Universitaires de Lille.

Bally, C. (1944) *Linguistique générale et linguistique française*, 2nd edition, Bern: Francke.

Barrett, R. (1995) "Supermodels of the World, Unite! Political Economy and the Language of Performance among African-American Drag Queens," in W. Leap (ed.) *Beyond the Lavender Lexicon: Authenticity, Imagination, and Appropriation in Lesbian and Gay Languages*, Luxembourg: Gordon and Breach, pp. 207–26.

—— (1997) "The 'Homo-genius' Speech Community," in A. Livia and K. Hall (eds) *Queerly Phrased: Language, Gender and Sexuality*, New York and London: Oxford University Press.

Barsky, R. F. (1994) *Constructing a Productive Other: Discourse Theory and the Convention Refugee Hearing*, Amsterdam: Benjamins.

—— (1996) "The Interpreter as Intercultural Agent in Convention Refugee Hearings," *The Translator* 2: 45–64.

Bassnett, S. (1980) *Translation Studies*, London and New York: Routledge; revised edition, 1991.

Bassnett, S. and A. Lefevere (eds) (1990) *Translation, History and Culture*, London: Pinter.

Bassnett, S. and H. Trivedi (eds) (1998) *Postcolonial Translation Theory*, London and New York: Routledge.

Bates, E. S. (1936) *Modern Translation*, London: Oxford University Press.

Baumhauer, O. A. (1986) *Die sophistische Rhetorik – Eine Theorie sprachlicher Kommunikation*, Stuttgart: Metzler.

Beerbohm, M. (1903) "Translation of Plays," *Saturday Review* (London) 96: 75–6.

Belloc, H. (1931) *On Translation*, Oxford: Oxford University Press.

—— (1931a) "On Translation," *Bookman* 74: 32–39, 179–85.

Benjamin, A. (1989) *Translation and the Nature of Philosophy*, London and New York: Routledge.

Benjamin, W. (1923) "Die Aufgabe der Übersetzung," in R Tiedemann and H. Schweppenhäuser (eds) *Gesammelte Schriften*, Frankfurt: Suhrkamp, 1980.

—— (1968) "The Task of the Translator," in *Illuminations*, ed. H. Arendt, trans. Harry Zohn, New York: Schocken, pp. 69–82.

Ben-Porat, Z., and B. Hrushovski (1974) *Structuralist Poetics in Israel*, Tel Aviv: Department of Poetics and Comparative Literature, University of Tel Aviv.

Ben-Shahar, R. (1983) "Dialogue Style in the Hebrew Play, both Original and Translated from English and French, 1948–1975," University of Tel Aviv, unpublished dissertation.

Bergeron, L. (1980) *Dictionnaire de la langue québécoise*, Montreal: VLB.

Bergstrom, M. (1989) "Communication and Translation from the Point of View of Brain Function," unpublished manuscript.

Berman, A. (1984) *L'Épreuve de l'étranger: Culture et traduction dans l'Allemagne romantique*, Paris: Gallimard.

—— (1985) "La Traduction comme épreuve de l'étranger," *Texte* 4: 67–81.

—— (1985a) "La Traduction et la lettre, ou l'auberge du lointain," in *Les Tours de Babel: Essais sur la traduction*, Mauvezin: Trans-Europ-Repress; Paris: Seuil, 1999.

—— (1992) *The Experience of the Foreign: Culture and Translation in Romantic Germany*, trans. S. Heyvaert, Albany, NY: State University of New York Press.

—— (1995) *Pour une critique des traductions: John Donne*, Paris: Gallimard.

Berman, R. (1978) "Postponing Lexical Repetition and the Like: A Study in Contrastive Stylistics," *Balshanut Shimushit* 1:2.

Bhabha, H. (1994) *The Location of Culture*, London and New York: Routledge.

Black, G. A. (1936) "James Thomson: His Translation of Heine," *Modern Language Review* 31: 48–54.

Blanchot, M. (1988) *The Unavowable Community*, trans. P. Joris, Barrytown, New York: Station Hill Press.

—— (1997) "Translating" (1971), in *Friendship*, trans. E. Rottenberg, Stanford, California: Stanford University Press.

Bloch, E. (1988) *The Utopian Function of Art and Literature: Selected Essays*, ed. and trans. J. Zipes and F. Mecklenburg, Cambridge, Massachusetts: MIT Press.

—— (1991) *Heritage of Our Times*, trans. N. Plaice and S. Plaice, Oxford: Polity.

Blum-Kulka, S. (1981) "The Study of Translation in View of New Developments in Discourse Analysis," *Poetics Today* 2:4.

—— (1983) "The Dynamics of Political Interviews," *Text* 3:2.

Booth, M. (1983) *Camp*, London: Quartet.

Borges, J. L. (1936) *Historia de la eternidad*, Buenos Aires: Viau y Zona.

—— (1999) *Selected Non-Fictions*, ed. E. Weinberger, New York: Viking Penguin.

Bory, J. L. (1969) *La Peau des Zèbres*, Paris: Gallimard.

Bower, A. (trans.) (1953) A. Camus, *The Rebel*, London: Hamish Hamilton.

Brecht, B. (1975) *La Bonne Âme de Se-Tchouan*, trans. J. Stern, Paris: L'Arche.

—— (1976) "Le Buffet impromptu ou la nôsse chez les propriétaires de bungalow," adapt. J. C. Germain, National Theatre School, unpublished manuscript.

—— (n.d.) "La Bonne Âme de Se-Tchouan," trans. G. Turp, National Theatre School, unpublished manuscript.

Brennenstuhl, W. (1975) *Handlungstheorie und Handlungslogik: Vorbereitungen zur Entwicklung einer sprachadäquaten Handlungslogik*, Kronberg: Athenäum.

Brisset, A. (1990) *Sociocritique de la traduction: Théâtre et altérité au Québec (1968–1988)*, Longueuil: Le Préambule.

—— (1996) *A Sociocritique of Translation: Theatre and Alterity in Quebec, 1968–1988*, trans. Rosalind Gill and Roger Gannon, Toronto: University of Toronto Press.

Bristow, E. K. (ed. and trans.) (1977) *Anton Chekhov's Plays*, New York: Norton.

Broch, H. (1966) *Création littéraire et connaissance*, trans. A. Kohn, Paris: Gallimard.

Broerman, I. (1984) "Die Textsorte 'Witz' im Portugiesischen," University of Heidelberg, unpublished dissertation.

Brower, R. (ed.) (1959) *On Translation*, Cambridge, MA: Harvard University Press.

Brown, P., and S. Levinson (1987) *Politeness. Some Universals in Language Usage*, Cambridge: Cambridge University Press.

Bruneau, C. (1955) *Petite Histoire de la langue française, I*, Paris: Armand Colin.

Buber, M., and F. Rosenzweig (1994) *Scripture and Translation*, trans. L. Rosenwald with E. Fox, Bloomington: Indiana University Press.

Burton, D. (1980) *Dialogue and Discourse*, London: Routledge and Kegan Paul.

Busch, W. (1987) "Die Kunst und der Wandel ihrer Funktion. Zur Einführung in die Themenstellung," in W. Busch and P. Schmook (eds) *Kunst – Die Geschichte ihrer Funktionen*, Weinheim and Berlin: Beltz.

Butler, J. (1990) *Gender Trouble: Feminism and the Subversion of Identity*, London and New York: Routledge.

Calzada Pérez, M. (1997) "Transitivity in Translating: the Interdependence of Texture and Context," Heriot Watt University, unpublished dissertation.

—— (2001) "A Three-way Methodology for Descriptive-Explanatory Translation Studies," *Target* 13(2): 203–39.

Camindade, M., and A. Pym (1995) *Les Formations en traduction et interprétation: Essai de recensement mondial*, Paris: Société Française des Traducteurs.

Campbell, G. (1789) *The Four Gospels*, London: Strahan and Cadell, vol. 1.

Camus, A. (1942) *L'Étranger*, Paris: Gallimard.

—— (1951) *L'Homme Revolté*, Paris: Gallimard.

—— (1951a) *Headam Hamored*, trans. Z. Arad, Tel Aviv: Am Oved.

—— (1953) *The Rebel*, trans. A. Bower, London: Hamish Hamilton.

—— (1953a) *Der Mensch in der Revolte*, trans. J. Streller, Hamburg: Rowohlt.

Camus, R. (1981) *Tricks*, Paris: P.O.L.

—— (1982) *Notes Achriennes*, Paris: P.O.L.

—— (1988) *Tricks* (édition définitive), Paris: P.O.L.

Cary, E. (ed.) (1959) "Notre enquête," *Babel* 5: 61–106.

Catford, J. C. (1965) *A Linguistic Theory of Translation: An Essay in Applied Linguistics*, London: Oxford University Press.

Cecchetti, G. (1959) Review of Mandelbaum (1958), *Comparative Literature* 11: 262–8.

Chamberlain, L. (1988) "Gender and the Metaphorics of Translation," *Signs* 13: 454–72.

Chamberland, P. (1969) *L'Afficheur hurle*, Montreal: Éditions Parti Pri.

Chan, S-W and D. Pollard (eds) (1995) *An Encyclopedia of Translation: Chinese–English/English–Chinese*, Hong Kong: The Chinese University of Hong Kong Press.

Chekhov, A. (1967) *Œuvres*, Paris: Gallimard.

—— (1983) *Uncle Vanya*, trans. M. Tremblay and K. Yaroshevskaya, Montreal: Lemeac.

—— (1984) *Tri sestry*, in *Izbrannoje, Rasskazy, Povesti, Piesy*, Moscow: Provescene.

—— (n.d.) "Les trois sœurs," trans. R. Lalonde, National Theatre School, unpublished manuscript.

Chesterman, A. (ed.) (1989) *Readings in Translation Theory*, Helsinki: Oy Finn Lectura Ab.

—— (1997) *Memes of Translation: The Spread of Ideas in Translation Theory*, Amsterdam: Benjamins.

Cheyfitz, E. (1991) *The Poetics of Imperialism: Translation and Colonization from The Tempest to Tarzan*, New York and London: Oxford University Press.

Ciardi, J. (trans.) (1954) D. Alighieri, *The Inferno*, New York: Mentor.

Cicero, M. T. (1949) *De inventione, De optimo genere oratorum, Topica*, trans. H. M. Hubell, Cambridge, MA: Harvard University Press.

Cooper, W. A. (1928) "Translating Goethe's Poems," *Journal of English and Germanic Philology* 27: 470–85.

Copeland, R. (1991) *Rhetoric, Hermeneutics, and Translation in the Middle Ages: Academic Traditions and Vernacular Texts*, Cambridge: Cambridge University Press.

Cotroneo, R. (1995) "Sostiene Tabucchi," *L'Espresso*, 2 June, pp. 104–8.

Cox, L., and R. Fay (1994) "Gayspeak, the Linguistic Fringe: Bona Polari, Camp, Queerspeak and Beyond," in S. White (ed.) *The Margins of the City: Gay Men's Urban Lives*, Aldershot: Arena.

Creagh, P. (trans.) (1995) *Declares Pereira: A Testimony*, London: Harvill.

Creed, B. (1998) "Film and Psychoanalysis," in J. Hill and P. Gibson (eds) *The Oxford Guide to Film Studies*, Oxford: Oxford University Press, pp. 77–90.

Crisp, Q. (1968) *The Naked Civil Servant*, London: Cape.

Cronin, M. (1996) *Translating Ireland: Translation, Languages, Cultures*, Cork: Cork University Press.

—— (2000) *Across the Lines: Travel, Language, Translation*, Cork: Cork University Press.

—— (2003) *Translation and Globalization*, London and New York: Routledge.

D'Ablancourt, N. P. (1972) *Lettres et préfaces critiques*, ed. R. Zuber, Paris: Marcel Didier.

Danan, M. (1991) "Dubbing as an Expression of Nationalism," *Meta* 36: 606–14.

—— (1999) "Hollywood's Hegemonic Strategies: Overcoming French Nationalism with the Advent of Sound," in A. Higson and R. Maltby (eds) *"Film Europe"* and *"Film America": Cinema, Commerce and Cultural Exchange 1920–1939*, Exeter: University of Exeter Press, pp. 225–48.

Daniell, D. (2003) *The Bible in English*, New Haven, CT: Yale University Press.

Davidson, D. (1984) *Inquiries into Truth and Interpretation*, Oxford and New York: Oxford University Press.

Davis, K. (2001) *Translation and Deconstruction*, Manchester: St Jerome.

De Geest, D. (1992) "The Notion of 'System': Its Theoretical Importance and its Methodological Implications for a Functionalist Translation Theory," in H. Kittel (ed.) *Geschichte, System, Literarische Übersetzung / Histories, Systems, Literary Translations*, Berlin: Schmidt, pp. 32–45.

Delabastita, D. (1989) "Translation and Mass Communication: Film and TV Translation as Evidence of Cultural Dynamics," *Babel* 35(4): 193–218.

De Linde, Z. and N. Kay (1999) *The Semiotics of Subtitling*, Manchester: St Jerome.

De Man, P. (1986) "'Conclusions': Walter Benjamin's 'The Task of the Translator'," in *The Resistance to Theory*, Minneapolis: University of Minnesota Press.

Denham, J. (ed. and trans.) (1656) *The Destruction of Troy, An Essay upon the Second Book of Virgil's Æneis. Written in the year, 1636*, London: Humphrey Moseley.

Derrida, J. (1979) "Living On/Border Lines," trans. J. Hulbert, in *Deconstruction and Criticism*, New York: Continuum, pp. 75–176.

—— (1985) "Des Tours de Babel," trans. J. Graham, in J. Graham (ed.) *Difference in Translation*, Ithaca, New York: Cornell University Press, pp. 165–248.

—— (1985a) *The Ear of the Other: Otobiography, Transference, Translation*, trans. P. Kamuf, New York: Schocken.

—— (1999) "Qu'est-ce qu'une traduction 'relevante'?" in *Quinzièmes Assises de la Traduction Littéraire (Arles 1998)*, Arles: Actes Sud, pp. 21–48.

—— (2001) "What Is a 'Relevant' Translation?" trans. L. Venuti, *Critical Inquiry* 27: 174–200.

De Saint-Exupéry, A. (1946) *Le Petit Prince*, Paris: Gallimard.

—— (1962) *The Little Prince*, trans. K. Woods, Harmondsworth: Penguin.

Diemert, B. (1996) *Graham Greene's Thrillers and the 1930s*, Montreal and Buffalo: McGill-Queen's University Press.

Dryden, J. (1680) "Preface to *Ovid's Epistles*," in E. N. Hooker and H. T. Swedenberg, Jr (eds) *The Works of John Dryden*, vol. I, Berkeley and Los Angeles: University of California Press, 1956.

Dubois, J. (1978) *L'Institution de la littérature*, Paris: Fernand Nathan.

Duvert, T. (1969) *Interdit de Séjour*, Paris: Les Editions de Minuit.

—— (1973) *Paysage de Fantaisie*, Paris: Les Editions de Minuit.

—— (1974) *Le Bon Sexe Illustré*, Paris: Les Editions de Minuit.

—— (1980) *L'Enfant au Masculin*, Paris: Les Editions de Minuit.

Dyer, R. (1977) "It's Being So Camp as Keeps Us Going," *Body Politic* 10: 11–13.

Ebel, J. G. (1969) "Translation and Cultural Nationalism in the Reign of Elizabeth," *Journal of the History of Ideas* 30: 593–602.

Edmondson, W. (1981) *Spoken Discourse: A Model for Analysis*, London: Longman.

Edwards, O. (1957) "Cynara," *Times of London*, July 11, p. 13.

Essmann, H., and A. P. Frank (1991) "Translation Anthologies: An Invitation to the Curious and a Case Study," *Target* 3: 65–90.

Even-Zohar, I. (1975) "Decisions in Translating Poetry," *Hasifrut* 21: 32–45. [Hebrew]

—— (1990) *Polysystem Studies*, Poetics Today 11:1.

Fairclough, N. (1992) *Discourse and Social Change*, Cambridge: Polity.

Fang, A. (1953) "Some Reflections on the Difficulty of Translation," in A. F. Wright (ed.) *Studies in Chinese Thought*, Chicago: University of Chicago Press, pp. 263–85; reprinted in Brower (1959), pp. 111–33.

Fawcett, P. (1996) "Translating Film," in G. T. Harris (ed.) *On Translating French Literature and Film*, Amsterdam: Rodopi.

—— (1997) *Translation and Language: Linguistic Theories Explained*, Manchester: St Jerome.

Fillmore, C. (1981) "Ideal Readers and Real Readers," *Proceedings of the 32nd Georgetown Round Table on Language and Linguistics*, Washington, DC: Georgetown University Press.

Fish, S. (1980) *Is There a Text in This Class?: The Authority of Interpretive Communities*, Cambridge, MA: Harvard University Press.

Fitts, D. (ed. and trans.) (1956) *Poems from the Greek Anthology*, New York: New Directions.

—— (1959) "The Poetic Nuance," in R. Brower (ed.) *On Translation*, Cambridge, MA: Harvard University Press, pp. 32–47.

Flores, S. (trans.) (1975) T. Duvert, *Strange Landscape*, New York: Grove.

Forster, L. (1958) "Translation: An Introduction," in Smith, *Aspects of Translation: Studies in Communication 2*, London: Secker and Warburg., pp. 1–28.

Foucault, M. (1964) "Les Mots qui saignent," *L'Express*, 29 August, p. 21.

Fowler, R. (1986) *Linguistic Criticism*, Oxford: Oxford University Press; 2nd edition, 1996.

—— (1996) "On Critical Linguistics," in C. R. Caldas-Coulthard and M. Coulthard (eds) *Texts and Practices: Readings in Critical Discourse Analysis*, London and New York: Routledge.

France, P. (ed.) (2000) *Oxford Guide to Literature in English Translation*, Oxford: Oxford University Press.

Fraser, J. (1993) "Public Accounts: Using Verbal Protocols to Investigate Community Translation," *Applied Linguistics* 14: 325–43.

—— (1996) "The Translator Investigated: Learning from Translation Process Analysis," *The Translator* 2: 65–79.

Frawley, W. (1984) "Prolegomenon to a Theory of Translation," in W. Frawley (ed.) *Translation: Literary, Linguistic, and Philosophical Perspectives*, Newark: University of Delaware Press, pp. 159–75.

Frere, J. H. (1820) Review of T. Mitchell's Aristophanes, *Quarterly Review* 46: 474–505.

Fujinami F. (1977) *Nyūsu Kameraman – Gekidō no Shōwashi o Toru* ("News Cameraman – Shooting the Turbulent History of the Shōwa Era"), Tokyo: Chūūkōronsha.

Gais et Lesbiennes Branchés (1995) "How to Say *It* in French," Website: http:// www.france.qrd.org/fqrd/texts/words.html.

Gambier, Y. (1994) *Language Transfer and Audiovisual Communication: A Bibliography*, Turku: University of Turku.

—— (ed.) (1996) *Les transferts linguistiques dans les médias audiovisuels*, Villeneuve d'Ascq: Presses Universitaires du Septentrion.

Gardt, A. (1987) "Literarisches Übersetzen in den Fremdsprachenphilologien," in A. Wierlacher (ed.) *Perspektiven und Verfahren interkultureller Germanistik*, Munich: Iudicium, pp. 551–6.

—— (1989) "Möglichkeiten und Grenzen einer pragmatischen Übersetzungstheorie," *TEXTconTEXT* 4: 1–59.

Garneau, M. (1973) *L'Animalhumain*, Montreal: Fédération des coopératives Étudiantes.

—— (1974) *Langage 5*, Montreal: L'Aurore.

Garvin, P. L. (ed. and trans.) (1955) *A Prague School Reader on Esthetics, Literary Structure and Style*, Washington, DC: Washington Linguistic Club.

Gasché, R. (1988) "Saturnine Vision and the Question of Difference: Reflections on Walter Benjamin's Theory of Language," in R. Naegle (ed.) *Benjamin's Ground: New Readings of Walter Benjamin*, Detroit: Wayne State University Press.

Genet, J. (1948) *Notre-Dame des Fleurs*, Paris: L'Arbalète.

Gentile, A., U. Ozolins, and M. Vasilakakos (1996) *Liaison Interpreting: A Handbook*, Melbourne: Melbourne University Press.

Gentzler, E. (1993) *Contemporary Translation Theories*, London and New York: Routledge; 2nd edition, Clevedon: Multilingual Matters, 2000.

Germain, J. C. (1972) *Diguidi, diguidi, ha! ha! ha!, suivi de, Si les Sansoucis s'en soucient, ces Sansoucis-ci s'en soucieront-ils? Bien parler, c'est se respecter!* Montreal: Leméac.

Gerow, A. A. (1996) "Writing a Pure Cinema: Articulations of Early Japanese Film," University of Iowa, unpublished dissertation.

Gerzymisch-Arbogast, H. (1987) *Zur Thema-Rhema-Gliederung in amerikanischen Wirtschaftsfachtexten. Eine exemplarische Analyse*, Tübingen: Narr.

Gilbert, S. (trans.) (1946) A. Camus, *The Stranger*, New York: Alfred Knopf.

Gill, B. (1955) "The Uses of Love," *New Yorker*, 5 March, pp. 114–15.

Glinz, H. (1973) *Textanalyse und Verstehenstheorie I*, Frankfurt: Athenäum.

Gobard, H. (1976) *L'Aliénation linguistique*, Paris: Flammarion.

Gobin, P. (1978) *Le Fou et ses doubles*, Montreal: Presses de l'Université de Montréal.

Godard, B. (1986) "Translator's Preface," in N. Brossard, *Lovhers*, Montreal: Guernica.

Goethe, J. W. V. (1819) *West-Östlicher Divan*, ed. H. Birus, Frankfurt: Deutscher Klassiker, 1994.

Goffman, E. (1976) "Replies and Responses," *Language in Society*, 5: 257–313.

Golino, C. (1959) Review of Mandelbaum (1958), *Italian Quarterly* 3: 76.

Gombrowicz, W. (1976) *Trans-Atlantique*, trans. C. Jelenski and G. Serreau, Paris: Denoël.

Gomery, D. (1980) "Economic Struggle and Holywood Imperialism: Europe Converts to Sound," *Yale French Studies* 60: 80–93.

Goodspeed, E. J. (1945) *Problems of New Testament Translation*, Chicago: University of Chicago Press.

Graham, J. (ed.) (1985) *Difference in Translation*, Ithaca, New York: Cornell University Press.

Green, J. (1974) *Jeunesse*, Paris: Plon.

Greene, T. (1982) *The Light in Troy: Imitation and Discovery in Renaissance Poetry*, New Haven, CT: Yale University Press.

Gresset, M. (1983) "De la traduction de la métaphore littéraire à la traduction comme métaphore de l'écriture," *Revue française d'études américaines* 18 (November).

Grice, H. P. (1975) "Logic and conversation," in P. Cole and J. Morgan (eds) *Syntax and Semantics 3: Speech Acts*, New York: Academic Press.

Grosse, E. U. (1976) *Text und Kommunikation: Eine linguistische Einführung in die Funktion der Texte*, Stuttgart: Kohlhammer.

Gutt, E.-A. (1991) *Translation and Relevance: Cognition and Context*, Oxford: Blackwell; 2nd edition, Manchester: St Jerome, 2000.

Habermas, J. (1998) *On the Pragmatics of Communication*, ed. M. Cooke, Cambridge, Massachusetts: MIT Press.

Halliday, M. (1985) *An Introduction to Functional Grammar*, London: E. Arnold.

Halliday, M. and R. Hasan (1976) *Cohesion in English*, London: Longman.

Hantsch, I. (1972) "Zur semantischen Strategie der Werbung," *Sprache im technischen Zeitalter* 42: 93–112.

Harras, G. (1978) *Kommunikative Handlungskonzepte, oder: Eine Möglichkeit, Handlungsabfolgen als Zusammenhänge zu erklären, exemplarish an Theatertexten*, Tübingen: Niemeyer.

Harris, B. (1990) "Norms in Interpretation," *Target* 2: 115–19.

—— (ed.) (1997) *Translating and Interpreting Schools*, Amsterdam: Benjamins.

Harvey, K. (2003) *Intercultural Movements: American Gay in French Translation*, Manchester: St Jerome.

Haseloff, O. W. (1969) *Kommunikation*, Berlin: Colloquium Verlag.

Hass, V. P. (1955) Review of Ash (1955), *Chicago Sunday Tribune*, 24 April, p. 6.

Hatim, B. (1997) *Communication across Cultures: Translation Theory and Contrastive Text Linguistics*, Exeter: University of Exeter Press.

—— (1998) "Translation Quality Assessment: Setting and Maintaining a Trend," *The Translator* 4: 91–100.

—— (2001) *Teaching and Researching Translation*, London: Longman.

Hatim, B. and I. Mason (1990) *Discourse and the Translator*, London: Longman.

—— (1997) *The Translator as Communicator*, London and New York: Routledge.

Hayashi C. (1931) "Tōkii ni Kan Suru Hashirigaki" ("A Quick Note on the Talkie"), *STS* 5(10 May): 39.

Heidegger, M. (1968) *Questions I*, Paris: Gallimard.

—— (1975) *Early Greek Thinking*, ed. and trans. D. F. Krell and F. A. Capuzzi, New York: Harper and Row.

Heinold, E., G. Keuchen, and U. Schultz (1987) *Bücher und Büchermacher: Was man von Verlagen wissen sollte*, Heidelberg: Decker and Müller.

Hemingway, E. (1938) *The Short Stories of Ernest Hemingway*, New York: Scriners.

Herding, K. (1987) "Realismus," in W. Busch and P. Schmook (eds) *Kunst: Die Geschichte ihrer Funktionen*, Weinheim and Berlin: Beltz, pp. 674–713.

Hermans, T. (ed.) (1985) *The Manipulation of Literature: Studies in Literary Translation*, London: Croom Helm.

——— (1991) "Translational Norms and Correct Translations," in K. van Leuven-Zwart and T. Naaijkens (1991), pp. 155–69.

——— (1995) "Toury's Empiricism Version One," *The Translator* 1: 215–23.

——— (1999) *Translation in Systems: Descriptive and System-oriented Approaches Explained*, Manchester: St Jerome.

Hjort, A. M. (1990) "Translation and the Consequences of Scepticism," in S. Bassnett and A. Lefevere (eds) *Translation, History and Culture*, London: Pinter, pp. 38–45.

Hoby, Sir T. (trans.) (1900) B. Castligione, *The Book of the Courtier*, ed. W. Raleigh, New York: AMS Press, 1967.

Hocquenghem, G. (1972) *Le Désir Homosexuel*, Paris: Editions Universitaires.

Holmes, J. S. (1988) *Translated! Papers on Literary Translation and Translation Studies*, Amsterdam: Rodopi.

Holz-Mäntärri, J. (1984) *Translatorisches Handeln: Theorie und Methode*, Helsinki: Suomalainen Tiedeakatemia.

— (1985) "Strukturwandel in den Translations-Berufen," *Juhlakääntäjä / Jubileums-Översättaren* 9: 30–5.

— (1988) "Funktionskonstanz: eine Fiktion?" unpublished manuscript.

—, H.-J. Stellbrink, and H. J. Vermeer (1986) "Ein Fach und seine Zeitschrift," *TEXTconTEXT* 1: 1–10.

Hönig, H., and P. Kussmaul (1982) *Strategie der Übersetzung*, Tübingen: Narr.

Horguelin, P. (ed.) (1981) *Anthologie de la manière de traduire*, Montreal: Linguatech.

House, J. (1977) "A Model for Assessing Translation Quality," *Meta* 22: 103–9.

——— (1977/81) *A Model for Translation Quality Assessment*, Tübingen: Narr.

House, J. and S. Blum-Kulka (eds) (1996) *Interlingual and Intercultural Communication: Discourse and Cognition in Translation and Second Language Acquisition Studies*, Tübingen: Narr.

Howard, R. (trans.) (1996) R. Camus, *Tricks* (1981), New York and London: Serpent's Tail.

Hrushovski, B. (1971) "The Major Systems of Hebrew Rhyme from the Piyut to the Present Day (500 AD–1970): An Essay on Basic Concepts," *Hasifrut* 2: 721–49. [Hebrew]

Hudson, A. (ed.) (1978) *Selections from English Wycliffite Writings*, Cambridge: Cambridge University Press.

Hutcheon, L. (1985) *A Theory of Parody: The Teachings of Twentieth-Century Art Forms*, New York: Methuen.

Hutchins, J., and H. Somers (1992) *Introduction to Machine Translation*, London: Academic Press.

Iwasaki, A. (1930) "Tōkii to Musankaikyū ("Talkies and the Proletariat"), *Shisō* 93 (February): 71–207.

Izre'el, S. (1994) "Did Adapa Indeed Lose His Chance for Eternal Life?: A Rationale for Translating Ancient Texts into a Modern Language," *Target* 6: 15–41.

Jackson, J. (1960) "Structural Characteristics of Norms," in N. B. Henry (ed.) *The Dynamics of Instructional Groups: Sociopsychological Aspects of Teaching and Learning*, Chicago: University of Chicago Press, pp. 136–63.

Jacobs, C. (1975) "The Monstrosity of Translation," *MLN* 90: 755–66.

Jacobs, G. (1996) "Lesbian and Gay Male Language Use: A Critical Review of the Literature," *American Speech* 71: 49–71.

Jakobson, R. (1969) "Linguistics and Poetics," in T. Sebeok (ed.) *Style in Language*, Cambridge, MA: MIT Press, pp. 350–77.

Jameson, F. (1981) *The Political Unconscious: Narrative as a Socially Symbolic Act*, Ithaca, New York: Cornell University Press.

Jerome (1980) *Liber de optimo interpretandi (Epistula 57)*, ed. G. J. M. Bartelnik, Lugundi Batavorum: Brill.

Jowett, B. (trans.) (1891) "Preface," in *The Dialogues of Plato*, 2nd edition, Oxford: Oxford University Press.

Kamijima K. (1995) *Jimaku Shikakenin Ichidaiki* ("Biography of a Subtitler"), Tokyo: Pandora.

Kaspar, R. (1983) "Die Biologische Grundlagen der evolutionären Erkenntnis-theorie," in K. Lorenz and F. M. Wuketits (eds) *Die Evolution des Denkens*, Munich and Zurich: Piper, pp. 125–45.

Kelly, J. N. D. (1975) *Jerome: His Life, Writings, and Controversies*, New York: Harper and Row.

Kelly, L. G. (1979) *The True Interpreter: A History of Translation Theory and Practice in the West*, Oxford: Blackwell.

Kenny, D. (1998) "Creatures of Habit? What Translators Usually Do with Words," in S. Laviosa (ed.) *The Corpus-Based Approach*, *Meta* 43(4): 515–23.

—— (2001) *Lexis and Creativity in Translation*, Manchester: St Jerome.

Kidd, J. (1997) *Guidelines for Translators*, revised by J. Doolaege, Paris: UNESCO.

King, T. (1994) "Performing 'Akimbo': Queer Pride and Epistemological Prejudice," in M. Meyer (ed.) *The Politics and Poetics of Camp*, London and New York: Routledge, pp. 23–50.

Kittel, H. (ed.) (1992) *Geschichte, System, Literarische Übersetzung / Histories, Systems, Literary Translations*, Berlin: Schmidt.

—— (1995) "Anthologies of Literature in Translation: The Göttingen Research Project," in H. Kittel (ed.) *International Anthologies of Literature in Translation*, Berlin: Schmidt, pp. 271–8.

Knox, R. A. (1957) *On English Translation*, Oxford: Oxford University Press.

Koller, W. (1979) *Einführung in die Übersetzungswissenschaft*, Heidelberg: Quelle and Meyer.

—— (1989) "Equivalence in Translation Theory," in A. Chesterman (ed. and trans.) *Readings in Translation Theory*, Helsinki: Oy Finn Lectura Ab, pp. 99–104.

Koskinen, K. (2000) "Institutional Illusions: Translating in the European Union Commission," *The Translator* 6(1): 49–65.

Kramer, L. (1978) *Faggots*, London: Minerva.

Kristal, E. (2002) *Invisible Work: Borges and Translation*, Nashville, TN: Vanderbilt University Press.

Krysinski, W. (1983) "Tchekhov, Tremblay, Brassard ou comment changer la vie par le théâtre," *Avant Première* 9(3): 10–11.

Kushner, T. (1992) *Angels in America, Part One: Millennium Approaches*, London: Royal National Theatre and Nick Hearn Books.

Labov, W. (1972) *Language in the Inner City: Studies in the Black English Vernacular*, Philadelphia: University of Pennsylvania Press.

Ladmiral, J. R. (1979) *Traduire: Théorèmes pour la traduction*, Paris: Payot.

—— (1986) "Sourciers et ciblistes," *Revue d'esthétique* 12: 422–33.

Lakoff, R. (1975) *Language and Women's Place*, New York: Harper and Row.

Lalonde, M. (1974) *Speak White*, Montreal: L'Hexagone.

—— (1979) *Défense et illustration de la langue québécoise*, Paris: Seghers-Laffont.

Lambert, J. (1990) "Le sous-titrage et la question des traductions: rapport sur une enquête," in R. Arntz and G. Thome (eds) *Übersetzungwissenschaft: Ergebnisse und Perspektiven*, Tübingen: Narr, pp. 228–38.

—— (1995) "Translation, Systems and Research: The Contribution of Polysystem Studies to Translation Studies," *TTR Traduction, Terminologie, Rédaction: Études sur le texte et ses transformations* 8(1): 105–52.

Lambert, J., L. D'hulst, and K. van Bragt (1985) "Translated Literature in France, 1800–1850," in T. Hermans (ed.) *The Manipulation of Literature: Studies in Literary Translation*, London: Croom Helm, pp. 149–63.

Lane-Mercier, G. (1997) "Translating the Untranslatable: The Translator's Aesthetic, Ideological and Political Responsibility," *Target* 9: 43–68.

Larbaud, V. (1946) *Sous l'invocation de saint Jérôme*, Paris: Gallimard: 1997.

Larose, R. (1989) *Théories contemporaines de la traduction*, Quebec: Presses de l'Université du Québec, 2nd edition.

Lasswell, H. D. (1964) "The Structure and Function of Communication in Society," in L. Bryson (ed.) *The Communication of Ideas: A Series of Addresses*, 2nd edition, New York: Cooper Square, pp. 37–51.

Lattimore, R. (ed. and trans.) (1951) *The Iliad of Homer*, Chicago: University of Chicago Press.

—— (1959) "Practical Notes on Translating Greek Poetry," in R. Brower (ed.) *On Translation*, Cambridge, MA: Harvard University Press, pp. 48–56.

Laviosa, S. (ed.) (1998) *The Corpus-Based Approach*, *Meta* 43(4).

Leap, W. (1996) *Word's Out: Gay Men's English*, Minneapolis: University of Minnesota Press.

Lecercle, J.-J. (1990) *The Violence of Language*, London and New York: Routledge.

Lefevere, A. (ed. and trans.) (1977) *Translating Literature: The German Tradition from Luther to Rosenzweig*, Assen: Van Gorcum.

—— (1992) *Translation, Rewriting, and the Manipulation of Literary Fame*, London and New York: Routledge.

—— (ed. and trans.) (1992a) *Translation/History/Culture: A Sourcebook*, London and New York: Routledge.

Lenk, H. (ed.) (1977) *Handlungstheorien interdisziplinär*, Munich: Fink.

Lescure, J. (trans.) (1953) Giuseppe Ungaretti, *Les cinq livres*, Paris: Editions de Minuit.

Leuven-Zwart, K. M. van (1989) "Translation and Original: Similarities and Dissimilarities, I," *Target* 1: 151–81.

—— (1990) "Translation and Original: Similarities and Dissimilarities, II," *Target* 2: 69–95.

Leuven-Zwart, K. M. van and T. Naaijkens (eds) (1991) *Translation Studies: The State of the Art*, Amsterdam: Rodopi.

Levenston, E. (1976) "Towards a Comparative Stylistics in English and Hebrew," *English Teacher's Journal* (Israel) 15: 16–22.

Levine, S. J. (1991) *The Subversive Scribe: Translating Latin American Fiction*, St. Paul, Minnesota: Graywolf Press.

Levý, J. (1965) "Will Translation Theory be of Use to Translators?" in R. Italiaander (ed.) *Übersetzen*, Frankfurt: Athenäum, pp. 77–82.

—— (1967) "Translation as a Decision Process," in *To Honor Roman Jakobson II*, The Hague: Mouton, pp. 1171–82.

—— (1969) *Die literarische Übersetzung: Theorie einer Kunstgattung*, trans. W. Schamschula, Frankfurt: Athenäum.

Lewandowski, T. (1973–5) *Linguistisches Worterbuch I–III*, Heidelberg: Quelle and Meyer.

Livia, A., and K. Hall (eds) (1997) *Queerly Phrased: Language, Gender, and Sexuality*, New York and London: Oxford University Press.

Locke, W. N., and A. D. Booth (1955) *Machine Translation of Languages*, New York: Wiley.

Lorenz, K., and F. M. Wuketits (eds) (1983) *Die Evolution des Denkens*, Munich and Zurich: Piper.

Lörscher, W. (1991) *Translation Performance, Translation Process, and Translation Strategies*, Tübingen: Narr.

—— (1996) "A Psycholinguistic Analysis of Translation Processes," *Meta* 41: 26–32.

Lucas, I. (1994) *Impertinent Decorum: Gay Theatrical Manoeuvres*, London: Cassell.

Luther, M. (1960) "On Translating: An Open Letter," trans. C. M. Jacobs, rev. E. T. Bachmann, in *Works*, ed. E. T. Bachmann, Philadelphia: Muhlenberg Press, vol. 35, pp. 179–202.

MacDuff, P. (1984) "Monique Mercure/Mère Courage," *En Scène* 2(2): 14–15.

MacIntyre, A. (1988) *Whose Justice? Which Rationality?*, Notre Dame, IN: University of Notre Dame Press.

Mahony, P. (1980) "Toward the Understanding of Translation in Psychoanalysis," in *Psychoanalysis and Discourse*, London: Tavistock, 1987, pp. 3–15.

Malmkjær, K. (1992) Review of Gutt (1991), *Mind and Language* 7(3): 298–309.

—— (1993) "Underpinning Translating Theory," *Target* 5: 133–48.

Malone, J. (1988) *The Science of Linguistics in the Art of Translation: Some Tools for the Analysis and Practice of Translation*, Albany: State University of New York Press.

Manchester, P. T. (1951) "Verse translation as an interpretive art," *Hispania* 34: 68–73.

Mandelbaum, A. (ed. and trans.) (1958) G. Ungaretti, *Life of a Man*, Milan: Scheiwiller, London: Hamish Hamilton, and New York: New Directions.

—— (ed. and trans.) (1975) *Selected Poems of Giuseppe Ungaretti*. Ithaca, New York: Cornell University Press.

Marcel, J. (1982) *Le Joual de Troie*, Montreal: E.I.P.

Marsolais, G. (1977) "Traduire et monter Mademoiselle Julie," *Cahiers de la Nouvelle Compagnie Théâtrale* 11(2): 11–12.

Martel, F. (1996) *Le Rose et le Noir: Les Homosexuels en France depuis 1968*, Paris: Seuil.

Martin, J. R., C. Matthiessen and C. Painter (1997) *Working with Functional Grammar*, London: E. Arnold.

Mason, I. (1994) "Discourse, Ideology and Translation," in R. de Beaugrande, A. Shunnaq and M. Heliel (eds) *Language, Discourse and Translation in the West and Middle East*, Amsterdam: Benjamins, pp. 23–34.

Massardier-Kenney, F. (1997) "Towards a Redefinition of Feminist Translation Practice," *The Translator* 3(1): 55–69.

Mathews, J. (1959) "Third Thoughts on Translating Poetry," in R. Brower (ed.) *On Translation*, Cambridge, MA: Harvard University Press, pp. 67–77.

Matthiessen, F. O. (1931) *Translation: An Elizabethan Art*, Cambridge, MA: Harvard University Press.

Maupin, A. (1980) *Tales of the City*, London: Corgi.

May, E. T. (1988) *Homeward Bound: American Families in the Cold War*, New York: Basic Books.

May, R. (1994) *The Translator in the Text: On Reading Russian Literature in English*, Evanston, IL: Northwestern University Press.

Meerschen, V. de (1982) "La Traduction française, problèmes de fidélité et de qualité," in *Traduzione-Tradizione*, Milan: Dedulo.

Merrick, J., and B. T. Ragan (1996) *Homosexuality in Modern France*, New York and Oxford: Oxford University Press.

Meschonnic, H. (1973) *Pour la poétique II*, Paris: Gallimard.

Meyer, M. (ed.) (1994) *The Politics and Poetics of Camp*, London and New York: Routledge.

—— (1994a) "Introduction: Reclaiming the Discourse of Camp," in M. Meyer (ed.) *The Politics and Poetics of Camp*, London and New York: Routledge, pp. 1–22.

Mikriammos, P. (trans.) (1981) G. Vidal, *Un Garçon Près de la Rivière*, Paris: Persona.

Millet, K. (1971) *Sexual Politics*, London: Hart-Davis.

Milligan, E. E. (1957) "Some Principles and Techniques of Translation," *Modern Language Journal* 41: 66–71.

Miron, G. (1970) *L'Homme rapaillé*, Montreal: Presses de l'Université de Montréal.

Morgan, B. Q. (1959) "A Critical Bibliography of Works on Translation: 46 BC–1958," in R. Brower (ed.) *On Translation*, Cambridge, MA: Harvard University Press, pp. 271–93.

Morgenthaler, E. (1980) *Kommunikationsorientierte Textgrammatik. Ein Versuch, die kommunikative Kompetenz zur Textbildung und Textreception aus natürlichem Sprachvorkommen zu erschliessen*, Düsseldorf: Schwann.

Morin, M., and C. Bertrand (1979) *Le Territoire imaginaire de la culture*, Montreal: Hurtubise HMH.

Mossop, B. (1988) "Translating Institutions: A Missing Factor in Translation Theory," *TTR* 1(2): 65–71.

—— (1990) "Translating Institutions and 'Idiomatic' Translation," *Meta* 35 (2): 342–55.

Mounin, G. (1955) *Les Belles Infidèles*, Paris: Cahiers du Sud.

—— (1963) *Les problèmes théoriques de la traduction*, Paris: Gallimard.

Munday, J. (2001) *Introducing Translation Studies: Theories and Applications*, London and New York: Routledge.

Mura C. (1933) "Ozu Yasujirō no Geijutsu Taido" ("Ozu Yasujirō's Artistic Attitude"), *STS* 13: 25.

Murray, S. O. (1979) "The Art of Gay Insulting," *Anthropological Linguistics* 21: 211–23.

Nabokov, V. (1941) "The Art of Translation," *New Republic* 105: 160–2.

—— (1955) "Problems of Translation: *Onegin* in English," *Partisan Review* 22: 496–512.

Nagid, N. L. (1955) "The Decadent Life," *Commonweal*, 13 May, pp. 163–6.

Navarre, Y. (1976) *Les Dernières Clientes*, in *Théâtre* II, Paris: Flammarion, pp. 139–224.

Neubert, A., and G. Shreve (1992) *Translation as Text*, Kent, Ohio: Kent State University Press.

—— (1994) "Foreword: 'A House of Many Rooms': The Range of Translation Studies," in D. Y. Kadish and F. Massardier-Kenney (eds) *Translating Slavery: Gender and Race in French Women's Writing, 1783–1823*, Kent, OH: Kent State University Press.

Newman, F. W. (1861) *Homeric Translation in Theory and Practice*, London: Williams and Norgate.

Newman, S. S. (1955) "Vocabulary Levels: Zuni Sacred and Slang Usage," *Southwestern Journal of Anthropology* 11: 345–54.

Newmark, P. (1977) "Communicative and Semantic Translation," *Babel* 23: 163–80.

—— (1982) *Approaches to Translation*, Oxford: Pergamon.

—— (1988) *A Textbook of Translation*, Hempel Hempstead: Prentice Hall.

—— (1991) "The Curse of Dogma in Translation Studies," *Lebende Sprachen* 36: 105–8.

New Yorker (1988) "Briefly Noted," 2 May, p. 119.

Nida, E. (1945) "Linguistics and Ethnology in Translation Problems," *Word* 1: 194–208.

—— (1964) *Toward a Science of Translating, With Special Reference to Principles and Procedures Involved in Bible Translating*, Leiden: Brill.

Nida, E. and C. Taber (1969) *The Theory and Practice of Translation*, Leiden: Brill, reprinted 1982.

Nietzsche, F. (1882) *The Gay Science*, trans. W. Kaufmann, New York: Vintage, 1974.

Niranjana, T. (1992) *Siting Translation: History, Poststructuralism, and the Colonial Context*, Berkeley and Los Angeles: University of California Press.

Nord, C. (1988) *Textanalyse und Übersetzung. Theoretische Grundlagen, Methode und didaktische Anwendung einer übersetzungsrelevanten Textanalyse*, Heidelberg: Groos; 2nd edition, 1991.

—— (1991) *Text Analysis in Translation*, Amsterdam and Atlanta: Rodopi.

—— (1996) "Text Type and Translation Method: An Objective Approach to Translation Criticism," *The Translator* 2: 81–8.

—— (1997) *Translation as a Purposeful Activity: Functionalist Approaches Explained*, Manchester: St Jerome.

Norton, G. P. (1984) *The Ideology and Language of Translation in Renaissance France and their Humanist Antecedents*, Geneva: Droz.

Nouss, A. (ed.) (1997) *Walter Benjamin's Essay on Translation: Critical Translations*, *TTR Traduction, Terminologie, Rédaction: Études sur le texte et ses transformations* 10(2).

O'Brien, J. (1959) "From French to English," in R. Brower (ed.) *On Translation*, Cambridge, MA: Harvard University Press, pp. 78–92.

O'Gorman, N. (1959a) "Language and Vision," *Poetry* 93: 329–32.

—— (1959b) *The Night of the Hammer*, New York: Harcourt Brace.

Okaeda S. (1988) *Sūpa Jimaku Nyōmon – Eiga Honyaku no Gijutsu to Chishiki* ("Introduction to Subtitles – Film Translation Technology and Knowledge"), Tokyo: Baburu Puresu.

—— (1989) *Jimaku Honyaku Kōgi no Jikkyō Chūkei* ("On-the-Spot Transmission of Subtitle Translation Lectures"), Tokyo: Gogakushunjusha.

O'Neill, E. (1959) *Three Plays*, New York: Vintage.

—— (n.d.) "Désir sous les ormes," trans. M. Dumont and M. Grégoire, National Theatre School, unpublished manuscript.

Orr, C. W. (1941) "The Problem of Translation," *Music and Letters* 22: 318–32.

Ortega y Gasset, J. (1937) "La Miseria y el esplendor de la traducción," in *Obras Completas: Tomo V (1933–1941)*, Madrid: Revista de Occidente, 1947, pp. 427–48.

—— (1992) "The Misery and the Splendor of Translation," trans. E. G. Miller, in R. Schulte and J. Biguenet (eds) *Theories of Translation: An Anthology of Essays from Dryden to Derrida*, Chicago: University of Chicago Press, pp. 93–112.

Ota T. (1939) "Supa Impozu ni Okeru Nihongo no Hinkon" ("The Poverty of Japanese Language of Spoken Titles"), *Nihon Eiga* 4:5(May): 51.

Paepcke, F. (1979) "Übersetzen als Hermeneutik," in P. Lehmann and R. Wolff (eds) *Das Stefan-George-Seminar 1979*, Heidelberg: Lambert Schneider.

—— (1986) "Textverstehen–Textübersetzen–Übersetzungskritik," in M. Snell-Hornby (ed.) *Übersetzungswissenschaft: eine Neuorientierung: Zur Integrierung von Theorie und Praxis*, Tübingen: Francke, pp. 106–32.

Panneton, G. (1946) "La transposition en traduction," University of Montreal, unpublished thesis.

Pannwitz, R. (1917) *Die Krisis der europäischen Kultur*, Nuremberg: H. Carl.

Pastre, G. (1997) "Linguistic Gender Play amongst French Gays and Lesbians," in A. Livia and K. Hall (eds) *Queerly Phrased: Language, Gender and Sexuality*, New York and London: Oxford University Press.

Penelope, J., and S. J. Wolfe (1979) "Sexist Slang and the Gay Community: Are You One Too?" *Michigan Occasional Paper*, No. XIV.

Phillips, H. P. (1959) "Problems of Translation and Meaning in Field Work," *Human Organization* 18: 184–92.

Phillips, J. B. (1953) "Some Personal Reflections on New Testament Translation," *Bible Translator* 4: 53–9.

The Phoenix of Sodom, Or the Vere Street Coterie (1813), London: J. Cook.

Pinter, H. (1971) *Old Times*, London: Methuen.

—— (n.d.) *Zman Avar*, trans. R. Kislev, unpublished manuscript.

Plett, H. F. (1975) *Textwissenschaft und Textanalyse*, Heidelberg: Quelle and Meyer.

Popovic, A. (1970) "The Concept of 'Shift of Expression' in Translation Analysis," in J. S. Holmes, F. de Haan and A. Popovic (eds) *The Nature of Translation*, The Hague: Mouton, pp. 78–87.

Pound, Ezra (1934) *The ABC of Reading*, New York: New Directions.

—— (1954) *Literary Essays*, New York: New Directions, and London: Faber and Faber.

Pratt, M. L. (1986) "Interpretive Strategies/Strategic Interpretations: On Anglo-American Reader-Response Criticism," in J. Arac (ed.) *Postmodernism and Politics*, Minneapolis: University of Minnesota Press, pp. 26–54.

—— (1987) "Linguistic Utopias," in N. Fabb, D. Attridge, A. Durant, and C. McCabe (eds) *The Linguistics of Writing: Arguments between Language and Literature*, Manchester: Manchester University Press.

Proust, M. (1924) *À la Recherche du Temps Perdu,* vol. VI, *La Prisonnière (Sodome et Gomorrhe* III), Paris: Nouvelle Revue Française.

Pulsifer, G. (1994) "Hot Off the Press: Gay Men's Publishing," in E. Healey and A. Mason (eds) *Stonewall 25: The Making of the Lesbian and Gay Community in Britain*, London: Virago.

Pusey, J. R. (1983) *China and Charles Darwin*, Cambridge, MA: Harvard University Press.

Pym, A. (1995) "European Translation Studies, 'Une science qui dérange,' and Why Equivalence Needn't Be a Dirty Word," *TTR Traduction, Terminologie, Rédaction: Études sur le texte et ses transformations* 8(1): 153–76.

—— (1996) "Venuti's Visibility," *Target* 8: 165–77.

—— (1997a) *Pour une éthique du traducteur*, Arras: Artois Presses Université, and Ottawa: Presses de l'Université d'Ottawa.

—— (1997b) "Koller's *Äquivalenz* Revisited," *The Translator* 3: 71–9.

—— (1998) *Method in Translation History*, Manchester: St Jerome.

—— (2000) *Negotiating the Frontier: Translators and Intercultures in Hispanic History*, Manchester: St Jerome.

Quine, W. V. O. (1960) *Word and Object*, Cambridge, MA: MIT Press.

Rabin, C. (1958) "The Linguistics of Translation," in A. H. Smith (ed.) *Aspects of Translation: Studies in Communication 2*, London: Secker and Warburg, pp. 123–45.

Rafael, V. (1988) *Contracting Colonialism: Translation and Christian Conversion in Tagalog Society under Early Spanish Rule*, Ithaca, New York: Cornell University Press.

Raymond, J. (1955) "Two First Novels," *New Statesman and Nation*, 21 May, pp. 727–8.

Rechy, J. (1963) *City of Night*, New York: Grove.

Rehbein, J. (1977) *Komplexes Handeln: Elemente zur Handlungstheorie der Sprache*, Stuttgart: Metzler.

Reichert, K. (1996) "'It Is Time': The Buber–Rosenzweig Bible Translation in Context," in S. Budick and W. Iser (eds) *The Translatability of Culture: Figurations of the Space Between*, Stanford, CA: Stanford University Press, pp. 169–85.

Reiss, K. (1971) *Möglichkeiten und Grenzen der Übersetzungskritik. Kategorien und Kriterien für eine sachgerechte Beurteilung von Übersetzungen*, Munich: Hueber.

—— (2000) *Translation Criticism: The Potentials and Limitations: Categories and Criteria for Translation Quality Assessment*, trans. E. F. Rhodes, Manchester: St Jerome.

Reiss, K. and H. J. Vermeer (1984) *Grundlegung einer allgemeinen Translationstheorie*, Tübingen: Niemeyer, 2nd edition, 1991.

Rener, F. M. (1989) *Interpretatio: Language and Translation from Cicero to Tytler*, Amsterdam and Atlanta: Rodopi.

Richie, D. (1991) "Donald Richie on Subtitling Japanese Films," *Mangajin* 10: 16.

Riedl, R. (1983) "Evolution und evolutionäre Erkenntnis: Zur Übereinstimmung der Ordnung des Denkens und der Nature," in K. Lorenz and F. M. Wuketits (eds) *Die Evolution des Denkens*, Munich and Zurich: Piper, pp. 146–66.

Rieu, E. V., and J. B. Phillips (1954) "Translating the Gospels," *Bible Translator* 6: 150–9.

Rioux, M. (1974) *Les Québécois*, Paris: Seuil.

Robinson, C. (1995) *Scandal in the Ink: Male and Female Homosexuality in Twentieth-Century French Literature*, London: Cassell.

Robinson, D. (1991) *The Translator's Turn*, Baltimore, MD: Johns Hopkins University Press.

—— (1992) "The Ascetic Foundations of Western Translatology: Jerome and Augustine," *Translation and Literature* 1: 3–25.

—— (1996) *Translation and Taboo*, DeKalb: Northern Illinois University Press.

—— (1997) *Translation and Empire: Postcolonial Theories Explained*, Manchester: St Jerome.

—— (1997a) *What is Translation? Centrifugal Theories, Critical Interventions*, Kent, OH: Kent State University Press.

—— (ed.) (1997b) *Western Translation Theory from Herodotus to Niezsche*, Manchester: St Jerome.

—— (2001) *Who Translates? Translator Subjectivities Beyond Reason*, Albany: State University of New York Press.

—— (2003) *Performative Linguistics: Speaking and Translating as Doing Things with Words*, London and New York: Routledge.

Robinson, S., and D. Smith (1973) *A Practical Handbook of Canadian French*, Toronto: Macmillan.

Robyns, C. (1994) "Translation and Discursive Identity," *Poetics Today* 15: 405–28.

Rodowick, D. N. (1988) *The Crisis of Political Modernism: Criticism and Ideology on Contemporary Film Theory*, Berkeley and Los Angeles: University of California Press.

Rolo, C. J. (1955) Review of Ash (1955), *Atlantic*, April, pp. 84–6.

Rossi-Landi, F. (1983) *Language as Work and Trade. A Semiotic Homology for Linguistics and Economics*, trans. M. Adams *et al.*, South Hadley, MA: Bergin and Garvey.

Sagan, F. (1954) *Bonjour Tristesse*, Paris: Julliard.

Sager, J. C. (1994) *Language Engineering and Translation: Consequences of Automation*, Amsterdam: Benjamins.

Sager, S. F. (1982) "Das Zusammenwirken dispositioneller und institutioneller Momente im verbalen Verhalten," in K. Detering, J. Schmidt-Radefeldt, and W. Sucharowski (eds) *Sprache erkennen und verstehen*, Tübingen: Niemeyer, pp. 283–92.

Said, E. (1978) *Orientalism*, New York: Pantheon.

Sanders, M. (1992) "Training for Community Interpreters," in C. Picken (ed.) *ITI Conference 6 Proceedings*, London: Aslib.

Sarig, G. (1979) "Agreement and Disagreement: A Model for a Speech Act Assessment of Translations," unpublished thesis.

Savory, T. H. (1957) *The Art of Translation*, London: Jonathan Cape, and Boston: The Writer, 2nd edition, 1968.

Schadewaldt, W. (trans.) (1958) *Homer: Die Odyssee*, Hamburg: Rowohlt.

Schleiermacher, F. (1813) "Ueber die verschiedenen Methoden des Uebersetzens," in M. Rössler with L. Emersleben (eds) *Schriften und Entwürfe*, vol. 11 of H. Fischer, U. Barth, K. Cramer, G. Meckenstock, and K.-V. Selge (eds) *Kritische Gesamtausgabe*, Berlin and New York: Walter de Gruyter, 2002, pp. 67–93.

Schulte, R., and J. Biguenet (eds) (1992) *Theories of Translation: An Anthology of Essays from Dryden to Derrida*, Chicago: University of Chicago Press.

Schwartz, B. (1964) *In Search of Wealth and Power: Yan Fu and the West*, Cambridge, MA: Harvard University Press.

Schweda Nicholson, N. (1994) "Professional Ethics for Court and Community Interpreters," in D. L. Hammond (ed.) *Professional Issues for Translators and Interpreters*, Amsterdam: Benjamins.

S., D. (1973) *"La Dialectique peut-elle casser les briques?" Image et Son* 276–7 (October): 110–11.

Séguinot, C. (1996) "Some Thoughts about Think-Aloud Protocols," *Target* 8: 75–95.

Shackman, J. (1984) *The Right to be Understood: A Handbook on Working with, Employing and Training Community Interpreters*, Cambridge: National Extension College.

Shakespeare, W. (1962) *The Oxford Complete Works*, ed. W. J. Craig, London: Oxford University Press.

—— (1978) *Macbeth*, trans. M. Garneau, Montreal: VLB.

Sheffy, R. (1992) "Repertoire Formation in the Canonization of Late 18th Century German Novel," University of Tel Aviv, unpublished dissertation.

Shimizu S. (1985) *Eiga Jimaku no Gojūnen* ("Fifty Years of Film Subtitling"), Tokyo: Hayakawa Shobō.

—— (1988) *Eiga Jimaku no Tsukurikata Oshiemasu* ("Teaching the Way to Make Movie Subtitles"), Tokyo: Bunshun Bunko.

—— (1992) *Eiga Jimaku wa Honyaku de wa Nai* ("Film Subtitling Is Not Translation"), ed. N. Toda and T. Ueno, Tokyo: Hayakawa Shobō.

Shlesinger, M. (1989) "Extending the Theory of Translation to Interpretation: Norms as a Case in Point," *Target* 1: 111–15.

Shuttleworth, M., and M. Cowie (1997) *Dictionary of Translation Studies*, Manchester: St Jerome.

Silverman, K. (1983) *The Subject of Semiotics*, Oxford: Oxford University Press.

Simon, S. (1994) *Le Trafic des langues: Traduction et culture dans la littérature québécoise*, Montreal: Boréal.

—— (1996) *Gender in Translation: Cultural Identity and the Politics of Transmission*, London and New York: Routledge.

—— (1999) "Translation as a Mode of Engagement: A Cultural and Ethical Agenda," *The Translator* 5(1): 113–17.

Simon, S. and D. Homel (1988) *Mapping Literature: The Art and Politics of Translation*, Montreal: Véhicule.

Simon, S. and P. St-Pierre (eds) (2000) *Changing the Terms: Translating in the Postcolonial Era*, Ottawa: University of Ottawa Press.

Simpson, P. (1993) *Language, Ideology and Point of View*, London and New York: Routledge.

Smith, A. H. (ed.) (1958) *Aspects of Translation: Studies in Communication 2*, London: Secker and Warburg.

Snell-Hornby, M. (1988) *Translation Studies: An Integrated Approach*, Amsterdam: Benjamins.

—— (1990) "Linguistic Transcoding of Cultural Transfer? A Critique of Translation Theory in Germany," in S. Bassnett and A. Lefevere (eds) *Translation, History and Culture*, London: Pinter, pp. 79–86.

Sontag, S. (1964) "Notes on 'Camp'," in *Against Interpretation and Other Essays*, New York: Delta, 1967, pp. 275–92.

Souter, A. (1920) *Hints on Translation from Latin into English*, London: Society for Promoting Christian Knowledge.

Sperber, D., and D. Wilson (1986) *Relevance: Communication and Cognition*, Oxford: Blackwell.

Spitzer, L. (1970) *Études de style*, trans. A. Conlon, M. Foucault and E. Kaufholz, Paris: Gallimard.

Spivak, G. (1992) "The Politics of Translation," in *Outside in the Teaching Machine*, London and New York: Routledge, 1993.

Stam, R., and E. Shohat (1985) "The Cinema after Babel: Language, Difference, Power," *Screen* 26 (3–4): 35–59.

Starke, S. (1999) *Behind Inverted Commas: Translation and Anglo-German Cultural Relations in the Nineteenth Century*, Clevedon: Multilingual Matters.

Steiner, G. (1975) *After Babel: Aspects of Language and Translation*, London, Oxford and New York: Oxford University Press, 3rd edition, 1998.

Steiner, T. R. (ed.) (1975a) *English Translation Theory 1650–1800*, Assen: Van Gorcum.

Stemmer, G. (1981) *Kohäsion im gesprochenen Diskurs deutscher Lerner des Englischen*, Bochum: Seminar für Sprachlehrforschung.

Störig, H. J. (ed.) (1963) *Das Problem des Übersetzens*, Darmstadt: Wissenschaftliche Buchgesellschaft.

Storr, F. (1909) "The Art of Translation," *Educational Review* 38: 359–79.

Strindberg, A. (1985) *Mademoiselle Julie*, trans. B. Vian, Paris: L'Arche.

—— (n.d.) "Mademoiselle Julie," adapt. G. Marsolais, National Theatre School, unpublished manuscript.

Sturge, K. (1997) "Translation Strategies in Ethnography," *The Translator* 3: 21–38.

Sturrock, J. (1991) "On Jakobson on Translation," in T. A. Sebeok and J. Umiker-Sebeok (eds) *Recent Developments in Theory and History: The Semiotic Web 1990*, Berlin: Mouton de Gruyter, pp. 307–21.

Sullivan, A. (1996) *Virtually Normal: An Argument about Homosexuality*, London: Picador.

Tabucchi, A. (1994) *Sostiene Pereira: Una testimonianza*, Milan: Feltrinelli.

Tachibana T. (1930) *Tokiitsu* ("Authoritative Knowledge of the Talkie"), Tokyo: Shiroku Shoin.

Tamura Yukihiko, "*Morocco*," *Kinema Junp Shobō.*, 1 February 1931.

Tanaka J. (1980) *Nihon Eiga Hattatsu-shi II* ("The History of the Development of Japanese Cinema II"), Tokyo: Chuokoronsha.

Tancock, L. W. (1958) "Some Problems of Style in Translation from French," in A. H. Smith (ed.) *Aspects of Translation: Studies in Communication 2*, London: Secker and Warburg, pp. 29–51.

Tennyson, A. (1972) *Selected Poetry*, ed. C. Ricks, London: Longman.

Times of London (1958) "Perplexities and Poetry," 6 November, p. 13C.

Tirkkonen-Condit, S. (1992) "A Theoretical Account of Translation: Without Translation Theory?" *Target* 4: 237–45.

Toda N. (1994) *Jimaku no Naka ni Jinsei* ("A Life in Subtitles"), Tokyo: Hakusuisha.

Toury, G. (1977) *Translation Norms and Literary Translations into Hebrew*, Tel Aviv: Porter Institute for Poetics and Semiotics.

—— (1980) *In Search of a Theory of Translation*, Tel Aviv: Porter Institute for Poetics and Semiotics.

—— (1985) "Translational Solutions on the Lexical Level and the Dictionary," in J. Tomaszczyk and B. Lewandowska-Tomaszczyk (eds) *International Conference on Meaning and Lexicography: Abstracts*, Lodz: University of Lodz.

—— (1985a) "A Rationale for Descriptive Translation Studies," in T. Hermans (ed.) *The Manipulation of Literature: Studies in Literary Translation*, London: Croom Helm, pp. 16–41.

—— (1995) *Description Translation Studies – and Beyond*, Amsterdam and Philadelphia: Benjamins.

Translation Bureau (1984) *Contractor's Guide: Translation*, Ottawa: Department of the Secretary of State.

Tremblay, M. (1969) "L'Intelligence de rire de soi-même," *L'envers du décor* (II) 1 (November): 3.

—— (1974) *Bonjour là, bonjour*, Montreal: Leméac.

Trinh. T. Minh-Ha (1992) *Framer Framed*, London and New York: Routledge.

Trudeau, D. (1982) *Léandre et son péché*, Montreal: Hurtubise.

Turp, G. (1984) "Pourquoi retraduire *Mère Courage et ses enfants?*" *En Scène* 2(2).

Tymoczko, M. (1999) *Translation in a Postcolonial Context: Early Irish Literature in English Translation*, Manchester: St Jerome.

—— (2000) "Translation and Political Engagement: Activism, Social Change and the Role of Translation in Geopolitical Shifts," *The Translator* 6 (1): 23–49.

Tytler, A. F. (1978) *Essay on the Principles of Translation*, ed. J. F. Huntsman, Amsterdam: John Benjamins.

Underhill, R.M. (1938) *Singing for Power*, Berkeley, CA: University of California Press.

Updike, J. (1960) *Rabbit Run*, New York: Fawcett.

—— (1965) *Shafan Brax*, trans. E. Kaspi, Tel Aviv: Am Oved.

Van Dijk, T., and W. Kintsch (1983) *Strategies of Discourse Comprehension*, New York: Academic Press.

Van Hoof, H. (1991) *Histoire de la traduction en occident: France, Grande-Bretagne, Allemange, Russie, Pays-Bas*, Paris and Louvain-la-Neuve: Duculot.

Venuti, L. (1986) "The Translator's Invisibility," *Criticism* 28: 179–212.

—— (1991) Review of Benjamin (1989), Cheyfitz (1991), and Robinson (1991), *Textual Practice* 6: 316–24.

—— (ed.) (1992) *Rethinking Translation: Discourse, Subjectivity, Ideology*, London and New York: Routledge.

—— (1995) *The Translator's Invisibility: A History of Translation*, London and New York: Routledge.

—— (1996) "Unequal Developments: Current Trends in Translation Studies," *Comparative Literature* 49: 360–8.

———— (1998) *The Scandals of Translation: Towards an Ethics of Difference*, London and New York: Routledge.

—— (2003) "Translating Derrida on Translation: Relevance and Disciplinary Resistance," *Yale Journal of Criticism* 16(2): 237–62.

Vercier, B. (1996) "An Interview with Renaud Camus," in B. Mahuzier, K. McPherson, C. A. Porter and R. Saronak (eds) *Same Sex/Different Text? Gay and Lesbian Writing in French*, *Yale French Studies* 90, New Haven, CT: Yale University Press, pp. 7–21.

Vermeer, H. J. (1970) "Generative Transformationsgrammatik, Sprachvergleich und Sprachtypologie," *Zeitschrift für Phonetik* 23: 385–404.

—— (1972) *Allgemeine Sprachwissenschaft: Eine Einführung*, Freiburg: Rombach.

—— (1978) "Ein Rahmen für eine allgemeine Translationstheorie," *Lebende Sprachen* 23: 99–102.

—— (1979) "Vom 'richtigen' Übersetzen," *Mitteilungsblatt für Dolmetscher und Übersetzer* 25 (4): 2–8.

—— (1983) *Aufsätze zur Translationstheorie*, Heidelberg: Groos.

—— (1986) *Voraussetzungen für eine Translationstheorie: Einige Kapitel Kultur- und Sprachtheorie*, Heidelberg: Groos.

—— (1989) "Skopos and Commission in Translational Action," trans. A. Chesterman, in A. Chesterman (ed.) *Readings in Translation Theory*, Helsinki: Oy Finn Lectura Ab, pp. 173–87.

—— (1992) *Skizzen zu einer Geschichte der Translation*, Frankfurt: Verlag für Interkulturelle Kommunikation.

Vidal, G. (1948) *The City and the Pillar*, London: Panther, revised edition, 1965.

Vieira, E. (1984) "Comparative Stylistics Applied to Translation from English to Portuguese," conference paper.

Vinay, J.-P. and J. Darbelnet (1958) *Stylistique comparée du français et de l'anglais*, Paris: Didier.

—— (1995) *Comparative Stylistics of French and English: A Methodology for Translation*, trans. and ed. J. C. Sager and M.-J. Hamel, Amsterdam: Benjamins.

Vincendeau, G. (1988) "Hollywood Babel: The Coming of Sound and the Multiple-Language Version," reprinted in A. Higson and R. Maltby (eds) *"Film Europe" and "Film America": Cinema, Commerce and Cultural Exchange 1920–1939*, Exeter: University of Exeter Press, pp. 207–48.

Vodička, C. F. (1964) "The History of the Echo of Literary Works," in P. L. Garvin (ed. and trans.) *A Prague School Reader on Esthetics, Literary Structure and Style*, Washington, DC: Georgetown University Press, pp. 71–81.

Von Flotow, L. (1991) "Feminist Translation: Contexts, Practices and Theories," *TTR Traduction, Terminologie, Rédaction: Études sur le texte et ses transformations* 4(2): 69–84.

—— (1997) *Translation and Gender: Translating in the "Era of Feminism"*, Manchester: St Jerome.

Vossler, K. (1932) *The Spirit of Language in Civilization* (1925), trans. O. Oeser, London: Routledge.

Waard, J. de, and E. Nida (1986) *From One Language to Another: Functional Equivalence in Bible Translating*, Nashville, TN: Nelson.

Wadensjö, C. (1998) "Community Interpreting," in M. Baker (ed.) *Encyclopedia of Translation Studies*, London and New York: Routledge, pp. 33–7.

Wagner, E., S. Bech and J. Martinez (2002) *Translating for the European Union Institutions*, Manchester: St Jerome.

Ward, M. (trans.) (1988) A. Camus, *The Stranger*, New York: Alfred Knopf.

Weinberg, H. (1985) *Booze, Cigars, and Movies*, New York: Anthology Film Archives.

Weinmann, H. (1977) "Narcisse et l'autre: Pour un ethnotype québécois," *Voix et images* 3(2) (December): 266–76.

Weissbrod, R. (1989) *Trends in the Translation of Prose Fiction from English into Hebrew, 1958–1980*, University of Tel Aviv, unpublished dissertation.

West, C. B. (1932) "La théorie de la traduction au XVIIIe siècle," *Revue Littérature Comparée* 12: 330–55.

Wexler, P. N. (1974) *Purism and Language: A Study in Modern Ukrainian and Belorussian Nationalism*, Bloomington, IN: Indiana University Press.

White, E. (1988) *The Beautiful Room Is Empty*, London: Picador.

—— (1994) "Out of the Closet, On to the Bookshelf," in *The Burning Library: Writings on Art, Politics and Sexuality*, London: Chatto and Windus, pp. 275–83.

—— (1997) "AIDS Awareness and Gay Culture in France," in J. Oppenheimer and H. Reckitt (eds) *Acting on AIDS: Sex, Drugs and Politics*, London and New York: Serpent's Tail, pp. 339–45.

Williams, J., and A. Chesterman (2002) *The Map: A Beginner's Guide to Doing Research in Translation Studies*, Manchester: St Jerome.

Wilson, A. (1952) *Hemlock and After*, Harmondsworth: Penguin.

Wilson, D., and D. Sperber (1988) "Mood and Analysis of Non-declarative Sentences," in J. Dancy, J. Moravcsik and C. C. W. Taylor (eds) *Human Agency: Language, Duty and Value*, Stanford, CA: Stanford University Press, pp. 77–101.

Wilson, E. (1946) "Books," *New Yorker*, 13 April, pp. 99–100.

Wilss, W. (1977) *Übersetzungswissenschaft: Probleme und Methoden*, Stuttgart: Klett.

—— (1982) *The Science of Translation: Problems and Methods*, Tübingen: Narr.

—— (1988) *Kognition und Übersetzen. Zu Theorie und Praxis der menschlichen und der maschineller Übersetzung*, Tübingen: Niemeyer.

Zuber, R. (1968) *Les "Belles Infidèles" et la formation du goût classique: Perrot d'Ablancourt et Guez de Balzac*, Paris: Colin.

Index